Monetary Policy Frameworks in a Global Context

The analysis of any monetary policy framework necessarily extends beyond the confinements of the central bank, and may depend upon many factors such as: its form of government, its financial and legal systems, the level of expertise in monetary policy matters that exist inside and outside the central bank. This broad ranging collection focuses on the monetary policy frameworks used by central banks and governments in their attempt to achieve their goals, of which price stability has become increasingly popular.

Monetary Policy Frameworks in a Global Context proceeds from general to the specific. General lessons are drawn in a Report prepared for the 1999 Central Bank Governors' symposium held at the Bank of England. This includes one of the broadest-ever surveys of monetary policy framework characteristics, covering 94 monetary frameworks. Within this rich sample, there exist monetary frameworks with many different forms and combinations of policy targets as well as institutional arrangements that incorporate varying degrees of accountability, independence, and transparency and a myriad of analytical methods that inform key decisions. The report seeks to identify where the search for best monetary policy practice has found common ground, and also distinguishes circumstances that might lead countries to choose frameworks that depart from the norm.

The second part of the book contains specific lessons drawn from renowned monetary policy researchers and practitioners, and the rich diversity of experiences assessed provide a wide perspective on how the evolution of monetary policy frameworks over the last 30 years has depended upon:

- Structural differences
- Varying degrees of indexation and nominal rigidities that affect the speed of transmission from monetary policy to inflation
- Institutional arrangements and analytical constraints that influence the way in which monetary policy can respond

This original and comprehensive text will be of great value to professional economists and students of economics and banking alike. And the data collected are likely to provide a rich information source for applied researchers and all those following global trends in monetary framework practice and design.

Lavan Mahadeva is adviser for Modelling and Forecasting at the Bank of England and **Gabriel Sterne** is an adviser for Monetary Analysis at the Bank of England. Their work at the Bank of England's Centre for Central Banking Studies is to provide technical assistance and establish collaborative research with economists from a very broad range of economies, and together they have worked in around 20 countries in recent years.

Monetary Policy Frameworks in a Global Context

Edited by
Lavan Mahadeva and **Gabriel Sterne**

London and New York

First published 2000
by Routledge
2 Park Square, Milton Park, Abingdon, Oxon, OX14 4RN

Simultaneously published in the USA and Canada
by Routledge
270 Madison Ave, New York NY 10016

Routledge is an imprint of the Taylor & Francis Group

Transferred to Digital Printing 2007

© 2000 Bank of England

Typeset in TimesTen Roman by Wearset, Boldon, Tyne & Wear

British Library Cataloguing in Publication Data
A catalogue record for this book is available from the British Library

Library of Congress Cataloging in Publication Data

Mahadeva, Lavan
  Monetary policy frameworks in a global context/Lavan Mahadeva
    and Gabriel Sterne. p. cm.
  Includes bibliographical references and index.
  1. Monetary policy—Decision making. 2. Financial institutions—
    Decision making. I. Sterne, Gabriel. II. Title.

HG230.3 M34 2000
332.4′6—dc21

00–028254

ISBN 0-415-22618-X (hbk)
ISBN 0-415-23768-8 (pbk)

Printed and bound by CPI Antony Rowe, Eastbourne

Contents

List of figures

Monetary policy in a dollarised economy

Balassa-Samuelson effect and monetary targets

PART IV

Inflation expectations in Japanese monetary policy

List of tables

Contributors and e-mail addresses

(Organisations were correct at the time of writing.)

Samuel Alfaro	Banco de México	salfaro@banxico.org.mx
Michael Atingi-Ego	Bank of Uganda	michaelatingiego@hotmail.com
Gil Bufman	Private economic consultant	Bufman@isdn.net.il
Andrew Crockett	General Manager, Bank for International Settlements	
Uros Cufer	Bank of Slovenia	Uros.cufer@bsi.si
Alex Cukierman	Tel Aviv University	
Maxwell Fry	Director, Centre for Central Banking Studies, Bank of England	
Charles Goodhart	Monetary Policy Committee, Bank of England	
Masahiro Higo	Institute for Monetary and Eonomic Studies, Bank of Japan	Masahiro.higo@boj.or.jp
Seamus Hogan	Bank of Canada	Seamus_hogan@hc-sc.gc.ca
Miroslav Hrnčíř	Executive Director, Czech National Bank	
DeAnne Julius	Monetary Policy Committee, Bank of England	
Marion Kohler	Bank of England	marion.kohler@bankofengland.co.uk
Oscar Landerretche	Central Bank of Chile	olanderr@condor.bcentral.cl
Leonardo Leiderman	Senior Director, Bank of Israel	leo.leiderman@db.com
Lavan Mahadeva	Centre for Central Banking Studies, Bank of England	lavan.mahadeva@bankofengland.co.uk
David G. Mayes	South Bank University and Bank of Finland	David.mayes@bof.fi
Felipe Morandé	Chief Economist, Central Bank of Chile	Fmorande@condor.bcentral.cl
Adam S. Posen	Institute for International Economics	Aposen@att.net

Zenón Quispe Misaico	Central Bank of Peru	zquispe@bcrp.gob.pe
Sandra Roger	Centre for Central Banking Studies, Bank of England	
Klaus Schmidt-Hebbel	Central Bank of Chile	Kschmidt@condor.bcentral.cl
Moisés J. Schwartz	Director of Economic Studies, Banco de México	schwartz@banxico.org.mx
Kateřina Šmídková	Czech National Bank	Katerina.smidkova@cnb.cz
Gabriel Sterne	Centre for Central Banking Studies, Bank of England	gabriel.sterne@bankofengland.co.uk
Matti Virén	Bank of Finland	matti.viren@bof.fi

Acknowledgements

This project has been truly collaborative. With regard to the survey, the care and attention with which central bankers from 94 central banks have completed the questionnaire, surpassed even our most optimistic expectations. Several of these individuals have also offered helpful comments on previous drafts of the Report. We would like to offer our sincerest gratitude to each of the following:

Fatmir Z. Xhaferi (*Bank of Albania*), Andrew Powell (*Banco Central de la Republica Argentina*), Sargsyam Tigran (*Central Bank of Armenia*), Glenn Stevens (*Reserve Bank of Australia*), Martin Schurz and Fritz Fritzer (*Oesterreichische Nationalbank*), John Rolle (*The Central Bank of the Bahamas*), Naser Al-Belooshi (*Bahrain Monetary Agency*), Faruqud-din Ahmed and Syed Ahmed Khan (*Bangladesh Bank*), Roland Craigwell (*Central Bank of Barbados*), Vincent Perilleux and Ivo Maes (*Banque Nationale de Belgique*), Keith Arnold (*Central Bank of Belize*), Peter Nicholl (*Central Bank of Bosnia & Herzegovina*), Julia Majaha-Jartby (*Bank of Botswana*), Svetsoslav Veleslavov Gavrisky (*Bulgarian National Bank*), Jean-Pierre Aubry (*Bank of Canada*), Felipe Morande and Oscar Landerretche (*Banco Central de Chile*), Fai-nan Perng (*The Central Bank of China*), Ou Hong (*The People's Bank of China*), Katja Gattin (*Croatian National Bank*), Takis Kanaris (*Central Bank of Cyprus*), Ales Capek (*Czech National Bank*), Tom Wagener (*Danmarks Nationalbank*), Prof. Remsperger and Dr Konig (*Deutsche Bundesbank*), Wendell Samuel (*Eastern Caribbean Central Bank*), Maritza Cabezas (*Central Bank of Ecuador*), Juan Penalosa (*Banco de Espana*), Klaus Masuch (*European Central Bank*), Ragaa Khalil (*Central Bank of Egypt*), Ilmar Lepik and Reet Reedik (*Bank of Estonia*), Uday Singh (*Reserve Bank of Fiji*), Jarmo Kontulainen (*Bank of Finland*), Thierry Grunspan (*Banque de France*), Khatuna Jincharadze (*National Bank of Georgia*), Kwabena Duffuor (*Bank of Ghana*), Lucas D. Papademos (*Bank of Greece*), Gobind Ganga (*Bank of Guyana*), Priscilla Chiu (*Hong Kong Monetary Authority*), Birgir Isleifur Gunnarsson and Arnor Sighvatsson (*Central Bank of Iceland*), Dr A. Vasudevan, Mr K. Kanagasabapathy, Dr G.S. Bhati and Dr H. Joshi (*Reserve Bank of India*), Bambang Wahyudi (*Bank*

Indonesia), John O'Neill and Paul McBride (*Central Bank of Ireland*), Efrat Katz and Ed Offenbacher (*Bank of Israel*), Giancarlo Morcaldo (*Bank of Italy*), Sogue Diarisso (*Bank of Jamaica*), Hiromi Yamaoka (*The Bank of Japan*), Ghassan Ifram (*Central Bank of Jordan*), Daulet Ismailov (*National Bank of Kazakstan*), Mr M. Kanga (*Central Bank of Kenya*), Hyung Moon Kang (*The Bank of Korea*), Sami H. Al-Anbaee (*Central Bank of Kuwait*), Elmira Toktomambetova, Jury Bushman, Saule Seizbaeva, Marina Titova (*National Bank of the Kyrgyz Republic*), Helmuts Ancans (*Bank of Latvia*), Ghina H. Jaroudi (*Banque Centrale de la Republique Libanaise*), Reinoldijus Sarkinas (*Bank of Lithuania*), Zoran Jovanovski (*National Bank of the Republic of Macedonia*), Ismael Alow (*Central Bank of Malaysia*), Emanuel Ellul (*Central Bank of Malta*), Mr R. Sooben (*Bank of Mauritius*), Javier Salas Martin del Gampo (*Banco de Mexico*), Leonid P. Talmmaci (*National Bank of Moldova*), Mr D. Ganbat (*Bank of Mongolia*), Antonio Pinto de Abreu (*Bank of Mozambique*), Thomas K. Alweendo (*Bank of Namibia*), Jan Kakes (*De Nederlandsche Bank*), Mary Hoffman and Antulio Bomgin (*Federal Reserve Bank of New York*), Donald Brash, Aaron Drew and Bruce White (*Reserve Bank of New Zealand*), Dr Ojo (*Central Bank of Nigeria*), Ole Bjorn Roste (*Norges Bank*), Hugo Perea and Susana Ishisaka (*Banco Central de Reserva Del Peru*), Ryszard Kokoszczynnski (*National Bank of Poland*), Maximiano Pinheiro (*Bank of Portugal*), Eugen Radulescu (*National Bank of Romania*), Viktor Gerashchenko (*The Central Bank of Russia*) Ms Celine Sia and Mr Tan Kim Eng (*The Monetary Authority of Singapore*), Ms Schmidt (*South African Reserve Bank*), Hennadige Thenuwara, (*Central Bank of Sri Lanka*), Mathias Zurlinden (*Banque Nationale Suisse*), Hans Dillen (*Sveriges Riksbank*), Dr Massawe and Nicodemus Mboje (*Bank of Tanzania*), Mrs Wai-quamdee (*Bank of Thailand*), Mrs Ketu'u (*National Reserve Bank of Tonga*), Mehtap Kesriyeli (*Central Bank of the Republic of Turkey*), Hudaiberdy Orazov (*Central Bank of Turkmenistan*), Michael Atingi-Ego (*Bank of Uganda*), Mr Stelmakh (*National Bank of Ukraine*), Jose L. Formoso (*Central Bank of Uruguay*), Nguyen Thi Kim Thanh (*State Bank of Vietnam*), Kablan Yao Sahi and Charles Konan Banny (*Central Bank of West African States*), and Noah Mutoti (*Bank of Zambia*).

We circulated a pilot questionnaire that was completed by CEFTA (Central European Free Trade Association) countries, and we are grateful to our colleagues in these central banks for their comments when we discussed the results at a workshop in Budapest in September 1998. We would also like to thank participants of a workshop on intermediate targets of monetary policy, here at the Bank of England in November 1998. We refer in this paper to many of the country experiences and research issues presented during that week. In particular several participants at the seminar worked with us for extended periods here in London to research the papers for this workshop, some of which are contained in this volume. These are Michael Atingi-Ego, Oscar Landerrechte, Zenón Quispe, Kateřina Šmídková, László Varró and Marion Kohler.

Our particular thanks go to Bill Allen who read every contribution to the book and made invaluable comments on each; and also to Lorraine Yuille for her excellent assistance in many aspects of this project. We would also like to acknowledge our discussants at the Central Bank Governors' symposium: Donald Brash, Chon Chol Hwan, and Josef Tosovsky.

Many people have helped by commenting on the questionnaire and drafts, as well as by providing administrative assistance with various aspects of the project. These include Bill Alexander, Kath Begley, David Buffham, Christine Chaplin, Alec Chrystal, Lucy Clary, Peter Doyle, Jeremy Fry, Karen Corbin, Graeme Danton, Pauline Findlay, Innes Davis, Andrew Haldane, Neal Hatch, Tony Ison, Robert Heath, Glenn Hoggarth, Marion Kohler, Stephen Millard, Edward Offenbacher, Nikki Panons, Adrian Penalver, Joanna Place, Kateřina Šmídková, Andy Snewin, Chang Shu, Peter Sinclair, Jonathan Sterne, Glenn Stevens, Tony Yates and John Vickers. We are also grateful to Suzanne Peake (Editorial Services, Annapolis, Md) and her colleagues Jennifer Burton, Michael Coleman, Maria Coughlin, Nedalina Dineva, Kelly Lutz, Linda O'Doughda and Jeanne Pinault. We are grateful to everybody at Routledge and Wearset who have contributed to the successful publication of this book.

Any mistakes remain our own, and we stress that the scores given to monetary frameworks in this volume represent our own interpretations of information provided by central banks and other sources. They do not represent the views of any central bank.

Foreword

Since the Bank of England's 300th birthday celebrations in 1994, its annual Central Bank Governors' Symposium has developed into a structured investigation of particular central banking topics. The Bank's first symposium, held in 1994, concentrated primarily on the history and nature of central banking in the industrialised countries (Capie, Goodhart, Fischer and Schnadt 1994). To complement the resultant work, a report on central banking in developing countries was produced for the second symposium, held during the 1995 meeting of governors (Fry, Goodhart and Almeida 1996). More recently, the symposium has concentrated on specific central banking issues. In 1996 it discussed how a government should best meet its borrowing requirements and what roles central banks might usefully play (Fry 1997). The 1997 symposium report focused on financial regulation (Goodhart, Hartmann, Llewellyn, Rojas-Suarez and Weisbrod 1998), and in 1998 the subject was payment systems (Fry, Kilato, Roger, Senderowicz, Sheppard, Solis and Trundle 1999).

The 1999 symposium turned to the theme of monetary policy frameworks and the role of central banks. I asked DeAnne Julius, a member of the Monetary Policy Committee of the Bank of England, to join forces with the team from the Centre for Central Banking Studies in a project coordinated by its Director, Professor Maxwell Fry. I asked the authors of the report to consider monetary policy frameworks in a global perspective, rather than focusing on any particular type of economy. The Report is therefore based on a detailed survey that brought together new comparative information on the monetary policy frameworks of 94 developing, transitional, and industrial economies – and that I think is a first. So, as was the case last year, this Report is a truly international product. The Bank of England is very grateful to all those central banks that have helped in the preparation of that product.

One particular development highlighted in the report is the rapid increase during the 1990s in the number of economies in all stages of development using explicit targets as a focal point for monetary policy, whether for the exchange rate, money, or inflation. The Report shows how targets are used and interpreted in different ways in different countries. It is clear, not only from the report, but also from the comments of Governors attending the Symposium, that the use of targets has gone hand-in-hand with a greater emphasis on communication among central banks, governments, and the private sector.

The preparation for the 1999 symposium was combined, as in the previous year, with a workshop run by the Centre for Central Banking Studies. Twenty-eight central banks sent experts to exchange views with each other as well as with leading experts from the International Monetary Fund (IMF), the Bank for International Settlements (BIS) and a number of distinguished academics. This was followed by a three-month research project involving representatives of the central banks of Chile, the Czech Republic, Hungary, Peru, and Uganda as well as the Bank of England. The success of the workshop and research project has led to a significant departure from previous years in that this year's symposium report and proceedings are accompanied in this book by a group of papers that were first presented at the workshop. The papers provide a wealth of detailed experience to follow the global picture painted by the survey.

This book exemplifies the spirit of learning through diversity in experiences. The authors come from countries ranging from Canada to Uganda. And the contributions come not only from distinguished experts with vast experience in formulating monetary policy, but also from researchers who are considerably newer in the field. We have found this to be an interesting and fruitful exercise, as, I hope, will readers of this book.

Eddie George
Governor of the Bank of England

General introduction

Lavan Mahadeva and Gabriel Sterne

Monetary policy framework designers were particularly busy during the last decade. Some countries made historic shifts toward currency union. Others were pushed by currency crises towards greater exchange-rate flexibility, developing their domestic nominal anchors to guide expectations more effectively and develop credibility.

The spur for this book was the sixth annual Central Bank Governors' Symposium held at the Bank of England in June 1999, where over 50 central bank governors met to share views on the important global developments of monetary policy frameworks. At the Symposium, Josef Tošovský of the Czech National Bank framed the key issue in the choice of framework design in nautical terms: As 'navigators aboard the good ship *Monetary Policy*', we search not just for an explicit target to provide a nominal anchor, but for institutional arrangements that constitute a harbour for safe anchorage.

After the inflation of the 1970s and 1980s, price stability is now the dominant and widely agreed objective of monetary policy, but as this book shows there are numerous routes to it. We now observe many different forms and combinations of policy targets as well as institutional arrangements that incorporate varying degrees of accountability, independence, and transparency and myriad analytical methods that inform key decisions. These reforms have had widespread success; by the end of the 1990s, global inflation was lower than at any time since the breakdown of Bretton Woods in the early 1970s. No matter what route was taken, the 1990s saw steadier prices almost everywhere. Annual inflation stood at a 25-year low in many countries by the end of the 1990s.

At the outset of this project, we set ourselves the objective of identifying areas where the search for best monetary policy practice has found common ground, for industrialised, transitional, and developing economies alike. We also sought to distinguish circumstances that might lead countries to choose frameworks that depart from the norm. When is it best to target inflation, or money, or exchange rates? What consensus exists on the ideal degrees of independence, accountability, and transparency for the central bank? When might the use of certain types of macroeconomic models and other forms of analysis be most appropriate?

In answering such questions, this book proceeds from the general to the specific. General lessons are drawn from one of the broadest-ever surveys of monetary policy framework characteristics, examined in a report by Maxwell Fry, DeAnne Julius, Lavan Mahadeva, Sandra Roger, and Gabriel Sterne (FJMRS). The Report draws from a vast database, covering 94 monetary frameworks in a diverse range of developing, transitional, and industrialised economies. The 15 papers that follow the Report draw specific lessons from the experiences of individual countries and report and research on specific issues.

Monetary policy strategies

Andrew Crockett assesses monetary framework options and cross-country differences in transmission mechanisms. In framework design, he finds that 'one size does not necessarily fit all'. He contrasts the potential benefits of the three types of targeting, discussing conditions under which one of the three might outperform the others.

Exchange-rate targeting has often been instrumental in braking inflation expectations, Crockett observes. This is corroborated by FJMRS (Chapter 2): there are virtually no instances in recent history of developing and transitional economies achieving low and stable inflation other than through exchange-rate targeting. Why then, does exchange-rate targeting sometimes end in currency crisis? One reason identified by Crockett is the challenge of devising an 'exit strategy' from fixed exchange rates. When their currency comes under pressure, the authorities are reluctant to abandon the peg until they are forced to do so. Very few countries have reaped the benefits from an exchange-rate peg before moving gradually to greater flexibility. Poland is one that has done so, however, and Chapter 7 of FJMRS looks at Poland's journey from fixed exchange rate to inflation targeting. Chile is another; Landerretche, Morandé, and Schmidt-Hebbel provide a detailed assessment of this case.

Exchange-rate targeting appears capable of delivering either the most stable or, if the regime breaks down, the least stable prices. So what of the alternative anchors, money and inflation targeting? Crockett finds these may succeed in some circumstances, but 'only if the authorities are willing to follow through with the necessary policy decisions, both in the realm of monetary policy and in the realm of fiscal and structural policies'.

Kydland and Prescott (1977) identified the problem of *time-consistency* in decision-making. The best long-run policy is to avoid inflation. But if authorities tend to think only of the here and now, they can be tempted by the temporary gain that some surprise inflation can bring. This conflict between reputation and temptation was explored further by Barro and Gordon (1983a, 1983b), Backus and Driffill (1985a, 1985b), Barro (1986), and Vickers (1986). One answer to the problem is the appointment of independent central bankers disposed to be anti-inflationary (Rogoff, 1985). More recently Walsh (1995) and Waller and Walsh (1996) have advocated organising the incentive structures of central bankers through a formal contract.

The practice of central banking is as much shaped by theory as the other way round (Blinder, 1998). In this spirit, Alex Cukierman's paper in this volume, 'Establishing a Reputation for Dependability by Means of Inflation Targets', weaves a new and important element of realism into the theoretical discussion of how to achieve low inflation at low cost to output. As in some earlier literature, the public is unsure about the commitment of policy-makers to pre-announced low inflation. Cukierman allows policy-makers to exercise only an imperfect control of inflation; they are constrained from pursuing inflation not just by an output cost but also because final outcomes are partly uncertain. This makes it more difficult for dependable policy-makers to establish their credentials and tends to stretch the process of learning about their dependability over time. Lucky shocks help dependable policy-makers to demonstrate their commitment to low inflation and to quickly achieve it. On the other hand unlucky shocks, by ruining the reputation of weak policy-makers, pushes them towards short sighted discretionary policies. Cukierman shows that better methods of inflation control and longer horizons encourage both weak and dependable policy-makers to control inflation more actively. Since they like to reveal their identity, dependable policy-makers will, in many cases, choose more precise methods than weak policy-makers, who like to hide their identity. Gradual (rather than 'cold turkey') inflation stabilisation is more likely to be observed when initial reputation is reasonably high and the policy-maker is sufficiently concerned about the future. The emphasis of the paper, as in much of this book, lies in describing the interaction between the environment (which can at times be harsh and at times benevolent to the policy-maker) and the institutions.

The literature to which Cukierman's paper adds a new dimension has consistently focused on how to provide all the main players with incentives to commit to and deliver low inflation. Getting these incentives right in practice is an important theme of Charles Goodhart's paper 'The Role of the Monetary Policy Committee: Strategic Considerations'. Goodhart builds on his experience as a member of the Bank of England's Monetary Policy Committee (MPC) to argue that, in the UK case, the inflation target has provided a good basis for building a constituency for low inflation. Although the Bank of England has operational independence, it is the UK government that sets the inflation target, currently at 2.5%. These arrangements make it hard for government to repudiate the measures that central bankers deem necessary to achieve the target, and stop governments from indulging in surprise inflation. The government can achieve higher inflation only through increasing the published inflation target, which by definition would not be a surprise. Thus the potential for time-inconsistencies in monetary policy are minimised. As to providing incentives to commit to the inflation target, Goodhart goes further than most. In discussing the individual accountability and incentive structure for MPC members in the United Kingdom, he expresses a desire to see his salary structure adjusted such that it includes a pecuniary reward that depends upon the closeness of inflation to the target, a view that he acknowledges is not necessarily shared by his colleagues on the MPC.

The question of how best to ensure commitment and co-ordination between the central bank and government when circumstances render clear specification of such contracts more complicated is a theme discussed in several of the papers in this book.

Mixed strategies and uncertain transmission mechanisms

Another important theme in this book is how the practice of monetary policy is shaped by the difficult task of identifying structural changes as and when they occur. Gil Bufman and Leo Leiderman develop an illustrative model that is a useful departure point. It outlines how optimal monetary policy can be described by an interest-rate rule if the sole objective is to keep expected future inflation at target. In the rule, the real interest rate reacts to deviations of current inflation from target, the level of output (y), and a representative exogenous indicator variable (x) of future inflationary pressure. The coefficients in this rule depend only on the economic structure in their simplified economy:

$$i = \pi_t + b_1(\pi_t - \pi^*) + b_2(y_t) + b_3(x_t).$$

Bufman and Leiderman emphasise that the rule does not imply a strict relationship between interest rates and inflation. Movements in the indicators of future inflation, such as fiscal policy, could also require a policy response. This rule may need to be interpreted flexibly, because structural breaks may change the weights of movements in the indicators: b_1, b_2, and b_3 may vary over time.

Structural breaks, far from being unusual events, are commonplace in many of the countries discussed in this book. In reviewing the past monetary policy regimes of the Czech Republic, Hrnčíř and Šmídková report that the Czech National Bank found it difficult to use any one single current variable to provide signals for monetary policy when different shocks and structural breaks were continually occurring. They argue that a broader set of indicators had to be relied upon; the correct interpretation of any one indicator's movements (the weights on the rule) vary from policy round to policy round.

As mentioned, one problem for monetary policy is that it is very hard to identify when structural change is taking place. That is true even when using the better-quality data that are available in industrialised countries.

Analogously, Goodhart argues that unadulterated model-based forecasts (based on relationships that were reliable in the past) cannot by themselves be trusted as a basis for policy-making. Credibility is maximised when policymakers' judgement is based on rational economic argument that is laid bare to the public.

Several contributions to this volume make plain that understanding the idiosyncrasies of a country's transmission mechanism also plays a key role in the success of monetary policy. For example, how does the transmission mechanism affect the time-horizon at which inflation should be targeted? Recent research suggests that targeting inflation about two years ahead would minimise the volatility of output and inflation in the United Kingdom (Batini and Haldane, 1999). Batini and Haldane suggested that the optimal horizon, *ceteris paribus*, should match the horizon at which wages and import prices pass monetary policy reactions through to inflation.

Mahadeva and Kateřina Šmídková's paper applies the Batini and Haldane model-based method to the case of the Czech Republic. The Czech Republic and the United Kingdom are both open-economy inflation targeters. But there seems to be a quicker passthrough of prices in the Czech Republic, in part because wage bargaining is more centralised and thus nominal movements more co-ordinated. Mahadeva and Šmídková's results for the Czech Republic confirm that the optimal targeting horizon is significantly shorter than the four to six-quarter horizon that seems suitable for the United Kingdom, which, if applied in the Czech Republic, would bring excessive volatility to output and inflation. They also show that the cost of targeting too short an horizon falls more upon inflation volatility in the Czech Republic while resulting in relatively more output instability in the United Kingdom. Targeting too short an horizon leads to excessive short-term interest-rate volatility in both cases. But because of its speedier price passthrough, short-run policy errors feed quickly to prices in the Czech Republic and affect output less.

Oscar Landerretche, Felipe Morandé, and Klaus Schmidt-Hebbel's discussion of Chile, another inflation-targeting economy, also addresses the effect of the speed of price passthrough in determining the costs of inflation stabilisation. Chile is highly indexed. The authors argue that the large inflation inertia that this creates can lead to substantial output costs. A credible inflation-targeting regime can help counteract inflation inertia by providing an anchor for inflation expectations. The authors use a structural model to show that, despite inflation inertia, the more credible an inflation target, the lower the output costs on a disinflation path. Supporting empirical evidence suggests that the announcement of an inflation target did contribute to the relatively very smooth disinflation that Chile underwent from 1990 to 1998.

The nature and scale of shocks that economies face also vary dramatically among countries. But it is surprising how similar the issues facing policy-makers can be. Michael Atingi-Ego analyses the policy implications of two major sources of uncertainty in Uganda: volatility in money-demand velocity and supply shocks, most notably large food-price movements that depend heavily on weather conditions. He uses a small structural model of Uganda to compare an alternative to the current procedure of setting base money as an operating target. Atingi-Ego shows that setting an operating target for interest rates instead would reduce output uncertainty in the face of velocity instability. It is interesting that this finding on velocity shocks, similar to that hypothesised by Poole in 1971 and supported by experience in many industrialised countries, applies to Uganda. But the optimal choice of operating target in the face of extremely volatile food-price movements is less clear-cut. Both types of shock can occur continually; Atingi-Ego therefore suggests that the Bank of Uganda's policy reaction should be based upon identifying the source of every inflation movement on a case-by-case basis, irrespective of the domestic monetary target in place.

Several countries' monetary policies are complicated by widespread dollarisation. Zenon Quispe discusses the case of Peru, where, despite several years of low and stable inflation, about 70% of deposits are still held in US dollars. As dollars are not used for transactions, there is some leeway for the Bank of Peru to implement monetary policy to affect inflation. As evidence, Quispe estimates Vector Auto Regressions (VARs) to show that reserve money shocks are indeed responsible for inflation, with these policy shocks being identified across several different identification schemes. And as long as solés and dollars are imperfect substitutes, sterilised foreign-exchange intervention can allow the Bank of Peru to reduce short-term exchange-rate volatility. Quispe stresses that because of a sizable external debt, this degree of control is enjoyed by the central bank only because fiscal policy is constrained and co-ordinated with monetary policy.

Marion Kohler's paper discusses the circumstances under which unbalanced sectoral productivity growth acts as a constraint on monetary policy. Because of the Harrod-Balassa-Samuelson effect, if the nominal exchange rate is fixed, faster productivity growth in tradables than non-tradables implies relatively high inflation. Kohler tests for the presence of this effect across a panel of 28 countries from 1960 to 1997. Her estimates uncover a link between relative productivity growth and relative prices, but its size varies country by country, with the extent of nominal wage flexibility in different sectors, for example. Furthermore, Kohler finds that there are countries where non-tradable productivity outpaces tradable productivity. In such cases, if the exchange rate were held constant, this would impart deflationary pressure on overall prices. Sectoral productivity growth differences would have to be quantified on a country-by-country basis if they are to be used to justify a persistent inflation differential.

In sum, some flexibility is needed in an uncertain world. The key tasks in judging an appropriate discretionary response are to identify shocks as they happen and then to estimate how they feed through to inflation. These papers use a variety of methodologies (structural models, structural VARS, cross-country panel estimates) to identify shocks. Parallel processes take place in the monetary policy decision-making in central banks. For example, the Swedish Riksbank is required to declare in public why it *expects* to miss its inflation target; the Riksbank may therefore need to identify the shock before it is fully observable. The authorities must decide whether a capital inflow is due to rising productivity (and is thus non-inflationary) or whether it calls for a monetary policy reaction.

As global inflation has receded, supply-side shocks may become increasingly important relative to monetary shocks in a number of economies, leading to further complications in policy implementation. Available data are silent on the sources of long-run productivity–technical progress, long-run employment, and long-run capital stock. Data on real variables (GDP, employment) arrive with a substantial lag and with error in many countries. In contrast, a monetary expansion is easier to identify and explain (with a burgeoning budget deficit, for example).

Even when the first-round effects of supply shocks are observable, their second-round effects may need to be evaluated. Prominent examples of supply-side shocks discussed in this book include movements in administered prices in Slovenia (Uros Cufer, Mahadeva, and Sterne), food prices in Uganda (Atingi-Ego) and administered and import prices in the Czech Republic (Hrnčíř and Šmídková, Mahadeva and Šmídková). Evaluating the second-round effects, and deciding on the optimal policy reaction, are problematic tasks.

This leads to another difficulty. If incorrect identification leads to a mistaken policy response, aggregate output and employment will be affected, with some consequences for inflation. Furthermore, most supply-side shocks have uneven sectoral impact. If price and wage stickiness are not uniform across sectors, as Kohler emphasises, different sectors may flash different signals for policy.

Finally, what if an unexpected supply shock brings a disinflating country closer to its long-run inflation target? Bufman and Leiderman highlight the difficult choice of whether to profit from the opportunistic disinflation or defend a short-run inflation target.

While much of the evidence in the papers in this book suggest that rigid adherence to domestic policy targets may not be *necessary* to anchor inflation expectations, Masahiro Higo's paper 'What can inflation expectations and core inflation tell us about monetary policy in Japan?' presents complementary evidence that successful stabilisation of current measured inflation rates in Japan has not been *sufficient* to stabilise inflation expectations. Higo employs three distinct techniques to measure inflation expectations in Japan, and uses his results to argue that the limited extent to which policy has controlled inflation expectations may have contributed to relatively high volatility in Japanese real growth rates and asset prices.

Higo assesses the possibility of adopting inflation targeting in Japan, and argues that while inflation targeting might help to stabilise inflation expectations, it is unlikely to provide a panacea for Japan's economic challenges. A key question posed by Higo is similar to that posed by Batini and Haldane (1999) for the United Kingdom and by Mahadeva and Šmídková for the Czech Republic: To what extent would forward-looking inflation targets help to smooth output volatility? The answer depends in part on the links among policy, inflation expectations, asset prices, and real output. Although Higo does not claim to provide a comprehensive analysis of each of these links, his perspective provides fresh insights into an economy that has experienced prolonged recession in recent years.

Evolution of domestic nominal targets into flexible tools

Any monetary policy aspires both to anchor long-term inflation expectations and to react efficiently and effectively to economic shocks. The FJMRS survey suggests that policy-makers across a very broad range of countries have striven to achieve these goals by affording central banks greater instrument independence, while central banks themselves have sought to widen support for low inflation through greater openness and accountability.

The momentum for transparency and openness in monetary policy is obvious to all, but where it began is disputed. Certainly the inflation-targeting countries, starting with New Zealand, provided impetus with numerous framework innovations in transparency and accountability that have now been adapted in many other countries around the world (see Haldane (1995); and Bernanke, Laubach, Mishkin, and Posen (1999).

Yet, as Adam Posen points out, there are strong arguments for citing the Bundesbank as an earlier pioneer of central bank transparency. He attributes one of the most enduring stories of successful macroeconomic management, the Bundesbank's performance in the 41 years between its founding and European monetary unification, partly to the transparency and flexibility of the German monetary framework, and not just to the more commonly cited factors of formal independence from political control, a legal mandate committing it to price stability as the ultimate policy goal, and monetary targets. Independence, after all, cannot be sustained in the long run without political support.

Posen provides a thorough assessment of the Bundesbank's use of monetary targets to signal its intent and explain its policies to the market and the public. Such actions include annual money-target announcements, setting and publicising a medium-term inflation goal (of 2%), and providing the information about its policies and economic outcomes necessary for assessing its performance.

In Posen's words, 'When it comes to being flexible in a disciplined manner, communication is necessary, and when it comes to communication, more is more.' In absorbing Posen's carefully dissected lessons from the Bundesbank's history, it is striking that many of the Bundesbank's actions and statements in recent decades were remarkably similar in spirit to those now adopted by inflation-targeting countries, be they industrialised, developing or transitional economies. Examples include the announcement of clear medium-term inflation goals, publication of forward-looking analysis, discussion of risks to forecasts, and openness in its expression of concern when the central bank feel its forecast is particularly uncertain. These elements of transparency were all evident in the Bundesbank's reaction to German Monetary Union, a shock that created great uncertainty. And through its explanations and its track record the Bundesbank managed with great success to keep expectations anchored.

These lessons Posen draws from the Bundesbank are corroborated on a global basis by the results from FJMRS. A particularly striking trend identified by their survey is the rapid growth in the use of explicit targets to guide policy during the 1990s. In 1998, 95% of the central banks in the survey were using some explicit target or monitoring range, compared to only 57% in 1990. Yet their statistical analysis of inflation- and money-target misses during this period confirms the view that, overall, targets were implemented flexibly.

The optimal monetary policy response will always depend upon the source of the shock that leads to a deviation from target, as well as the size of target deviation. Thus central banks do not generally use their money or inflation targets as rigid rules. Yet without such rules, how can policy-makers achieve credibility sufficient to anchor expectations when shocks knock inflation or money off track? Goodhart discusses a variety of ways in which the Bank of England's Monetary Policy Committee (MPC) aims to achieve this goal in the United Kingdom. He closes by answering a question that many in central banking, as in other walks of life, often evade. 'Should we fail to remain close to target?' When the MPC miss the target by more than 1%, the Governor, as Chairman of the MPC, is required to write an open letter to the Chancellor. But Goodhart stresses that the letter will not necessarily be a sign of failure; the explanations and prescriptions will depend upon the nature of the shock. When indirect taxes were raised, the letter would say, 'Chancellor, you did it yourself'. When supply shocks explain the deviation, the letter could argue that restoring inflation to target quickly could have entailed excessive output costs.

The contracting approach to monetary policy is not the only route to price stability. Nor is it universally applicable. As Goodhart notes, two of the world's most successful central banks, the Bundesbank and the Federal Reserve, have arrived there by other means. And contracting becomes more complicated during times of disinflation: the direction for policy will not necessarily be clear, for example, when inflation falls below the short-term target but remains above the long-term target.

In many countries, therefore, formal contracts may have to give way to other methods of ensuring that government and the central bank work in harmony. This institutional aspect of monetary framework design is important in many countries because the central bank is constrained in its capacity to deliver price stability with its monetary policy instruments alone. Until problems such as inflationary finance for fiscal deficits, banking sector instability, and poor financial sector development are resolved together, the central bank's ability to set interest rates to stabilise inflation may be seriously limited.

The challenge was expressed at the Governors' Symposium by Dr Matthew Chikaonda, Governor of the Reserve Bank of Malawi who argued, '[W]hat we need to do is to cross over to the other side of the harbour, the fiscal side, and bring those guys on board.' FJMRS link the rapid expansion of the use of explicit targets to a growing desire for transparency and accountability coupled with a desire to co-ordinate macroeconomic management with government. Inflation targets may be useful in that regard. In around 70% of frameworks with inflation targets, government has some role in setting the target, which implies it also has some responsibility for co-operating with the central bank if the target is to be met.

The increasingly widespread use of explicit targets for domestic variables as a key element of monetary strategy makes available a wealth of detail about how the use of such targets can be adapted to meet particular economic, institutional, and historical circumstances. Samuel Alfaro and Moisés Schwartz identify several ways in which inflation targeting has been adapted to Mexican conditions. The move towards the adoption of explicit inflation targets in Mexico has implied defining objectives more narrowly. But in Mexico as elsewhere, objectives are not as narrow as a single inflation number; policy may sometimes have to react to the impact of volatile capital flows on interest rates and the exchange rate, even when that means accommodating higher inflation. This, together with the unpredictable behaviour and effects of administered prices, means that targets have occasionally been overshot.

The new Mexican framework has evolved from an earlier regime of quantitative intermediate money targets. Yet money forecasts still have a role to play. A key element of transparency in the monetary framework is the publication each year of a forecast of the daily path of the monetary base, consistent with the inflation objective. The forecast provides information that the central bank and markets can use as a high-frequency benchmark. To varying degrees, both the inflation targets and the money forecasts may be thought of as benchmarks rather than rigid pre-commitments.

The paper also provokes the question of what a 'fully fledged inflation-targeting framework' is. The authors suggest that the Banco de Mexico has yet to operate such a procedure in full, since there remain a variety of factors affecting inflation that are outside the control of monetary policy. Yet in spite of more widespread shocks than are common in industrialised countries targeting inflation, the Mexican framework has delivered a relatively smooth path for disinflation and a means for communication among various players in the economy.

Target specification and implementation

Several papers in this volume emphasise that understanding the reason for missing a target may be more important than the precise magnitude of the miss. Seamus Hogan's paper 'Core Inflation as an Indicator in Monetary Policy Rules' focuses on the potential inclusion of such indicators by the Bank of Canada in Taylor-type rules. He defines two measures of core inflation. The first removes temporary price-level shocks; the second removes all influences on the inflation rate not due to expectations or an output gap. Empirical work using the measures of core inflation employed by the Bank of Canada suggests that those measures do provide a better indicator of future inflation pressures than the quarterly headline inflation rate over a two-year horizon, but that the improvement is modest.

Several countries have tried to increase the flexibility with which they use policy targets by excluding specific items or groups of items from the targeted price index. Uros Cufer of the Bank of Slovenia, along with Mahadeva and Sterne, assess the circumstances under which certain items should be excluded from a targeted price index. They argue that policy-makers try to achieve the best trade-off between the clarity and comprehensiveness of the consumer price index. Excluding a price from the overall index can add to clarity of the index if the exclusion provides a more accurate indication of the present and future monetary policy stance. But the exclusion is costly: as the index becomes narrower it becomes less representative of the costs of living. The authors suggest a variety of econometric tests that might be used in general to evaluate these costs and benefits.

David Mayes and Matti Virén's paper is a comprehensive assessment of the potential advantages and pitfalls in using a Monetary Conditions Index (MCI) as a supplementary transparency device to aid in monetary policy explanation. They provide a thorough theoretical, econometric, and practitioners' examination of MCIs. For economies being buffeted by large shocks arising in international financial markets, an index that sums the exchange-rate and interest-rate contributions to inflation may be a practicable way of continuing to inform the markets of the central bank's thinking about the policy stance. Other advantages are that the MCI can be easier to calculate than a full model-based forecast, since it summarises the pressure on the economy from monetary sources in a single number, and it can be updated continuously. But they point out that there are also potential disadvantages to the device as one must have a view of the source of the shocks hitting the economy to understand the MCI's implications on any particular occasion.

Mayes and Virén's paper contains a mine of information on MCIs. They provide a context of how MCIs might be used to inform policy in small open economies by assessing the experiences in Canada, Finland, New Zealand, Norway and Sweden. And they also illustrate the extent to which the difficulties of estimation can be addressed by conducting new estimates for 12 EU countries over the period 1972 to 1997.

Experience of three inflation targeters in reducing inflation

The FJMRS report argues that the increased use of explicit targets is part of a move toward greater transparency in monetary policy. Yet there may be good reasons why targets cannot on their own fully describe the direction of monetary policy. For example, in the early years of inflation targeting, it was questioned whether the framework would be suitable for disinflating countries where the target may have to be revised periodically. This volume's studies of the inflation-targeting countries of Chile, the Czech Republic, and Israel provide some intriguing answers to this pressing question.

One common feature of these three countries is that (formal or informal) co-ordinated wage-setting prevails in the public sector. In each case, this would suggest a need for a publicly announced inflation target to anchor expectations during disinflation. But these economies are also small and open: the exchange rate is in all cases a potentially important source of shocks as well as the main transmitter of monetary policy. Given these conditions, Bufman and Leiderman explain that in Israel, inflation targeting can best be seen as a process that has evolved from an earlier disinflationary phase when inflation and the exchange rate were both targeted to provide a stronger overall nominal anchor. As the domestic anchors became more effective in Israel and Chile, conflicts over the exchange-rate bands have been resolved increasingly through inflation objectives taking precedence. This strategy of treating the exchange rate as a flexible target has minimised the possibility of providing markets with one-way exchange-rate bets. Chile successfully evolved its dual-target approach, with the exchange-rate band gradually losing weight in policy until the adoption of free float in 1999.

In Chile, the Czech Republic, and Israel, the unpredictable nature of the shocks that led to lower inflation has given rise to the question of whether targets should be revised occasionally to accommodate opportunistic disinflation. Bufman and Leiderman stress the need to preserve the integrity of the new target along this disinflation path through co-ordination with the fiscal authority and wage bargainers.

Miroslav Hrnčíř and Šmídková argue that in spite of the many macro-economic instabilities associated with it that would have bedevilled any policy framework, the inflation-targeting regime has furthered Czech monetary policy because of the institutional changes it has wrought. For example, they document how the new regime was used to promote transparency and explanation. They suggest that the Czech inflation target provided an institutional anchor as well as a nominal anchor, another step forward in a transitional economy in which other aspects of the reform strategy are revised frequently. The decisions of other players in the macroeconomy can be co-ordinated around the only publicly announced target.

Conclusion

The rich diversity of experiences assessed in this book provides a wide perspective on the evolution of monetary frameworks over the past 30 years. During that time there has emerged an increasingly strong public constituency for low inflation. The legal objectives of central banks have become increasingly focused on price stability, backed up by an ever-widening use of numerically specified inflation objectives. And policy-makers have sought to anchor long-term inflation expectations by granting many central banks a greater degree of independence.

The diversity in frameworks reflects the desire among policy-makers to react flexibly to a wide variety of shocks, while not undermining the anchor for long-term inflation expectations. To this end, the trend in the 1990s has been for greater communication within central banks, between central banks and governments, and between policy-makers and the private sector. A motto for central bankers suggested by Mervyn King (page 184 in this volume) is 'do as you say and say as you do'. Nowadays, the vast majority of central banks base their communication around some explicitly defined objective, an inflation target being the most popular type in the late 1990s.

Macroeconomic policy-makers have evolved their frameworks by fusing successful strategies from different types of frameworks. A pioneer of the strategy to anchor expectations though targets and communication was the Bundesbank, and more recently other inflation-targeting countries have taken on the mantle. Similarly, the US Federal Reserve was a pioneer of forward-looking policy, yet forecasts have become increasingly important in inflation-targeting countries and elsewhere. And inflation targets themselves are now used far more widely than in the small group of industrialised economies that first made them the centrepiece of their monetary frameworks: of the 93 central banks in the FJMRS study that existed in 1998, well over half used inflation targets. Indeed, as Arminio Neto, Governor of the Banco Central do Brasil (page 202 in this volume) argues, 'it is very hard not to move toward inflation targeting once you have chosen to float'. And while much literature exists that attempts to identify the circumstances under which policy-makers should choose either inflation or money targets, a final striking example of framework fusion is that one of the most popular target combinations is to declare numerical targets for both money and inflation. The papers in this book suggest this may be a natural move for many central banks in countries that have chosen not to target the exchange rate. Central banks, after all, have relatively abundant access to data and analytical techniques with which to analyse the monetary sector, but it is generally inflation that is the most visible vehicle available for guiding private-sector expectations and communication with government.

As the medium-term incentives to deliver price stability become better established, it becomes easier to respond flexibly to short-run shocks without undermining credibility. An early reservation about inflation targeting was that relatively benign conditions in the industrialised economies up to the mid-1990s meant that the framework remained fairly untested by severe recessions and supply shocks. But the experiences described in this volume of New Zealand, Chile, the Czech Republic, and Israel, along with those of many other developing and transitional economies using inflation targets, show that the targets' value in providing a medium-term focal point on which macroeconomic policy-makers can co-ordinate and commit has not been severely undermined even in the face of adverse shocks.

The possibility that explicit targets can be implemented flexibly undermines the view that strict prerequisites need to be in place before targets are adopted. Countries with unstable velocity have found intermediate money targets to be useful, just as countries with supply shocks and no detailed macroeconometric model have found inflation targets to be useful. FJMRS argue that 'it is better to have narrow objectives and be obliged to explain misses rather than having imprecise objectives that make success or failure difficult to measure'. Adoption of explicit domestic targets, then, provides momentum for a heightened role for explanation in monetary strategy and an important role for the now-thriving cottage industry of research that assesses optimal target specification, policy rules, and monetary conditions, examples of which are contained in this book. Whichever target is adopted, it is highly unlikely that the optimal strategy will always be to maintain policy exactly on target. And a target miss coupled with a convincing explanation for the miss is unlikely to significantly undermine credibility.

Thus, while the labels of inflation targeting, money targeting, and exchange-rate targeting are a convenient means by which to distinguish broad differences among framework types, the evidence presented in this book suggests that in a global context frameworks are better thought of in terms of a wide array of underlying characteristics. It is, after all, the use of flexible strategies that has contributed to inflation's historically low levels at the end of the 1990s. As Adam Posen concludes in his paper, 'the central bank must encourage the public discussion of monetary policy to take the form of a substantive interchange rather than just a numerical assessment'. This holds true in all countries striving for domestic nominal anchors, no matter what is the structure of the economy that their central banks have inherited from their history.

Bibliography

Backus, D. and Driffill, J. (1985a), 'Inflation and reputation', *American Economic Review*, vol. 75, pp. 530–38.

Backus, D. and Driffill, J. (1985b), 'Rational expectations and policy credibility following a change in regime', *Review of Economic Studies*, vol. 52, pp. 211–21.

Barro, R.J. (1986), 'Reputation in a model of monetary policy with incomplete information', *Journal of Monetary Economics*, vol. 17, pp. 3–20.

Barro, R. (1986), 'Rules versus discretion', in *Alternative Monetary Regimes*, Campbell, C.D. and Dougan, W.R., Baltimore, (eds) Johns Hopkins University Press.

Barro, R.J. and Gordon, D.B. (1983a), 'A positive theory of Monetary Policy in a natural rate model', *Journal of Political Economy*, vol. 91, pp. 589–610.

Barro, R.J. and Gordon, D.B. (1983b), 'Rules, discretion and reputation in a model of monetary policy', *Journal of Monetary Economics*, vol. 12, pp. 101–21.

Batini, N. and Haldane, A. (1999), 'Forward looking rules for monetary policy', *Bank of England Working Paper, No 91*, January.

Bernanke, B., Laubach, T., Mishkin, F. and Posen, A. (1999), *Inflation Targeting: Lessons from the International Experience*, Princeton, New Jersey: Princeton University Press.

Blinder, A. (1998), *Central Banking in Theory and in Practice*, Cambridge, Massachusetts: MIT Press.

Haldane, A.G., (ed.) (1995), *Targeting Inflation*, London: Bank of England.

Kydland, F.E. and Prescott, E.C. (1977), 'Rules rather than discretion: the inconsistency of optimal plans', *Journal of Political Economy*, vol. 85, No 3, June 1977, pp. 473–91.

Rogoff, K. (1985), 'The optimal degree of commitment to an intermediate monetary target', *Quarterly Journal of Economics*, vol. 100(4), November, pp. 1169–90.

Vickers J.S. (1986), 'Signalling in a model of monetary policy with incomplete information', *Oxford Economic Papers*, 38, pp. 443–55, and in *Prices, Quantities and Expectations*, Sinclair, P.J.N. (ed.) (1987), Oxford: Oxford University Press, pp. 471–84.

Waller, C.J. and Walsh C.E. (1996), 'Central bank independence, economic behaviour and optimal term lengths', *American Economic Review*, vol. 86, pp. 1139–53.

Walsh, C. (1995), 'Optimal contracts for central bankers', *American Economic Review*, vol. 85, pp. 150–67.

Part I

Key issues in the choice of monetary policy framework

Maxwell Fry, DeAnne Julius,
Lavan Mahadeva, Sandra Roger and
Gabriel Sterne*

*Originally Prepared for the Central Bank Governors' Symposium at the Bank of England, 4 June 1999. DeAnne Julius is a member of the Bank of England's Monetary Policy Committee. Maxwell Fry, Lavan Mahadeva, Sandra Roger and Gabriel Sterne all worked at the Centre of Central Banking Studies at the Bank of England at the time the Report was written. Parts of the Report reflect personal opinions and hence we provide the names of the leading authors for each Chapter. Chapter 1: Maxwell Fry; Chapters 2 to 6: Gabriel Sterne; Chapter 7: DeAnne Julius. Lavan Mahadeva provided analytical and written input throughout the report. Sandra Roger was responsible for collating and analysing the questionnaire responses.

1 Introduction

1.1 Overview

A monetary policy framework comprises 'the institutional arrangements under which monetary policy decisions are made and executed' (McNees, 1987, p. 3). Necessarily, therefore, analysis of any monetary policy framework extends considerably beyond the confines of the central bank. Indeed, only in a few countries is much of the monetary policy framework decided by the central bank itself. Monetary policy frameworks are normally politically determined, and may well depend, for example, on the country's financial institutions, and the degree of expertise in monetary policy matters that exists both inside and outside the central bank, as well as other institutional economic features.

This chapter focuses on several aspects of the monetary policy frameworks used by central banks and governments in their attempts to achieve their various goals, among which price stability is becoming increasingly popular. Chart 1.1 gives us a flavour of what our 94 surveyed central banks said their objectives were, apart from price stability.

One should note, however, that the stated immediate objectives of monetary policy in a number of developing countries still include rapid economic growth, as well as the sectoral allocation of credit, full employment, etc. (Fry, 1995, 1997; Fry, Goodhart and Almeida, 1996). Another trend worth noting is the increasing popularity of explicit, i.e. publicly announced, targets, be they for the exchange rate, money, or inflation, in all types of economies. One of the reasons for using explicit targets is the role they can play in securing credible monetary policy. In this report we analyse the empirical links among targets and central bank independence, accountability, and the transparency of monetary policy in differing economic circumstances.

Much of the analysis presented in this report is based on data collected through a questionnaire completed by 94 central banks in a remarkably diverse group of economies, listed in Table 1.1. We are extremely grateful to our fellow central bankers for providing this information. These data enable analysis of how monetary policy frameworks as well as monetary

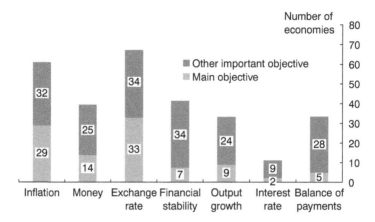

Answers to question: 'Please rank objectives (other than price stability) that the central bank pursues'
Source: Bank of England Survey of monetary frameworks.

Chart 1.1 Monetary policy objectives other than price stability

policy actions and outcomes are determined by an array of different economy characteristics.

By comparing experiences in a broad range of economies, we show how the detailed characteristics of a monetary policy framework depend upon:

1   Structural differences, e.g. the structure of the financial sector, types and amounts of debt, openness to trade, commodity dependence, fiscal discipline, etc.
2   Varying degrees of indexation and other nominal rigidities that affect the speed of transmission from monetary policy instruments to inflation.
3   Institutional arrangements and analytical constraints (such as data availability) that influence the way in which monetary policy can respond.

Empirical analyses of these relationships are presented in subsequent chapters of this report.

1.2   Post-war origins

During the 1945 to 1970 period, one could distinguish two distinct types of monetary policy framework. The first was based on the Bretton Woods system. Under these arrangements, a considerable part of the monetary policy framework of members of the International Monetary Fund (IMF) was determined, or at least constrained, by the Fund's Articles of Associ-

Table 1.1 Economies included in the survey

Industrialised		Transitional		Developing			
1.	Australia	1.	Albania	1.	Argentina	31.	Nigeria
2.	Austria	2.	Armenia	2.	Bahamas	32.	Peru
3.	Belgium	3.	Bosnia Herzegovina	3.	Bahrain	33.	Sierra Leone
4.	Canada	4.	Bulgaria	4.	Bangladesh	34.	Sri Lanka
5.	Denmark	5.	Croatia	5.	Barbados	35.	South Africa
6.	Finland	6.	Czech Republic	6.	Belize	36.	Tanzania
7.	France	7.	Estonia	7.	Botswana	37.	Thailand
8.	Germany	8.	Georgia	8.	Chile	38.	Tonga
9.	Greece	9.	Hungary	9.	China	39.	Turkey
10.	Hong Kong	10.	Kazakhstan	10.	Cyprus	40.	Uganda
11.	Iceland	11.	Kyrgyz	11.	Eastern Caribbean	41.	Uruguay
12.	Ireland	12.	Latvia	12.	Ecuador	42.	Vietnam
13.	Israel	13.	Lithuania	13.	Egypt	43.	West African MU
14.	Italy	14.	Macedonia	14.	Fiji	44.	Zambia
15.	Japan	15.	Moldova	15.	Ghana		
16.	Korea	16.	Poland	16.	Guyana		
17.	Netherlands	17.	Russia	17.	India		
18.	New Zealand	18.	Romania	18.	Indonesia		
19.	Norway	19.	Slovakia	19.	Jamaica		
20.	Portugal	20.	Slovenia	20.	Jordan		
21.	Singapore	21.	Turkmenistan	21.	Kenya		
22.	Spain	22.	Ukraine	22.	Kuwait		
23.	Sweden			23.	Lebanon		
24.	Switzerland			24.	Malta		
25.	Taiwan			25.	Malaysia		
26.	United Kingdom			26.	Mauritius		
27.	United States			27.	Mexico		
28.	Euro Area			28.	Mongolia		
	(European			29.	Mozambique		
	Central Bank)			30.	Namibia		

ation. Members were expected to maintain fixed exchange rates to the US dollar and, after the resumption of general convertibility to permit all foreign-exchange dealings for current-account transactions under Article 8 of the Articles of Association. In countries where there were no exchange controls, or existing controls failed to insulate the economy from the rest of the world, there was in practice at most limited scope for an independent national monetary policy. In this period most countries imposed exchange controls on capital movements but in many cases they did not provide lasting insulation from external influences on monetary policy.

In the second typical monetary policy framework, fiscal exigencies dominated monetary policy (see Box 6A in Chapter 6). Many developing countries opted out of Article 8, maintaining exchange controls to insulate their economies from world prices. They could then extract more revenue from their financial systems through financial repression and the inflation tax

(Fry, 1997, 1998). Consequently, these countries experienced high inflation and currency depreciation. In such countries, the monetary policy framework was designed in practice to raise government revenue from the inflation tax. Higher government deficits led to higher inflation, as the government turned to its central bank as its revenue source.

For at least a decade after the collapse of the Bretton Woods system in the early 1970s, monetary policy frameworks changed surprisingly infrequently. While some countries adopted floating exchange rates, smaller countries as well as several European economies continued with pegged exchange rate systems. Even the floaters made few formal changes to their monetary policy frameworks. This may well have been due to the general view that monetary policy was not very effective. Furthermore, only 25 years ago, Karel Holbik (1973, p. xxv) could write of monetary policy in 12 OECD countries (including Germany): 'There is hardly a central bank in existence which does not conform to, co-operate with, and support national economic, social and other objectives. All central banks are sensitive to governmental authority.'

All this has changed dramatically over the past two decades. Much more attention has been devoted to devising appropriate monetary policy frameworks essentially to secure price stability in industrial, developing, and transitional countries. This follows the increasingly widespread acceptance of the view that price stability fosters improved economic performance.

So price stability has been adopted by more countries as the sole, or at least primary, objective of monetary policy since the early 1980s, a trend that has accelerated during the 1990s. Specifically, the early 1990s witnessed a rapid rise in the number of industrialised countries that adopted explicit inflation targets pursued by relatively independent central banks. Somewhat ironically, however, explicit inflation targets are now becoming popular in developing and transitional economies just when industrialised economies in Europe have moved towards monetary union, the ultimate form of fixed exchange rate target.

1.3   What monetary policy can and cannot do

To devise a logical framework for the conduct of monetary policy, it is first essential to know what monetary policy can and cannot do. In most industrial countries, by far the most important instrument of monetary policy is a short-term interest rate set by the central bank to influence financial conditions that, in turn, affect aggregate demand. In some other countries, particularly where financial markets are not well developed, the central bank exerts its influence through reserve requirements applied to commercial banks and administrative controls over commercial bank interest rates and the allocation of credit.

Chart 1.2, drawn from the answers in the survey, shows how most mone-

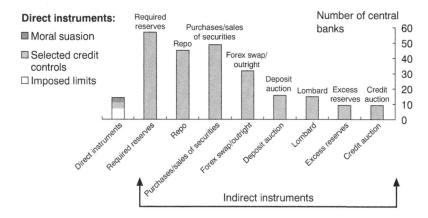

Source: Bank of England Survey of monetary frameworks.

Chart 1.2 Operating instruments of monetary policy

tary policy is now implemented using indirect operating instruments of monetary policy. Of the sample of 94 economies, 61% use required reserves, 48% use repos to manage or influence short-term interest rates and 52% operate through buying or selling securities. Only 11 countries from our sample of 94 use direct controls on interest rates or credit allocation.

The standard monetary model has the central bank interest rate affecting aggregate demand in the economy: a lower interest rate increases the quantity of reserve money demanded as banks find profitable uses for the extra reserves that boost aggregate demand, while when interest rates are increased, banks find the cost of funds now exceeding potential returns, and the demand for reserve money decreases.

Alan Blinder (1998) stresses that a logical monetary policy must start with an objective function and at least one macroeconomic model showing how at least one monetary policy instrument affects the economy. Blinder (1998, Ch. 1) shows convincingly that effective monetary policy must be based on at least one macroeconomic model and the underlying concept of dynamic programming – 'think ahead in order to make today's decision' (Blinder, 1998, p. 14). In other words, the policy-maker should work out a path from the present to the desired future situation.

The dynamic programming approach can help to avoid overshooting which might otherwise result from time lags in economic reactions. The alternative static approach, 'looking out the window' in Blinder's terminology (p. 16), of tightening monetary policy if the current inflation rate is too high and loosening policy if it is too low, is bound to result in monetary policy being kept tight or loose for too long. Blinder concludes that 'the dynamic programming way of thinking is not sufficiently ingrained into the habits of monetary policy makers, who too often just "look out the window" and base policy judgements on present circumstances. I believe this is a fundamental mistake and is one reason why central banks often overstay their policy stance' (Blinder, 1998, p. 23).

Blinder illustrates the dynamic-programming strategy with the 'pre-emptive strike' adopted by the US Federal Reserve (Fed) in early 1994 in which monetary policy was tightened before inflation rose. Blinder points out that one practical difficulty is the central bank will appear to be implementing unnecessarily restrictive monetary policy. If successful, the pre-emptive strike ensures that inflation does not increase (so critics will complain that tighter monetary policy was unnecessary!) And, of course, perfect pre-emptive monetary policy implies that no observable relationships will be observed between monetary policy actions and macro-economic variables. For example, if monetary policy successfully maintains inflation at exactly $2\frac{1}{2}\%$, it would be impossible to detect the effect of any policy instruments on inflation – the dependent variable is a constant.

As Charles Goodhart (1994, pp. 1424–25) stresses, monetary policy cannot control in any mechanistic way the quantity of reserve money through control over an interest rate. There are just too many shocks to the demand for reserve money to enable such control within any reasonable range of interest rates. So the central bank is always obliged to adjust the supply of reserve money to demand at some acceptable interest rate, i.e. to offer an elastic supply of reserve money. Nevertheless, influence over the quantity of reserve money through short-term interest-rate control should be achievable over time, if not immediately, in virtually all market-based banking systems.

Debate still continues over the appropriate objectives of monetary policy, in large part because of disagreement over what monetary policy can and cannot achieve. On the one hand, some advocate that monetary policy can and should be targeted at employment and economic growth in addition to price stability.[1] The alternative view is that monetary policy should be directed solely at price stability.

The apparent conflict between these two views is resolved if it can be established that monetary policy is conducive to high employment and growth only if it maintains stable prices. In such a case, price stability is a necessary condition for sustained economic growth and there is no conflict between the two objectives: they always imply the same policy.

The debate has a long history. It suffices to say here that it has a major influence on choices of monetary policy framework. At present, the pendulum has swung in favour of the second view: an increasing number of recent central bank laws establish price stability as the predominant, if not the exclusive, monetary policy objective. This, however, reflects a growing belief that there is in fact no conflict between price stability and sustain-

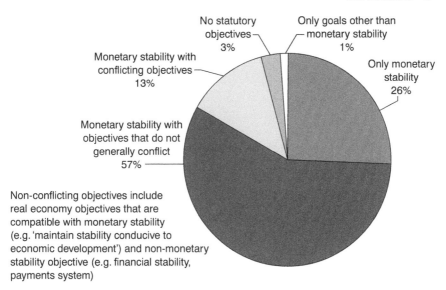

No statutory objectives
3%

Only goals other than monetary stability
1%

Monetary stability with conflicting objectives
13%

Only monetary stability
26%

Monetary stability with objectives that do not generally conflict
57%

Non-conflicting objectives include real economy objectives that are compatible with monetary stability (e.g. 'maintain stability conducive to economic development') and non-monetary stability objective (e.g. financial stability, payments system)

Source: Bank of England Survey of monetary frameworks.

Chart 1.3 Categories of Statutory Objectives

able economic growth, and that inflation is likely to be harmful to long-term growth prospects. Chart 1.3 demonstrates that price and currency stability (monetary stability) is primary among the statutory objectives of most central banks. In fact, debate over the objectives of monetary policy has to a large extent been replaced by debate over how to maximise economic growth.

Views on what monetary policy can do have changed radically during the twentieth century. While Irving Fischer's (1922) quantity theory suggested that monetary policy's primary effect was on changes in the price level through changes in the quantity of money, Keynesians as represented in the UK Radcliffe Report (1959) found a far less clear-cut role for the quantity of money in the macroeconomy. Also, those who advocated economic planning techniques saw no independent role for monetary policy. Milton Friedman and the other monetarists, who stressed the importance of the causal relationship running from money growth and inflation, challenged the Keynesian view, as well as the rationale for economic planning. Two landmarks in this literature were Bill Phillips' (1958) empirical work on the relationship between the rate of change in wages and the unemployment rate in the United Kingdom and the subsequent article by Paul Samuelson and Robert Solow (1960) on the cost of reducing inflation in terms of lower economic growth.

In 1958, Bill Phillips demonstrated the existence of a stable relationship

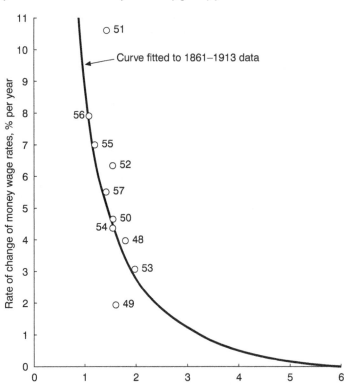

Figure 1.1 Original Phillips curve

between unemployment and the rate of change in wages in the United Kingdom over the past century, shown in Figure 1.1 (Phillips, 1958, p. 288). He used this relationship to estimate the maximum level of aggregate demand and hence minimum level of unemployment consistent with price stability. He perceived that some combinations of lower unemployment rates and concomitant positive inflation rates fell inside a 'no-go zone' for macroeconomic policy and should therefore be avoided.

Within four years of its invention, Paul Samuelson and Robert Solow (1960) had inverted Phillips' analysis to suggest that a range of 3%–4% inflation was the necessary price of bringing unemployment down to 3% in the United States. Samuelson and Solow represented the Phillips curve as a relationship between price inflation and unemployment rather than between wage inflation and unemployment. This transformation was consistent with Phillips' own claim that low productivity growth in the United Kingdom permitted nominal wages to rise by only 2% for price stability to be maintained. In other words, it was reasonably safe to assume productiv-

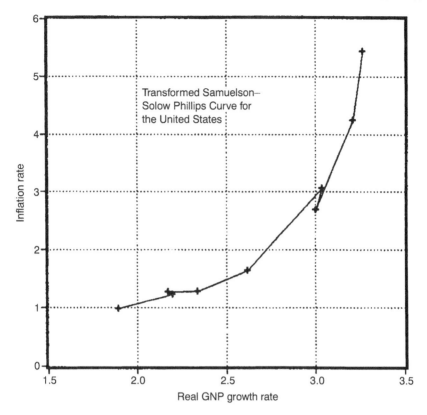

Figure 1.2 Transformed Samuelson–Solow Phillips curve for the United States

ity growth of 2%. So the *y*-axis of the United Kingdom Phillips diagram was recalibrated at a price inflation rate two percentage points lower than the corresponding rate of wage inflation.

Combining assumptions of constant productivity growth and constant labour force growth enabled Arthur Okun (1962) to derive a monotonic relationship between growth and unemployment. In this way, the downward-sloping Phillips curve is transformed into an upward-sloping relationship between inflation and growth: higher growth can be achieved at a cost of higher inflation. Figure 1.2 illustrates this transformed Phillips curve for the United States between 1961 and 1969, starting with 1% inflation and less than 2% growth in 1961. For virtually all developing countries, Phillips curves can be represented only in this form, because there are no unemployment data.

In the 1960s, the economics profession in general accepted the proposition that a stable trade-off existed between inflation and growth: higher growth could be achieved at the cost of higher inflation. But, as anticipated by Phillips himself (Phillips, 1958), no sooner had policy-makers started to exploit the Phillips curve relationship than it disappeared. The generally accepted explanation is the expectations-augmented Phillips curves expounded by Milton Friedman (1968) and Edmund Phelps (1967). David Hume provided one of the clearest expositions of this relationship in 1752:

> Accordingly we find, that in every kingdom, into which money begins to flow in greater abundance than formerly, every thing takes a new face; labour and industry gain life; the merchant becomes more enterprizing; the manufacturer more diligent and skillful; and even the farmer follows his plough with greater alacrity and attention.... To account, then, for this phænomenon, we must consider, that tho' the high price of commodities be a necessary consequence of the encrease of gold and silver, yet it follows not immediately upon that encrease; but some time is requir'd before the money circulate thro' the whole state, and make its effects be felt on all ranks of people. At first, no alteration is perceiv'd; by degrees, the price rises, first of one commodity, then of another; till the whole at last reaches a just proportion, with the new quantity of specie, which is in the kingdom. In my opinion, 'tis only in this interval or intermediate situation, betwixt the acquisition of money and rise of prices, that the encreasing quantity of gold and silver is favourable to industry.
>
> (Hume, 1752, pp. 46–47)

So within a decade of its discovery, the Phillips curve had come under theoretical attack. Within two decades, the relationship had indeed disappeared. From an upward-sloping relationship between inflation and growth, the transformed Phillips curve had become vertical. No long-run trade-off between inflation and growth could be detected in the data collected after 1970.

Over the past two decades, the Phillips curve has rotated: simple bivariate regressions, cross-section and pooled time series, now detect negative relationships between inflation and growth for various country groups in both long and short runs. One study finds negative-sloping long-run expectations-augmented Phillips curve relationships between inflation and growth in developing countries (Fry, 1995, Ch. 10).

Far from there being any exploitable trade-off in the medium and longer terms between inflation and higher output levels, the more widely accepted view today is that, in the longer term, this relationship is negative, i.e. more inflation is associated with lower growth (Barro, 1995; De Gregorio, 1994; Fischer, 1994). While the deleterious effects of hyperinflation on growth, with the dislocations caused to saving patterns and to the monetary and pricing mechanisms, are fairly obvious, it appears that inflation has a negative effect on growth even at low or moderate levels.

A wide variety of potential channels for both negative and positive effects running from inflation to growth, and vice versa, exist. In developing countries, fixed non-adjustable nominal interest and exchange rates may have been particularly harmful (Fry, 1995, Ch. 8). As inflation rises, lower real interest rates resulting from fixed nominal rates reduce credit availability and distort resource allocation, while a fixed exchange rate prices exports out of world markets. Both effects are growth-reducing.

Another explanation for the negative relationship between inflation and growth lies in the fact that a higher level of inflation is generally associated with a greater variability of inflation and hence a greater riskiness of longer-term unindexed contracts. As John Locke (1695, p. 189) wrote:

> I see no reason to think, that a little bigger or less size of the pieces coined is of any moment, one way or the other. ... The harm comes by the change, which unreasonably and unjustly gives away and transfers men's properties, disorders trade, puzzles accounts, and needs a new arithmetic to cast up reckonings, and keep accounts in; besides a thousand other inconveniences.

The negative relationship between growth and inflation detected in recent years might also be attributable to the worldwide supply shocks of the 1970s and 1980s: a leftward shift in the supply curve lowers quantity and raises price. But the period 1988–1995 was not characterised by large supply shocks, and demand shocks affect price and quantity in the same direction, and yet the negative relationship appears to be even stronger over this more recent period. In any event, the available evidence from industrial, transitional, and developing economies does not support the belief that monetary policy can accelerate growth or reduce unemployment at the cost of a higher inflation rate. Hence, monetary policy frameworks should clearly not be based on the assumption that there is any such trade-off.

1.4   Who determines the monetary policy framework?

A crucial element of a country's monetary policy framework is how it is determined. Invariably, the basic legal framework is to be found in a country's central banking law. In some cases, the legislation is so outdated or unclear as to have been greatly augmented by convention and precedent. In several recent instances, monetary policy frameworks have been defined in new central bank legislation.

At one end of the spectrum, the framework may retain all policy decisions for the government, as was the case in the United Kingdom prior to 1997. In such a case, the government sets the goals of monetary policy and manages the instruments used to achieve them. Towards the other end of the spectrum the central bank may enjoy substantial, though not unlimited discretion to define the goals of monetary policy, as well as the autonomy to manage the instruments of monetary policy. The US Federal Reserve System provides an example of such independence. An increasingly widespread practice is for the government to be involved in setting the goals, while the central bank manages the instruments to achieve the goals, i.e. the central bank possesses instrument or operational independence but not goal independence.

1.5   Rules versus discretion

An important issue related to who determines the monetary policy framework is whether the central bank is obliged to pursue fixed rules in its conduct of monetary policy or is free to use discretion. Milton Friedman (1960, p. 87) stresses that monetary policy takes effect with long and variable lags: '... there is much evidence that monetary changes have their effect only after a considerable lag and over a long period and that the lag is rather variable'.

Since these lags are also unpredictable, it is impossible to achieve desired results by implementing monetary policy in a discretionary fashion. So, given imperfect knowledge about the way the economy works together with the danger that policy-makers might take inappropriate actions either out of ignorance or to further ends such as re-election that are unlikely to be in the general interest of the public, one can make a case in favour of adopting a monetary policy rule, such as annual growth in the money stock of $x\%$. In this way, pro-cyclical monetary policy would be avoided. While not perfect, a rule may well deliver more stability than discretion will in practice.

The modern debate over rules versus discretion focuses on the time-inconsistency problem (Barro, 1986; Kydland and Prescott, 1977). The concept of time inconsistency can be illustrated in the case of patents. A patent encourages invention, which increases social welfare. Once the invention has taken place, however, social welfare can be increased by reneging on the patent right so that the patented good can be produced competitively. So too with monetary policy there is an incentive to renege on any commitment (the rule) to price stability and to generate unanticipated inflation in order to increase output, albeit only temporarily.

This dilemma also exists in monetary policy conduct. *Unexpected* increases in the price level increase real economic activity temporarily, i.e. an expectations-augmented Phillips curve exists. Economic expansions, even though temporary, provide utility, but inflation is costly. The policy-maker has an incentive to generate unexpected inflation in order to achieve higher growth. However, individuals in the economy are rational and understand the policy-maker's incentives as well as the way the economy works. So people expect that the policy-maker will produce some inflation in order to raise output. In equilibrium, actual inflation is anticipated correctly on average. So to maximise social welfare, the policy-maker creates unanticipated inflation to the point where the marginal cost of inflation equals the marginal benefit of unanticipated inflation (Barro, 1986, pp. 16–19).

Under such circumstances the equilibrium inflation rate is relatively high, as of course is the cost of inflation. In this case, the policy-maker can improve social welfare by making a commitment to deliver low inflation. If such commitment is credible, individuals will anticipate low inflation and the equilibrium will be one of low and stable inflation but with the same amount of surprise inflation on average (zero) as before.

The ability to enforce of the commitment is all-important to ensure credibility. Without credibility of the commitment, individuals would understand the policy-maker's incentive to cheat and the low-inflation equilibrium would not be stable; the welfare-maximising policy-maker would return the economy to the previous high-inflation discretionary equilibrium.

Even with a model that incorporates the desire of policy-makers to create inflation surprises, Persson and Tabellini (1993, p. 77) show that 'the optimal central-bank contract, when feasible, does not entail any loss of welfare nor any sacrifice of stabilization policies ... In general, the design of optimal monetary institutions does not seem to entail any trade-off between credibility and flexibility'.

As an alternative to securing a credible commitment from the policy-maker, various other enforcement devices have been proposed to counter-act the perceived inflationary bias in monetary policy:

   i Free banking that allows commercial banks to compete by issuing their own money. In conjunction with rational expectations and strong legal enforcement of contracts (both explicit and implicit), competition should ensure that the public accepts only commercial bank money that offers a competitive real return on deposits. In this model, there is no central bank and no official monetary policy.
  ii A monetary constitution, 'a regime prescribed by constitutional law and changeable in its main lines only by constitutional amendment' (Yeager, 1992, p. 731). The idea here is that the obstacles to changing the constitution will reinforce adherence to a monetary constitution that presumably incorporates price stability as its main or sole goal.
 iii Ensuring that central bankers benefit, perhaps financially, from maintaining a reputation for establishing and sustaining price stability.
  iv Appointment of conservative central bankers (Rogoff, 1985).
   v Use of principal-agent contracts to make central bankers' remuneration decline as inflation rises (Walsh, 1995). Under this approach, the legislature creates an independent central bank and assigns it, by law, the objective of price stability (Persson and Tabellini, 1993).
  vi Assuming that central bankers are not motivated by financial incentives, use of inflation targeting as constrained discretion. Ben

Bernanke, Thomas Laubach, Frederic Mishkin and Adam Posen (1999, pp. 4–6) argue that inflation targeting is a framework, not a rule:

By imposing a conceptual structure and its inherent discipline on the central bank, but without eliminating all flexibility, inflation targeting combines some of the advantages traditionally ascribed to rules with those ascribed to discretion.

(Bernanke, Laubach, Mishkin and Posen, 1999, p. 6)

Blinder (1998, pp. 36–48) attacks the case for monetary policy rules in various ways. One simple device is to ask the question: If there is an inherent inflationary bias in discretionary monetary policy, why has inflation been reduced in so many countries since 1980? He then demolishes two of the three proposed solutions to this inflationary bias – reputation, principal-agent contracts, and the deliberate appointment of conservative central bankers. While reputation is undoubtedly important in practice, Blinder objects to the on–off way it is introduced in Barro's model. Contracts between the government and the central bank that imposed financial penalties for inflationary bias do not address the fact that most central bank policy-makers would be far better off financially in alternative employment. If financial incentive was not the overriding consideration in accepting the job, why would financial incentive affect behaviour in the job? While more tolerant to Rogoff's suggested solution in the form of appointing conservative central bankers, Blinder (1998, pp. 47–48) points out that there is a danger in appointing central bankers who are too conservative.

Blinder (1998, pp. 50–51) concludes that academic research has assisted practitioners in choosing an appropriate monetary policy instrument (interest rates), but has provided, in the main, misleading answers in the debate revolving around time-inconsistency and rules versus discretion, and has left the issue of defining a neutral monetary policy unresolved.

1.6   Central bank independence

An important objection to central bank independence in democracies is based on the fact that central bankers are not elected to office and are not therefore directly accountable to the electorate for their actions. One solution to this so-called 'democratic deficit' is to ensure that the central bank is accountable to the electorate and that its affairs are transparent.

Blinder (1998, Ch. 3) accepts the proposition that in a democratic society the central bank should have instrument but not goal independence. Because monetary policy-making necessitates a long time horizon and often requires an initial cost before the benefit is reaped, impatient politicians would be tempted to seek short-term gain at the expense of longer-term benefits. But to pursue the goals set by government central bankers need independence not only from government itself but also from financial markets. When extracting information for monetary policy purposes from financial markets, Blinder believes that it is all too easy to fall into the trap of 'following the market'.

While advocating central bank independence, Blinder (1998, pp. 62–66) claims that there is no evidence that such independence increases credibility of monetary policy announcements and so improves the short-run trade-off between inflation and unemployment in OECD countries. Perhaps, however, a wider search for credible macroeconomic policy announcements is warranted. In 1975, for example, Taiwan launched a stabilisation plan. That year its inflation fell from 47% to 5%, while the economic growth rate increased from 1% to 5%. In 1976 inflation fell further to 2.5%, while growth accelerated to 13.9%. Just sometimes, useful additional data points are available outside the OECD countries.

Note

1 This view was presented forcefully by Kenneth Clarke, the former UK Chancellor of the Exchequer, to the House of Lords Treasury Select Committee on 18 March 1999. He maintains that economic policy should be aimed at steady, sustainable growth and that 'everything else is subordinate'.

2 A historical examination of inflation stability under alternative monetary frameworks

> Inflation is like sin: every government denounces it and every government practises it.
>
> (Sir Frederick Leith-Ross, *Observer*, 1957)[1]

2.1 Introduction

Monetary stability[2] is a legal objective of 90 of the 94 central banks in the Bank of England's Survey of monetary policy frameworks. This chapter provides measures of the extent to which central banks from a broad group of economies met this objective between 1970 and 1996. These measures have been developed based on the premise that monetary stability is closely associated with periods of stability in inflation. Thus this chapter measures, first, the extent to which periods of *stable* inflation are linked to *low* inflation, and second, the extent to which periods of stable inflation are linked to the choice of monetary policy framework.

The approach used here may be regarded as complementary to, though a step removed from the literature that seeks to establish a theoretical and empirical basis for assessing the costs and benefits of price stability.[3] Some empirical estimates of the costs of inflation stress the role of inflation in causing welfare losses through exaggerating the distortionary effects of the tax system. Such studies include Feldstein (1979) for the United States, and Bakhshi, Haldane, and Hatch (1998) for the United Kingdom.[4] Other studies have, with varied success, used aggregate cross-country, time-series data to illustrate an inverse relationship between inflation and growth. Several authors, such as Barro (1995), have found a link between high inflation and low growth, but that the link is tenuous at lower rates of inflation (below 10%). The study in this chapter does not attempt to measure the costs of inflation directly. Where the results presented identify circumstances of inflation instability, for example, it is not to be assumed that this is bad for output, as this study does not assess any trade-off between output and inflation stability.[5]

Nowadays, however, most policy-makers need little convincing that stable inflation is a good thing. The basic measure of stability used here is the number of occasions since 1970 that a country has achieved a five-year period of inflation stability (defined in more detail below). Such stability usually cannot be achieved without successful fiscal and monetary discipline. A degree of luck in avoiding any external shocks is also helpful. Information about where, when, and how periods of stable inflation have been achieved helps illuminate how characteristics of monetary frameworks contribute to stability in inflation.

2.2 A brief history of inflation diversity

This is a study of diversity, and Chart 2.1 helps to shift the focus from the global average inflation performance to the performance of countries with unaverage experience.

The chart illustrates the cross-sectional distribution of inflation rates across 91 economies for which continuous inflation data exist between 1970 and 1998. For example, the lowest line on the chart is the 5th percentile of the global inflation distribution, and the lowest point on this 5th percentile line shows that in 1993, 5% of countries in the sample had inflation below −3% (i.e. deflation of over 3%). In contrast, the upper line represents the 95th percentile. In some years, this line goes off the scale. For example, in 1985, 5% of countries had an annual inflation rate of more than 163%.

Inflation fell sharply across a very wide distribution of economies after 1994, and such reductions mirror the rapid increases in inflation following the oil price shocks of the 1970s. Inflation within the group is lower now than it has been since the start of the 1970s. Chart 2.1 illustrates the differential impact of various global events in the last three decades. The

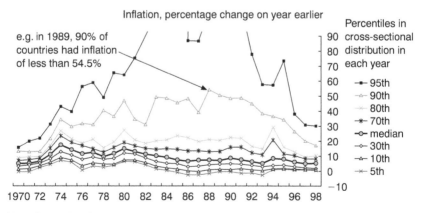

Note: Data taken from 91 developing and industrialised economies for which data are available in each year 1970 to 1998. Data for 1997 and 1998 includes estimates
Source: World Development Indicators (World Bank) and International Financial Statistics (IMF)

Chart 2.1 Cross-sectional distribution of inflation rates in 91 economies, 1970 to 1998

oil price increases of the mid- and late-1970s show up in rises in inflation across the whole distribution of countries. In contrast, the international debt crisis of the early 1980s and the 'tequila crisis' of the mid-1990s affect the skew of the distribution; the impacts of these crises are more visible for high-inflation than low-inflation economies. Regarding the Asian crisis of 1997–98 and the Russian crisis of 1988, there is hardly a sign that these resulted in increased inflation in any part of the distribution.

2.3   The circumstances of inflation stability

It is hard to distinguish from the chart the effects of exogenous shocks from those of the monetary framework. The following analysis partially remedies this problem by seeking to establish some of the properties of economies that have achieved periods of inflation stability, by examining how stability is related both to the rate of inflation and the monetary policy framework.

2.3.i   Data and methodology

The starting point is to identify periods of stable inflation using data for 96[6] economies between 1970 and 1996. The analysis does not include transitional economies, as their time series is not long enough. Data for monetary frameworks came from Cottarelli and Giannini (1997), supplemented by IMF annual publications and the Bank of England survey.

The first step is to identify episodes when inflation remained in particular ranges for consecutive years. A proposition to be tested is that if inflation is in a very low range (e.g. below 4%), it is more likely to remain within that range for a number of years than if it is in a higher (and wider) range of, say 12% to 20%. The measure of stability used is the number of years that inflation remained in a specific range.

Drawing on the entire data set, we count the number of years countries maintain inflation in specific ranges. We specify the ranges by splitting the sample according to percentiles in the entire distribution of inflation. Of the 2,520 annual observations:

1	20% are less than 3.8%	*hence:*	the very low inflation range is defined is as <3.8%
2	40% are less than 7.4%,		the low inflation range is defined as 3.8% to 7.4%
3	60% are less than 11.5%		the medium inflation range is defined as 7.4% to 11.5%
4	80% are less than 19.7%		the high inflation range is defined as 11.5% to 19.7%
5	20% are higher than 19.7%		the very high inflation range is defined as >19.7%

2.3.ii Are periods of stable inflation associated with low inflation?

One possible argument for a policy that aims for low inflation is that if policy starts to let inflation rise, even if only to still-moderate levels, it may become increasingly difficult to keep the lid on further increases. Using this logic, it may be that the best way of securing stable inflation is to keep it permanently at low rates, reasonably close to zero. This proposition forms the basis of the first statistical experiment in this chapter. The test assesses the extent to which inflation is more or less likely to remain in any particular range. Table 2.1 and Chart 2.2 summarise the results. The first row of the table illustrates that once inflation fell below 3.8%, there was a relatively high probability it would stay there for long episodes.[7] Table 2.1 may be read as follows: row 1 shows that there were 504 observations of inflation below 3.8%. Of these, 402 (80% of the total) were part of a two-year episode in a particular country in which inflation remained below 3.8% in both years. 338 (67%) were part of an episode when inflation ran below 3.8% for three years and so on. Based on the sample, if inflation was below 3.8% for one initial year, the probability that it would stay below 3.8% was:

- 49% for at least 5 consecutive years
- 22% for at least 10 consecutive years
- 14% for at least 14 consecutive years

In stark contrast to the results for the stability of inflation within the *very low* range, the second, third, and fourth rows of Table 2.1 show that inflation does not remain in the ranges of *low*, *medium* or *high* inflation for nearly so long. For example, of the 503 to 504 observations in these ranges:

- If inflation ran between 3.8% and 7.4% in one year, the probability that it would stay in the range for at least 5 consecutive years was 15%
- If inflation ran between 7.4% and 11.5% in one year, the probability that it would stay in the range for at least 5 consecutive years was 11%
- If inflation ran between 11.8 and 19.7% in one year, the probability that it would stay in the range for at least 5 consecutive years was 16%

Chart 2.2 strikingly illustrates the same result, that inflation has been markedly more stable when it was less than 3.8% than in any of the other ranges. The lines representing the higher ranges are of a similar shape. Thus there have been no significant differences in the stability of inflation within these other ranges.

Instances of inflation remaining in a stable range above 3.8% are very few. Only four economies experienced inflation in a low-, medium- or high-inflation range for at least ten years. The *very high* inflation range (higher than 19.7%) is too broad for firm inferences to be drawn regarding

Table 2.1 The historical probability of inflation remaining within various ranges over a given number of years

Inflation range	Percentiles	obs[1]	Probability of remaining in range over the given number of years (per cent)															
			1	2	3	4	5	6	7	8	9	10	11	12	13	14	15	16
1. less than 3.8%	0 to 20th	504	100	80	67	53	49	41	36	28	26	22	18	14	14	14	3	0
2. 3.8 to 7.4%	20th to 40th	504	100	64	42	26	15[2]	12	8	8	8	4	4	0				
3. 7.4 to 11.5%	40th to 60th	503	100	60	33	17	11	8	4	2	0							
4. 11.5 to 19.7%	60th to 80th	504	100	63	39	22	16	11	7	6	3	3	3	3	3	3	0	
5.a. 19.7% to 50%	80th to 94th	344	100	60	39	29	20	12	12	8	5	3	0					
5.b. 50 to 100%	94th to 97th	90	100	70	41	28	24	19	0									
5.c. Over 100%	97th to 100th	83	100	87	75	71	57	45	30	30	30	30	30	17	17	17	0	
Memo: −1 to 3.8%	2.7th to 20th	436	100	76	65	48	43	36	32	24	24	19	15	10	10	10	3	0

Notes:
Based on data for 96 developing and industrialised economies for which data were available in each year from 1970 to 96.
[1] The total number of observations in each range in the entire sample
[2] For example, of the total observations in which inflation was in the range 3.8% to 7.4%, 15% of them formed part of a period in which inflation remained in that range for at least five years.

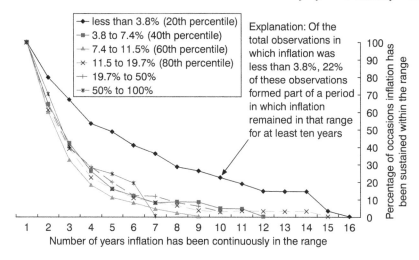

Legend:
- less than 3.8% (20th percentile)
- 3.8 to 7.4% (40th percentile)
- 7.4 to 11.5% (60th percentile)
- 11.5 to 19.7% (80th percentile)
- 19.7% to 50%
- 50% to 100%

Explanation: Of the total observations in which inflation was less than 3.8%, 22% of these observations formed part of a period in which inflation remained in that range for at least ten years

Percentage of occasions inflation has been sustained within the range

Number of years inflation has been continuously in the range

Chart 2.2 How inflation has been sustained within different ranges (% terms)

the stability of inflation within the entire range. Observations of higher inflation were therefore subdivided into three further categories: inflation of 19.7% to 50%, 50% to 100%, and more than 100%. The results are presented in the rows 5a–c of Table 2.1. They show that even for such a broad inflation range as 19.7 to 50%, a relatively small probability existed of inflation persisting in the range for very long.

The final (memorandum) row in Table 1 confirms that the result that very low inflation is more stable is not merely a statistical property of the lowest inflation range having no lower bound. The absence of a lower bound to the 0 to 20th percentile inflation range means that, in contrast to other ranges, inflation can only exit the range in one direction. Yet when an arbitrary lower bound of −1% inflation is imposed, the result once again is that inflation is markedly more stable when it is low.

2.4   Inflation stability and monetary frameworks

In this section we seek to identify the relative success of particular monetary policy frameworks in achieving episodes of stable inflation. For the purposes of this chapter, an episode of inflation stability is somewhat arbitrarily defined as one in which inflation remains in a specific range for a minimum of five years. Table 2.2 presents the 70 occasions in the study that met this criterion.[8] Reflecting the results discussed above, a relatively high number of these, 27 in total, secured episodes of very low and stable inflation.

As the table clearly shows, exchange rate targeting countries made up the majority of those achieving episodes of stable inflation: 39 of the 70

Table 2.2 Episodes of stable inflation (in a range for at least 5 years) 1970 to 96

Framework	*Inflation range (%)*				*very high*		*Totals*
	very low <3.8	*low* 3.8 to 7.4	*medium* 7.4 to 11.5	*high* 11.5 to 19.7	19.7 to 50	50 to 100	
Exchange rate targeting (1st year of 5 year episode follows country name)	**18** Belgium, 86 Bahrain, 83 C. African Rep., 86 Denmark, 90 France, 86 Ireland, 90 Malta, 70 Niger, 85 Oman Panama, 83 Saudi Arabia, 78 Senegal, 87 Thailand~, 83 Togo, 87 Norway~, 83 Malaysia~, 68 Singapore~, 83 Korea~, 83	**9** Bahrain, 82 Cyprus, 89 Denmark, 83 Finland, 87 Italy, 86 Korea, 92 Spain, 87 Sweden, 85 Thailand, 88	**6** Botswana, 82 Denmark, 75 Netherlands, 71 Philippines~, 92 Sweden, 74 Trinidad, 85	**6** Kiribati, 74 Lesotho, 77 Mali, 78 N. Zealand, 75 Trinidad, 78 Tunisia, 79	**0**	**0**	**39**

							Totals
Inflation targeting	**4** Canada, 92 Finland, 90 UK, 92 New Zealand, 91	**0**	**0**	**0**	**0**	**0**	**4**
Money/credit targeting	**2** Germany, 86 Switzerland, 83	**2** Canada, 83 Germany, 71	**2** Australia, 78 Canada, 73	**3** Greece, 75 Italy, 74 Spain, 79	**0**	**0**	**9**
Discretionary framework	**3** Australia, 91 Japan, 82 US, 92	**0**	**1** India, 90	**2** Turkey, 70 S. Africa, 79	**9** Brazil, 70 Colombia, 74 Ecuador, 83 Ghana, 86 Guinea, 87 Iceland, 73 Israel, 73 Paraguay, 84 Turkey, 81	**3** Peru, 78 Turkey, 88 Uruguay, 72	**18**
Totals	**27**	**11**	**9**	**11**	**9**	**3**	**70**

Note:
The first year of the sequence follows the country's name. If the regime changed during the period, the framework given is the one used for most of the period.
~ These countries were not using explicit exchange rate targets but have been categorised by Ohno (1998) as using 'soft-dollar' pegs.

stable-inflation episodes occurred when the country was targeting the exchange rate for all or most of the episode. If very high inflation observations are excluded, two thirds of stable-inflation episodes were achieved through exchange rate targeting.

Industrialised countries have been far more successful in achieving episodes of stable inflation within ranges of very low, low or medium inflation: There were 29 industrialised country episodes of such stable inflation, versus 18 for developing economies[9] (see Table 2.2). Among those industrialised economies are the world's three largest: the United States, Japan and Germany. Also included are 12 countries that have at some point since 1970 tied their exchange rates to one or other of these larger economies (Belgium, Denmark, Finland, France, Ireland, Italy, Korea, Netherlands, Norway, Singapore, Spain and Sweden). Switzerland, Germany, Australia and Canada all used money targeting to achieve medium to very low stable-inflation episodes, beginning between 1971 and 1986. More recently, Canada, Finland, New Zealand and the United Kingdom achieved inflation stability through inflation targeting. The United States, Japan and Australia (in the 1990s) achieved episodes using a discretionary policy framework.

The 14 episodes of low or very low stable inflation in developing economies have all been achieved through exchange-rate targeting. These episodes include Bahrain (twice), Central African Republic, Cyprus, Malaysia, Malta, Niger, Oman, Panama, Saudi Arabia, Senegal, Thailand (twice) and Togo. There is no precedent for a developing economy having achieved very low or low stable inflation through relying on domestic policy anchors (although India achieved stable inflation in the medium range in the 1990s using a discretionary policy that was based on managing – as opposed to pegging – its exchange rate).

2.5   Conclusions and interpretation

The analysis provides some clear results, but cloudier policy conclusions.

The results have established, first, that low inflation (below 3.8%) has been strongly associated with periods of stable inflation. Very low rates of inflation appear to provide inflation with its most natural home in so far as once inflation is low, it has been more likely to stick there than it has to become stuck at higher rates. Stable periods of higher inflation have been much less frequent in the last three decades. Second, over the past three decades, low stable inflation has occurred predominantly in Germany, the United States and Japan, and in the countries that successfully fixed their exchange rates to these large economies. More recently, it has also been achieved by inflation-targeting countries and by Switzerland using money targeting. Third, it is particularly striking that there are no examples of a developing economy achieving a five-year period of very low or low inflation (under 7.4%) other than through fixing the exchange rate. In other words, there are no precedents in these data for developing and transitional economies successfully using a domestic nominal anchor to achieve price stability.

We are, however, hesitant to draw conclusions for the future from these results. The analysis has been based on the past experience of two variables – inflation and a summary measure of the policy framework. Policy pursues price stability in order to achieve higher long-term growth in living standards, but the above assessment does not consider output and the underpinnings of low-inflation episodes. Neither has this study addressed the issues of what happens when countries leave periods of stable inflation. Are the periods of stable inflation underpinned by sound financial policies? If not, did the periods end turbulently?

The prominent role of fixed exchange rates in providing episodes of stable inflation provides a counterbalance to the results of Eichengreen (1999), who vividly illustrates the problems in emerging smoothly from them. His results, demonstrating that there are very few precedents for a smooth exit from a fixed exchange rate regime, together with the results presented here, indicating that there are no precedents for developing countries achieving periods of stable inflation *other* than through fixed exchange rates, paint a rather gloomy picture.

The gloom, however, is offset by the likelihood of improving inflation performance within individual countries thanks to the advances made in the technology of monetary frameworks, ranging from reduced provision for fiscal deficit finance to greater accountability and transparency of policy.

In summary, the balance of arguments holds that the lack of precedents for periods of stable inflation being achieved in developing countries through methods other than exchange-rate targeting does not necessarily imply that such economies will be unable to achieve stable inflation in the future by means of domestically oriented monetary policies.

Notes

1 For this and other quotes on inflation see MacFarlane and Mortimer-Lee's (1994) light-hearted look at 'Inflation over 300 years'.
2 Includes price stability and currency stability.
3 See Briault (1995) for a survey of the theoretical justifications for low inflation.
4 Many of the features in the UK tax system identified in the article as having major effects on the welfare costs of inflation were changed in the 1998 Budget.
5 Yates (1998) demonstrates that there is no conclusive evidence regarding the shape of the Phillips curve, though relatively more studies exist showing that the output costs of reducing inflation are greater at *lower* rates of inflation. In any case, the Phillips curve and output gap are not easily measurable concepts in the majority of developing and transitional economies. In fact, only 25% of central banks in developing and transitional economies in the Bank of England survey have recently considered these concepts in detail.
6 We have full data on the framework used in each year for the 96 economies, but full inflation data for five of these is lacking.

7   The test is subject to the criticism that the lower range does not have a lower bound, making it statistically less likely for there to be exits from the range.
8   Some countries appear more than once in the table, reflecting episodes of stable inflation.
9   Based on classifications used in Table 1.1 in Chapter 1.

3 The use of explicit targets for monetary policy

Practical experiences in 93 economies in the 1990s

> I find myself wondering if this swing of the pendulum to more autonomy [of central banks] can really be sustained. No matter how hard we work at disclosure, as long as there are perceptions that the central bank is making judgements about some important policy trade-off ... I wonder whether we all won't get pushed to far more narrowly defined objectives.
>
> (Gordon Thiessen, Governor, Bank of Canada,
> speaking in 1994 at the Tercentenary Symposium of the Bank of England
> on 'The Future of Central Banking'[1])

3.1 Introduction

Following the breakdown of the Bretton Woods system of exchange rates, policy-makers have employed a variety of monetary frameworks to increase the credibility of monetary policy.[2] The key characteristic of the frameworks is often an explicit target for monetary policy, and this chapter assesses the use of such targets in a range of economies in the 1990s. The analysis is based on data provided by the 93[3] central banks that responded to the Bank of England questionnaire.

Explicit monetary policy targets have become more widely used in the 1990s than at any time since the Bretton Woods era. In the survey of 93 central banks,[4] 95% (all but five economies) were using some form of explicit target or monitoring range in 1998.[5] This contrasts sharply with 1990, when only 57% had an explicit target or monitoring range.[6] So Governor Thiessen's prediction, that objectives might become increasingly narrowly defined, appears to have been fulfilled across this broad sample. So does the role he suggested for an explicit target – that of helping to define an institutional relationship between the central bank, the government and the population.

This chapter addresses in detail the use of explicit targets. The first section argues that the choice of policy target rests not just on the likelihood and utility of hitting a single number. Other important roles for explicit targets may include defining informal or formal contractual relationships between institutions, and focusing analysis on particular economic indicators.

The second section examines the targets that have been adopted in the 1990s by the 93 countries sampled, and the degree of flexibility with which they have been implemented. The announcement of an explicit target can represent full commitment to a particular outcome, or it may be no more than a benchmark used to explain deviations from the target. The sample provides extremes of experience that include rigidly fixed exchange rates on the one hand, and loose monitoring ranges for some or all of the exchange rate, money, and inflation on the other.[7] In the case of domestic monetary targets, the data used in this chapter relating to the deviations of outcomes from targets indicate that, in many cases, targets have been implemented flexibly.

3.2   A review of the arguments for different explicit targets

The changes between 1990 and 1998 reported by the survey respondents show a marked shift towards some form of explicit monetary policy target. And most of the central banks that said their monetary frameworks targeted a particular variable specified the exchange rate, money, or inflation. The choice depends on a number of diverse although interrelated factors. The following six factors are among those that influence the choice of policy target.

(i)   The role of the targeted variable and the impact of different shocks on the transmission mechanism from policy instruments to inflation

Much of the literature[8] on the choice of target has focused on the stability of the relationship between the target and the final objective of monetary policy. In turn this relationship depends partly on structural economic changes. For example, rapid financial liberalisation can lead to instability in the velocity of money; this was one explanation for industrialised countries (such as Australia and Canada) dropping money targets in the 1980s. More recently, some transitional and developing economies have followed suit because of similar problems.[9] Conversely, Issing (1997) argues that stable policy in Germany has contributed to more stable velocity of money.

Similarly, aggregate supply shocks can undermine inflation targets. In the case of Uganda, Atingi-Ego (in this volume) stresses the impact not only of the unpredictable velocity of money, but also of volatility in domestic food prices, which is related to rainfall.[10] And the closeness of the relationship between the exchange rate and the final policy objective may also depend upon structural factors; for example, exchange rates may be more closely related to consumer prices in small open economies where most consumer goods are imported.[11]

Though these structural factors remain important, the diversity of experience in the choice of explicit target illustrates that the choice also depends on a range of other factors.

(ii) The role of the target in defining a relationship between the central bank, the government, external institutions, and the private sector

An important function of explicit inflation targets has been to define the roles of the government and the central bank in the monetary policy strategy. The global experience offers a variety of approaches, ranging from demarcation of responsibilities to drawing together institutions to formulate targets. Chart 3.1 represents the responses of 93 central banks when asked whether they or the government set the explicit target in 1998, or whether the target was set jointly.

In a contractual approach, the government sets a target and provides the central bank with operational independence to pursue the target. Of the countries which describe themselves as 'inflation-targeting' only Israel and the United Kingdom have adopted a framework in which the government alone sets the target. Government sets the inflation target in 13 other cases although none of them were described by the central bank as 'inflation-targeting frameworks'. Government has had a relatively bigger role in the setting of exchange rate targets: it has a role in setting the target in 80% of the economies with exchange rate targets[12] (see Chart 3.1). Sometimes, however, it is difficult to specify objectives that are narrow enough to define a contract clearly.

Some countries, for example, have important objectives for financial stability or balance of payments, as well as inflation targets. And for countries that are undertaking disinflation, there are often at least two inflation targets: one for the current period and one for the long run (see further discussion in Section 3.6.iii below).

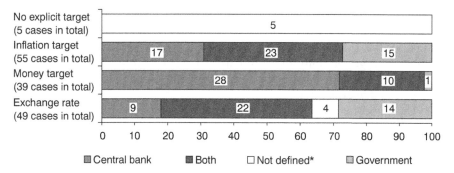

Note: From a sample of 93 central banks describing their practices in late 1998 (with some revisions for changes made in 1999, but not including changes in EMU countries): The figures in the bars indicate the number of economies with this arrangement. The length of the bars indicate the percentage set under different arrangements.
* These mainly include countries that are defined by the IMF as having a fixed exchange rate, but do not announce an explicit target.
Source: Bank of England survey of monetary frameworks

Chart 3.1 Who sets explicit targets and monitoring ranges for the exchange rate, money, and inflation?

Where contracts become complicated, an alternative approach may be for the government and the central bank to agree on an explicit target, in order to emphasise joint ownership of the monetary strategy. In 23 out of 55 cases (42% of central banks with explicit inflation targets), the government and the central bank jointly set the inflation target. These include seven central banks where the framework is described as inflation-targeting (Armenia, Australia, Canada, Jamaica, Mexico, Mongolia, and New Zealand). The comments on pages 187 and 194 of Donald Brash and Gordon Theissen, Governors of the Reserve Bank of New Zealand and the Bank of Canada, illustrate that joint responsibility has been important in improving monetary and fiscal co-ordination in these economies.

In contrast, in the 24 economies whose central banks described their regime as money-targeting (see Table 5.2), the targets were set jointly in only three cases – Bangladesh, Guyana, and Russia. Assumptions about inflation, output, and velocity developments are a prerequisite for setting money targets, and central banks have a comparative advantage in researching monetary and banking developments that may cause changes in velocity. Thus governments have been more likely to use an exchange rate or inflation target to instruct the central bank to meet an explicit target or to emphasise joint ownership of the programme.

Where the institutional arrangements have been designed to afford a high degree of central bank autonomy, progress towards price stability may have been achieved through 'target independence', whereby the central bank sets its own explicit objectives. Intermediate money targets have frequently been used in this way: in 28 out of 39 cases the central bank alone has set the money target. And six money-targeting central banks – in Germany, Kenya, Moldova, South Africa, Switzerland, and Zambia – had full independence over all targets and instruments. In contrast, of the 16 central banks in the survey describing their framework as inflation-targeting, only those in Chile, the Czech Republic, and Sweden have, according to the survey's measures, full independence to set both targets and instruments.

The importance of targets in defining relationships between different agents in the economy goes beyond that of the central bank and the government. For countries with IMF programmes, levels of money and credit aggregates are used as performance criteria that must be met to ensure continued financial support from the Fund. Cottarelli and Giannini (1998) argue that, where policy-makers in developing countries have little anti-inflationary credibility, adopting a Fund programme may be the most effective means of enhancing the credibility of a disinflationary strategy.

(iii)   The role of targets and forecasts in explaining outcomes

Targets and forecasts may be used either as means of pre-committing to a particular outcome or as benchmarks for explaining deviations from predicted outcomes. Mexico uses a combined approach. Alfaro and Schwartz (in this volume) describe how the annual programme of the Banco de México involves setting an annual inflation target, which, subject to certain shocks, represents a pre-commitment. The programme also incorporates a forecast for the daily path of the monetary base, given the information available in early January of each year, which represents a benchmark. The benchmark provides a basis for comparing developments during the year with those anticipated at the start of the year.

(iv) The skills and experience within the central bank

Central banks have limited budgets for analytical resources. Budgetary constraints are particularly binding in poorer countries, because less money is available, and skilled staff are scarce.[13] Skills may include knowledge of reserve money programming, of broad money targeting, of inflation targeting or analysis of the implications of implementing crawling exchange rate bands. So there may be some 'transaction costs' from buying into one or an other domestic monetary framework, both in terms of re-education within the central bank, and in terms of explaining policy to the public. This may help to explain why many central banks take an evolutionary approach to changing monetary frameworks, with radical shifts generally taking place only in response to external shocks and crises.[14]

(v) The extent to which 'policy technology' gives policy-makers confidence in their ability to influence targeted variables in a predictable fashion

Central banks require comprehensive data and powerful analytical tools to be confident that they are setting instruments optimally. But in many countries, data can be patchy, infrequent, and available only for short-time series, and rapid structural change may wrap very wide confidence intervals around estimated relationships between macroeconomic variables.

Whether the availability of good data and analytical techniques should affect the choice of target is controversial. On the one hand, inflation targeting in industrialised economies has benefited from the existence of macroeconometric forecasting models. But such models are difficult to estimate accurately where data are inadequate, and if analytical capacity is limited.[15] This might seem to suggest that countries that lack good data and analytical capacity should not be setting inflation targets. On the other hand, poor analytical capacity undermines implementation of *any* domestic target.

Money targets, for example, also depend implicitly upon an inflation projection, whether or not the projection is cast in terms of a forecast, target, or desired outcome. One possible solution to poor knowledge about domestic transmission may be to announce an exchange-rate peg, but even the choice of peg may increase the costs of disinflation if there is limited knowledge of the equilibrium exchange rate.[16] Analytical limitations may indeed influence the optimal choice of target, but it is not clear that the influence will be in a particular direction in all cases.

(vi) Attempts to impose discipline on fiscal and monetary policy

Chapter 2 shows that exchange-rate targeting was the only regime that delivered five-year periods of low, stable inflation in developing economies between 1970 and 1996. And Crockett (in this volume) argues that 'although exchange-rate targeting has frequently ended in currency crisis, it cannot be denied that exchange-rate pegs have also often been instrumental in braking inflation expectations'. Much of the credit for this must be due to the widespread understanding that exchange rate pegs imply strict constraints on credit expansion. Exchange-rate pegs have frequently acted as a means of engendering fiscal and monetary discipline. Because the private sector can understand what is at stake, inflation expectations can be rapidly lowered when the peg is implemented.

3.3 Explicit targets in the 1990s

The past three decades have seen marked swings in choices of explicit targets and monitoring ranges[17] (see Chart 3.2). Table 3.1 provides detailed information about the periods in which exchange-rate, money,

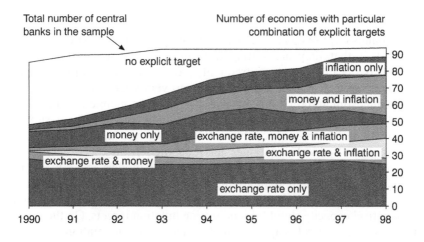

Note: Money targets include all targets for different definitions of money and credit period.
Source: Bank of England survey of monetary frameworks, Cottarelli and Giannini (1997) and IFS (various issues)

Chart 3.2 Explicit targets in the 1990s

Table 3.1 Chronology of the adoption and removal of explicit targets and monitoring ranges in the 1990s

A: Explicit targets and monitoring ranges as of Jan. 1990 (dates adopted and dropped in brackets)

	Exchange rate (31 economies from a total of 84)		Money (14 economies from a total of 84)		Inflation (4 economies from a total of 84)	
Developing	**17**		**4**		**3**	
	Cyprus (60s–)	Bahrain (80–)	India (85–)	Mozambique (87–)	Malaysia (70s–)	Tanzania (80s–)
	Egypt (60s–91)	Belize (80s–)	South Africa (86–)	Nigeria (87–)	Mozambique (87–)	
	Fiji (60s–)	E. Caribbean (83–)				
	Tonga (60s–)	Hong Kong (83–)				
	W. Afr. States (60s–)	Chile (86–)				
	Malta (71–)	Mexico (88–94)				
	Bahamas (73–)	Kuwait (90–)				
	Barbados (75–)	Mozambique (?–95)				
	Jordan (75–)					
Industrialised	**14**		**10**		**1**	
	Norway (60s–94)	France (79–)	Greece (50s–)	UK (77–97)	New Zealand (88–)	
	Belgium (71–)	Italy (79–96)	USA (late 70s–)	Spain (78–94)		
	Netherlands (71–)	Austria (81–)	Germany (75–)	Korea (79–)		
	Denmark (72–)	Taiwan (85–)	Switzerland (75–)	Italy (84–)		
	Ireland (72–)	Israel (86–)	France (77–)	Taiwan (89–)		
	Finland (78–96)	Spain (89–)				
	Portugal (78–)	Iceland (89–)				

B. Adoption of explicit targets during the 1990s (dates adopted and dropped[1] in brackets)

	Exchange rate		Money		Inflation	
Total Adopted	**31**		**33**		**50**	
Total Dropped	**12**		**7**		**0**	
Developing	Argentina (91–)	Vietnam (94–)	Guyana (90?–)	China (94–)	Chile (91–)	Peru (94–)
	Indonesia (92–97)	Uruguay (95–)	Kenya (90?–)	Malta (94–)	Egypt (91–)	Uruguay (95–)
	Lebanon (93–)	Malaysia (98–)	Turkey (90–92)	Mauritius (94–)	India (91–)	Zambia (95–)
	Namibia (93–)	Turkey (98–)	Ghana (92–)	Vietnam (94–)	Indonesia (92–)	Jamaica (96–)
	Ecuador (94–)		Jordan (92–)	Tanzania (95–)	Uganda (92–)	Mauritius (96–)
			Uganda (92–)	Zambia (95–)	Guyana (93–)	Sierra Leone (96–)

Table 3.1 Continued

			Developing		
			Indonesia (93) Bangladesh (94–)	Jamaica (96–) Armenia (98–)	Nigeria (93–) Vietnam (93–) Bangladesh (94–) Ecuador (94–) Mexico (94–)	W. Afr. States (97–) China (98–) Kenya (98?–) Lebanon (98–) Turkey (98–)
Transitional	Poland (90–) Estonia (92–) Croatia (Oct–Dec 93) Czech Rep. (93–97) Slovakia (93–) Latvia (94–) Lithuania (94–) Hungary (95–)	Russia (95–98) Macedonia (96–) Bosnia-Herz. (97–) Bulgaria (97–) Turkmenistan (97–) Mongolia (98–) Ukraine (98–)	Poland (91–97) Ukraine (91–) Macedonia (92–95) Mongolia (92–) Albania (93–) Czech Rep. (93–97) Kyrgyz (93–) Russia (93–)	Slovakia (93–) Moldova (94–) Georgia (95–) Kazakhstan (97–) Romania (97–) Slovenia (97–) Turkmenistan (97–) Armenia (98–)	Poland (92–) Albania (93–) Macedonia (93–) Russia (93–) Slovakia (93–) Croatia (94–) Armenia (95–) Georgia (96–)	Kyrgyz (96–) Moldova (96–) Kazakhstan (97–) Mongolia (97–) Romania (97–) Slovenia (97–) Turkmenistan (97–) Czech Rep (98–)
Industrialised	Norway (60s–94) Finland (78–96) Portugal (78–96) Italy (79–96)	Sweden (90–92) UK (90–92) Greece (95–)	Portugal (91–92)		Greece (90?–) Taiwan (90?–) Canada (91–) Israel (91–) UK (92–) Australia (93–)	Finland (93–) Sweden (93–) France (94–) Spain (94–) Italy (95–) Korea (98–)

¹ Targets dropped include all economies from Table 3.1.A and 3.1.B, including Norway and Finland who resumed later. The full list is provided in the text. Russia is included as a drop, since in 1998 it operated a managed exchange rate with a corridor wider than 30%.

C. Explicit targets as at late 1998 (with dates they were adopted)

	Exchange Rate (50 economies from a total of 93)	Money (40 economies from a total of 93)	Inflation (54 economies from a total of 93)
	22	**18**	**25**
Developing	Cyprus (60s–) Fiji (60s–) Tonga (60s–) W. African Sts (60s–) E. Caribbean (83–) Hong Kong (83–) Chile (86–) Argentina (91–)	India (85–) South Africa (86–) Mozambique (87–) Nigeria (87–) Indonesia (93–) Bangladesh (94–) China (94–) Malta (94–)	Malaysia (70s–) Tanzania (80s–) Mozambique (87–) Chile (91–) Mexico (94–) Peru (94–) Uruguay (95–) Zambia (95–)

	Malta (71–) Bahamas (73–) Barbados (75–) Jordan (75–) Bahrain (80–) Belize (80s–) Kuwait (80s–)	Lebanon (93–) Namibia (93–) Ecuador (94–) Vietnam (94–) Uruguay (95–) Malaysia (98–) Turkey (98–) **13**	Kenya (90?–) Guyana (90?–) Ghana (92–) Jordan (92–) Uganda (92–)	Mauritius (94–) Vietnam (94–) Tanzania (95–) Zambia (95–) Jamaica (96–)	Egypt (91–) India (91–) Uganda (92–) Indonesia (92–) Guyana (93–) Nigeria (93–) Vietnam (93–) Bangladesh (94–) Ecuador (94–)	Jamaica (96–) Mauritius (96–) Sierra Leone (96) W. Afr. States (97–) China (98–) Kenya (98?) Lebanon (98–) Turkey (98–)
Transitional	Poland (90–) Estonia (92–) Slovakia (93–) Latvia (94–) Lithuania (94–) Hungary (95–) Russia (95–) **15**	Macedonia (96–) Bosnia-Herz. (97–) Bulgaria (97–) Turkmenistan (97–) Mongolia (98–) Ukraine (98–) **13**	Ukraine (91–) Macedonia (92–95) Mongolia (92–) Albania (93–) Kyrgyz (93–) Russia (93–) Slovakia (93–)	Moldova (94–) Georgia (95–) Kazakhstan (97–) Romania (97–) Slovenia (97–) Turkmenistan (97–) Armenia (98–) **14**	Poland (92–) Albania (93–) Macedonia (93–) Russia (93–) Slovakia (93–) Croatia (94–) Armenia (95–) Moldova (96–)	Georgia (96–) Kazakhstan (97–) Kyrgyz (96–) Mongolia (97–) Romania (97–) Slovenia (97–) Turkmenistan (97–) Czech Rep. (98–) **16**
Industrialised	Norway (60s–94) Belgium (71–) Netherlands (71–) Ireland (72–) Denmark (72–) Portugal (78–) Finland (78–96) Italy (79–96)	France (79–) Austria (81–) Taiwan (85–) Israel (86–) Spain (89–) Iceland (89–) Greece (95–) **15**	Greece (50s–) Germany (75–) Switzerland (75–) France (77–)	Korea (79–) USA (late 70s–) Italy (84–) Taiwan (89–)	New Zealand (88–) Greece (90?–) Taiwan (90?–) Canada (91–) Israel (91–) UK (92–) Australia (93–) **8**	Finland (93–) Sweden (93–) France (94–) Italy (95–) Spain (94–) Korea (98–) **13**

Data from 92 responses to the Bank of England survey of Monetary Frameworks. A full list of the economies in the sample is given in Chapter 1. In 1998, the only economies in our sample that reported no explicit targets or monitoring ranges were Botswana, Japan, Singapore, Sri Lanka and Thailand. We defined Cyprus, Fiji, Norway, and Tonga as having explicit exchange rate targets as although no particular number is announced, the targets are either legal ones or they are sufficiently strong to be defined by the IMF as 'fixed to another currency'. In the case of exchange rate pegs, years in which devaluations took are included, as are years in which the currency targeted was changed. Germany and Switzerland have explicit long-term objectives for inflation but these are not included in the Table. Some authors, such as Bernanke, Laubach, Mishkin and Posen (1999) regard these as 'precursors to inflation targeting'. A '?' is included for Greece and Taiwan because we are not sure if inflation targets were used before 1990.

Sources: Bank of England Survey of Monetary Frameworks and Cottarelli and Giannini (1997).

and inflation targets were adopted, used, and dropped in all 93 economies in the sample and for every year in the 1990s.

The data indicates three particular trends:

- *Explicit targets have become much more widespread in the 1990s than in the previous two decades*   The use of explicit targets – for the exchange rate money, or inflation – grew in the 1990s. Their use is now more widespread than at any time since Bretton Woods.[18] Between 1990 and 1998, the percentage of economies with explicit exchange-rate targets increased from 37% to 54%. The percentage of countries with an explicit money target increased from 17% to 43%. The number of countries with inflation targets increased over tenfold, from 5% to 58% of the sample.[19] Of the 54 countries that had inflation targets in 1998, 11 (12% of all countries) had inflation targets only; while of the six countries that had explicit inflation targets in 1990, only one (New Zealand) described it as the centrepiece of its monetary framework.

- *Many countries in the sample use more than one explicit target*   There has been a long-standing economic literature, which treats targets as alternatives, yet central bank practices in the 1990s confound that treatment. In 1998, nearly half the economies in the sample announced an explicit target (or monitoring range) for more than one of the exchange rate, growth in money or credit, and inflation, compared with only 8% in 1980. In 1998, each country published an average of 1.5 targets for these variables.

- *In the 1990s (up to 1998), there were 114 examples of an economy announcing a new explicit target for any of the exchange rate, money and inflation, while only 19 economies dropped an explicit target*   In other words, more new targets were adopted than there are economies in the sample. Of the targets dropped, 12 were exchange rate targets: Egypt (1991); Finland, Italy, Norway, the United Kingdom and Sweden (1992); Croatia (1993); Mexico (1994); Mozambique (1995); Czech Republic and Indonesia (1997) and Russia (1998). The majority of these changes were in response to a currency crisis. Seven countries dropped money targets (or monitoring ranges) during the period: Portugal and Turkey (1992); Spain (1994); Macedonia (1995); Czech Republic, Poland, and the United Kingdom (1997). Generally, this represented an acknowledgement that money growth was not at the top of the central bank's hierarchy of indicators. There were no cases of a country dropping its explicit inflation target in the 1990s,[20] with the exception of countries joining the European single currency.

3.4   Flexibility and uncertainty in the implementation of inflation and money growth targets

Policy-makers may sometimes regard it as acceptable to miss their target. In the analysis that follows, a larger miss is associated with a relatively flexible approach to policy targeting. An important caveat, however, is that even when policy attempts to adhere rigidly to targets, transmission lags may imply that policy is unable to restore a variable to its targeted path within a given period. The data used here cannot distinguish between these two possibilities.

Charts 3.3 and 3.4 show the average performance relative to target and

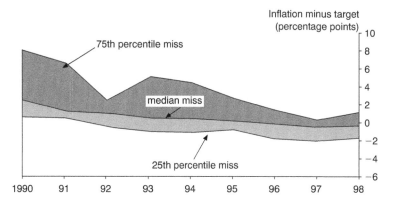

Note: Money targets include all targets for different definitions of money and credit period.
Source: Bank of England survey of monetary frameworks, Cottarelli and Giannini (1997) and IFS

Chart 3.3 The distribution of inflation target 'misses' in the 1990s

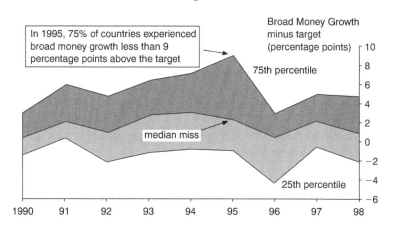

Note: See Table 3.2 for the number of observations in each year.
Source: Bank of England survey of monetary frameworks

Chart 3.4 The distribution of broad money target 'misses' in the 1990s

Table 3.2 Number of observations of inflation and broad money target misses in each year, and the median target

	Number of observations for inflation target misses[a]	Median inflation target	Number of observations for money target misses[a][b]	Median money target
1990	7	3.5	14	9.25
1991	11	5	16	10.75
1992	14	9	19	10.5
1993	23	10	23	12
1994	30	8	27	12.5
1995	37	8	29	13.2
1996	44	7	30	14.8
1997	50	7.3	33	15
1998	53	6.5	26	11.6

[a] Some outcomes for 1998 were not yet available from central banks. Where possible these outcomes have been estimated using IMF data.
[b] These are predominantly targets for broad money. Narrower measures were only included only when no broad money target was used.

Source: Bank of England survey of monetary frameworks

the distribution of misses for broad money growth and inflation targets.[21] In each year of the 1990s the charts show the median miss, plus the value of the miss for the country at the 25th and 75th percentile of the distribution. Thus the shaded area encloses the outcomes for the half of the sample with the smallest misses above and below the target ('accurate' observations). The analysis focuses on the median rather than the mean, because the distribution is skewed by a very small number of wide target misses.

The number of observations varies from year to year, as do the median target levels (see Table 3.2). For both money and inflation targets, the number of observations is particularly small in 1990–92; we focus on the results between 1993 and 1998, when there are between 23 and 53 observations in each year.

The data raise several questions:

*   *To what extent does the increased use of explicit targets indicate a more rigid approach to monetary policy?*

For inflation targets between 1993 and 1998, the average width of the range of target misses between the 25th and 75th percentile is 3.9 percentage points (see Chart 3.3). Chart 3.4 illustrates country experience with broad money growth targets. Between 1993 and 1998, the average width of the range enclosed by the 25th percentile miss and the 75th percentile miss is 7.3 percentage points. These data suggest that broad money targets have not been treated as rigid rules.

The cross-sectional evidence presented here is complementary to the time series evidence that assesses the likelihood of adhering to particular inflation outcomes. The time series evidence from the 1980s and earlier suggests a humbling degree of inaccuracy in central banks' capacity to meet targets. Haldane and Salmon (1995) estimate a model for inflation in a particular country (the United Kingdom) and observe errors based on historical experience.[22] They find that, on the basis of UK data between 1960 and 1994, in some of their simulations there is 'only a 50% probability of adhering to a target range of 6 percentage points'. As a result, Haldane (1995) suggests that the central bank faces a trade-off between 'credibility and humility'.[23]

The cross-sectional evidence from our survey suggests that, in the 1990s, central banks have done considerably better in meeting both inflation *and* money targets than might have been expected from model-based analysis of earlier experience.[24] Nevertheless, the results from Table 3.3.A show that the median absolute miss in the 1990s was 1.5 percentage points, i.e. there was approximately a 50% success rate in adhering to an inflation-target range of ± 1.5 percentage points in the 1990s.[25] For countries setting an inflation target of less than 3.5%, there has been around a 50% probability of adhering to a much narrower range of ± 0.7 percentage points. For money targets and outcomes, Table 3.3.B suggests greater accuracy than that predicted by models based on time-series data. For explicit money targets, there was approximately a 50% success rate in achieving an outcome within 3.1 percentage points of the target.

Why do the time-series and cross-country evidence differ? One possibility is that judgement combined with models markedly improves the accuracy of policy. Another is that, whereas the time series results are based on estimates over several decades, the results from the Bank of England survey refer only to the 1990s, when there may have been fewer exogenous (non policy induced) shocks that induced inflation volatility. This explanation is consistent with the view that the 1990s provided a relatively shock-free environment conducive to building credibility through the use of explicit targets.[26]

• *Are the results suggestive of bias – i.e. do outcomes tend to overshoot or undershoot the target on average?*

To the extent that unexpected shocks even out over the sample period, the results suggest that central banks have, on average, been realistic in setting inflation targets. Chart 3.3 suggests that since 1994 inflation outcomes have not been obviously biased in either direction relative to target. In the years since 1993, the median miss has been within +0.5% to −0.5%. And in the sample as a whole, the median miss is zero (see Table 3.3.A). In contrast, money growth has tended to overshoot the target. Part of the explanation may be that central banks have consistently underestimated falls in veloc-

Table 3.3 Summary of misses from inflation and broad money targets in countries that announced explicit targets in the 1990s

Table 3.3.A Summary of misses from inflation targets
Total number of annual observations = 269. Total number of countries = 56

Percentile	All	Low target observations			High target observations
		0–25	25–50	50–75	75–100
Range of Targets (percentage points)		Less than 3.5	3.5–7.2	7.2–13.5	Above 13.5
Median miss	0	−0.4	0	0.3	1.3
Median absolute miss	1.5	0.7	1.0	2.2	6.7

Table 3.3.B Summary of misses from money targets
Total number of annual observations = 217. Total number of countries = 37

Percentile	All	0–25	25–50	50–75	75–100
Range of Targets (percentage points)		less than 6.5	6.5–12.3	12.3–17.0	Above 17.0
Median miss	1.8	0.3	1.8	2.7	3.5
Median absolute miss	3.1	1.8	3.0	3.0	6.5

Table 3.3.C Comparison of misses from inflation and money targets in economies where both were announced in the same year
Total number of annual observations = 143. Total number of countries = 31

Observations for:	All observations		Low target observations[a]		High target observations[a]	
	inflation	money	inflation	money	inflation	money
Median absolute miss	1.5	3.2	0.8	2.3	4.4	6.2

[a] The 'high' and 'low' groups were divided according to the magnitude of the sum of the inflation and money target in that year.

Table 3.3.D Summary of misses from inflation targets for economies with IMF programmes
Total number of annual observations = 107. Total number of countries = 29

Percentile	All	0–50	50–100
Range of Targets (percentage points)		less than 7.2	more than 7.2
Median miss	0	0	0.4
Median absolute miss	4.4	2.8	6.6

Table 3.3.E Summary of misses from money targets for economies with IMF programmes
Total number of annual observations = 80. Total number of countries = 19

Percentile	All	0–50	50–100
Range of Targets (percentage points)		less than 12.5	more than 12.5
Median miss	3.9	2.6	4.0
Median absolute miss	5.9	4.6	6.75

Source: Bank of England survey of monetary frameworks

ity. Chart 3.4 provides evidence that money targets have been overshot more often than undershot. Table 3.3.B shows that the median money target miss for the entire sample was +1.8 percentage points.

- *To what extent do the results depend upon the rate of inflation when the targets are being set?*

The sample contains examples of targets announced when inflation is low, and examples of explicit targets announced as part of a policy plan to reduce inflation from high rates. High inflation that occurs because of adverse shocks or because there are pressing policy objectives other than low inflation is likely to make it harder to achieve monetary targets. Table 3.3.A contains the median misses from explicit inflation targets in the 1990s for all observations. It also divides the sample into four groups, according to the size of the target. One quarter of observations represent countries targeting a rate of inflation of under 3.5%; half are below 7.2%; and three quarters are below 13.5%. Table 3.3.B provides analogous information, based on the experience of explicit targets for money growth. The data used in each section of the table are set out in two rows. The first relates to the median miss, which may be greater or less than zero depending upon whether targets are relatively more likely to be overshot or undershot. The second gives the median absolute misses, irrespective of whether the outcome was above or below the target.

Each section of Table 3.3 shows that misses are higher when the targets are higher, both for inflation and for money growth. Overall, the table shows that misses remain roughly in proportion to the level of the target. There are more than 67 observations spread over the entire sample length for annual inflation targets of less than 3.5%. They illustrate that the median miss is −0.4 percentage points (the minus sign indicating that low-inflation countries have undershot the target more often than overshooting it).[27] Low-inflation countries have established a track record of accuracy in hitting targets, with little evidence of systematic over or under-shooting. For countries with higher targets, Table 3.3.C confirms that misses have been larger and outcomes are more likely to be above target.

Money-growth targets exhibit a similar pattern of misses, increasing in magnitude for higher-target observations. The size of the absolute miss is not as clearly related to the size of the target as is the case for inflation. This is because several economies, such as Taiwan, have had considerable success in anticipating shifts in velocity and meeting money targets, even when the targets are set at relatively high growth rates.

The final question raised by the data is:

- *Are monetary and inflation targets implemented with equal or differing degrees of flexibility?*

Table 3.3.C provides information on countries that had explicit inflation and money-growth targets in the same year. This makes it possible to compare the flexibility with which inflation and money targets are implemented in countries that announce both. An important caveat is that the misses not only could be attributable to greater flexibility in policy, but also could arise because of the differing impact of demand, supply, and velocity shocks on money and inflation targets. If policy is not able to restore the variable to target within the period because of relatively long transmission lags, then even attempts to adhere rigidly to targets may not succeed in eliminating target misses.

The results show that inflation misses were less than half of those for money targets. The median inflation target miss (in absolute terms) for countries that announce both inflation and money targets is 1.5 percentage points, compared with 3.2 percentage points for broad money growth. The results are consistent with the view that over a broad range of countries, the mix of shocks leads to greater deviations from money targets than inflation targets. In particular, velocity shocks may have led to relatively larger deviations from money targets. The results may also reflect the priority that policy-makers give to inflation targets over money targets, in the event of a conflict between them.

The results also illustrate that, in practice, it is difficult to assert that inflation targets imply any more or less discretion than do money targets. It might be thought that inflation targets are more discretionary in the short term. Cottarelli and Giannini (1997) note that money targeting is 'characterised' by the announcement of a short-term intermediate target, either in the form of a monetary aggregate or of a (typically crawling) peg.[28] Policy instruments typically affect money aggregates sooner than inflation, and hence policy-makers wishing to adhere to money targets may have to act sooner and with less discretion.[29] Yet money target outcomes have deviated from target by more than inflation outcomes, indicating that money targets are either harder to hit or are interpreted more flexibly. This would support the view that policy may be set pragmatically irrespective of the published target.

Finally, Tables 5.3.D and 5.3.E show a similar pattern of results in the sub-group of countries that were using IMF programmes during the sample. During the 1990s, the median inflation target miss was zero, and the median absolute miss was 4.4 percentage points. For money targeters, the median miss was 3.9 percentage points and the median absolute miss of 5.9 percentage points. There is therefore, some evidence of consistent overshooting of money targets for countries with IMF programmes, just as there is in the sample as a whole.

3.5   Rules versus discretion revisited

The debate about rules versus discretion in monetary policy can be traced back several decades.[30] The arguments are well summarised by Guitian

(1994). He describes how, under a successful rules-based policy, 'the predictability of policy should help offset the unpredictability of the environment'. In contrast, a successful discretionary approach involves using 'policy adaptability as a means of keeping an uncertain environment under control'.

The choice of intermediate target for monetary policy has usually been framed in terms of the controllability of a particular variable and the stability of the relationship between that variable and the final objective.[31] Yet it is hard to explain some countries' choice of targets using such a framework. Why do so many liberalising countries with poor data and unstable velocity use money targets? Why do other countries that have poor data and are vulnerable to supply shocks use explicit inflation targets? Are 'explicit targets' in some cases better described as benchmarks for variables, against which outcomes can be usefully measured and deviations analysed?

In the light of this debate, explicit targets for domestic nominal variables can be seen as part of a communications device, an attempt to maximise the benefits of both rule-based and discretionary approaches. The choice of target depends not only on the role of the candidate variable in the transmission mechanism, but also on the issues of transparency and governance in monetary policy. We note above the increase in the number of economies that announced targets for more than one variable. Chart 3.2 above illustrates that the fastest-growing 'regime' is the combined use of explicit money and inflation targets. In 1998 this combination was used by 25% of the sample, more than the combined total of inflation targets only (12%) and money targets only (5%). The use of dual targets is consistent with the view that targets sometimes represent benchmarks. Policy-makers use explicit targets because they find that it is better to have narrow objectives and explain misses, rather than having imprecise objectives that make success or failure difficult to measure.

Many authors assessing the international context of monetary frameworks have reinforced the message of compromise between explicit targets and flexibility. In summarising the debate between rules and discretion, Guitian reminds us that 'there is an exception to every rule'. Similarly Bernanke, Laubach, Mishkin, and Posen (1999) describe inflation targets as 'a framework not a rule' and 'constrained discretion'.[32] Responses to our survey also illustrate the flexibility in money targeting. Indian policy-makers describe their framework as 'money targeting with feedback', and the Swiss respondent described their framework as 'money targeting with an escape clause'. The Swiss response also informs us how a central bank may implement such 'constrained discretion':

> Overall, money targeting provided a useful framework to explain current policy and deviations from targets. Target misses were explained in detail and attributed to specific shocks. Deviations

resulted in a policy response but not necessarily within the same year. The combination between a long-term commitment to price stability and short-run policy discretion was reaffirmed in 1989 by the change from annual targets to multi-year targets. Since then the SNB [Swiss National Bank] has tried to use the flexibility provided by a multi-year target without letting the deviations get out of hand. The multi-year target itself may be described as an ideal path that would be valid in the absence of shocks, i.e. with output matching potential and inflation equal to the inflation target.

The increasingly widespread use of explicit targets over the past decade reflects the progress of the debate between rules and discretion. Explicit targets can be used to demonstrate that a particular variable ranks high on the hierarchy of indicators, even if it is acceptable to miss the 'target'.

3.6   An anatomy of policy targets

Whatever the reasons for policy-makers missing their targets, and particularly money growth targets, the earlier sections of this chapter illustrate that domestic policy targets have not in general been implemented strictly, in a rules-like manner. Yet without such rules, how will credibility be earned? In the long run, the answer lies in central bank actions, but until such time as central bank actions have earned sufficient stripes, policy-makers may be concerned about the prospect of large target misses undermining their credibility. Therefore, this section assesses the features of target design that are intended to improve flexibility while minimising the possibility of substantial misses.[33]

3.6.i   *Choosing a band width for inflation and money targets*

One way of acknowledging the uncertainties involved in attempting to meet explicit inflation and money targets is to express the target as a range rather than a point. Target ranges represent an attempt to counter general rather than specific uncertainty in the policy environment. The survey asked respondents whether their targets were expressed as points, ranges, or ceilings, and why. Chart 3.5 shows an even use of points and ranges for both money and inflation targets.

The advantages and disadvantages of ranges and points mentioned by respondents mirror those summarised in Yates (1995). The great majority of those using ranges viewed them as providing greater flexibility, while several disinflating central banks argued that ceilings could capture flexibility and also provide a trigger point for policy action. But other responses represented the view that in practice ranges may not increase flexibility, by much. The Swiss National Bank noted that a point target might not inhibit flexibility as few would expect a point target to be met

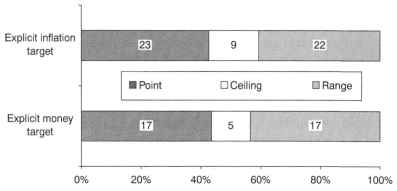

Percentage of economies using each technique (numbers of economies in boxes)

Source: Bank of England survey of monetary frameworks

Chart 3.5 Design of explicit targets: points, ceilings, or ranges

continuously, and that missing a range may be more damaging to credibility than missing a point target. And if the range boundary represents an
inflexible trigger point for policy changes, it may undermine the *raison
d'être* of the range, i.e. to express uncertainty and flexibility.

Furthermore, any increased flexibility from the use of a range may be
offset by losses to policy clarity. The survey results (see Charts 3.3 and 3.4)
indicate that, in a global context, the majority of outcomes are above
target, so it would be understandable if the public did not necessarily view
the range as providing information that is symmetrical about the mean. In
Albania, however, there was no perceived trade-off, since an inflexible
rules-based approach (through the use of a point target) was judged beneficial in providing an anchor in an otherwise unstable financial environment.

3.6.ii Exemptions from explicit inflation and money targets

Excluding particular measurable components from a targeted price index
or money aggregate can be a way of cushioning the policy impact of specific shocks.[34] Food prices, for example, may be too volatile; administered
prices may be unresponsive to policy, and the direct impact of higher
interest rates on credit-financed items will increase their cash flow cost. If
these items are included in a target inflation index, it could be seen as
giving an inappropriate policy signal. Similarly, the definitions of money
targets used for policy vary significantly across economies, with foreign
currency deposits for example being either included or excluded depending partly upon its effect on the predictability of the velocity of money.

The exclusions from price indices for targeting purposes differ significantly across inflation-targeting countries. Cufer, Mahadeva, and Sterne (this volume) argue that, in considering an exclusion, policy-makers face a trade-off between the clarity and comprehensiveness of the consumer price index. For comprehensiveness, the index should include a range of products whose prices fully describe changes in the cost of living. In particular, excluding a price that in the long run moves differently from the rest means that policy is not targeting changes in the overall cost of living. But for clarity, the exclusion may remove noise from the index and thus help to increase its usefulness as an inflation indicator.

In many transitional economies, administered prices play an important role, and changes are usually akin to a supply shock. If monetary policy is not thought to be a major determinant of administered prices' movements in the medium term, that lends support to the argument that they should be excluded. Comprehensiveness argues for inclusion. And the arguments for exclusion are subject to the qualification that administered prices affect price formation in the rest of the economy, and so their effect should be taken into account in formulating monetary policy.

3.6.iii   *Time horizons over which targets are to be achieved*

Targets have the potential to communicate both long-term preferences and the desired adjustment path in the face of economic shocks. Yet in practice, targets do not usually fulfil both roles. The most common occurrence in setting either money or inflation targets is for the central bank or ministry of finance to announce, once a year, a single number for the forthcoming year. Yet this does not always square with the desire to use targets both to anchor long-term expectations and to steer expectations through what may be a bumpy ride towards price stability. Nor is an annual process necessarily consistent with the transmission lags of monetary policy, which appear to vary greatly from country to country. The use of targets alone may therefore open a 'transparency gap' that can be filled using other instruments of communication.

When inflation is low and relatively stable, governments or central banks may enjoy the luxury of setting targets that do not change much over time. In these countries, a target of say '2% inflation at all times' represents an attempt to anchor long-run expectations even when a shock to the economy temporarily diverts a variable from its long-term path. Chart 3.6 illustrates that only 17% of inflation targets (including those of Australia, Canada, Finland, Sweden and the UK) and 9% of money growth targets (including those of France and Switzerland) set the same target number year after year. Such targets may provide information about long-term preferences rather than a planned adjustment path. In the event of a shock moving inflation or money away from target, the long transmission lags imply that the target by itself is insufficient to provide an indication of

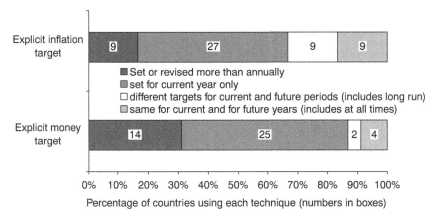

Note: Numbers of frameworks in the boxes, percentage of each target set according to a particular time horizon measured on the axis. The shorter-term arrangements represented by boxes on the left.
Source: Bank of England survey of monetary frameworks

Chart 3.6 Time horizon of inflation and money targets in the surveyed frameworks

how quickly policy will restore inflation or money towards the target. Additional instruments of communication, such as forecasts, are frequently used to fill this transparency gap.[35]

Two thirds of inflation targets and 87% of money targets are set or revised at least annually and are not specified for more than one year ahead (Chart 3.6). In determining the nature of any potential transparency gap left open by targets in these economies, it helps to consider roughly how long it takes for policy instruments to impact on the target variable. There is enormous diversity in the perceived transmission lags across the different economies. Chart 3.7 represents the relationship between changes in the operating instrument (e.g. interest rates), the operating target (e.g. base money), and the final objective (e.g. inflation). Specifically, Chart 3.7 indicates respondents' estimates for: (i) the time taken to impact fully on inflation, and (ii) the full impact upon inflation.

The bars in Chart 3.7 represent the average transmission length; the points illustrate the average strength of the relationship. The results provide a loose but illuminating means of cross-country comparison. A strong caveat is that although the results represent central bank views about the transmission mechanism in their economies, no attempts are made to ensure consistency across countries, either in terms of the model used or the approach to the experiment.[36] Differences may reflect several factors, including: (i) structural differences between economies; (ii) differences in framework;[37] and (iii) differences in estimation and simulation

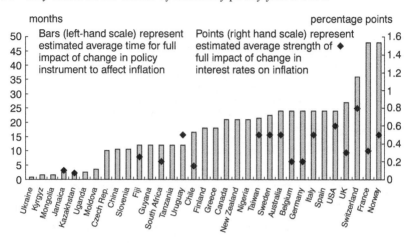

Source: Bank of England Survey of Monetary Frameworks.

Chart 3.7 Estimated average length and strength of transmission mechanisms

procedures. Furthermore, not all respondents reported the strength of the effect on inflation of changes in instruments. And in order to allow comparability across countries, we report only results for those that specified the strength in terms of a relationship between a short-term interest rate and inflation. Nevertheless, the chart illustrates that the perceived average length of time taken for instruments to affect inflation ranges from 1 to 50 months in different economies.

The wide dispersion of lags in transmission mechanisms contrast sharply with the homogeneity of the frequencies and time horizons over which targets are set. Thus targets communicate different aspects of short-run and long-run policy intentions in the various economies. It is not, however, possible to specify targets in such a way that they specify precise guidance of how policy should react to shocks and the time horizon over which price stability should be restored. Thus target specification leaves open different forms of 'transparency gaps', which are described below.

First, when transmission lags are longer than the target-horizon, then there is limited capacity for policy to bring inflation back on track within the target horizon. In this case a transparency gap may be filled by regular publication of a forecast that can indicate expected progress in bringing inflation back to target

When transmission lags are much shorter than the target horizon, the transparency gap is of a different nature. In this case the target may not in itself provide a reason for instruments to be changed immediately to achieve the target. In an extreme example of a disinflating economy, where the transmission length is just, say, one month, then to achieve a given inflation target in a year's time, policy changes could in principle be delayed for eleven months and policy tightened sharply in the last month of the target year.[38] Thus, as in this example the target specification leaves a transparency gap in the sense that the target may not provide a guide as to exactly when policy should be changed. And if in this example inflation starts off well above price stability, then the target is likely to be revised in a year's time. Then there is a 'two-way' transparency gap, as the target does not bind policy in either the very short or long run.

Such transparency gaps might be closed by publishing multi-period targets that set out a convergence path for inflation (see Hrnčíř and Šmídková (in this volume), and by publishing short- and long-term forecasts (with the long run target below the short-run one). A sixth of all countries specify distinct short- and long-run targets when announcing inflation targets, including Chile, Croatia, the Czech Republic, Israel, Jamaica and Poland.

Yet a potential difficulty of this approach is that the difference between setting targets and instruments becomes blurred. Government involvement in setting such intricate multi-period targets is likely to severely erode instrument independence. What should happen if inflation falls between the short- and long-run target (as happened in 1998 in Chile, the Czech Republic, Israel, and Poland)? In terms of a contracting approach to price stability,[39] for example, it is considerably more difficult for the government to specify in advance a transparent contract when there is a possibility that short-term and long-term targets might point policy in different directions. The papers in this volume by Hrnčíř and Šmídková (for the Czech Republic), Landerretche, Morandé, and Schmidt-Hebbel (for Chile), and Bufman and Leiderman (for Israel) show how each of these economies have approached this issue. Specifying targets for disinflation as ceilings rather than as points or ranges may help to resolve the problem, since an outcome for inflation below the short-term ceiling but above the long-term goal does not imply any conflict between the short- and long-term targets. The distance between a short-term inflation ceiling and a long-term target of close to zero may, however, be so large as to undermine the clarity of the target.

Several recent papers have highlighted the importance of forward-looking policy in minimising instabilities arising from any mismatch between transmission mechanism length and the time horizon of targets. For the United Kingdom, see Batini and Haldane (1999), and for a similar approach in the Czech Republic, see Mahadeva and Šmídková (this volume). The papers seek to address how far forward policy should look, and what the costs are for looking too far forward, or not far enough. They use small macroeconometric models and observe what happens to output and inflation volatility in response to shocks, when policy tries to bring inflation back to target relatively quickly or relatively slowly. Goodhart (this volume) reproduces some of the results for the United Kingdom.

Mahadeva and Šmídková's model for the Czech Republic is also contained in this volume. The results illustrate that in order to minimise the volatility in output and inflation, it is optimal for policy to react to forecasts for inflation between three and five quarters ahead in the Czech Republic[40] rather than the longer reaction time in the United Kingdom.

These authors also look at the costs of targeting inflation at too short or too long time horizons. For the United Kingdom, Batini and Haldane calculate that targeting at too short time horizons tends to lead to excessive volatility in output, while targeting at too long time horizons tends to lead to excessive volatility in inflation. Remarkably, the results are reversed for the Czech Republic. In practice, the relative costs of targeting inflation at a very short or long horizon depends upon the extent of factors such as real versus nominal range stickiness.

3.6.iv   *Combining dimensions of flexibility*

In a growing number of economies the focus of policy has shifted towards price stability (Cottarelli and Giannini, 1998), and central banks have been innovative in their attempts to use targets to guide policy and expectations appropriately. At the same time, central banks have been careful to protect credibility by providing (in targets) the flexibility to respond to shocks. The methods described above have sometimes been combined to maximise such flexibility. The Reserve Bank of Australia, for example, states that its target needs to be met on average over the cycle, rather than at a particular time;[41] therefore its 'thick-point' target of between 2% and 3% provides flexibility in the timing of dimension rather than in the breadth of the target range.

Yet whichever combination of points, lines, bands, tubes, and cones most aptly describes the specified evolution of targets over time, and whichever exclusions are made, it is unlikely that a target alone will be a sufficient communications device. The optimal policy response is likely to depend as much upon the source of a shock as it does on the deviation of a particular variable from target.

The answer, as argued by several authors, including King (1997), lies in explanation. Published forecasts may be used to fill the transparency gaps that are left open by the specification of targets for particular points in time. Frequently specified money targets coupled with publicly specified price stability objectives may be used to fulfil a similar role.

Similarly, forecasts may better express uncertainty than embodying uncertainty in an explicit target range. Forecasts may be more flexible than targets for illustrating how policy is reacting to specific current and previous shocks, since they tend to be revised more frequently and can be formulated to show expected developments in important variables period by period. Forecasts are also potentially more flexible than target ranges for expressing uncertainty, since they can be defined to express a policy-maker's best estimates of circumstance-specific risks. The Czech Republic, Finland, Iceland, Ireland, Sweden, and the United Kingdom have moved to an increasingly explicit treatment of risks in published inflation forecasts. Mexico publishes confidence intervals around its published money-base forecasts.

Targets, therefore, are an important, but not comprehensive means of communicating preferences. This is a point taken up by King (1996), who argues that:

> The search for a simple policy rule to guide the transition is an illusion. But central banks can try to accelerate the learning process by 'teaching by doing'; in other words making clear their own preferences and explaining their own view of how the economy behaves.

(page 444)

3.7 Summary and conclusions

Throughout the world, monetary policy objectives in the 1990s have become increasingly focused on more precisely defined objectives that are consistent with central banks' statutory objectives of price and monetary stability. From the wealth of experience evident in the responses to the questionnaire, it is clear that explicit targets are being used more than at any time since Bretton Woods, and the publication of targets for domestic aggregates has never been more widespread. This represents a marked convergence in the approach to policy.

The results have illustrated that countries have been far more successful in minimising the deviation of outcomes from target than might have been expected on the basis of experience in the 1960s, 1970s, and 1980s. This may be partly attributable to a relatively low incidence of external shocks (such as hikes in commodity prices) that contributed to higher global inflation in previous decades. But it is also likely to reflect the value of an explicit target as a forward-looking guide to central bank action.

The variety of combinations of published targets and the varying degrees to which targets are met illustrate their possible use as either a pre-commitment or a communication device. Such diversity reflects widely differing economic and institutional circumstances in the various countries in the survey.

The greater use of explicit targets does appear to be part of a broader move to build credibility through transparency. In the long run, credibility is built primarily by actions and achievements. But a strong message from the survey is that defining objectives more narrowly, and making an effort to explain the outcome of targeted variables more clearly, can be an important contribution to central bank credibility and policy.

Notes

1 See Capie, Goodhart, Fischer, and Schnadt (1994), p. 258.
2 See Cottarelli and Giannini (1997) for a detailed assessment of the experience since Bretton Woods.
3 The ECB also completed the survey in 1999, after other central banks. But the information used here related to the period before 1999.
4 The survey aimed to include variety of countries. However, some sample selection bias may remain. For example, small open developing economies that target the exchange rate are under represented.
5 The exceptions are Botswana, Japan, Sri Lanka, and Thailand, but not the United States. In 1998 the Federal Reserve still published a monitoring range for broad money growth.
6 Of the countries in the survey, nine did not exist in 1990; so 58% relates to 84, not 93 monetary frameworks.
7 Chapter 4 measures the degree to which policy in different countries focuses on different objectives.
8 Starting with Poole (1970).
9 See Hrnčíř and Šmídková (this volume) for an assessment of velocity developments in the Czech Republic. Their paper also illustrates the difficulties of specifying an inflation target in the presence of supply shocks.
10 Similarly, Alfaro and Schwartz (this volume) argue that many of the shocks that affect price developments in Mexico are beyond the immediate control of monetary policy. These include developments in the exchange rate, wages, controlled prices, and external inflation.
11 See Crockett (this volume) for a more detailed assessment of the effect of structural factors on the choice of target.
12 Excluding those countries that did not provide details about who set the exchange-rate target.
13 Fry, Goodhart, and Almeida (1996), pp. 90–96, show that in developing countries, the proportion of graduate staff increases with a country's income.
14 Changes to the monetary framework are analysed in greater detail in Chapter 7.
15 In response to the question 'Have researchers in your bank considered the Phillips curve and output gaps in the last five years?' only 24% of the transitional and developing countries responded that they had been considered in detail.
16 See Christoffersen and Doyle (1998).
17 In the remainder of the chapter we refer to 'targets' rather than 'targets and monitoring ranges'. Nevertheless, we acknowledge that some countries, including the United States, have stated that monitoring ranges have limited importance in terms of guiding monetary policy.
18 This result is made clear by comparing our data with that presented in Cottarelli and Giannini (1997).
19 There are governments that publish forecasts for inflation in their annual budget that may or may not represent an explicit target for monetary policy. We regard them as explicit targets of monetary policy only if a central bank responded that there was an explicit inflation target.
20 Some countries that joined the European single currency may have dropped formal targets for domestic inflation in 1999.
21 Data are responses to the Bank of England questionnaire. We tried to make data consistent by asking for information about when the target was set in the year prior to which the target referred. Target revisions during the course of the year were excluded, even when such data were provided. Where there is a

target range, we use the average as the reference point. Where the target is specified as a ceiling, we treat the ceiling as the reference point.

22 Haldane and Salmon use a small macro model, add to it a policy rule, and then solve the system by feeding in a set of shocks calibrated from the historically estimated residuals. They control for policy-induced volatility. Their results are in line with time-series results for other countries estimated at the same time.

23 Haldane (1995), p. 203.

24 Though the cross-sectional analysis used here has the disadvantage of being unable to explain such good performance.

25 This is the median absolute miss for the entire sample – shown in the first column of Table 3.3.A.

26 It is less clear how the proliferation of explicit targets has helped to create such a shock-free environment.

27 Some of these targets are ceilings, so a marginal undershoot may not be indicative of systematic target undershooting.

28 This argument about the nature of the implementation of intermediate money targets does not necessarily conflict with the view that inflation is purely a monetary phenomenon in the long term.

29 Although if inflation targeting implies rigid adherence to an inflation forecast, it may limit the scope for discretion even when policy does not attempt to hit the current inflation rate. Goodhart (this volume) assesses how targeting future inflation may still leave scope for discretion in policy decision.

30 Simons (1948) stresses the policy benefits of stable money rules, which are also promoted by Friedman (1960).

31 See, for example, Cukierman (1995).

32 See Guitian (1994), p. 36, and Bernanke, Laubach, Mishkin, and Posen (1999), pp. 293 and 299.

33 A quick comparison between the contents of academic journals and central bank working paper series will show that issues in the different behaviour of various price and money aggregates are of far more interest to central banks than they are to academics. In our sample, 59% of central banks in industrialised economies reported that they had published research relating to 'price specification issues'.

34 In spite of the appeal of wholesale price measures as a better proxy for competitiveness, India is the only economy that announces targets for this measure, as opposed to consumer prices. Similarly, nominal GDP targets have had no takers, their potential superiority in absorbing supply shocks being outweighed by the practical considerations of transparency and data availability.

35 Goodhart (this volume) provides a vivid description of remaining sources of ambiguity, including the relative benefits of targeting the mean, median, or mode of inflation forecasts.

36 For example, we did not specify for how long instruments were to be changed in the policy simulation.

37 The exchange-rate channel tends to be fast in many economies: if the exchange rate is fixed, the transmission mechanism may be longer.

38 Such a possibility would be much more likely where target inflation was defined as the month-to-month change in the price index, rather than the 12-month change

39 See Chapter 4.

40 Batini and Haldane estimate that, for the United Kingdom, the optimal forecast horizon is considerably longer. Another significant difference between the United Kingdom and the Czech Republic is the direction of the arrow. In the United Kingdom it goes in the opposite direction, meaning that when the fore-

casting horizon is too short, output (rather than inflation) is relatively more volatile. The differences may reflect differing strengths of particular shocks, different forms of nominal and real rigidities, and the relative importance of the various transmission channels. In the Czech Republic the exchange-rate channel is particularly important.

41 The ECB has explained that its reference values for inflation and money have a similar property.

4 The devil in the detail of monetary policy frameworks

Issues and measures of monetary framework characteristics

4.1 Introduction

Central banks' monetary policy frameworks attempt to marry the long-run objective of securing low and stable inflation with the shorter term objective of reacting efficiently and flexibly to economic shocks. Methods of dealing with trade-off between the short- and long-run objectives vary widely, as the survey results show.

Monetary policy regimes are commonly given labels, such as exchange-rate, money, or inflation targeting, yet such labels can obscure important differences among superficially similar frameworks. The approach used here provides a context for assessing the great diversity that is evident in objectives, policy processes, analysis and institutional arrangements in monetary frameworks.

In seeking to explain differences in inflation outcomes and credibility, researchers have identified a role for various factors both across time and place. Academic literature, for example, has demonstrated why independent central banks could reduce inflation in the long run by removing the inflation bias from macroeconomic policy (see e.g. Rogoff (1985), Walsh (1995)). Empirical evidence supports the view that central bank autonomy has resulted in lower inflation (see Alesina and Summers (1993) and Lybek (1999)). Experience and results are continuing to influence the monetary arrangements that are in place today, and the changes that have taken place may have contributed to marked reductions in inflation across a wide range of countries. Chapter 2 of this Report illustrated, that in 1997 in a sample of 91 developing and industrialised economies, 90% had inflation less than 10%, the highest proportion for 25 years.

Researchers are still some way from identifying and explaining all the detailed and complex relationships between monetary frameworks and economic performance. An important objective of this Report is to measure and interpret the diversity in monetary frameworks. The novelty in the approach lies in a breadth of coverage that stretches beyond previous studies in two dimensions. First, the survey attempts to capture the diverse factors that influence the choice of framework by measuring across a very broad range of framework characteristics. The survey assesses the extent to which the central bank focuses on various objectives, most particularly the exchange rate, money and inflation. And it relates these policy choices to institutional factors such as central bank independence, transparency and accountability, structural factors such as the importance of financial stability issues, and the nature of the analysis conducted by the central bank.

The second dimension in which the survey extends the work of previous studies is in the number of frameworks measured.[1] This maximises the possibility of capturing and explaining diversity of experience. Diversity is a defining feature of the responses of the 94 central banks in the sample. Countries with vastly different structures have chosen similar frameworks. For example France and St Kitts both belong to currency unions. Conversely, countries whose economies have similar structures have chosen different frameworks. For example, the advanced transition economies of central Europe and the Baltic states have a diversity of monetary policy frameworks, in spite of the fact that their economic structures are in many respects similar and each of their long-term objectives all to some extent relate to macroeconomic integration with the European Union.

In drawing on the knowledge (both factual and judgmental) of well over 100 central bankers from all over the world, the broad coverage of the report maximises the size of the data bank of experiences from which to draw lessons. Nevertheless breadth of coverage also has potential disadvantages. One is that measures of certain characteristics such as independence lack the depth of previous studies (e.g. Grilli, Masciandaro, and Tabellini (1991) and Cukierman (1992)). Another weakness is that some of the measures depend upon subjective opinions, of both the authors of the Report and the respondents to the survey. This subjectivity may perhaps reduce the accuracy of some of the measures (see Mangano (1998)).[2]

4.2   Key objectives of the survey and the survey process

Those who are expert in both the theory and practice of central banking[3] are generally quick to stress that the art of central banking is a good deal more complicated than the theory of textbooks. With monetary policy frameworks, the devil is in the detail. A primary objective of the survey is therefore to 'measure' the key characteristics of monetary frameworks in a way that is broadly consistent across a highly diverse group of economies and arrangements. Such an objective is motivated by the desire, foremost, to provide policy-makers with a means of placing their monetary framework in a global context. A second objective is to interpret such measurements, using the explanations provided by the 94 central banks whose staff completed the questionnaire.

The questionnaire circulated to around 114 central banks set out the questions that the project was aiming to answer as follows:

- How broad is the spectrum of frameworks, even within groups of economies that share the same explicit target?
- To what extent is it meaningful to classify economies according to the variable used as an explicit target?
- To what extent is the choice of framework limited by economic and financial factors, institutional factors, and the capacity to analyse these factors?
- To what extent are developments in monetary frameworks being shared across developing, transitional and industrialised economies?
- What common ground is there in the search for best practices in monetary framework design?

The survey process lasted over a year. At the outset, a pilot survey was sent to CEFTA[4] central banks and the results discussed at a Workshop in Budapest in September 1998. The full survey was then sent to a further 109 central banks in late 1998. Seventy-seven responses were collated in time to be reported at the Central Bank Governors' Symposium held at the Bank of England in June 1999, the minutes of which are included in this publication (pp. 182–205). In total 94 institutions completed the questionnaire. Each was invited to comment upon the findings of the Report, and 37 made detailed comments upon the interpretation of their own frameworks, and about the Report's content. These comments were incorporated and the results finalised in late 1999. The results, although based on the information provided by central banks, rest heavily on the judgement of the authors. They do not necessarily reflect the views of any of the participating central banks.

4.3   Measuring the characteristics of monetary policy frameworks: issues and results

Monetary policy would be simple if, first there existed a single objective; second, there was a single instrument and third, policy-makers had available a model that accurately, comprehensively and transparently described the transmission mechanism of monetary policy. In practice, there is sometimes more than one objective, more than one instrument from which to choose, and uncertainty about the economic outlook. In order to improve understanding of the interactions between objectives, constraints and the choice of policy framework instruments the survey sought to measure as fully as possible the characteristics of frameworks. It therefore measured:

The extent to which each country focuses on:
1   Exchange rate objectives
2   Money objectives

3   Inflation objectives

Institutional factors:
4   Independence of the central bank
5   Accountability of the central bank to government and parliament
6   Policy explanations: the extent to which the central bank provides the public with information about the goals and reactions of policy

Structural factors:
7   The importance of particular financial stability issues in the setting of monetary policy instruments

Analytical factors
8   The extent to which the central bank uses various indicators of inflation expectations
9   The extent to which the central bank uses models and forecasts
10   The importance of analysis of money and the banking system to the choice of the monetary framework.

From the survey results we compiled a score between zero and a hundred per cent for each of the 10 categories, based on the weighted sum of responses to individual questions according to the criteria shown in Tables 4.1 to 4.10 below. The survey responses provided a factory of framework facts and many of these statistics can be drawn from the numbers in the right-hand side of each table. These columns illustrate the distribution of answers in all economies, and in each of industrialised, transitional and developing economies. The detailed scores for each framework are provided in Appendix Tables A.1 to A.11. The scoring of frameworks in such a way involves subjectivity, so the next section considers in detail issues in measuring each characteristic.

4.3.i   Issues in measuring monetary policy focus

How is it possible to define inflation and money targeting?

'Inflation targeting' and 'money targeting' are labels attached to particular monetary frameworks. Yet it is not always clear what are their exact distinguishing features. Box 4.A illustrates some of the core features of inflation and money targeting frameworks in industrialised economies as defined by various authors. Factors that make definition difficult include:[5]

(i) Definitions that focus on the explicit variable targeted may not fully capture policy preferences   In considering money, inflation and exchange rates for the 94 central banks in the sample group, the average central bank announces a target for 1.5 variables. Furthermore, some economies may focus policy on a variable for which they do not announce an explicit

target. Peru, for example, announces an explicit target for only one vari-able – inflation, yet it operates a money-targeting framework as a means of achieving the inflation target (see Quispe and Mahadeva, in this volume).

(ii) Definitions that distinguish regimes according to the time frame of pub-lished targets and forecast horizon may be a useful benchmark for industri-alised economies, but are unlikely to be appropriate universally   Cottarelli and Giannini (1997) argue that differences between money and inflation targeting depend upon the time-dimension over which an explicit target constrains policy. When adhered to, money targets tend to constrain policy in the short run, but not the long run (since they are periodically revised). However, inflation targets tend to constrain policy in the long run, but allow for flexibility in the way policy adjusts inflation towards the target.[6]

Often inflation targets are set for more than one year, but money targets for only one year ahead (see Chapter 3). But this is not always the case. Switzerland, for example, announces multi-year money targets. Con-versely, there is wide diversity across countries in the time it takes for policy instruments to affect inflation, which suggests that caution is needed in defining different frameworks according to the perceived difference in time horizons. The survey responses suggest that the time taken for policy instruments to affect inflation may be less than three months in some developing and transitional economies. In that context does a target one year ahead represent a short-, medium- or long-term commitment? (see Chart 3.7 above). In industrialised economies, where the lags are generally thought to be much longer, multi-year targets and forecasts may be used to influence expectations of how monetary policy will be conducted between the time at which policy changes and the time when policy has had its full impact. In economies with shorter transmission horizons, multi-year targets may have a smaller role in helping to influence expectations about monetary policy.

(iii) Some definitions overstate the relative importance of analytical methods to a particular framework   In labelling frameworks, a number of IMF Working Papers[7] have stressed both the importance of macroecono-metric models in inflation targeting economies, and the problems in build-ing and using such models in developing and transitional economies. Yet the argument that accurate model-based forecasts are a more important prerequisite for inflation targeting than in money-targeting or discre-tionary frameworks is difficult to defend. The survey results illustrate that judgmental forecasts remain of prime importance for a wide range of economies. In frameworks described by central banks as inflation target-ing, the survey results indicate that judgmental forecasts are used just as frequently as model-based forecasts. Inflation targeting has re-emphasised the role of forward-looking policy, but looking to the future is important in any policy framework.

Box 4.1 Definitions of Different Characteristics of Money and Inflation Targets

Study	*Main Distinction Identified between Money and Inflation Targeting*
Leiderman and Svensson (1995)	With reference to New Zealand, Canada, United Kingdom, Sweden and Finland the authors wrote 'These inflation targeting regimes have two characteristics:

    (i) An explicit quantitative inflation target (specifying the index, the target level, the tolerance interval, the time frame, and possibly situations under which the inflation target will be modified or disregarded).

    (ii) The absence of an explicit intermediate target for monetary aggregates or exchange rates.'

| Masson, Savastano and Sharma (1997) | The authors mention four essential ingredients of inflation targeting: |

    (i) 'explicit quantitative targets for the rate of inflation some period(s) ahead'

    (ii) 'clear and unambiguous indications that the attainment of the inflation target constitutes the overriding objective of monetary policy in the sense that it takes precedence over all other objectives'

    (iii) 'a methodology ("model") for producing inflation forecasts that uses a number of variables and indicators containing information on future inflation'; and

    (iv) 'a forward-looking operations procedure in which the setting of policy instruments depends upon the assessment of inflation pressures and where the inflation forecasts are used as the main intermediate target'

| Cottarelli and Giannini (1997) | 'Inflation Targeting' is not purely the announcement of some short-run inflation target by the government – something that to different degrees occurs in most countries – but the announcement of a targeted inflation path extending up to a few years ahead, coupled with the setting up of procedures for public monitoring of how the monetary authorities pursue their objective' |

[Money targeting] is 'characterised by the announcement of a short-term intermediate target, either in the form of a monetary aggregate or of a (typically crawling) peg'.

The above arguments suggest that attaching labels to frameworks can easily be misleading. This discussion of the difficulties in classifying monetary policy frameworks has focused on inflation targets. Yet classification problems also apply to money and exchange rate targets. Economies using a money-targeting framework, for example, do not always use their target to anchor policy, particularly in the face of unexpected velocity shocks.[8] And the survey results illustrate that several economies whose exchange rate regime is classified by the IMF[9] as 'fixed to another currency' do not classify themselves as exchange rate targeters (see Table 5.2 in Chapter 5). Sometimes this may be because capital controls allow the central bank to target both a domestic and exchange rate objective. And in the case of East-Asian economies before 1998, Ohno (1999) illustrates just how close was the pre-crisis link between the dollar and several of the currencies in the 'soft dollar' zone.[10]

4.3.i.a Measures of monetary policy focus: questions, issues, and answers

In terms of the Report's attempts to categorise economies according to their targets or objectives, the approach differed in at least one of the following ways from previous studies:[11]

i *Objectives are defined over three rather than just one dimension.* An important aspect of the methodology is that each country's objectives are measured over the exchange rate, money growth and inflation. For most frameworks, the short-term objective function depends on several variables rather than just one.

ii *The survey attempted to measure <u>the degree</u> to which a country's policy focused on a particular objective, rather than assuming that policy frameworks could be classified as 100% committed to a single objective.* In some, but not all industrialised countries, 'labelling' of the monetary framework is feasible.[12] In other countries, frameworks often contain a mixture of exchange rate, money and inflation targeting, so it is difficult or impossible to assign a simple label to the framework.

iii *The survey isolated measures of objectives from other characteristics commonly associated with particular frameworks.* For example, inflation targeters in industrialised economies often use model-based inflation forecasts, but the survey treated measures of policy objectives and analytical techniques as separate characteristics, rather than as two parts of the same package.

In attempting to measure the degree to which policy focuses on each of the exchange rate, money and inflation (at least in the short term; they are perhaps less likely to conflict in the long term), the survey used answers to questions that were consistent across each of these variables. The questions asked were as follows:[13]

1 *How does each central bank categorise its regime?* A central bank's own categorisation of its monetary framework should provide a good indication of its priorities. The questionnaire therefore asked each central bank to categorise its regime as one of exchange rate targeting, money targeting, inflation targeting, discretionary, balance of payments

targeting, pursuing some other target, or whether the framework could not be summarised as targeting a single variable.

2   *Is there an explicit target for the exchange rate, money or inflation?*[14] Table 3.1 in the previous chapter shows which countries in the survey announced targets for which variables. But what might at first sight appear to be an explicit target may in fact not represent a leading characteristic of the framework. For example, in the US the Federal Reserve publish monitoring ranges for monetary growth that do not represent targets: the Federal Reserve Board Chairman Alan Greenspan announced, in testimony to a Senate Committee (1993) that the Fed was giving 'less weight to monetary aggregates as guides to policy'. In a similar vein, some countries publish a variety of targets and monitoring ranges, some of which represent only a loose guide to policy preferences. And although many governments publish inflation targets in their annual budgets and financial statements, it is not always clear whether these have an important role in monetary policy. We include such targets only when the central banks report them.

3   *How does each central bank rank its monetary policy objectives (other than statutory objectives)?* We asked central banks to rank policy objectives. The answers provide information not only on the targeted variable(s), but also on other preferences that can guide policy in the face of the variety of shocks that face different economies.

4   *Which variables have priority if there is a policy conflict?* This question attempts to measure any flexibility in the approach to the main focal point of policy. Our measure gave the highest score for a particular objective when it always wins the day in policy conflicts. It also awarded a score to variables that sometimes guide policy even if they are not the main target. We note, however, that our measures will capture not only preferences, but also the likelihood of policy conflicts. Where no policy conflicts were anticipated or reported, the scores were set so as to mirror the rank of policy objectives.[15]

4.3.ii   Issues in measuring institutional characteristics of monetary policy framework (independence, accountability and transparency explanations)

4.3.ii.a   Measuring central bank independence

There have been many authoritative studies on independence (Chapters 1 and 6 of this Report refer to some[16]). The difficulties in measuring independence have been well known for years and the following summary provided in Cukierman (1992) rings true:

Actual, as opposed to formal, central bank independence depends on

Table 4.1 Measure of policy focus on exchange-rate objectives

Questions	Question weight	Scores	Categories of answers, distribution of results	All economies	Industrialised	Transitional	Developing
1. If you were to categorise your framework as one of the following, which would it be?	1	100	mentioned exchange rate only	**26**	11	7	8
		50	not categorised as one target but mentioned exchange rate targeting with one other objective	**6**	2	1	3
		33	Not categorised as exchange rate targeting but mentioned in the context of two other objectives	**3**	1	1	1
		0	did not mention exchange rate	**59**	14	13	32
2. To what extent is the exchange rate fixed to another currency?	1	100	explicit point target, or described by IMF as 'fixed to another currency'	**18**	1	6	11
		75	explicit band narrower than 6%, or described by IMF as 'limited flexibility'	**13**	3	1	9
		50	explicit band of 30% or less	**15**	11	2	2
		25	no explicit target (but public knowledge that target exists), or IMF described as managed floating	**21**	3	10	8
		0	freely floating	**27**	10	3	14
3. Please rank monetary policy objectives (other than price or monetary stability) the central bank pursues (1 = first priority), indicate if there is no fixed target.	1	100	exchange rate first objective	**33**	13	7	13
		50	exchange rate mentioned as an objective	**35**	5	11	19
		0	otherwise	**26**	10	4	12
4. In your current monetary framework, is there scope for other variables to prevail over the target in the event of policy conflicts	1	100	exchange rate always prevails over *all other objectives*	**17**	6	5	6
		75	exchange rate always prevails over *money and inflation objectives*	**6**	1	1	4
		50	exchange rate usually prevails	**12**	8	1	3
		25	exchange rate sometimes prevails	**38**	6	10	22
		0	exchange rate rarely or never prevails	**21**	7	5	9

Table 4.2 Measure of policy focus on money objectives

Questions	Question weight	Scores	Categories of answers, distribution of results	All economies	Industrialised	Transitional	Developing
1. If you were to categorise your framework as **one** of the following, which would it be?	1	100	money targeting	**23**	4	5	14
		50	could not categorise as one target but mentioned money targeting with one other objective	**6**	1	1	4
		33	Mentioned in context of two other objectives	**2**	1	1	0
		0	Otherwise	**63**	22	15	26
2. Do you have a specific, numerical, publicly announced target or monitoring range for money or credit?	1	100	Yes	**39**	8	12	19
		0	No	**55**	20	10	25
3. Please rank monetary policy objectives (other than price or monetary stability) the central bank pursues (1 = first priority). Indicate if there is no fixed target.	1	100	money first objective	**14**	2	5	7
		50	money mentioned as an objective	**26**	5	7	14
		0	otherwise	**54**	21	10	23
4. In your current monetary framework, is there scope for other variables to prevail over the target in the event of policy conflicts? If so, how often does money prevail as a target?	1	100	money always prevails over *all other objectives*	**0**	0	0	0
		75	money always prevails over *the exchange rate and inflation* objectives	**1**	0	0	1
		50	money usually prevails	**19**	3	4	12
		25	money sometimes prevails	**21**	3	5	13
		0	money rarely or never prevails	**53**	22	13	18

Table 4.3 Measure of policy focus on inflation objectives

Questions	Question weight	Scores	Categories of answers, distribution of results	All economies	Industrialised	Transitional	Developing
1. If you were to categorise your framework as one of the following, which would it be?	1	100 50 33 0	inflation targeting could not categorise but mentioned inflation in the context of one other objective mentioned inflation in the context of two other objectives Otherwise	15 8 3 68	6 3 1 18	4 3 1 14	5 2 1 36
2. Do you have a specific, numerical, publicly announced target or monitoring range for inflation or credit?	1	100 0	Yes No	55 39	13 15	16 6	26 18
3. Please rank monetary policy objectives (other than price or monetary stability) the central bank pursues (1 = first priority). Indicate if there is no fixed target.	1	100 50 0	Inflation first objective Inflation mentioned as an objective Otherwise	30 33 31	8 11 9	8 6 8	14 16 14
4. In your current monetary framework, is there scope for other variables to prevail over the target in the event of policy conflicts? If so, how often does inflation prevail as a target?	1	100 75 50 25 0	Inflation always prevails over *all other objectives* Inflation always prevails over *the exchange rate and inflation* objectives Inflation usually prevails inflation sometimes prevails inflation rarely or never prevails	4 6 10 40 34	3 2 4 12 5	1 3 3 6 9	0 1 3 22 18

the degree of independence conferred on the bank by law, but also on a myriad of less structured factors such as informal arrangements between the bank and other parts of the government, the quality of the bank's research department, and the personalities of key individuals in the bank and other policymaking organs like the Treasury.

(1992, page 369)

Authors have taken different approaches to measuring central bank independence. Several, including Cukierman, acknowledge the problems and try to cast the net of measures widely in order to take account of as many as possible. Yet even highly disaggregated measures remain subjective. Mangano (1998) illustrates the wide 'interpretation spread' in the various components of indices that measure central bank independence. Fry (1998) judges independence by asking, 'Do actions speak louder than words?' For developing economies he measures independence according to the extent to which a central bank neutralises the effects of increased credit demands by the government on the money supply by reducing credit to the private sector.

The approach taken here follows that of Cukierman (1992) and Grilli, Masciandaro, and Tabellini (1991). We define an overall measure of independence over a range of characteristics covering legal objectives, goals, instruments, finance of the government deficit and term of office of the Governor. The approach remains vulnerable to the criticism of subjectivity, particularly insofar as the measures depend upon the responses of central banks (Chapter 6 contains further analysis of the issue).

4.3.ii.b Measures of central bank independence

The survey's measures of central bank independence cover a broad range of factors. The scoring and the distribution of responses are shown in Table 4.4. Chapter 6 interprets the results in greater detail. The questions related to central bank independence were as follows:

- *To what extent do statutory objectives provide the central bank with a clear focus on price stability?* The approach follows Cukierman's in measuring the strength of the unequivocal legal mandate to price stability. The approach treats statutory monetary objectives as potentially conflicting with price stability when objectives such as employment or growth are stated separately without being qualified by statements such as 'without prejudice to monetary stability'. Financial stability objectives are not interpreted as potentially conflicting with monetary stability.
- *To what extent does the central bank determine the setting of explicit policy targets?* Another measure of independence ('goal independ-

ence' rather than 'instrument independence') is the extent to which, in practice, the central bank sets its own policy targets. The survey scores independence according to whether only the central bank, only the government, or both, have a role in setting any explicit target.[17]

In constructing this measure of goal independence, the survey does not distinguish between exchange rate, money and inflation targets. The survey awards a score of 1 if the central bank is the only institution to set a target at its own discretion; 0.5 if both the government and the central bank have some role in setting at least one of these targets; and 0 if the government is the only institution to set at least one of these targets at is own discretion. The score does not depend upon which party sets which target (if there is more than one target).[18]

- *To what extent does the central bank determine the adjustment of monetary policy instruments ('instrument independence')?* The questionnaire asked each central bank to state the extent to which they or government decide on changes to monetary policy instruments. Among central banks that reported having full control over the full range of policy instruments, the score was higher for those in which no government representative had voting rights on changes to monetary policy instruments.
- *Limits on government borrowing from the central bank.* Successive authors have identified these limits as highly important in explaining inflation, particularly in developing economies (e.g. Fry, Goodhart and Almeida (1996)). The survey attempts to measure both the breadth of the limits, and also the degree to which they are used and enforced.
- *How long is the governor's term of office?* The survey uses information from Pringle (1999) and awards a higher score to those central banks whose governors are appointed for longer fixed terms.

4.3.iii.a   *Issues in interpreting accountability and policy explanations*

Accountability and transparency have become buzzwords amongst policy-makers in the late-1990s. In the field of monetary policy, the theoretical work of Persson and Tabellini (1993), Walsh (1995) and Svensson (1997), coupled with practical experience of several central banks, has demonstrated the possibility of governments maintaining low inflation through contracts with the central bank incorporating targets. Central bank accountability to government and parliament is key to the success of these contracts. Similarly, transparency and in particular the explanation of policy decisions, have an important role in reducing uncertainty by increasing the public's understanding of the contracts (Schaling, Hoeberichts and Eijffinger (1998)).

To the extent that transparent and accountable policies can demonstrate the authorities' commitment to an 'anti-surprise' policy, they may reduce

Table 4.4 Measures of central bank independence

Questions	Question weight	Scores	Categories of answers, distribution of results	All economies	Industrialised	Transitional	Developing
1. To what extent do statutory objectives provide the central bank with a clear focus on price stability?	1	100	only goal is price, monetary or currency stability	24	9	9	6
		75	price stability + financial stability objectives and non-conflicting monetary stability objectives	54	13	13	28
		50	Price stability plus conflicting objectives	12	4	0	8
		25	no statutory objectives	3	1	0	2
		0	only goals other than price stability	1	1	0	0
2. To what extent does the central bank determine the setting of policy targets?	1	100	only central bank sets an explicit target (for either inflation, money or the exchange rate) OR there are no explicit targets	27	7	6	14
		50	both central bank and government have a role in setting an explicit target (for either inflation, money or the exchange rate)	55	17	14	24
		0	only government sets a target (for either inflation, money or the exchange rate)	12	4	2	6
3. To what extent does the central bank determine the adjustment of monetary policy instruments?	2	100	central bank decides on changes in instruments and no representative of government attends the meeting of monetary policy makers, other than as an observer	63	23	18	22
		65	central bank decides on changes to instruments and a representative of government attends the meeting of monetary policy makers	15	3	3	9
		33	central bank and government have a role in setting instruments	12	2	0	10
		0	central bank role in setting instruments is limited	4	0	1	3
4. To what extent are there limits on central bank financing of the fiscal deficit?	2	100	prohibited, never used, or amounts so small and for short periods independence in no way affected	46	26	11	9
		75	narrow, well enforced limits exist	15	1	5	9
		50	limits exist that are usually enforced	25	1	4	20
		25	wide limits exist and some procedures exist when limits are missed	7	0	2	5
		0	no limits or little enforcement	1	0	0	1

5.	How long is the term of office of the Governor?	0.5					
	8 years or above	100	5	3	1	1
	7 years	86	11	5	6	0
	6 years	71	21	6	9	6
	5 years	57	37	9	4	24
	4 years	43	6	2	1	3
	3 years	29	5	1	0	4
	term can exceed 3 years	14	9	2	1	6
	Memo: Can the Central Bank formulate and implement policy without government constraint? (Scores are authors' interpretation of general answer provided)	0				
	independent with no qualification	100	36	16	10	10
	independent with any qualification	75	31	10	6	15
	independent with significant qualification	50	11	1	4	6
	limited independence	25	14	1	2	11
	not possible, or requires sanction of other person/body	0	2	0	0	2

any inflationary (and deflationary) bias from policy. As pointed out by Blinder (1998) and Goodhart (in this volume), such incentives have the potential to reduce the relevance of a generation of macroeconomic literature that is based around the premise that policy-makers have the incentive to boost output by involving short-term surprises to inflation.

Defining distinct measures of independence, accountability and policy explanations is, however, difficult. It is not always clear into which of independence, accountability and explanation the various potential measures should be allocated. A central bank report may, by example, contribute to both transparency and accountability. Few authors have published separate indices for these concepts. Amongst those who have done so are Briault, Haldane and King (1996), who constructed an index of accountability in monetary policy for industrialised economies and compared it with an index of goal independence. Lybek (1999) included measures of accountability in his index of autonomy (and accountability) of central banks in transitional economies in the former Soviet Union. And Hochreiter and Kowalski (1999) also explored aspects of accountability in central and eastern European countries. We are not aware of previous studies that have conducted indices of policy explanations, although Masson, Savastano and Sharma (1997) include measures of policy explanations, accountability and analysis in their index of inflation targeting characteristics for five developing economies.

Likewise, independence and accountability are distinct parts of the same (implicit or explicit) contract between central bank and government. The capacity for the Minister of Finance to overrule the central bank may reduce independence just as, in a democracy, it increases accountability. In particular countries, it may be possible to identify separate characteristics of a framework that represent independence, accountability and transparency. For example, there may exist an explicit contract in which the government sets a particular target, and the central bank both has the independent authority to change instruments to meet the target, and is accountable to government or parliament if it misses the target.

It is considerably more difficult to provide separable measures of independence and accountability when stretching the measure to cover many economies, including those where contracting is not a feature of the monetary framework. Where there is no explicit contract that distinguishes the roles of government and the central bank, measures of *increased* accountability may sometimes flow indistinguishably along the same veins as measures of *reduced* independence. Thus although independence and accountability are not merely inverses of each other, some features of monetary frameworks have opposite implications for independence and accountability. Our definition of accountability focuses on the extent to which the central bank has to explain its actions directly to government, and if there are specified circumstances in which the government may intervene in the process of monetary policy formulation.

In spite of the problems discussed above, the measures presented can be useful in highlighting the differences in the combination of independence and accountability that prevail in economies, according to their institutional arrangements.[19]

The measure of policy explanations used in the survey focuses on the information published by the central bank that could help the public to understand policy, analysis and forecasts of the central bank. This is not a comprehensive definition of the transparency of a monetary framework. Such a definition would have to include aspects of a monetary framework that are *inherently* transparent. For example, currency boards in the sample may be regarded as inherently transparent (and accountable). Indeed, policy-makers' motives for offering explanations of policy may be a substitute for the failure of past actions to provide credibility (Briault, Haldane and King (op cit.)). Box 4.2 addresses broader issues in assessing whether or not it is possible to measure transparency across a broad spectrum of monetary frameworks.

Box 4.2 Is transparency measurable?

A monetary policy becomes increasingly transparent when those outside the central bank are provided with fuller access to the information necessary to understand both the goals of policy and the means by which policy-makers react to changes in economic conditions. The striking trend towards greater explanation of policy evident in this report is one important manifestation of greater transparency. Yet there are many ways in which transparency can be manifested, not least since actions as well as words affect transparency. The survey provides measures of these various factors in its measures of policy explanations, independence and accountability of central banks, and the degree to which policy focuses on particular objectives.

Yet the Report does not attempt to produce an overall index of transparency by weighting together each component, mainly because the appropriate weights are highly variable across countries. In particular the measures of policy explanations in the survey are most relevant for floating, rather than fixed, exchange rate countries. The framework of a small open economy with a credible exchange rate peg may be inherently easy to understand; the transparency of the regime comes primarily from the ability of market participants and the public to continuously observe and test the credibility of the target. And some currency boards, such as Hong Kong, have made strenuous efforts towards transparency, for example by publishing short-term liquidity forecasts. In short, although the questions in this survey are not adequate to capture the degree to which a fixed exchange-rate regime is transparent, such a policy is very likely to be clear and easy to understand so long as the currency peg is widely perceived to be secure.

Even where the exchange rate is flexible, there may be several factors other than those measured in the survey that affect transparency. Market participants and others may find it easier to understand long-term policy preferences when the legal and institutional framework provides clear incentives for policy-makers, and when the central bank has clarified its preferences by making policy choices according to a predictable pattern over a number of years. The Bundesbank, for example, has a long-established record for delivering low inflation. Conversely, the monetary policy of other countries may have been predictably expansionary before elections.

In particular, the public may understand policy-makers' objectives, and predict their likely reaction to short-term disturbances, by observing actual policy changes, regardless of how much explanation is offered. In circumstances where policy instruments and targets are changed frequently, the central bank may reveal its preferences to the public more clearly through actions rather than words. And in the case of money-targeting central banks such as the Bundesbank, the intermediate money target may have had a strong role in communicating with the public in a way that is not captured by the survey's focus on published forecasts (see Posen, in this volume).

As a complement to measures of policy explanations, it would be possible to construct an index measuring the 'inherent' transparency of a framework, using answers to questions asked in the survey that include 'How frequently is policy changed?' 'How often are data for the target and outcomes observable?' and using information on the reliability with which policy has achieved stability in the past. Yet the interpretation of each measure would be complicated. For example, although frequent policy changes may communicate regular updates in policy preferences, they will not necessarily add to transparency when they are made in a highly uncertain environment (see Martin and Salmon (1999)). And defining what constitutes a policy change is not simple. Some countries change operational instruments daily, yet it is unlikely that a single such change would reveal policy preferences to the same extent as the outcome of a regular monthly meeting of policy-makers. Similarly, frequent target revisions may provide more information about policy preferences, but they may be an indication of reduced clarity in policy-setting in so far as they reflect difficulties in forecasting accurately.

In measuring overall transparency, an alternative to the survey's approach of measuring as many as possible of 'transparency' inputs is to assess the effect of transparency on the relationship between policy announcements and market responses. If policy is highly transparent, then the 'news' contained in policy announcements should be reduced, and the yield curve may shift less when policy actions are revealed. Haldane and Read (1999) find some evidence that transparency reforms in the UK and USA reduced conditional yield curve volatility. For Canada, Muller and Zelmer (1999) find that increasing transparency may have helped markets to anticipate monetary policy actions.

Recent discussions undertaken under the auspices of the BIS and IMF attempted to develop a framework for analysing monetary policy transparency.[20] Such discussions and our results gave the clear impression of an increasing desire among policy-makers to provide the public with the necessary tools and access to assess policy objectives, operating targets, reaction functions and the decision making process.

4.3.iii.b   *Measures of accountability*

The survey measured how far the central bank has a legal or informal responsibility to explain and defend its policies to government and parliament, and to involve parliament in policy decisions.[21] At one end of the spectrum this relationship may involve informal meetings between the Governor and Finance Minister. At the other end, it may involve government intervening frequently in the formulation and implementation of monetary policy (the opposite of central bank independence).

The survey distinguishes two forms of accountability. The first relates to accountability to a specific target. Monetary policy contracts between governments and central banks, whether informal or formal, are likely to be clearer if they incorporate a numerical target. The survey therefore measures accountability according to the existence of such a target, whether or not government has a role in setting it, and what procedures came into play if it is missed. The second form of accountability is a more general measure, relating to governmental and parliamentary monitoring of the central bank.

In some respects these measures of accountability remain controversial, for example in that they automatically award scores for the existence of explicit targets. In 1998 there was no explicit target in Japan, yet the Governor of the Bank of Japan appeared 106 times before Parliament during the 1998 fiscal year. In that sense the survey measurement techniques might underestimate the accountability of a framework such as Japan's. Future surveys might profit by looking in greater depth at parliamentary monitoring.

Potentially important aspects of both accountability and independence are clauses that allow politicians to override the central bank, sometimes only in pre-specified circumstances. Responses to the survey describe how these can be used. These are summarised for each framework in a memorandum item at the end of the accountability and independence measures (Appendix Table A.6). Although these clauses are potentially important, they were not taken into account in the overall scores for either independence or accountability because of difficulties in finding a measure that is consistent across economies. Several respondents said that although they were in place, override clauses were unlikely ever to be used.[22] In currency boards, the question of an override clause has relatively little relevance, since it might be difficult to overrule the currency board without endangering its existence.[23] Thus although an override clause may be important in particular frameworks, we elected not to include it in the scores calculated here.

4.3.iii.c   Measures of policy explanations

The overall measure of how fully policy decisions are explained is shown in its disaggregated detail in Table 4.6. It attaches equal weight to the efforts made in explaining: (i) policy decisions; (ii) assessments of the economy; and (iii) forecasts and forward-looking analysis. The component questions of each are assessed below:

- *Explaining policy decisions*   We measured policy explanations according to three factors. The first covers *timeliness*. The questionnaire asked how soon after a meeting of policy-makers are explanations provided. The survey attached the highest weight to the question *how frequently does the central bank provides explanations of policy decisions in its published bulletins.* We also asked about *breadth of coverage*: Are policy decisions explained in both regular assessments and in timely minutes of meetings? And does the central bank publish the votes of individual policy-makers within the committee? Voting patterns may add to the capacity of the public is assessing the balance of the decision, but we attached a lower weight to this question, in part because publication of voting patterns will not necessarily illuminate the reasons for the decision. And there are other means of communicating the 'balance' of the decision. For example, the Federal Reserve sometimes communicates a 'bias' towards changing policy in a particular direction.
- *Publicly explaining forecasts*   Our measures include questions regarding the frequency of forward-looking analysis in bulletins, i.e. the extent to which the central bank publishes and explains forecasts, explains risks to the forecast, and explains past forecasting errors. In assessing the importance of various aspects of forward-looking analysis, the survey attaches most weight to the extent to which there is forward-looking analysis in bulletins, because information about such analysis is readily available. There is, however, a strong element of

Table 4.5 Accountability of the central bank to government

Questions	Question weight	Scores	Categories of answers, distribution of results	All economies	Industrialised	Transitional	Developing
Accountability to a specific target							
1. Is there a specific published target?	1	100 0	yes no	**83** **11**	25 3	22 0	36 8
2. Does government have a role in setting any central bank target?	1	100 0	yes no	**67** **27**	21 7	16 6	30 14
3. Do procedures exist for when the target is missed?	1	100 50 0	recognised formal procedures exist informal procedures exist, or if central bank reports instruments set in conjunction with government no	**17** **31** 46	8 5 15	4 6 12	5 20 19
Accountability to Government or in general							
1. Central Bank subject to monitoring by legislature	3	100 50 0	yes irregularly, or if instrument independence limited no	**70** **6** 18	19 4 5	21 1 0	30 1 13
Memo: Procedures written when government can overrule	0	100 50 0	formally written down informally no	**20** **3** **71**	6 0 22	2 0 20	12 3 29

Table 4.6 Measure of policy explanations

Questions	Question weight	Scores	Categories of answers, distribution of results	All economies	Industrialised	Transitional	Developing
Explanation of Policy decisions (weights refer to sub-total – each has a weight of 1/3 in total score for policy explanations)							
1. Central bank provides explanations on day policy changed?	1.5	100 0	Yes No	**76** **18**	25 3	21 1	30 14
2. Explanations provided when policy-makers meet and *do not change* policy	0.3	100 50 0	Yes Sometimes no	**15** **5** **74**	4 2 22	9 1 12	2 2 40
3. Policy decisions Discussed in standard bulletins and reports	2	100 50 0	at least twice a year at least annually no	**61** **12** **21**	21 2 5	15 2 5	25 8 11
4. Minutes of policy Meetings published	1	100 50 0	within a month of meeting more than a month after no	**12** **5** **77**	7 2 19	2 2 18	3 1 40
5. Voting patterns published	0.5	100 0	yes no	**6** **88**	5 23	1 21	0 44
Published forward-looking analysis							
6. Forward-looking analysis in standard bulletins and reports	2	100 50 25 0	more than annually at least annually unspecified otherwise	**39** **24** **10** **21**	18 4 2 4	7 4 4 7	14 16 4 10

No.	Item	Weight	Category					
7.	Form of publication	1.5	words, one of numbers and graphs	100	35	16	5	14
			one of words, numbers and graphs	50	25	8	6	11
			unspecified	25	13	0	4	9
			none	0	21	4	7	10
8.	Risks to forecast published	1	words and one of numbers and graphs	100	9	7	2	0
			one of words, numbers and graphs	50	23	9	4	10
			none	0	62	12	16	34
9.	Discussion of past forecast errors	1	yes	100	21	8	3	10
			sometimes	50	9	7	2	0
			no	0	64	13	17	34

Assessment and Analysis

No.	Item	Weight	Category					
10.	Analysis in standard bulletins and reports	2	more than annually	100	86	28	20	38
			at least annually	50	7	0	2	5
			otherwise	0	1	0	0	1
11.	Frequency of speeches	1.5	at least monthly	100	39	20	11	8
			at least quarterly	66	26	6	5	15
			less than quarterly/occasional	33	29	2	6	21
			never, almost never	0	0	0	0	0
12.	Working papers and other research publications	1	more than 10 each year	100	35	18	5	12
			more than 5 each year	66	19	9	3	7
			more than 2/occasional	33	18	1	8	9
			never	0	22	0	6	16

subjectivity in the responses. Some respondents interpreted publishing an intermediate money target as providing forward-looking analysis. Such a target, after all, must be based upon output and inflation projections. The survey attached less weight to those answers that depend upon publication and discussion of explicit forecasts than to analysis published in bulletins, since in some countries, intermediate targets (either for money or the exchange rate) may act as substitutes for published forecasts.

- *Explaining assessment and analysis*   The survey attached most weight to analysis provided in bulletins and in the speeches made by senior members of staff. A lower weight was attached to the frequency with which the central bank publishes research since such research may not always be related to the current conjuncture.

4.3.iv   Issues and the measurement of the importance of financial stability issues

Financial stability issues can be important for monetary policy in particular circumstances. Volatile asset prices, domestic and overseas financial sector insolvency, and credit rationing may each affect monetary policy decisions. The questionnaire asked how far these various financial stability issues affected both the choice of framework and the setting of policy instruments. The questions and a summary of the answers are shown in Table 4.7.

4.3.v   Issues and the measurement of analysis conducted in central banks

Many authors have agreed that the choice of a framework depends upon the degree of policy technology available (see section 4.3 above). If, for example, data inadequacies mean that policy-makers have limited knowledge of how their actions affect monetary stability, this may reduce the sacrifice of monetary autonomy involved in giving up control over domestic instruments when fixing the exchange rate. Similarly, data inadequacies may also affect the choice of domestic framework. The force of arguments for money targets may increase in circumstances where data for money and the banking system are more reliable and frequent than for other sectors of the economy.

4.3.v.a Measuring the use of inflation expectations

One of the measures of a successful monetary policy is its ability to engender expectations of low future inflation, even in the face of short-term shocks. Some inflation-targeting central banks in particular have placed emphasis on measuring and monitoring measures of inflation expectations,

Table 4.7 Measure of influence of financial stability issues in the setting of monetary policy instruments

Questions	Question weight	Scores	Categories of answers, distribution of results	All economies	Industrialised	Transitional	Developing
1. Asset price volatility	1	100	vital,	6	0	1	5
		66	important	15	5	6	4
		33	relevant	45	19	5	21
		0	not important	28	4	10	14
2. Domestic financial sector insolvency	1	100	vital,	27	1	7	19
		66	important	21	4	9	8
		33	relevant	23	11	2	10
		0	not important	23	12	4	7
3. Reports of credit rationing by domestic financial sector	1	100	vital,	10	0	3	7
	66	important	18	3	6	9	
		33	relevant	29	11	7	11
		0	not important	37	14	6	17
4. Financial sector insolvency overseas	1	100	vital,	4	0	0	4
		66	important	18	2	8	8
		33	relevant	25	10	6	9
		0	not important	47	16	8	23

partly in keeping with the forward-looking nature of the targets. The survey assessed three means by which central banks may assess the degree to which different groups in the economy predict likely inflation outcomes, and weights each equally (Table 4.8). The first measure uses information from financial markets; the second uses surveys of producers and consumers in the economy; the third uses information from outside forecasting agencies. In each case, respondents provided information as to whether (a) the information source was used, and (b) how frequently the measure was published. The survey treats publication as a proxy both for the importance attached to the analysis, and its quality.

4.3.v.b   Measuring the use of models and forecasts

The questionnaire asked for information regarding the use of various modelling and forecasting techniques. In measuring separately the nature of analysis and the focus of policy, the survey is able to provide new evidence on these issues. The survey attached most weight to the use of a structural model, which is judged according to the frequency with which it is used to produce forecasts, and also its size. Vector Auto Regression-based models have become an increasingly widely used tool in the central bank's kit, particularly with regard to short-term forecasts, and the weights attached to their use are also relatively high.

The survey attaches less weight to the other three analytical methods shown in Table 4.9. Theory based models such as computable general equilibrium models are not yet much used in the conjunctural work of most central banks. In reporting the use of these models, however, some central banks took an apparently wider interpretation of 'theory-based' than we intended in the question.[24] Similarly, although judgement remains of the highest importance in the 'art' of policy setting the answers suggest that the definition of 'off-model data-based forecasts' was interpreted in different ways by different central banks, providing some concern regarding the consistency of the answers.

Finally, some central banks benefit from access to a wide range of other forecasts from financial, academic and other institutions; hence the survey also took account of the use of such forecasts in compiling an overall score.

4.3.vi   Measuring the importance of analysis of money and the banking sector

This final characteristic measured by the survey rests on subjective responses to questions asking each central bank to assess the importance to the monetary policy framework of three methods of assessing the role of money and the banking sector, namely money demand equations, analysis of monetary survey data, and analysis of the effect of policy

Table 4.8 Measures used in analyses of inflation expectations

Questions	Question weight	Scores	Categories of answers, distribution of results	All economies	Industrialised	Transitional	Developing
1. Market information	1	100	used and published at least quarterly	12	7	2	3
		75	used and published	13	7	2	4
		50	used but not published	17	8	4	5
		0	not used	52	6	14	32
2. Surveys of consumers/producers/others	1	100	used and published at least quarterly	17	8	2	7
		75	used and published	7	4	2	1
		50	used but not published	16	9	3	4
		0	not used	54	7	15	32
3. Surveys of outside forecasts	1	100	used and published at least quarterly	14	8	3	3
		75	used and published occasionally	8	4	1	3
		50	used but not published	17	7	5	5
		0	not used	55	9	13	33

Table 4.9 Measures of use of models and forecasts

Questions	Question weight	Scores	Categories of answers, distribution of results	All economies	Industrialised	Transitional	Developing
1. Does the central bank use a model with at least 10 endogenous variables or 10 behavioural equations?	1	100 0	yes no	**31** **63**	20 8	4 18	7 37
2. Structural macroeconomic models and forecast	1	100 50 0	at least quarterly less than quarterly not used	**38** **20** **36**	20 7 1	6 6 10	12 7 25
3. VAR-based models and forecasts	1	100 50 0	at least quarterly less than quarterly not used	**28** **14** **52**	11 7 10	7 3 12	10 4 30
4. Other agencies' models and forecasts	0.5	100 50 0	at least quarterly less than quarterly not used	**28** **21** **45**	15 8 5	8 6 8	5 7 32
5. Short term off-model data-based forecasts	0.5	100 50 0	at least quarterly less than quarterly not used	**57** **19** **18**	23 4 1	15 3 4	19 12 13
6. Theory-based models and forecasts (e.g. dynamic stochastic models, computable general equilibrium models, real business cycle models)	0.5	100 50 0	at least quarterly less than quarterly not used	**16** **16** **62**	5 7 16	5 5 12	6 4 34

Table 4.10 Measures of the importance of analysis of money and the banking sector

Questions	Question weight	Scores	Categories of answers, distribution of results	All economies	Industrialised	Transitional	Developing
1. Money demand equations	1	100	vital	**9**	2	2	5
		66	very important	**25**	7	6	12
		33	fairly important	**35**	9	7	19
		0	not or not very important	**25**	10	7	8
2. Analysis of data from the monetary survey	1	100	vital	**20**	0	5	15
		66	very important	**36**	6	10	20
		33	fairly important	**24**	14	6	4
		0	not or not very important	**14**	8	1	5
3. Analysis of banking sector or impact of changes in policy instruments on commercial bank interest rates and credit provision	1	100	vital	**20**	4	6	10
		66	very important	**45**	9	11	25
		33	fairly important	**26**	12	5	9
		0	not or not very important	**3**	3	0	0

instruments on commercial bank interest rates and credit provision. The survey weighted the responses to each of the three questions equally. A summary of responses is shown in Table 4.10.

4.4 Conclusion

Measuring characteristics of monetary policy frameworks by reference to the results of a survey of central banks is prone to subjectivity and to measurement error. Our judgement is however that they are unlikely to blur the larger picture to a great extent. The following chapter will attempt to use the information gathered to paint as clear as possible a picture of global developments in monetary frameworks.

Notes

1 Most previous studies have focused on a more limited sub-set of characteristics or a more limited group of economies, most frequently industrialised economies. Fry, Goodhart and Almeida (1996), however, look at a wide range of characteristics for central banks in developing economies.
2 In that regard our efforts to impose consistency in the answers imply that measures represent our interpretations of each central banker's own interpretation of his or her monetary framework.
3 See for example Goodhart (1994) and Blinder (1998).
4 CEFTA (Central European Free Trade Association) includes Czech Republic, Hungary, Poland, Slovenia and Slovakia.
5 These problems should not be seen as a criticism of the above definitions of inflation targeting, but rather an attempt to identify difficulties in applying such definitions universally.
6 See Goodhart, in this volume.
7 For example, Masson, Savastano and Sharma (1997), Debelle and Hoon Lim (1998) (Philippines), Christoffersen and Wescott (1999) (Poland), and Hoffmaister (1999) (Korea).
8 Issing (1997) observes that the Bundesbank frequently chose to miss its money target in the 1980s and 1990s.
9 In its monthly International Financial Statistics (e.g. March 1999, p. 8).
10 Under these arrangements, several East Asian economies ensured there was very limited nominal exchange rate depreciation with respect to the dollar, yet did not announce a specific exchange rate target.
11 Such as Masson, Savastano and Sharma (1997) and Cottarelli and Giannini (1997).
12 See Bernanke, Laubach, Mishkin and Posen (1999), Clarida and Gertler (1997) and Issing (1997) for views on the extent to which the Bundesbank targeted money in the years leading to 1999.
13 The exact questions asked are included in the Tables 4.1–4.10.
14 In the case of exchange rates we also asked for details of the target, and used IMF classifications of exchange rate arrangements to supplement information provided by each central bank.
15 In measuring the extent to which policy focuses on the exchange rate in countries that subsequently entered EMU, the responses led to some significant differences in scores. For example, the exchange rate was not always reported to be the first objective of policy, in part because the exchange rate has been

changed in the past when it conflicted with domestic macroeconomic objectives. However, the scoring system imposed some consistency across these
countries based on the assumption that in the run up to EMU, the exchange
rate had the first rank in terms of policy objectives in all cases except Germany.
Similarly, the minimum score for the exchange rate in assessing policy conflicts
was 0.5, i.e. it usually prevails. In terms of the self-description of the regime,
not all countries described their regime as exchange rate targeting. No adjustments were made to these answers.

16 A special issue of Oxford Economic Papers in July 1998 includes 11 articles on
many of the issues.

17 For countries participating in the European Exchange Rate Mechanism in
1998, the Ecofin Council was responsible for setting the parity grid, though the
central banks were involved to varying degrees in the negotiations of these
parities. For the sake of consistency, the survey places each ERM country in
the category of those where both government and the central bank set the
target. This was by far the most common categorisation, though it does not
accord with the views of every central bank.

18 Separating the roles of each institution for setting each target has the benefit of
taking account of the different role each variable has in the transmission
mechanism, but since transmission mechanisms are so diverse across
economies, that solution is not ideal. For example, fixing the exchange rate in a
country where there are capital controls and limited financial market development constrains monetary policy far less than in a country where there are no
capital controls and active financial markets. Similarly the length of transmission time affects the way money and inflation targets affect policy. An alternative might have been to measure the role of central bank and government in
setting each target separately, but we did not find this method improved our
ability to explain independence in estimates contained in Chapter 6.

19 Lybek (1999) tackles these problems by defining a single index that represents
both autonomy and accountability. This, however, may to some extent sacrifice
the possibility of capturing the distinct roles that independence and accountability may bring to the contract between government and the central bank.

20 See BIS (1999), Summary of Reports on The International Financial Architecture, October, Basle.

21 This definition enables us to separate accountability of the central bank to the
population, a relationship that is embodied in our measure of transparency.
However, we do not capture particular measures that may make the government accountable to Parliament and the population at large, an omission that
may be important in some cases.

22 In Israel and New Zealand, for example, the clause has never been used. And
in Australia the clause is sufficiently demanding such that it provides accountability yet reinforces the central bank's independence.

23 There are exceptions to this assertion. The gold standard was equivalent to a
currency board after 1844, and was overridden several times without being
abolished.

24 We intended the question to illustrate the extent to which central banks were
simulating compulsive general equilibrium models and similar theoretical
models. However, we suspect some responses interpreted 'theory-based' to
include standard structural models.

5 The devil in the detail of monetary policy frameworks (2)

Interpreting measures of framework characteristics

5.1 Introduction

Chapters 3 and 4 presented measures of the different aspects of monetary frameworks. The aim of this chapter is to put them together and identify a 'big picture' for the 94 central banks and currency boards in our sample. The scores derived from the survey responses are provided in Appendix 1 (Tables A.1 to A.11). They represent our interpretation of the information provided by each central bank, and do not necessarily represent the views of any particular central bank.

In particular this chapter discusses relationships among:

- the various objectives on which monetary policy focuses
- independence, accountability, and transparency
- policy objectives, institutional and structural aspects of the framework, and the way in which analysis is conducted

5.2 Methodological issues

Based on scoring methods described in detail in Chapter 4, the cross-country cross-correlation matrix of monetary policy framework characteristics shown in Table 5.1 summarises the broad relationships among the categories measured in the survey. The table covers the 93 economies in the sample.[1]

There are two particular reasons for caution in interpreting the matrix. First, the correlations cannot necessarily be interpreted as causal relationships because they omit other relevant explanatory variables and because the direction of causality is rarely unambiguous. Second, there is the statistical issue of how simple correlation coefficients should be interpreted for variables that are not derived from a normally distributed sample.[2] In spite of these caveats, we refer frequently in this chapter to the results shown in the correlation matrix, as it is a useful tool with which to identify interesting questions for further explanation.

Table 5.1 Correlations between measures of framework characteristics in 93 monetary frameworks

	Exchange rate	Money	Inflation	Discretion	Independence	Accountability	Explanations	Financial stability	Inflation expectations	Models and forecasts	Money and banking
A. Exchange-rate focus	1.00	-0.54	-0.68	-0.46	-0.09	0.03	-0.26	-0.29	-0.29	-0.07	-0.40
B. Money focus	-0.54	1.00	0.07	0.41	-0.05	-0.08	-0.12	0.26	-0.06	-0.14	0.58
C. Inflation focus	-0.68	0.07	1.00	0.18	0.15	0.09	0.30	0.14	0.43	0.15	0.13
D. Discretion* (high score implies more discretion)	-0.46	0.41	0.18	1.00	-0.09	-0.25	-0.10	0.42	0.06	-0.18	0.38
E. Independence	-0.09	-0.05	0.15	-0.09	1.00	0.06	0.42	-0.14	0.32	0.47	-0.13
F. Accountability of central bank to government	0.03	-0.08	0.09	-0.25	0.06	1.00	0.14	0.03	0.21	0.11	-0.07
G. Policy explanations	-0.26	-0.12	0.30	-0.10	0.42	0.14	1.00	-0.05	0.47	0.50	-0.01
H. Importance of financial stability issues in setting instruments	-0.29	0.26	0.14	0.42	-0.14	0.03	-0.05	1.00	-0.03	-0.02	0.52
I. Analysis of inflation expectations	-0.29	-0.06	0.43	0.06	0.32	0.21	0.47	-0.03	1.00	0.49	-0.15
J. Analysis using models and forecasts	-0.07	-0.14	0.15	-0.18	0.47	0.11	0.50	-0.02	0.49	1.00	-0.18
K. Importance of analysis of money and banking sector	-0.40	0.58	0.13	0.38	-0.13	-0.07	-0.01	0.52	-0.15	-0.18	1.00
memo:											
Inflation (average 1997 and 1998, includes estimates)	0.04	0.00	-0.01	0.00	-0.16	0.09	-0.17	0.08	-0.02	-0.08	-0.07
Inflation rank (1 = lowest inflation rate in the sample)	-0.30	0.31	0.23	0.18	-0.09	0.04	-0.23	0.20	-0.12	-0.19	0.14

*Discretion depends only on the scores for exchange rate targeting, money targeting, and inflation targeting. Discretion is a decreasing function of the maximum score and an increasing function of the sum of the other two.

Note: A coefficient of 0.17 is significant at the 90% confidence level; a coefficient of 0.20 is significant at the 95% level.

5.3   Policy focus

The survey responses provide new evidence with which to assess how central banks around the world direct policy towards their objectives. In particular, the survey sheds light on the capacity of monetary framework labels such as money and inflation targeting to distinguish adequately among frameworks, and examines the extent to which exchange-rate strategies are being pushed towards more extreme choices of freely floating or rigidly fixed exchange-rate arrangements.

5.3.i   Policy focus and framework labels

It is convenient to attach simple labels to frameworks such as 'inflation targeting', 'money-targeting' and 'exchange rate targeting'. But as discussed in previous chapters, labels can be misleading. Logically, a label might be thought of as an assertion of which variable it is that dominates a central bank's policy reaction function. But in practice only a small minority of economies treat their targets as rigid rules – and nearly all of these are exchange-rate targeters – so a label cannot in reality predict how policy will react to a given shock. In the short run, almost all central banks may treat domestic targets flexibly. In the long run, by contrast, almost all central banks are likely to aim for monetary stability, as defined by their legal objectives.

There is therefore scope for labels to be misinterpreted. Money targeting has been associated with 'monetarism' – a particular view about economic relationships – when in fact money targets may be used in some economies because money data are more timely and reliable than data for the real economy (see below). Inflation targeting has become associated with the use of macroeconometric forecasting models (see various Working Papers mentioned in the previous chapter). Yet those central bank governors with the most experience in using inflation targets regard it as one of their greater advantages that they can refocus both the internal policy process within the central bank and the central bank's relations with government, the parliament and the private sector (see the Minutes of the Central Bank Governors' Symposium 1999, pages 182–205, this volume).

Rather than categorise economies into neat lists of labelled frameworks, this study attempts to capture the degree to which policy focuses on a particular variable by asking four questions relating to each type of target. These are combined to form a single score – between zero and 100 – for each economy for each variable. The scoring system, described in detail in Chapter 4, is based upon: (i) whether a target is announced; (ii) whether the central bank defines its framework in terms of targeting a particular variable; (iii) how the central bank ranks policy priorities in practice; and (iv) which variables prevail in policy conflicts. The scores are shown in the Appendix, Tables A.1 to A.4. The scores give an indication of the degree to which policy focuses on its principal objective, and of how far policy may be diverted toward other objectives.

The tables in Appendix 1 give a fuller picture of what governs short- and medium-term policy focus (in the long term, policy is almost invariably directed by a legal mandate to achieve price stability). For the great majority of countries, the indices show that policy is sometimes diverted from its prime focus. The measures of policy focus suggest that only 10% of frameworks in the sample have a policy that focuses 100% on only one of the exchange rates, money or inflation. In the other 90%, the responses show evidence of discretion. For example, money targeters may rank inflation as important in setting the target, while inflation targeters may pay close attention to the exchange rate. Prospects for domestic inflation may affect decisions about exchange rate pegs.

Some of the potential pitfalls of a 'labels' approach are illustrated in Tables 5.2 and 5.3. Table 5.2 compares the categorisation of regimes according to: (i) the variable for which a numerical target is published; and (ii) self-classification by policy-makers. In terms of how central banks in the sample classify their frameworks, Table 5.2 (column D) shows that just under a third of respondents do not classify their framework as targeting one variable in particular. Of those that do classify their regimes as targeting one particular variable, exchange rate targeting is the most popular self-classification (28% of the sample), followed by money-targeting (24%) and inflation-targeting (16%).

There is, however, by no means a one-to-one correspondence between such self-classifications and the variables for which policy targets are announced. Thus some of the pitfalls of a labelling approach illustrated in the table include:

- *Not all targets are announced*: Table 5.2 illustrates that 7% of economies do not publish targets or reference values for the variable they classify themselves as targeting. Of these, Cyprus, Ghana, Egypt and Peru do not announce money targets, yet classify their frameworks as money-targeting; Botswana classifies its framework as inflation-targeting but does not announce inflation targets; and Singapore classifies its framework as exchange-rate targeting but does not announce an exchange-rate target.
- *Fourteen per cent of countries publish a target for only one variable, but do not classify themselves as targeting that variable* (see Table 5.2). Croatia, Ecuador, Egypt, Peru, and Sierra Leone, for example, publish inflation targets only, but do not classify themselves as inflation-targeting. The United States announces a monitoring range for money but does not classify itself as money-targeting. And The Bahamas, Botswana, Cyprus, Belize, Fiji, Kuwait and Tonga all have exchange rate targets but do not classify their regime as exchange-rate targeting.
- *Central banks that publish both inflation and money targets, but not*

Table 5.2 Matrix showing central bankers' self-classifications of their monetary frameworks[1] and also the targets they publish

Targets published shown in rows 1 to 7.	Self-classification shown in columns A. to D.			
	A. Framework classified as exchange rate targeting	B. Framework classified as money-targeting	C. Framework classified as inflation-targeting	D. Cannot be summarised as such[2]
Total of 94 frameworks (% of total)	28	24	16	32
1. Explicit target only for 'framework' variable	Argentina Austria Bahrain Barbados Belgium Bosnia Herz. Bulgaria Denmark E. Caribbean Estonia Hong Kong Hungary Iceland Ireland Latvia Lithuania Namibia Netherlands Norway Portugal	Germany South Africa[3] Switzerland	Australia Canada Czech Rep. Israel Mexico New Zealand Sweden UK	Bahamas (exch.) Belize (exch.) Fiji (exch.) Kuwait (exch.) Tonga (exch.) USA (money) Croatia (inflation) Ecuador (inflation) Sierra Leone (inflation)
2. Explicit target for one variable other than 'framework' variable (explicit target in brackets)		Cyprus (exchange rate) Egypt (inflation) Peru (inflation)	Botswana (exchange rate)	
3. Explicit target for exchange rate and money	Malta			Jordan

4. Explicit target only for exchange rate and inflation	Lebanon Macedonia Uruguay			Chile[3] Poland	Finland Malaysia Spain West Afr. States
5. Explicit target only for money and inflation		China Guyana Indonesia Kazakhstan Kenya Korea Mauritius	Moldova Nigeria Russia Romania Slovenia Tanzania Zambia	Albania Armenia Jamaica	Georgia India Kyrgyz Mozambique Slovakia Turkey Turkmenistan Uganda
6. Explicit targets for exchange rate, money and inflation	Greece	Bangladesh Taiwan		Mongolia	France Italy Ukraine Vietnam
7. No explicit target	Singapore	Ghana			Japan Sri Lanka Thailand ECB

[1] Respondents were asked If you were to categorise your framework as one of the following, would you describe it as: (1) money targeting; (2) inflation targeting; (3) discretionary; (4) exchange rate targeting; (5) balance of payments targeting; (6) other (please specify); (7) cannot be summarised as one of above; (8) none of the above?

[2] This column includes various classifications, such as 'discretionary' and combinations of the other categories.

[3] Known changes since the survey was completed include: Chile has dropped its exchange-rate band, South Africa has announced it will implement inflation targets

exchange-rate targets, do not classify their frameworks uniformly. Of these 25 economies, 14 classify themselves as money-targeting and 3 as inflation-targeting, and 8 choose not to classify themselves according to a single label (see row 5 of Table 5.2).

- *It is not possible to distinguish between money, and inflation-targeting frameworks by observing which countries publish inflation targets, because virtually all countries that classify themselves as money targeters also publish inflation targets, guidelines or reference values for inflation (column B).* These include the central banks of Germany (up to 1998) and Switzerland, which clearly state their medium-term inflation preferences, even though they do not describe them as inflation targets (see Posen in this volume). It is not surprising that so many money-targeting central banks announce inflation targets. To establish a money target, countries need to work back from an inflation and growth target or forecast. If the inflation projections are being missed yet money targets are on track – for example because of a velocity shock – there is no intrinsic reason why the intermediate target should take precedence over such inflation and output projections (see the evidence in Chart 3.3 in Chapter 3).

- *Differences between money and inflation targeting do not necessarily reflect differences in a central bank's reaction function.* King (p. 182, this volume) argues that 'an inflation target is not a new view of monetary economics or the monetary transmission mechanism'. The evidence in Tables 5.2 and 5.3 lends support to his claim. While 24% of respondents classified their regime as money-targeting (Table 5.2), only 1% reported that money always prevailed over inflation and exchange-rate objectives in the event of policy conflicts. The survey results indicate that in the event of velocity shocks, both money and inflation targeters are likely to focus on inflation objectives.

- *There are around four times as many central banks with explicit inflation targets as there are central banks that categorise themselves as 'inflation targeting'* (Table 5.3). 60% of economies announce inflation targets and 33% rank the variable as the main objective of policy, yet only 13% classify themselves as 'inflation targeting'.

The results highlight some potentially misleading consequences of labelling particular frameworks as 'inflation-targeting', 'exchange rate targeting', or 'money targeting'. Many frameworks have some of the characteristics of each, suggesting the need for a broader approach to assessing the extent to which the various objectives of monetary policy are, in the short and medium term, better described as complementary or as alternatives.

We take this broader approach, using the overall policy focus scores for each economy in Appendix Tables A.1 to A.4. The first four rows of the correlation matrix (Table 5.1) show the extent to which measures of policy focus are correlated with each other and with a proxy for discretion,[3] for

Table 5.3 Policy priorities in 93 economies

% of economies that:	exchange rate	money	inflation
Classified themselves as targeting the variable	27	25	13
Published an explicit target for the variable	50	43	60
Stated primary objective to be the variable	36	15	33
Stated this variable always prevails over other two	25	1	11

all 93 frameworks. Table 5.1 shows that the money-focus score and the score for discretion are positively with a correlation coefficient of 41%. The results are consistent with evidence presented in the previous chapter relating to target misses. It is evident that money is not generally used as an exclusive target, and that money targeting does not preclude policy from focusing on other objectives as well.

The increasing tendency of policy-makers in money-targeting economies to announce such inflation projections as targets or reference values may have contributed to making policy preferences more transparent in these economies. In the 1990s a growing number of countries with IMF programmes have announced inflation objectives reflecting their increasing importance in Fund-supported programmes. This represents a change in emphasis from practices in the 1980s, when Fund-supported programmes gave relatively more prominence to the role of money and credit targets in adjustment programmes.[4]

Central banks classifying their regimes as inflation targeting appear to focus strongly on inflation, but not to the complete exclusion of other priorities. They have a 14% focus on the exchange rate and a money-focus score of 12% (Table 5.2.B). Overall, Table 5.1 shows an insignificant correlation between the focus on inflation and money. Yet this may be misleading. If frameworks with a strong exchange-rate focus are removed from the sample, the coefficient becomes significantly negative, suggesting that, in general, for non-exchange-rate targeters, money and inflation are alternative points of policy focus. In Australia, Canada, the Czech Republic, Mexico, New Zealand, Sweden, and the United Kingdom, the focus on inflation largely excludes any focus on the exchange rate or money, except insofar as these variables affect inflation.

5.3.ii   To what extent do currency arrangements take extreme forms?

The past two decades have seen extensive reductions in capital controls and increases in the size and volatility of international capital movements. This development has in some cases made fixed but adjustable exchange-rate pegs harder to sustain (King, 1999). To what extent has this forced countries to make the stark choice between adopting a free exchange rate float and an extremely rigid currency peg, such as a currency board or monetary union?

Exchange-rate targeting is in some ways the least discretionary framework. This is confirmed by its highly negative correlation (−0.46) with discretion shown in Table 5.1. The correlation between the exchange-rate and money focus across all 93 frameworks examined in Table 5.1 is −0.54, and between the exchange-rate and inflation focus it is −0.68, suggesting that the exchange rate focus is an alternative rather than a complement to other possible frameworks. These aspects of the survey responses are illustrated in Charts 5.1.A and 5.1.B. The scatter-graphs plot scores for

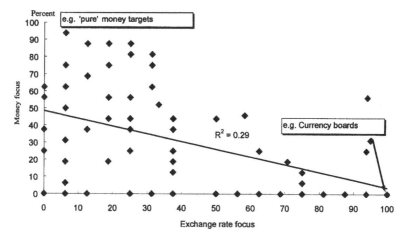

Chart 5.1.A Scores for exchange rate and money focus

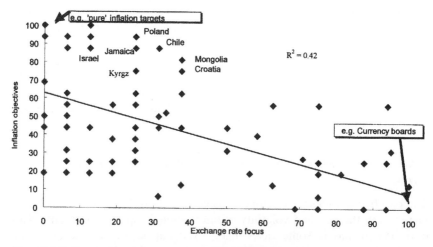

Chart 5.1.B Scores for exchange rate and inflation objectives

exchange-rate focus against those for money focus (5.1.A) and inflation focus (5.1.B). Some observations are clustered at the extremes of the two scatter plots,[5] supporting the view that these objectives are alternatives in most cases.

There remain, however, a significant number of economies whose exchange-rate objectives do not eliminate the possibility of policy also focusing on money and inflation. Table 5.3, for example, illustrates that while 50% of the survey respondents publish some explicit target for the exchange rate, only half of these claim that the exchange-rate objective always prevails over inflation and money.

Dual objectives are feasible in a variety of circumstances. The scatter plots in Charts 5.1 A–C illustrate that there are numerous exceptions to a single-minded approach to exchange-rate targeting. In some cases, capital controls allow policy some scope to pursue domestic and external object-ives independently. In others, the exchange-rate peg may be both highly credible and complementary to domestic objectives, thereby reducing the possibility of policy conflicts. Spain and Finland, for example, were both inflation targeters that more recently refocused policy towards exchange-rate objectives ahead of joining the European single currency. The increased emphasis on exchange-rate targets did not appear to present significant conflicts with inflation objectives in the lead-up to EMU. Finally, exchange-rate focus may be used in conjunction with domestic objectives when it is managed sufficiently flexibly to minimise tensions between domestic and external objectives.

In small, open economies with liberalised capital markets, exchange-rate changes may feed quickly through to domestic prices, so that inflation and exchange-rate objectives may evoke similar policy responses in all but the very short term. In the process of disinflation, Chile, Poland, and Israel

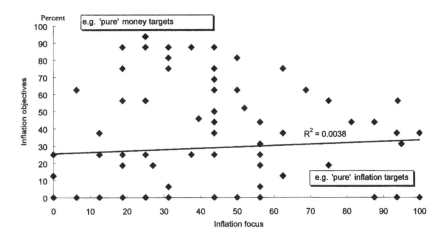

Chart 5.1.C Money and inflation objectives

have used formal exchange-rate bands in conjunction with inflation targets in order to exploit the benefits of the link and to anchor inflation expectations during disinflation. A potential difficulty in this strategy is the possibility of providing markets with 'one-way risk' to speculators that may lead to currency attacks and sharp exchange-rate adjustment. In Chile, policy-makers have emphasised that inflation objectives take priority over exchange-rate objectives, and this has helped to create two-way exchange-rate risk. The approach has helped Chile to secure a remarkably smooth disinflation (see Landerretche, Morandé, and Schmidt-Hebbel, this volume).

Several inflation-targeting countries have acknowledged the importance of the exchange rate by calculating and using Monetary Conditions Indices (MCIs), which attempt to indicate the relative contribution of interest rates and exchange rates to the stance of monetary policy. Mayes and Virén (in this volume) assess the history and use of MCIs. They argue that MCIs may have a role as a transparency device, particularly in small, open economies where the exchange rate plays a pivotal role in monetary transmission.

5.3.iii   The shape of monetary policy objectives

The survey responses suggest that policy objectives are better viewed as a shape representing different objectives, and the priorities attached to them, rather than a point representing a single objective. Chart 5.1.D shows the shape of monetary policy focus in central European countries and measures the degree to which policy focuses on the exchange rate, money, and inflation. For economies with similar structures and with similar long-term goals related to integration in the EU, there is a striking diversity in the present framework shapes. The Czech Republic became the first transitional economy to adopt inflation targeting, having experienced instability in the velocity of money and then an exchange-rate crisis in 1997 (see Hrnčíř and Šmídková, this volume). Poland has shifted from exchange-rate to inflation targeting more gradually (see Chapter 7), retaining an exchange-rate target, though with a fluctuation band that has become wider over time. Slovenia has achieved disinflation through money targeting combined with capital controls and a managed exchange rate. Hungary has achieved a more gradual stabilisation than other countries in the region by using exchange-rate bands, while Slovakia announced targets or bands for each of the exchange rate, money, and inflation.

The tables and charts leave the impression that the differences among the self-assessments of monetary policy frameworks are not fully explained by either the type of targets announced or by central bank reaction functions. This is partly because inflation and money targets have purposes that are not confined to their role in the transmission mechanism.

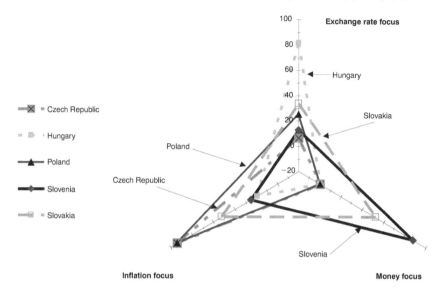

Chart 5.1.D The shape of monetary frameworks in central Europe

Perceived differences in self-assessments may also be partly explained by the role of the policy framework or target in defining the relationships among the different agencies involved in policy formulation and implementation. These institutional issues are discussed further in the sections below.

5.4   The relationship between policy objectives and institutional characteristics of monetary policy frameworks (independence, accountability, and transparency)

In the 1980s and 1990s, many countries have given greater independence to their central banks.[6] And some countries have stressed the importance of the accountability and transparency of monetary policy, characteristics that may offer a counterbalance to increased independence.

5.4.i   Stylised facts about independence in different types of economies

Central banks are now more independent than ever. The summary results presented in Chapter 8 show that central banks now regard independence as the most important aspect of the monetary framework. Two thirds of the sample have full independence to change interest rates, with no government influence (Table 4.4). Among industrialised and transitional economies, 80% have this independence; for developing economies, however, the figure is just 50%.

This difference between developing and transitional economies may be explained in part by the fact that generally central bank legislation in transitional economies is recent in origin and provides a degree of independence consistent with current thinking on central banking, which includes a powerful consensus in favour of instrument independence. Differences also show up in obligatory central bank financing of the government deficit. In industrialised economies such financing is very rare, and in nearly three quarters of transitional economies governments either do not use obligatory central bank financing or keep it within very narrow, tightly enforced limits. This compares with just over 40% in developing economies.

When granting operational independence to central banks, some countries have also required minimum standards of accountability and transparency. These have included the setting of explicit inflation targets and procedures to be invoked when the outcome deviates from target. Accountability and transparency motivate central banks to deliver on their words, while also helping the public to form expectations that inflation will turn out in line with stated objectives.

Transparency and accountability in monetary policy are not new issues,[7] but they have become much more prominent issues in recent years, both in international attention and in specific actions by individual countries. It is hard to estimate precisely how far explaining policy to the public can help to lower inflation expectations, yet markets have generally reacted very positively to announcements of increased central bank independence and to the release of economic assessments.[8] Recently, the IMF published 'Experimental Case Studies on Transparency Practices'[9] which illustrates a number of circumstances in which greater transparency can improve outcomes.

5.4.ii   Stylised facts about accountability and policy explanations in different types of economies

In spite of the very marked shift towards increased independence of central banks, Table 4.5 in the previous chapter shows that most governments have kept at least one hand on the steering wheel of monetary policy, in their role as target setters. Seventy-one per cent of governments have either a sole or joint role in setting an explicit target for at least one of the exchange rate, money, or inflation. And where there is no explicit target, for example in Japan (see Higo, this volume), accountability is sometimes achieved through very frequent parliamentary monitoring.

The origins of the push toward transparency lie both inside and outside central banks. By their nature, markets thirst for information, and analysts within central banks enjoy, and are motivated by seeing the fruits of their labour published as economic assessments in print or on web pages. One argument against too much explanation is that credibility may be undermined when policy forecasts prove to be incorrect or targets are missed. Yet if targets are treated flexibly, forecasts can fill 'transparency gaps' left by the inability of targets to describe fully central bank preferences and intentions.

The great majority (91%) of central banks publish monetary analysis at least quarterly (see Table 4.6 in Chapter 4). Most include forward-looking analysis. Thirty-seven per cent of central banks publish forecasts in the form of both numbers (or graphs) and words. Single-point forecasts almost always turn out to be incorrect, but the fear of embarrassment caused by forecasting mistakes appears to be waning; 23% publish regular discussions of past forecasting errors. Forecasts can be used to convey central bank uncertainty, and 9% of central banks now publish formal assessments of uncertainty in their forecasts, in the form of both graphs (or numbers) and words. Those central banks that do not publish assessments, analysis and forecasts are concentrated among the exchange-rate targeters, for whom credibility, transparency, and accountability of policy generally may be achieved through the capacity of market participants and the public to observe and test the credibility of the target continuously (see Chapter 4).

5.4.iii   Relationships between institutional characteristics and policy focus

Institutional characteristics may be seen as a prerequisite or, alternatively, a consequence of adopting particular regimes. Masson, Savastano, and Sharma (1997), for example, argue that independence may be a prerequisite of inflation targeting. The results of our study do not support the view that independence and accountability affect the choice of monetary policy target. They do not show any significant correlation between independence and accountability on the one hand, and the focus of policy on the exchange rate, money, or inflation on the other (see Table 5.1). There is scope for independence to improve the effectiveness of policy, irrespective of whether or not a particular variable is targeted. Similarly, even when there is limited independence, there is scope for using published targets to increase the clarity and transparency of the framework.

The scores for the focus of policy on inflation objectives are significantly correlated with the scores for policy explanations. Inflation targets need to be supported by more explanation than other targets, since the time delay between policy action and its effect on inflation is longer than that between policy action and its effect on money or the exchange rate.[10] Money and exchange rates targets are 'intermediate' and provide information supplementary to the final objective of price stability. Emphasis on explaining policy, however, is by no means confined to those industrialised economies that target inflation. Frameworks that incorporate a high degree of policy explanation include those in Barbados, the Czech Republic, Chile, Estonia, Japan, Italy, Korea, Switzerland, Uganda, and the United States. This group includes developing and, transitional as well as industrialised economies, and frameworks that are discretionary or money targeting, or that have a currency board as well as inflation targeters.

Previous chapters referred to two approaches to achieving price stability. The legislative approach involves a very high degree of central bank independence and limited accountability of the central bank to government. In this environment, explanations are often used as a substitute for mandatory accountability. In Chile and Germany (up to 1998), independent central banks make strong efforts to communicate with the public and government, even though the central bank is subject to limited formal procedures ensuring accountability to government. The contracting approach to achieving price stability is consistent with a 'democratic' view that accountability should accompany independence (Briault, Haldane, and King, 1996).

National practices are diverse. Chile and Israel, for example, both have apparently similar monetary policy frameworks, employing exchange-rate targets in conjunction with inflation targeting.[11] Yet Chile's framework features a high degree of central bank independence (including goal independence) and a low degree of central bank accountability to government. Israel, in contrast, has taken an approach that involves a high degree of accountability coupled with instrument, but not goal, independence. The experiences of both economies are examined in papers in this volume. Table 5.1 illustrates that in the sample as a whole, there is no significant correlation between our measures of accountability and independence. Thus, while some central banks have very high degrees of independence with limited accountability, there are many countries that have each achieved high levels of both independence and accountability. These include Canada, the Kyrgyz Republic, Mexico, New Zealand, and Sweden.

5.5 Financial stability issues and other aspects of the monetary policy framework

Financial stability is among the core functions of most central banks, and recent financial crises have had important spillover effects on monetary stability. The survey asked about the importance of financial stability issues in the setting of monetary policy instruments. The financial stability issues specified were: (i) domestic financial sector insolvency; (ii) overseas financial sector insolvency; (iii) reports of credit rationing; and (iv) asset price volatility. A problem in interpreting the responses is that although the questions are standardised across countries, their interpretations by respondents may have varied substantially.

There is a significant positive correlation between the importance of financial stability issues and discretion. Could this reflect a trade-off between maintaining financial stability and targeting specific monetary objectives? After all, when central banks act as lender of last resort, it may be at the expense of creating a temporary expansion of the money supply (see Goodhart and Schoenmaker, 1993).

Yet there are positive correlations between financial stability concerns and focus on money and (to a lesser extent) inflation objectives (see Table 5.1). This finding apparently contradicts the view that financial stability concerns may conflict with targeting of specific monetary objectives. The positive correlation may be attributable to four factors. First, an explicit domestic nominal anchor may help to stabilise inflation expectations so that the expectations on which asset prices are based are less volatile. Second, central banks with financial stability concerns are perhaps more likely than other central banks to pay particular attention to monetary aggregates. Third, IMF programmes that are launched in response to financial crisis will in many cases involve money targets; and as noted above, they increasingly involve inflation objectives also. Fourth, money targets are typically interpreted flexibly, as the survey responses show, so that they provide scope for the central bank to react to financial stability concerns.

5.6   The relationship between measures of analysis conducted and other aspects of the monetary framework

The success of a monetary framework that retains any degree of exchange-rate flexibility depends upon the analysis that supports it. The questionnaire therefore asked about the analysis of three separate issues. The first is the extent to which central banks monitor and use various measures of inflation expectations (financial markets, surveys, and outside forecasts). The second relates to the extent to which different methods are used to forecast economic variables (e.g. off-model forecasts, VARs,[12] structural models, theoretical models and outside forecasts). Third, we asked central banks about the importance of money-demand equations and other means of analysing the role of the financial sector in the transmission mechanism.

The results are shown in detail in Appendix, Tables A.9 to A.11, and the extent to which these characteristics are correlated with other aspects of monetary frameworks is shown in rows I to K of Table 5.1. Some of the correlations in the table are as expected: the more important inflation objectives are, the greater the score for analysis of inflation expectations. The more important money objectives are, the greater the importance attached to analysis of money demand and the banking system. Yet the use of models and forecasts is not significantly related to the choice of monetary framework. Knowledge of how policy actions affect the economy is always useful, irrespective of the policy target.

Policy explanations however, are strongly correlated with both analysis of inflation expectations and the use of models and forecasts. It is easier for central banks to explain why outcomes are deviating from target when they have access to analysis that makes them confident in their explanations.

The survey sought to measure the extent to which central banks focused on particular areas of analysis by asking about their research on particular subjects. The questionnaire set out a list of subjects and asked each respondent if their central bank had: (i) published research in that area; (ii) considered it in detail; (iii) considered it; or (iv) not considered that subject much. The results, summarised in Table 5.4, illustrate some marked differences between industrialised economies and the other group of developing and transitional economies.[13] Two of the main difference are as follows:

- The average industrialised-economy central bank had published[14] work in 59% of the categories identified in the table in the past five years, compared with 26% in developing and transitional economies. The difference is likely to be attributable both to a higher concentration of research resources in industrialised economies and to significantly more and better data on which to use them. While industrialised economies have researched across the broad range of subjects, analysis in developing and transitional economies has focused on some core areas of the economy, including money, banking, the balance of payments,[15] the exchange rate, and fiscal policy. The data in Table 5.4 show that at least 50% of respondents in developing and transitional economies reported that these areas had been at least considered in detail.
- There appear to be large gaps in the analysis of the real sector in developing and transitional economies. For example, only 8% of respondent banks had published research on labour markets and there had been similarly little analysis of consumption and investment. In large part this reflects lack of data. For example, the September 1999 edition of the IMF's *International Financial Statistics* included no recent quarterly data[16] at all for any item in the National Accounts for 80% of the developing and transitional economies included in our study, compared with only 15% of the industrialised economies.

These results may help to explain why so many developing economies categorise themselves as money-targeting rather than inflation-targeting. Inflation-targeting central banks generally forecast inflation by assessing the impact of real disequilibria in domestic goods markets (through the output gap) and labour markets (through the NAIRU).[17] These assessments are made using analysis that is often supported by a variety of theoretical and econometric models (see Chapter 4.3.v above). For example, all the industrialised economies that classify themselves as inflation-targeting have published research on the Phillips curve and the output gap,[18] whereas

Table 5.4 Focus of research in central banks

To what extent have researchers in each central bank considered the following issues in the last five years?	1. Published	2. Considered in detail	3. Considered	4. No or not much considered	% published		Overall ranking in priorities		
					Industrialised	Developing and transitional	All countries	Industrialised	Developing and transitional
% of Total	**36**	**22**	**25**	**17**	**59**	**26**			
Monetary policy framework	59	24	10	7	93	44	**1**	1	2
Behaviour of banks	43	30	24	2	59	37	**2**	7	3
Balance of payments (incl. cap. flows)	46	28	20	7	41	48	**3**	14	1
Analysis of financial instruments	44	29	18	9	67	35	**4**	2	6
Money-demand equation	49	17	24	10	74	38	**5**	4	7
Exchange rate and regime	40	29	24	7	52	35	**6**	10	4
Financial fragility issues	39	28	29	4	52	33	**7**	11	4
Fiscal sector	32	28	28	12	41	29	**8**	13	8
Transmission mechanism	39	17	30	14	63	29	**9**	6	9
Modelling and econometrics	37	22	23	18	70	22	**10**	2	10
Price specification	30	17	34	19	59	17	**11**	8	11
Commodity prices and terms of trade	24	19	33	23	48	14	**12**	16	12
Investment and corporate sector	23	19	30	28	48	13	**13**	14	13
Consumption and personal sector	23	16	30	31	56	10	**14**	12	14
Phillips curve and output gap	24	18	16	42	67	6	**15**	4	16
Labour market	24	9	31	36	63	8	**16**	9	15

Notes: The precise categories are provided in Question An.4 of the questionnaire, reproduced in Appendix A.2.
The rankings are based on a weighted sum average score of the three columns given by:
Priority of research topic = (number of countries in column 1) * 3 + (column 2) * 2 + (column 3) * 1.
The overall rankings are strongly influenced by the results for developing and transitional economies because there was considerably more variance across categories in their analytical focus. In industrialised economies, for example, there was no category had been at least considered in detail by more than 70% of economies.

only 6% of developing and transitional economies reported having published such research. And finally, the inflation reports of central banks from economies such as the Czech Republic, Hungary, Israel, Poland, Sweden, and the United Kingdom[19] all give prominence to assessing the relative strength of demand and supply.

Thus the weight placed on analysing the various aspects of the transmission mechanism differs sharply across economies. In a developing economy with limited data on the real economy and much more frequent and reliable data for the exchange rate and money supply, these latter variables are more likely to remain permanently close to the top of the hierarchy of indicators, even if neither is targeted directly. In such circumstances, it makes sense to use annual data for real and nominal output to derive quarterly or monthly forecasts and targets for variables such as money. This approach may be appropriate whether or not the central bank (or IMF) takes a 'monetarist' view of the economy.

5.7   Interpreting the results

In measuring and comparing characteristics, we have attempted both to summarise developments in monetary frameworks across a very broad range of economies and to identify a wide range of factors that are important in the choice and operation of monetary policy frameworks. An important conclusion from the previous chapter is that any explicit domestic target may at times be treated flexibly. The complementary message from this chapter is that in assessing individual monetary frameworks, their characteristics should be looked at one-by-one. It would be a mistake to imagine that certain groups of characteristics belong together, or that some characteristics (such as the use of forecasting models) are prerequisites to the successful implementation of others (for example, inflation targets).

In themselves, domestic targets may not always protect national economies from all unforeseen domestic and external shocks (see Tošovsky in the Minutes (page 191) following this Report). This is the case even when targets are accompanied by constructive relationships between the central bank and government and the central bank has access to the latest analytical techniques. Nevertheless, such targets may help in adjusting the economy to the impact of the shocks in a wide range of circumstances. Chilean monetary policy has brought about a very smooth disinflation, in spite of Chile's previous history of highly volatile inflation and a sometimes-turbulent international environment (Landerretche, Morandé, and Schmidt-Hebbel, this volume). A number of factors played an important role, including inflation targets, exchange rate bands, goal and instrument independence, the possibility of imposing reserve requirements on certain capital inflows, sound fiscal policy, a good inflation-forecasting record, and some favourable productivity shocks. It is the combination of these characteristics rather than a focus on any one of them that has helped to reduce inflation expectations.

The evidence is that policy-makers have learned much from experience since the early 1970s. Nowadays, inflation is seen as a symptom of economic ills rather than as all or part of a potential cure, and there appears to be a much broader constituency favouring low inflation than at any time since the breakdown of Bretton Woods. These changes are manifested in inflation outcomes around the world, and in the results of this survey.

Arguably the most important trend has been the design of frameworks that minimise the possibility of major players having incentives that conflict with price stability. In some countries, governments may have sometimes had an incentive to increase output above potential to buy short-term popularity. One of the most important contributions of inflation and exchange-rate targets has been to minimise such incentives by securing government commitment to a key aspect of policy design. Those central bank governors who have the longest experience of inflation targets have stressed the role of targets in defining constructive relationships between central banks and governments (see the Minutes of the Central Bank Governers' Symposium, this volume).

Similarly, central banks whose targets, forecasts, models, and analysis are published have an incentive to ensure they are of the highest quality. Thus, in order to achieve both flexibility and credibility, many central banks have sought to bolster their analytical capacity and increase the quantity and quality of their published work. This is consistent with a goal of implementing flexibility in a credible fashion.

Finally, recent currency and banking crises have refocused attention on the need to design frameworks and policies in ways that minimise the incentives for market participants to take risks that endanger monetary stability. In the area of exchange-rate policy, there are examples of frameworks that appear to have secured some of the benefits of using exchange-rate bands in terms of stabilising inflation expectations, but have not created the perception in markets of a one-way currency being available.

For the time being, it appears that central banks have learnt much about how to use their powers over framework characteristics in a highly diverse fashion that suits their own needs. In spite of, or perhaps because of, this diversity, today's monetary frameworks are contributing to a global environment of lower and more stable inflation.

Notes

1 The ECB response, which was circulated after the others in 1999, is excluded to avoid double-counting.
2 The variables used here are discrete and are bounded between 0 and 1. Nevertheless, we use standard correlations as our preferred measure of how two characteristics are related across countries. Of the alternatives, the rank correlation measures ignore important information about the quantitative difference

between two countries' scores. Another alternative would be to use an ordered probit model. But this would only offer us different information compared to the standard correlation coefficient in so far as the relationship between the characteristics is not linear. With most of our data set, our experiments suggest that there are enough discrete categories of scores for the probit-fitted values to be quite close to a linear relationship.

3 Our definition of discretion is shown in Appendix Table A.1.

4 See Cottarelli and Giannini (1998).

5 The trend-line is not intended to assert any causal relationship, but is useful because there are several repeat observations that are not visible on the graph.

6 The following chapter contains an assessment of what independence means to central banks.

7 For example, Bernanke, Laubach, Mishkin, and Posen (1999) emphasise that the Bundesbank has for many years made great efforts to explain policy to the public through published reports and speeches of senior members of staff. Another example is the gold standard, which was a highly transparent monetary policy framework.

8 See Haldane and Read (1999) for an assessment of how transparency may reduce the effect of changes in policy instruments on market interest rates, a possibility that makes an interesting counter-argument to arguments made by the Federal Reserve in earlier decades (see the influential work of Goodfriend, 1986).

9 IMF, April 1999.

10 Though inflation may still represent an intermediate target, to the extent that the targeted price measure is not a complete indicator of the long-run aggregate price level.

11 Chile dropped its explicit exchange rate band in 1999.

12 Vector Auto Regression models.

13 Central banks show much greater variation in research focus when categorised by economy type than by type of framework. This in part reflects the breadth of the research categories. Several central banks have published in almost all of these areas, irrespective of their framework.

14 In this case 'published' could be interpreted in a broad sense, including central bank working papers and bulletins, and also external publications by central bank staff.

15 The balance of payments is the only category in which greater proportions of developing and transitional economies have published research relative to industrialised economies.

16 For any of the previous four quarters.

17 See, e.g., 'Economic Models at the Bank of England' (1999), Bank of England, p. 32.

18 The central banks reporting such published research are the inflation-targeting (or former inflation-targeting) countries of Australia, Canada, Chile, Finland, Mexico, New Zealand, Spain, Sweden, and the UK, plus the following economies that do not classify themselves as inflation targeting: Belgium, Ghana, Greece, Iceland, Ireland, Italy, Japan, Korea, Norway, Peru, Portugal, Switzerland, and the USA.

19 Other central banks publish very similar documents with titles other than 'Inflation Report'.

6   What does independence mean to central banks?

6.1   Introduction

Central banks have for many years held forthright views on their independence. As long ago as 1929, Montagu Norman, Governor of the Bank of England wrote that:

> I look upon the Bank as having the unique right to offer advice and to press such advice even to the point of nagging; but always of course subject to the supreme authority of the government.[1]

The tables have turned since Governor Norman's day to the point where it is governments that often hesitate before nagging central banks in public, in case this undermines the credibility of the framework.

Various studies have constructed and assessed detailed measures of central bank independence[2] and others have criticised them for being subjective.[3] This chapter attempts to use subjectivity to its advantage by asking central banker respondents for their impressions about central bank independence using two approaches. The first approach interprets responses to the general, subjective question, How would you define central bank independence? As far as we know, this simple approach has not been used before, yet it reveals which aspects of independence really matter to central banks. The second method involves asking central bankers how independent their own institution's are, and using the answers to construct an index of self-assessment of independence. We then attempt to explain which objective indicators of central bank independence explain the subjective self-assessment using ordered probit regressions.

6.2   A direct method of understanding what independence means to central bankers

Chart 6.1 summarises responses to the question, How would you define central bank independence? We translated the general responses into the categories shown in the chart, which is ordered with categories representing goal independence on the left, instrument independence in the centre, and other aspects that may affect policy setting on the right-hand side. We used 60 responses[4] with each country represented in at least one and, as it turned out, at most of seven categories. It is evident from the data underlying the chart that most responses reflect each country's own experience, and it is under this premise that we interpret the responses.

By far the most important factor by which most central banks define independence is the capacity to set instruments and operating procedures; 80% of central banks across a broad range of economies mentioned this in their responses (see Chart 6.1).[5] In practice the effectiveness of formal arrangements providing central banks with instrument independence may, however, be undermined by a number of factors that are represented by bars towards the right-hand side of the graph. These include the capacity of governments to: (i) be represented on central bank boards; (ii) borrow from central banks; (iii) exert general pressure on central banks; and (iv) exert influence on the staffing of central banks. The absence of fiscal dominance remains a defining characteristic of central bank independence in developing economies (Fry, 1998 and Box 6.A). Dr Courtney Blackman, former Governor, Central Bank of Barbados, is among those who stress that rules on deficit finance are particularly important in developing countries where financial markets are not fully developed and cannot punish government attempts to extract excessive seigniorage revenues.[6]

Extensive recent academic literature, prompted in part by Walsh (1995), has stressed the difference between goal and instrument independence. Almost all central banks considered instrument independence to be an important aspect of independence. By contrast, goal independence tends to be important to central banks in particular circumstances. Chart 6.1 shows that in their identification of the defining factors of independence only 22% of respondents mentioned the ability to set targets, objectives or goals, while 38% defined independence by stressing the importance of legal objectives. The relative importance of these two measures of goal independence depends, as usual, upon circumstances.

Central banks are likely to feel more independent when they are able to act to meet clearly defined statutory objectives. The 38% of respondents who defined independence by relating it to the central bank's statutory objectives[7] generally fall into two categories. First, they are central banks whose mandate and statutory objectives have been revised in recent years, such as recently formed central banks in transitional economies and European central banks affected by the Maastricht Treaty and other EU legislation. These responses suggest that governments and central banks are more likely to focus upon legal objectives when these objectives are fresh and pertinent, having been recently debated. The second group that are more likely to define independence according to statutory objectives are

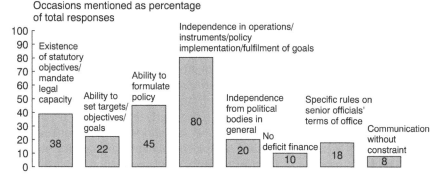

Factors mentioned by central bankers as important in the definition of independence

*The responses are the authors' categorisation of answers to the question 'How would you define central bank independence?' There were 60 usable responses (23 from industrialised economies and 37 from developing and transitional economies). Respondent cited an average of 2.9 categories in industrialised economies and 2.2 in developing and transitional economies.

Chart 6.1 How central bankers define independence*

central banks in money and exchange rate targeting countries. Money and exchange rates are generally referred to as 'intermediate' targets, and as such are likely to complement statutory objectives that focus on the final goal of price stability.

In contrast, the country groups that did not mention statutory objectives comprised, first, inflation-targeting central banks, where the explicit inflation targets are often used to convey directly the message in statutory objectives and second, developing countries, whose statutory objectives more frequently do not defend them from either deficit finance obligations or general government intervention in monetary policy.

Which central banks define independence according to the capacity to set their own targets or objectives? They are predominantly central banks that use a domestic nominal anchor, and six of the eleven responses for this definition came from central banks that have used explicit inflation targets recently as part of a disinflation process. As argued in Chapter 3, the responsibility to set inflation targets may be of heightened importance during disinflation. This is illustrated vividly by one such respondent who posed the rhetorical question, What good is instrument independence if the Parliament or Cabinet sets politically motivated goals that are binding?

The responses from inflation-targeting central banks reflect how the relationship between government and central bank is strongly influenced by whether or not inflation is already acceptably low. Central banks in inflation-targeting countries with low inflation did not generally regard the ability to set the target as important in assessing their own independence. This suggests that when inflation is low, there is little scope for disagreement about what the target should be. Indeed, three inflation-targeting central banks in low-inflation economies stated explicitly that independence could be defined in terms of the central bank's capacity to meet a *mutually* agreed target. Such responses may reflect how successfully the responsibility for monetary policy has been shared between government and the central bank. The arrangements may not only allow government to control the long-run direction of policy, but they can also help to remove any incentive for the government to create surprise inflation (Goodhart, this volume). If government attempts to boost output in the short run and forces a target revision against its central bank's published advice, the blatant transparency of such an act is likely to remove the surprise from 'surprise inflation'. This in turn may reduce any output effects and make such a policy ineffective.

In contrast, other responses illustrate that when inflation is high, it has proved to be more difficult for government and the central bank to split responsibilities for inflation targeting and instruments. In the context of Walsh-type models, this may be because in the presence of a high degree of shocks, the temptation may be to revise the contract *ex post*, thus negating the contract's benefits. What should happen, for example, if inflation falls below the annual target, but remains above the long-run target for inflation (as happened in 1998 in the Czech Republic, Israel, Poland, and, to a lesser extent, Chile)? The optimal response may depend upon the source of the shock that caused the inflation target to be missed, and in some circumstances an option might be to permit inflation to fall below its short-run target, so that it can reach its long-run target quicker.[8] In high-inflation countries this policy dilemma highlights the difficulties in specifying narrow central bank objectives that provide the basis for an accountable contract between the central bank and government.[9]

In 80% of countries where the monetary policy framework is based on an exchange rate target, government has a role in setting the exchange-rate target (see Chapter 3), yet the lack of freedom to set an exchange-rate target does not appear to influence how a central bank defines independence. A number of exchange rate and money-targeting countries also describe independence as the capacity to formulate monetary policy. Our interpretation of 'formulate' is that it is a 'catch-all' term that could refer to goals and instruments, depending upon the circumstances in which it is used, therefore we do not infer any particular significance from these answers.[10]

6.3   An indirect approach to explaining central bank perceptions of their independence

The second approach to gauging what independence means to central banks involves using more objective[11] measures of independence to explain responses to the subjective question, 'To what extent can your central bank formulate and implement policy without the constraint of government?' The details of all questions are shown in Table 4.4 in Chapter 4. The objective measures of independence include the extent to which statutory objectives focus clearly on price stability, the capacity of central banks to define explicit targets independently, the degree of instrument independence, freedom from obligatory finance of the government deficit and the length of the Governor's appointment. We use regression analysis to determine which of these best explains the self-assessment of independence.

Table 6.1 shows simple correlations between the measures of independence. The top row also shows the extent to which the central banks' self-assessment of their independence can be related to each of the objective measures of independence. Self-assessment of independence is strongly associated both with the degree of measured instrument independence and the absence of any deficit finance obligation. In contrast, the extent to which statutory objectives focus on price stability, and the capacity to set targets are each only weakly correlated with self-assessments of independence.

In Table 6.1, the only measures of independence that appear to be correlated significantly with inflation rates in the previous two years are freedom from deficit finance obligation and the self-assessment of independence. These results, however, are influenced by the endogeneity of each of the variables. It could be that the high inflation has led to high (and increased) independence in some economies.

The results from the simple correlation matrix are corroborated in regressions of the perception of independence in the other measures, as shown in Table 6.2. We present results for all countries and for developing, transitional, and industrialised economies. In each case, our ability to explain central banks' assessments of their independence vary is reasonably good.

For the entire sample of countries, the results confirm that central banks' self-assessment of independence is fairly well explained by the degree of instrument independence and the limits on deficit finance. The capacity to set targets and the nature of statutory objectives, though correctly signed, are both insignificant at the 10% level. The regressions vividly illustrate differences between different types of economies. The results for developing countries are similar to those of the entire sample – the absence of deficit finance and instrument independence explains the self-assessment variable. When we group together developing and transitional economies, the results show that limits on deficit finance are the most important influence on the perception of independence.

For industrialised economies, variables are less significant, which probably reflects insufficient variance in the regressors. Almost all industrialised economies have been granted a large degree of instrument independence and do not finance fiscal deficits, and so the variation in the regressors is too small to produce positive results. The term of office of the

Table 6.1 Correlations between measures of independence

	Self-assessment	Target	Instrument	Absence of deficit finance	Statutory objectives	Long term of office of Government	memo (1): average inflation 1997–98	memo (2): inflation rank 1 = lowest
Self-assessment	**100%**	**10%**	**46%**	**50%**	**10%**	**25%**	−16%	−14%
Target-setting capacity	10%	**100%**	11%	−10%	17%	**−7%**	−2%	14%
Instrument independence	46%	11%	**100%**	**36%**	14%	**22%**	−15%	5%
Absence of deficit finance	50%	−10%	36%	**100%**	5%	**13%**	−13%	−37%
Statutory objectives	10%	17%	14%	5%	**100%**	**21%**	2%	17%
Long term of office of Governor	25%	−7%	22%	13%	21%	**100%**	−10%	−6%

Notes: A high score indicates greater independence.
A coefficient of 0.17 is significant at the 90% confidence level; a coefficient of 0.20 is significant at the 95% level.

Table 6.2 Regressions of central bank self-assessments of independence on tangible measures of independence

Dependent variable is self-assessment of independence

Country type	Degree of statutory independence	Target setting capacity	Instrument independence	Deficit finance independence	Term of office of Governor	Observations	Chi² (prob)	Pseudo-R^2[1]
All countries	0.61 (0.107)		1.08** (0.014)	2.07*** (0.000)	1.07* (0.056)	94	41.3 (0.000)	0.163
Developing			1.35*** (0.010)	1.70** (0.014)		44	14.5 (0.001)	0.113
Transitional				2.20** (0.030)		22	4.86 (0.291)	0.087
Industrialised		1.89** (0.026)			2.21 (0.052)*	28	9.5 (0.009)	0.182

Notes: Using an ordered probit regression.
*Indicates significance at the 10% level, **Significant at 5%, ***Significant at 1%
Probability values in brackets indicate at what level of significance the statistic would be no different from zero.
[1] We use an ordered probit method, and for such a technique, a pseudo-R^2 in the region of 0.1 is satisfactory. The Chi² statistic provides a test of the overall explanation of the regression and is highly significant in all cases (Maddala, 1997).

Governor and the capacity to set targets are the only significant variables in this regression.

6.4   Independence and rules versus discretion

Is it possible to go on to argue that independence in terms of limited deficit financing obligations is a necessary condition for a central bank to operate a flexible monetary policy strategy (such as the money and inflation targeting discussed in Chapter 3 or the mixed strategies discussed in Chapter 5)? Without independence from financing the government, is a rigid commitment to an exchange rate target or an IMF programme the most feasible option to achieve economic stability?

Quispe and Mahadeva (this volume) provide the example of Peru in the 1990s to suggest that limits on deficit finance are a precondition for a flexible monetary policy. The Central Bank of Peru has reduced inflation through a mixed strategy of using base money growth as an intermediate target, publishing an inflation target as a transparency device, and using as instruments CD (certificate of deposit) interest rate and foreign exchange market interventions. Although Quispe explains how this strategy is successful in a heavily asset-dollarised Peru, he points out that this success is contingent on the strict limits that had been placed on the government's ability to require deficit finance from domestic banks, foreign banks, or the central bank.

Without these budgetary controls, however, other forms of independence may grant some success to a flexible monetary policy strategy. Box 6.A explains how a central bank acting independently can reduce credit to the private sector as a response to high public-sector financing demands. In the event that the central bank does not have the variety of policy *choices* provided by independence, it may yet be able to have an independent *voice* with which to place public pressure on the government to limit future fiscal dominance. Chart 6.1 illustrates that a minority of central banks view independent communication as a defining factor in overall independence. With free communication, the central bank may be able to identify and publish how much of undesirable inflation is due to the finance of the deficit, increasing the possibility that government is seen as responsible for any inflationary pressure it has created.

6.5   Conclusions

This analysis of the survey results leads to three main conclusions:

i   Central banks define independence as an absence of factors that constrain their ability to set instruments in pursuit of objectives.
ii The results throw interesting light on 'goal independence'. The ability to set targets independently of the government was not generally con-

sidered to be important in countries targeting inflation in low-inflation economies. For disinflating countries, however, it has proved harder to devise clear 'instrument-independent' relationships between central bank and government based on inflation targets, in which government sets a clear target and the central bank sets instruments to meet the target.

iii Finally, the results shed some light on the capacity of measures of independence to explain performance. Posen (1998) is among those to have pointed out that cross-country measures of independence are not always good indicators of performance. Our results provide some reasons why. The factors that affect perceived central bank independence are highly diverse. They include laws, instruments, targets, and government deficit finance. And the relative importance of each of these factors may vary markedly across countries, time, and circumstances.

Box 6A Fiscal dominance and central bank independence in developing countries

In many developing countries, monetary policy has been dominated by fiscal exigencies. There are four primary ways in which governments can finance their deficits:

1 Monetising the deficit by borrowing at zero cost from the central bank.
2 Borrowing at below-market interest rates by thrusting debt down the throats of captive buyers, primarily commercial banks.
3 Borrowing abroad in foreign currency.
4 Borrowing at market interest rates from voluntary domestic private-sector lenders.

The typical OECD country finances about 50% of its deficit from voluntary non-bank domestic sources, while the typical developing country finances only about 8% of its deficit from this source (Fry, 1997, Ch. 1). Evidence suggests that the more a government uses the country's financial system to finance its deficit, the less independent will be the central bank. The fiscal dominance hypothesis holds that both the magnitude of the government's deficit and the methods by which it is financed determine central bank independence.[12] Greater reliance on the inflation tax and financial repression are associated with less central bank independence, while greater recourse to voluntary domestic financial markets is associated with greater central bank independence.

There exists one type of freedom or independence in their balance sheets that all central banks may exploit, at least to some extent. To pursue a monetary target, the central bank in any open economy operates to control domestic credit expansion. Hence, if the government's demands would otherwise produce inflationary domestic credit expansion, the central bank could react by reducing credit to the private sector.

A central bank that turns to the government and says, 'While we can't resist your financing demands, we will neutralise them by squeezing the private sector and we will tell the private sector exactly why we have to squeeze credit' is surely acting more independently than one that simply lets domestic credit rise by the full extent of any extra government borrowing from the banking system.[13] If the central bank behaves consistently in this way by punishing the government through the lobby for private-sector credit, it may exert indirect pressure on the government to reduce its deficit or to finance it in less inflationary ways.

The measure of central bank independence used in Fry (1998) is the central bank's reaction to increased credit demands by the central government. The monetary policy reaction function is specified in terms of the change in domestic credit scaled by GDP, the intermediate target of monetary policy in most open economies. Among various explanatory variables is the change in net domestic credit to the government scaled by GDP. A complete neutralisation of the government's extra borrowing requirements would imply a coefficient of zero for this variable in this monetary policy reaction function. Partial neutralisation would produce a coefficient greater than zero but less than 1. This neutralisation coefficient is interpreted as a measure of central bank independence. In fact, the estimated monetary policy reaction functions show that larger deficits and greater reliance by governments on the inflation tax and financial repression are associated with less central bank independence.

Notes

1 Royal Commission on Indian Currency and Finance. Mins. of Ev., vol. v (1926) Non-Parl. Qn. 14597.
2 See for example Cukierman (1992); Grilli, Masciadaro and Tabellini (1991); and Eijffinger and Scaling (1993).
3 Mangano (1998).
4 Some central banks in our questionnaire did not complete this question; answers from others were excluded because they referred explicitly only to the independence of their own central bank.
5 From the responses, instrument independence could be subdivided into independence to implement, operate, and set policy instruments, yet we found little in the answers that would help us explain the implications of such a subdivision.
6 See Capie, Goodhart, Fischer, and Schnadt (1994), pp. 255–56.
7 Typical responses included: 'The extent to which the central bank can act effectively to fulfil its statutory objectives without political interference' and

'The ability of the central bank to pursue statutory objectives without undue influence from other government officials or private parties'.

8 This is often termed 'opportunistic disinflation', a term used by Blinder (1994).

9 Debates on the question include an illuminating exchange of views between Stanley Fischer and Donald Brash, Governor, Reserve Bank of New Zealand. See Capie, Goodhart, Fischer and Schnadt, 1994, pp. 302 and 310). Fischer states the view that: 'The Bank's inflation goals for the next three years should be announced, after consultation with the Treasury.' In response, Brash argues that although the RBNZ is not goal independent, the framework works because it is one where 'I can force the hand of the Minister if and only if the Minister is seeking to fudge on the price stability objective, while the Minister can force my hand (by sacking me) if and only if I am seeking to fudge on the self-same objective'.

10 Cukierman (1992), p. 372 defines policy formulation as 'concerning the resolution of conflicts between the executive branch and the central bank and the degree of participation of the central bank in the formulation of monetary policy and in the budgetary process'. He distinguishes this from the extent to which the final objectives as stated in the central bank charter focus on price stability.

11 We recognise that subjectivity remains even in the 'more objective' measures. But for convenience we continue with the use of the word 'objective'.

12 The theoretical literature, e.g. Canzoneri and Diba (1996), Sargent and Wallace (1981), Woodford (1995, 1996), focuses only on the size and sustainability of the government deficit. With the exception of Masciandaro and Tabellini (1988), however, there appears to be no empirical work on the relationship between deficits and central bank independence (Eijffinger and De Haan, 1996).

13 Using a similar approach, Eijffinger, Van Rooij, and Schaling (1996) estimate monetary policy reaction functions with changes in money market interest rates as the dependent variable to measure central bank independence in industrial countries. However, they take the country dummies rather than the shift parameters as their measure of central bank independence.

7 Redesigning the monetary policy framework
Practical considerations

7.1 Introduction

Events of the last two years have shifted the spotlight of public attention in many countries onto the framework for setting monetary policy. The sudden collapse of exchange-rate pegs in several Asian countries in 1997 demonstrated the fragility of frameworks that rely on an exchange-rate anchor for inflation control in today's world of massive private capital flows. Financial ruptures in Indonesia, and subsequently Russia, eroded public faith in the ability of bankers to protect the value of their money and in the safety of their savings. Meanwhile, in Europe in January 1999, 11 countries moved to unite their currencies into a single new entity, the euro, managed by a new European Central Bank (ECB).

In the United Kingdom, which has chosen to remain for the present outside the Euro zone, the Government has given the 300-year-old Bank of England 'instrument independence' to achieve an inflation target laid down by the Chancellor. This inflation-targeting framework follows in the footsteps of those developed in other countries such as New Zealand and Canada. The details differ from country to country, but in the United Kingdom, the Government has appointed four independent economists, including one of this Report's authors, to the new nine-member Monetary Policy Committee (MPC), which sets interest rates. The degree of press and public attention to monetary policy that this move has provoked – as well as the continuing interest in the Committee itself – has surprised many on the MPC.

All of this demonstrates that the choice of monetary policy framework is no longer a technical, academic topic to be debated behind closed doors leading off the corridors of power. There is an active public interest in the subject, which is only fitting in view of the widespread costs that result when the framework for delivering price stability fails. In today's world, public accountability and political sovereignty are central elements in the design of a country's monetary policy framework. This chapter considers those aspects, alongside some of the more traditional economic ones, in addressing four questions:

1 *Why* do countries redesign or change their monetary policy frameworks?
2 *When* should countries do this?
3 What are the practical considerations in the *choice* of a new framework?
4 What are the practical considerations in the *design* of a new framework?

The results of the survey of 94 central banks conducted during the course of 1998/99 throw interesting light on these questions. Those reported experiences, as well as our own involvement in the new monetary policy framework here in the UK, lead to the conclusions presented in the final section.

7.2 Why do countries redesign their monetary policy frameworks?

As in most human endeavours, the impetus for change in monetary policy regimes often comes from necessity: until something breaks, it is not fixed. For example, the advent of inflation targeting in the United Kingdom in 1992 grew directly out of the failure of exchange-rate targeting for sterling within the European Monetary System. It was not part of a careful transition strategy or contingency plan.[1] In a speech by the then-Chancellor one month after sterling left the Exchange Rate Mechanism (ERM), the new strategy was articulated:

> ... (leaving the ERM) ... marked a watershed. Though the aims of government policy remain the same, we are now in an entirely different policy environment. We are outside the ERM and are likely to remain so for some time. And with a floating pound we have had more flexibility to reduce interest rates without prejudice to our goal of permanently low inflation.... This does not mean that the Government has gone soft on inflation. But the dramatic progress we have made in getting inflation down does allow me now to give greater weight to securing an early resumption of growth.
>
> (Lamont, 1992)

The British economy did begin to recover shortly thereafter from its longest recession since the 1930s. But the credibility of monetary policy, and of the government more generally in the eyes of the voters, suffered a major blow.

A second example is the adoption of money targeting by the US Federal Reserve Board at a secret meeting of the Open Market Committee in October 1979, shortly after Paul Volcker was appointed. That change in monetary policy target was in response to inflation reaching double-digit levels and the dollar's rapid decline. Commenting on the change from interest rates to money targeting, Volcker said later:

> ... the general level of interest rates reached higher levels than I or my colleagues had really anticipated. That, in a perverse way, was one benefit of the new technique; assuming that those levels of interest were necessary to manage the money supply, I would not have had support for deliberately raising short-term rates that much ... Most disconcerting of all, while the money supply behaved more or less as we had intended for the rest of the year, the inflationary momentum actually had increased by early 1980. With consumer prices rising at an annual rate of around 15% for a few months, there was a palpable sense of growing political panic as well as economic distress.
>
> (Volcker and Gyohten, 1992)

The US economy subsequently entered a deep recession that carried the unemployment rate to a post-war high of over 11% in 1982. But the tide was turned on inflation, and the credibility of the central bank was restored as the economy embarked on a long upswing that lasted through the rest of the decade.

The UK and US experiences illustrate two of the main reasons for a change in monetary policy framework. In the United Kingdom, and more recently in Korea, Indonesia, and Brazil, the change was forced, rather suddenly, by external developments. This is often the case with countries that abandon exchange-rate targeting (but see the next section). The regime had been successful in controlling inflation, but imbalances elsewhere in the economy eventually made it unsustainable. In the United States, and in countries such as Argentina and Brazil during the earlier part of this decade, the change of framework was prompted by the failure of the previous monetary policy regime to control inflation. A change of framework – to money targeting in the United States; to exchange-rate locks in Argentina and Brazil – was needed to bring inflation under control and to rebuild the credibility of the central bank so that inflationary expectations could be subdued.

The survey shows that changes in monetary policy framework (or at least target) have been widespread, especially in industrialised countries, since the 1970s. Charts 7.1 and 7.2 below show how the broad monetary policy frameworks of the total survey population have evolved over the past three decades.[2] There is a distinct difference between developing and industrialised country sub-sets, so these are shown separately. In developing countries (Chart 7.1), roughly half of the sample use exchange-rate targeting. However, this has shown a steady decline since the break-up of the Bretton Woods system in the early 1970s. The number of exchange-rate targeters without capital controls has remained broadly stable over that period, while the number with capital controls has steadily diminished. Only a small number of developing countries relied upon explicit money

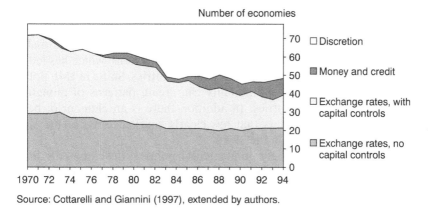

Chart 7.1 Distribution of monetary frameworks in developing economies

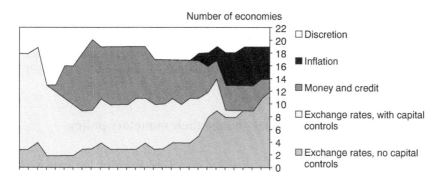

Chart 7.2 Distribution of monetary frameworks in industrialised economies

or credit targets.[3] The big increase since the mid-1970s has been in discretionary frameworks, i.e. without explicit targets.

By contrast, in the 22 industrialised economies in this sample, discretionary frameworks have been less widely used since the late 1970s.[4] The number of exchange-rate targeters has remained broadly stable since then, although the share with capital controls shrank rapidly in the early 1980s and has since disappeared. Short-term intermediate targets (mostly money) have also become less popular, while inflation targets have gained converts since their introduction in 1989 by New Zealand. Some might argue that inflation targeting is simply a structured form of discretionary monetary policy.

These charts above suggest that there may be broader forces at work in the change of monetary policy frameworks than simply the individual country pressures of external or domestic circumstances discussed above.

For example, the integration of global capital markets over the past two decades has made it more difficult to sustain effective capital controls as a feature of the monetary policy framework. The same trend has probably contributed to the instability of money demand functions, which has led to the abandonment of money targets by some countries. Shifts in IMF policy towards certain forms of conditionality can create patterns of monetary policy changes across countries. In addition there is an element of best-practice learning from others that has clearly sparked some of the shift towards inflation targeting in the 1990s.

There are also cases where fundamental political developments have provoked a change in monetary policy framework. The reshaping of Europe since the collapse of the Soviet Union in 1989 left a policy vacuum in the transitional economies, sometimes coupled with severe inflationary pressures, that had to be filled. The abandonment of the rouble was an obvious rupture in regime for some transitional economies. At the same time, among the countries of western Europe, it was largely a political drive towards the creation of an 'ever closer union' that provided the impetus for the single currency.

In sum, there are many reasons – both positive and negative – for a country to decide to change its monetary policy framework. It is not as infrequent an occurrence as one might think in either industrialised or developing countries.

7.3   When should countries change their monetary policy framework?

Although the survey does not provide direct evidence of the reasons for change of the monetary policy framework, a perusal of the dates and directions of changes suggests that most were in reaction to adverse circumstances. Countries mostly jumped when pushed. This is true particularly with regard to countries that dropped exchange rate targets (see p. 38 in Chapter 3). For those countries demoting the importance of money targets, the situation varied a bit more. Several economies maintained explicit money targets or monitoring ranges for some time after they ceased to have a fixed position at or even close to the top of the policy-makers' hierarchy of indicators. The United Kingdom, for example, kept them until 1997, and the United States of America still had them in 1998.

More concrete evidence is provided in Eichengreen (1999), who looks at the subset of countries moving from pegged exchange rates to exchange-rate flexibility over the last 20 years, compared to two control groups: those that continued to peg and all other developing countries.

Eichengreen concludes:

> ... exits have not been happy events. Typically, growth has slowed in the period leading up to the exit. In the year the exit takes place,

growth is negative and significantly below that in both the non-exit cases and in countries with lasting pegs. Export growth also slows, falling significantly below that in both comparison groups in the year preceding the exit.... Countries have generally waited to exit until reserves are falling.... There is a clear sense that policymakers are reluctant to face the facts: they fear that exiting from a pegged rate regime will undermine confidence, destabilise the financial system, and depress the economy, with adverse political repercussions. ... Officials' consequent reluctance heightens the fragility of the financial system, leading to an unnecessarily high incidence of crises, since the necessary move to greater flexibility only occurs when the markets force it upon the authorities.

(Eichengreen, 1999)

With hindsight, it appears that when changes in monetary policy regime have been made, they generally have been delayed longer than would have been optimal if the real economic costs of change could have been foreseen accurately. Of course, the difficulty with this observation is that it does not take into account those cases where the costs of change were avoided because, in the end, the authorities were able to ride out the storm without a change in regime. The benefits of riding out the storm are likely to take the form of heightened credibility and to manifest themselves only in the longer term, when they are likely to be hard to distinguish from other influences. Because regime change itself is, or at least is perceived to be, costly, the authorities generally will delay too long. This is particularly true when the defence of the existing regime requires public statements committed to its continuation. Contingency planning for change, in such circumstances, becomes more difficult.

There are examples of countries that have managed a smooth change in monetary policy regime with few economic costs and potentially large avoided costs of having to change under pressure. Chile, Israel, and Poland have all moved from exchange-rate pegs to flexible rates in a series of steps over several years.[5] In Poland, for example, a US dollar peg was initially used as part of a stabilisation programme to curtail inflation beginning in 1990. The next step was to change the peg from the dollar to a basket of currencies, in 1991. Five months later, the fixed-basket peg was replaced by a crawling peg that remained in place for four years as inflation came steadily down. Most restrictions on capital-account transactions were abolished and capital inflows began to rise. In 1995, the authorities shifted from a crawling peg to a crawling band where fluctuations of $\pm 7\%$ were permitted. Three years later the band was widened to 10%. This step-by-step adjustment of the monetary policy framework has proceeded in parallel to the reduction of inflation in Poland and its continued success in attracting foreign investment. The fixed peg initially signalled its determination to pursue stabilisation, make a clear break from the past and build public confidence in the discredited domestic currency. The crawling peg allowed it to bring domestic inflation down gradually toward the rates of its trading partners. The crawling bands introduced an element of exchange-rate risk for domestic industry as well as foreign investors, and widening the bands increased the degree of market-determined behaviour in the exchange rate. Because inflation has continued on a downward path, and because the liberalised capital account has helped to attract foreign inflows, the credibility of the monetary authorities has remained high with both foreign investors and domestic constituencies.

The Polish case demonstrates how a proactive redesign of the monetary policy framework can be successful both in preventing crises from developing and in supporting the wider objectives of economic growth and structural change in a transition economy. The broader answer to the question of 'when to change' is 'sooner rather than later'. And it is never too soon to start work on a contingency plan for the next change, even if no date is yet in mind.

7.4   Practical considerations in the choice of a new monetary policy framework

The choice of an alternative monetary policy framework to what a country has at the moment involves at least five practical considerations. Some of these seem obvious, yet they are often neglected in the economic literature, which tends to focus on the intricacies of policy design rather than the broader context of policy choice.

The first consideration is the policy history of the country: what has worked or failed already. Reference is often made to Germany's pre-war history of hyperinflation as a key pillar of the country's strong political support for the independence of the Bundesbank (Kennedy, 1991). In the US case discussed earlier, the failure of a purely discretionary monetary policy to contain inflation in the 1970s led to the choice of an announced money-growth target as a commitment device. Once the new framework had achieved its objective, however, it was possible to move back gradually to a more eclectic and discretionary framework, culminating in the explicit abandonment of monetary targets, as reported in the minutes of the December 1998 Federal Reserve Board meeting. In the UK case, the uncomfortable history of abandoned exchange rate targets has made the public debate over joining the euro particularly contentious compared to that in other European countries. Revisiting the terrain of past policy failures, even if the circumstances have materially changed, is difficult to manage. Perhaps this is what drives the continual evolution of monetary policy.

The second consideration is the starting point for inflation. How far is the country from price stability when the change of monetary policy framework is made? For Britain in 1992, for Thailand and Korea in 1997, and for Brazil in 1999, inflation was close to its desired level when the previous policy regime failed. This makes it easier to manage inflation expectations during the transition, which provides more scope for the introduction of a semi-discretionary, rather than a tightly rule-based, policy framework. Inflation targeting, in particular, can be introduced with a higher probability of success if a country is already close to the target.[6]

If, on the other hand, inflation is significantly above its desired level, then it is necessary to brake, rather than reinforce, inflation expectations. This strengthens the case for 'shock therapy' rather than gradualism, and for rule-based or highly transparent regimes. Among the transition economies, both the Czech Republic's choice of gradual policy change and Poland's choice for sudden stabilisation can be explained, at least in part, by their vastly different inflation rates at the outset. Both choices proved successful in supporting economic development over the initial years of transition.

A third practical consideration is the international evidence on what works in similar countries. This does not always provide a clear steer. As noted in Chapter 4, 'diversity is a defining feature of the responses of the 94 central banks in the sample'. Countries with quite different economies choose similar frameworks and vice versa. It would be interesting to determine the relationship among monetary policy frameworks and political (rather than economic) structures. For example, federal or multi-state political structures appear to have more independent central banks than do highly centralised states. However, we do not have sufficient political data to draw conclusions in this area.

An obviously relevant economic comparison is with a country's major trading partners. For a small country, asymmetrical exchange-rate targeting is likely to work best when the bulk of its trade is with a single large country (or currency bloc) that has a low inflation rate. Failing this, it is possible to target a currency basket. Symmetrical exchange-rate targeting, as in the European Monetary System, requires a degree of mutual political commitment that is rarely found without an overarching political structure. Despite the difficulties of cross-country comparison, the lessons from others' experience with different policy regimes should not be ignored.

A fourth, and related, consideration is the set of economic characteristics of the country. How large and how open is its economy? How commodity-dependent? What is the role of the banking sector? How deep and how internationally integrated are the capital markets? Questions such as these are important in comparing the potential suitability of alternative monetary policy frameworks. Money or credit targeting, for example, is likely to be relatively ineffective in a small, open economy where private investment is financed through the stock market as well as the banking system, and where foreign banks and investment managers play a significant role. Hong Kong is perhaps an extreme example of this case; an exchange-rate target makes much more sense for it. In many respects,

China has the opposite set of economic characteristics, which makes money or credit a much more suitable intermediate target for monetary policy.

Finally, it is important to consider a country's political characteristics in the choice of monetary policy framework (as well as in its design, as discussed below). The constitutional structure will influence the appropriate degree of independence for the central bank. Where the structure is one of countervailing powers, as in the United States, there is ample support for an independent central bank with long terms for its Governors and explicit relationships between it and the legislative and executive arms of government. In a system of parliamentary sovereignty without constitutional checks and balances, the democratic legitimacy of the central bank may rest on its receiving marching orders, at least in terms of the policy target, from the government in power. In order to preserve the advantages of central bank independence in the pursuit of price stability, in such cases it may be preferable to have a highly transparent target – whether for the exchange rate or for inflation – and a mechanism for public accountability. However, it should also be recognised that the general standards for transparency and accountability in government vary considerably across countries. Those applied to the central bank should not be inconsistent with those applied to other arms of government in that country.[7]

7.5   Practical considerations in the design of a new monetary policy framework

Whatever framework is chosen for monetary policy, many design details will have to be determined. These can make or break the new system. Yet the economic literature provides little guidance on questions such as the relative merits of committee versus individual decisions, or how committee decisions should be taken. This section describes the results of the Bank of England survey on such details and suggests a few considerations that may be relevant in redesigning or changing them.

7.5.i   Individual or committee?

A policy-making committee is more common than an individual decision-maker. Chart 7.3 shows the distribution of responses to the survey question, 'Who takes the decision to change the main monetary policy instrument?' In only nine countries is the decision taken by an individual, while 79 countries use a committee structure. Slightly less than half of the committees have a procedure for voting, while the other half take a decision by consensus. Six of the 36 voting committees publish the votes of individuals.

The decision procedures have an important bearing on accountability. Only in the case where the votes are published is there an opportunity for

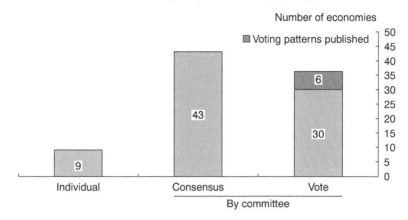

Note: the countries publishing individual votes are Japan, Korea, Poland, Sweden, the United Kingdom and the United States.
Source: Bank of England Survey of monetary frameworks.

Chart 7.3 Monetary policy decision procedure

individual accountability. Indeed, in the case of the United Kingdom, all members of the Monetary Policy Committee are called before the parliamentary committee that scrutinises economic policy for public questioning on their votes and the reasoning behind them. This degree of individual accountability greatly heightens the chance of split votes in the Monetary Policy Committee, as it effectively prevents consensus even when the differences among members are small. However, it also sharpens debate within the Committee and ensures that all members devote careful attention to their task. After several early months of closely split votes, the British press and public became accustomed to the fine balance of judgement that is often involved in monetary policy decisions, and the financial-market commentators seem to appreciate the additional information that individual voting records provide. However, the system could lead to public confusion and an unproductive focus by the press on personalities rather than policy. The President of the European Central bank has also expressed concerns that individuals might face additional political pressure if their votes were known: so in the ECB, only the decision is published.

7.5.ii   Size of committee

As shown in Chart 7.4, most of the countries with monetary policy committees have between five and ten members on the committee. Just under 10% of respondents have more than ten members. The ideal size of a decision-making committee is large enough to include the relevant expertise and experience, but small enough for each member to contribute effectively and for there to be genuine challenge and interchange of views.

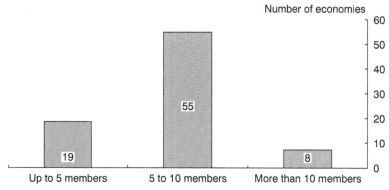

Source: Bank of England Survey of monetary frameworks.

Chart 7.4 Number of people in the Monetary Policy Board/Committee

Improvements in data collection and the growing sophistication and time-liness of economic statistics have reduced the need for large committee structures. In most countries, it is no longer necessary for regional or sectoral representatives to bring specific information from their constituencies to the committee as a whole; indeed, this can be counterproductive because it may bias the committee's decision in an inappropriate way.

7.5.iii   Composition of committee

A committee will take better decisions than an individual only if, first, its members bring diverse but relevant experience and, second, they engage in a process of 'creative challenge' so that the decision that results incorporates what they have learned from one another. Unlike many management committees in the private sector, there is no need to promote 'buy-in' of the monetary policy decision by those who would 'implement' it. Including representatives of those affected by a monetary policy decision on the committee would risk violating both of the requirements for better committee decisions by overloading it with people who lack the qualifications to contribute meaningfully to the debate.

Some countries have a political need for regional representatives on the policy-making board. In such cases it will be especially important to limit the total number of committee members and to ensure that all members are technically qualified professionals as well as regional representatives. An alternative approach is to separate the policy-making board from the board of governance for the central bank, and to include regional representation on the board of governance rather than the policy board. This is the route that the United Kingdom has taken.

While committee members need to share a certain degree of technical expertise, it is equally important that they bring diverse perspectives to their common task. A committee of clones, whether central bank professionals or economic model builders, is likely to prove unanimously incapable of spotting the unexpected threat that lies outside their area of competence, or recognising soon enough that their shared underlying assumptions may no longer be appropriate. Complacency and 'groupthink' prove the undoing of many established committees.

7.5.iv Frequency of meetings

Over 90% of respondents reported that their policy-makers met at least monthly to decide on the setting of policy instruments, and 43% met at least weekly (see Chart 7.5). The frequency of policy change was, of course, much lower (see Chart 7.6 below). 73% of the sample reported that they changed the main policy instrument no more frequently than quarterly.

The frequency of meetings will depend on the monetary policy framework as well as on the number and type of committee members. Exchange-rate targeting may require more frequent meetings – or at least the ability to hold meetings at short notice – simply because information on the target is updated frequently. Money targeting will generally have new information monthly, while updating an entire inflation forecast will rarely be justified by new data in a single month. There are also questions of feasibility. If the committee is large and includes part-time members who have other commitments, it would be quite difficult for the entire committee to meet as often as weekly, let alone daily.

Such mundane considerations can have major repercussions on the

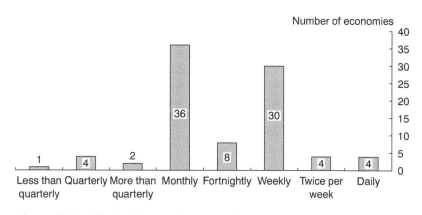

Source: Bank of England Survey of monetary frameworks.

Chart 7.5 How often do policy-makers meet to decide on the setting of policy instruments? (NB. Need more discrimination on which instruments)

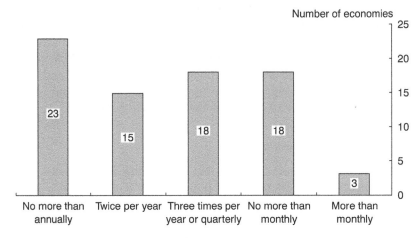

Source: Bank of England Survey of monetary frameworks.

Chart 7.6 How frequently is the main instrument changed?

ability of the central bank to attract the range and calibre of people it needs for an effective policy board. That is why the design details need to be considered at the outset and, if the initial set-up proves too constraining, modified later.

7.6   Conclusions

Central banks are inherently attracted to stability, be it price stability, financial stability, exchange-rate stability, or stability in their own operational framework. Yet experience shows that, in order to achieve the first two stability objectives, it has sometimes been necessary to endure change in the last. The past three decades have witnessed many changes in monetary policy regime in both industrialised and developing countries. Change has generally been provoked by one of three factors: the failure of the existing framework to control inflation; international financial flows that have undermined exchange-rate regimes; and intercountry political initiatives such as the European Exchange Rate Mechanism.

It is possible for a central bank to take two widely different attitudes towards a future change in its monetary policy framework. The most common approach is to stick to what it has, robustly defend it and refuse to contemplate change until change is forced upon it. While that approach has been successful in some countries for some periods of time, when change has come it has brought high economic and political costs. The other approach, more difficult and rare, is to anticipate change, plan for it, and proactively initiate it when the time is propitious. Countries that have succeeded with this strategy have received far less public attention than those that have failed with the former, but their examples are worth studying as well.

On the more specific questions of which framework to choose and which details to incorporate, the overall conclusion is that both should fit the circumstances of the country. There is no 'best-practice' framework for all. Relevant considerations include the size and openness of the economy, the degree of centralisation in the political structure, norms for transparency in the public sector, and the history of past monetary policy successes and failures.

Notes

1 According to journalist David Smith's book (1992): 'The Government's response to the ERM threat was not to prepare a contingency plan to cover the possible collapse of the system, or sterling's departure from it. Instead (Chancellor) Lamont and (Prime Minister) Major reinforced their commitment to the pound's continuation in the system at the existing central parity ...' p. 236.
2 There are no transitional economies in this sample, which contains a different group of countries from that used in the Bank of England survey. The way in which Cottarelli and Giannini (1997) distinguish money and inflation targeting frameworks is discussed in Box 4.1 on p. 62.
3 It is likely that the number of money or credit targeters has increased since the end of this data based on Cottarelli and Giannini (1997). It has not been possible to extend their breakdown past 1994.
4 The United States and Japan are noteworthy exceptions
5 Eichengreen (1999) presents these examples and others. Most of the following discussion on Poland comes from that source.
6 When that is not the case, some countries have set both long-run and short-run inflation targets, where the latter is close enough to the starting point for inflation to be clearly achievable.
7 One of the more difficult political issues faced by the European Central Bank, in common with other European Union institutions, is how to reconcile the quite different norms for transparency and accountability in different European member states.

8 Conclusions and summary

In 1900 only 18 countries had central banks and today the number is 172 (King, 1999). More than half of these participated in the survey on which this Report is based, and the central banks covered in the Report come from economies representing over 95% of the world's GDP.[1] In using information from such a broad cross-section of the world's central banks, the report has shed light on the role and workings of these important institutions: their priorities and processes in policy formulation; their relationships with government and the private sector; their analytical processes; and the important institutional and analytical constraints under which they operate. Above all the Report has sought to represent and interpret the views of central banks within an objective framework.

The final question in the survey asked central banks to reveal how important various factors were in their monetary framework. The results, shown in Table 8.1, are the final piece in our jigsaw. Columns A to D present the rankings given to features by the sample as a whole, shown as percentages for the total. Columns E and F show differences in the responses of industrialised and the other economies in terms of which features they consider vital components of their monetary framework. Finally, columns G to M use all the answers to rank the importance of each aspect of the framework according to the type of economy and framework.

Price stability is now the dominant ethos of monetary policy. Throughout the world, policy-makers have moved toward defining and publishing numerical objectives for policy in keeping with their central banks' statutory objectives of price and monetary stability. There is evidently a growing taste amongst policy-makers to specify targets for the key responsibilities of central banks, even when, as was shown in Chapter 3, such targets are used more frequently as a policy benchmark than a rigid rule. From the perspective of an observer of central banking even ten years ago, this represents a remarkable convergence in the approach to policy, and one that has contributed to delivering lower and more stable inflation throughout the world.

Table 8.1 shows that for central banks as a whole, the long-run goal of

Table 8.1 Important features of monetary frameworks by type of economy and framework

Responses to the question, 'How important are the following components of your monetary framework at the present time?'

| | % responses in each category | | | | % vital | | Ranking of importance of feature[1] | | | | | | | |
	A vital	B very important	C fairly important	D not important	E Industrialised	F Dev. and Trans	All	G Industrialised	H Developing	I Transitional	J Exchange rate	K Money	L Inflation	M Discretionary
% of total	**22**	**36**	**26**	**15**	**20**	**24**								
Number of economies in category							**89**	**26**	**42**	**21**	**30**	**18**	**16**	**25**
Inflation targets (informal or formal)	48	22	12	17	46	49	4	5	5	7	15	5	1	2
Money-growth targets (informal or formal)	27	28	13	31	15	32	14	16	10	12	20	1	17	10
Exchange-rate targets (informal or formal)	44	24	17	16	46	43	6	6	10	3	1	15	18	16
Balance of payments targets (informal or formal)	12	30	28	29	0	17	19	21	15	16	14	18	19	21
Output targets (informal or formal)	8	26	33	34	4	10	21	17	20	21	18	20	21	19
Macroeconomic forecasts	16	33	38	13	35	8	14	7	19	18	16	17	6	10
Market indicators of inflation	13	38	29	19	15	13	16	10	19	20	16	15	15	8
Money demand equations	11	27	36	26	8	13	20	13	21	18	19	11	19	18
Analysis of monetary-survey data	25	40	20	13	4	34	10	15	3	10	11	2	12	10
Analysis of banking sector	22	49	25	3	15	25	7	9	9	4	7	5	9	6
Analysis of domestic financial stability	33	40	18	9	15	40	5	11	1	7	4	7	8	4
Analysis of international financial stability	11	33	40	15	8	13	18	12	18	17	11	18	16	20
Analysis of real sector of the economy	9	54	36	1	15	6	11	8	16	14	9	14	5	14
Analysis of balance of payments	19	52	21	8	4	25	9	13	3	9	8	8	11	4
Transparency of policy	35	39	20	6	50	29	3	3	13	5	3	10	4	8
Accountability of policy	25	40	29	4	35	21	8	4	13	12	5	11	6	10
Independence of central bank	54	29	13	3	69	48	1	1	7	1	2	3	3	10
Maintenance of low inflation expectations	51	31	10	8	54	49	2	2	5	2	6	3	2	3
Constraints resulting from lack of data	20	31	30	18	0	29	13	19	10	6	10	20	9	16
Constraints resulting from fiscal policy	28	30	21	20	0	40	12	18	2	10	13	8	13	7
Constraints from structure of financial sector	18	37	18	27	4	24	16	20	7	14	16	13	14	15

[1] Ranking 1 is the most important. The rankings are based on a score given by: importance = 3 × %vital + 2 × % very important + 1 × fairly important.
[2] Allocation in groups is based on whether the exchange-rate, money, inflation, or discretion was the highest 'score' in Table A.1.

reducing or maintaining low inflation expectations was described as vital by more than half the respondents, and is more important to central banks than any particular target, formal or informal. In the long run, there is only one monetary policy objective, that of maintaining price stability, and very few central banks now have legal or other objectives that pose a potential conflict with this goal.

On what does policy focus during the journey toward the long-run goal of price stability? There is certainly evidence that a growing number of central banks have escaped from perennial concerns over external payments problems and also from the view that central banks should target output directly: balance of payments and output objectives are very close to the bottom of the list of central banks' current priorities mentioned in Table 8.1. There still exist a small minority of frameworks that specify growth and employment as valid monetary policy objectives. Overall, however, such objectives are increasingly seen as a consequence of rather than an alternative to low and stable inflation.

Financial stability concerns have emerged as a very important aspect of central banking. This is evident from the table (see row 11). In developing economies, such concerns appear to have made financial stability analysis even more important than any aspect of monetary stability. The resurgence of financial stability issues in the priorities of central banks has a familiar ring to it. And although the recent talk of the death of inflation may be premature, Chapter 2 of this report confirms that across a broad range of economies, inflation is lower than it has been since the early 1970s. In 1931, long before the high-inflation decades of the 1960s, 1970s and 1980s, the Macmillan Committee in the United Kingdom described a central bank as being 'called upon to keep the financial structure upon an even keel'. In 1953 Sayers[2] asserted that 'It is generally agreed nowadays that this public responsibility is the sole *raison d'être* of the central bank.'

There remains plenty of scope for debate as to how the goal of price stability can best be attained and maintained, and why, in a global context, there has been more success in achieving it now than at any time since the early 1970s (Chapter 2). This reflects in part an ongoing debate as to what monetary policy can and cannot do given both the world environment and each country's history, politics, and economic structure (Chapter 7). Much of the remaining debate is over the optimal speed of adjustment to price stability.

Changes in monetary policy design over the last 30 years have been an evolutionary rather than a revolutionary process. Outcomes partly reflect the ethos of the survival of the fittest and partly the constraint of the environment in which the monetary authority operates. A plethora of monetary policy frameworks has resulted, employing various combinations of a fixed set of characteristics, but nearly all with the common goal of price stability. A country seeking to develop its monetary policy by looking around at the experiences of other countries can integrate many different choices involving not only the degree to which policy focuses on explicit targets, but also which institutional devices can make its central bank transparent, accountable and independent.

In this Report, we have aimed to inform these choices by relating the institutional features of a monetary framework to the economic and political constraints in which it must operate by explaining the transparency, accountability and independence characteristics that each framework brings to monetary policy. Independence is viewed by central banks as the most important feature of their monetary framework (Table 8.1). Remarkably, central banks rank transparency as the third most important aspect of the monetary framework, a reflection of the very considerable changes in the role and outlook of central banks in recent decades.

The basis of our analysis was a survey of 94 central banks with a broad range of experiences and backgrounds. In trying to draw out lessons from this survey, we are careful to account for diversity. First, we do not assume *a priori* that any one feature of a framework, such as the variable targeted, can be understood in isolation: an appropriate monetary framework comes as a package rather than as a sum of parts. Second, we are careful to account for a country's idiosyncrasies.

As an example of the methodology, Chapter 3 analysed the choice of explicit monetary policy targets. Because many central banks use more than one explicit target, we determined for each country three scores that depend on the degree to which policy objectives depend on exchange rate, inflation, and money growth. The focus of monetary policy is then expressed as a three-dimensional shape rather than a point representing particular variable targeted. The alternative would have been to force each country into only one category. The characteristics identified depend on institutional features of the regime (what they publish, etc.) as well as what central banks themselves say they target.

In drawing lessons from the survey, we take account of what could be a dramatic change in the world environment. The information in Chapter 2 suggests that global inflationary history has entered a new phase (or is perhaps has returned to its pre-1970s state). Inflation differentials are narrowing as more countries fall into the category of having low and stable inflation. Chapter 2 illustrated that even in the high-inflation decades of the 1970s, 1980s and 1990s, low inflation (less than about 4%) has been a more permanent home for a country than are the higher ranges of inflation. So although in the past it has been true that no developing country has ever reached a low inflation state without a fixed exchange rate regime, there are good reasons to believe that the 1990s should witness the beginning of periods of inflation stability that break from that precedent.

What are the ingredients of a good framework that can operate in this environment? We can begin by comparing the recent changes in monetary policy across the wide sample of countries.

Perhaps the most visible change in the 1990s has been that announcing explicit targets for intermediate variables has become more widespread. During this period, 114 new explicit targets were adopted and only 19 dropped (Chapter 3). This has meant that elements of exchange-rate targeting, inflation targeting *and* money targeting are present in the way many central banks conduct monetary policy. Across our sample as a whole, there were on average over 50% more explicit targets being announced than there were central banks.

The increased prevalence in the announcement of explicit targets for money and inflation may have been both the result and a cause of lower inflation across many countries. The results in Chapter 3 illustrate that countries have been far more successful in minimising the deviation of outcomes from target than might have been expected on the basis of experience in the 1960s, 1970s and 1980s. This may, however, be in part due to a relatively low incidence of external shocks (such as hikes in commodity prices) that contributed to higher global inflation in previous decades. Of course it is possible that the relatively low incidence of external shocks is at least in part a consequence of low inflation.

The survey also revealed how these targets were used. Exchange-rate targeting is the least flexible strategy. The evidence is that when exchange rate targeting is the main objective, it is less amenable to combination with elements of other targets. Chapter 4 showed that exchange-rate targeters rarely allow money or inflation considerations to prevail in conflicts, and Chapter 5 shows that the more that a country focuses its monetary policy framework on exchange-rate objectives, the less money and inflation-targeting characteristics it has. Exchange-rate targeting can be characterised as a strategy that will gain credibility by making its outcomes transparent. Policy-makers are announcing that they can be trusted because policy failure will be visible and less excusable. Because defending an exchange rate is based on rules, it is difficult even behind the closed doors of the central bank to allow other objectives to impinge.

The evidence from this Report is that, as a generalisation, central banks treat money and inflation targets move flexibly (Chapter 3). Table 8.1 shows that inflation targets – be they informal or formal – are of great importance in money targeting regimes. Such targets not necessarily alternatives to be chosen by the followers of different theoretical approaches to monetary policy. In many of these regimes, particularly in developing economies, money-targeting refers to a policy process that makes use of frequently available data. It is a practical approach rather than a philosophy. And one of the most important uses of inflation targets as cited in Chapter 3, has been to define relationships among different institutions and agents in the economy in a way that it is difficult to do using money targets.

The survey shows that another important feature of both money and inflation targeting is their discretionary nature. In Chapter 4 it is argued that narrow discrepancies between target and outcome designate a strategy as more rules-based, whereas large discrepancies designate it as more discretion-based. That chapter shows that money and inflation targeting are used with significant flexibility, and that exchange-rate, inflation and money targets may be combined within a framework. For example, many countries combine inflation targeting with elements of exchange-rate and money targeting (e.g. Chile, Mexico and Peru). Although money targeting is on the wane in industrialised countries, it stills remains popular elsewhere where the changing structure of the real economy and associated data problems make it particularly difficult to assess the balance between demand pressures and supply potential. This could partly be because money targeting can be combined with other strategies. Elements of money targeting bring with it a focus on the money market, which enables the central bank to keep up its monitoring of financial stability (Chapter 5). It also offers accountability to the IMF.

Experience shows them that inflation and money targets are being widely used but not treated as rules. How then is credibility achieved with these frameworks? Our results show that this is achieved through a discretionary strategy employing combination of transparency and explanation. Policy-makers ask not just to be judged purely on results but instead commit themselves to inform the public about their thought processes so that agents may understand the difficulties of the economic environment. The recent eagerness to publish regular assessments, minutes of meetings, forecasts and even discussion of past forecast errors is not confined to inflation targeting central banks (see Chapter 5). The greater emphasis on explaining policy may also indicate a need to acquire internal discipline, for it brings focus to a central bank if it knows that not just its actions but also its thinking will be open to scrutiny.

Notes

1 Based upon World Bank Data contained in the World Development Report (1998/99).
2 *Central Banking After Bagehot.*

Appendix 1

Measures of monetary framework characteristics from the Bank of England questionnaire

The results represent the authors' interpretation of information provided by central banks. They do not necessarily represent the views of any central bank and have not necessarily been seen by the board or governors of any central bank. Some scores that are confidential have been left blank. Details of the calculation methods are provided in Chapter 4.

Table A.1 Summary scores for framework characteristics (% of maximum)

	Albania	Argentina	Armenia	Australia	Austria	Bahamas	Bahrain	Bangladesh	Barbados	Belgium	Belize	Bosnia-Herz.	Botswana	Bulgaria	Canada	Chile	China	Croatia	Cyprus	Czech Rep.	Denmark	Eastern Carib.	Ecuador
Short and medium-term policy focus																							
1. Exchange-rate focus	0	100	0	0	0	88	100	31	100	94	71	100	38	100	6	6	31	25	38	6	94	94	6
2. Money focus	38	0	38	0	0	0	0	75	0	0	19	0	13	0	0	0	88	88	19	0	0	0	31
3. Inflation focus	94	0	100	94	94	0	13	44	0	0	27	0	63	0	88	88	31	31	75	94	0	0	56
4. Discretion (high score implies more discretion)*	25	0	19	6	13	13	6	63	0	6	52	0	63	0	16	28	28	41	53	9	6	6	63
Institutional characteristics																							
4. Independence	66	79	76	73	68	39	54	56	24	77	43	81	65	79	91	93	68	79	79	98	88	49	93
5. Accountability of central bank to government	75	100	83	83	67	100	75	83	92	33	42	100	58	100	100	17	100	72	83	75	75	92	75
6. Policy explanations	40	53	65	78	27	50	18	39	73	68	48	35	53	46	79	83	63	42	48	86		48	59
Use and importance of forms of monetary analysis																							
7. Inflation expectations	0	0		92	89	0	0	25	0	50	6	0	100	0	92	17	17	83	0	33	42	0	75
8. Models and forecasts	11	0	28	33	33	17	0	6	0	61	6	0	6	33	89	56	56	72	11	89	56	22	39
9. Money and banking sector	22	44	89	22	0	67	44	56	44	11	33	11	67	33	44	33	33	78	56	44	11	44	78
Structural characteristics																							
10. Importance of financial stability issues	33	58	75	8	17	25	0	17	67	8	33	17	17	0	33	17	33	33	42	33	0	33	83
Memo																							
11. Inflation, av. '97–98, incl. estimates	27	0.7	11	0.6	1.1	0.9	0.6	5.8	3.2	1.3	0.1	12	7.7	552	1.3	5.6	1.0	5.3	2.9	9.6	2.0	2.4	33
12. Inflation rank (1 = lowest)	87	8	73	6	13	10	7	48	34	17	1	74	60	92	19	47	12	45	33	69	26	28	89

* This is intended as a particular rather than general measure of discretion. It depends only on the scores for exchange-rate focus, money focus, and inflation focus. Discretion is calculated as twice the maximum of these scores minus the sum of the other two. It is converted to an index between zero and 100, where a high score implies more discretion.

Table A.1 Summary scores for framework characteristics (% of maximum) – continued

	Egypt	Estonia	Fiji	Finland	France	Georgia	Germany	Ghana	Greece	Guyana	Hong Kong	Hungary	Iceland	India	Indonesia	Ireland	Israel	Italy	Jamaica	Japan	Jordan	Kazakhstan	Kenya
Short and medium term policy focus																							
1. Exchange-rate focus	13	100	50	63	58	25	13	0	94	19	100	81	75	6	6	75	13	50	25	0	63	25	13
2. Money focus	38	0	0	0	46	25	88	56	25	88	0	0	0	50	63	0	0	44	44	0	25	88	69
3. Inflation focus	44	0	31	56	40	56	19	19	25	25	0	19	19	44	50	19	88	44	88	50	13	44	44
4. Discretion (high score implies more discretion)*	81	0	66	66	84	69	28	53	31	34	0	28	34	75	66	34	19	94	47	50	56	47	59
Institutional characteristics																							
4. Independence	53	85	73	91	90	80	96	60	86	65	74	86	59	83	56	87	66	88	39	93	74	76	66
5. Accountability of central bank to government	83	100	17	92	83	83	17	58	33	42	92	83	92	67	83	83	100	58	42		75	83	67
6. Policy explanations	47	71	64	74	53	65	70	36	36	32	58	49	65	75	83	78	68	81	65	89	60	51	52
Use and importance of forms of monetary analysis																							
7. Inflation expectations	17	25	0	67	67	17	50	0	50	0	0	25	50	0	50	42	50	92	0	75	33	83	0
8. Models and forecasts	28	83	6	61	44	11	56	0	67	6	28	22	11	11	100	56	67	94	44	72	39	44	6
9. Money and banking sector	89	56	44	22	56	100	56	44	56	89	56	22	33	89	89	33	44	44	56	78	100	78	56
Structural characteristics																							
10. Importance of financial stability issues	92	33	0	8	50	75	33	0	8	33	0	0	8	67	83	8	33	33	8	50	58	67	25
Memo																							
11. Inflation, av. '97–98, incl. estimates	4.4	11	4.5	1.3	0.9	7.0	1.4	21	5.2	4.1	4.3	16	1.7	10	32	1.9	7.2	2.0	9.1	1.2	3.7	12	8.9
12. Inflation rank (1 = lowest)	42	72	43	18	11	56	20	83	44	39	41	79	21	71	88	23	57	25	66	14	37	75	65

* This is intended as a particular rather than general measure of discretion. It depends only on the scores for exchange-rate focus, money focus, and inflation focus. Discretion is calculated as twice the maximum of these scores minus the sum of the other two. It is converted to an index between zero and 100, where a high score implies more discretion.

Table A.1 Summary scores for framework characteristics (% of maximum) – *continued*

	Korea	Kuwait	Kyrgyz	Latvia	Lebanon	Lithuania	Macedonia	Malaysia	Malta	Mauritius	Mexico	Moldova	Mongolia	Mozambique	Namibia	Netherlands	New Zealand	Nigeria	Norway	Peru	Poland	Portugal	Romania	Russia
Short and medium-term policy focus																								
1. Exchange-rate focus	6	75	25	100	75	100	94	94	38	25	13	19	38	19	100	88	0	6	6	0	0	75	25	25
2. Money focus	75	13	56	0	6	0	0	0	25	88	0	88	44	44	0	0	0	94	0	63	0	0	88	81
3. Inflation focus	63	0	75	0	56	0	25	44	19	25	94	38	81	56	13	0	94	25	25	44	94	6	38	31
4. Discretion (high score implies more discretion)*	59	31	66	0	56	44	19	75	19	38	13	41	59	75	6	13	6	22	31	59	19	28	44	47
Institutional characteristics																								
4. Independence	73	63	87	98	68	89	80	85	83	70	82	80	70	71	50	91	89	42	57	89	86	85	77	76
5. Accountability of central bank to government	83	67	92	67	17	100	83	83	83	33	92	75	83	50	33	83	100	92	50	92	58	83	83	83
6. Policy explanations	88	38	49	74	29	63	56	71	67	20	69	67	61	66	56	79	92	37	89	38	69	78	60	58
Use and importance of forms of monetary analysis																								
7. Inflation expectations	17	0	50	0	33	0	0	67	33	0	92	33	50	0	0	58	92	0	33	25	67	50	33	67
8. Models and forecasts	78	56	44	11	67	67	11	17	67	22	56	28	33	17	22	100	100	11	67	78	78	89	6	78
9. Money and banking sector	100	78	78	22	89	44	67	56	44	78	11	78	44	67	56	33	22	89	0	33	56	22	78	67
Structural characteristics																								
10. Importance of financial stability issues	58	50	50	0	75	58	50	67	42	50	42	58	33	25	0	8	8	33	17	25	25	33	42	58
Memo																								
11. Inflation, av. '97–98, incl. estimates	6.0	0.4	20	6.5	6.2	7.0	7.0	0.8	4.0	2.8	6.8	7.3	23	7.8	7.5	2.1	1.2	9.3	2.4	7.9	14	2.5	21	21
12. Inflation rank (1 = lowest)	49	4	81	52	50	55	9	80	38	32	53	58	84	62	59	27	15	67	29	63	76	30	82	81

* This is intended as a particular rather than general measure of discretion. It depends only on the scores for exchange-rate focus, money focus, and inflation focus. Discretion is

Table A.1 Summary scores for framework characteristics (% of maximum) – *continued*

	Sierra Leone	Singapore	Slovakia	Slovenia	South Africa	Spain	Sri Lanka	Sweden	Switzerland	Taiwan	Tanzania	Thailand	Tonga	Turkey	Turkmenistan	Uganda	UK	Ukraine	Uruguay	USA	Vietnam	W. African S.	Zambia
Short and medium term policy focus																							
1. Exchange-rate focus	19	56	33	13	6	6	6	13	19	31	19	6	38	38	38	0	0	0	88	0	0	75	19
2. Money focus	19	0	52	88	75	75	19	0	75	81	56	6	38	25	38	63	0	44	0	25	25	0	56
3. Inflation focus	56	19	91	25	31	56	19	100	19	50	25	31	13	44	63	69	100	56	25	19	38	25	56
4. Discretion (high score implies more discretion)*	63	53	91	31	44	66	94	6	44	59	66	75	88	88	69	63	0	78	25	84	88	38	81
Institutional characteristics																							
4. Independence	62	90	90	86	85	80	54	97	90	85	60	82	52	70	36	81	77	63	70	92	42	47	66
5. Accountability of central bank to government	83	25	67	83	75	83	58	83	17	92	92	50	0	42	75	92	100	92	83	83	92	42	17
6. Policy explanations	47	49	49	54	70	59	48	95	86	72	51	67	30	24	33	69	94	69	4	95	31	46	57
Use and importance of forms of monetary analysis																							
7. Inflation expectations	0	0	0	0	17	50	17	100	33	17	0	0	0	33	50	33	100	75	0	83	67	0	33
8. Models and forecasts	0	83	39	50	78	50	11	78	50	67	0	83	11	11	33	22	94	56	39	89	11	44	0
9. Money and banking sector	56	22	67	100	67	56	56	33	56	67	56	67	56	22	44	89	56	67	22	33	56	67	89
Structural characteristics																							
10. Importance of Financial Stability issues	33	17	50	33	25	33	33	42	8	50	67	83	75	58	83	0	16	42	17	33	50	58	58
Memo																							
11. Inflation, av. '97–98, incl. estimates	25	0.4	6.4	8.8	7.7	1.9	9.5	0.2	0.3	1.3	14	6.8	2.7	85	584	3.5	3.3	10	15	1.9	5.5	4.2	26
12. Inflation rank (1 = lowest)	85	4	51	64	61	22	68	2	3	16	77	54	31	90	93	36	35	70	78	78	46	40	86

* This is intended as a particular rather than general measure of discretion. It depends only on the scores for exchange-rate focus, money focus, and inflation focus. Discretion is calculated as twice the maximum of these scores minus the sum of the other two. It is converted to an index between zero and 100, where a high score implies more discretion.

Tables A.2, A.3 and A.4 Focus of policy on exchange-rate, money-growth, and inflation objectives

Table A.2 Exchange rate focus

	Weight	Albania	Argentina	Armenia	Australia	Austria	Bahamas	Bahrain	Bangladesh	Barbados	Belgium	Belize	Bosnia-Herz.	Botswana	Bulgaria	Canada	Chile	China	Croatia	Cyprus	Czech Rep.	Denmark	Eastern Carib.	Ecuador
Weighted total (% of maximum)		**0**	**100**	**0**	**0**	**88**	**88**	**100**	**31**	**100**	**94**	**71**	**100**	**38**	**100**	**6**	**31**	**25**	**38**	**31**	**6**	**94**	**94**	**6**
1. Described as exchange rate targeting?	1	0	100	0	0	100	50	100	0	100	100	33	100	0	100	0	0	0	50	0	0	100	100	0
2. Degree to which exchange rate fixed?	1	0	100	0	0	50	100	100	75	100	75	100	100	75	100	0	50	25	25	75	25	75	100	0
3. Rank of objectives?	1	0	100	0	0	100	100	100	50	100	100	100	100	50	100	0	50	50	50	50	0	100	100	0
4. Objective prevails in policy conflicts?	1	0	100	0	0	100	100	100	0	100	100	50	100	25	100	25	25	25	25	0	0	100	75	25

Table A.3 Money focus

	Weight	Albania	Argentina	Armenia	Australia	Austria	Bahamas	Bahrain	Bangladesh	Barbados	Belgium	Belize	Bosnia-Herz.	Botswana	Bulgaria	Canada	Chile	China	Croatia	Cyprus	Czech Rep.	Denmark	Eastern Carib.	Ecuador
Weighted total (% of maximum)		**38**	**0**	**38**	**0**	**0**	**0**	**0**	**75**	**0**	**0**	**19**	**0**	**13**	**0**	**0**	**0**	**88**	**19**	**63**	**0**	**0**	**0**	**31**
1. Regime described as money targeting?	1	0	0	0	0	0	0	0	100	0	0	0	0	0	0	0	0	100	0	100	0	0	0	50
2. Published target/monitoring range?	1	100	0	100	0	0	0	0	100	0	0	0	0	0	0	0	0	100	0	0	0	0	0	0
3. Rank of objectives?	1	50	0	50	0	0	0	0	50	0	0	50	0	50	0	0	0	100	50	100	0	0	0	50
4. Objective prevails in policy conflicts?	1	0	0	0	0	0	0	0	50	0	0	25	0	0	0	0	0	50	25	50	0	0	0	25

Table A.4 Inflation focus

	Weight	Albania	Argentina	Armenia	Australia	Austria	Bahamas	Bahrain	Bangladesh	Barbados	Belgium	Belize	Bosnia-Herz.	Botswana	Bulgaria	Canada	Chile	China	Croatia	Cyprus	Czech Rep.	Denmark	Eastern Carib.	Ecuador
Weighted total (% of maximum)		**94**	**0**	**100**	**94**	**0**	**0**	**13**	**44**	**0**	**0**	**27**	**0**	**63**	**0**	**88**	**88**	**31**	**75**	**6**	**94**	**0**	**0**	**56**
1. Regime described as inflation targeting?	1	100	0	100	100	0	0	0	0	0	0	33	0	100	0	100	100	0	50	0	100	0	0	50
2. Published target/monitoring range?	1	100	0	100	100	0	0	100	100	0	0	0	0	0	0	100	100	100	100	0	100	0	0	100
3. Rank of objectives?	1	100	0	100	100	0	0	50	50	0	0	50	0	100	0	100	100	25	100	25	100	0	0	50
4. Objective prevails in policy conflicts?	1	75	0	100	75	0	0	0	25	0	0	25	0	50	0	50	50	25	50	25	75	0	0	25

Tables A.2, A.3 and A.4 Focus of policy on exchange-rate, money-growth, and inflation objectives – *continued*

	Weight	Egypt	Estonia	Fiji	Finland	France	Georgia	Germany	Ghana	Greece	Guyana	Hong Kong	Hungary	Iceland	India	Indonesia	Ireland	Israel	Italy	Jamaica	Japan	Jordan	Kazakhstan	Kenya
Table A.2 Exchange rate focus																								
Weighted total (% of maximum)		**13**	**100**	**50**	**63**	**58**	**25**	**13**	**0**	**94**	**19**	**100**	**81**	**75**	**6**	**6**	**75**	**13**	**50**	**25**	**0**	**63**	**25**	**13**
1. Described as exchange rate targeting?	1	0	100	0	50	33	0	0	0	100	0	100	100	100	0	0	100	0	0	0	0	0	0	0
2. Degree to which exchange rate fixed?	1	25	100	75	50	50	25	25	0	75	0	100	75	50	0	0	50	25	50	25	0	100	25	25
3. Rank of objectives?	1	0	100	100	100	100	50	0	0	100	50	100	100	100	0	0	100	0	100	50	0	100	50	50
4. Objective prevails in policy conflicts?	1	25	100	25	50	50	25	25	0	100	25	100	50	50	25	25	50	25	50	25	0	50	25	25
Table A.3 Money focus																								
Weighted total (% of maximum)		**38**	**0**	**0**	**0**	**46**	**25**	**88**	**56**	**25**	**88**	**0**	**0**	**0**	**50**	**63**	**0**	**0**	**44**	**44**	**0**	**25**	**88**	**69**
1. Regime described as money targeting?	1	100	0	0	0	33	0	100	100	0	100	0	0	0	0	100	0	0	0	0	0	0	100	100
2. Published target/monitoring range?	1	0	0	0	0	100	100	100	0	100	100	0	0	0	100	100	0	0	100	100	0	100	100	100
3. Rank of objectives?	1	0	0	0	0	50	0	100	100	0	100	0	0	0	50	0	0	0	50	50	0	0	100	50
4. Objective prevails in policy conflicts?	1	50	0	0	0	0	0	50	25	0	50	0	0	0	50	50	0	0	25	25	0	0	50	25
Table A.4 Inflation focus																								
Weighted total (% of maximum)		**44**	**0**	**31**	**56**	**40**	**56**	**19**	**19**	**25**	**25**	**0**	**19**	**19**	**44**	**50**	**19**	**88**	**44**	**88**	**50**	**13**	**44**	**44**
1. Regime described as inflation targeting?	1	0	0	0	50	33	0	0	0	0	0	0	0	0	0	0	0	100	0	0	0	0	0	0
2. Published target/monitoring range?	1	100	0	0	100	100	100	0	0	100	0	0	0	0	100	100	0	100	100	100	0	0	100	100
3. Rank of objectives?	1	50	0	100	50	0	100	50	50	0	0	0	50	50	50	100	50	100	50	100	100	50	50	50
4. Objective prevails in policy conflicts?	1	25	0	25	25	25	25	25	25	0	0	0	25	25	50	0	25	50	25	50	100	0	25	25

Tables A.2, A.3 and A.4 Focus of policy on exchange-rate, money-growth, and inflation objectives – *continued*

Table A.2 Exchange-rate focus

	Weight	Korea	Kuwait	Kyrgyz	Latvia	Lebanon	Lithuania	Macedonia	Malaysia	Malta	Mauritius	Mexico	Moldova	Mongolia	Mozambique	Namibia	Netherlands	New Zealand	Nigeria	Norway	Peru	Poland	Portugal	Romania	Russia
Weighted total (% of maximum)		**6**	**75**	**25**	**100**	**75**	**100**	**94**	**38**	**94**	**25**	**13**	**19**	**38**	**19**	**100**	**88**	**0**	**6**	**69**	**0**	**25**	**75**	**25**	**25**
1. Described as exchange rate targeting?	1	0	50	0	100	100	100	100	0	100	0	0	0	0	0	100	100	0	0	100	0	0	100	0	0
2. Degree to which exchange rate fixed?	1	0	75	25	100	100	100	100	75	100	25	0	0	75	0	100	50	0	25	50	0	50	50	25	25
3. Rank of objectives?	1	0	100	50	100	50	100	100	50	100	50	50	50	50	50	100	100	0	0	50	0	50	100	50	50
4. Objective prevails in policy conflicts?	1	25	75	25	100	50	100	75	25	75	25	0	25	25	25	100	100	0	0	75	0	0	50	25	25

Table A.3 Money focus

	Weight	Korea	Kuwait	Kyrgyz	Latvia	Lebanon	Lithuania	Macedonia	Malaysia	Malta	Mauritius	Mexico	Moldova	Mongolia	Mozambique	Namibia	Netherlands	New Zealand	Nigeria	Norway	Peru	Poland	Portugal	Romania	Russia
Weighted total (% of maximum)		**75**	**13**	**56**	**0**	**6**	**0**	**0**	**0**	**25**	**88**	**0**	**88**	**44**	**44**	**0**	**0**	**0**	**94**	**0**	**63**	**0**	**0**	**88**	**81**
1. Regime described as money targeting?	1	100	50	50	0	0	0	0	0	0	100	0	100	0	0	0	0	0	100	0	100	0	0	100	100
2. Published target/monitoring range?	1	100	0	100	0	0	0	0	0	100	100	0	100	100	100	0	0	0	100	0	0	0	0	100	100
3. Rank of objectives?	1	50	0	50	0	0	0	0	0	0	100	0	100	50	50	0	0	0	100	0	100	0	0	100	100
4. Objective prevails in policy conflicts?	1	50	0	25	0	25	0	0	0	0	50	0	50	25	25	0	0	0	75	0	50	0	0	50	25

Table A.4 Inflation focus

	Weight	Korea	Kuwait	Kyrgyz	Latvia	Lebanon	Lithuania	Macedonia	Malaysia	Malta	Mauritius	Mexico	Moldova	Mongolia	Mozambique	Namibia	Netherlands	New Zealand	Nigeria	Norway	Peru	Poland	Portugal	Romania	Russia
Weighted total (% of maximum)		**63**	**0**	**75**	**0**	**56**	**0**	**25**	**44**	**0**	**25**	**94**	**38**	**81**	**56**	**13**	**0**	**94**	**25**	**0**	**44**	**94**	**6**	**38**	**31**
1. Regime described as inflation targeting?	1	0	0	50	0	0	0	0	0	0	0	100	0	100	0	0	0	100	0	0	0	100	0	0	0
2. Published target/monitoring range?	1	100	0	100	0	100	0	100	100	0	100	100	100	100	100	0	0	100	100	0	100	100	0	100	100
3. Rank of objectives?	1	100	0	100	0	100	0	0	50	0	0	100	50	100	100	50	0	100	0	0	50	100	0	50	0
4. Objective prevails in policy conflicts?	1	50	0	50	0	25	0	0	25	0	0	75	0	25	25	0	0	75	0	0	25	75	25	0	25

Tables A.2, A.3 and A.4 Focus of policy on exchange-rate, money-growth, and inflation objectives – continued

Table A.2 Exchange rate focus

	Weight	Sierra Leone	Singapore	Slovakia	Slovenia	South Africa	Spain	Sri Lanka	Sweden	Switzerland	Taiwan	Tanzania	Thailand	Tonga	Turkey	Turkmenistan	Uganda	UK	Ukraine	Uruguay	USA	Vietnam	W. African S.	Zambia
Weighted total (% of maximum)		**19**	**56**	**33**	**13**	**6**	**63**	**6**	**13**	**19**	**31**	**19**	**6**	**38**	**38**	**38**	**0**	**0**	**25**	**88**	**0**	**25**	**75**	**19**
1. Described as exchange rate targeting?	1	0	100	33	0	0	50	0	0	0	0	0	0	0	0	0	0	0	0	100	0	0	50	0
2. Degree to which exchange rate fixed?	1	0	30	25	25	0	50	25	0	0	50	0	0	75	25	75	0	0	50	75	0	50	100	0
3. Rank of objectives?	1	50	50	50	25	0	100	0	50	50	50	50	50	50	100	50	0	0	50	100	0	50	50	50
4. Objective prevails in policy conflicts?	1	25	50	25	25	25	50	0	0	25	25	25	25	25	25	25	0	0	0	75	0	0	100	25

Table A.3 Money focus

	Weight	Sierra Leone	Singapore	Slovakia	Slovenia	South Africa	Spain	Sri Lanka	Sweden	Switzerland	Taiwan	Tanzania	Thailand	Tonga	Turkey	Turkmenistan	Uganda	UK	Ukraine	Uruguay	USA	Vietnam	W. African S.	Zambia
Weighted total (% of maximum)		**19**	**0**	**52**	**88**	**75**	**0**	**19**	**0**	**75**	**81**	**56**	**6**	**38**	**25**	**38**	**63**	**0**	**44**	**0**	**25**	**25**	**0**	**56**
1. Regime described as money targeting?	1	0	0	33	0	100	0	0	0	0	100	0	0	0	0	0	50	0	0	0	0	0	0	100
2. Published target/monitoring range?	1	0	0	100	100	100	0	0	0	100	100	100	0	0	100	100	100	0	100	0	100	100	0	100
3. Rank of objectives?	1	50	0	50	100	50	0	50	0	50	100	50	50	50	0	50	50	0	50	0	0	0	0	0
4. Objective prevails in policy conflicts?	1	25	0	25	50	50	0	25	0	50	25	25	25	50	0	0	50	0	25	0	0	0	0	25

Table A.4 Inflation focus

	Weight	Sierra Leone	Singapore	Slovakia	Slovenia	South Africa	Spain	Sri Lanka	Sweden	Switzerland	Taiwan	Tanzania	Thailand	Tonga	Turkey	Turkmenistan	Uganda	UK	Ukraine	Uruguay	USA	Vietnam	W. African S.	Zambia
Weighted total (% of maximum)		**56**	**19**	**52**	**25**	**31**	**56**	**19**	**100**	**19**	**50**	**25**	**31**	**13**	**44**	**63**	**69**	**100**	**56**	**25**	**19**	**38**	**25**	**56**
1. Regime described as inflation targeting?	1	0	0	33	0	0	0	0	100	0	0	0	0	0	0	0	50	100	50	0	0	0	0	0
2. Published target/monitoring range?	1	100	0	100	100	0	100	0	100	0	100	100	0	0	100	100	100	100	100	100	0	100	100	0
3. Rank of objectives?	1	100	50	50	0	100	50	50	100	50	50	0	100	50	50	100	100	100	50	0	50	50	100	100
4. Objective prevails in policy conflicts?	1	25	25	25	0	25	25	25	100	25	50	0	25	0	25	50	25	100	25	0	25	0	0	25

Tables A.5 and A.6 Independence and accountability

	Weight	Albania	Argentina	Armenia	Australia	Austria	Bahamas	Bahrain	Bangladesh	Barbados	Belgium	Belize	Bosnia-Herz.	Botswana	Bulgaria	Canada	Chile	China	Croatia	Cyprus	Czech Rep.	Denmark	Eastern Carib.	Ecuador
Table A.5 Independence																								
Weighted total (% of maximum)		**66**	**79**	**76**	**73**	**68**	**39**	**54**	**56**	**24**	**77**	**43**	**81**	**65**	**79**	**91**	**93**	**68**	**79**	**77**	**98**	**88**	**49**	**93**
1. Statutory objectives focus on price stability?	1	100	75	100	50	100	75	75	50	0	25	75	100	75	75	100	75	50	75	75	100	75	75	100
2. Target independence?	1	100	50	50	50	50	0	50	50	75	50	0	0	100	0	50	100	50	50	100	100	50	50	100
3. Instrument independence?	2	67	100	100	67	33	75	33	100	0	100	33	100	33	100	100	100	67	100	100	100	100	33	100
4. Central bank financing of gov. deficit?	2	25	75	50	100	100	75	75	25	25	100	50	100	75	100	100	100	100	75	50	100	100	50	100
5. Term of office of Governor	0.5	86	71	86	86	57	57	14	29	57	57	71	57	57	71	86	57	14	71	57	71	100	57	14
Table A.6: Accountability																								
Weighted total (% of maximum)		**75**	**100**	**83**	**83**	**67**	**100**	**75**	**83**	**92**	**33**	**42**	**100**	**58**	**100**	**100**	**17**	**100**	**83**	**58**	**75**	**75**	**92**	**75**
Accountability in terms of numerical target																								
Unweighted sub-total (% of maximum)	3	**50**	**100**	**67**	**83**	**83**	**100**	**100**	**67**	**83**	**67**	**83**	**100**	**17**	**100**	**100**	**33**	**100**	**67**	**17**	**50**	**100**	**83**	**50**
1. Numeric target published?	1	100	100	100	100	100	100	100	100	100	100	100	100	0	100	100	0	100	100	0	100	100	100	100
2. Government role in setting any target?	1	0	100	100	100	100	100	100	100	100	100	100	100	0	100	100	0	100	100	0	0	100	100	0
3. Procedures when target missed/changed?	1	50	100	0	0	50	100	100	0	50	0	50	100	50	100	100	0	100	0	50	50	100	50	50
Parliamentary monitoring of central bank	3	**100**	**100**	**100**	**100**	**50**	**100**	**50**	**100**	**100**	**0**	**0**	**100**	**100**	**100**	**100**	**0**	**100**	**100**	**100**	**100**	**50**	**100**	**100**
Memo: Procedures for government to override?	0	100	0	0	100	0	0	50	100	100	0	100	0	0	0	100	100	0	100	0	0	50	100	50

Tables A.5 and A.6 Independence and accountability – continued

	Weight	Egypt	Estonia	Fiji	Finland	France	Georgia	Germany	Ghana	Greece	Guyana	Hong Kong	Hungary	Iceland	India	Indonesia	Ireland	Israel	Italy	Jamaica	Japan	Jordan	Kazakhstan	Kenya
Table A.5: Independence																								
Weighted total (% of maximum)		**53**	**85**	**73**	**91**	**90**	**80**	**96**	**60**	**86**	**65**	**74**	**86**	**59**	**83**	**66**	**87**	**66**	**88**	**39**	**93**	**74**	**76**	**66**
1. Statutory objectives focus on price stability?	1	25	75	75	100	100	75	75	100	75	75	75	75	50	75	50	75	50	75	75	75	75	75	75
2. Target independence?	1	0	50	50	50	50	50	100	50	50	50	0	50	50	100	50	50	0	50	50	100	100	50	100
3. Instrument independence?	2	100	100	100	100	100	100	100	33	100	33	100	100	33	100	100	100	100	100	0	0	100	67	67
4. Central bank financing of gov. deficit?	2	50	100	50	100	100	75	100	50	100	100	100	100	100	75	50	100	75	100	50	100	50	100	50
5. Term of office of Governor?	0.5	43	57	100	86	71	86	100	43	71	57	14	71	29	29	57	86	57	100	57	57	57	71	43
Table A.6: Accountability																								
Weighted total (% of maximum)		**83**	**100**	**17**	**92**	**83**	**83**	**17**	**58**	**33**	**42**	**92**	**83**	**92**	**67**	**83**	**83**	**100**	**58**	**42**	**100**	**75**	**83**	**67**
Accountability in terms of numerical target																								
Unweighted sub-total (% of maximum)	3	67	100	33	83	67	67	33	17	67	83	83	67	83	33	67	67	100	67	83	100	50	67	33
1. Numeric target published?	1	100	100	0	100	100	100	100	0	100	100	100	100	100	100	100	100	100	100	100	100	100	100	100
2. Government role in setting any target?	1	100	100	100	100	100	100	0	0	100	100	100	100	100	0	100	100	100	100	100	100	0	100	0
3. Procedures when target missed/changed?	1	0	100	0	50	0	0	0	50	0	50	50	0	50	0	0	0	100	0	50	0	50	0	0
Parliamentary monitoring of central bank	3	**100**	**100**	**0**	**100**	**100**	**100**	**0**	**100**	**0**	**0**	**100**	**100**	**100**	**100**	**100**	**100**	**100**	**50**	**0**	**100**	**100**	**100**	**100**
Memo: Procedures for government to override?	0	50	0	100	0	0	0	0	0	0	0	0	0	0	0	0	0	0	0	100	0	0	0	0

Tables A.5 and A.6 Independence and accountability – continued

Table A.5: Independence

	Weight	Korea	Kuwait	Kyrgyz	Latvia	Lebanon	Lithuania	Macedonia	Malaysia	Malta	Mauritius	Mexico	Moldova	Mongolia	Mozambique	Namibia	Netherlands	New Zealand	Nigeria	Norway	Peru	Poland	Portugal	Romania	Russia
Weighted total (% of maximum)		**73**	**63**	**87**	**98**	**68**	**89**	**80**	**75**	**83**	**70**	**82**	**80**	**70**	**71**	**50**	**91**	**89**	**42**	**57**	**89**	**86**	**85**	**77**	**76**
1. Statutory objectives focus on price stability?	1	100	50	75	100	75	100	75	75	75	75	100	75	75	100	75	100	100	75	0	100	75	75	100	75
2. Target independence?	1	50	0	50	100	100	50	50	50	50	50	50	100	50	50	0	50	50	50	0	50	50	50	50	50
3. Instrument independence?	2	100	67	100	100	67	100	100	100	100	100	100	100	100	67	67	100	100	33	67	100	100	100	100	100
4. Central bank financing of gov. deficit?	2	50	100	100	100	50	100	75	100	100	50	75	50	50	75	50	100	100	25	100	100	100	100	100	100
5. Term of office of Governor?	0.5	43	57	86	71	71	57	86	57	29	57	71	86	57	57	29	86	57	57	71	57	71	57	100	43

Table A.6: Accountability

	Weight	Korea	Kuwait	Kyrgyz	Latvia	Lebanon	Lithuania	Macedonia	Malaysia	Malta	Mauritius	Mexico	Moldova	Mongolia	Mozambique	Namibia	Netherlands	New Zealand	Nigeria	Norway	Peru	Poland	Portugal	Romania	Russia
Weighted total (% of maximum)		**83**	**67**	**92**	**67**	**17**	**100**	**83**	**67**	**83**	**33**	**92**	**75**	**83**	**50**	**33**	**83**	**100**	**92**	**50**	**92**	**58**	**83**	**83**	**83**
Accountability in terms of numerical target																									
Unweighted sub-total (% of maximum)	3	67	33	83	33	33	100	67	33	67	67	83	50	67	100	67	67	100	83	100	83	67	67	67	67
1. Numeric target published?	1	100	0	100	100	100	100	100	100	100	100	100	100	100	100	100	100	100	100	100	100	100	100	100	100
2. Goverment role in setting any target?	1	100	100	100	0	0	100	100	0	100	100	0	0	0	100	100	100	100	100	100	100	100	100	100	100
3. Procedures when target missed/changed?	1	0	0	50	0	0	100	0	0	0	0	50	50	0	100	0	0	100	50	100	50	0	0	100	0
Parliamentary monitoring of central bank	3	**100**	**100**	**100**	**100**	**0**	**100**	**100**	**100**	**100**	**100**	**100**	**100**	**100**	**0**	**0**	**100**	**100**	**100**	**0**	**100**	**50**	**100**	**100**	**100**
Memo: Procedures for government to override?	0	0	0	0	0	0	0	0	100	100	0	0	0	0	0	0	100	100	0	100	0	0	0	0	0

Tables A.5 and A.6 Independence and accountability – continued

	Weight	Sierra Leone	Singapore	Slovakia	Slovenia	South Africa	Spain	Sri Lanka	Sweden	Switzerland	Taiwan	Tanzania	Thailand	Tonga	Turkey	Turkmenistan	Uganda	UK	Ukraine	Uruguay	USA	Vietnam	W. African S.	Zambia
A.5 Independence																								
Weighted total (% of maximum)		**62**	**90**	**90**	**86**	**85**	**80**	**54**	**97**	**90**	**85**	**60**	**82**	**52**	**70**	**36**	**81**	**77**	**63**	**70**	**92**	**42**	**47**	**66**
1. Statutory objectives focus on price stability?	1	75	75	100	75	75	100	50	100	50	75	75	25	75	75	75	100	75	100	75	75	50	50	75
2. Target independence?	1	50	100	100	50	100	50	100	100	100	50	50	100	75	50	100	50	0	50	50	100	50	50	100
3. Instrument independence?	2	100	100	100	100	100	67	33	100	100	100	67	100	100	100	0	100	100	67	100	100	33	33	100
4. Central bank financing of gov. deficit?	2	25	100	75	100	75	100	50	100	100	100	50	100	0	50	25	75	100	50	50	100	50	50	25
5. Term of office of Governor?	0.5	57	14	71	71	57	71	71	57	71	57	57	14	57	57	14	57	57	57	57	43	14	71	14
A.6 Accountability																								
Weighted total (% of maximum)		**83**	**25**	**67**	**83**	**75**	**83**	**58**	**83**	**17**	**92**	**92**	**50**	**0**	**42**	**75**	**92**	**100**	**92**	**83**	**83**	**92**	**42**	**17**
Accountability in terms of numerical target																								
Unweighted sub-total (% of maximum)	3	**67**	**0**	**33**	**67**	**50**	**67**	**17**	**67**	**33**	**83**	**83**	**0**	**0**	**83**	**50**	**83**	**100**	**83**	**67**	**67**	**83**	**83**	**33**
1. Numeric target published?	1	100	0	100	100	100	100	0	100	100	100	100	0	0	100	100	100	100	100	100	100	100	100	100
2. Government role in setting any target?	1	100	0	0	100	0	0	0	0	0	100	100	0	0	100	0	100	100	100	100	0	100	100	0
3. Procedures when target missed/changed?	1	0	0	0	0	50	0	50	100	0	50	50	0	0	50	50	50	100	50	0	100	50	0	0
Parliamentary monitoring of central bank	3	**100**	**50**	**100**	**100**	**100**	**100**	**100**	**100**	**0**	**100**	**100**	**100**	**0**	**0**	**100**	**100**	**100**	**100**	**100**	**100**	**100**	**50**	**0**
Memo: Procedures for government to override?	0	0	0	0	0	0	0	100	0	0	0	0	0	0	0	0	0	100	0	0	0	0	0	0

Table A.7 Policy explanations

	Weight	Albania	Argentina	Armenia	Australia	Austria	Bahamas	Bahrain	Bangladesh	Barbados	Belgium	Belize	Bosnia-Herz.	Botswana	Bulgaria	Canada	Chile	China	Croatia	Cyprus	Czech Rep.	Denmark	Eastern Carib.	Ecuador
Total score for explaining policy																								
Unweighted total (% of maximum)		40	53	65	78	27	50	18	39	73	68	48	35	53	46	79	83	63	42	48	86	80	48	59
Explaining policy decisions																								
Weighted sub-total (% of maximum)	1.5	66	66	91	66	0	66	0	38	66	66	38	19	47	66	88	75	66	34	38	91	85	28	69
1. Explanations on day policy changed		100	100	100	100	0	100	0	0	100	100	0	0	100	100	100	100	100	100	0	100	100	100	100
2. Explanations when policy-makers meet and make no change	0.3	0	0	100	0	0	0	0	0	0	0	0	0	0	0	50	0	0	0	0	100	100	0	50
3. Policy decisions discussed in publications	2	100	0	100	0	0	0	0	100	100	100	100	50	50	100	100	100	50	100	100	100	100	0	100
4. Minutes of policy meetings published (or similar)	1	0	0	100	0	0	100	0	0	0	0	0	0	0	0	100	50	100	0	0	100	0	0	0
5. Voting patterns published	0.5	0	0	0	0	0	0	0	0	0	0	0	0	0	0	0	0	0	0	0	0	0	0	0
Explanations in forecasts and forward-looking analysis																								
Weighted total (% of maximum)		0	0	43	68	0	25	0	25	73	64	45	0	32	0	50	73	64	0	25	68	73	43	50
1. Forward-looking analysis in bulletins	2	0	0	100	100	0	50	0	50	100	100	50	0	50	0	50	50	50	0	50	100	100	100	50
2. Form of publication	1.5	0	0	25	50	0	25	0	25	100	100	100	0	50	0	50	100	100	0	25	50	100	25	50
3. Risks to forecast published	1	0	0	0	0	0	0	0	0	50	0	0	0	0	0	50	50	0	0	0	50	50	0	0
4. Discussion of past forecast errors	1	0	0	0	100	0	0	0	0	0	0	0	0	0	0	50	100	100	0	50	50	100	0	100
Explanations in published assessments and research																								
Weighted total (% of maximum)		53	93	60	100	80	60	53	53	80	73	60	87	80	73	100	100	60	93	80	100	80	73	60
1. Analysis in published bulletins	2	100	100	100	100	100	100	100	100	100	100	100	100	100	100	100	100	50	100	100	100	100	100	100
2. Speeches	2	33	100	33	100	67	33	33	33	67	67	33	33	67	67	100	100	100	100	100	100	67	33	66
3. Working papers and other research	1	0	67	33	100	67	33	0	0	67	33	33	33	67	33	100	100	0	67	0	100	67	100	66

Table A.7 Policy explanations – continued

	Weight	Egypt	Estonia	Fiji	Finland	France	Georgia	Germany	Ghana	Greece	Guyana	Hong Kong	Hungary	Iceland	India	Indonesia	Ireland	Israel	Italy	Jamaica	Japan	Jordan	Kazakhstan	Kenya
Total score for explaining policy																								
Unweighted total (% of maximum)		47	71	64	74	53	65	70	36	36	32	58	49	65	75	83	78	68	81	65	89	60	51	52
Explaining policy decisions																								
Weighted sub-total (% of maximum)	1.5	66	66	66	66	66	66	66	28	28	0	57	57	47	66	72	66	72	66	66	94	47	72	38
1. Explanations on day policy changed	0.3	100	100	100	100	100	100	100	100	100	0	0	100	100	100	100	100	100	100	100	100	100	100	0
2. Explanations when policy-makers meet and make no change		0	0	0	0	0	0	0	0	0	0	0	0	0	0	100	0	100	0	0	0	100	100	0
3. Policy decisions discussed in publications	2	100	100	100	100	100	100	100	0	0	0	100	50	50	0	100	100	100	100	100	100	50	100	0
4. Minutes of policy meetings published (or similar)	1	0	0	0	0	0	0	0	0	0	0	100	50	0	0	0	0	0	0	0	0	0	0	0
5. Voting patterns published	0.5	0	0	0	0	0	0	0	0	0	0	0	0	0	0	0	0	0	0	0	100	0	0	0
Explanations in forecasts and forward-looking analysis																								
Weighted total (% of maximum)		23	59	59	64	0	64	50	25	0	36	23	25	82	59	91	82	32	77	43	73	73	0	64
1. Forward-looking analysis in bulletins	2	25	100	100	50	0	100	100	50	0	25	25	50	50	50	100	100	50	100	100	100	50	100	100
2. Form of publication	1.5	50	50	50	100	0	100	50	25	100	100	50	25	100	50	50	100	50	50	25	100	100	100	100
3. Risks to forecast published	1	0	50	50	0	0	0	0	0	0	0	0	0	0	50	50	50	0	0	0	0	100	0	0
4. Discussion of past forecast errors	1	0	0	0	0	0	0	0	0	0	0	0	0	100	100	100	50	100	100	0	50	100	0	0
Explanations in published assessments and research																								
Weighted total (% of maximum)		53	87	67	93	93	66	93	53	80	60	93	67	67	100	87	87	100	100	87	100	60	80	53
1. Analysis in published bulletins	2	100	100	100	100	100	100	100	100	100	100	100	50	100	100	100	100	100	100	100	100	50	100	100
2. Speeches	2	33	100	67	100	100	66	100	33	67	33	100	67	33	100	67	67	100	100	67	100	100	100	33
3. Working Papers and other research	1	0	33	0	67	67	0	67	0	67	33	67	100	67	100	100	100	100	100	100	100	0	0	0

Table A.7 Policy explanations – continued

	Weight	Korea	Kuwait	Kyrgyz	Latvia	Lebanon	Lithuania	Macedonia	Malaysia	Malta	Mauritius	Mexico	Moldova	Mongolia	Mozambique	Namibia	Netherlands	New Zealand	Nigeria	Norway	Peru	Poland	Portugal	Romania
Total score for explaining policy																								
Unweighted total (% of maximum)		88	38	49	74	29	63	56	71	67	20	69	67	61	66	56	79	92	37	89	38	69	78	60
Explaining policy decisions																								
Weighted sub-total (% of maximum)	**1.5**	**91**	**47**	**66**	**66**	**28**	**34**	**66**	**85**	**66**	**0**	**66**	**72**	**66**	**66**	**66**	**47**	**85**	**0**	**66**	**28**	**91**	**66**	**69**
1. Explanations on day policy changed	1.5	100	100	100	100	100	100	100	100	100	0	100	100	100	100	100	100	100	0	100	100	100	100	100
2. Explanations when policy-makers meet and make no change	0.3	100	0	0	0	100	100	0	0	0	0	0	100	0	100	0	0	0	0	0	0	100	0	50
3. Policy decisions discussed in publications	2	100	50	100	100	0	0	100	100	100	100	100	100	50	100	100	50	100	100	100	0	100	100	0
4. Minutes of policy meetings published (or similar)	1	50	0	0	0	0	0	0	0	0	0	0	0	100	0	0	0	0	0	0	0	50	0	0
5. Voting patterns published	0.5	100	0	0	0	0	0	0	0	0	0	0	0	0	0	0	0	0	0	0	0	100	0	0
Explanations in forecasts and forward-looking analysis																								
Weighted total (% of maximum)		**73**	**0**	**0**	**64**	**0**	**55**	**41**	**55**	**55**	**0**	**68**	**64**	**50**	**73**	**43**	**91**	**91**	**43**	**100**	**0**	**43**	**82**	**25**
1. Forward-looking analysis in bulletins	2	100	0	0	100	0	25	25	50	50	0	100	50	25	100	100	100	100	100	100	0	100	100	50
2. Form of publication	1.5	100	0	0	100	0	100	50	100	50	0	50	100	50	100	25	100	100	25	100	0	25	100	25
3. Risks to forecast published	1	50	0	0	0	0	100	0	50	50	0	0	0	50	50	0	100	50	0	100	50	0	50	0
4. Discussion of past forecast errors	1	0	0	0	0	0	0	100	0	0	0	100	0	100	0	0	50	50	0	100	0	0	50	0
Explanations in published assessments and research																								
Weighted total (% of maximum)		**100**	**66**	**80**	**93**	**60**	**100**	**60**	**73**	**80**	**60**	**73**	**67**	**67**	**60**	**60**	**100**	**100**	**67**	**100**	**87**	**73**	**87**	**87**
1. Analysis in published bulletins	2	100	100	100	100	100	100	100	100	100	100	100	100	100	100	100	100	100	100	100	100	100	100	100
2. Speeches	2	100	66	100	100	33	100	33	67	67	33	33	67	67	33	33	100	100	67	100	67	33	67	100
3. Working Papers and other research	1	100	0	0	67	33	100	33	33	67	33	100	0	0	33	33	100	100	0	100	100	100	100	33

Table A.7 Policy explanations – continued

	Weight	Russia	Sierra Leone	Slovakia	Slovenia	South Africa	Spain	Sri Lanka	Sweden	Switzerland	Taiwan	Tanzania	Thailand	Tonga	Turkey	Turkmenistan	Uganda	UK	Ukraine	Uruguay	USA	Vietnam	W. African S.	Zambia
Total Score for explaining policy																								
Unweighted total (% of maximum)		**58**	**47**	**49**	**54**	**70**	**59**	**48**	**95**	**86**	**72**	**51**	**67**	**30**	**24**	**33**	**69**	**94**	**69**	**4**	**95**	**31**	**46**	**57**
Explaining policy decisions																								
Weighted sub-total (% of maximum)		**34**	**38**	**28**	**28**	**66**	**28**	**53**	**85**	**66**	**72**	**38**	**38**	**38**	**0**	**66**	**66**	**83**	**72**	**0**	**94**	**28**	**50**	**47**
1. Explanations on day policy changed	1.5	100	0	100	100	100	100	100	100	100	100	100	0	0	0	100	100	50	100	0	100	100	100	100
2. Explanations when policy-makers meet and make no change	0.3	100	0	0	0	0	0	100	100	0	100	0	0	0	0	0	0	50	100	0	0	100	100	0
3. Policy decisions discussed in publications	2	0	100	0	0	100	0	50	100	100	100	100	100	100	0	100	100	100	0	0	100	0	50	50
4. Minutes of policy meetings published (or similar)	1	0	0	0	0	0	0	0	50	0	0	0	0	0	0	0	0	0	0	0	100	0	0	0
5. Voting patterns published	0.5	0	0	0	0	100	0	0	100	0	0	0	0	0	0	0	0	100	0	0	100	0	0	0
Explanations in forecasts and forward-looking analysis																								
Weighted total (% of maximum)		**55**	**43**	**59**	**41**	**50**	**50**	**45**	**100**	**91**	**45**	**50**	**64**	**0**	**0**	**0**	**55**	**100**	**50**	**0**	**91**	**32**	**0**	**50**
1. Forward-looking analysis in bulletins	2	25	100	50	25	50	100	50	100	100	25	100	100	0	0	0	25	100	100	0	100	50	0	100
2. Form of publication	1.5	100	25	50	50	50	50	100	100	100	100	50	100	0	0	0	100	100	50	0	100	50	0	50
3. Risks to forecast published	1	50	0	0	0	0	0	0	100	50	50	0	0	0	0	0	0	100	0	0	50	0	0	0
4. Discussion of past forecast errors	1	50	0	100	100	100	0	0	100	100	0	0	0	0	0	0	100	100	0	0	100	0	0	0
Explanations in published assessments and research																								
Weighted total (% of maximum)		**87**	**60**	**60**	**93**	**93**	**100**	**46**	**100**	**100**	**100**	**67**	**100**	**53**	**73**	**33**	**87**	**100**	**87**	**13**	**100**	**33**	**87**	**73**
1. Analysis in published bulletins	2	100	100	100	100	100	100	50	100	100	100	100	100	100	100	50	100	100	100	0	100	50	100	100
2. Speeches	2	100	33	33	100	100	100	33	100	100	100	67	100	33	33	33	67	100	67	33	100	33	67	33
3. Working Papers and other research	1	33	33	33	67	67	100	66	100	100	100	0	100	0	100	0	100	100	100	0	100	0	100	0

Table A.8 Financial stability

(overall score for the importance of FS issues in setting instruments)

	Weight	Albania	Argentina	Armenia	Australia	Austria	Bahamas	Bahrain	Bangladesh	Barbados	Belgium	Belize	Bosnia-Herz.	Botswana	Bulgaria	Canada	Chile	China	Croatia	Cyprus	Czech Rep.	Denmark	Eastern Carib.	Ecuador
Total Score for explaining policy																								
Weighted total (% of maximum)		**33**	**58**	**75**	**8**	**17**	**25**	**0**	**17**	**67**	**8**	**33**	**17**	**17**	**0**	**33**	**17**	**33**	**42**	**33**	**33**	**0**	**33**	**83**
1. Asset-price volatility	1	0	33	67	33	0	0	0	33	67	33	0	0	33	0	33	33	33	33	33	0	0	100	33
2. Domestic financial sector insolvency	1	33	100	100	0	33	100	0	33	67	0	100	67	33	0	33	0	33	100	100	100	0	0	100
3. Report of credit rationing	1	100	33	67	0	33	0	0	0	33	0	0	0	0	0	33	0	33	33	0	33	0	33	100
4. Overseas financial instability	1	0	67	67	0	0	0	0	0	100	0	33	0	0	0	33	33	33	0	0	0	0	0	100

	Egypt	Estonia	Fiji	Finland	France	Georgia	Germany	Ghana	Greece	Guyana	Hong Kong	Hungary	Iceland	India	Indonesia	Ireland	Israel	Italy	Jamaica	Japan	Jordan	Kazakhstan	Kenya
Weighted total (% of maximum)	**92**	**33**	**0**	**8**	**50**	**75**	**33**	**0**	**8**	**33**	**0**	**0**	**8**	**67**	**83**	**8**	**33**	**33**	**8**	**50**	**58**	**67**	**25**
1. Asset-price volatility	100	0	0	33	33	100	33	0	33	0	0	0	33	33	100	33	33	33	0	67	33	33	33
2. Domestic financial sector insolvency	100	33	0	0	67	100	33	0	0	67	0	0	33	100	100	0	33	33	33	67	100	67	67
3. Report of credit rationing	100	33	0	0	67	33	33	0	0	67	0	0	0	67	100	0	33	33	0	67	67	100	0
4. Overseas financial instability	67	67	0	0	33	67	33	0	0	0	0	0	0	67	33	0	33	33	0	0	33	67	0

Table A.8 Financial stability – continued

(overall score for the importance of FS issues in setting instruments)

	Weight	Korea	Kuwait	Kyrgyz	Latvia	Lebanon	Lithuania	Macedonia	Malaysia	Malta	Mauritius	Mexico	Moldova	Mongolia	Mozambique	Namibia	Netherlands	New Zealand	Nigeria	Norway	Peru	Poland	Portugal	Romania
Weighted total (% of maximum)		**58**	**50**	**50**	**0**	**75**	**58**	**50**	**75**	**42**	**50**	**42**	**58**	**33**	**25**	**0**	**8**	**8**	**33**	**17**	**25**	**25**	**33**	**42**
1. Asset-price volatility	1	67	33	33	0	100	33	67	100	33	0	100	67	33	0	0	33	33	33	33	33	0	33	0
2. Domestic financial sector insolvency	1	100	100	100	0	100	67	67	100	33	100	33	67	67	33	0	0	0	67	33	0	67	33	67
3. Report of credit rationing	1	0	67	67	0	0	67	67	67	33	100	0	67	33	67	0	0	0	33	0	67	0	33	33
4. Overseas financial instability	1	67	0	0	0	100	67	0	33	67	0	33	33	0	0	0	0	0	0	0	0	33	33	67

	Russia	Sierra Leone	Singapore	Slovakia	Slovenia	South Africa	Spain	Sri Lanka	Sweden	Switzerland	Taiwan	Tanzania	Thailand	Tonga	Turkey	Turkmenistan	Uganda	UK	Ukraine	Uruguay	USA	Vietnam	W. African S.	Zambia
Weighted total (% of maximum)	**58**	**33**	**17**	**50**	**25**	**25**	**33**	**33**	**42**	**8**	**50**	**67**	**83**	**75**	**58**	**83**	**0**	**16**	**42**	**17**	**33**	**50**	**58**	**58**
1. Asset-price volatility	67	0	33	67	0	33	33	33	67	33	67	33	67	33	67	67	0	33	33	0	33	33	33	33
2. Domestic financial sector insolvency	67	67	0	67	67	33	33	33	33	0	67	100	100	100	67	100	0	33	100	33	33	100	100	100
3. Report of credit rationing	67	0	33	33	0	33	33	67	33	0	33	100	67	100	33	100	0	0	0	33	33	33	67	33
4. Overseas financial instability	33	67	0	33	33	0	33	0	33	0	33	33	100	67	67	67	0	0	33	0	33	33	33	67

Tables A.9 to A.11 Use of analysis

Table A.9: Analysis of inflation expectations

	Weight	Albania	Argentina	Armenia	Australia	Austria	Bahamas	Bahrain	Bangladesh	Barbados	Belgium	Belize	Bosnia-Herz.	Botswana	Bulgaria	Canada	Chile	China	Croatia	Cyprus	Czech Rep.	Denmark	Eastern Carib.	Ecuador
Weighted total (% of maximum)		**0**	**0**	**0**	**92**	**0**	**0**	**0**	**25**	**0**	**50**	**0**	**0**	**100**	**0**	**92**	**17**	**83**	**0**	**0**	**33**	**42**	**0**	**75**
1. Use market information	1	0	0	0	0	0	0	0	0	0	50	0	0	100	0	100	50	75	0	0	0	75	0	75
2. Use surveys of consumers/producers/others	1	0	0	0	100	0	0	0	0	0	50	0	0	100	0	100	0	100	0	0	0	50	0	100
3. Use surveys of outside forecasts	1	0	0	0	100	0	0	0	75	0	50	0	0	100	0	75	0	75	0	0	100	0	0	50

Table 10: Forecasting and simulation methods

	Weight	Albania	Argentina	Armenia	Australia	Austria	Bahamas	Bahrain	Bangladesh	Barbados	Belgium	Belize	Bosnia-Herz.	Botswana	Bulgaria	Canada	Chile	China	Croatia	Cyprus	Czech Rep.	Denmark	Eastern Carib.	Ecuador
Weighted total (% of maximum)		**11**	**0**	**28**	**33**	**89**	**17**	**0**	**6**	**0**	**61**	**6**	**0**	**6**	**33**	**89**	**56**	**72**	**11**	**11**	**89**	**56**	**22**	**39**
1. Structural model exists (>10 equations)	1	0	0	0	0	100	0	0	0	0	100	0	0	0	0	100	0	0	0	0	100	100	0	0
2. Use structural macro-models and forecasts	1	0	0	50	100	100	0	0	0	0	50	0	0	0	50	100	100	100	0	0	100	100	50	100
3. Use VAR-based models and forecasts	1	0	0	0	0	100	0	0	0	0	50	0	0	0	50	100	100	100	0	0	100	100	50	50
4. Use theory-based models and forecasts	0.5	0	0	50	0	0	0	0	0	0	50	0	0	0	50	0	0	50	0	0	100	0	50	0
5. Use short-term off model, data-based forecasts	0.5	0	0	50	100	100	0	0	50	0	50	0	0	50	0	100	100	100	100	100	100	100	50	50
6. Use other agencies' models and forecasts	0.5	100	0	50	0	100	50	0	0	0	50	50	0	0	50	100	0	100	100	0	0	0	0	0

Table A.11: Analysis of money and banking sector (importance of aspects)

	Weight	Albania	Argentina	Armenia	Australia	Austria	Bahamas	Bahrain	Bangladesh	Barbados	Belgium	Belize	Bosnia-Herz.	Botswana	Bulgaria	Canada	Chile	China	Croatia	Cyprus	Czech Rep.	Denmark	Eastern Carib.	Ecuador
Weighted total (% of maximum)		**22**	**44**	**89**	**22**	**0**	**67**	**44**	**56**	**44**	**11**	**33**	**11**	**67**	**33**	**44**	**33**	**78**	**56**	**67**	**44**	**11**	**44**	**78**
1. Money-demand equations	1	0	33	67	0	0	0	0	33	0	0	0	0	33	0	33	33	33	33	33	33	0	33	100
2. Analysis of data from monetary survey	1	33	33	100	33	0	100	67	67	67	0	67	0	100	33	67	0	100	67	100	33	33	67	67
3. Effect of instruments on banking sector	1	33	67	100	33	0	100	67	67	67	33	33	33	67	67	33	67	100	67	67	67	33	33	67

Tables A.9 to A.11 Use of analysis – continued

Table A.9: Analysis of inflation expectations

	Weight	Egypt	Estonia	Fiji	Finland	France	Georgia	Germany	Ghana	Greece	Guyana	Hong Kong	Hungary	Iceland	India	Indonesia	Ireland	Israel	Italy	Jamaica	Japan	Jordan	Kazakhstan	Kenya
Weighted total (% of maximum)		**17**	**25**	**0**	**67**	**67**	**17**	**50**	**0**	**50**	**0**	**0**	**25**	**50**	**0**	**50**	**42**	**50**	**92**	**0**	**75**	**33**	**83**	**0**
1. Use market information	1	0	0	0	100	50	0	50	0	50	0	0	75	75	0	75	0	75	100	0	75	50	50	0
2. Use surveys of consumers/producers/others	1	50	75	0	100	100	0	50	0	0	0	0	0	75	0	0	50	0	75	0	75	0	100	0
3. Use surveys of outside forecasts	1	0	0	0	0	50	50	50	0	100	0	0	0	0	0	75	75	75	100	0	75	50	100	0

Table A.10: Forecasting and simulation methods

	Weight	Egypt	Estonia	Fiji	Finland	France	Georgia	Germany	Ghana	Greece	Guyana	Hong Kong	Hungary	Iceland	India	Indonesia	Ireland	Israel	Italy	Jamaica	Japan	Jordan	Kazakhstan	Kenya
Weighted total (% of maximum)		**28**	**83**	**6**	**61**	**44**	**11**	**56**	**0**	**67**	**6**	**28**	**22**	**11**	**11**	**100**	**56**	**67**	**94**	**44**	**72**	**39**	**44**	**6**
1. Structural model exists (>10 equations)	1	0	100	0	100	100	0	100	0	100	0	0	0	0	0	100	0	100	100	0	100	0	0	0
2. Use structural macro-models and forecasts	1	100	0	0	50	50	0	50	0	100	0	50	0	0	0	100	50	0	100	50	100	100	50	0
3. Use VAR-based models and forecasts	1	0	100	0	50	50	0	50	0	0	0	0	0	0	0	100	0	0	100	100	50	0	50	0
4. Use theory-based models and forecasts	0.5	0	100	0	0	0	0	0	0	100	0	50	0	0	0	100	0	0	50	0	0	0	50	0
5. Use short-term, off-model, data-based forecasts	0.5	50	50	0	100	100	100	0	0	100	50	50	100	50	100	100	100	100	100	100	100	100	100	50
6. Use other agencies' models and forecasts	0.5	0	50	50	50	0	0	100	0	0	0	50	100	50	0	100	100	100	100	0	50	50	50	0

Table A.11: Analysis of money and banking sector (importance of aspects)

	Weight	Egypt	Estonia	Fiji	Finland	France	Georgia	Germany	Ghana	Greece	Guyana	Hong Kong	Hungary	Iceland	India	Indonesia	Ireland	Israel	Italy	Jamaica	Japan	Jordan	Kazakhstan	Kenya
Weighted total (% of maximum)		**89**	**56**	**44**	**22**	**56**	**100**	**56**	**44**	**56**	**89**	**56**	**22**	**33**	**89**	**89**	**33**	**44**	**44**	**56**	**78**	**100**	**78**	**56**
1. Money-demand equations	1	67	33	33	67	67	100	67	0	33	67	67	0	33	100	100	33	33	67	33	67	100	67	33
2. Analysis of data from monetary survey	1	100	67	33	67	33	100	67	100	67	100	33	33	33	100	67	33	0	0	67	67	100	67	100
3. Effect of instruments on banking sector	1	100	67	67	0	67	100	33	33	67	100	67	33	67	67	100	33	67	67	67	100	100	100	33

Tables A.9 to A.11 Use of analysis – continued

Table A.9: Analysis of inflation expectations

	Weight	Korea	Kuwait	Kyrgyz	Latvia	Lebanon	Lithuania	Macedonia	Malaysia	Malta	Mauritius	Mexico	Moldova	Mongolia	Mozambique	Namibia	Netherlands	New Zealand	Nigeria	Norway	Peru	Poland	Portugal	Romania	Russia
Weighted total (% of maximum)		**17**	**0**	**50**	**0**	**33**	**0**	**0**	**67**	**33**	**0**	**92**	**33**	**50**	**0**	**0**	**58**	**92**	**0**	**33**	**25**	**67**	**50**	**33**	**67**
1. Use market information	1	0	0	50	0	0	0	0	100	0	0	75	0	50	0	0	75	75	0	100	0	50	50	100	100
2. Use surveys of consumers/producers/others	1	50	0	50	0	50	0	0	100	100	0	100	100	50	0	0	50	100	0	0	75	100	50	0	50
3. Use surveys of outside forecasts	1	0	0	50	0	50	0	0	0	0	0	100		50	0	0	50	100	0	0	0	50	50	0	50

Table 10: Forecasting and simulation methods

	Weight	Korea	Kuwait	Kyrgyz	Latvia	Lebanon	Lithuania	Macedonia	Malaysia	Malta	Mauritius	Mexico	Moldova	Mongolia	Mozambique	Namibia	Netherlands	New Zealand	Nigeria	Norway	Peru	Poland	Portugal	Romania	Russia
Weighted total (% of maximum)		**78**	**56**	**44**	**11**	**67**	**100**	**11**	**17**	**67**	**22**	**56**	**28**	**33**	**17**	**22**	**100**	**100**	**11**	**67**	**78**	**78**	**89**	**6**	**78**
1. Structural model exists (>10 equations)	1	100	100	0	0	0	100	0	0	100	0	0	0	0	0	0	100	100	0	100	100	0	100	0	100
2. Use structural macro-models and forecasts	1	100	100	0	0	100	100	0	50	50	0	100	50	0	0	50	100	100	0	100	100	100	100	0	100
3. Use VAR-based models and forecasts	1	50	0	100	0	50	100	0	0	100	100	100	0	50	0	0	100	100	0	0	100	100	100	0	0
4. Use theory-based models and forecasts	0.5	50	0	50	0	100	100	0	0	50	0	100	0	50	0	0	100	100	0	100	100	100	100	0	100
5. Use short-term, off-model, data-based forecasts	0.5	100	100	100	100	100	100	100	50	50	0	0	100	50	100	50	100	100	0	100	0	100	100	0	100
6. Use other agencies' models and forecasts	0.5	50	0	50	0	100	100	0	0	0	0	0	50	100	50	50	100	100	100	0	0	100	0	100	100

Table A.11 Analysis of money and banking sector (importance of aspects)

	Weight	Korea	Kuwait	Kyrgyz	Latvia	Lebanon	Lithuania	Macedonia	Malaysia	Malta	Mauritius	Mexico	Moldova	Mongolia	Mozambique	Namibia	Netherlands	New Zealand	Nigeria	Norway	Peru	Poland	Portugal	Romania	Russia
Weighted total (% of maximum)		**100**	**78**	**78**	**22**	**89**	**44**	**67**	**56**	**44**	**78**	**11**	**78**	**44**	**67**	**56**	**33**	**22**	**89**	**0**	**33**	**56**	**22**	**78**	**67**
1. Money-demand equations	1	100	67	67	0	67	0	67	33	0	67	0	33	0	67	33	33	0	100	0	67	33	0	33	67
2. Analysis of data from monetary survey	1	100	67	67	0	100	67	67	67	67	100	0	100	67	67	67	33	33	100	0	33	67	67	100	67
3. Effect of instruments on banking sector	1	100	100	100	67	100	67	67	67	67	67	33	100	67	67	67	33	33	67	0	33	67	67	100	67

Tables A.9 to A.11 Use of analysis – continued

	Weight	Sierra Leone	Singapore	Slovakia	Slovenia	South Africa	Spain	Sri Lanka	Sweden	Switzerland	Taiwan	Tanzania	Thailand	Tonga	Turkey	Turkmenistan	Uganda	UK	Ukraine	Uruguay	USA	Vietnam	W. African States	Zambia
Table A.9: Analysis of inflation expectations																								
Weighted total (% of maximum)		**0**	**0**	**0**	**0**	**17**	**50**	**17**	**100**	**33**	**17**	**0**	**0**	**0**	**33**	**50**	**33**	**100**	**75**	**0**	**83**	**67**	**0**	**33**
1. Use market information	1	0	0	0	0	0	50	50	100	50	0	0	0	0	0	50	100	100	75	0	50	100	0	0
2. Use surveys of consumers/producers/others	1	0	0	0	0	0	50	0	0	0	0	0	0	0	100	50	0	100	75	0	100	0	0	100
3. Use surveys of outside forecasts	1	0	0	0	0	50	50	0	100	0	50	0	0	0	0	50	0	100	75	0	100	100	0	0
Table 10: Forecasting and simulation methods																								
Weighted total (% of maximum)		**0**	**83**	**39**	**50**	**78**	**50**	**11**	**78**	**50**	**67**	**0**	**83**	**11**	**11**	**33**	**22**	**94**	**56**	**39**	**89**	**11**	**44**	**0**
1. Structural model exists (>10 equations)	1	0	100	0	0	100	0	0	0	100	100	0	100	0	0	0	0	100	50	0	100	0	100	0
2. Use structural macro-models and forecasts	1	0	100	100	50	100	50	0	100	100	100	0	100	0	0	100	0	100	50	50	100	0	50	0
3. Use VAR-based models and forecasts	1	0	50	0	50	100	100	0	100	50	0	0	100	0	0	0	0	100	100	100	100	0	50	0
4. Use theory-based models and forecasts	0.5	0	50	0	50	0	50	0	100	0	0	0	0	0	0	100	100	50	0	0	100	0	0	0
5. Use short-term, off-model, data-based forecasts	0.5	0	100	50	100	100	50	100	100	100	100	0	100	100	0	100	100	100	100	50	100	100	0	0
6. Use other agencies' models and forecasts	0.5	0	100	100	100	0	50	0	100	50	100	0	50	0	0	0	100	100	100	0	100	0	0	0
Table A.11: Analysis of money and banking sector (importance of aspects)																								
Weighted total (% of maximum)		**56**	**22**	**67**	**100**	**67**	**56**	**56**	**33**	**56**	**67**	**56**	**67**	**56**	**22**	**44**	**89**	**56**	**67**	**22**	**33**	**56**	**67**	**89**
1. Money-demand equations	1	33	0	67	100	67	33	33	33	100	67	33	67	33	33	0	100	33	67	33	0	33	67	67
2. Analysis of data from monetary survey	1	67	33	67	100	67	33	67	33	33	33	67	67	100	0	67	100	67	67	0	33	67	67	100
3. Effect of instruments on banking sector	1	67	33	67	100	67	100	67	33	33	100	67	67	33	33	67	67	67	67	33	67	67	100	100

Appendix 2

Monetary frameworks questionnaire

Bank of England
Centre for Central Banking Studies

Aim of the survey

Central banks' monetary policy frameworks consist of many characteristics. They aim to capture the best trade-off between low inflation expectations and efficacy in reaction to economic shocks. The leading characteristic of the framework is usually the choice of intermediate policy target. This survey aims to assess the role of intermediate targets and the wide array of other characteristics of a monetary framework. Such characteristics include central bank independence, transparency and accountability of the monetary framework, the nature of analysis conducted by the central bank, and the wider political and economic context in which the central bank operates.

The survey seeks to answer:

- How broad is the spectrum of frameworks even within groups of countries that share the same intermediate target?
- To what extent is it meaningful to divide countries according to the variable used as an intermediate target?
- To what extent are developments in monetary frameworks being shared across developing, transitional and industrialised economies?
- What common ground is there in the search for best practices in monetary framework design?

F.   Monetary framework specifics

F.1   Monetary policy framework

F.1	Please provide a general description of your monetary policy framework. This might include instruments and targets used, a brief description of the transmission mechanism, and constraints on monetary policy. It may also include central bank independence, and other broad issues that impact on the framework. Note that later questions will ask more about the details of your monetary framework.

F.2   Statutory objectives

F.2	Does the central bank have statutory objective(s)? Yes/No *Please specify.*

F.3   Ordering intermediate monetary policy objectives; resolving policy conflicts; record of compliance

F.3.i	Please rank monetary policy objectives (other than price or monetary stability) the central bank pursues (1 = first priority). For example, balance of payments, money growth target, exchange rate, inflation target, interest rates, output growth, stability of financial sector … Or, indicate if there is no fixed target.	
	Do rankings change over time? **Yes/No** and details	
F.3.ii	If you were to categorise your framework as **one** of the following, would you describe your monetary framework as: (please tick a box)	
	money targeting		details where appropriate:
	inflation targeting		
	discretionary		
	exchange rate targeting		
	balance of payments targeting		
	other (please specify)		
	cannot be summarised as targeting one variable		
	none of the above		
F.3.iii	Are these priorities conveyed to the public? **Yes/No**	
F.3.iv	In your **current** monetary framework, is there scope for other variables to prevail over the target in the event of **policy conflicts**? For example, in the event of important development in variables	

other than the target, policy-makers may choose either:

(i) *not to change* policy even when the target is expected to be met

(ii) *to change* policy even when the target is expected to be met

A specific example would be when a country that has an explicit inflation target chooses to miss the target in order to absorb output shocks. Inflation target may do this either by not changing policy when inflation is expected to be different from the target, or by changing policy when inflation is expected to be on target. Such variables might include indicators of recession, capital inflows, financial instability, asset prices, exchange rate changes, inflation ...

Please indicate below by answering yes in any box when that variable can prevail over the target, then describing in more detail below the table:

Type of Regime (columns) Type of indicator (rows)	Money targeters	Exchange rate targeters	Inflation targeters	Other target or discretionary (please specify)
Money	■			
Exchange Rate		■		
Inflation			■	
Others (please specify, e.g. recession, long-term growth, financial instability, fiscal policy, capital flows)				

	Please give details here to support your answers. How were the conflicts resolved?	
	If the monetary framework has been recently changed, how were any conflicts resolved under the **previous** framework?	
F.3.v	What is your overall record of compliance with policy targets?	
	What reasons were provided to the public when targets were missed?	
	Did you attribute the miss to an external (exogenous) shock or policy action?	
	Did deviations result in a policy response?	
	For exchange-rate targets, approximately for how long has the exchange rate peg or band been maintained? If the target has come under pressure, was the peg or band changed or were other policy measures taken?	

F.4   Intermediate money and credit targets

Please answer even if this is not the primary intermediate target

F.4.i	Do you have a specific, numerical, publicly announced target or monitoring range for money or credit? **Yes/No**
	Is it a point target or a range? What reasons have you provided for this choice?
	Did you have such a target in other years in the 1990s? **Yes/No**

	If no please go to F.5
F.4.ii	What has been the publicly announced target (or indicator or monitoring range) and outcomes in the 1990s?

	First Target/Indicator/Monitoring Range (delete as appropriate)		Second Target/Indicator/Monitoring Range (delete as appropriate)	
	Target	Outcome	Target	Outcome
1990				
1991				
1992				
1993				
1994				
1995				
1996				
1997				
1998				
1999				

F.4.iii	Who sets the target? (please tick a box)	
	Government	In which context and how frequently is the announcement made? (e.g. annual statement on monetary policy)
	Central Bank	
	Both	
	not applicable	

F.4.iv	**Time Specification of Target**
	Is the target for: (tick a box)
	• current period only (annual or quarterly?)
	• indefinite period (i.e. the same rate now and for future periods)
	• different targets set for current and future periods
	• other (please specify)
	Please give details of the above specification of target over time.

F.4.v	Is the target set according to a regular timetable? **Yes/No**
	How regularly?
	Is the target sometimes revised in between regular dates (for example because of unexpected shocks)? If yes, how frequently?
F.4.vi	When was the target first announced? Was this part of broader changes in monetary policy?
F.4.vii	Is your intermediate target described as the **current** annual rate of change in money/credit growth? Or is it more accurately described as a target for a *forecast* of money/credit growth? If it is the forecast, over what time horizon?
F.4.viii	Please, give details of monetary targets/indicators/monitoring ranges.

F.5 Inflation targets

Please answer even if this is not the primary intermediate target

F.5.i	Do you have a specific, numerical, publicly announced target for prices or inflation at the present time? **Yes/No**	
	Is it a point target or a range? What reasons have you provided for this choice?	
	Did you have such a target in other years in the 1990s? **Yes/No**	
	If no to both please move to question F.6	
F.5.ii	What has been the target in other years in the 1990s? How does this compare with the outcome?	
	Target for Current Year	Outcome
1990		
1991		
1992		
1993		
1994		
1995		
1996		
1997		
1998		

F.5.iii	Who sets the inflation target? (please tick a box)		
	Government		In what context is the announcement made? (e.g. annual statement of monetary policy)
	Central Bank		
	Both		
	not applicable		
F.5.iv	**Time Specification of Target**		
	Is the target for: (tick a box)		
	• current period only (annual or quarterly?)		
	• indefinite period (i.e. the same rate now and for future periods)		
	• different targets set for current and future periods		
	• other (please specify)		
	Please give details of the above specification of target over time.		
F.5.v	Is the target set according to a regular timetable?		
	How regularly?		
	Is the target sometimes revised in between regular dates (for example because of unexpected shocks)? If yes, how frequently?		
F.5.vi	When was the target first announced? Was this part of broader changes in monetary policy?		
F.5.vii	Is your intermediate target described as the **current** annual rate of change in inflation? Or is it more accurately described as a target for a **forecast** of inflation? If it is the forecast, over what time horizon?		
F.5.viii	Any further details about specification of target over this period (e.g. why changes were made)?		

F.6   Specification of price index

F.6.i	On what price measure does policy most frequently focus (e.g. CPI, GDP deflator, export prices)?
	If a price basket is used, are any items excluded from the measure on which policy focuses most? (e.g. administered prices, energy prices). Are they always excluded or only under particular circumstances (e.g. terms of trade shock)?
	Have there been recent changes?
F.6.ii	What proportion of your price index is administered (i.e. set by government or government agency)? (sales taxes should not be included as administered since they are not necessarily passed on to consumers by firms).

F.7 Exchange rate target

If there has been no exchange rate target in the 1990s please go to F.8

F.7.i	Indicate the years in which you *announced* you were targeting the exchange rate	If it was publicly announced, indicate *the specific target* (or target band/crawling peg)
1990		
1991		
1992		
1993		
1994		
1995		
1996		
1997		
1998		
F.7.ii	Who sets the target? (please tick a box)	
	Government	Details:
	Central Bank	
	Both	
	not applicable	
F.7.iii	What is the number (or bandwidth) for the target? What reasons have you provided for choosing the width of the band and the currencies to which you peg?	
F.7.iv	Any further details about exchange rate targets?	

F.8   IMF programmes

Indicate years in the 1990s in which monetary policy have been operating under the direct influence of an IMF programme (e.g. SBA, SAF, and SAL).

	Type of Programme (date introduced and date expired)	Which macro variables were subject to a specific target under the agreement?	Which of the targeted macro variables were *publicly announced?*
1990			
1991			
1992			
1993			
1994			
1995			
1996			
1997			
1998			

T.   Transparency of the monetary framework

In this survey **transparency of framework** refers to elements that may increase the private sector's understanding of the framework.

Transparency Issue 1: Information the private sector receives by observing policy decisions

Background: The private sector knows that the central bank believes changes in monetary conditions justify a change to the operational instrument when the central bank:

- announces a change in policy
- announces no change in policy following a publicised meeting of its monetary policy committee.

T.1 Meeting of monetary policy makers

T.1.i	What is the main operating instrument of monetary policy? (e.g. repo rate, reserve requirements, Treasury Bill rate)?
	What operating instruments are used?
T.1.ii	Do the monetary policy-makers meet according to a set timetable? **Yes/No**
T.1.iii	With what frequency do they meet? annually/quarterly/monthly/weekly/daily/other (please specify)
T.1.iv	Where possible, give other details of the meeting process including: • The duration of meeting and other related meetings in the process. • A description of any formal documentation and presentations made at the meetings
T.1.v	Please describe the policy-making committee. How many members of any committee. Which institutions or departments do they represent?
T.1.vi	Does the public know in advance that monetary policy-makers are meeting to decide whether or not to change policy?
T.1.vii	What is the usual frequency of policy changes? **or** How many times (approximately) have the operational instrument or instruments been changed in the last *12 months?*
T.1.viii	Other details about the process of deciding upon changes to policy (e.g. an indication of usual size of any changes to policy).
T.1.ix	Details and dates of major recent changes to procedures.

Transparency Issue 2: Information the central bank provides that explains its assessment of monetary conditions

T.2.i	On the day of a change to the policy instrument, does the central bank convey information to the public that explains the change in policy? If so, please describe:
T.2.ii	If **no** policy change is made following a meeting of the policy-makers, does the central bank or government explain the decision to the public?

T.2.iii	Does the central bank publish minutes (summary discussion) of the policy-makers' meetings?		
	If so, how long after the meeting are they released?		
	Do the policy makers reach theirs decisions by vote/consensus or does one individual decide on policy (e.g. Governor or Finance Minister)?		
T.2.iv	If the decision is decided by vote, are the voting patterns published? **Yes/no** With what delay?		
	Are the votes of individual members of the committee published? **Yes/no**		

Assessments of monetary policy stance conveyed to the public in regular reports? The following questions seek to establish the nature of Central Bank Reports and Bulletins

T.2.v	Name of publication	1	2	3
	Main area(s) covered			
	How frequently is it published?			
	Does it contain tables of data?			
	Does it contain analysis?			
	Does it contain a forecast or forward looking analysis			
	Does it contain discussion of policy decisions?			
	Name of publication	4	5	6
	Main area(s) covered			
	How frequently is it published?			
	Does it contain tables of data?			
	Does it contain analysis?			
	Does it contain a forecast or forward looking analysis			
	Does it contain discussion of policy decisions?			
T.2.vi	Any other details concerning nature of publications.			
T.2.vii	How frequently does the governor or other senior members of central bank staff give speeches related to monetary policy?			
T.2.viii	Approximately how many working papers and other research papers were published in the last year? If this was not a typical year please indicate how many are published usually.			
T.2.ix	Details and dates of major recent changes in procedures to explain policy (e.g. new report/working paper series introduced)?			

Forecasts
Please note there is a separate question on forecasting methodology in the section on analysis in central banks.

T.2.x	Do you publish forecasts of any macro-economic variables? (Please note that in section An.2 below we ask questions about forecasting irrespective of whether or not you publish) Yes/No Details	Are forecasts most frequently published in the form of:	**Please tick**
		Numbers	
		graphs	
		words	
T.2.xi	For Inflation?		Yes/No
	For output?		Yes/No
	For money aggregates? (which ones?)		Yes/No
	Other (please specify)		Yes/No
T.2.xii	Over what time horizon is the forecast *published*?		
T.2.xiii	Do you publicly comment and assess risks to the forecast? **yes/no** Details:	Are risks published in the form of	
		numbers	
		graphs	
		words	
T.2.xiv	Do you publicly comment upon and explain past forecasting errors?		
T.2.xv	How frequently are forecasts for the target variable published?		

T.3   Transparency in foreign exchange operations

T.3.i	How frequently do you publish data for foreign exchange reserves and with what lag?
T.3.ii	Do these data include a description of interventions on futures markets? **Yes/No** Please give details such as frequency (indicate if forward interventions do not exist).

T.4 For all countries: Please give details of other measures not described in your survey responses that may affect the transparency of policy (e.g. lectures for students, radio appearances, press notices).

I. Independence and accountability

Note: In this survey accountability refers to accountability of the central bank to the government. We identify accountable actions as those where the main audience is the central government rather than the private sector. When the private sector is the main audience we classify this as transparency rather than accountability.

I.1.i	How would you define central bank independence?
I.1.ii	To what extent can your central bank formulate and implement monetary policy without the constraint of government?

I.2 Instrument independence

I.2.iii	Who decides on the adjustment of monetary policy instruments? Please give details if appropriate.
I.2.iv	What happens if government bond sales fail to cover the government's deficit (e.g. reduce expenditure or borrow from central bank or from abroad)?
I.2.v	Under what circumstances does the central bank provide finance of the government deficit? What are the limits?
I.2.vi	If there are limits, what happens if and when they are exceeded?
I.2.vii	Does government exert control over other monetary policy decisions (there are further related questions in the accountability section below)?

A. Accountability of monetary framework

Accountability Issue 1: Parliamentary involvement

The following questions relate to actions that the central bank may take to involve government and parliament in its decision making process. Such actions are not necessarily required by parliament.

A.1.i	Is your central bank subject to external monitoring by Parliament? Yes/no
A.1.ii	If yes, please give details.
A.1.iii	Please give dates and details of major changes to procedures in recent years?

Accountability Issue 2: Government influence over central bank inter-mediate target

This aspect of accountability is related (inversely) to goal and instrument independence of central banks.

A.2.i	What procedures are used in the event of the central bank missing its policy target? For countries with no policy target, have there (or could there feasibly be) circumstances in which the central bank is forced to account for its actions owing to adverse developments in the macro-economy?
A.2.ii	Are the procedures the same when the target is undershot as when it is overshot?
A.2.iii	Is there a clause that allows the central bank monetary policy decisions to be overridden in the event of certain policy shocks? **Yes/No** Details.
A.2.iv	Are the circumstances in which the central bank may be overridden written down explicitly in central bank law or elsewhere?
A.2.v	Details and dates of recent changes.

A.3	Are there any other significant ways in which policy-makers are accountable?

FS. Financial stability and monetary policy

At the present time, are the following factors important

	Asset price volatility	Domestic financial sector insolvency	Reports of credit rationing by domestic financial sector	Financial sector insolvency overseas
• FS.1.i in your choice Monetary Policy framework?				
Vital				
Important				
Relevant				
Not important				
• FS.1.ii in the setting of policy instruments?				
Vital				
Important				
Relevant				
Not important				
FS.2	Further details on how financial stability issues impact on the setting of Monetary Policy, and how it is organised in your bank?			

An   Analysis and policy technology

An.1   Measuring inflation expectations

An.1.i	• Do you estimate inflation expectations using information derived from financial markets (e.g. yield curve)? **Yes/No** and brief details.		
	How frequently do you publish this information? (please tick a box)		
	monthly		Details
	quarterly		
	occasionally		
	never		
	other		
An.1.ii	• Do you estimate inflation expectations using surveys of consumers/producers/others? **Yes/No** and brief details.		
	How frequently do you publish this information? (please tick a box)		
	monthly		Details
	quarterly		
	occasionally		
	never		
	other		
An.1.iii	• Do you estimate inflation expectations using surveys of outside forecasts? **Yes/No** and brief details.		
	How frequently do you publish this information? (please tick a box)		
	monthly		Details
	quarterly		
	occasionally		
	never		
	other		

An.2   *Forecasting inflation and assessing the monetary stance*

		Please tick a box:			
An.2	Does the central bank rely upon the following model-based projections of macro-economic variables produced by its staff?	At least quarterly	Less than quarterly	Never	Rank (1 to 5) 1 = most important
An.2.i	VAR based models and forecasts of macroeconomic variables?				
An.2.ii	Theory-based models or forecasts of macroeconomic variables? (e.g. dynamic stochastic models, computable general equilibrium models, real business cycle models)				
An.2.iii	Structural macroeconometric models and forecasts of macroeconomic variables				
An.2.iv	Does the central bank rely upon the models and forecasts of other agencies?				
An.2.v	Short-term off-model data-based forecasts				
An.2.vi	Please describe briefly the main models used by the central bank? (E.g. how many core equations?) How many endogenous variables? Is there a formal treatment of risks to your inflation forecast (for example through different forecast scenarios)?				
An 2.vii	How do you forecast the fiscal deficit?				
	use own forecast		Details		
	use government forecast				
	use other forecast (please specify)				
	other				
	N/A				

An 2.viii	Treatment of exchange rate and interest rates over the forecast horizon			
		Exchange rate	Interest rate	Details
	Model consistent rational expectations			
	Expectations derived from financial markets			
	Fixed nominal rates			
	Fixed real rates			
	Policy rule (e.g. Taylor rule)			
	Backward looking rule (e.g. adaptive expectations, autoregressive process)			
	Other (please specify)			
	Judgement			
	N/A			

An.3   Estimates of transmission mechanism

An.3.i	What is the operating instrument (e.g. 2-week repo rate, T-Bill)? What is your operational target (if this is different from the instrument)? Note that this question is repeated from question T.1.i in order to ensure clarity in the remainder of this question.	
An.3.ii	On average, what is the relationship between changes in your operating instrument (e.g. interest rates), the operating target (e.g. base money) and the final objective (e.g. inflation)? Specifically, what are your estimates for:	
	Time taken to impact fully on inflation?	The full impact upon inflation? (e.g. what percentage point reduction in inflation for every 1 percentage point increase in official rates)
	Time taken to impact most strongly on other policy target/indicator?	Full impact on other policy target/indicator?
Please provide other details supporting your answers. For example, how stable is the relationship?		

An.4 Analysis and research issues

An.4	Have researchers in your bank considered the following issues in the last five years?			
	No or not much	Considered	Considered in detail	Considered in detail and published in some form
An.4.i Price Specification Issues (e.g. trimmed mean, bias in consumer price index, behaviour of alternative price indices, asset prices, Balassa-Samuelson effect)				
An.4.ii Labour markets				
An.4.iii Fiscal sector				
An.4.iv Balance of payments (including capital flows)				
An.4.v Choice of exchange rate regime and identifying equilibrium exchange rates				
An.4.vi Money demand equations				
An.4.vii Consumption and personal sector				
An.4.viii Commodity Price Behaviour and other terms of trade related				
An.4.ix Investment and company sector				
An.4.x Modelling and econometrics				
An.4.xi Transmission Mechanism				
An.4.xii Financial Stability issues				
An.4.xiii Behaviour of banks				
An.4.xiv Analysis of monetary instruments and markets (e.g. extracting information from markets)				
An.4.xv Monetary policy framework				
An. 4.xvi Phillips Curve and Output Gaps				
An.4.xvii Others (please specify)				
An.5 Specific analysis on which bank has focused recently.				

S.　Summary of important features of monetary framework

Issue: Other parts of the survey describe the different characteristics of the monetary framework. Answers to this part of the survey are intended to give an indication of the relative importance of each characteristic.

S.1　How important are the following components of your monetary framework at the present time?

	Please tick a box in each row	Not or not very important	Fairly important	Very important	Vital
S.1.i	Inflation targets (informal or formal)				
S.1.ii	Money growth targets (informal or formal)				
S.1.iii	Exchange rate targets (informal or formal)				
S.1.iv	Balance of payments targets (informal or formal)				
S.1.v	Output targets (informal or formal)				
S.1.vi	Macroeconomic forecasts				
S.1.vii	Market indicators of inflation				
S.1.viii	Money demand equations				
S.1.ix	Analysis of monetary survey data from monetary survey				
S.1.x	Analysis of banking sector or impact of changes in policy instruments on commercial bank interest rates and credit provision				
S.1.xi	Analysis of domestic financial stability				
S.1.xii	Analysis of international financial stability				
S.1.xiii	Analysis of the real sector of the economy				
S.1.xiv	Analysis of the balance of payments				
S.1.xv	Transparency of policy				
S.1.xvi	Accountability of policy				
S.1.xvii	Independence of Central Bank				
S.1.xviii	Reducing inflation expectations or maintaining low inflation expectations.				
S.1.xix	Constraints on analysis resulting from lack of data				
S.1.xx	Constraints on monetary policy resulting from fiscal policy				
S.1.xxi	Constraints on monetary policy resulting from structure of financial sector				

S.2   Please give details of other important aspects of your
monetary framework not yet covered

```


```

**And finally, please provide copies of articles, or references for recent
articles about your country's monetary framework.**

Appendix 3

Minutes of the Bank of England's 6th Central Bank Governors' Symposium

4 June 1999

The subject for the morning session was 'Monetary Policy Frameworks in a Global Context'. The discussion was based on the Report written by Maxwell Fry, DeAnne Julius, Lavan Mahadeva, Sandra Roger, and Gabriel Sterne. The proceedings were introduced and chaired by Eddie George, Governor of the Bank of England. Before Gabriel Sterne and DeAnne Julius presented some of the Report's findings, Mervyn King assessed some of the Bank of England's own experiences in inflation targeting since 1992.

Mervyn King   I thought I would start by saying something about what an inflation target is, and also what it isn't. And in my view an inflation target is not a new view of monetary economics or the monetary transmission mechanism. There is, I think, a view held by all central banks, irrespective of whether their framework is based upon an inflation target or other nominal anchor. This broad consensus is that inflation is a monetary phenomenon, and there is no long-term trade-off between output and employment on the one hand and inflation on the other. But there is a short-term trade-off. With open economies, exchange rates move around in a way that can create difficulties for countries pursuing domestic targets, and similarly, capital flows can create difficulties for countries trying to hold fixed exchange rate regimes. And that view of the economy is common to all central banks irrespective of the framework.

But the essence of an inflation target is that it is a particular type of monetary framework. Now it is worth asking, what is meant by the word 'framework'? Why do we talk of frameworks for monetary policy? As I said, this is not a question of economic theory but is about how monetary policy actually works in practice. It is a matter of how we think about setting policy and about how we explain policy to the economic actors whose behaviour influences and indeed determines the outcomes we are trying to control. I want to separate my remarks into two parts: internal to the central bank, and external when we speak to the rest of the community.

In terms of the internal benefits of an inflation target, it does give everyone in the central bank a very clear view as to what the domestic anchor for policy is. It is a common-sense approach to say that what we are trying to achieve is price stability, so let us be very clear and judge our success or failure by what happens to inflation. There is also one additional advantage internally: the inflation target enables us to separate the discussion of policy objectives from our monthly technical discussion about what decisions on short-term interest rates or reserves of the banking system are needed in order to hit the objective. In our Monetary Policy Committee, one of the benefits we have seen in the past two years is that as a committee we work successfully together even when there are differences of view or judgement. The process works because we do not question each other about the objective. We have a very clear objective, which is the inflation target. And when there is a discussion about what that target should be, it takes place outside the Committee. In our case, the Government sets the target, but it could be set in other ways too. It is the separation which I think is crucial, as this the internal technical discussion to take place inside the central bank.

Regarding the external discussion – explaining decisions to the community of economic actors outside – again I think that an inflation target has two real benefits. The first one is very simple and obvious, but needs to be repeated again and again. Placing emphasis on an inflation target makes clear to the public what monetary policy can achieve and what it cannot. In much of the discussion one sees in the press, in every country in the world, there is often a great confusion about what monetary policy can hope to achieve. It is very easy for people outside the central bank to assume that if we are successful in bringing about broad price stability, then we have the ability to influence all manner of things connected with output, or the way in which different sectors of the economy relate to each other. And it seems to be fundamental to get across to the public that the objective of monetary policy is solely to do with price stability in the long run.

The other benefit in terms of explanation is that it is extremely helpful to have an objective that clearly helps in explaining our policy decisions. And the great advantage of an inflation target is that ordinary people can understand what it is we are trying to achieve. There are many arguments for and against the use of monetary targets, but it is more difficult to explain to the population at large that a particular interest-rate decision was made in order to control the growth of a monetary aggregate. It is easier, I think, to explain if you can relate the decisions to something that is visible and comprehensible, and an inflation target has that great advantage.

Now one brief word on our own experience on this, because we did not adopt an inflation target as a result of a theoretical discussion about what was the optimal target – we did it because we left, completely unexpectedly and unplanned, the Exchange Rate Mechanism in September 1992. We were then left with the need to construct a new framework. We had tried an exchange-rate link and it had not worked, so we were looking for a domestic nominal anchor. And we learnt a great deal from the experience of New Zealand, which had introduced and had been operating an inflation target. But we also looked at what we thought were broadly successful central banks around the world, and let me take the examples of the Bundesbank and the Federal Reserve. Neither had an inflation target: one had a monetary target and the other had no quantified specific target at all, though it had general commitment to price stability and high employment. But, we asked ourselves, what sort of discussion took place in the Bundesbank Council and the FOMC? And it seemed to us that a good description of what they actually did was that they looked ahead to where inflation was likely to go in the absence of a policy change. And then they decided whether or not the likely inflation outcome was acceptable. If not, then they adjusted policy to correct that outlook, accepting that the main contribution of monetary policy was to influence the rate of inflation. And whatever targets were used in their publications, that broad description of how they behaved was common to both the Bundesbank and the Fed. So, we thought, if that is what you actually do inside a central bank, why not be explicit about it? Why not describe policy in terms of an inflation target?

And the second argument is related to us somewhat lacking in credibility when we left the Exchange Rate Mechanism. Indeed, inflation expectations as measured in financial markets rose quite sharply from one day to the next, as people felt that our anchor had gone. We wanted to acquire credibility and you cannot do that easily without a track record. But you can do something on the way to developing a track record. We felt that by being transparent – by explaining not only what the target was but also how we thought about the economy – we could actually acquire some credibility. So if we were doing things privately, we should say what we were doing. Our motto became 'do as you say and say as you do', and that guided the construction of our framework with an inflation target and a high degree of transparency.

In terms of economics, there are two key elements of our approach. One is the need to look ahead. One cannot influence or control inflation in the next few months because that is largely predetermined irrespective of whether you have inflation or monetary targets. The second is to stress the uncertainty involved. I think that, by being as open and transparent about the uncertainty as possible, we have acquired some credibility and respect from commentators – we are not making false claims about what we can do. We publish fan charts that describe our view about where the economy will go both in terms of output and inflation, and in so doing we stress always the balance of risks – a phrase that is perhaps the most common one in our discussion of policy. In the end, we would describe an inflation target as a way of operating constrained discretion. It is inevitable that any policy framework is going to contain an element of discretion. There is no rule that anyone has invented or will invent that will enable policy to be set mechanically. But completely unfettered discretion lacks real credibility because markets are uncertain about how policy will be set. So we felt it important to constrain the discretion in terms of the objective of policy through an inflation target.

One of the frequent questions we are asked about an inflation target is, 'what does this mean for output; are you ignoring output altogether?' There are two answers we give to that. The first is that we do not believe in targeting output for a number of reasons. One is that we do not have the technical knowledge or ability to fine-tune movements in output. But a more important reason is that perhaps we do not want to constrain output growth. If productivity growth does rise, whether through miracles or simply through changes in the economy, then we have no wish to hold output down. But the best way to discover that is by trying to keep inflation on track with its target, and then to let output grow as fast as it can, consistent with the inflation target.

In terms of the short run, our view is that you cannot fine-tune output, but you can help to reduce the fluctuations in output. The best way to reduce fluctuations in output is to try to target inflation looking ahead. And we adopt a rough and ready time horizon of about two years, given our knowledge of the transmission mechanism. And if we make this very clear to people in the economy, they will increasingly believe that inflation will gradually be brought back to the inflation target looking two years ahead, irrespective of the shocks that will inevitably occur from time to time. That means that inflation expectations become less sensitive or volatile to short-term shocks to the economy, and it provides a framework of predictability for the outcome of inflation, which enables people to plan. So we think we can make a contribution to creating greater stability in output, not by targeting output directly but by making sure we look two years or so ahead and keep inflation close to the target.

So in conclusion, I think it would be very interesting to hear the views of others with inflation targets as well as of those without. But in our view it is not a new theory of monetary economics, it is not a panacea, it is not a magic ingredient, but it is a sort of healthy way of living. It is like a diet; in fact it is more than a diet, it is a way of life, a holistic diet. It does not prevent serious illness or financial crisis, and it requires the application of intelligent judgement on a regular basis. But once you live with this healthy diet, once you are used to living with an inflation target, it makes you feel better.

PRESENTATIONS OF THE REPORT

Gabriel Sterne, Adviser at the Centre of Central Banking Studies, Bank of England and **DeAnne Julius** of the Bank of England's Monetary Policy Committee then presented some of the main findings from the Report. They were followed by three discussants: Governor Donald Brash of the Reserve Bank of New Zealand; Governor Chon Chol Hwan of the Bank of Korea; and Governor Josef Tošovský of the Czech National Bank.

Dr Don Brash (New Zealand) I think the survey is a very interesting one and could indeed provide a mine of information for central banking studies for a considerable period. It will not surprise anybody that I am an enthusiastic advocate of having an explicit, publicly announced inflation target, and preferably one agreed with government. I think that Mervyn King has highlighted a lot of the logic of that position, but let me just briefly summarise it from my perspective also.

First, it is now pretty clear that the best contribution that monetary policy can make to the real economy is to keep inflation low and stable. The debate is now restricted to an argument about whether it is possible to have a target which is too low. As many of you will know, there is a debate about target ranges between those who want a zero-to-two target – in other words bias-adjusted price stability – and those, such as Paul Krugman and Stanley Fischer who think that it would be preferable to have some small positive rate of inflation, perhaps a 1% to 3%. I guess there is a small amount of literature that suggests that a slightly higher target might be preferable. But nobody, as far as I know, has suggested a long-run target that is above 8% and the great majority of targets are clearly well below that. So this suggests that in one way or another, monetary policy should try to keep inflation low and stable with two qualifications, which I will come back to in a moment.

My second point is that the two ways by which many countries have traditionally tried to deliver low and stable inflation have been found to have potentially serious problems. These two approaches are, of course, targeting some money aggregate and, secondly, targeting some exchange rate, usually that of a country with an established track record of low inflation.

Targeting a money aggregate has been found by most countries, perhaps all countries, to be difficult to do and not very effective in delivering low and stable inflation – I say that notwithstanding the outstandingly good inflation record of a country like Germany. Many people believe that Germany has delivered low inflation *despite* ostensibly targeting money aggregate ranges rather than *because* it was targeting money aggregates. Certainly, we have found that deregulation and liberalisation have both in recent years made interpreting money aggregates extremely difficult. We have had situations where broad money is rising very slowly while narrow money is rising very rapidly, and we have had situations that have been quite different, and both situations seem to be consistent with continuing very low levels of measured inflation.

Exchange-rate targeting has worked for some countries at some times but can involve huge risks, even with the use of capital controls, as recent events in East Asia suggest. My own view is that exchange-rate targeting makes good sense if you fully adopt the currency you are targeting, or if, like Hong Kong, you have a currency-board arrangement which is very tough and is supported by an institutional framework that makes it very difficult indeed to attack. But if you do not have that kind of arrangement, you are in my view living pretty dangerously.

So I think, in a sense, because both money aggregates and exchange rates have been found to have difficulties, inflation targeting has to some extent been adopted by default – we have moved from the intermediate targets to targeting inflation directly. But, of course, this does not mean that an inflation-targeting central bank can ignore money aggregates and it does not mean that it can ignore the exchange rate.

The third point in my argument is that in announcing the inflation target rather than just having it implicit inside the central bank, there is the huge benefit of enabling the government and the public to hold the central bank accountable for the use of its power. It constrains central-bank behaviour in the way that Mervyn King indicated and it conditions the public's expectations. Clearly, it is much easier for the public to understand an inflation target than it is for the public to understand a money-aggregate target.

A fourth point relates to the virtue of having a target agreed with the government. I believe that it is in fact hugely beneficial and I do not accept the argument expressed by some; that having the government involved in some way degrades the independence of the central bank. To me, having the target agreed with the government and known to the public greatly reduces the risk of government criticism of the central bank as long as the inflation rate is, and seems likely to remain, above the floor of the inflation target. Our experience now goes back more than ten years, during which time we have had two recessions, one quite brief and one quite prolonged. And at no point has the government, either in public or in private, criticised us for having policy too tight. Having the target agreed with the government might also have the beneficial effect of improving fiscal policy, and that has certainly been the case in New Zealand. If the government stipulates an inflation target that it wants the central bank to deliver, it implicitly states that, if fiscal policy is eased in a way that is inconsistent with that inflation target, the central bank will of necessity tighten monetary policy. And of course vice versa. We have had a couple of quite dramatic illustrations of that, and I would argue that having an inflation target agreed in public and agreed with the government has made an important contribution to the quite marked improvement in fiscal policy that we have experienced in the last ten years. So whatever policy rule is adopted, whatever forecasting model is used, I strongly favour an announced explicit numerical inflation target. I can see lots of benefits and no costs that I can think of.

Let me just briefly suggest two qualifications to having an inflation target, or at least two qualifications to the public perception that an inflation outcome that is always inside the inflation target is optimal. I think all the inflation-targeting central banks that I am familiar with recognise that there are circumstances where it is acknowledged that breaching the inflation target is in fact optimal. First, there are supply shocks, where it is judged inappropriate to keep the inflation rate inside the agreed target. In our case, the supply shocks that have traditionally affected us the most dramatically have been sharp changes in the price of some international commodity, most obviously oil, and we have clear acknowledgement in our contract with the government that if the measured inflation rate departs from the agreed range in response to that totally exogenous kind of shock, then we can legitimately breach the target. Another circumstance, which I think applies to many countries, particularly developing countries, is where there is a sharp rise in the price of a domestic food item, perhaps in response to a drought or other crop failure, although in that circumstance one would expect the inflation rate to quickly return to the target when next year's crop presumably returns to normal. In all these circumstances, the objective of policy should presumably be to avoid the price-level changes feeding through into generalised inflationary pressures.

The second circumstance that I have been troubled about is a circumstance that has really been triggered in my thinking by an article in the 1998 annual report of the Cleveland Fed.* Some of you may have seen the article. It basically suggests that in the presence of strong productivity growth, it may be appropriate for a central bank to deliver inflation that is actually below zero. The article talks about the United States in the 1920s and, by analogy, the United States in the 1990s, where positive CPI inflation has been consistent with growth in money aggregates and very strong growth in US asset prices. The argument of the article is that perhaps central banks have not been sufficiently ambitious in the face of that very strong productivity growth. That's a qualification which most of us do not need to be too concerned about. In the case of New Zealand we are content to keep inflation between 0% and 3%.

Prof. Chol-Hwan Chon (South Korea) Thank you, Mr Governor. It gives me great pleasure to have this opportunity to discuss monetary policy frameworks with distinguished fellow governors. Professor Fry and his co-authors have performed an excellent analysis of the characteristics of monetary policy frameworks and compared their relative usefulness from

---

*Beyond Price Stability: A Reconsideration of Monetary Policy in a Period of Low Inflation.

various angles. The Report will, I believe, serve as a valuable reference for the conduct of monetary policy, since it incorporates the experiences of a vast number of countries. Before starting, I would like to congratulate them on their successful work. In particular, I applaud Professor Fry for his valuable contribution to the work. His courage and passion will surely be rewarded.

In today's presentation, I would like to focus on Korea's recent experiences in the conduct of monetary policy, rather than making specific comments on the paper. As you are all well aware, the Korean economy went through great difficulties following the currency crisis that broke out in late 1997. Now, though, it is making a steady recovery in the aftermath of the crisis. Korea undertook various policy measures to bring about overall economic reform and restructuring. These involved major changes in the monetary policy framework. I think Korea's experiences in this regard may be helpful to other countries.

Once the currency crisis broke out, the Korean government put in place a package of financial reforms to cope with it. These included the reorganisation of the central bank. As a result, the monetary policy framework has taken on a new form. Perhaps most notably, the Bank of Korea Act was revised, with effect from April 1998. As a result, the independence of the central bank in conducting monetary policy was considerably enhanced. In particular, the Governor of the Bank of Korea has taken over as chairman of the monetary policy committee. The central bank's responsibility for maintaining price stability was also strengthened by introducing inflation targeting and stipulating the sole objective of monetary policy as the attainment of price stability. The Bank of Korea now sets a target range for inflation in consultation with government and announces it towards the end of each year.

For 1998, the first year of the new framework, the Bank of Korea set its inflation target at the relatively high level of 9% plus or minus 1%, in terms of the annual rate of increase of the consumer price index (CPI). This reflected the sharp depreciation of the Korean won. But in fact, consumer prices were more stable than had been anticipated. They rose by only 7.5% due mainly to the deeper than expected economic recession. For this year, the target range of inflation has been set at 3% plus or minus 1%.

However, in operating inflation targeting, we have to address certain issues. First, the Bank of Korea sets its target range for inflation in terms of headline inflation rather than underlying inflation. This implies that we do not separate out the price changes due to temporary factors when setting the target range. However, in evaluating whether price stability has been achieved, we exclude one-off factors influencing prices. These include wild swings in agricultural product prices caused by abnormal weather and price hikes resulting from tax changes. At present, the Bank is pursuing a research project to develop a new underlying inflation measure, which is objective in nature, linked in closely to monetary policy, and predictable to a significant degree of accuracy.

Second, the Bank of Korea sets an inflation target for each year. Considering the time lags between monetary policy and inflation, however, it is desirable to set inflation targets over a two to three-year horizon. A forward-looking monetary policy should then be carried out to achieve the medium-term inflation target.

One point I would like to make is that the current monetary policy framework of Korea may not be categorised as strict inflation targeting like the United Kingdom's or New Zealand's. Even though the Bank of Korea now explicitly announces an inflation target every year, there still remain the legacies of monetary targeting. Under the IMF programme, the Bank is required to announce the target range for the growth rate of broad money (M3). However, we fully intend to move forward to take advantage of the contribution that an inflation-targeting regime can make to achieve low and stable inflation.

In order to heighten the accountability of monetary policy, the revised Bank of Korea Act requires the Bank to submit a report on the implementation of its monetary policy to the National Assembly at least once a year. The Governor of the Bank should then attend the National Assembly and answer its questions.

I think that the authors of the Report made a valid point that transparency is just as important for the effectiveness of monetary policy as the independence and accountability of the central bank. The Bank of Korea has thus tried to signal its intentions to the market clearly and with greater transparency. The report describes Korea as being a country with a highly transparent framework. In fact, the Bank of Korea promptly discloses relevant information concerning monetary policy to enhance transparency. For example, decisions of the monetary policy committee are made public right after the meeting. And the Governor of the Bank of Korea frequently delivers speeches or gives interviews to explain monetary policy direction.

Up to this point, I have talked about changes in the monetary policy framework. Besides this, though, there have also been substantial changes in how monetary policy operates in practice. Before the currency crisis, the Bank of Korea used reserve money as its main operating target. Since the mid-1990s, however, the stability of the monetary aggregates has declined, reflecting financial liberalisation and market opening. Instead, the role of price variables, such as the interest rates, has been progressively heightened. This means that monetary policy in Korea is expected to be more effective when it is based on a price variable like the interest rate rather than a monetary aggregate.

Since the Korean economy was hit by the currency crisis, exchange-rate stability has become a crucial concern for the monetary authority. Under this circumstance, the Bank of Korea had no option but to engineer a sharp rise in interest rates in order to rebuild foreign reserves as quickly as possible. After that, in line with the trend of foreign-exchange market stability, the Bank of Korea cautiously lowered the money-market rate. Consequently, the overnight money-market rate has come to serve as an important operational target in addition to reserve money. While still closely monitoring monetary aggregates, the Bank places more emphasis on interest-rate movements. For example, each month its Monetary Policy Committee sets and announces the desirable direction of short-term rates for the month.

I have kept my explanation of the monetary policy framework in Korea since the currency crisis as brief as possible. The authors of the Report have my heartfelt agreement in saying that, 'as an art, central banking is a good deal more complicated than the textbook theory suggests'. Such sentiments strengthen my belief in the value of today's Symposium as an opportunity to share our experiences of central banking.

In closing, I would like to express my sincere thanks to Governor Eddie George for offering me this opportunity to serve as a discussant for the symposium. Thank you very much for listening so attentively.

Mr Josef Tošovský (Czech Republic) I would also like to join my colleagues in congratulating Professor Maxwell Fry and his team on this report. This Report is very useful as well as topical, and we can learn a lot from this expertise.

Please forgive me if my address today is somewhat maritime in nature. Coming from the landlocked Czech Republic, I probably have as little authority here in the UK to talk about seafaring as I do to discuss the sport of cricket. Nevertheless, we central bankers frequently use terms with a nautical flavour – anchors, rolling horizons, floating exchange rate and so on and perhaps this is appropriate in view of our role as navigators aboard the good ship, *Monetary Policy*.

Let me first start with sharing my experience. After reading this Report, which utilises a new extended survey of 77 countries, one can get an impressive picture of what I would call a 'prototype' central bank, meaning, how the bank can define its position within society, how it chooses its monetary framework, how it sets explicit targets, what instruments it employs, and how it communicates its strategy to the general public. Compared with the results, our central bank fits the picture perfectly. It is quite encouraging to learn also that the problems we have faced, and also the problems we will probably face in the future when making decisions, are very similar to those of the 'prototype' bank, because it means that solutions are searched for globally, and sharing of experiences among central bankers can help a lot.

If we compare the experience of the sample of the 77 countries' monetary frameworks to that of the Czech National Bank, it can be demonstrated that we went through a very typical process during the last decade. In the first half of this decade, our monetary strategy was based on two intermediate explicit targets, for money and the exchange rate. We abandoned them – or dare I say, they abandoned us – and at the end of the decade, a new strategy of inflation targeting was adopted.

Similarly, one can demonstrate that the problems that the Czech National Bank faced during this decade were similar to those of the sample. There was overshooting of monetary targets in 1995, collapse of the currency peg in 1997, and we undershot the inflation target in 1998. I would like at this time to speak about the anchors in general and a little bit more about this Report.

The report shows a trend. The surveyed central banks want to offer a nominal anchor to their economies. In the past, they have often searched for these anchors abroad by borrowing credibility through the exchange-rate peg. Now they produce their anchor at home, with their own explicit inflation target. I do not play down the role of anchors because they are important for effective and credible decision-making. But is this enough? The problem is that we live in a globalised world-economy with massive capital flows, which therefore means quite a high degree of volatility to which small open emerging economies are especially exposed. The evidence of problems is clear. Many small open emerging economies went through financial crisis in the last few years. We have also noticed the reactions of the international community and institutions like the IMF.

My question could also be, is it enough or do we need another step? A small economy, especially an emerging one, has several characteristics that together can create an environment for which an anchor might not be enough for strong protection. First, the scope of capital flows is large with respect to both the domestic financial sector and the central bank. Second, the financial sector is emerging, which means that players are inexperienced, some instruments are missing, and hedging, if available, can be costly. Third, there is an underdeveloped institutional infrastructure.

This implies that a central bank may be forced to react to consequences of exchange-rate volatility with its instruments in order to hit its targets when the state of the domestic economy itself would not call for such a reaction. Practically, in this non-standard condition, neither homemade nor external anchors alone appear to work satisfactorily enough to secure stability. There is a risk of boom-and-bust patterns, and the issue is how to avoid an undesirable transmission of the exchange rate and price instability into output instability, with all of its social and political consequences.

What is my vision of a harbour? A harbour can represent institutionalised links between the currency of an emerging economy and a major anchor currency. It may have different forms or grades ranging from *ex-ante* concluded provisions for *ad hoc* support in case of distress, to a more extended arrangement of regional co-operation. Such an arrangement is not, however, possible without the credible commitment of both parties and all the corresponding conditionalities. I can imagine certain building blocks required for such a harbour. On the side of an emerging-market economy, I can imagine that it could include the completion of the institutional framework, policy convergence, and of transparency of decision-making. At the same time, it is vital that the counter-party should lend a helping hand and should be ready to help and make commitments and arrangements in the course of the adjustment stages. This would diminish the probability of currency instability. In fact, it would help in the convergence process of the given emerging economy, as well as increase the prospect of its success.

QUESTION AND ANSWER SESSION

Eddie George I suggest that we try to structure our discussion. We want to continue to move from the aggregate experience of the survey to your own experiences, and we would be extremely interested to hear those. I suggest there are three issues that you might think of in representing to us your own experience. The first issue is that in terms of the clear trend in the aggregate data toward explicit targets, I noticed that it was not an absolute trend, and I would be very interested if people have reservations about this move toward explicit targets in terms of your own experience. The second issue relates to the choice of targets. There was quite an emphasis in the early part of the presentations on inflation targets and I felt it was appearing as if this was a great lobby group. But I think Josef Tošovský raised a very interesting question about how reliant one could be upon an inflation target in certain circumstances and raised questions about how you reconcile that with exchange rate stability. And a third area for discussion is aspects of the structure of explicit targets, which could apply to inflation, or money or exchange rates.

What we really want to do is simply learn of your experiences and your reactions to the aggregate picture and to the comments that have been made so penetratingly by our discussants. So who would like to lead off our open discussion?

Mr Abdulla Al-Attiya (Qatar) I would like to thank our panellists for an excellent presentation. My question is can we argue that target inflation has been successful because of lower worldwide inflation and because of world integration?

Mervyn King Well, it has clearly played a role. I would distinguish, I think, between lower world inflation and greater world integration. I think in many ways the greater integration over the past ten years, particularly in capital markets, has created problems for many countries with rapid reversals of capital flows, so that has not been easy. Lower world inflation has clearly helped but not every country has had lower inflation, and I think that in order to converge on low and stable inflation a credible domestic nominal anchor was necessary. And in those countries that adopted inflation targets, it almost seemed to energise the efforts and provide a focus for the willingness of the authorities really seriously to pursue low and stable inflation.

If there had not been falling world inflation, would inflation targets have been as successful? It might have been more difficult. But equally, without the inflation targeting approach, lower world inflation would not have necessarily enabled countries to maintain low and stable inflation expectations and to bring inflation down and keep it down. The effort of changing expectations in the domestic economy needs not just lower world inflation but also the domestic nominal anchor.

Eddie George I would agree with that. I have to say that as far as the UK is concerned, we have bucked the world trend in terms of low inflation in the past, and we could very easily have done it again now.

Mr Gordon Thiessen (Canada) On the issue of whether the world-wide decline in inflation really overstates the achievement of inflation targets, I guess there were some of us who were in early enough before the inflation rate had gone down all that much. There is no question that the targets really did help us bring our inflation below that of the US. I think it is just another indication that the target system really did work very well. But in assessing inflation targets, we do not just want to look at the success of bringing down inflation, although that is terribly important. I think you were saying, Don, and also you, Mervyn, it changes the way you make decisions and the way you describe decisions and I must say from my own personal point of view it has changed enormously my relationship with the House of Commons standing committee. Having an agreed target just changes the whole nature of these discussions and I think makes monetary policy more credible, more understandable, and less an issue of controversy than it was before. I think that it is a huge step forward.

Mr Baledzi Gaolathe (Botswana) Thank you very much, Mr Chairman. I was interested to hear that in the UK the Government has responsibility for setting the target. And then the Bank tries to implement policy to achieve the target. I assume that there are advantages and disadvantages and I would like a little bit more comment on that. In our case, in recent years we have started setting targets, but the initiative and the responsibilities are on us, the central bank. Although the act under which we operate gives us that independence, we have found that we cannot succeed without pulling the government in because the fiscal side is crucial. You cannot really influence inflation to the level you want using only monetary instruments, in a situation such as ours. So we have set these targets and sat down and agreed them with the government.

In terms of target-setting, two aspects stand out. For the past two years we have been producing a monetary policy statement which provides the public with guidelines of where we are going. But we do not necessarily provide the figures in detail. We might say that we want single digit inflation. But with the government, we sit down and agree whether it should be 5% or 6% and so on. The number depends on what our colleagues in other southern African parts are doing. That is one complication we have encountered. And having said that, we find that such an approach enables us to debate these things with government and the private sector. Eventually I think they will begin to understand.

Tan Sri Ali Abul Hassan bin Sulaiman (Malaysia) I have two observations to make and a question to raise. The first observation is that it is not really the monetary framework, but the commitment of the government that is of the greatest importance. There are cases where inflation targets or monetary growth targets have been set, but the central banks are helpless because they are forced to finance some of the government deficits. So the role of fiscal policy becomes very important. I think, within the context of a developing economy, given the need to achieve economic growth and the possibility of fiscal expansion, the need for close co-operation between the government and the central bank is very important. The second point I want to raise is that the Fry Report says that those developing economies that have low and stable inflation have been those with fixed exchange rate regimes. But clearly in the case of Malaysia, we generally had low and stable inflation even when we were on a floating exchange rate regime. An important factor that made this possible was the fiscal discipline on the part of the Malaysian government.

Finally, inflation targeting is based on a country's forecast inflation rate. In the case of a developing economy, forecasting inflation can sometimes be very difficult because of lack of information. Moreover, there are so many variables that are beyond the control of the authorities, particularly where the economy is an open one or where the economy depends a great deal on commodity pricing. The question therefore is: How relevant is inflation targeting in the absence of a wide access to information?

Dr Christian Stals (South Africa) This is a very useful study prepared by Dr Julius and the Centre for Central Banking Studies. I think, as it was said a few times this morning, monetary policy framework is very much about presentation, transparency, explanation, and so on, and sometimes I have a little bit of a problem by trying to classify the various monetary policy frameworks followed by countries as different frameworks. I think there is only one particularly defined monetary policy framework: it can begin with an inflation target, and if you have an inflation target you have to control the growth in the money supply, and if you have to control the growth in the money supply you have some kind of restriction on bank credit extension, and if you have to control bank credit extension then you have a liquidity policy, and if you have a liquidity policy you have an interest-rate policy, and if it's all successful, then you have a stable exchange rate. So deciding in the end which one of those elements of the framework you use as a reference point or as an intermediate target or as a final target, as Governor Brash quite rightly pointed out, you cannot ignore the other elements of that framework.

This brings me then to our own experience. We used a money-supply anchor. And again, as one of the panellists already said, the money supply abandoned us, rather than us abandoning the money-supply anchor. I think globalisation has had a very important effect on our own situation, where for about three years in succession we had unacceptably high rates of increase in the money supply, a persistent decline in the rate of inflation, and a very substantial decline in the conventional velocity of circulation of the money supply. But if you try to explain why that link between increases in the money supply and inflation broke down in our situation, it is globalisation: a huge expansion in velocity and turnover in financial markets.

Because the money supply became less useful for monetary policy purposes, and then we have to start looking at the alternatives, and obviously inflation targeting could become very effective. Our own experience is that we are gradually moving to inflation targeting, but we are looking for the support and commitment of the government. We think it is important, as Governor Brash said, that it should not be a commitment not only of the central bank but also of the government. The reason in our own situation is that there are many other inflationary pressures working in the economy – fiscal policy, labour policy, and trade policy. These create inflationary pressure and make it extremely difficult for a central bank to fight inflation unless you have a commitment of overall macroeconomic policy to a lower rate of inflation. I hope we will get to that stage, where it will give us more credibility, also in the objectives of inflation targeting, as it is not only a central bank objective but is all of our objectives.

Dr Mathew A.P. Chikaonda (Malawi) I think most of us in developing countries would agree with Dr Julius when she emphasised the point of finding a design that must fit our individual circumstances. To me that meant that everyone must behave in that system. The central bank will easily lose credibility if we go too quickly to these announced targets where there is not serious commitment from all segments.

So in terms of policy designs, I would be interested if this study were to be extended a bit, to look at countries that have an ESAF programme which include specific targets – like 10% inflation by this year; by end of programme, 5%. And then within the same structures you will find that in certain countries central bank independence is already there, at least within the legal framework. But is this enough to deliver on our targets?

For that I would like to extend Governor Tošovský's analogy of a harbour a little bit. I think what we need to do is to cross over to the other side of the harbour, the fiscal side, and bring those guys on board. We need to find a way to say that the guys on the other side of the harbour should be on board, and I think the Governor for Malaysia was pretty much making a similar point. Meanwhile, in spite of the very good views I have heard about inflation targeting, for some of us there is still some haze surrounding monetary policy, and until this haze clears, I think we will stick to a policy of constructive ambiguity on the part of the central bank.

Mr K. Dwight Venner (Eastern Caribbean) Let me thank Professor Fry and his team for this excellent study. There have been significant externalities from this study. When we got the questionnaire, a group of us sat down and did a tremendous job of trying to answer the questions and also to put in context how we looked at our monetary policy framework. And I can assure you that they have written several papers on it and if that is the only benefit, then I think it has been tremendous and we may want to share some of this with you.

When it comes to policy frameworks, there is a great dependence on the state of the particular society; for example whether the economy is developed or developing. There you would have to go back to an overall policy framework, taking in all the policies of the particular country, which in turn depend on the political evolution, the legal frameworks for accountability. I think this comes through in the summary of the Report.

Such differences are particularly important because there is a division of responsibility in economic policy. Fiscal policy, incomes policies and structural policies are the province of the central government. Monetary policy may or may not be the province of the central bank. That depends on the level of independence. Some central banks acquire independence for peculiar reasons. And let me mention two here. One, it depends on the constitution of the country – federalist countries seem to have more independence in the central monetary authorities than others. For examples in the case of the European Central Bank (the ECB), and our own institution, the ECCB, because we have many members and no member has a veto, there is a passing of influence from the single country to the whole, to the authority. Which brings us the question of targeting. Again, the target you pick may depend on historical circumstances. In our case our target is the exchange rate. It was not a conscious choice in a sense but coming from a relationship when we were first pegged to the pound sterling and then to the US dollar. Given the consequences of massive depreciations elsewhere in the region, the public at large had a feeling that devaluations were not good. And therefore you have the public, in a sense, picking a target. They do not want a depreciation of the rate because the rate ends up in high inflation. But if you peg, as a small country, to a country that is pursuing a low inflation rate, then you end up secondarily with an inflation target. So the target is picked for you in the first instance; it is then reinforced by the public experience of what this can do; and if you link to a country that has a low inflation rate then you do end up with that as well.

Mr Joseph Yam (Hong Kong) Just a few points. I think that, generally speaking, discretion in the monetary policy framework breeds uncertainty and undermines credibility, notwithstanding a high degree of transparency. There are, of course, exceptions, but I doubt if there are a lot of central bank governors with eyebrows as thick as the eyebrows of the Governor of the Bank of England or as eloquent as Alan Greenspan's 'Greenspeak'.

There is an advantage to reducing the degree of discretion. Even though your objective is inflation targeting or money targeting, I was wondering whether anyone has considered reducing further the discretion that you have, by introducing, for example, a response equation determining changes in interest rates by looking at forecasts of inflation, or measures of inflation expectations – rather than depending on the wisdom of the monetary policy committee so much. That is the point about discretion. I think in terms of the overall monetary framework; there are obviously advantages in having a target over not having a target, and I think the macro trend is certainly moving toward targets. And in the choice of the target, obviously inflation is becoming a very popular target. But as pointed out by a number of people, for small open economies it may be better to have an exchange-rate target. Unfortunately, an exchange-rate target can be attacked, whereas an inflation target or a money target cannot be attacked. So there are certain costs one will have to bear.

Dr Marion Williams (Barbados) First let me congratulate the central bank for a most interesting study. It has thrown light on many issues that have been entertaining our minds over the last number of years. What I would like to comment on is the fact that incomes policy and wages policy up to many years ago would have been the focal point of any discussion about inflation targeting. Over the last several years it has become possible to speak of inflation targeting without really concentrating a great deal on incomes policies and on the role of the unions. I believe this has a great deal to do with the fact that this is an age of globalisation and that countries are now exposed to pressures of competitiveness from other countries, so that in fact the power of the unions is not as great as it has been in earlier years. But I believe, however, that incomes policy are still, in a sense, out of the hands of the central banks and, to a large extent, of governments.

So I am wondering how countries that are not as open as, for example, the UK, manage or would manage to use an inflation target where the unions are strong and where control of wages does not particularly rest in the hands of policy-makers. Perhaps the applicability of inflation targeting for some countries might not be as relevant as for other countries like the UK or perhaps the US.

Mr Daudi Ballali (Tanzania) Thank you, Governor George, I would like to join the other governors in applauding the study, which is extremely useful and a good basis for this discussion and it has stimulated our thoughts on how we ourselves do in our own countries. Now while we also in Tanzania target inflation, we have a problem. The problem is that the government is so large in comparison to the rest of the economy. Therefore, before I can agree to target inflation, there is usually a need to decide on the size of the deficit. So when the Treasury asks what is the size of reduction in the inflation rate that is achievable in the coming year, I just say, 'if you can give me the size of the deficit, then I can say what is achievable'. Therefore, in our case the starting point is to agree on the inflation rate and then the size of the deficit.

In the recent past of course, and particularly in Africa, we have been helped because we have had Fund-supported programmes. Now of course, many of these programmes forecast the reduction of the government deficit. So it has been a little easier for us to achieve the inflation targets, and in the case of Tanzania, we have achieved a single digit this year for the first time in a quarter of a century. But I wonder what inflation would be if there was not this additional influence of an overall macroeconomic programme. I would therefore be interested to know how countries with inflation targets have fared without a very strong commitment from the government to contain the deficit.

Mr Tito Mboweni (South Africa) I must say that I found the paper very interesting and stimulating. The first point of concern for me is one that Dr Julius also raised, the institutional design in the development and implementation of monetary policy. I am a bit concerned, for example, that in the UK structure, this individual accountability for the members of the Monetary Policy Committee to Parliament could be a mistake in the sense that it might impinge to a large extent on the independence of the Bank. Why do I say so? If I know that I am individually accountable to Parliament for the decisions which I have to make in the monetary policy committee, and I know that the standing committee is full of left-wing labour members who are likely to give me a hard time, my behaviour in the Monetary Policy Committee might be influenced by what I am likely to face in that House of Commons Committee. I think that even though people will not admit it openly, it does influence their behaviour in the Monetary Policy Committee.

A second issue. I am happy that there was a survey to find out which ones of these committees vote and which ones make decisions by consensus. But I am not quite sure what point is being made by the voting. What is the difficulty with debating the issues until you come to final conclusions?

Dr Hanna Gronkiewicz-Waltz (Poland) I think that what was said by Josef Tošovský about harbour was important, but I am afraid that the world changes so quickly nowadays that even if you stop in a harbour you must leave it quickly. So I frankly think that I do not believe in harbours except in the eternal life. However, when we have changed our monetary targets, on each occasion we were thinking about price stability as the main goal. I think that we had quite a pragmatic approach because we wanted to avoid problems that have included credit growth, capital inflows, and appreciation. So until now, after ten years, I can say that we have been lucky.

But because we shifted to inflation targeting quite recently, in 1998, I have two questions for Mervyn King or Eddie George. First, what is the best range for the target? I ask because I am afraid that in 1998 the range was a little bit too narrow in our case. And second, what are the obstacles to direct inflation targeting? Who do you warn not to undertake inflation targeting? Which economy and in what circumstances?

Mr Emanuel Ellul (Malta) Our economy is very small and open and we have an exchange rate that has been fixed to a basket of currencies for over 25 years. So we must ensure that our real effective exchange rate remains competitive. In this regard, at present the main threat to inflation in our country is from the domestic side. In the last three or four years the problem was the relatively large fiscal deficit. This deficit last year was around 10% of GDP, so we have to be extremely careful how we try to tackle this. Yet in spite of the heavy government deficit, the domestic economy experienced a slowdown in demand, and this helped to ease inflationary pressures in the last 18 months.

However, things can change very dramatically for us and one thing that we have realised is that in a small economy like ours, it is not possible to have a completely independent monetary policy. You have to look at what is happening with your trading partners, since this can influence your decisions dramatically. We are lucky because we are living in a region where our main trading partners happen to be the EU countries, which have low inflation as their major target. I think that this has served us quite well, as imported inflationary pressures are subdued.

Mr Winston Dookeran (Trinidad and Tobago) Just briefly to indicate our own assessment in Trinidad and Tobago. About a year or so ago we undertook an assessment as to monetary targeting in general and, more specifically, on the issue of inflation targeting as an objective of the Trinidad monetary policy framework. The essential point that emerged was that we must target those variables and objectives that are controllable. In that respect, inflation appears not to be as controllable as we would like, particularly in light of fluctuations in our terms of trade. More importantly, the overriding price that needs to be controlled is the external price of the currency.

In that context, we started from your premise that initially a country must identify which variables are within its control and which variables are outside its control, and then decide how best to fulfil the core function – which is essentially to protect the value of the currency while maintaining the competitiveness of the economy. Taking account of the fact that we are a very open economy, that we need to focus on a more ambiguous policy framework, without tying ourselves to a very specific inflation target.

We found that the studies and discussions of the Symposium have helped put the arguments in a global context, taking into account the far greater integration of the financial markets.

Mr Álmos Kovàcs (Hungary) Dr Julius spoke of history suggesting change in monetary frameworks, even though credibility benefits from stability in monetary policy implementation. And I wonder if, after reaching inflation targeting, there will be a need for any further change. That is a very attractive possibility.

However, I think it is important to examine the preconditions for implementing inflation targeting, and I very much do agree with those who emphasise that there is a minimum level of prerequisites to fiscal policy, and I would add incomes and wage policy. I think that aggressive inflation targeting, and by that I mean teaching a lesson to players in the economy through high interest rates, could lead to strong output effects. So I think that it is very important to reach that minimum level of consistency between policy and policy environment. And here comes the question – what happens if this consistency will not be valid anymore? What happens if there are very high nominal wage increases in an inflation-targeting environment? Can the central bank use further tightening in that case?

I have a more general question concerning the fact that sometimes the real rate of interest may be higher after introducing targeting. I wonder whether the study would continue looking into that effect. Finally, I would like to add that I very much agree with Governor Tošovský that in a small open economy, it is very important that the actual volatility coming from global financial flows should be kept within limits, and I wonder if there could be some international arrangement to help countries. In that sense it would be a good idea, because some countries cannot afford to endure high volatility as much as others do.

Mr Julian Francis (Bahamas) I first of all wanted to join the others in congratulating the Bank on this excellent study and, as Governor Venner said, just the exercise of responding to this questionnaire was really a very worthwhile exercise for our institution. While not at all questioning the legitimacy of this study, I would like to join a certain number of governors who have already commented in perhaps asking about the feasibility of inflation targeting in an economy such as ours – a small open economy, characterised by fixed exchange rates and dominated by large economies in close proximity.

Indeed, this study might be a first step to another study that tries to answer the question – under what circumstance should one attempt to move to inflation targeting? I believe that it would be a very interesting exercise and one on which one can certainly build. Once again I would like to thank the Bank of England for giving us this opportunity to look at it.

Dr Arminio Neto (Brazil) Just briefly on this last issue, we are just going through this discussion in Brazil, as we are now about a month away from formally launching our own inflation-targeting framework. And what I have found in the debate in Brazil is really that there are two issues that seem to get mixed up in the same debate. One question is what is the proper exchange-rate regime? And the other question is, if you decide you want to float, what do you do? Do you target inflation or not? And what we have realised in Brazil is that if you keep those two separate, it is very hard not to move towards inflation targeting once you have chosen to float. That has been our decision. Once that point has been reached, we have a short-term issue that we need to deal with. And I think it is a similar situation in Korea, and that is how to fit what is a medium to long-term process into the short-term needs of an IMF programme.

Dr Don Brash (New Zealand) May I make three points very briefly? First, on the question of incomes policy and unions, a deregulated, non-unionised workforce makes inflation targeting that much easier. But if you have a highly unionised workforce, it clearly does not make it impossible. When our inflation target was introduced, the trade union movement basically denounced it, and called the central bank Governor all kinds of unflattering names. But at the same time, they told their members that, as long as this undesirable policy was in place, the unions would have to restrain their wage demands, otherwise unemployment was going to go up. And I think inflation targeting really meant that unions recognised that they were no longer influencing the inflation rate, they were influencing the unemployment rate, and I think that was a very important learning point.

My second point regards volatility of the exchange rate. Certainly in our experience with a clean float, we found that inflation targeting has been very helpful in reducing week-to-week and month-to-month volatility – and in fact our volatility against the US dollar is lower than that of any of the major floating-rate currencies except the Canadian dollar, which is much more closely integrated with the US economy than we are. In terms of the big cyclical swing in the real exchange rate, we have been through a very large cyclical swing recently. I had thought there might be something flawed about inflation targeting in that it produced that kind of very large cyclical swing in the real exchange rate. But looking around at other countries with a whole range of different exchange-rate regimes, I find that the cycle in the real exchange rate that we have had has been typical. And even Hong Kong, with a pegged exchange rate to the US dollar, has had a rise in its real exchange-rate, which has been very similar indeed to our floating exchange rate. So I do not think that is a reason against inflation targeting.

The third point, very briefly, is on the role of government. I agree with all those who have commented that having the government on outside is crucial. If the government can be persuaded to publicly endorse the inflation target, a large part of the battle is over. We had the experience very early on when the government substantially eased fiscal policy. Within 48 hours we had tightened monetary policy. The media focused on this very substantially and the basic message was that the New Zealand government had just discovered they could no longer buy elections by easing fiscal policy, because the central bank would send voters the bill in the form of higher mortgage rates. And the opposition party campaigned on a platform that promised lower interest rates if they became government, not by interfering with the monetary policy framework, but by tightening fiscal policy. And that was a turning point in the whole debate on economic policy in New Zealand, when the governments recognised that they could not any longer treat monetary policy and fiscal policy as entirely independent. Given the inflation targets, fiscal policy was to some extent constrained.

Eddie George Perhaps I could pick up on that myself, because I thought that was a very interesting part of the discussion – the constraints as a result of the relationship with the government on the one hand and the relationship with the labour leaders on the other. And I think from our experience you had to have an acceptance within society as a whole of the importance of a price stability objective. It would have been inconceivable that we could have moved to inflation targeting without having first developed that understanding. And I think that the absolute precondition for a move in this direction is that there should be that kind of understanding; otherwise it is very difficult to make the policy work. Of course in a democratic society you would not get that sort of agreement without it. But the really important, thing I think, is that when the Conservative government first adopted a target, in so doing they were accepting the objective of price stability. And after the election, the inflation target was confirmed by the new Labour government, who also confirmed it in the form of giving the Bank operational independence to implement that target.

Then it seems to me that once that has been accepted at the political level and embodied in statute, or in the government endorsing or imposing a monetary or inflation target on the central bank, then this is a symptom which means that you can expect to have greater co-ordination on the fiscal side. And that is why the explicit endorsement by the political authorities in the country is absolutely crucial, in our experience, in implementing this regime.

Mr Josef Tošovský (Czech Republic) What you mentioned now is perhaps the most important issue in the framework of inflation targeting: expectations. Inflation targeting helps to reach a certain consensus on the inflation outlook between trade unions, on the one hand, and the Government and of course central bank on the other. Gaining such agreement on the mix of policies – income policy, fiscal policy, and monetary policy – should be beneficial because it should reduce the cost of this inflation. Sometimes, for a country that has never gone through hyperinflation, it may be more difficult to persuade the politicians that to keep low inflation or to go ahead with disinflation is so important. This is one of my comments.

My second comment is: I would like to invite you all into the club of inflation targeters, but one must be careful. It requires a lot of modelling as well as communication skills. Moreover, inflation targeting changes the central bank completely. In our case, there were changes in organisation structure, in procedures, and in responsibilities and accountability of individual people in the central bank, including the board. So one breaks down the barriers and communicates very effectively with the general public. The 'kitchen' of monetary policy has to be open, showing what ingredients were used when the staff was preparing the forecast and what was behind a particular decision. Later it is possible to admit to any second-best decisions, but it is good to know what the circumstances were when a certain decision was made. It is necessary to open the kitchen, maybe revealing some technical problems, or inconsistencies, or lack of expertise. So, I would warn against the hurried approach because credibility could then be eroded.

I would welcome you in joining the club, but you should know that this nominal anchor is also not a panacea for small open emerging economies.

Mervyn King There are so many good questions that I think the right solution is for me to sit here answering them, while you all go and have lunch. I thought I might just make one brief comment, and this goes back to something that Chris Stals said. In one profound sense, there is only one framework in terms of how we think about policy, and indeed you can describe all monetary policies as a combination of two approaches. One is a medium-term inflation target and the other is the way in which the central bank responds to short-term shocks to the economy. But I do think there is something different about the way in which inflation targets alter both the central bank internally, as Josef has just said, and also the relationship between the central bank and the rest of society, as Gordon Thiessen stressed. And sharing one's analysis, sharing one's thinking – opening the kitchen in Josef's words – are, I think, are very important. For many years, it is possible to go to restaurants that have a good track record and you do not worry about opening the kitchen: the restaurant does not worry because it already has credibility, and the customers do not worry because they are happy with previous experiences. But it does not take more than one restaurant that poisons the customers to lead to a situation in which more transparency is needed. And actually, I think the feeling expressed by Gordon Thiessen and others certainly fits our experience, once you change that relationship between a central bank and the rest of society not only do you feel better about it but so does society as well.

Appendix 4

Central Bank Governors' Symposium participants

HEADS OF DELEGATION

Mr Eddie George
Governor
Bank of England

Mr Julian Francis
Governor
Central Bank of Bahamas

Dr Mohammed Farashuddin
Governor
Bangladesh Bank

Dr Marion Williams
Acting Governor
Central Bank of Barbados

Mr Keith Arnold
Governor
Central Bank of Belize

Mrs Cheryl-Ann Lister
Chairman
Bermuda Monetary Authority

Mr Baledzi Gaolathe
Governor
Bank of Botswana

Dr Arminio Fraga Neto
Governor
Banco Central de Brasil

Mr Gordon Thiessen
Governor
Bank of Canada

Mr Afxentis Afxentiou
Governor
Central Bank of Cyprus

Mr Josef Tošovskỳ
Governor
Ceska Narodni Banka

Mr Dwight Venner
Governor
Eastern Caribbean Central Bank

Mr Momodou Clarke Bajo
Governor
Central Bank of The Gambia

Dr Emanuel Ossei-Kumah
Deputy Governor
Bank of Ghana

Mr Joseph Yam
Chief Executive
Hong Kong Monetary Authority

Mr Álmos Kovàcs
National Bank of Hungary
Magyar Nemzeti Bank

Mr Birgir Gunnarsson
Governor
Central Bank of Sedlabanki Islands

Mr Jagdish Capoor
Deputy Governor
Reserve Bank of India

Mrs Audrey Anderson
Deputy Governor
Bank of Jamaica

Mr Micah Kiprono Cheserem
Governor
Central Bank of Kenya

Prof Chol-Hwan Chon
Governor
Bank of Korea

HE Salem Abdul-Aziz Al-Sabah
Governor
Central Bank of Kuwait

Mr Stephen M. Swaray
Governor
Central Bank of Lesotho

Dr Mathew A.P. Chikaonda
Governor
Reserve Bank of Malawi

Mr Tan Sri Ali Abul Hassan
Bin Sulaiman
Governor
Bank Negara Malaysia

Mr Emanuel Ellul
Governor
Central Bank of Malta

Mr Rameswurlall Basant Roi
Governor
Bank of Mauritius

Mr Adriano Afonso Maleiane
Governor
Banco de Mocambique

Mr Tom Alweendo
Governor
Bank of Namibia

Dr Donald Brash
Governor
Reserve Bank of New Zealand

Mr Oluwole Oduyemi
Deputy Governor
Central Bank of Nigeria

HE Hamood Sangour Al-Zadjali
Executive President
Central Bank of Oman

Dr Hanna Gronkiewicz-Waltz
President
Narodny Bank Polski

Mr Abdulla Al-Attiya
Governor
Qatar Central Bank

Mr Rick Houenipwela
Governor
Central Bank of Solomon Islands

Mr Tito Mboweni
Governor Designate
South African Reserve Bank

Dr Christian Stals
Governor
South African Reserve Bank

Mr Amarananda Jayawardena
Governor
Central Bank of Sri Lanka

Mr Martin Dlamini
Governor
Central Bank of Swaziland

Mr Daudi T.S. Ballali
Governor
Bank of Tanzania

Mr Siosiua T. Utoikamanu
Governor
National Reserve Bank of Tonga

Mr Victor V. Gerashchenko
Chairman
Central Bank of Russia

Mr James Sanpha Koroma
Governor
Bank of Sierra Leone

Mr Yong Guan Koh
Managing Director
Monetary Authority of Singapore

Mr Winston Dookeran
Governor
Central Bank of Trinidad and Tobago

Mr Antonio Casas Gonzalez
Governor
Banco Central de Venezuela

Mr Joaram Kahenano
Executive Director Operations
Bank of Uganda

Dr Abraham Mwenda
Deputy Governor
Bank of Zambia

HE Sultan Bin Nasser Al-Suwaidi
Governor
Central Bank of the United Arab
Emirates

Dr Leonard Ladisius Tsumba
Governor
Reserve Bank of Zimbabwe

Bank of England

Mr Clementi
Deputy Governor

Mr Jenkinson
Deputy Director

Mr Mervyn King
Deputy Governor

Mr Andrew G. Haldane
Ms Juliette Healey

Dr DeAnne Julius
Monetary Policy Committee

Dr Marion Kohler
Dr Lavan Mahadeva
Ms Joanna Place

Mr Bill Allen
Deputy Director

Ms Sandra Roger
Mr Gabriel Sterne

Others

Mr Moses Palaelo
Director Financial Institutions
Bank of Botswana

Miss Josie Wong
Adviser (London)
Hong Kong Monetary Authority

Mr Momodou A. Ceesay
Director of Research
Central Bank of The Gambia

Mr Aviral Iain
Executive Director to the Governor
Reserve Bank of India

Mr Herbert Carr
Principal Administrative Officer
Central Bank of The Gambia

Mrs Faith Stewart
Senior Director
Bank of Jamaica

Dr H.A.K. Wampah
Chief Economist
Bank of Ghana

Mr Maurice J.P. Kanga
Director of Research
Central Bank of Kenya

Mr Eddie Yue
Administrative Assistant to the
Chief Executive
Hong Kong Monetary Authority

Mr Mark L. Lesiit
Personal Assistant to the Governor
Central Bank of Kenya

Mr Hak-Ryul Kim
Chief Secretary (London Office)
Bank of Korea

Mr Chang-Hun Song
Deputy Chief Representative
(London Office)
Bank of Korea

Mr Nabil H. Al-Saqabi
Manager, Governor's Office
Central Bank of Kuwait

Mr Charles S.R. Chuka
General Manager
Reserve Bank of Malawi

Mrs Angela Mjojo
Bank Officer
Reserve Bank of Malawi

Mrs Latifah Merican Cheong
Assistant Governor
Bank Negara Malaysia

Mr Herbert Zammit Laferla
Deputy General Manager
Central Bank of Malta

Mr Vikramdass Mehendra Punchoo
Senior Research Officer
Bank of Mauritius

Mr Antonio Pinto De Abreu
General Manager
Banco de Mocambique

Mrs Ilda Elizabete Comiche
Division Chief
Banco de Mocambique

Mr Mihe Gaomab
Special Assistant
Bank of Namibia

Mr M.R. Rasheed
Director, Foreign Operations
Central Bank of Nigeria

Dr O.J. Nnanna
A. Director, Governor
Central Bank of Nigeria

Mr O. Ezewu
Special Assistant to the Deputy
Governor
Central Bank of Nigeria

Mr N.C. Nimzing
Manager, Foreign Exchange
Department
Central Bank of Nigeria

Dr Bogustaw Grabowski
Member of the Monetary Policy
Council
Narodny Bank Polski

Mr Pawet Durjasz
Director of Research Department
Narodny Bank Polski

Sh Fahad Faisal Al-Thani
Head of Banking and Issue
Department
Qatar Central Bank

Mr Patrick Samu
Divisional Head, Research
Department
Bank of Sierra Leone

Mr Ravi Menon
Director, Planning Policy and
Communications
Monetary Authority of Singapore

Mr Timothy Thahane
Deputy Governor
South African Reserve Bank

Ms Ranee Fernanado
Addl. Director/Bank Supervision
Central Bank of Sri Lanka

Mr Siva Sivagananthan
Banking and Financial Consultant
Central Bank of Sri Lanka

Mr Albert M. Mhlanga
Director of Investment and
Exchange
Central Bank of Swaziland

Mr John B. Kimaro
Manager
Bank of Tanzania

Miss Seneti Aho
Manager, Corporate Service
Department
National Reserve Bank of Tonga

Mr A.W. Walugember Musoke
Director Public Relations
Bank of Uganda

Mr German Uteras
Vice President of International
Operation
Banco Central de Venezuela

Dr Danny H. Kalyalya
Director
Bank of Zambia

Bibliography

Agenor, P.R. and Monteil, P.J. (1996), *Development Macroeconomics*, Princeton, New Jersey: Princeton University Press.

Alesina, A. and Summers, L. (1993), 'Central bank independence and macroeconomic performance: some comparative evidence', *Journal of Money, Credit and Banking*, Vol. 25, pp. 151–62.

Alfaro, S. and Schwartz, M. (2000), 'The recent experience of monetary policy in Mexico', this volume.

Atingi-Ego, M. (2000), 'Setting monetary policy instruments in Uganda', this volume.

Bakhshi, H., Haldane, A. and Hatch, N. (1998), 'Some costs and benefits of price stability in the United Kingdom', *Bank of England Working Paper No. 78.*

Balassa, B (1964), 'The purchasing power doctrine: a reappraisal', *Journal of Political Economy,* December.

Bank of England (1999), *Economic Models at the Bank of England*, London: Bank of England.

Bank for International Settlements (1998), *Summary Reports on the International Financial Architecture.* Basle: BIS.

Barro, R. (1995), 'Inflation and economic growth', *Bank of England Quarterly Bulletin*, May.

Barro, R. (1986), 'Rules versus discretion', in *Alternative Monetary Regimes*, Campbell, C.D. and Dougan, W.R. (eds) Baltimore: Johns Hopkins University Press.

Batini, N. and Haldane, A. (1999), 'Forward looking rules for monetary policy', *Bank of England Working Paper No. 91*, January.

Bernanke, B., Laubach, T., Mishkin, F. and Posen, A. (1999), *Inflation Targeting: Lessons from the International Experience*, Princeton, New Jersey: Princeton University Press.

Bleaney, M. and Fielding, D. (1999), 'Exchange rate regimes, inflation and output volatility in developing countries', *CREDIT Research Paper No. 994*, University of Nottingham.

Blinder, A. (1998), *Central Banking in Theory and in Practice*, Cambridge, Massachusetts: MIT Press.

Blinder, A. (1994), 'On sticky prices: academic theories meet the real world', in *Monetary Policy*, Mankiw, N.G., (ed.) Chicago: University of Chicago Press.

Briault, C. (1995). 'The costs of inflation', *Bank of England Quarterly Bulletin*, Vol. 35, February, pp. 33–45.

Briault, C., Haldane, A. and King, M. (1996), 'Independence and accountability', *Bank of England Working Paper No. 49.*

Canzoneri, M.B. and Behzad, D. (1996), 'Fiscal constraints on central bank independence and price stability', Georgetown University, Washington DC, June.

Capie, F., Goodhart, C., Fisher, S. and Schnadt, N. (1994), 'The future of central banking', Tercentenary Symposium of the Bank of England, Cambridge University Press.

Christoffersen, P.F. and Doyle, P. (1998), 'From inflation to growth: eight years of transition', *IMF Working Paper WP/98/100.*

Christoffersen, P.F. and Wescott, R.F. (1999), 'Is Poland ready for inflation targeting?', *IMF Working Paper WP/99/41,* March.

Clarida, R., Gali, J. and Gertler, M. (1998), 'Monetary policy rules in practice: some international evidence', *European Economic Review*, Vol. 42, pp. 1033–67.

Clarida, R. and Gertler, M. (1997), 'How the Bundesbank conducts monetary policy', in *Reducing Inflation: Motivation and Strategy*, Romer, C.D. and Romer, D.H., (eds) Chicago: University of Chicago Press. Also *NBER Working Paper No. 5581*, May 1996.

Cottarelli, C. and Giannini, C. (1998), 'Inflation, credibility, and the role of the International Monetary Fund', *IMF Paper PPAA/98/12.*

Cottarelli, C. and Giannini, C. (1997), 'Credibility without rules? Monetary frameworks in the post-Bretton Woods era', *IMF Occasional Paper No. 154.*

Crockett, A. (2000), 'Monetary policy objectives emerging markets in light of the Asian crisis', this volume.

Cufer, U., Mahadeva, L. and Sterne, G. (2000), 'Specifying an inflation target: the case of administered prices and other candidates for exclusion', this volume.

Cukierman, A. (2000), 'Establishing a reputation for dependability by means of inflation targets', Paper presented at Workshop on Choice of Intermediate Monetary Policy Targets, Bank of England, Centre for Central Banking Studies, November 1998.

Cukierman, A. (1995), 'Towards a systematic comparison between inflation targets and monetary targets', in *Inflation Targets*, Leiderman, L. and Svensson, L., eds. London: CEPR.

Cukierman, A. (1992), *Central Bank Strategy, Credibility, and Independence: Theory and Evidence*, Cambridge, Massachusetts: MIT Press.

Cukierman, A. and Leiderman, L. (1996), 'Transparency and the evolution of exchange rate flexibility in the aftermath of disinflation', in *Financial Factors in Economic Stabilization and Growth*, Blejer, M., Eckstein, Z., Hercowitz, Z. and Leiderman, L., (eds) Cambridge University Press.

Cukierman, A., Webb, S.B. and Neyapti, B. (1994), 'Measuring central bank independence and its effect on policy outcomes', *Occasional Paper No. 58*, International Center for Economic Growth, San Francisco.

Debelle, G. and Hoon Lim, C. (1998), 'Preliminary considerations of an inflation targeting framework for the Philippines', *IMF Working Paper WP/98/39.*

Eichengreen, B. (1999), 'Kicking the habit: moving from pegged rates to greater exchange rate flexibility', *Economic Journal*, March, pp. C1–C14.

Eijffinger, S. and Schaling, E. (1993), 'Central bank independence in twelve industrial countries?', *Banca Nazionale del Lavoro Quarterly Review*, Vol. 184, pp. 49–89.

Eijffinger, S.C.W. and De Han, J. (1996), 'The political economy of central bank independence', *Special Papers in International Economics*, 19 May.

Eijffinger, S.C.W., Van Rooij, M. and Schaling, E. (1996), 'Central bank independence: a panel data approach', *Public Choice*, Vol. 89, pp. 163–82.

Enoch, C. (1998), 'Transparency in central bank operations in the foreign exchange market', *IMF Paper WP/98/2*, March.

Feldstein, M. (1979),'The Welfare Cost of Permanent Inflation and Optimal Short-Run Economic Policy', *Journal of Political Economy*, Vol. 87, No. 4, pp. 749–68.

Fisher, I. (1922), *The Purchasing Power of Money*, MacMillan.

Fischer, S. (1993), 'The role of macroeconomic factors in growth', *Journal of Monetary Economics*, Vol. 32, pp. 485–512.

Forder, J. (1998), 'Central bank independence – conceptual clarifications and interim assessment', *Oxford Economic Papers*, Vol. 50, p. 307.

Freedman, C. (1994), 'The use of indicators and of the monetary conditions index in Canada', in *Frameworks for Monetary Stability Policy Issues and Country Experiences,* Balino, T. and Cottarelli, C., (eds) Washington DC: International Monetary Fund.

Friedman, M. (1960), *A Programme for Monetary Stability*, New York: Fordham University Press.

Froyen, R.T. (1974), 'A test of the endogeneity of monetary policy', *Journal of Econometrics*, 2 July, pp. 175–88.

Fry, M.J. (1998), 'Assessing central bank independence in developing countries: do actions speak louder than words?', *Oxford Economic Papers*, Vol. 50, No. 3, pp. 512–29.

Fry, M.J. (1998a), 'Saving investment, growth and financial distortions in the Pacific Basin and other developing areas', *International Economic Journal*, Vol. 12, Spring, pp. 1–24.

Fry, M.J. (1997), *Emancipating the Banking System and Developing Markets for Government Debt*, London: Routledge.

Fry, M.J. (1995), *Money, Interest and Banking in Economic Development*, 2nd edn. Baltimore: Johns Hopkins University Press.

Fry, M.J., Goodhart, C.A.E. and Almeida, A. (1996), *Central Banking in Developing Countries: Objectives, Activities and Independence*, London: Routledge.

Fry, M.J. and Lilien, D.M. (1986), 'Monetary policy responses to exogenous shocks', *American Economic Review*, Vol. 76, May, pp. 79–83.

Fry, M.J., Lilien, D.M. and Wadhwa, W. (1988), 'Monetary policy in Pacific Basin developing countries', in *Monetary Policy in Pacific Basin Countries*, Cheng, H-S., (ed.) Boston: Kluwer Academic Publishers.

'G day Goldilocks', (1996), *The Economist*, March 6, p. 96.

Ghosh, A.R., Guile, A.M., Ostry, J.D. and Wolf, H.C. (1995), 'Does the nominal exchange rate regime matter?', *IMF Working Paper WP/95/121*.

Goodfriend, M. (1986), 'Monetary mystiques: secrecy and central banking', *Journal of Monetary Economics*, Vol. 17, pp. 63–97.

Goodhart, C.A.E (2000), 'The role of the Monetary Policy Committee: strategic considerations and operational independence', this volume.

Goodhart, C.A.E (1994), 'What should central bankers do? What should be their macroeconomic objectives and operations?', *Economic Journal*, Vol. 104, pp. 1424–36.

Greenspan, A. (1993), 'Testimony before the Committee on Banking, Housing, and Urban Affairs, United States Senate', *Federal Reserve Bulletin*, pp. 342–8.

Grilli, V., Masciadaro, D. and Tabellini, G. (1991), 'Political and monetary institutions and public financial policies in the industrial economies', *Economic Policy*, Vol. 6, pp. 341–92.

Guitian, M. (1994), 'Rules or discretion in monetary policy: national and international perspectives', in *Frameworks for Monetary Stability Policy Issues and Country Experiences,* Balino, T. and Cottarelli, C., (eds) Washington DC: International Monetary Fund.

Haldane, A.G., (ed.) (1995), *Targeting inflation*, London: Bank of England.

Haldane, A.G and Read, V. (1999), *Monetary Policy Surprises and the Yield Curve*, London: Bank of England.

Haldane, A.G. and Salmon, C.K. (1995), 'Three issues on inflation targets', in *Targeting Inflation,* Haldane, A.G., (ed.) London: Bank of England.

Higo, M. (2000), 'What can inflation expectations and core inflation tell us about monetary policy in Japan?', this volume.

Hoffmaister, A.W. (1999), 'Inflation targeting in Korea: an empirical exploration', *IMF Working Paper WP/99/7*, January.

Hogan, S. (2000), 'Core inflation as an indicator in monetary policy rules', this volume.

Holbik, K. (1973), *Monetary Policy in Twelve Industrial Countries*, Boston: Federal Reserve Bank of Boston.

Hrnčíř, M. and Šmídková, K. (2000), 'Inflation targeting in the Czech Republic', this volume.

IMF (1999) 'Experimental case studies on transparency practices', Washington: International Monetary Fund.

Issing, O. (1997), 'Monetary targeting in Germany: the stability of monetary policy and of the monetary system', *Journal of Monetary Economics*, Vol. 39, No. 1, pp. 67–79.

Kaminsky, G.L. and Reinhart, C.M. (1998), 'On crises, contagion and confusion', Paper prepared for Duke University conference 'Globalization, Capital Market Crisis and Economic Reform'.

Kennedy, E. (1991), 'The Bundesbank: Germany's central bank in the international monetary system', *Chatham House Paper,* London: Pinter Publishers.

King, M.A. (1999), 'Challenges for monetary policy: new and old', *Bank of England Quarterly Bulletin*, Vol. 39, No. 4, pp. 397–415.

King, M.A. (1998), 'The UK economy and monetary policy: looking ahead', *Bank of England Quarterly Bulletin*, November, pp. 283–6.

King, M.A. (1997), 'The inflation target five years on', *Bank of England Quarterly Bulletin*, November, pp. 434–42.

King, M.A. (1997), 'Monetary policy and the exchange rate', *Bank of England Quarterly Bulletin,* May, pp. 225–8.

King, M.A. (1996), 'How should central banks reduce inflation? Conceptual issues', *Bank of England Quarterly Bulletin*, Vol. 36, No. 4, pp. 434–48.

Kohler, M. (2000), 'The Balassa-Samuelson effect and monetary targets', this volume.

Kohler, M. (1998), 'Optimal currency areas and customs unions: are they connected?', *Bank of England Working Paper*, Series No. 89.

Kydland, F.E. and Prescott, E.C. (1977), 'Rules rather than discretion: the inconsistency of optimal plans', *Journal of Political Economy*, Vol. 85, No. 3, June 1977, pp. 473–91.

Lamont, N. (1992), *The Chancellor's Mansion House Speech,* 29 October 1992. London: HMT.

Landerretche, O., Morande, P. and Schmidt-Hebbel, K. (2000), 'Inflation targets and stabilisation in Chile (1991–98)', this volume.

Leiderman, L. and Bufman, D. (2000), 'Monetary policy and disinflation in Israel', Paper presented at Workshop on Choice of Intermediate Monetary Policy Targets, this volume.

Leiderman, L. and Svensson, L., (ed.) (1995), *Inflation Targets*, London: CEPR.

Lohmann, S. (1992), 'Optimal commitment in monetary policy', *American Economic Review*, Vol. 82, pp. 237–86.

Lybek, T. (1999), 'Central bank autonomy, and inflation and output performance in the Baltic States, Russia, and other countries of the former Soviet Union, 1995–97', *IMF Working Paper WP/99/4*, January.

MacFarlane, H. and Mortimer-Lee, P. (1994), 'Inflation over 300 years', *Bank of England Quarterly Bulletin*, Vol. 34, No. 2, May.

McNees, S.K. (1987), 'Prospective nominal GNP targeting: an alternative framework for monetary policy', *New England Economic Review*, September/October 1987, pp. 3–9.

Maddala, G.S. (1983), *Limited-dependent and Qualitative Variables in Econometrics*, Cambridge: Cambridge University Press.

Mahadeva, L. and Šmídková, K. (2000), 'Modelling the transmission mechanism of monetary policy in the Czech Republic', this volume.

Mangano, G. (1998), 'Measuring central bank independence: a tale of subjectivity and of its consequences', *Oxford Economic Papers*, Vol. 50, pp. 468–92.

Martin, B. and Salmon, C. (1999), 'Should uncertain monetary policy-makers do less?', *Bank of England Working Paper*, series No. 99.

Masciandaro, D. and Tabellini, G. (1988), 'Monetary regimes and fiscal deficits: a comparative analysis', in *Monetary Policy in Pacific Basin Countries*, Cheng, H-S, (ed.) Boston: Kluwer Academic Publishers.

Masson, P., SavastaNo. M.A. and Sharma S. (1997), 'The scope for inflation targeting in developing economies', *IMF Working Paper No. 130*.

Mayes, D. and Virén, M. (2000), 'Exchange rate considerations in a small open economy: a critical look at the MCI as a possible solution', this volume.

Muller, P. and Zelmer, M. (1999), 'Greater transparency in monetary policy: impact on financial markets', Bank of Canada Technical Report No. 86.

Mundell, R.A. (1999), 'Exchange rate arrangements during the transition economies', mimeo.

Nargis, B. and Kent, C. (1998), 'Inflation targeting in a small open economy', Reserve Bank of Australia, RDP 9807.

Ohno, K. (1999), 'Exchange rate management in developing Asia: a reassessment of the pre-crisis soft dollar zone', *ADBI Working Paper 1*, Asian Development Bank, Tokyo.

Okun, A.M. (1962), 'Potential GNP: its measurement and significance', *Proceedings of the Business and Economics Statistics Section of the American Statistical Association*, pp. 98–104.

Persson, T. and Tabellini, G. (1993), 'Designing institutions for monetary stability', *Carnegie Rochester Conference Series on Public Politic*, 39, pp. 53–84.

Phillips, A.W. (1958), 'The relation between unemployment and the rate of change of money wage rates in the United Kingdom, 1861–1957', *Economica*, Vol. 25.

Poole, W. (1970), 'Optimal choice of monetary policy instruments in a simple stochastic macro model,' *Quarterly Journal of Economics*, Vol. 84, May 1970, pp. 197–216.

Posen, A. (1998), 'Central bank independence and disinflationary credibility: a missing link', *Oxford Economic Papers*, Vol. 50, p. 335.

Posen, A. (2000) 'Lessons from the Bundesbank on the occasion of its early retirement', this volume.

Pringle, R., ed. (1999), *The Morgan Stanley Dean Witter Central Bank Directory*, London: Central Banking Publications Ltd.

Quispe, Z. and Mahadeva, M. (2000), 'Monetary policy in a dollarised economy: the Peruvian case', this volume.

Radcliffe Report (1959), *Report of the Committee on the Working of the Monetary System*, London: Her Majesty's Stationery Office.

Reuber, G.L. (1964), 'The objectives of Canadian monetary policy, 1949–61: empirical "trade-offs" and the reaction function of the authorities', *Journal of Political Economy*, Vol. 72, April, pp. 109–32.

Rich, G. (1998), 'Inflation and money stock targets: is there really a difference?', *Paper Presented at International Conference on the Conduct of Monetary Policy*, Central Bank of China, Taipei, 12–13 June.

Rogoff, K. (1985), 'The optimal degree of commitment to an intermediate monetary target', *Quarterly Journal of Economics,* 1 November, pp. 169–90.

Samuelson, P.A. and Robert, M.S. (1960), 'Analytical aspects of anti-inflation policy', *American Economic Review*, Vol. 50, No. 2, May 1960, pp. 177–94.

Sargent, T.J. and Wallace, N. (1981), 'Some unpleasant monetarist arithmetic', *Federal Reserve Bank of Minneapolis Quarterly Review*, Fall, pp. 1–17.

Sayers, R.S. (1957), 'Central banking after Bagehot', Oxford: Clarendon Press.

Schaling, E., Hoeberichts, M. and Eijffinger, S. (1998), 'Incentive schemes for central bankers under uncertainty: inflation targets versus contracts', *Bank of England Working Paper*, No. 88, November.

Simons, H.C. (1936), 'Rules versus authorities in monetary policy', *Journal of Political Economy*, Vol. 44, February 1936, pp. 1–30. Reprinted in *Economic Policy for a Free Society*, Simons, H.C., Chicago: University of Chicago Press, 1948.

Spearman, C. (1904), 'The proof and measurement of association between two things', *American Journal of Psychology*.

Svensson, L. (1997), 'The optimal inflation targets, "conservative" central banks and linear inflation contracts', *American Economic Review*, Vol. 87, March, pp. 98–111.

Volcker, P.A. and Gyohten, G. (1992), *Changing Fortunes: the World's Money and the Threat to American Leadership*, New York: Random House.

Walsh, C. (1995), 'Optimal contracts for central bankers', *American Economic Review*, Vol. 85, pp. 150–67.

Woodford, M. (1996), *Control of the Public Debt: a Requirement for Price Stability?*, Princeton: Princeton University.

Woodford, M. (1995), 'Price-level determinacy without control of a monetary aggregate', *Carnegie-Rochester Conference Series on Public Policy*, 43, December, pp. 1–46.

Yates, A. (1998), 'Downward nominal rigidity and monetary policy', *Bank of England Working Paper*, Series No. 82, August.

Yates, A. (1995), 'On the design of inflation targets', in *Targeting Inflation*, Haldane, A.G., (ed.) London: Bank of England.

Yeager, L.B. (1992), 'Monetary constitutions', in *The New Palgrave: a Dictionary of Money and Finance*, Eatwell, J., Milgate, M. and Newman, P., (eds) London: Macmillan.

Part II
Monetary policy strategies

Monetary policy objectives in emerging markets in light of the Asian crisis

Andrew Crockett

1 Introduction

The Asian crisis has prompted a reconsideration of the issue of how to formulate monetary policy in emerging markets. Many countries have been forced to abandon exchange-rate anchors, and in the process have discovered costly imbalances in their banking and financial systems. These countries are now in the process of seeking an alternative framework for monetary policy. Should this framework involve a return to an exchange-rate target at a more realistic rate? Or the use of monetary aggregate targeting? Or an inflation target? This paper will attempt to explore some of the issues relevant to this choice without, however, recommending a single solution.

2 Policy frameworks in emerging markets

The issue of the choice of monetary policy framework has acquired prominence in emerging markets in response to several recent developments. First, countries that have been forced to abandon pre-existing currency pegs have sensed a need for a nominal anchor to guide market expectations and gain credibility. Second, many emerging markets and transition economies have achieved low and steady inflation and have relatively well-developed financial markets. This suggests that they may be ready to move beyond a monetary policy framework based on exchange-rate pegging to one that exploits their increased control over domestic monetary conditions. Finally, the fact that inflation targeting has generally worked well in those countries that have adopted it is encouraging others to consider whether it could be equivalently effective in their own particular institutional and historical setting.

However, there are important differences among countries, both in economic environment and financial structure. One difference lies in the external shocks to which economies may be exposed. Another is in financial structure, which affects the transmission mechanism that translates economic disturbances to inflationary consequences. And past inflationary history influences the formation of expectations, which are particularly important in determining how quickly an original price impulse is translated into an underlying increase in inflation.

In general, less developed countries tend to have monetary transmission mechanisms that are harder to control. They often have larger agricultural and primary producing sectors, for which prices are set in international markets. They have less well-developed financial systems, so that inflation is less responsive to incremental changes in monetary conditions. And they frequently (though not always) have a history of relatively high inflation. It is useful, therefore, to consider the monetary transmission mechanism in a little more depth.

3   The transmission mechanism of monetary policy

Monetary policy affects inflation through various channels, often classified as the interest-rate channel, the wealth channel, the exchange-rate channel, and the credit-availability channel. The relative importance of these channels can vary depending on the financial structure of the economy. Less developed financial structures may make the effects of monetary policy less predictable. For example, thin markets raise the volatility of money-market interest rates. This reduces the sensitivity of economically important interest rates to the policy actions of the authorities.

The *interest-rate channel* of monetary policy relies on the elasticity of demand and supply of funds to changes in market interest rates. In highly developed financial markets, small changes in the interest rates at which the authorities supply (or drain) the interbank money market are quickly translated into rates paid by ultimate borrowers and lenders. Market expectations about the authorities' future behaviour influence developments at longer maturities along the yield curve.

For a central bank with strong credibility in a developed financial centre, the process may work as follows: With information that the economy is expanding above the rate of growth of productive potential, the central bank may act to raise interest rates in the money market. If the situation of above-normal demand pressure is expected to persist for some time, market participants will reason that monetary policy is likely to remain restrictive, with higher overnight interest rates. Rates will therefore tend upwards along the maturity spectrum for as long as the overheating is expected to persist.

In turn, higher rates are likely to influence demand for investment at the margin, as borrowers in interest-sensitive sectors (housing, long-term investment, inventories) scale back current spending in order to await a more favourable financing environment.

In less developed financial markets, the interest-rate channel will probably not work in the idealised fashion just described. Lack of competition in the banking sector may render lending rates less flexible to changes in monetary policy instruments. This effect may be compounded when state-owned banks play a dominant role in the financial system. Lastly, if securities markets are underdeveloped, one means by which interest-rate policy affects spending and savings decisions in industrialised countries will be cut off.

Similarly, *the asset-price channel*, which can play an important role in generating wealth effects in countries with sizable securities markets, is much less important in countries where financial wealth is more limited in relation to GNP.

By contrast, *the exchange-rate channel* can be very powerful in small open economies. In many emerging markets, it is no exaggeration to say that the foreign exchange rate is the single most important price. It affects not only the price of imports and exports but prices of a wide range of domestically produced and consumed agricultural products whose prices are set in international markets. Expenditure-switching effects tend to be important in small open economies, and wealth effects can result from foreign exchange market developments when households or firms have significant quantities of foreign currency denominated assets or debt.

For countries with inflationary histories, exchange-rate movements can have a powerful effect on expectations. In a number of Latin American countries, for example, domestic prices used to be adjusted automatically in line with movements in the exchange rate, reflecting the fact that currency depreciation is the best single leading indicator of domestic inflation.

The role of the exchange-rate channel in influencing inflation via expectations is a factor that differentiates many emerging and transition economies from more advanced economies. Because of the potential for self-fulfilling expectations (or multiple equilibria), the exchange rate can display instability. This can be a justification for targeting the exchange rate in an effort to brake inflationary expectations. However, if the underlying causes of inflation are not tackled, depreciation is bound to become necessary sooner or later.

The fourth transmission channel of monetary policy is the *credit-availability channel*. This can also be more important in emerging and transition economies than in countries with more developed and diversified financial sectors. In emerging markets, banks tend to play a relatively larger role in financial intermediation. There are fewer alternative sources of finance. The role of credit availability may be increased by the existence of officially sanctioned interest-rate ceilings or by credit controls or guidelines.

The fact that credit availability plays an important role means that the price of credit, and so the influence of conventional monetary policy, is correspondingly less. The influence of monetary policy can be even further reduced by the existence of official development banks, interest-rate subsidies, and government-owned banks. However, deregulation can moderate the impact of these forms of market intervention.

4   The inflation process and economic structure

Quite apart from the transmission channels of monetary policy, the inflationary process itself may operate in a less easily controllable manner in emerging and transition economies.

High past inflation, combined with indexation and weak credibility of monetary policy, can make prices more sensitive to shocks and create unstable inflation expectations. Moreover, exogenous shocks may themselves be of greater importance in small open economies. These factors mean that domestic inflationary forces are less easily kept in check through modest adjustments in domestic monetary conditions.

Another feature of developing economies is the greater importance of administratively controlled prices. If these represent a large proportion of goods and services in the consumer price index, adjustments in them can obscure the impact of monetary policy on underlying inflation. In addition, when prices are being liberalised, inflation can appear high (and lead to pressure for compensating wage adjustments) although in reality what is happening is a one-time adjustment of relative prices.

Emerging and transition economies often have a rather different economic structure than advanced industrial economies. This can have implications for the choice of monetary policy framework. For example, some (though by no means all) emerging markets have a greater concentration of output and exports in a relatively small number of sectors. This can make the economy more vulnerable to sector-specific shocks. Such a consideration reduces the appropriateness of adjustment instruments, such as monetary policy, that have a generalised impact on the whole economy. An example is countries that are heavily dependent on raw material production. Long-term shifts in the real price of raw materials may require corresponding movements in the equilibrium real exchange rate. This can make a policy targeted on the exchange rate, or even the domestic consumer price index, less appropriate.

5   Implications for the monetary policy framework

The key conclusion from the foregoing is that the choice of monetary policy framework will be influenced by the economic environment and the nature of the monetary transmission mechanism. Since countries face different economic environments and have different economic and financial structures, it should not come as a surprise to find different choices of anchor for domestic monetary policy. One size does not necessarily fit all.

Is it possible to go beyond this finding and reach any conclusions about which policy regime is appropriate for a country with given structural characteristics? Firm conclusions would probably not be warranted, but the considerations discussed above do provide some suggestions.

5.1 Monetary targeting

Monetary targeting may have more usefulness in certain emerging and transition economies than in advanced industrial economies. Where other channels of finance are relatively undeveloped (this is often the case in the less developed economies), monetary targets may serve as a proxy for the growth of overall credit. As noted above, the credit-availability channel of monetary policy is likely to be relatively more important in less developed financial systems. Monetary targets can also help discipline the budget, which is at least a subsidiary reason why the IMF typically sets conditions for the rate of growth of monetary and credit aggregates.

A negative reason for emerging economies to stick with monetary targets may be the difficulties of applying exchange-rate or inflation targeting. Exchange-rate targeting has the well-known drawback of causing external disequilibria to build up, if domestic cost-inflation cannot be brought under control. Inflation targeting may lack credibility in a high-inflation environment, thus failing to achieve one of its main objectives, which is to influence domestic price expectations.

Whatever the weaknesses of monetary targeting in economies with advanced financial systems (where the demand-for-money function has proved to be unstable), these weaknesses are attenuated when the financial system is dominated by banks and initial inflation is high. It is a widely observable fact that a durable reduction in inflation is nearly always accompanied by a reduction in the rate of growth of monetary aggregates.

5.2 Exchange-rate targeting

Although exchange-rate targeting has frequently ended in currency crisis, it cannot be denied that exchange-rate pegs have also often been instrumental in braking inflation expectations. It may be the case that a properly managed exchange-rate peg is a useful policy framework for an emerging market at a certain stage in its policy development.

The exchange rate can often have large economic effects in an emerging market. This will be the case when a large part of domestic output is influenced by international prices, or where inflationary expectations are conditioned by the exchange rate. Given the political and economic sensitivity of price changes in low- and middle-income societies, policy-makers may wish to have some ability to moderate externally generated price disturbances.

They are unlikely to be willing or able to manage the exchange rate solely through adjustments in domestic interest rates. This is a key difference from economies with more advanced financial systems, in which domestic interest rates tend to have a more predictable (though still not perfectly predictable) impact on capital flows and the exchange rate. The experience of East Asian countries shows clearly the role of extrapolative expectations in the exchange market, and the consequent risk of exchange-rate overshooting.

There are counter-arguments, however, suggesting that exchange-rate targeting may be less desirable in emerging and transition economies. These economies are more likely to experience relatively large disturbances to equilibrium real exchange rates. Unless domestic costs are highly flexible, which is unlikely, there is value in having some means of allowing the exchange rate to adjust.

In economies with rapid productivity growth, there is a need for real exchange rate appreciation. This can be achieved either through allowing the nominal exchange rate to appreciate, or through a rate of domestic inflation that is higher than that in partner countries. If the authorities prefer lower domestic inflation, they will have to permit a measure of exchange-rate flexibility.

A final situation in which exchange-rate targeting may be unwise is when credibility is weak, and the authorities are unable to take the necessary supporting measures to make the exchange rate stick. In such a case, an exchange-rate target will allow disequilibria to build up and eventually provoke a speculative attack.

Some observers have suggested that exchange-rate targeting can be a useful policy tool in the early stages of a determined anti-inflation strategy, but that it should subsequently be replaced with a domestically oriented policy anchor. There is much to commend this approach in principle. The difficulty is practical: very few countries have been able to formulate a successful 'exit strategy' from fixed exchange rates. While the system is working well, the political authorities usually see little reason to replace it. And when the currency comes under pressure, the authorities are unwilling to accept a policy defeat by abandoning the peg.

All in all, the experience of the Asian and other crises suggest that exchange-rate targeting is a risky strategy. Its usefulness is limited to those cases where the authorities have the desire and the credibility to allow other adjustment channels (e.g. domestic prices and activity) to take the strain of adjusting to external disturbances.

5.3   *Inflation targeting*

There are four broad requirements for the success of an inflation-targeting regime:

- A track record of relatively low and stable inflation, which provides the credibility that enables the announcement of a target to stabilise expectations rather than act as a focus for speculative attack.
- Well-developed financial markets, which allow the authorities to influence the balance of supply and demand in the economy through indirect instruments that bring about incremental changes in monetary conditions.

- An independent central bank that is believed by market participants to have the operational autonomy to pursue the inflation target.
- A supportive macroeconomic and structural environment, in which the budget remains under control and key domestic prices (especially wages) are responsive to changes in supply and demand conditions.

Several emerging market economies have made considerable progress in achieving these preconditions. It may therefore be appropriate for them to consider inflation targeting as a policy anchor.

It is important to realise, however, that this is not an easy policy option. Observed inflation rates in emerging markets are liable to be buffeted by relatively large disturbances. There needs to be a credible strategy to deal with such disturbances, which may include some combination of allowing departures from targeted inflation in certain clearly specified circumstances, and firm monetary policy action in others. As already noted, the domestic economy must have enough flexibility to adapt to a monetary policy oriented primarily at inflation control.

6 Conclusion

It is usually desirable for countries to have a defined strategy, or anchor, for domestic monetary policy. The nature of this anchor may differ according to the circumstances in which a country finds itself. Of the three broad types of anchor, exchange-rate targeting may be appropriate in the early stages of stabilisation or when the authorities are willing and able to use other adjustment mechanisms to adjust to shocks. But fixed exchange rates have well-known drawbacks if these alternative adjustment mechanisms are insufficiently flexible. Monetary targets have advantages when the demand for money is stable and when the credit availability channel of monetary policy transmission is important. Inflation targets have proved effective when the financial structure and central bank credibility are developed enough to be a stabilising factor in the formation of expectations.

In all cases, however, the policy anchor will be successful in achieving low and stable inflation only if the authorities are willing to follow through with the necessary policy decisions, both in the realm of monetary policy and in the realm of fiscal and structural policies.

The role of the Monetary Policy Committee

Strategic considerations

Charles Goodhart

1 Operational independence

When the (new) Labour Government was elected in May 1997, one of the first acts of the Chancellor of the Exchequer, Gordon Brown, was to give the Monetary Policy Committee (MPC) of the Bank of England operational autonomy to vary interest rates, but not goal independence (i.e. the right to set its own target). The objective specified for the MPC was to achieve, by varying interest rates, a $2\frac{1}{2}$% rate of inflation in a selected version of the Retail Price Index (RPI), the RPIX. In effect, this version is the RPI excluding the effects of interest-rate changes themselves, an adjustment achieved primarily by removing most of the effects on the RPI of changes in the cost of housing.

In the United Kingdom, as contrasted, for example, with the Federal Reserve System (Fed) in the USA, the Bundesbank in Germany up till now, and the European System of Central Banks (ESCB) in the Euro-zone, the government has selected, and retains the right to vary, a numerically quantified target. The government may keep the same index to target but vary the chosen numerical objective, or it may choose another price index for its inflation target, such as the Harmonised Index of Consumer Prices (HICP), which is favoured in the Euro-zone. The government also retains the right to change the nature of the target altogether, for example, to an exchange-rate target.

There is a vast literature on arguments for, and a few against, central bank independence. In this paper I will only emphasise the importance of the theoretical analysis that, in the medium and longer run, monetary policy can affect only inflation and other nominal variables such as the exchange rate, and not real variables. It follows from this analysis that in the medium or longer run, the MPC can be held responsible only for achieving a nominal objective, though in the shorter run the MPC can try to maintain a stable path for output while continuing to aim for its medium-term nominal objective. Having a single *quantified* objective greatly facilitates delegation to agents who can then be held accountable, because it is relatively easy to see whether or not the MPC has succeeded in achieving the objective. Quantification is also important because without it legislators will often make 'price stability', or some close synonym, the main objective, but then leave it to the central bank to interpret what that may mean.

While the MPC is different from the Fed and the ECB in not having goal independence, it shares this attribute with a number of other central banks that have operational independence, such as the Bank of Canada and the Reserve Bank of New Zealand.

2 Arguments for goal dependence

There are a number of arguments for keeping the designation and control of the objective in the hands of the elected government:

(i) Central bank officials and members of the MPC are not elected. If they nevertheless determine objectives, something of a 'democratic deficit' results. When the government sets the target, it effectively transforms the MPC into a technical agency, charged solely with achieving an objective that the government has mandated.

(ii) The fact that the government has willed the objective that the MPC is to achieve means that it is much harder for the government to distance itself or repudiate the measures that central bankers feel are necessary to achieve it. When the government sets the objective, it is in effect tied in to accepting the measures chosen by the MPC or central bank as best able to achieve that objective, or else it must explain in some detail why these technical means are inappropriate. This situation should increase and improve co-ordination and co-operation between the government and the MPC. By setting the objective, the government becomes tied in to accepting the means necessary to achieve that end. Thus the effective co-ordination between the monetary authority and the government is likely to be considerably improved when the government is also responsible for setting the objective.

(iii) The fear that the government might set an objective that is in some sense too lax and expansionary, involving too high a rate of inflation, is in my view misplaced. If the government were to announce publicly that it wanted a higher rate of inflation, that information would be almost instantaneously incorporated in all wage and price decisions, so that all the government would achieve would be a higher rate of inflation, with no expansionary effect on output. The argument that there is an upward inflationary bias in monetary policy (the time-inconsistency, or Barro-Gordon, argument) depends on a belief that the monetary authorities can fool the public. This is impossible if the inflation target is set publicly, as is the case in the United Kingdom.

(iv) The existence of a publicly known, quantified objective, set externally by the government, is a major factor in the achievement of transparency and accountability. Wherever there are multiple objectives, and/or objectives are imprecise and not known with certainty, it is much harder to hold the monetary authority accountable for their achievement, and transparency is lost. A quantified *monetary* target will not really suffice to resolve these problems because a monetary target is never the ultimate objective; if velocity should behave in an unexpected way, one would want one's monetary authorities to succeed in maintaining price stability, even if that meant missing a monetary target. On this point see Estrella and Mishkin (1997).

3   Arguments against goal dependence

(i) The most common arguments against having the government set monetary policy objectives are based primarily on a pathological generalised fear of any government involvement whatsoever. Similarly, some believe that the establishment of a target by government actually compromises the credibility of the target, in contrast to the reaction expected if the monetary authority were to set targets for itself.

(ii) Another argument is that the existence of a government-set, quantified, and publicly announced target might decrease the discretionary powers of the monetary authorities, notably in the case of an adverse supply shock. This is a serious point, one that has been addressed in various ways by countries that use government-set targets. For example, should an adverse supply shock occur in the United Kingdom, the MPC would have the ability to allow inflation to go outside the 1% band (discussed later in this paper), and then write a letter to the Chancellor explaining why this is preferable to trying to hold inflation rigidly to the objective initially set.

(iii) The final argument is that neither of the two most successful central banks in the world, i.e. the Fed and the Bundesbank, have had to deal with a quantified numerical objective set by the executive government. If they have been successful without an externally mandated objective, why could not lesser central banks be so as well? Part of the answer is that other central banks were, indeed, historically less successful in target-setting on their own.

4   Governance structure

With its objective set for it by the government, the Monetary Policy Committee of the United Kingdom is free to use its technical expertise to try to vary interest rates so as to make the forecast rate of inflation come exactly into line, on average, with the target. But why give such decisions to a *committee*, which includes outsiders who are not officials of the Bank of England, and not just to the Bank of England itself? Within a corporate body, there has to be a means of reaching final decisions; decisions made by the Bank ultimately are expressed by the Governor. Giving responsibility to the Bank alone, then, would in effect make the Governor solely responsible for monetary policy decisions, as is the case in New Zealand and Canada.

There are, indeed, arguments for giving the final decision effectively to the person of the Governor. This system provides exact clarity of responsibility, leads to greater ease of decision-making, and lessens internal dissent.

There are also, however, a number of arguments in favour of committee-based decision-making. First, when a single person is responsible for a decision, it is arguable that there have been 'too many eggs placed in one basket'. We all have our personal idiosyncrasies, and we all have our various mental shortcomings and other flaws. Moreover, giving the decision to a committee provides a degree of protection for a Governor who might otherwise be exposed to considerable personal and political pressures, and even in some extreme cases to personal abuse. With the decision in the hands of a committee, there is also likely to be greater discussion of different views. Not only is it at least arguable that diversity of views itself is desirable, but the airing of these views provides greater transparency of the inevitable arguments for one course of action or another. Whenever policy is roughly on track, it can be assumed to represent a balance among arguments for the different courses of action. A pretence of unanimity, when in fact the arguments for and against one course or another are surely finely balanced, does not lead to greater public understanding of the issues, or to real transparency of outcomes.

5   The make-up of the committee

Monetary policy is now set by a committee in most countries – for example the Bank of Japan, the Fed, and the ESCB – and where this system is not used, a committee usually offers advice to the Governor, even when the final responsibility rests in the hands of the Governor alone. What, then, is the basis for membership in such a committee? This is perhaps easiest to establish in a federal system, such as the USA or Germany, where membership consists of a combination of presidents of the local regional banks and senior officials of the central federal bank. In a unitary state, however, should membership in the committee be based on representation of certain regions or sectors, such as manufacturing or the City of London? Or should the membership consist of technical experts, who have a comparative advantage in being able to ascertain, for example, the interest rates most likely to achieve the mandated objective? The disadvantage and danger of having *representatives* as members of the committee is that they are bound to give some priority in their decisions to a partial view of the aggregate picture. In the United Kingdom, the membership of the MPC is chosen not in terms of the representation of geographical regions or particular industries, but on the basis of personal expertise. The members of the MPC are individually and personally accountable for their expert ability and knowledge and for applying them in order to achieve the mandated objective.

The members of the UK Monetary Policy Committee are appointed to three-year terms by the Chancellor (apart from the Governor and his two deputies, who are there by reason of their position). The three-year length of appointment has been criticised as too short (by, for example, the Treasury Subcommittee of the House of Commons). One argument holds that three years is too short a time to establish a verifiable track record of successful, or otherwise, voting patterns. Others have argued that three years is too short to enable an appointed member to behave with sufficient independence, if reappointment is to be a possibility. (I must add, however, that personally I have never observed any lack of independence in my colleagues.) There is also the question of whether or not government appointees should also be confirmed by the Treasury Subcommittee of the House of Commons. This issue concerns the relative roles of the executive and legislature, a topic on which an outsider is not in a good position to pass comment.

Another issue is the balance between the number of inside members and external members. In the UK MPC there are five internal officials, that is, from the Bank of England, and four external members. It was once suggested that the internal members would always vote together as a bloc, which might frustrate the ability of the externals to make their case strongly. This fear has been shown to be misplaced in two respects. First, the internal members have not always voted together, and no pressure is placed on them to do so. Second, the ability of any member, whether external or internal, to make the case for a preferred course of action in public, notably through the Minutes, means that every case will get a full hearing, even if it is not supported by a majority of members.

Finally, there is the question of the incentive structure for members. There are very clear incentives to do one's best. Votes are individually recorded, and members have a strong incentive and desire to be seen to get their judgements exactly right. To some extent, the possibility of reappointment after three years may also act as an incentive to seek to record a vote most likely to result in the inflation outcome mandated. Even so, I tend to support the position, most notably presented in the academic literature by Walsh (1995), that there can be advantages in a pecuniary reward. A relatively small basic salary with a potentially large bonus depending on the closeness with which the objective is hit, would in my view be a desirable feature; most central bankers and members of monetary policy committees, however, do not take this view.

6   Accountability of the Monetary Policy Committee

The UK MPC is surrounded by institutional arrangements that enhance both accountability and transparency.

The Minutes are now published with a relatively short lag of two weeks, representing the minimum time necessary to get the discussion of the issues at the MPC drafted with clarity and completeness. Until the autumn of 1998, the Minutes were produced with a longer lag and published only after the subsequent meeting. This procedure followed the example of the Federal Open Market Committee in the USA and was intended to ensure that the Minutes were not just read in order to predict voting in next meeting. But there was criticism that the delay was excessive. One disadvantage of late publication was the occasional difficulty members experienced in giving evidence to the Treasury Committee, since their last publicly *reported* position might be one that they no longer held. The earlier publication of the Minutes, accomplished while memories were still fresh, has led commentators to examine the issues more closely. The Minutes disclose how each member has voted. They also report the substance and general themes of discussion, without identifying any particular theme with an individual, in order to allow discussion to remain uninhibited. (So far I have noticed few inhibitions in my colleagues.)

In addition to the monthly Minutes, the MPC prepares a forecast once a quarter, the gist of which is subsequently presented publicly in the *Inflation Report*. MPC members do not actually run the equations themselves, but work with the staff of the Bank to set the assumptions, explore and examine cases where the equations are not working well, deal with special cases that the equations cannot fully incorporate, and make such other adjustments as are necessary to produce a final forecast with which they, the MPC members, both individually and collectively agree. There may, of course, be cases where some element of the forecast, or indeed the forecast in its entirety, is not acceptable to a member or members of the MPC. Such reservations are noted in the *Inflation Report*, and, if necessary, a dissenting member or members could even have a separate forecast published to indicate where the disagreement lay. In the absence of such disagreements, both the forecast and the resulting *Inflation Report* are the responsibility of the MPC as a whole; the key elements of the forecast and much of the analysis underlying it are presented publicly in the *Inflation Report* and are open to public criticism and challenge. The suite of models and their associated equations have also been published.

In addition to publishing the Minutes and the *Inflation Report*, the MPC is required to appear before both the Treasury Committee of the House of Commons and the recently appointed Monetary Committee of the House of Lords. These committees, which have the benefit of professional advisers, can and do grill members of the MPC for periods of several hours at a time, at least once a quarter. Moreover, the Court of the Bank of England has overall responsibility for ensuring that the procedures and resources applied by the MPC are suitable for the conduct of their responsibilities. Finally, most members of the MPC are appointed by the Chancellor following an Act of Parliament, and the MPC is ultimately responsible to the government for carrying out the mandate it is given.

Taken all in all, the MPC is both accountable and transparent.

7   What goal has the MPC been set?

As indicated earlier, the choice of goal for the MPC remains entirely in the hands of the Chancellor. The general consensus, however, is that monetary policy should aim at a medium-term goal, and that in the medium and longer run the only variables that monetary policy can clearly affect are nominal variables, not real variables. The choice of target should therefore be limited to nominal variables, of which there are many alternatives.

Some (such as Sir Samuel Brittan) would prefer a nominal income objective. The advantages and disadvantages of a nominal income objective, as contrasted with an inflation target, have been rehearsed at length elsewhere and it is not the purpose to continue that debate here. In practice, the Chancellor has chosen an inflation target in the form of a $2\frac{1}{2}\%$ rate of increase in the RPIX for the indefinite future.

Even within the restricted range of price indices and their associated inflation targets, there is a wide range of possible choices, including three RPI measures (RPI, RPIX, and RPIY), the harmonised index of consumer prices (HICP), and more, including variants of any particular RPI index with trimmed or truncated distributions. Without going into the issue of which index might be optimal, it may be worth noting that should a different index be chosen, it would require a commensurate adjustment in the inflation target to maintain a constant monetary policy.

Even so, all the main price indices cover the prices of current goods and services and exclude asset prices, such as the prices of houses, land, and financial assets such as equities. It is debatable both in theory and practice whether it is appropriate to restrict attention to the prices of current goods and services, excluding those of assets. As is well known, the rate of growth of Japanese consumer prices has been both low and stable over the last decade. But it is highly dubious whether Japanese monetary policy could be said to have been exemplary. The bubble in asset prices in Japan from the late 1980s up to about 1990, and the collapse of asset prices during the 1990s, have both seriously affected the Japanese economy, and could be taken as a measure of failings in Japanese monetary policy. But whether asset prices are formally included in the relevant price index or not, all central bankers will keep a wary eye on the development of such asset prices. Exactly how monetary policy might respond to large fluctuations in asset prices, however, remains a difficult and uncertain subject.

There are other difficult issues as well. For example, the Chancellor has required the MPC to hold inflation to $2\frac{1}{2}$% indefinitely. That leaves open the question on what horizon the MPC should concentrate. Because of lags in the operation of monetary policy, the MPC clearly cannot seek to control inflation over the next few months: that is already determined. Nor would it be sensible for the MPC to try to aim too far into the distant future, say more than three years hence: any monetary action taken now would have worked itself out by then, and the future developments of the fundamentals of the economy are too uncertain to try to look that far ahead. In practice, the MPC tends to concentrate on a window of up to two years ahead, 6 to 24 months into the future. Even here there are some difficult problems. The Chancellor has required the MPC to maintain $2\frac{1}{2}$% at all times, but the predicted path for inflation before remedial action is rarely expected to be constant over time, as in Chart 1a. Instead it may look more like the path shown in Chart 1b, which provides $2\frac{1}{2}$% on average but is clearly increasing over time, so that the bias would presumably be to tighten monetary policy to prevent inflation from trending continually upward. But what should the policy response be if the projected path for inflation is as in Chart 1c, where inflation is on average below $2\frac{1}{2}$% over the next two years, but the trend is upward toward the end? Given that the expected path for inflation is likely to show various twists and turns, an effective plan for achieving an exact average of $2\frac{1}{2}$% indefinitely is rarely easy to formulate.

8   Operational issues: the quarterly calendar

Table 1 shows the quarterly calendar for the MPC in the spring of 1999. Each month there are three regular meetings, with the 'Pre MPC' providing a full-day briefing by the staff for the MPC on recent developments that might have a bearing on the future path of inflation. The meetings of the Committee itself are held usually on the Wednesday and Thursday after the first Monday of each month, but these dates can be varied to avoid particular difficulties with the calendar as represented, for example, by Easter and the New Year, or by international meetings that the Governor has to attend. The Minutes are published on the Wednesday a fortnight later. In the month in which the quarterly forecast is completed, a series of about six meetings are held prior to the MPC meetings themselves, in order to agree on the forecast. Several other meetings are held to decide on the wording of the *Inflation Report*, which is then published on the Wednesday following that month's MPC meeting.

9   The importance of the forecast

The quarterly forecast is crucial to the policy decisions made in the month in which it is completed. The timetable during this forecast month is compressed and stressful for both staff and MPC members.

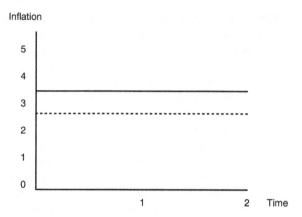

Chart 1a

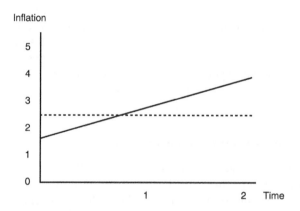

Chart 1b

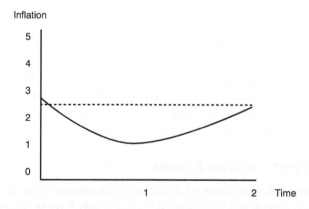

Chart 1c

Table 1 MPC Calendar, Spring 1999

01 Jan 99		**01 Mar**	
04 Jan	**Pre MPC**	02 Mar	
05 Jan		03 Mar	**MPC**
06 Jan	**MPC**	04 Mar	**MPC**
07 Jan	**MPC**	05 Mar	
08 Jan		08 Mar	
11 Jan		09 Mar	
12 Jan		10 Mar	
13 Jan		11 Mar	
14 Jan		12 Mar	
15 Jan		15 Mar	
18 Jan		16 Mar	
19 Jan		17 Mar	Feb. MPC minutes published
20 Jan	Dec. MPC minutes published	18 Mar	
21 Jan		19 Mar	
22 Jan		22 Mar	
25 Jan		23 Mar	
26 Jan		24 Mar	
27 Jan		25 Mar	
28 Jan		26 Mar	
29 Jan	**Pre MPC**	29 Mar	
01 Feb		30 Mar	
02 Feb		31 Mar	
03 Feb	**MPC**		
04 Feb	**MPC**		
05 Feb			
08 Feb			
09 Feb			
10 Feb	**Inflation report**		
11 Feb			
12 Feb			
15 Feb			
16 Feb			
17 Feb	Jan. MPC minutes published		
18 Feb			
19 Feb			
22 Feb			
23 Feb			
24 Feb			
25 Feb			
26 Feb	**Pre-MPC**		

Because of the long lags before monetary policy measures, in the shape of interest-rate changes, affect output and subsequently inflation, it is impossible for the MPC to control current inflation, or at least impossible without such huge changes in interest rates, operating via exchange rates, as would lead to instability in the real economy. So it is not possible to control current inflation, only to forecast inflation rates. But one might ask are not forecasts (i) uncertain (which they certainly are), and (ii) manipulable? Forecasts are, indeed, manipulable in that they are, and should be, subject to off-model judgement, since no formal econometric model can take into account fully the entire range of subjective judgements that those involved in the forecast can bring to bear. Forecasts are certainly not manipulable in the political sense that the numbers are chosen to accord with 'political' preferences of MPC members, if indeed they have any. Any such 'political' adjustment would be (i) *ex post* unavailing and would cause a loss in credibility, and (ii) would be known to too many, and too independent, observers. Any adjustment not made on the basis of rational and reasoned economic arguments would soon become publicly known and would shatter the credibility of the MPC.

The need once every quarter to produce a forecast, therefore, acts as strong discipline for the MPC. If it should appear that the forecast path for inflation will not meet the mandate, then there is pressure on the MPC to vary interest rates such that the forecast can be changed to one in which inflation is brought closer to the target with a plausible path for interest rates. In practice, in its forecast the MPC has followed the convention of taking interest rates as constant from the latest chosen level. However, that path need not necessarily be constant; it could, for example, mimic the forward rates already evident in markets. In so far as the MPC and its forecast are credible, its conditionally assumed path for interest rates and market forward rates should not diverge too markedly.

The main structure and components of the models that are used to make the forecast were exhibited publicly (Bank of England, 1999), so it is unnecessary to discuss the structure and nature of the forecasting exercise further here. In any case it is a large subject, which deserves a paper all to itself. Briefly, however, the forecast is driven primarily by a short-run, sticky wage/price, extended Keynesian model with long-run classical (money neutrality) characteristics. Given the sticky wage/price nature of the system in the short run, interest-rate changes lead to shifts in real interest rates, which have real effects. There are powerful, but inherently uncertain, effects on real exchange rates. Among the many difficult issues involved is the nature of the interface between the longer-term classical and the shorter-term Keynesian structures, especially when the velocity of the monetary aggregates is subject to shifts, as has been the case in the course of the last few decades, so that demand-for-money functions remain uncertain. This uncertainty is especially strong in the other financial intermediaries (OFI) sector, and this is where the main growth (and fluctuations) in broad money (M4) has been in the last few years. Moreover, the money/wealth/consumption nexus is less than completely understood.

A particularly appealing feature of the MPC forecast is that it attempts to emphasise the distribution of outcome probabilities rather than the single most likely point to be reached. It is possible to describe a forecast as an attempt to estimate a vector of outcomes Y in terms of a vector of exogenous and predetermined variables X in the following equation:

Y = bX + u
where u = $N(0,\sigma^2)$ and $E\sigma^2 = K$ (K constant)

In the MPC forecast, $Eu \neq 0$ and $E\sigma^2 \neq K$. The historical variances and covariances are estimated; and at the same time primarily subjective estimates, provided by the MPC as a whole, are made of probable risks and of future variances relative to the estimated past average variances in these econometric relationships.

As is common with most such forecasting models, the equations have been estimated on the assumption of additive, stochastic shocks. There has, however, been a considerable amount of work during the last couple of years on assessing the implications of taking into account Brainard multiplicative uncertainty. (A working paper by Martin and Salmon, and my own Keynes lecture, reprinted in the Bank of England's *Quarterly Bulletin* in February 1999, relate to this subject.)

10   Mean, median, or mode

The existence of skew, caused by the introduction of asymmetric risks into the forecast by the MPC, has the consequence that the mean outcome is not equal to the median or the mode. (The mode is the most probable outcome.) Which should you aim for? This depends in part on your own objective function. Take, for example, the possibilities of missing the inflation target by 1% or by 3%. How do you rate the loss from these alternative deviations? If you regard them as equally bad, because 'a miss is as good as a mile', then you should aim for the mode. If you think that missing by 3% rather than by 1% is nine times worse, then you should aim for the mean. If you think missing by 3% rather than 1% is just three times worse, then you should aim for the median. I am myself a median man.

But the best choice also depends on the circumstances. If the skew is caused by a low-probability event, which, if it should happen, would have a very large effect on the economy, then there is an argument for waiting to see whether that eventuality actually occurs. For example, if the event has only a 2% probability of occurrence but would drastically alter the prospective path of output and inflation, it would seem rather odd to adjust policy in advance to take account of that low-probability/high-effect eventuality. You would prefer to wait, if possible, to see whether the event actually occurred. Also relevant, of course, will be the question of whether the prospective event is one to which it is feasible to adjust after it occurs through a change in interest rates. So, if the main difference between the mean and the mode is due to a peso problem, in other words, a low-probability event having a large effect (e.g. a Japanese financial meltdown) to which one can react *ex post facto*, and the MPC meets every month, there is a case for paying more attention to the mode (see Vickers (1998)).

11 Between quarterly forecasts

The market learns of the MPC forecast from the *Inflation Report*. (The fan charts for prospective output and inflation, as published in the February 1999 *Inflation Report*, are shown in Chart 2.) The market can also be assumed to 'know' the assumed constant path for short-term interest rates; and the MPC runs a subsidiary forecast on the basis of the market's implied expectations for short-term interest rates. In the meantime, the market can interpret 'news' as it arrives and judge its likely effect on our forecast. The market should, then, adjust forward rates to take account of how it expects the MPC to react. If the market is reasonably correct in anticipating the MPC's reaction, then interest-rate adjustments made by the MPC will tend simply to ratify those that the market will have put in place already. As Mervyn King has described, interest-rate adjustments in this case should become relatively 'boring', and that is indeed what the MPC would like to happen.

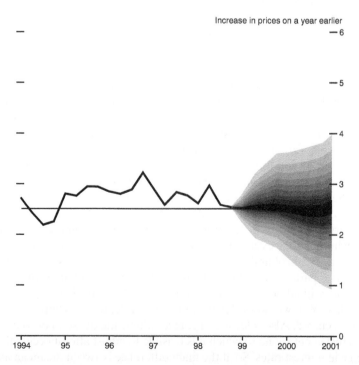

Chart 2a Inflation projections based on constant nominal interest rates at 5.5%

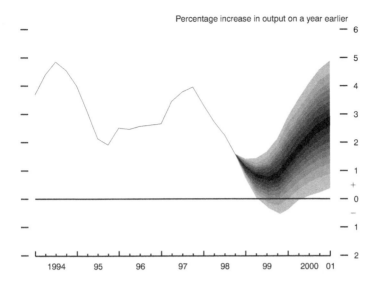

Percentage increase in output on a year earlier

Chart 2b GDP projection based on constant nominal interest rates at 5.5%

12   Instruments

The decision taken at each meeting of the MPC is whether or not to vary the short-term interest rate. All central banks now make the choice of a short-term interest rate their key decision. Once upon a time, there was considerable academic discussion and argumentation about the supposed advantages for monetary policy of deciding, instead, on a target path for the monetary base, and seeking to control this directly via open market operations. That debate has since subsided, and there is now general acceptance that adjustment of short-term interest rates is *the* instrument of monetary policy, with the monetary base allowed to adjust endogenously to allow the system's demand for monetary base money to be satisfied exactly at the interest rate chosen by the authorities.

Some discussion of other potential subsidiary instruments for monetary policy did take place at the September 1997 meeting of the MPC, as reported in the Minutes published in November 1997. The three instruments considered were the following:

(i) Changes in commercial bank reserve requirements (a form of tax on banks);
(ii) Overfunding (although debt management had been transferred to a special subsidiary branch of the Treasury in the United Kingdom); and
(iii) Direct intervention in the foreign-exchange market, either sterilised or unsterilised.

The Minutes of this meeting indicated that there were considerable problems with all three subsidiary techniques. It was noted that intervention could be desirable under particular circumstances, but if undertaken, it should be publicly reported after the event. At the time of the writing of this paper, there have been no cases of use of any of these alternative instruments. Moreover, there has been surprisingly little discussion of these alternatives, either in the press or among academic commentators.

Until June 1998, all changes in interest rates had been increases of 25 basis points. It was explicitly noted in the October 1997 meeting (Minutes published in December 1997) that changes in official interest rates could be of any size, either less than or greater than a quarter percentage point. The fact that all moves between May 1997 and June 1998 were of 25 basis points was happenstance. In late 1998 and early 1999, there were three cuts of interest rates of half of one percentage point, or 50 basis points; on occasion there were dissenting members who would have liked even larger cuts. So it is clear that the MPC is willing to consider rate changes of any size that seems appropriate should a change be required to bring the inflation forecast into line with the mandated target.

13   Should we fail to remain close to target?

When the MPC started with its objective, inflation was fairly close to the mandated target (in June 1997 the RPIX was about $2\frac{3}{4}\%$ above the previous year). Any subsequent failure to stay close to the target would presumably be due to some shock that the MPC had failed to forecast. Shocks of various sizes are inevitable, so at some future point, the MPC is bound to be unable to prevent the RPIX from falling more than one percentage point from the target of $2\frac{1}{2}\%$ on either side. However, the variance of inflation has been falling alongside the decline in the mean value of inflation over the last two decades (see Chart 3). The coefficient of variation for inflation, i.e. the variance divided by the mean, has remained rather stable; the decline in the mean has been associated with an equivalent or even greater decline in the variance of inflation. Indeed, the variance of inflation has fallen to quite remarkably low levels in the course of the last two years. It is possible that this is a beneficial result of the adoption of inflation targeting. But it may well be the case that the variance of inflation has fallen equally in countries that have not adopted inflation targets.

When the MPC misses the target by more than 1% (i.e. when the RPIX goes above $3\frac{1}{2}\%$ or below $1\frac{1}{2}\%$ at an annual rate), the MPC is required to write a letter to the Chancellor. The letter must state what happened and provide the plans of the MPC for bringing inflation back to the target level. No such letter has been required to date.

But if and when a letter does need to be written, it will not necessarily be a sign of failure. For example, the 1 percentage point margin could be breached as a result of actions to vary indirect taxes taken by the Chancel-

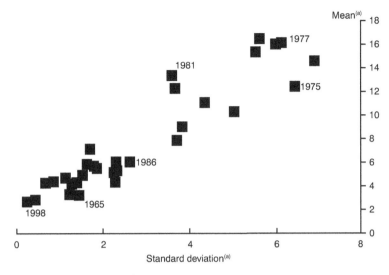

(a) Figures for third quarter of each year

Chart 3 First two moments of RPIX Inflation (1965–1998)

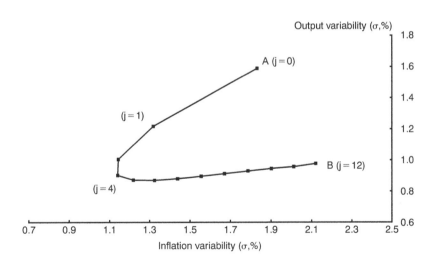

Chart 4 Output-Inflation Volatility Frontier

lor himself. In which case, the letter would simply say 'Chancellor, you did it yourself'. Moreover, There could also be supply shocks, such as oil price changes, the first-round effect of which would be economically undesirable for the MPC to try to prevent. When such supply shocks occur, and indeed whenever inflation deviates beyond the 1% margins, there is a question of the short-run trade-off between the volatility of output and that of infla-tion. In the face of supply shocks, and with monetary policy only taking effect after a relatively long lag, too quick an attempt to regain the infla-tion target would cause greater output variance. On the other hand, too much concern with maintaining stable output over the short run might cause greater inflation variance around the target.

In practice, it seems that technical considerations relating to the lag struc-ture within the economy largely determine the optimal speed of adjustment, i.e. the trade-off between the volatility of output and that of inflation is not smoothly curved, but quite sharply angled toward a rectangular corner solution, as indicated by Batini and Haldane in their 1999 working paper (Chart 4). So the scope for the application of preferences between smooth-ing output and smoothing inflation is probably quite slight.

For the time being the requisite margins have not been broken. Indeed, the stability of inflation around the mandated target level has been quite remarkable, although the extent of stability, and the closeness of inflation to the target, undoubtedly represent a degree of good fortune as well as reasonably good management.

Bibliography

Bank of England (1999), 'Economic models at the Bank of England'.

Batini, N. and Haldane, A. (1999), 'Forward looking rules for monetary policy', *Bank of England Working Paper No. 91*, January.

Estrella, A. and Mishkin, F. (1997), 'Is there a role for monetary aggregates in the conduct of monetary policy?', *Journal of Monetary Economics*, 40(2), pp. 279–304.

Goodhart, C. (1999), 'Central bankers and uncertainty', *Bank of England Quar-terly Bulletin*, February, pp. 102–14.

Martin, B. and Salmon C. (1999), 'Should uncertain monetary policy-makers do less?' *Bank of England Working Paper*, No 99, August.

Vickers, J. (1998) 'Inflation targeting in practice: the UK experience', *The Bank of England Quarterly Bulletin*, November, pp. 368–75.

Walsh, C. (1995), 'Optimal contracts for central bankers', *American Economic Review*, Vol 85, pp. 150–67.

Establishing a reputation for dependability by means of inflation targets[1]

Alex Cukierman[2]

1 Introduction

The recent quest for price stability in conjunction with the breakdown of traditional nominal anchors induced several countries to introduce inflation targets.[3] Under this system of targeting policy-makers preannounce a target or a target range for the rate of inflation. Although some details of the targeting method vary across countries, a common motivation for this arrangement is to influence inflationary expectations early on.

Since deviations between announced and actual rates of inflation are possible and, as a practical matter, are not uncommon, the mere announcement of an inflation target does not generate immediate credibility. On the other hand, the announcement of targets usually has *some* effect on inflationary expectations. This imperfect credibility of inflation targets may be due to the fact that policy-makers are not necessarily committed to achieve those targets. But in the presence of imperfect control of inflation by policy-makers, such deviations could also be due to bad luck. When individuals understand that actual inflation performance is due to a mixture of both elements they give some, but usually not full, credence to preannounced targets. The size of the effect of announced targets on expectations depends on the past record of policy-makers, which I will call 'reputation'. This reputation is valuable because it enables policy-makers to influence inflationary expectations and, through them, real variables by merely making an announcement.

This paper develops a framework that makes it possible to evaluate some of the factors that affect the reputation of policy-makers and the speed with which this reputation is built up or depleted, as well as to identify the effect of reputational considerations on policy choices and on the formation of inflationary expectations. The analytical framework features two basic ingredients that appear to characterise most real life inflation targeting frameworks. First, the public is uncertain about whether the target represents a commitment or is just cheap talk. Second, is that policy-makers possess some but not perfect control over inflation.

The first element is modelled by assuming that there are two types of policy-makers, denoted 'dependable' (D) and 'weak' (W) (or opportunistic), respectively. Both policy-makers possess the same objective function. The only difference between them is that the dependable policy-maker is truly committed to the target he announces whereas the weak one is not and chooses, therefore, his policy actions according to what is expedient *ex-post*, after expectations have been embedded into wage contracts. The public is unsure about the identity of the policy-maker in office and the reputation of policy-makers for dependability is, accordingly, the probability assigned by the public that type D is in office. The second ingredient is modelled by assuming that there is a (white noise) random deviation between the inflation planned by policy-makers and the actual rate of inflation. Differences in dependability between policy-maker types are generally due to differences in the power or ability of policy-makers and to the value they put on being dependable. One of the factors that determines the ability of monetary policy-makers to live up to preannounced targets is the actual level of central bank independence. Although this level is affected by the central bank charter, it is also affected by other less formal and visible factors.[4]

A main objective of the paper is to identify some of the factors that determine the speed and the direction of changes in reputation. This obviously requires a dynamic framework. For simplicity and pedagogical reasons, I focus on a horizon of two periods. Although somewhat limited, this framework captures, in a relatively simple manner, many of the factors that operate in longer time horizons and provides a simple and unified introduction to signalling games in monetary policy. The paper also provides theoretical underpinnings for the view that dependability and the precision of inflation control are often positively related. The first six sections of the paper simply assume that this is the case. The seventh section shows that, when policy-makers are allowed to choose the precision of control procedures, dependable policy-makers often pick more precise control procedures than their opportunistic counterparts. This provides a more solid foundation for the assumption made in the first six sections.

During the mid-1980s Backus and Driffill (1985) and Barro (1986) produced longer time horizon models that provide a dynamic analysis of the evolution of reputation. The model in this paper is aimed at a similar objective but it differs from those earlier frameworks in two basic respects. First, the public's doubts about the nature of the policy-maker in office are due here to the fact that policy-makers do not control inflation perfectly, while in those earlier papers uncertainty is due to the fact that policy-makers are using mixed strategies.[5] Second, unlike in those earlier papers, this paper explicitly features a preannouncement of inflation targets. Incorporation of such a preannouncement in the analysis seems essential for understanding the factors that govern the evolution of reputation under inflation targeting regimes.

Cukierman and Meltzer (1986a) provide an infinite-horizon analysis of the evolution of inflationary expectations within a framework in which the public is uncertain about the relative importance attributed by policy-makers to employment versus price stability considerations, and in which there is imperfect control of inflation. But, this framework still does not feature a preannouncement of targets. The earliest formal discussion of announced targets appears, as far as I know, in Cukierman and Meltzer (1986b).[6] But in that framework the announcement is not a fully free choice variable and the public's uncertainty is about the shifting preferences of policy-makers rather than about their commitment ability, as is the case in the present paper.[7]

The paper's framework makes it possible to analyse the effects of various parameters like initial reputation, the rate of time preference of policy-makers, the precision of inflation control, and the relative importance attributed to price stability versus employment considerations on the equilibrium policies of the two policy-maker types and on the probability of a shock treatment.[8] A sample of results follows. First, better inflation control by dependable policy-makers makes the policy plans of both policy-maker types more conservative. Since, in a wider sense, better inflation control is positively related to the transparency of policy, the broader implication of this result is that more transparency induces policy-makers to make less inflationary policy plans.

Second, the higher initial reputation, the less inflationary the policy of opportunistic policy-makers. The intuitive reason is that, when reputation is high, weak policy-makers stand to lose more from being revealed as weak. Finally, the probability of a shock treatment rises or falls with policy-makers' concern for the future, depending on whether initial reputation is low or high.

The basic model, the equilibrium concept, and the trade-offs facing the two policy-maker types are presented in section 2. Equilibrium strategies in the second and last period of the game and the evolution of reputation are characterised in section 3. Intertemporal considerations and equilibrium strategies in the first period are discussed in section 4. The impact of initial reputation and of other parameters on policy choices and on the evolution of reputation is discussed in section 5. The effect of alternative parameters on the probability of full separation between the two policy-maker types is discussed in section 6. A basic maintained assumption of the analysis in the first six sections is that dependable policy-makers have better control of inflation than their opportunistic counterparts. Section 7 provides deeper underpinnings for this assumption by showing that, if allowed to pick the precision of inflation control, dependable policy-makers often prefer to establish more precise control procedures than their weak counterparts. This is followed by concluding remarks.

2   The model

The common objective function of policy-makers is given by

$$A(\hat{\pi}_1 - \pi_1^e) - \frac{(\hat{\pi}_1)^2}{2} + \delta\left(A(\hat{\pi}_2 - \pi_2^e) - \frac{(\hat{\pi}_2)^2}{2}\right). \tag{1}$$

Here $\hat{\pi}_j$ and π_j^e, $j = 1,2$ are actual and expected inflation in period j respectively, A is a parameter that is directly related to the relative importance of employment versus price stability considerations and δ is a discount factor, between zero and one, that measures the relative importance attributed by policy-makers to the present in comparison to the future.[9] Let π_j be the rate of inflation planned by the policy-maker in office for period j. This rate is implicitly determined by the policy instruments at his disposal. Throughout the paper I treat this planned rate as the policy instrument under his control without specifying explicitly the relation between underlying instruments (like the overnight interest rate) and the planned rate of inflation. The relation between actual and planned inflation is given by

$$\hat{\pi}_i = \pi_i + \epsilon_i, i = D,W \tag{2}$$

where ϵ_i possesses a uniform distribution with support in the range $(-a_i, a_i)$, $i = D,W$, and $a_W > a_D > 0$. The first inequality reflects the presumption that W is less dependable than D, also in the sense that he institutes procedures that lead to relatively poorer control of inflation.[10] Section 7 below provides deeper theoretical underpinnings for this assumption. At least in the case of the dependable policy-maker equation (2) involves, as in Svensson (1997), targeting of the policy-maker's inflation forecast rather than of actual inflation.

The timing of moves within each period is as follows: first the policy-maker announces the inflation target for that period. Then inflationary expectations are formed and embedded into (at least partially) nominal wage contracts. Following that, the policy-maker picks the rate of inflation he plans for the period. Finally, the control error ϵ_i realises and determines, along with the policy plans, actual inflation $\hat{\pi}_j$. The timing of moves is illustrated in Figure 1. At the beginning of the game the policy-maker in office is either D or W and he remains in office during *both* periods. Initial reputation, which is equal to the probability assigned by the public to the event that a dependable policy-maker is in office is denoted by β_1 and is inherited from the past. Reputation at the beginning of the second period (β_2) is determined endogenously as a function of the policy choice and of the realisation of random external circumstances.

Throughout most of the paper I deliberately refer to a policy-maker (or policy-makers) without specifying explicitly whether monetary policy decisions are made by the central bank or the political establishment. In

| Target, π_j^t, is announced | Expectations, π_j^e, are formed | Planned inflation, π_j, is chosen | Inflation control error, ε_j, (j = 1,2) is realised |

Figure 1 Timing of moves within each period

most countries both institutions have some input into those choices with the central bank having more influence the larger its independence.[11] The equilibrium choices of different policy-makers derived below should be viewed as generally arising from the, at times conflicting, desires of the central bank and of the political establishment. One way to interpret the difference between the dependable and the weak policy-makers is in terms of central bank independence. It is well known that, in addition to the letter of the law, this independence is affected by numerous informal relations between the central bank and its political masters that are usually not fully revealed to the public. Since politicians normally feel less compelled to abide by preannounced targets than the central bank the 'dependable policy-maker' can be thought of a central banker that has enough power to abide by the target, in spite of political pressures whereas the 'weak policy-maker' can be thought of as a central bank that cannot resist the pressures of politicians to behave in a discretionary manner.[12]

2.1 Full separation versus gradual learning and the equilibrium concept

By definition, a dependable policy-maker always plans to achieve the target rate of inflation. Hence, under him, any deviation between the target and actual inflation is due to events that he did not expect when he chose his instrument. But the weak type plans to adhere to the target only if this is expedient *ex-post*. Hence, under a weak policy-maker, actual inflation may deviate from the target by deliberate design as well as because of unexpected events. Even when he does not plan to achieve the target, the weak policy-maker need not be revealed as such. This is due to imperfect control of inflation by both policy-makers. But each policy-maker type can influence, *ex-ante*, the probability that his identity will be revealed at the beginning of the second period by planning a higher or a lower rate of inflation, taking as given what the public expects from him and from his counterpart.

Other things being the same, a dependable policy-maker would like to maximise the probability of full identification and a weak one would like to minimise it. But neither of them necessarily finds it optimal to achieve such extreme outcomes. The reason is that, in order to distinguish himself with probability one from his weak counterpart at the beginning of the second period a dependable policy-maker has to disinflate more

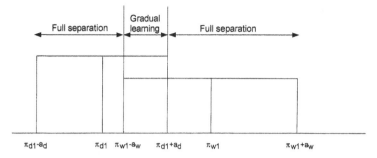

Figure 2 Strategies of dependable and of weak policy-makers in the first period
and the corresponding distributions of inflation

aggressively in the first period and therefore to produce a larger recession.
Similarly, in order to reduce the probability of separation in the second
period as much as possible, the weak policy-maker has to emulate D not
only in pronouncements but also in actions in the first period. And this
involves a current employment cost that he is not always willing to incur.

The trade-offs facing the two policy-maker types in the first period are
illustrated in Figure 2. Given the choice of planned inflation, π_{i1}, by each
type in the first period, the figure shows the *actual* rates of inflation that
could arise under each of them. The left-hand rectangle represents rates of
inflation that could arise under a D type and the right-hand rectangle represents rates of inflation that could arise under a W type. If D is in office
and (actual) inflation falls to the left of the rectangle of the weak policy-
maker his dependability is revealed with probability one at the beginning
of the second period. But if inflation falls in the range of overlap between
the two rectangles there is no sharp separation. In this case individuals
update their views about the probability β using Bayes rule. As will be
shown below, since D has better control of inflation than W, the reputation of the policy-maker in office increases in this case.

If W is in office and inflation in the first period falls to the right of the
rectangle representing the distribution of inflation under a D type, the
identity of the weak policy-maker is revealed with probability one. But if
the realisation of inflation under him is in the overlapping area there is no
sharp separation and his reputation increases in the same manner as it
would have increased had a D type been in office. Since the choice of
planned rates of inflation determines the extent of overlap between the
two distributions each policy-maker can affect the probability of full separation by choice of planned inflation in the first period.

The equilibrium concept I use is a subgame perfect Bayesian Nash equilibrium. For non-game theory specialists, this simply means that at each
stage of the game, each policy-maker type (when in office) chooses his
strategy by taking the structure of the public's beliefs about his strategy

and that of the other type as given, so as to maximise the expected value of his objectives *from that point and on*. In addition, the public updates β by Bayes rule whenever possible and forms its inflationary expectation as the expected value of actual inflation which is conditional on the target announced at the beginning of the period. Subgame perfection implies that we can start by finding equilibrium in the second period.

Figure 2 implicitly assumes that the equilibrium values of planned inflation are such that the probability of full separation is smaller than one, and that the weak policy-maker experiences a trade-off between improving his first and his second-period objectives. Whether this is the case or not depends on the values of the underlying parameters. Here I focus on the case in which the equilibrium probability of full separation is strictly between zero and one and there is some trade-off between W's first and second-period objectives. Conditions on the underlying parameters which assure that this is the case are discussed in part 1 of the appendix and before the end of section 4 below. Those conditions also imply that the policy plan of the opportunistic policy-maker in the first period is more inflationary than that of his dependable counterpart. Further detail appears in part 1 of the appendix.

3 Equilibrium in the second period

In the second and last period the policy-maker in office faces a one-period problem that is similar to the one-period problem with perfect control that appears in Cukierman and Liviatan (1991) and in chapter 16 of Cukierman (1992). Provided his identity has not yet been revealed, a W type always announces the same inflation target as his dependable counterpart would have since otherwise he is unmasked already at the beginning of period two.[13] Such a strategy is individually optimal since full revelation would have curtained his ability to stimulate employment in the second period. Using the superscript 't' to denote an announced target, this implies that:

$$\pi_{w2}^t = \pi_{d2}^t. \tag{3}$$

But since he is not really committed to the target, and since this is the last period, the weak policy-maker chooses his instrument, π_{w2}, so as to maximise the expected value (over the distribution of ϵ_{w2}) of the following expression:

$$A(\pi_{w2} + \epsilon_{w2} - \pi_2^e) - \frac{(\pi_{w2} + \epsilon_{w2})^2}{2}. \tag{4}$$

The solution to this problem is:

$$\pi_{w2} = A \tag{5}$$

which is the well known discretionary solution when the public knows with certainty that the regime is indeed discretionary. The weak type also chooses this rate in the case in which he has been revealed as weak at the beginning of the second period. The only difference is that, in this case, it does not matter (for the public's inflationary expectation) what target he announces since the public knows with certainty that, no matter what he announces, the policy-maker is going to set monetary instruments so as to achieve, on average, the discretionary rate A.

At the beginning of period two the public believes there is a probability β_2 that the policy-maker in office is dependable. Consequently, expected inflation is given by

$$\pi_2^e = \beta_2 \pi_{d2}^t + (1 - \beta_2)A. \tag{6}$$

I turn now to a characterisation of the optimal strategy of a dependable policy-maker. The main difference between him and his weak counterpart is that he chooses the target subject to the dependability constraint:

$$\pi_{d2} = \pi_{d2}^t. \tag{7}$$

More precisely, D picks π_{d2} so as to maximise the expected value (over the distribution of ϵ_{d2}) of the following expression

$$A(\pi_{d2} + \epsilon_{d2} - \pi_2^e) - \frac{(\pi_{d2} + \epsilon_{d2})^2}{2} \tag{8}$$

subject to the process of expectation formation in equation (6) and the dependability constraint in equation (7). The solution to this problem is

$$\pi_{d2} = \pi_{d2}^t = (1 - \beta_2)A. \tag{9}$$

Note that the dependable policy-maker partially accommodates the public's suspicions concerning his dependability and that the degree of accommodation is stronger, the lower the reputation. This is due to the fact that a D type always creates a recession and, given actual inflation, the recession is more severe the lower his reputation.[14]

The choice of equilibrium strategies in the first period depends, among other things, on the difference between the expected, as of period one, equilibrium values of the second-period objective functions in the presence and in the absence of full separation. The expectation of equilibrium values of second-period objectives can be calculated by inserting the appropriate equilibrium strategies into equations (4) and (8). The resulting expressions are:

$$V_{w2}(NS) = A^2\beta_2^2 - \tfrac{1}{2}(A^2 + \sigma_w^2), \quad V_{w2}(S) = -\tfrac{1}{2}(A^2 + \sigma_w^2) \tag{10}$$

$$V_{d2}(NS) = -\tfrac{1}{2}(1 - \beta_2^2)A^2 - \frac{\sigma_d^2}{2}, \quad V_{d2}(S) = -\frac{\sigma_d^2}{2}. \tag{11}$$

Here $V_{i2}(S)$ and $V_{i2}(NS)$ stand, respectively, for the equilibrium expected values of objectives of policy-maker i when there is, and when there is no, full separation at the beginning of the second period, respectively. Note that $V_{w2}(NS) > V_{w2}(S)$, inducing W to try to reduce the probability of separation and $V_{d2}(NS) < V_{d2}(S)$, inducing D to try to raise the probability of sharp separation.[15]

3.1 The evolution of reputation and of inflationary expectations

When the realisations of external shocks are such that there is full separation, $\beta_2 = 0$ if W is in office and $\beta_2 = 1$ if D is in office. When there is no separation, reputation is adjusted according to Bayes' rule which states that:[16]

$$\Pr[D \mid \hat{\pi}_1] = \frac{\Pr[\hat{\pi}_1 \mid D]\Pr[D]}{\Pr[\hat{\pi}_1 \mid D]\Pr[D] + \Pr[\hat{\pi}_1 \mid W]\Pr[W]} \tag{12}$$

where $\Pr[J \mid \hat{\pi}_1]$, $J = D,W$, is the probability that type J is in office conditional on the realisation of the first-period inflation, $\hat{\pi}_1$, $\Pr[\hat{\pi}_1 \mid J]$, is the probability that the rate of inflation $\hat{\pi}_1$ has been produced by a policy-maker of type J, and $\Pr[J]$ is the initial probability that type J is in office.[17] Noting that $\Pr[D] = 1 - \Pr[W] = \beta_1$, $\Pr[\hat{\pi}_1 \mid D] = \frac{1}{2a_d}$, $\Pr[\hat{\pi}_1 \mid W] = \frac{1}{2a_w}$ and inserting those relations into equation (12) yields:

$$\beta_2 = \frac{\beta_1}{\beta_1 + \dfrac{a_d}{a_w}(1 - \beta_1)}. \tag{13}$$

Since $a_d < a_w$, reputation in the second period is higher than in the first one. The speed with which reputation goes up, when there is no full separation, is inversely related to the ratio $\frac{a_d}{a_w}$.

Inserting the equilibrium value of π_{d2} into equation (6), inflationary expectations in period two can be expressed as

$$\pi_2^e = (1 - \beta_2^2)A. \tag{14}$$

4 Equilibrium in the first period

Equilibrium choices in the first period take into consideration the effects of those choices both on the values of objectives in the first period as well as on the probability of full separation at the beginning of the second period and, through this probability, on the value of second-period objectives. The weak policy-maker mimics the dependable one in the announcement of targets in the first period as well and for the same reason. But he picks his first-period instrument, π_{w1}, so as to maximise the expected value (over the distributions of ϵ_{w1} and of ϵ_{w2}) of the following expression:

$$V_w(.) \equiv A(\pi_{w1} + \epsilon_{w1} - \pi_1^e) - \frac{(\pi_{w1} + \epsilon_{w1})^2}{2}$$

$$+ \delta\left[-\frac{1}{2}(A^2 + \sigma_w^2) + \Pr(NS/W)\beta_2^2 A^2\right] \qquad (15)$$

where $\Pr(NS/W)$ is the probability of no separation under a weak policy-maker. This probability is given by

$$\Pr(NS/W) = \frac{1}{2a_w}[\pi_{d1} - \pi_{w1} + a_d + a_w]. \qquad (16)$$

The last term that is premultiplied by δ in equation (15) is a weighted average of the equilibrium values of W's objectives in the second period under full, and under no full, separation where the weights are the probabilities of those two events.

Maximising equation (15) with respect to π_{w1} and rearranging, the optimal strategy of a weak policy-maker in the first period is given by:

$$\pi_{w1} = A - \delta\frac{(\beta_2 A)^2}{2a_w}. \qquad (17)$$

Thus, when the horizon is longer than one period, even the inflation planned by a weak, or opportunistic, policy-maker is lower than the one period discretionary rate of inflation A. The reason is that, in the first period, due to the existence of intertemporal considerations, the weak policy-maker tries to balance the current costs of restrictive monetary policy with the benefits of better chances to maintain his future reputation for dependability. How much π_{w1} is lower than π_{w2} depends on several factors, all of which have clear intuitive interpretations. For example, the difference between the two planned rates of inflation is larger, the larger are the discount factor, δ, and second-period reputation, β_2. The reason is that, when either of those two factors is larger, the weak policy-maker stands to lose more from sharp separation at the beginning of the second period.

Since initial reputation is β_1, inflationary expectations in the first period are a weighted average, with weights β_1 and $(1 - \beta_1)$, of the first-period target and of the rate of inflation planned by a W type. More precisely

$$\pi_1^e = \beta_1\pi_{d1}^t + (1 - \beta_1)\pi_{w1}. \qquad (18)$$

I turn now to the decision problem of a dependable policy-maker in the first period. Unlike his weak counterpart, he is bound by the preannounced target. Therefore, already at the announcement stage, he weights the relative impact of the announcement on expectations and on actual inflation. Inserting the dependability constraint, $\pi_{d1} = \pi'_{d1}$, and equation (18) into equation (1), D's problem is to pick π_{d1} so as to maximise the expected value (over the distributions of ϵ_{d1} and of ϵ_{d2}) of the following expression:

$$V_d(.) \equiv A[\pi_{d1} + \epsilon_{d1} - (\beta_1\pi_{d1} + (1 - \beta_1)\pi_{w1})] - \frac{(\pi_{d1} + \epsilon_{d1})^2}{2}$$

$$- \frac{\delta}{2}[\sigma_d^2 + \Pr(NS/D)(1 - \beta_2^2)A^2] \tag{19}$$

where

$$\Pr(NS/D) = \frac{1}{2a_d}(\pi_{d1} - \pi_{w1} + a_d + a_w) \tag{20}$$

is the probability of no separation when a dependable policy-maker is in office. The solution to this problem is:

$$\pi_{d1} = (1 - \beta_1)A - \frac{\delta}{4a_d}(1 - \beta_2^2)A^2. \tag{21}$$

As was the case with the weak policy-maker, the rate of inflation planned by the dependable policy-maker in the presence of intertemporal considerations is lower than the rate of inflation he plans in the absence of intertemporal considerations ($\pi_{d1} < (1 - \beta_1)A$).[18] The difference between those two planned rates is larger the higher the discount factor and, in contrast to the W type, the lower β_2. The reason for the effect of the discount factor is the same as in the case of W. Since the future is relatively more valuable when the discount factor is higher it pays to invest more in reputation. The reason for the effect of β_2 is that when second-period reputation in the absence of full separation is expected to be low a dependable policy-maker (unlike a weak one) stands to gain a lot from full separation. Note that if δ and A are sufficiently large, a dependable policy-maker may even plan to create a deflation in the first period (in spite of the obvious first-period cost of such a policy) in order to establish his dependability beyond doubt.

The equilibrium characterised above for the first-period planned rates of inflation implicitly assumes that the probability of full separation is smaller than one and that the weak policy-maker faces a tradeoff between his first-period objectives and the desire to hide his identity. I refer to the first requirement as 'uncertain or probabilistic separation'. Part 1 of the appendix presents conditions on the underlying parameters of the economy and of policy-makers objectives under which this is indeed the case.[19]

To sum up, we have established that, given the condition in part 1 of the appendix, the first-period equilibrium strategies of the two policy-maker types, inflationary expectations in the first period, and the dynamic evolution of reputation when there is no full separation are given, respectively, by

$$\pi_{w1} = A - \delta\frac{(\beta_2 A)^2}{2a_w} \tag{22}$$

$$\pi_{d1} = (1 - \beta_1)A - \frac{\delta}{4a_d}(1 - \beta_2^2)A^2$$

$$\pi_1^e = \beta_1\pi_{d1}^t + (1 - \beta_1)\pi_{w1}$$

$$\beta_2 = \frac{\beta_1}{\beta_1 + \frac{a_d}{a_w}(1 - \beta_1)}.$$

Those results are reproduced here for compact reference in the following sections, which deal with comparative statics.

5   The effects of initial reputation and of other parameters on equilibrium strategies and on the evolution of reputation

The main results are summarised in the following series of propositions. The propositions are usually followed by an intuitive discussion of their results.

Proposition 1   *In the case of no full separation second-period reputation, β_2, is higher the higher initial reputation, β_1, and the lower the ratio $\frac{a_d}{a_w}$.*

Proof   By differentiating the expression for β_2 in (22).

The proposition states that there is some degree of persistence in the evolution of reputation. Other things equal, second-period reputation is higher the higher initial reputation.

Proposition 2   *The higher the precision of inflation control under a dependable policy-maker (the lower is a_d) the more conservative the policy plans of **both** policy-maker types in the first period (both π_{d1} and π_{w1} are lower).*

Proof   In part 2 of the appendix.

The response of the weak type is due to the fact that, given initial reputation, a lower value of a_d means that second-period reputation is higher implying that he stands to lose more from full separation. As a consequence, the weak type plans a more restrictive policy when the quality of inflation control by dependable policy-makers is better. Essentially, by raising transparency, better inflation control on the part of dependable policy-makers makes it more costly, at the margin, for weak policy-makers to indulge in achieving their first-period objectives.

The response of a dependable policy-maker to increased precision in his inflation control is a combination of two opposing factors. On one hand the increase in second-period reputation induces him to be more expansionary since he stands to gain less from full separation. On the other hand, the increase in precision also increases the effect of a marginal reduction in his planned inflation on the probability that he will succeed in establishing his dependability beyond doubt. This induces him to be more conservative. The proposition states that the second effect dominates. Hence, the overall effect of an increase in the precision of inflation control by a dependable policy-maker is to reduce the inflation he plans. The broader implication of this result is that more transparency by dependable types induces all policy-makers to be less inflationary.

How does the precision of inflation control by an opportunistic type affect policy plans? The effect on his own policy is generally ambiguous. An increase in a_w triggers two opposing effects on W's policy plans. On one hand he can indulge in more short-run output stimulation by planning higher inflation since the marginal risk he takes of being revealed is lower when his control precision is lower. On the other hand, since second-period reputation is higher when a_w is higher, W stands to lose more from full revelation. This moderates his expansionary tendencies. By contrast, as can readily be seen from an examination of equation (21), the effect of an increase in a_w on D's policy plans is unambiguously positive. This is summarised in the following proposition.

Proposition 3 *A higher precision of inflation control by the opportunistic type induces the dependable type to be more conservative in the first period (π_{d1} is lower).*

Intuitively, for a given policy plan by D, a higher precision of inflation control by W reduces reputation and induces the dependable policy-maker to make a stronger effort to reveal his dependability to the public. Thus, an increase in the transparency of policy plans of weak types induces dependable types to be less inflationary.

The following two propositions report the effects of initial reputation on the policy plans of the two types.

Proposition 4 *The higher initial reputation, β_1, the more conservative is the policy plan of the weak policy-maker in the first period (π_{w1} is lower).*

Proof By using proposition 1 in the expression for π_{w1} in equation (22).

The intuition is the same as that of proposition 2. Since second-period reputation is directly related to first-period reputation, the weak policy-maker stands to lose more from sharp separation. He, therefore, plans a more moderate rate of inflation when initial reputation is higher in order to reduce the probability that he will be fully revealed as weak.

A similar logic would seem to imply that when initial reputation is higher the dependable policy-maker will inflate at a higher rate since he stands to gain less from sharp separation. But this abstracts from the effects of initial reputation on first-period's objectives. As can be seen from the appropriate expression in equation (22) the direct effect (as opposed to its effects through β_2) of initial reputation is to *reduce* the rate of inflation planned by a dependable policy-maker. The reason is that, the higher the initial reputation, the less costly it is for him in terms of first-period objectives to reduce inflation. This is due to the fact that the higher the initial reputation, the higher the impact of the first-period inflation target on expectations and the smaller, therefore, the first-period recession caused by the fact that a D type takes the target seriously. The upshot is that the effect of a higher initial reputation on the planned policy of a dependable policy-maker is generally ambiguous and depends on whether the present or the future dominates his objectives. The following proposition provides conditions under which the impact is positive or negative.

Proposition 5   *The rate of inflation planned by a dependable policy-maker is an increasing function of initial reputation if and only if*

$$\delta > \frac{2a_w\left(\beta_1 + \frac{a_d}{a_w}(1 - \beta_1)\right)^3}{A\beta_1} \equiv \delta_c. \tag{23}$$

Proof   In part 3 of the appendix.

The proposition states that when the future is sufficiently important, an increase in initial reputation induces the dependable policy-maker to be, on balance, more inflationary. The converse holds when the future is not so important (the discount factor δ is below the threshold δ_c). Intuitively, when δ is sufficiently, large an increase in β_1 raises the future marginal benefit of an increase in planned inflation by more than it reduces the current marginal benefit of such an action. And when δ is smaller than the threshold, the opposite is true.

The threshold, δ_c, is a decreasing function of A, implying that when the relative importance attributed by policy-makers to employment versus price-stability considerations is higher, the range of discount factors for which future objectives dominate is wider. This is due to the fact that the future marginal benefit of an increase in planned inflation is proportional to A^2, whereas the current marginal benefit of such an action is only linear in A. Hence, the larger A, the wider the range of discount factors for which future objectives dominate the impact of an increase in initial reputation on the rate of inflation planned by dependable policy-makers.

6   Determinant of the probability of full separation

Due to imperfect control of inflation, full separation, or a shock treatment, as this is sometimes called in the literature on inflation stabilisation, is a random event that may or may not materialise. But policy-makers can influence the probability of full separation via the choice of their planned inflation rates in the first period. The further apart the planned rates of inflation of the two types, the larger the probability of full separation. From equation (22), the difference between the strategies of the two types is

$$
\pi_{w1} - \pi_{d1} = A\beta_1 + \frac{\delta A^2}{2}\left[\frac{1}{2a_d} - \left(\frac{1}{a_w} + \frac{1}{2a_d}\right) \frac{\beta_1^2}{\left(\beta_1 + \frac{a_d}{a_w}(1 - \beta_1)\right)^2} \right].
$$

(24)

Since the probability of full separation is an increasing function of the difference between the policies planned by the two policy-makers in equation (24), it is possible to find the effect of various parameters on this probability by differentiating this equation with respect to each of those parameters. The following propositions report the effect of the discount factor and the degree of 'liberalism' of policy-makers on the equilibrium probability of a shock treatment.

Proposition 6   *(i) The probability of a shock treatment increases or decreases with the discount factor, δ, depending on whether initial reputation is lower or higher than a threshold, β_{1c}, that is given by*

$$
\beta_{1c} \equiv \frac{\dfrac{a_d}{a_w}\sqrt{\dfrac{1}{1 + 2\dfrac{a_d}{a_w}}}}{1 - \left(1 - \dfrac{a_d}{a_w}\right)\sqrt{\dfrac{1}{1 + 2\dfrac{a_d}{a_w}}}}.
$$

(25)

(ii) When initial reputation is equal to β_{1c} the probability of a shock treatment does not depend on the discount factor.

Proof   In part 4 of the appendix.

The proposition implies that when the future becomes more important, dependable policy-makers are more likely to induce a shock treatment when reputation is low than when it is high. The intuition underlying the proposition is as follows. An increase in the discount factor makes the future more important and induces *both* policy-makers to inflate at a lower rate. When reputation is low the reduction in planned inflation by D is larger than the reduction in planned inflation by W because, with a low reputation, D stands to gain relatively more from full separation than W stands to lose from it at the margin. As a consequence, the probability of separation goes up. When reputation is high, W stands to lose relatively more than what D stands to gain from full separation. Hence, when the future becomes more important, W makes a relatively stronger effort to prevent full separation and the probability of such an event goes down.

Proposition 7   *An increase in A raises the probability of a shock treatment if $\beta_1 \leq \beta_{1c}$.*

Proof   In part 5 of the appendix.

The proposition implies that a shock treatment is more likely to be observed when initial reputation is low and policy-makers are liberal in the sense that the relative emphasis they put on employment is high. The proposition reveals the existence of an interesting interaction between the magnitude of A and the size of initial reputation. A larger A implies that the inflation bias is larger so that the incentive of the dependable policy-maker to induce a sharp separation is stronger, and the incentive of the weak policy-maker to prevent it is stronger as well. In general, therefore, the total effect is ambiguous. When initial reputation is small, the first effect dominates since the dependable policy-maker stands to gain substantially from sharp separation and the weak one does not lose much from it. When reputation is high the second effect dominates since the weak policy-maker now stands to lose more from sharp separation than what his dependable counterpart might gain from it.

Note, however, that the condition in Proposition 7 is not necessary. In other words, an increase in A may raise the probability of a shock treatment even when $\beta_1 > \beta_{1c}$. A condition that is both necessary and sufficient is given in part 4 of the appendix.

7   A deeper motivation for the positive association between dependability and the precision of inflation control

To this point, this paper has maintained the basic assumption that the precision of inflation control by dependable policy-makers is better than that of their opportunistic counterparts. This section explores the extent to which the association between dependability and the precision of inflation control is due to deliberate choices by two different policy-maker types and, in the process, provides deeper foundations for this assumption. The intuition underlying such a presumption is that, since they gain from establishing their identity, dependable policy-makers would like to pick control procedures that raise the probability of separation while their opportunistic or weak counterparts would like to reduce this probability since they lose from having their identity revealed. To the extent that an increase in the precision of inflation control raises the probability of separation, D types have an incentive to raise this precision while W types have an incentive to reduce it.

I endogenise the choice of precision by adding, prior to the beginning of the game described in Figure 1, a preliminary stage in which the policy-maker in office chooses the precision of inflation control for the duration of his term in office. In doing that, he takes as given the public's beliefs about the equilibrium choices of both policy-maker types. Note that prior to separation the public does not know what the actual precision is, but it does know the equilibrium individually optimal levels of precision for each policy-maker type. In the preliminary stage the policy-maker in office chooses the precision, a_j, $j = D,W$, taking into consideration this structure of beliefs and subgame perfection. That is, he takes into consideration that, once the choice of a_j has been made, his subsequent choices of first and of second-period planned inflation proceed optimally taking a_j as given. To characterise the individually optimal choices of precision, we first calculate the impact of a change in a_j on the probability of no separation in the first period. From equations (16) and (20), the marginal impacts of an increase in a_j on the probability of no full separation when policy-maker j, $j = D,W$, is in office are given respectively by[20]

$$\frac{\partial \Pr(NS/W)}{\partial a_w} = \frac{1}{2a_w^2}\left[A\beta_1 + \frac{\delta A^2}{4a_d}(1 - \beta_2^2) - \frac{\delta A^2}{a_w}\beta_2^2 - a_d\right] \qquad (26)$$

and

$$\frac{\partial \Pr(NS/D)}{\partial a_d} = \frac{1}{2a_d^2}\left[A\beta_1 + \frac{\delta A^2}{2a_d}(1 - \beta_2^2) - \frac{\delta A^2}{2a_w}\beta_2^2 - a_w\right]. \qquad (27)$$

Differentiating equation (15) with respect to a_w and equation (19) with respect to a_d, and using equations (26) and (27) we obtain, respectively:

$$\frac{\partial V_w(a_w)}{\partial a_w} = -\frac{1 + \delta}{3}a_w + \frac{\delta A^2\beta_2^2}{2a_w^2}\left[A\beta_1 + \frac{\delta A^2}{4a_d}(1 - \beta_2^2) - \frac{\delta A^2}{a_w}\beta_2^2 - a_d\right]$$
$$(28)$$

and

$$\frac{\partial V_d(a_d)}{\partial a_d} = -\frac{1 + \delta}{3}a_d - \frac{\delta A^2(1 - \beta_2^2)}{4a_d^2}$$

$$\left[A\beta_1 + \frac{\delta A^2}{2a_d}(1 - \beta_2^2) - \frac{\delta A^2}{a_w}\beta_2^2 - a_w\right]. \qquad (29)$$

Equations (28) and (29) represent, respectively, the marginal impacts of a change in the own precision of inflation control on the expected value of objectives of each of the two policy-maker types. In principle there could be four types of solutions. In one, the equilibrium values of both a_d and a_w are internal; and, in another, both of them are equal to the minimal technologically feasible value of a denoted $\underline{a}$.[21] It is also conceivable that either $a_d = \underline{a}$ and the solution for a_w is internal, or that the reverse configuration holds. A full characterisation of the mapping from parameter values to types of equilibrium solutions is beyond the scope of this paper. But even without doing that, it is possible to establish that there is a reasonably strong presumption that the opportunistic policy-maker chooses less precise control procedures than his dependable counterpart. More precisely, I show below that this is always the case when the equilibrium solutions for the levels of inflation control are internal and that it is also the case for a whole range of parameter values when the dependable policy-maker picks the highest possible level of precision that is technologically feasible.[22]

Assuming that the exogenous parameters are such that there are positive internal equilibrium solutions for both a_d and a_w equations (28) and (29) can be equated to zero and rearranged to yield the (implicit) reaction functions of the two policy-makers' types in the (a_d, a_w) space:[23]

$$a_w^3 = \frac{3}{2} \frac{\delta}{1+\delta} (A\beta_2)^2 \left[A\beta_1 + \frac{\delta A^2}{4a_d}(1 - \beta_2^2) - \frac{\delta A^2}{a_w}\beta_2^2 - a_d \right]$$

$$\equiv \frac{3}{2} \frac{\delta}{1+\delta} (A\beta_2)^2 N_w \tag{30}$$

and

$$a_d^3 = \frac{3}{2} \frac{\delta}{1+\delta} A^2(1 - \beta_2^2) \left[\frac{\delta A^2}{2a_w} \beta_2^2 + a_w - A\beta_1 - \frac{\delta A^2}{2a_d}(1 - \beta_2^2) \right]$$

$$\equiv \frac{3}{2} \frac{\delta}{1+\delta} A^2(1 - \beta_2^2) N_d. \tag{31}$$

Although those two equations do not provide explicit solutions for each precision level in terms of the precision level of the other policy-maker they determine implicitly (along with equation (13) for β_2) the equilibrium levels of inflation control by the two policy-maker types.

Proposition 8   *When the equilibrium solutions for a_d and for a_w are internal the equilibrium level of a_w is larger than that of a_d.*

Proof Since the solutions for a_d and for a_w are internal N_d and N_w are both positive, which implies:

$$\frac{\delta A^2}{2a_w} \beta_2^2 + a_w > A\beta_1 + \frac{\delta A^2}{2a_d} (1 - \beta_2^2)$$

and

$$A\beta_1 + \frac{\delta A^2}{4a_d} (1 - \beta_2^2) > \frac{\delta A^2}{a_w} \beta_2^2 + a_d.$$

The last two equations imply that

$$\frac{\delta A^2}{2a_w} \beta_2^2 + a_w > \frac{\delta A^2}{a_w} \beta_2^2 + a_d. \tag{32}$$

Equation (32) is satisfied only if $a_w > a_d$.

When the exogenous parameters are such that the dependable policy-maker chooses the corner solution at $\underline{a}$ it can be shown that, provided initial reputation and $\underline{a}$ are both sufficiently small, the equilibrium level of a_w is larger than $\underline{a}$. Those conditions are jointly sufficient but not necessary. Together with Proposition 8, this result supports the presumption that, in a non-negligible number of cases, dependable policy-makers have an incentive to choose more precise inflation control procedures than their weak or opportunistic counterparts. In summary, the underlying basic intuition is that, by choosing less precise control procedures, weak policy-makers reduce the (undesirable to them) probability of being revealed as weak. Conversely, by choosing more precise control procedures, dependable policy-makers raise the (desirable to them) probability of being revealed as dependable.

8 Concluding remarks

An important general lesson of the paper is that, in the presence of intertemporal considerations, the policies of both types of policy-makers depend on the level of reputation and on the relative precision of inflation control by different types of policy-makers.[24] In particular the higher the transparency of policy plans under a dependable policy-maker (i.e. the tighter his control of inflation), the more conservative the policy plans of the two policy-maker types. The broader implication of this result is that better precision of inflation control induces less inflationary policies. The paper also establishes a theoretical presumption for the view that dependability and the precision of inflation control are often positively related. This is basically due to the fact that, dependable policy-makers like to raise the probability of being revealed as such, whereas opportunistic policy-makers like to reduce the probability of being revealed as opportunistic or weak, since this ruins their reputation and destroys the effectiveness of inflation targets as a device for influencing expectations.

The paper also contains results concerning the speed with which dependability is built up or depleted. There are two cases. When there is no sharp separation and learning is gradual, the speed of learning is directly proportional to the relative precision of inflation control by dependable policy-makers. The speed of learning is also higher on average as the probability of sharp separation increases, which depends in turn on the policy plans of the different policy-maker types. When reputation is sufficiently low, an increased concern for the future (an increase in the discount factor), raises, or reduces, the probability of sharp separation and with it the average speed of learning, depending on whether initial reputation is low or high. The results depend on the level of initial reputation for the following reasons. By making the future more important, an increase in the discount factor motivates both policy-maker types to be less inflationary. When reputation is low, the incentive of the dependable policy-maker to moderate inflation is larger than that of his weak counterpart since he stands to gain a lot from a sharp separation while the weak type does not risk much in terms of lost reputation. The exact opposite is true when initial reputation is sufficiently high since, in this case, the dependable type has little to gain, and the weak one has a lot to loose, from sharp separation.

More broadly, those results imply that, when policy-makers become more concerned with the future, shock treatments are more likely if initial reputation is low, and that gradual stabilisations are more likely to be observed when initial reputation is already non-negligible. Stabilisation of many high inflations in Latin America during the eighties appear to fit the first pattern and many episodes of inflation stabilisation in developed economies seem to fit the second one.[25]

Another result is that a higher initial level of reputation moderates the inflationary tendencies of weak policy-makers. The broader implication is that, once reputation has been established, even an opportunistic policy-maker may find it expedient to deliver a reasonably low level of inflation. Furthermore, to the extent that government involvement in the public setting of inflation targets increases initial reputation, the above-mentioned result implies that such an involvement moderates inflation when monetary policy-makers are not dependable.

Melnick and Liviatan (1998) have recently documented the fact that the inflationary process in Israel tends to behave as a step function. The type of model proposed here may be used to 'explain' such steps in terms of full separation of the policy-maker type due to lucky or unlucky random economic events. More precisely as long as shocks are small, there is no full separation – reputation changes in relatively small increments and so does policy.

As a consequence inflation remains within the 'same step'. But when there is a sufficiently extreme shock full separation occurs triggering a jump in both planned and actual inflation. Recall from equation (22) that the policies of both policy-makers depend on reputation. When there is a dependable policy-maker in office and he happens to experience a 'lucky' downward shock to inflation, his identity is fully revealed, inducing him to also adjust planned inflation downward in a stepwise fashion. Similarly, when there is a weak policy-maker in office, and he happens to experience an 'unlucky' upward shock to inflation his identity, and therefore the discretionary nature of policy, is fully revealed, inducing him to fully indulge in discretionary policies. This creates an upward step in the rate of inflation. Thus, under a weak policy-maker, an unlucky inflationary draw can push inflation to a self-fulfilling higher step and, under a dependable policy-maker, a lucky inflation draw can pull inflation to a self-fulfilling lower step.

I have assumed that policy-makers announce a point target. In practice, a target range rather than a point target is often announced. Note, however, that individuals in the model understand that the point target that is announced really means that actual inflation falls within some range. Thus the point target is interpreted, in any case, by individuals in the model as a range.[26]

To preserve analytical simplicity I have restricted the supports of the control errors to finite ranges by assuming that they possess uniform distributions. Had those supports been unbounded, as in the case with normal distributions, for example, full separation would not have been possible and the area of gradual learning in Figure 2 would stretch over the entire range between minus and plus infinity. Although the uniform distribution assumption may therefore be construed as a limitation of the model, I believe it should not be taken too seriously for two reasons. First, the uniform distribution can always be sufficiently stretched out to approximate a wide support. Perhaps more importantly, it is likely that, as a rule of thumb, individuals treat very low and very high levels of reputation, respectively, as full reputation and no reputation at all, even if Bayes formula implies that reputation has not quite reached the extreme values of one and zero. Thus, uniform distributions may better describe the actual evolution of individual beliefs than distributions with full supports.

To preserve analytical simplicity, I also have taken the level of inflation planned by each policy-maker to be the 'policy instrument'. Since, currently, many central banks use some short-term interest as the main policy instrument, it would be interesting to map the level of planned inflation from this paper into an interest-rate instrument. Such a formulation would hopefully make it possible to derive propositions on some of the basic factors that influence the difference in the interest-rate policy of different policy-maker types. Since it would have to recognise the potential role of the interest rate as a signal of dependability, such a reformulation is not likely to be an immediate extension of this paper and is left for future work.

9   APPENDIX

9.1   Statement and derivation of a condition for probabilistic separation and for the existence of a trade-off between W's first and second-period objectives

Claim: (i) A sufficient condition for probabilistic separation and for the existence of an equilibrium trade-off between W's first and second-period objectives is:

$$a_d + a_w + \frac{\delta A^2}{2a_w} \beta_2^2 > \beta_1 A + \frac{\delta A^2}{4a_d} (1 - \beta_2^2) > a_w - a_d + \frac{\delta A^2}{2a_w} \beta_2^2 \qquad (33)$$

where

$$\beta_2^2 = \frac{\beta_1^2}{\left(\beta_1 + \dfrac{a_d}{a_w}(1 - \beta_1)\right)^2}.$$

(ii) The condition in equation (33) implies $\pi_{w1} - \pi_{d1} > a_w - a_d > 0$.
Proof   (i) After some rearrangement, the left-hand inequality implies (using the equilibrium expressions for π_{w1} and for π_{d1} in equation 22)

$$\pi_{w1} - a_w < \pi_{d1} + a_d.$$

This inequality, in conjunction with Figure 2, implies that the probability of separation is smaller than one. In other words, there is probabilistic separation.

Rearrangement of the right-hand inequality in equation (33) and use of the equilibrium expression for π_{d1} yields

$$\pi_{w1} - a_w > \pi_{d1} - a_d. \qquad (34)$$

Equation (34) in conjunction with Figure 2 implies that W faces an equilibrium trade-off between his first-period and second-period objectives. For if he did not, he would have reduced π_{w1} at least down to the level of $\pi_{d1} - a_d$ in order to reduce the probability of being revealed as weak.

(ii) The result follows by rearrangement of the right-hand inequality in equation (33) and by use of the expressions for π_{d1} and for π_{w1} in equation (22).

9.2   Proof of proposition 2

The effect of a_d on π_{w1} follows from direct examination of the expression for π_{w1} in equation (22). Differentiating the expression for π_{d1} in equation (22) with respect to a_d and rearranging:

$$\frac{\partial \pi_{d1}}{\partial a_d} = \frac{\delta A^2 (1 - \beta_1)}{4 a_d a_w \left(\beta_1 + (1 - \beta_1)\dfrac{a_d}{a_w}\right)^2} \left[(1 - \beta_2)\beta_1 + \frac{a_d}{a_w}(1 - \beta_1)\right].$$

Since this expression is unambiguously positive a decrease in a_d reduces π_{d1}.

9.3 Proof of proposition 5

Differentiating the equilibrium expression for π_{d1} from equation (22) with respect to β_1

$$\frac{\partial \pi_{d1}}{\partial \beta_1} = A\left(\frac{\delta A \beta_1}{2a_w\left(\beta_1 + (1 - \beta_1)\dfrac{a_d}{a_w}\right)^3} - 1\right).$$

Rearrangement shows that this expression is negative, zero or positive as δ is smaller than, equal to, or larger than δ_c in equation (23).

9.4 Proof of proposition 6

Differentiating equation (24) with respect of δ,

$$\frac{\partial(\pi_{w1} - \pi_{d1})}{\partial \delta} = \frac{A^2}{2}\left[\frac{1}{2a_d} - \left(\frac{1}{a_w} + \frac{1}{2a_d}\right)\frac{\beta_1^2}{\left(\beta_1 + \dfrac{a_d}{a_w}(1 - \beta_1)\right)^2}\right].$$

Rearrangement of this expression reveals that the difference $\pi_{w1} - \pi_{d1}$ is an increasing or decreasing function of δ depending on whether β_1 is smaller or larger than β_{1c}. When $\beta_1 = \beta_{1c}$ this difference is independent of δ.

9.5 Proof of proposition 7 and an extension

(1) Differentiating equation (24) with respect to A

$$\frac{\partial(\pi_{w1} - \pi_{d1})}{\partial A} = \beta_1 + \delta A\left[\frac{1}{2a_d} - \left(\frac{1}{a_w} + \frac{1}{2a_d}\right)\frac{\beta_1^2}{\left(\beta_1 + \dfrac{a_d}{a_w}(1 - \beta_1)\right)^2}\right].$$

(35)

The proof of proposition 5 implies that if $\beta_1 \leq \beta_{1c}$ the term in brackets on the right-hand side of (35) is non-negative. It follows that, for $\beta_1 \leq \beta_{1c}$, an increase in A raises the probability of separation.

A necessary and sufficient condition for the probability of a shock treatment to increase in A is (rearranging equation (35)):

$$\frac{1}{2a_d} - \left(\frac{1}{a_w} + \frac{1}{2a_d}\right)\frac{\beta_1^2}{\left(\beta_1 + \dfrac{a_d}{a_w}(1 - \beta_1)\right)^2} + \frac{\beta_1}{\delta A} > 0.$$

Notes

1 Reprinted with minor changes from: Economics of Governance, February 2000.

2 The Eitan Berglas School of Economics, Tel Aviv University, Tel Aviv 69978, Israel and Center, Tilburg University, 5000 LE, Tilburg, The Netherlands. I am grateful to two anonymous referees, to Nissan Liviatan and to Carmit Segal for useful suggestions. Earlier versions of this paper were presented at the Bank of Israel conference on 'Inflation, macroeconomic policy, and the transmission mechanism', July 1998, at the CCBS academic workshop on 'Intermediate policy targets in developing, industrialized and transitional economies', Bank of England, November 1998 and at the European Central Bank. E-mail: alexcuk@ccsg.tau.ac.il

3 Those include, among others, Canada, the UK, New Zealand, Australia, Spain, Sweden, Finland and Israel. Extensive descriptions of recent country experiences with inflation targeting and related issues appear in Leiderman and Svensson (1995), Haldane (1995) and in Bernanke *et al.* (1999).

4 The formal model is closely related to that in Cukierman, 1995, which is, in turn, a hybrid of the framework in Cukierman and Liviatan (1991) (or chapter 16 of Cukierman (1992)) and Cukierman and Liviatan (1992). The two middle references contain a more detailed discussion of possible reasons for the difference in commitment ability between the two policy-maker types. See also section 3 of chapter 8 in Walsh (1998).

5 Personally, I find the notion that the public is uncertain about the nature of policy-makers because they do not exercise perfect control over inflation more realistic than the notion that this is due to strategic randomisation by policy-makers.

6 From an analytical point of view, this paper is an extension of Cukierman and Meltzer (1986a) to the case in which the policy-maker makes a noisy, but unbiased, announcement of inflation in each period. An in depth treatment and comparison of those various alternative frameworks appears in chapters 8, 9, 10, and 14 of Cukierman (1992).

7 A discussion of the consequences of this distinction appears in chapter 16 of Cukierman (1992). See also Vickers (1986).

8 A shock treatment is a situation in which a dependable policy-maker deliberately plans to reduce inflation by a lot in order to establish his commitment ability with the public beyond any doubt. Such a strategy is sometimes also referred to as 'cold turkey'.

9 More precisely, A is the product of this relative preference with the slope of the short-run Phillips trade-off.

10 As we shall see later this presumption implies that the average level of inflation and its uncertainty are positively related. This implication is consistent with a lot of empirical evidence.

11 A detailed analysis of the effect of independence on policy choices under imperfect information appears in chapter 18 of Cukierman (1992).

12 The current relationship (1998/99) between the Bank of Israel and the Israeli government can be reasonably characterised in these terms.

13 See also endnote 14 below.

14 Note that this choice of strategy by D relies on the presumption, embedded in equation (6), that whenever he reduces the announced target by 1% inflationary expectations go down by β_2%. An off-equilibrium assumption that supports this choice by D, is

$$\pi_j^e = \begin{cases} \beta_j \pi_j^t + (1 - \beta_j)A, & if \ \pi_j^t \geq \pi_{dj} \\ \pi_{wj} & if \ \pi_j^t < \pi_{dj} \end{cases}$$

where π_{dj} is the equilibrium strategy of D in period j and $j = 1,2$. This assumption states that, as long as the announced target is above the (publicly known) equilibrium strategy of D, inflationary expectations are formed as an appropriate weighted average of the rates of inflation expected from D and from W, respectively. But, if the target is over-ambitious in the sense that it is even lower than the inflation expected from a dependable type, the public concludes that such an announcement could have come only from an opportunistic type who does not intend to live up to the target. The public expects, therefore, the higher inflation rate, π_{wj} in this case.

Notice that this off-equilibrium assumption also supports W's strategy to always announce the same target as his dependable counterpart. At first blush it would seem that since the announcement does not commit him, W should announce a zero inflation. But the off-equilibrium assumption above makes this choice undesirable since the public's expectation reverts to π_{wj}, for any announced target below π_{dj}, raising rather than reducing inflationary expectations.

15 I am using the terms 'separation' and 'full separation' interchangeably.

16 A statement of Bayes' theorem can be found in most texts on statistical theory. See for example pp. 55–8 of DeGroot (1975).

17 The more statistically inclined reader should replace the term 'probability' everywhere in this sentence by the term: 'probability density'.

18 In the absence of intertemporal considerations $\delta = 0$ so that $\pi_{d1} = (1 - \beta_1)A$.

19 For other ranges of values of the underlying parameters, equilibrium may be of the conventional separating variety in which the probability of separation is one. Depending on parameter values, the weak policy-maker may or may not face a trade-off between his first period objectives and the desire to minimise the probability of being revealed *even when the probability of separation is smaller than one*. I focus here on the first type of equilibrium since it seems to be the most relevant for understanding reality.

20 Note that those marginal impacts include only the non-expectational effects of a_j on the probability of no separation since each policy-maker type takes the public's beliefs regarding a_d and a_w, and therefore also about the choices of π_{d1} and π_{w1}, as given. In other words, those marginal impacts include, besides the direct effect of a change in a_j on the probability of separation, only the effect via the subsequent adjustment in the first period planned rates of inflation π_{j1}, by each type.

21 Although in practice $\underline{a}$ is probably strictly positive nothing in the analysis precludes it from being 0.

22 One may wonder why it does not always pay D to choose $\underline{a}$. The reason is that, for uniform distributions of ϵ_i, the choice of a lower value of a given the strategy and the precision of inflation control by the weak type does not always increase the probability of full separation for the dependable type. It does increase it when, as is the case in Figure 2, the equilibrium policies of the two types are sufficiently distant from each other. More precisely when $\pi_{d1} < \pi_{w1} - a_w$. But when the reverse inequality holds, a decrease in a_d is counterproductive from D's point of view since it reduces his chances to fully separate himself from his opportunistic counterpart.

23 This assumption implies that N_d and N_w are both positive.

24 This contrasts with a single period model in which only the policy of dependable policy-makers depends on reputation (see section 3).

25 'Cold turkey' Latin American stabilisations during the 1980s and the 1985 'shock' Israeli stabilisation are discussed in Bruno *et al.* (1988) and in Cukierman, Kiguel and Liviatan (1992). The work of Ball (1994), (1997) suggests that the stabilisation of inflation in many developed economies has been substantially more gradual. A related discussion regarding the factors that affect the choice of stabilisation type appear in Cukierman and Liviatan (1992).
26 Additional discussion of the relative merits of a point target versus a target range appears in chapter 12 of Bernanke *et al.* (1999).

Bibliography

Backus, D. and Driffill, J. (1985), 'Inflation and reputation', *American Economic Review*, 75, pp. 530–38.

Ball, L.N. (1994), 'What determines the sacrifice ratio?' in Mankiw, G.N. (ed.) *Monetary Policy*, Chicago, University of Chicago Press.

Ball, L.N. (1997), 'Disinflation and the NAIRU', in Romer, C.D. and Romer, D.H. (eds) *Reducing Inflation: Motivation and Strategy*, University of Chicago Press, Chicago.

Barro, R.J. (1986), 'Reputation in a model of monetary policy with incomplete information', *Journal of Monetary Economics*, 17, pp. 3–20.

Bernanke, B.S., Laubach, T., Mishkin, F.S. and Posen, A.S. (1999), *Inflation Targeting – Lessons from the International Experience*, Princeton University Press, Princeton, NJ.

Bruno, M., Di Tella, G., Dornbusch, R. and Fischer, S. (eds) (1988), *Inflation Stabilization: The Experience of Israel, Argentina, Brazil, Bolivia and Mexico*, MIT Press. Cambridge, MA.

Cukierman, A. (1992), *Central Bank Strategy, Credibility and Independence: Theory and Evidence*, MIT Press. Cambridge, MA.

Cukierman, A. (1995), 'Towards a systematic comparison between inflation and monetary targets' in Leiderman, L. and Svensson, L. (eds) *Inflation Targets*, CEPR. London.

Cukierman, A. and Liviatan, N. (1991), 'Optimal accommodation by strong policymakers under incomplete information', *Journal of Monetary Economics*, 27, 1 January, pp. 99–127.

Cukierman, A. and Liviatan, N. (1992), 'The dynamics of optimal gradual stabilizations', *The World Bank Economic Review*, 6 September, pp. 439–58.

Cukierman, A., Kiguel, M. and Liviatan, N. (1992), 'How much to commit to an exchange rate rule? Balancing credibility and flexibility', *Revista de Analisis Economico*, 7, June, pp. 73–90. Reprinted in Siklos, P. (ed.) *Varieties of Monetary Reforms*, Kluwer Academic Publishers, 1994.

Cukierman, A. and Meltzer, A. (1986a), 'A theory of ambiguity, credibility and inflation under discretion and asymmetric information', *Econometrica*, 54, September, pp. 1099–128.

Cukierman, A. and Meltzer, A. (1986b), 'The credibility of monetary announcements', in Neumann, M.J.M. (ed.) *Monetary Policy and Uncertainty*, Nomos-Verlagsgesellschaft, Baden-Baden, pp. 39–68.

De Groot, M.H. (1975), *Probability and Statistics*, Addison-Wesley Publishing Company.

Haldane, A.G. (1995), *Targeting Inflation*, Bank of England, London.

Leiderman, L. and Svensson, L.E.O. (1995), *Inflation Targets*, CEPR, London.

Liviatan, N. and Melnick, R. (1998), 'Inflation and disinflation by steps in Israel', Discussion Paper No. 98.01, Research Department, Bank of Israel, January.

Svensson, L.E.O. (1997), 'Inflation forecast targeting: implementing and monitoring inflation targets', *European Economic Review*, 41, pp. 1111–46.

Vickers, J. (1986), 'Signalling in a model of monetary policy with incomplete information', *Oxford Economic Papers*, 38, pp. 443–55.

Walsh, C.E. (1998), *Monetary Theory and Policy*, The MIT Press, Cambridge MA.

Part III

Transmission mechanisms and monetary frameworks

Modelling the transmission mechanism of monetary policy in the Czech Republic

Lavan Mahadeva
and Kateřina Šmídková[1]

1 Introduction

In December 1997, the Czech Republic became the first transitional economy to adopt an inflation-targeting (IT) framework for its monetary policy. This was an important change in monetary policy procedure. The IT framework requires that many types of information be analysed and explained to the public.[2] The central bank must communicate both the weights attached to each macroeconomic indicator and explain how these weights evolve as the economy develops.

This paper attempts to develop a general picture of the monetary transmission mechanism, following the move to an IT framework, and examines what this mechanism means for the Czech IT framework. More specifically, we address two questions about the design of the Czech IT framework:

i   What is the optimal inflation-targeting horizon for forward-looking policy?
ii How steep should be the disinflating path for the targeted rate of inflation?

The first question is familiar to other inflation targeting countries. Batini and Haldane (1999(a))[3] found that policy rules with a forecast horizon for quarterly inflation of about three to six quarters appeared to minimise output and inflation volatility in the United Kingdom. When translated into annual inflation rates, this time period is similar to the one- to two-year targeting horizon[4] that is often referred to in the United Kingdom (see Budd, 1998). Batini and Haldane's findings provide a useful benchmark for comparison of results from the Czech Republic; the two countries have different economic structures but similar monetary policy frameworks.

The approach taken in this paper is to calibrate and estimate a small, aggregate, forward-looking model of the Czech monetary policy transmission mechanism. We answered the first question above by comparing the consequences of different forecast horizons for setting interest rates when this model was hit by shocks.

For much of its recent history the Czech Republic has not targeted a constant rate of inflation: inflation has been converging towards EU rates. It is natural then to ask the second question: what is the optimal rate of disinflation to be targeted? Our results can be interpreted as telling us about targeting too rapid and too slow disinflations; we estimate what different rates of disinflation imply for output and trade balances.

Several empirical problems relate to model-based analysis of the Czech economy. Few findings have been established from past research, and the short samples of available data are plagued by structural breaks. One particular example of a coefficient for which no consensus estimate exists is the effect of the output gap on inflation in the Phillips curve. This coefficient is very important because different estimates, all equally justifiable empirically, could significantly affect the estimated short-run output costs of lowering inflation. In order to provide some guidance as to what the inherent uncertainty in Phillips curve estimates could mean for monetary policy, this paper reports on various simulations using different values for this important but unknown coefficient.

Section 2 describes how we constructed our experiments with a model, a policy rule and a set of structural shocks. Sections 3 and 4 present our results on the forecast horizon and timing of disinflation, respectively. Section 5 presents some concluding remarks.

2 Method

This paper aims to explore, first, the consequences of targeting inflation at different horizons and, second, the effect of disinflating at different speeds. The analytical tools to conduct these 'what-if' experiments on monetary policy are presented in this section. We describe how the transmission mechanism, the monetary policy reaction, and the structural shocks faced by the economy were modelled for this paper.

2.1 The model of the Czech transmission mechanism

Batini and Haldane (1999(a)) and Svensson (1999) contain references to the predecessors and theoretical foundations of the small, open economy monetary policy model that we construct. But it is worth reminding ourselves of one reason why this class of models is suitable when working with Czech data.

It is important that the model is semi-structural, particularly in the sense that the transmission mechanism is written independently of the policy regime. Using a structural model partially protects from the Lucas critique. A reduced-form model – unrestricted VARs for example – would be more open to the risk of reflecting the influence of previous Czech monetary policy regimes (see Šmídková and Hrnčíř in this volume), which are of no interest in this paper. Also, in the rapidly changing environment of the Czech economy in transition, untreated estimates on past data can be a poor guide to the present and future. A more structural approach allows priors about economic theory to be imposed on the calibrations to reflect transition. The price to pay is that the paper's results are conditional on these assumptions. The small model comprises the following equations and base-line parameter values:

$$y_t = \ln(\exp dd_t + \exp x_t - \exp m_t) \tag{1}$$

$$dd_t = dd_t^s + c_{10} + c_{11}(i_t - \exp \text{inf}_t) + c_{12}(dd_{t-1} - dd_{t-1}^s) + \epsilon_{1t} \tag{2}$$
with $c_{10} = 0.03$, $c_{11} = -0.37$ and $c_{12} = 0.51$.

$$m_t = c_{20} + c_{21}dd_{t-1} + c_{22}(pf_{t-1} + e_{t-1} - p_{t-1}) + c_{23}\Delta dd_t + \epsilon_{2t} \tag{3}$$
with $c_{20} = 2.82$, $c_{21} = 0.93$, $c_{22} = -0.82$ and $c_{23} = 0.51$.

$$x_t = c_{30} + c_{31}yf_t + c_{32}(pf_t + e_t - p_t) + c_{33}x_{t-1} + \epsilon_{3t} \tag{4}$$
with $c_{30} = -55.17$, $c_{31} = 1.95$, $c_{32} = 0.27$ and $c_{33} = 0.60$.

$$\Delta e_t = c_{40}\left(E_{t-1}\Delta e_t^e - \frac{i_{t-1} - if_{t-1}}{4} + c_{41}\right) + \epsilon_{4t} \tag{5}$$
with $c_{40} = -0.80$ and $c_{41} = -0.02$.

$$e_T = e_{T-1} \tag{6}$$

$$\Delta_4 p_t = \exp \text{inf}_t + c_{50}(\Delta_4 p_{t-1} + c_{51}(\Delta_4 pf_{t-1} + \Delta_4 e_{t-1})) \tag{7}$$
$$+ c_{52}(y_{t-1} - y_{t-1}^s) + \epsilon_{5t}$$
where $c_{50} = -0.47$, $c_{51} = 0.3$ and $c_{52} = 0.5$ or 0.15.

$$\Delta_4 p_T = c_{31}(\Delta_4 pf_T + \Delta_4 e_T) \tag{8}$$

$$\exp \text{inf}_t = c_{70}E_t\Delta_4 p_{t+1}^e + (1 - c_{70})\Delta_4 p_{t-1} \tag{9}$$
where $c_{70} = 0.2$.

The operator Δ_4 indicates the difference between the present value and the value of four quarters ago, and Δ indicates the difference with last quarter's value. The variable $E_t z_{t+s}^e$ refers to the rational expectation of the variable z at time t+s, calculated at time t. The parameters were either calibrated or estimated using data from 1994Q1–1997Q4. Our calibrations are described in the text below. The details of the estimations are in an appendix to this paper.

Since the model is highly aggregated, the simultaneous system can be described as a GDP block, an exchange-rate block, a domestic-price block, and an inflation-expectations block. The model contains two terminal conditions that relate expectations to long-run assumptions on exchange rate and inflation. The model is then closed with a policy rule to be discussed at the end of this section.

Equation (1) in the GDP block is the familiar identity that links real private-sector GDP to the aggregate of real domestic demand, imports, and exports. For simplicity, we excluded government expenditure from demand and output variables. In what follows, we are therefore assuming that the government's behaviour is exogenous.

Equation (2) is the IS curve. Aggregate private-sector domestic demand (dd_t) depends on the cost of borrowing, which depends on a measure of the short-term *extante* real rate of interest $(i_t - \exp \inf_t)$ and its lagged value. Domestic demand is affected relative to its steady-state level (dd_t^s) where that steady state is estimated by a simple time trend.

The Czech economy is very open – exports plus imports have steadily increased to reach about 130% of GDP in 1997 – and it is interesting to include an indicator that shows whether inappropriate monetary policy destabilises trade as well as inflation or growth. The import and export equations, numbered (3) and (4), respectively, summarise how trade is linked to growth and inflation through income and price effects. In equation (3), the level of imports (m_t) depends on domestic demand, with the real exchange rate $(e_t + pf_t - p_t)$ also being influential.[5] Similarly, the demand for Czech exports (x_t) is both price- and income-elastic, with world demand (yf_t) being especially important. The relatively short dynamics in both equations reflects a quick pass-through of exchange-rate changes onto volumes.

Two important compromises were made in modelling the trade sector. First, imports (and exports) of goods and services were not treated separately. Second, as there is no adequate Czech export price data, only export volume adjustments are explicitly incorporated.

In the exchange-rate block, the dynamic adjustment equation (5) is used to forecast the nominal exchange rate (e_t). The long run is based on the uncovered interest-parity relationship, which equates the expected exchange-rate change to the nominal interest rates at home and abroad $(i_t$ and if_t, respectively) and a constant risk premium, (c_{41}). The parameters of this exchange rate equation are calibrated rather than estimated because the Czech exchange rate data was fixed for much of the estimation period. The risk premium is equal to the average interest rate differential from 1995 to 1997. The value of the other parameter, (c_{40}), determines the extent to which the exchange rate is a random walk as opposed to being given by the interest parity condition. Our base-line calibration implies that any deviation of the exchange rate from uncovered interest parity is temporary – 80% of the short-run disequilibrium disappears by the following quarter. Our checks on this calibration indicated that our results were not affected seriously by using any value where between 30% to 90% of the disequilibrium was eliminated in the first quarter.[6]

The real exchange rate in the Czech Republic has been appreciating at about 5% per year since 1993. This partly reflects the combination of different rates of productivity growth and the equalising of nominal wages between the traded and non-traded goods sectors. Appreciation could also be due to a gradual lowering of the risk premium on koruna-denominated assets. To incorporate this trend and to acknowledge that it is likely to persist, we introduce a constant nominal exchange rate as a terminal condition in equation (6). This would imply that the foreign-exchange market expects the upward trend in real exchange rates to persist as long as inflation in the Czech Republic is higher than that of its trading partners.

The main characteristics of consumer prices (p_t) in a very open transitional economy should be incorporated in the price block. For example, our intuition was that Czech prices are very sensitive to the domestic price of imports,[7] and the exchange-rate effect via import prices would be a major channel of monetary policy transmission in our model. To support our crucial calibrations, we used monthly data to test how consumer prices are determined by foreign prices and with what lags. The details are in the appendix, but the main findings can be summarised as follows:

1   A first step was to estimate how domestic and foreign prices are cointegrated. The bulk of results indicate that in the long run, about one third of any increase in annual import price inflation was passed on to annual Czech consumer price inflation. This was used as a terminal condition for inflation expectations in equation (8).
2   Our estimates also confirm that this import price pass-through is quick. This long-run effect of about a third is reached after about three to six months.
3   The autoregressive lag structure of domestic consumer prices is also important for our results. We estimated this lag length in a VAR using monthly data on domestic consumer prices, disaggregated into its economically interesting components – net inflation and regulated price inflation – with import price inflation as an exogenous variable. The statistical tests on lag length indicate that only recent (at most one quarter ago) past inflation affects current inflation.

Turning to other influences on prices, the GDP output gap measures the extent to which real private sector GDP (y_t) is over the full-capacity level (y_t^s), at which there is pressure on wages and prices. A researcher of western industrialised economies could calculate full-capacity output by using capital stock and employment data to fit a production function. But for the Czech economy, we do not have the luxury of reliable data on the factors that contribute to the non-standard pricing and production decisions over transition. We have instead chosen to approximate the

GDP output gap by fitting a simple log-linear trend to GDP from 1994 to 1997.

In the event, a significant statistical estimate of the influence of this GDP output gap on inflation could not be obtained. Several explanations for this failure are plausible. First, the output gap could be seriously mismeasured. But the measure used, although imperfect, is correlated with other measures of demand pressure, such as the balance of payments–GDP ratio. A second view is that the output-gap effect is simply dormant. In our small sample of past data, the inflation profile could have been dominated by measurement error and transitional shocks. And the type of excess domestic-demand pressures that emerged could have dissipated mostly into trade deficits rather than manifesting as a GDP gap. If these influences were to die away, the output gap effect *would* become more prominent in the future, and imposing a zero coefficient could then prove misleading.[8]

In the face of this uncertainty about the coefficient on the output gap in a Phillips curve equation, this paper allows for a broad range of possibilities by presenting the results from two very different calibrations. In our baseline scenario, the initial effect of a 1% increase in the output gap is to raise inflation by 0.5%, *ceteris paribus*. This value is comparable to an upper bound reported for other countries.[9] We re-ran our simulations with an alternative value for this parameter that approximates the lowest value reported for other countries. For this alternative scenario, a 1% increase in the output gap causes inflation to rise by only 0.15%.

All the price-setting influences are combined in a Phillips curve – equation (7). The functional form that seems best to capture the lag structure assumes that the difference between annual inflation and next-period expected inflation is a function of the lagged private-sector GDP gap and the last-period's deviation of inflation from its long-run relationship with import price inflation. If private-sector domestic demand is in equilibrium, expectations are consistent with actual inflation, and annual inflation is constant, the annual CPI inflation rate will then be described by the long-run relationship with import price inflation.

Due to the absence of adequate labour market data for the Czech economy, we chose not to incorporate wages and employment into the model explicitly. The inflation-expectation block reflects our attempt to model wage-setting behaviour implicitly. Czech wages, particularly in the public sector, have traditionally been set to adjust for future inflation (OECD, 1998). So equation (9) assumes that expectations of annual inflation are a weighted average of forward-looking, model-consistent expectations and adaptive expectations.[10]

The weight on forward-looking as opposed to backward-looking expectations (parameter c_{70}) was calibrated at 0.2. That does seem to be a robust approximation of Czech inflation expectations. Simulations with different values in the plausible range from 0 to 0.5 did little to change the results of the paper. When agents were assumed to have predominantly forward-looking expectations of annual inflation in forming their view on the real interest rate and current inflation, the inflation profile became implausibly unstable.

A cursory summary of the model would describe it as emphasising that the transmission of monetary policy occurs through the exchange rate in the Czech Republic. That seems to be true of the direct effect of the exchange rate on inflation (via import prices). But the indirect effect of policy-induced exchange-rate changes (on the trade balance, and so on output) will only feed through onto prices if the Phillips-curve relationship is significant.

Monetary policy in the model also works through the inflation-expectations and real-interest-rate channels. When are these last two domestic channels important monetary policy transmitters? As inflation is sticky and slow to adjust, inflation expectations are not likely to shift much in response to temporary monetary policy movements. It will be persistent, long-run monetary policy changes that can affect inflation through altering long-run expectations. The real-interest-rate channel describes how nominal interest changes affect the real *exante* interest rate, and subsequently consumption and investment. But the extent to which lower domestic demand affects GDP depends on any offsetting trade imbalances. Whether lower GDP then goes on to reduce inflation further depends on the Phillips-curve link.

A simulation from the model may serve as a guide to the importance of these channels, to the role played by the output gap coefficient in the Phillips curve, and to the model's properties. In this simple experiment, we temporarily raised interest rates by one percentage point for 1995 above its historical values. Chart 1 compares simulations in which the coefficient on the output gap in the Phillips curve is 0.5 to simulations in which the coefficient is zero.

In the experiment with a zero coefficient on the Phillips curve, the only channels through which monetary policy can affect *inflation* are the direct effect of the exchange rate on import prices and inflation expectations. In this zero-coefficient simulation, the import-price and inflation-expectation channels' contribution together is to lower inflation by about 0.45% after a 1% interest-rate rise. That is about half of the 1% maximum fall in inflation when the output gap coefficient is at its largest value. A rough indication of how important these channels are in our simulations is that at their maximum strength, the real interest rate and trade channels together achieve about as much inflation reduction as the import price effect and inflation expectations. Since the interest rate move is temporary, inflation expectations are not likely to be much altered; the largest part of the 0.45% fall in inflation will be due to the import-price effect.

The simulation also shows how the effect of monetary policy in output

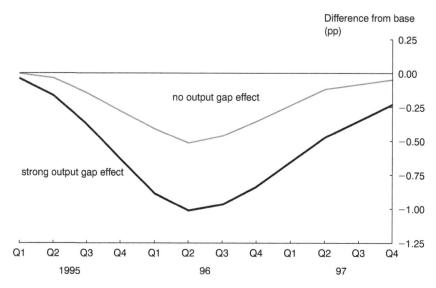

Chart 1a Annual inflation after a 1% interest rate rise for 1995Q1–95Q4

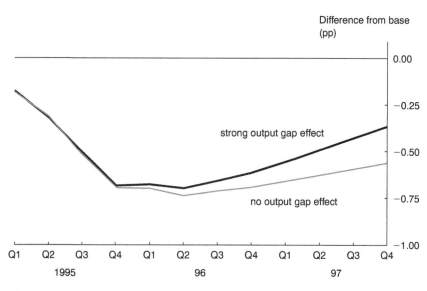

Chart 1b The private-sector GDP gap after a 1% interest rate rise for 1995Q1–95Q4

depends on the output gap coefficient. Lower values of the coefficient reduce the interest rate's influence on inflation and heighten the output costs of the policy tightening; i.e. the trade-off between inflation and output is unequivocally worse with lower coefficient values.[11] Output instability may be as extensive as it is with a weaker Phillips curve may be because the policy rule is switched off in this illustrative experiment. But it could also demonstrate that when the interest-rate rise and consequent exchange-rate appreciation are not matched by an adequate fall in prices, the real exchange rate and the real interest rate both rise. That affects both trade and domestic demand. This sensitivity to the output gap coefficient can thus be expected to feature in the results.

Chart 1 also gives us some idea of the speed of monetary policy transmission. It takes interest rates about one-and-a-half years to exercise their full effect on inflation, irrespective of the output gap coefficient. This transmission is quicker than what we can judge from comparative illustrative simulations for the United Kingdom (Bank of England, 1999). Section 3 explores what this could mean for the forecast horizon.

2.2 The policy rule

A second stage in setting up our experiment is to develop a hypothetical rule for setting interest rates that can be incorporated into the model. This rule is a stylised description of our counterfactual Czech monetary policy. We use it as a yardstick – comparing across different rules approximates a comparison across the monetary policies that they represent.

Our rule can then be written as

$$i_t = c_{80}i_{t-1} + (1 - c_{80})(\text{target}_t + if_t - \Delta_4 pcf_t + \gamma(\Delta_4 p_{t+j} - \text{target}_{t+j}))$$
(10)

with base-line parameter values $c_{80} = 0.2$, $j = 4$, and $\gamma = 3$, and the target reflecting a linear rate of disinflation from 9% in 1994 to 2% in 2008.

As a stylised representation of inflation targeting, our interest rate setting rule combines three elements. First, it depends on policy-makers' expectations of the deviation of future inflation ($\Delta_4 p_{t+j}$) from the target rate (target_{t+j}). The choice of horizon (j) at which this is done and the way to set a falling target rate are the subjects of this paper. The expectation of future inflation is calculated as the rational expectation that is consistent with this model. Although shocks remain unanticipated, the incorporation of model-consistent expectations confers some advantage on policy-makers over the public-sector price-setters, whose expectations are largely backward-looking; less advantage is gained over foreign-exchange market participants, whose expectations are more forward-looking.

Another factor in the rule is the equilibrium anchor for interest rates. The assumption adopted was that the Czech real interest rate ($i_t - t \arg et_t$)

would be equal to the world real interest rate ($if_t - \Delta_4 pcf_t$) when the final objective, inflation, is at its target. For consistency, both foreign and domestic real rates in this rule are assumed to be *expost* and in terms of consumer prices.

A low weight on the third component, past interest rates, reflects the assumption that it is less costly to alter nominal interest rates in transitional economies. Czech inflation is expected to trend downward over time and, given the extra difficulties of managing disinflation, Czech policymakers are allowed more leeway in changing nominal interest rates. In our stylised rule, the weight on last quarter's rate, (c_{80}), is 0.2. That is less than the value of 0.5 typically in use in Taylor rule for the United Kingdom and the United States. Furthermore, different values in the range of 0 to 0.5 do not change the qualitative rankings that comprise the results.

2.3 The shocks

The final elements in our experiments are the shocks that hit the economy. The mix should resemble the disturbances that the Czech economy plausibly could face in the future. Many sources of volatility could be unique to transitional economies. For example, the economy could be shocked by repeated corrections in relative prices towards their free-market proportions.[12] But the Czech economy also experiences shocks more typical of other economies: changes in the world demand for Czech goods, falls in commodity and oil prices, and variations in the foreign exchange market perception of the risk in holding koruna-denominated assets.[13]

Given these considerations, we decided to allow for shocks to the following five endogenous variables: domestic demand, imports, exports, the nominal exchange rate, and inflation. These shocks are represented by ϵ_{1t}, ϵ_{2t}, ϵ_{3t}, ϵ_{4t}, and ϵ_{5t}, in equations 2, 3, 4, 5, and 7, respectively. But we wanted to add an extra emphasis to price disturbances arising from abroad, as world prices have been a major source of exogenous external supply-side shocks for the Czech economy; an additional shock from foreign import prices is also included.

In the absence of alternatives, the statistical standard errors of the residuals in our estimated equations were used to scale the variances of the shocks to the endogenous variables. The import price shock was scaled by the variance of foreign import prices, adjusted for trends and structural breaks. Table 1 reports these calibrations.

The simulations were carried out on Winsolve software[14] for the period 1994 to 1997. The rational (or model-consistent) expectations were calculated by a Stacked Newton numerical algorithm. The non-linear parts of the model were also solved numerically by the Newton–Raphson method. The simulations were repeated using 100 draws of antithetic, unanticipated shocks with the predetermined variances above and zero covariances.

Table 1 Scaling of the shocks

Sources of uncertainty	Standard errors (percentage points)
Equation uncertainty	
Inflation	0.7
IS curve	3.8
Imports	5.2
Exports	8.2
Exchange rate	2.0
Exogenous variable uncertainty	
Foreign price of imports	6.0

2.4 Caveats

Although the simulations seem to be a reasonable depiction of the Czech transmission mechanism, many limitations remain in the aggregate structure of the model and its calibrations. One important omission is that we have not incorporated credit, money, or wealth effects. Their potential influence cannot be quantified and incorporated easily in this type of model. In particular, it is difficult to find an adequate aggregate measure of credit and money over this period of intense financial innovation.

Nor have we considered how the central bank's instrument, the policy interest rate, transmits to market interest rates, especially on instruments of longer maturities. Instead, this structure is collapsed into one interest rate: the three-month maturity interbank rate. If there were a slow and imperfect transmission to market interest rates, and especially if this were to depend on the policy rule in place, our results would certainly be affected.[15]

More generally, we are not confident that there is an adequate role for expectations in our model. Future research could improve on our findings by incorporating data on published inflation forecasts and also by looking for a forward-looking element in the nominal wage-setting behaviour. A more disaggregated consideration of expectations of price shocks could also be important. Some transitional shocks could be anticipated by agents (e.g. tax reforms) and others not (e.g. the timing of regulated price adjustments).

As far as possible, the robustness of results for different calibrations is mentioned in the paper. But this study does not address the monetary policy implications of model uncertainty in sufficient depth. That would require asking how policy should be altered to cope with stochastic parameters as well as (additive) stochastic shocks as recent articles by Sack (1998) and Martin and Salmon (1999) discuss for the United States and the United Kingdom respectively.

Finally, there are no covariances in the shocks. Allowing for covariance could alter the weights of the different sources of inflation and output volatility and affect the relative performance of rules. The zero-covariance assumption was made in the absence of alternatives. The statistical residuals from our equations did not indicate a significant covariance, although that could easily arise from the poor quality of Czech data. The short data sample does not permit VAR estimates, the other popular way to obtain these estimates.

The results of the simulations could be sensitive to these considerations to a lesser or greater degree. Nevertheless, this paper should be taken as a first step toward addressing inflation-targeting issues for the Czech Republic. Further research could return to improve upon its preliminary conclusions.

3   The search for the optimum forecasting horizon

In principle, targeting inflation at either too short or too long a horizon can be destabilising for both output and inflation.[16] Targeting too short a horizon – reacting to current or even past inflation – runs the risk of using large interest-rate changes to react unnecessarily to temporary movements in inflation. Targeting inflation too far forward in the future runs the risk of allowing damaging inflationary (or deflationary) pressure to build up. The horizons that lie between these extremes are then all possible optima where lower inflation volatility can be procured only with more output volatility.[17] But this theoretical discussion begs the question, how long is too long? And how short is too short? In this section, a first answer is provided for the Czech Republic.

A stochastic simulation is first performed on the model using a policy rule that reacts to current inflation, setting $j = 0$ in equation (10). The experiment is then repeated with ever longer horizons, estimating the unconditional means and variances of output and inflation at each stage.[18] In this initial set of experiments, all the parameters were set at their baseline values. The output gap coefficient in the Phillips curve was set at its maximum value of 0.5. Table 2 reports the outcomes of our experiments over the period 1994Q1–1996Q4 for horizons of up to six quarters ahead. As shall be discussed, the consequences of longer forecasting horizons did not need to be reported in the Czech case.

Arguably, the costs and benefits of different horizons are better understood in terms of inflation and output volatilities than by their mean values. Chart 2 plots the locus that joins the inflation and output volatility pairs from using each forecast horizon. The arrow directs the eye toward longer horizons.

The chart illustrates that the optimal forecast horizon for the Czech economy should be around a year. The inflation and output volatilities for horizons of one to five quarters ahead are bunched together and closest to

Table 2 Inflation and output outcomes with different forecast horizons and a strong output-gap effect[*]

Horizon (in quarters)	Inflation		GDP output gap	
	Mean	Std deviation	Mean	Std deviation
0	8.24	6.52	0.64	5.39
1	8.32	4.19	0.78	4.10
2	8.44	3.79	0.88	4.50
3	8.58	3.87	0.99	4.74
4	8.78	4.09	1.40	5.04
5	9.17	4.58	1.50	5.62
6	10.28	7.61	1.45	7.54

[*] Inflation volatility is measured in terms of the standard deviation of the annual inflation rate from its target path because that is what is relevant for welfare costs. Output volatility is measured in terms of the standard deviation of an output gap for similar reasons. It is the volatility of overall consumer price inflation that is reported, although the Czech National Bank target an inflation rate that is net of the first-round effect of regulated price changes. As regulated price inflation is exogenous in the model, conclusions based on comparisons across simulations should be equally valid for net inflation.

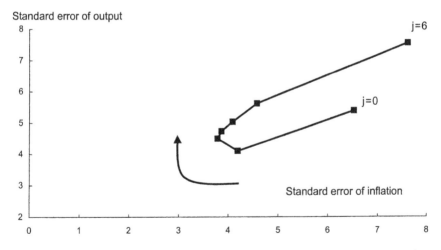

Chart 2 Trade-off between output and inflation variability at different forecasting horizons

the origin. Given the inevitable inaccuracies in our calibrations, one should be cautious in ranking the outcomes within this range. But less than one or more than five-quarter-ahead horizons can be fairly confidently considered sub-optimal in terms of inflation and output volatility. The estimate of optimal policy horizon for the United Kingdom of around two years is likely to be too long a horizon for the Czech inflation-targeting regime.

Why is the favourable horizon shorter in the Czech case? Our intuition is that the Czech Republic has quicker price dynamics than the UK.[19] The Czech economy is very open, and as we measured it, the exchange-rate pass-through is quite fast. It is true that, at least in the public sector, administered wage-setting is a common practice in the Czech Republic. But, following a tradition from the former socialist regime, wage negotiations are more or less co-ordinated at a national level (OECD, 1998) and thus may even act to speed up the transmission of nominal changes.[20] In the absence of more comparative research on nominal rigidities, our results suggest that the target horizon to be incorporated in the Czech monetary policy framework should be somewhat shorter than what is appropriate in the United Kingdom.

There is another intriguing difference between our results and those of Batini and Haldane: in the United Kingdom version of Chart 2, the arrow was pointing in the opposite direction. Taking our results at face value, targeting too recent inflation destabilises inflation more than output in the Czech case, whereas for the United Kingdom, the price of too short a horizon is paid mainly in terms of output volatility. We can hypothesise why the Czech case is different. The slope at the short-horizon end of the locus in general depends on the nominal versus real cost of *short-term* interest-rate volatility. Because the import price effect of monetary policy is quick in the Czech Republic, this short-term volatility of interest rates is passed immediately on to Czech prices without affecting real variables as much. At the longest horizons, the slope of the locus depends on the nominal versus real cost of *longer-term*, persistent interest-rate changes. Persistent unsynchronised movements in interest rates, exchange rates, and inflation rates can be relatively more destabilising for real variables.

The experiment above assumed that the output-gap effect was strong, even though there is little justification for or against any particular value. What would it mean for the targeting horizon if the Phillips-curve effect were much weaker? To answer this question, the experiment was repeated with a smaller output gap coefficient, setting $c_{52} = 0.15$. Table 3 reports the results of simulations with this lower coefficient, and Chart 3 plots the results.

The implications for the optimal forecast horizon do not vary substantially. The locus clearly shifts to the left but its shape stays the same. The optimal horizon can be expected to lie in the same range of two to five quarters.

Why is there such a large shift to the left? Why does a weaker Phillips-curve relationship mean more output instability at all horizons? Some clues may be found in the model's interest-rate impulse responses presented in Chart 1 in the previous section. There it was shown that breaking the Phillips-curve link means that policy-induced nominal exchange- and

Table 3 Inflation and output outcomes with different forecast horizons and a weak output-gap effect

Horizon (in quarters)	Inflation		GDP output gap	
	Mean	Std deviation	Mean	Std deviation
0	8.24	5.54	1.12	5.65
1	8.29	3.76	1.24	4.77
2	8.38	3.28	1.36	4.98
3	8.48	3.27	1.48	5.15
4	8.60	3.37	1.84	5.38
5	8.87	3.43	1.88	5.93
6	9.45	5.15	1.54	7.67

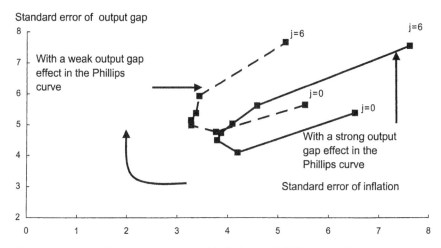

Chart 3 Trade-off between output and inflation variability over different forecasting horizons

interest-rate changes are less synchronised with domestic price movements. With less synchronised nominal variables, the real exchange rate and real interest rate, and consequently real output, can be destabilised.

Other unreported calibrations were carried out to check that the qualitative results do not change for other key parameters of the model and the policy rule.[21] For example, charts similar to Charts 2 and 3 would result from simulations with different degrees of forward-looking behaviour in the exchange-rate and inflation-expectation equations (within what is described as a plausible range in the previous section). In the policy rule, more interest-rate smoothing (a higher c_{80} in equation (10)) and less concern about deviation from target (a lower γ in equation (10)) bunches the outcomes of experiments together. That is hardly surprising; both parameters make interest rates less responsive to the deviations of expected inflation from target. But most importantly for this paper, different values do not change the shape of these trade-off curves.

4   The search for the optimal disinflation strategy

For many transitional countries the key issue is how quickly the inflation rate should converge to lower rates of inflation.[22] In the third simulation exercise, we have tried to find out what our model suggests about the relative costs of different disinflation strategies that could be embodied in a downward-sloping inflation target. We first define the criteria according to which we compare the strategies. Then we describe the alternative strategies themselves.

For this exercise, our set of indicators was expanded to include the ratio of net exports to GDP. Although the trade-off between volatility of inflation and output is still the most important outcome, the experiment now also provides some measure of whether a trade-balance crisis could jeopardise the process of disinflation for a central bank in a small open economy.

To simulate seven different strategies for disinflation, we defined seven alternative paths for the variable target$_t$ in our policy rule, equation (10). These are shown in Chart 4. A starting point of 9% in 1994 and a terminal point of a 2% in 2008 for the target rate are common to all paths. But quite early on there are large differences in the target paths. The slowest

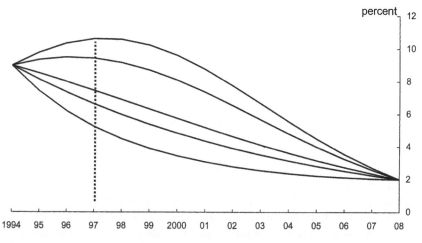

Chart 4 Different target paths for annual inflation

paths allow for a rise in inflation while the quickest paths get through much of convergence without delay. We measure the consequences of disinflation for the initial stage only, over the period 1994Q1 to 1996Q4. The exercise then tells us about the early costs and benefits of rapid versus slow purely policy-induced disinflations. We will return to what this could mean for our results below.

The seven strategies were tested with the same method as the previous exercises. The analogy is straightforward. In the first simulations, the parameter j in our policy rule was varied. Now, j is fixed to reflect a four-quarter horizon, and it is the target rate of inflation that is varied according to the different disinflation paths depicted in Chart 4.

The results of the simulations are reported in Tables 4 and 5 as the unconditional means and standard deviations for inflation, the output gap, and net exports for the two alternative assumptions about the output gap coefficient.

The more lenient, slower paths are better at limiting the volatility of inflation around their higher target rates. What is also interesting is that the tables suggest that quicker disinflation is associated with lower but more stable output gaps early on in transition. This trade-off becomes stark when the Phillips-curve relationship is weaker.

Chart 5 compares inflation and output volatility across the locus of disinflation paths. The arrow now points from fast to slow speeds of targeted disinflation. When there is a strong Phillips-curve relationship there is not

Table 4 Inflation, output, and net export outcomes with different disinflation speeds and a strong output-gap effect[*]

Disinflation speeds	Inflation		GDP output gap		Net exports	
	Mean	Std deviation	Mean	Std deviation	Mean (% of GDP)	Std deviation (billion Korunas, 1995 prices)
Fast	6.25	4.21	0.54	5.00	5.87	5.81
	7.15	4.13	1.05	5.01	5.77	5.45
	7.66	4.09	1.34	5.04	5.71	5.24
Linear	8.23	4.05	1.88	5.10	5.64	5.01
	8.84	4.00	2.01	5.20	5.57	4.77
	9.52	3.94	2.39	5.35	5.50	4.53
Slow	11.06	3.83	3.25	5.82	5.33	4.21

[*] Although the standard deviation of net exports is included for completeness, it may not describe trade flow volatility usefully, in a very open economy with a high-income elasticity of import demand. For example, a large shock that lowered exports would typically lower incomes and so also imports. The shock could even reduce the standard deviation of net exports.

Table 5 Inflation, output, and net export outcomes with different disinflation speeds and a weak output-gap effect

Disinflation speeds	Inflation		GDP output gap		Net exports	
	Mean	Std deviation	Mean	Std deviation	Mean (% of GDP)	Std deviation (billion Korunas, 1995 prices)
Fast	6.05	3.43	0.67	5.25	6.35	5.10
	6.90	3.39	1.40	5.29	6.32	4.65
	7.38	3.37	1.82	5.38	6.31	4.38
Linear	7.91	3.34	2.28	5.52	6.29	4.09
	8.49	3.31	2.78	5.74	6.27	3.78
	9.13	3.28	3.32	6.03	6.24	3.45
Slow	10.58	3.21	4.57	6.92	6.19	2.90

much grounds for discriminating against any disinflation path except the slowest, at least in terms of inflation and output volatility. With the weak Phillips curve, and a subsequent heightening of output costs, the moderate (near linear) or fastest disinflations are preferable.

Chart 6 links inflation volatility with our indicator of the trade balance – the average net exports to GDP ratio. The arrow again points from fast to slow speeds of targeted disinflation. The chart shows that the fastest disinflations are the least harmful for net exports; this follows because faster

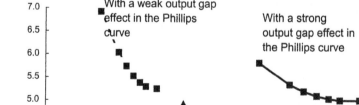

Chart 5 Trade-off between output and inflation variability at different disinflation speeds

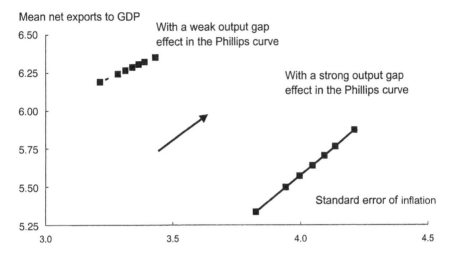

Chart 6 Trade-off between inflation variability and trade balance at different disinflation speeds

disinflations imply lower output gaps and large output gaps a tendency to
spill over into trade imbalances, through a greater demand for imports.

To summarise the results of our disinflation simulations, policy rules
that aim at moderate or fast disinflations seem to be superior to those
aiming at slower disinflation. This conclusion is based only on estimated
outcomes over the early years of disinflation. With faster disinflations,
costs can be expected to concentrate in the early stage of convergence,
while with slower disinflations, they are probably postponed for later.
Thus, comparing the costs over the total disinflation period is, if anything,
likely to favour faster disinflations.

5 Conclusions

This paper makes a first step towards asking the questions that are important for inflation targeting in the Czech Republic. A small model is presented to capture what constrains policy in a small, open, transitional
economy. The transmission mechanism of the Czech Republic is thus
analysed in a way that should be informative to monetary policy. Our
main finding is that the transmission mechanism in the Czech Republic is
substantially quicker than that, for example, in the United Kingdom, with
the import price effect being relatively important in transmitting at least
temporary interest-rate changes.

We have two main conclusions about the Czech Republic from stochastic simulations with this model. First, the optimal targeting horizon is
probably less than a year. Second, postponing the initial disinflation does

not imply significant gains in terms of lower output volatility or a smaller external imbalance.

Clearly the results are sensitive to some of the calibrations and this is brought out by repeating simulations for different values of these parameters. This exercise should guide the reader as to what part of the structure merits further investigation and monitoring. In particular, the output gap effect on inflation is a very important calibration in the model simulations and it was not possible to estimate this parameter due to a lack of data. We hope that the results presented here at least prove that it is possible to discover some features of the transmission mechanism of a transitional economy like the Czech Republic and thus provide some basis for decisions about the most suitable Czech policy framework.

APPENDIX

Table 6 Data list*

Name	Description
PRIBOR	Czech Interbank Market Rate (Three month maturity, annualised, end of month)
P	Consumer price index
PNET	Net consumer prices
PREGUL	Regulated consumer prices
PF	A weighted average of the German and US export prices, with weights 0.65 and 0.35, respectively
IF	A weighted average of the German and US money-market interest rates, with weights 0.65 and 0.35, respectively (three month maturity, annualised, end of month)
YF	A weighted average of German and US real GDP, with weights 0.65 and 0.35, respectively
PCF	A weighted average of the German and US consumer prices with weights 0.65 and 0.35, respectively
E	A weighted average of the Czech koruna-DM and Czech koruna USD exchange rate with weights 0.65 and 0.35, respectively. A rise indicates a depreciation
DD	Real private sector domestic demand. The sum of private consumption, investment and stock-building (all in real terms)
Y	Real private sector GDP. DD + X − M
X	Real exports (goods and services)
M	Real imports (goods and services)

* Source: IFS and Czech National Bank.

Estimates of the parameters of the model of the Czech economy are presented in the rest of the appendix.

The price system and a Phillips curve: some useful results with monthly data

Three features of the Phillips curve that are important to the model's properties are the long-run pass-through between import prices and consumer prices and the lag structure of this pass-through. Because there is a lack of quarterly data points, these relationships are investigated using monthly data.

The long-run pass-through between import prices and consumer prices

The Johansen and Juselius test of cointegration is well known. The Pesaran, Shin, and Smith (1996) test has the advantage of being robust to whether the variables are I(1) or I(0). It is based on two statistics: a Wald test and an F-statistic whose critical values have been tabulated by the authors.

The Pesaran *et al.* test accepts the null hypothesis of cointegration whereas the Johansen-Juselius test rejects cointegration. The former single-equation tests can be favoured if annual import price inflation is weakly exogenous. Some evidence is reported below that this is indeed the case. Whether the inflation series are I(0) or I(1) cannot be accurately determined using statistical criteria. As the Pesaran *et al.* test is robust to either possibility, we are more inclined to accept the null hypothesis that the series are cointegrated.

The long-run coefficients of the relationship between the two series are estimated by a variety of techniques. First, the coefficient estimates from a Vector Error Correction Mechanism with two lags in each variable are reported. The t-statistics are based on Newey–West standard errors so as

Table 7 Cointegration tests between annual CPI inflation and annual import price inflation[†]

	Null hypothesis	*Alternative hypothesis*	*Sample estimate*	*No. of observations*
Johansen–Juselius	R = 0 R <=1	R = 1 R = 2	**11.47** **4.16***	32
Pesaran *et al.* Wald statistic	Cointegrated if variables I(0) or I(1)		**6.06****	44
Pesaran *et al.* F statistic	Cointegrated if variables I(0) or I(1)		**12.12****	44

[†] * significance at 10%. ** significance at 5%.
Note: R is the number of cointegrating vectors.

Table 8 Estimates of the long-run relationship between annual CPI inflation and annual import price inflation[†]

	No. of observations	Estimate of c51	Asymptotic t-stat
Johansen	32	**0.18**	1.70
Inders	43	**0.48**	1.73
ARDL IV	43	**0.38**	2.06**
Engle–Granger	32	**0.50**	

[†]* significance at 10%. ** significance at 5%.

to be more robust to any serial correlation arising from estimating annual inflation on a monthly frequency. A second set of values are provided by Inder's (1993) version of the Phillips–Hansen fully modified estimator (1990) which may have good small-sample properties. Third, the Pesaran Instrumental Variable method (ARDL IV) may be useful because (i) it should have good small-sample properties, and (ii) is robust to whether the inflation rates are difference-stationary or stationary. Finally, the results from a simple OLS estimation of the inflation rates, which would be consistent with the Engle–Granger approach, are reported.

The range of estimates of the long-run elasticity from import prices to consumer prices is 0.18 to 0.5 with the upper end more reliable if import prices are weakly exogenous.

To test the exogeneity of import prices, Vector Error Correction Mechanisms between annual domestic price inflation and annual import inflation were estimated with lag lengths varying from 1 to 4. In each case, the coefficient of the cointegrating equation involving these two series and a constant in the dynamic import price inflation equation is insignificant and incorrectly signed. This can be taken as convincing evidence of the weak exogeneity of import prices. As the estimates of the long-run relationship that assume import prices are exogenous are more likely to be valid, we calibrated the parameter c51 in equation (7) to be 0.3.

Lag structure

The dynamics of domestic consumer price inflation is tested with the following assumptions: (i) based on the above finding discussed immediately above, annual import price inflation is supposed to be weakly exogenous; and (ii) consumer prices are disaggregated into their regulated and net price components, as this more general form is expected to provide more information about the structure.

The lag structure between the price components indicates a short pass-through, as a lag of two months is favoured by the criteria in Table 9.

Table 9 Choice of lag length in a monthly VAR with annual net price inflation and regulated price inflation (1994M1–1997M12)[†]

No. of lags in VAR	AIC	SBC	Q-stat test of serial correlation in residuals of net price inflation equation
2	−12.084	−11.762	insignificant
3	−11.916	−11.434	26.66*
4	−11.776	−11.134	insignificant
12	−11.660	−10.860	insignificant

[†] Annual import price inflation is exogenous. * significance at 10%. ** significance at 5%.

The IS curve

$$dd_t = dd_t^s + c_{10} + c_{11}(i_t - \exp \inf_{t+1}) + c_{12}(dd_{t-1} - dd_{t-1}^s) + \epsilon_{1t}. \qquad (2)$$

Table 10 Estimates of the IS curve[†]

TSLS, 1994Q1–1997Q4 Coefficient	Estimates	Std. error	t-stat
C10	0.027	0.008	3.39**
C11	−0.37	0.177	−2.06**
C12	0.51	0.135	3.67**
R2	0.38	Durbin Watson	1.8
RBAR2	0.30		
Equation std. Error	0.034		
Sum of squared residuals	0.02		
No. of observations	16		
LM test of 4th order serial correlation (chi sqrd 4)	1.79		
Ramsey RESET (chi sqrd 1)	0.23		

[†] Actual inflation was used instead of unobservable expected future inflation. Lagged inflation and lagged growth were used as instruments. * significance at 10%. ** significance at 5%.

The import and export equations

$$m_t = c_{20} + c_{21}dd_{t-1} + c_{22}(pf_{t-1} + e_{t-1} - p_{t-1}) + c_{23}\Delta dd_t + \epsilon_{2t}. \tag{3}$$

$$x_t = c_{30} + c_{31}yf_t + c_{32}(pf_t + e_t - p_t) + c_{33}x_{t-1} + \epsilon_{3t}. \tag{4}$$

Table 11 Estimates of the import and export equations[†]

OLS, 1994Q1–1997Q4 Coefficient	Estimate	Std. error	t-stat	Coefficient	Estimate	Std. error	t-stat
C20	2.82	0.70	−0.88	**C30**	−55.17	21.63	−2.55
C21	0.93	0.13	3.56**	**C31**	1.95	2.66	2.67**
C22	−0.82	0.32	−2.77**	**C32**	0.27	0.23	1.17
C23	0.51	0.24	2.15**	**C33**	0.60	0.19	3.02**
R2	0.91	Durbin Watson	2.13		0.32	Durbin Watson	2.91
RBAR2	0.89				0.23		
Equation std. error	0.052				0.082		
Sum of squared residuals	0.033				0.107		
No. of observations	16				16		
LM Test of 4th order serial correlation (chi sqrd 4)	1.37				8.37*		
Ramsey RESET (chi sqrd 1)	0.05				0.04		

[†] * significance at 10%. ** significance at 5%.

The Phillips curve

$$\Delta_4 p_t = \exp \inf_{t+1} + c_{50}(\Delta_4 p_{t-1} + c_{51}(\Delta_4 p f_{t-1} + \Delta_4 e_{t-1})) + c_{52}(y_{t-1} - y^s_{t-1})$$
$$+ \epsilon_{5t} \tag{7}$$

where c_{51} is calibrated at 0.3 and c_{52} is calibrated first at 0.5 and then 0.15.

Table 12 Estimates of the Phillips curve[†]

TSLS, 1994Q1–1997Q4 *Coefficient*	*Estimates*	*Std. error*	*t-stat*
C50 Constant not significant	−0.47	0.134	−3.50**
R2	0.50	Durbin Watson	2.30
RBAR2	0.43		
Equation std. error	0.007		
Sum of squared residuals	0.001		
No. of observations	16		
LM test of 4th order serial correlation (chi sqrd 4)	4.36		
Ramsey RESET (chi sqrd 1)	1.53		

[†] Using lagged inflation and growth as instruments. * significance at 10%. ** significance at 5%.

Notes

1 We would like to thank Nicoletta Batini and Jagjit Chadha for helpful comments and suggestions. The views and opinions are those of the authors alone and do not represent the Czech National Bank or the Bank of England.
2 'One of the main features of the inflation targeting strategy is its transparency. In the regimes of exchange rate targeting and monetary targeting, inflation targets are usually implicit. Moreover the speed and timing of the disinflation process are not specified properly in those regimes. In the inflation targeting regime, the central bank, through its inflation report, openly announces its disinflation intentions and acquaints the public as much as possible with the implementation of its policy' ('Introduction' in *Inflation Report*, April 1998, Czech National Bank).
3 See also Batini and Haldane (1999(b)).
4 The optimum forecast horizon is conceptually different to the optimum targeting horizon. The former strictly refers to how far in the future is the expected inflation that interest rates should react to in a policy rule. The latter refers to the point at which expected inflation and the target are in line in policy discussions. Estimating the former should provide us with some approximate guide as to where the latter lies.
5 Although re-exporting seems to be a feature of the Czech economy, we did not find that exports were separately significant in the import equation.

6 It could be argued that any degree of dynamic exchange adjustment is inappropriate to model exchange rates on quarterly data; uncovered interest parity should hold at all times. But a fully forward-looking exchange rate makes the model of this open, transitional economy unstable. And our results emphasise how quickly monetary transmission through the exchange rate occurs in the Czech Republic. By slowing it down artificially, we are, if anything, providing further support for our findings.

7 The hypothesis is based on several observations. There are no substitutes for imported raw materials and some intermediate-good inputs. And although in the final-goods markets for tradables there is enough competition between domestically produced goods and imports to mean that these domestic producers are forced to be price-takers, in the non-tradable goods sector production cost increases are passed on to consumers.

8 An absence of stable Phillips curves estimated on 1970s US and Western European data did not negate the emergency of more robust relationships in the 1980s. See, for example, Di Nardo and Moore (1999).

9 As an example, Britton and Whitley (1997) report the following values for output gap parameter in Phillips curve: 0.5 in the United Kingdom, 0.2 in France and 0.3 in Germany.

10 Indeed one of the reasons that the CNB chose inflation targeting was the feeling that it was important to anchor inflation expectations in wage-setting with a transparent framework (CNB, *Inflation Report*, April 1998).

11 Theoretical models of the Phillips curve associate a lower coefficient for the output gap with more nominal rigidities. For example the coefficient would rise with a higher cost of nominal price adjustment. More nominal rigidities mean more real effects of monetary policy.

12 The transitional shocks and their consequences are described by several studies. See for example Hájek (1997).

13 An assessment of the importance of external shocks is reviewed in inflation reports. See, for example, *Inflation Report*, July 1998 and October 1998, Czech National Bank.

14 Richard Pierse, University of Surrey, United Kingdom.

15 Svensson (1988) develops a small model in this mould that explicitly incorporates interest rate transmission and allows for expectations of monetary policy to influence this channel.

16 For the problem of targeting too short a horizon, see the voluminous literature on forward-looking versus current or backward-looking rules (e.g. Svensson (1997)). Difficulties with using too long a horizon are usually explained with reference to Woodford (1994) and Bernanke and Woodford (1997).

17 The precise optimum horizon would depend on the society's relative welfare preferences over output and inflation volatility.

18 The unconditional standard deviations of the variables of interest were estimated by the following method: first we estimated the standard deviation across time for each simulation and then we averaged these estimates across simulations.

19 Erceg *et al.* (1999) relate the trade-off between output and inflation volatility to wage and price stickiness.

20 Vávra (1999) suggests that Czech wage-setting displays real rigidity but not as much nominal rigidity. See Grubb *et al.* (1983) for a distinction between real and nominal rigidity in wage setting.

21 In order to establish a constraint for one parameter in the policy rule, we have to assume a particular functional form for the policy rule and near optimal values for the other parameters. In principle it is possible to vary more than one policy parameter according to a grid and so explore the policy-makers'

constraint in many dimensions but we leave this as a topic for further research.
22 Sargent (1982) and Gordon (1982) provide contrasting evidence about the costs of disinflation. Ireland (1997) reconciles their views in a model with large fixed costs of price adjustments. He suggests that an optimal strategy might be to target a quick disinflation initially and replace with a gradual disinflation once the lower inflation rates are reached. This strategy would be represented by our fastest disinflation paths.

Bibliography

Bank of England (1999), 'The transmission mechanism of monetary policy', *Bank of England Quarterly Bulletin*, Vol. 30, No. 2, May.

Batini, N. and Haldane, A.G. (1999(a)), 'Forward-looking rules for monetary policy', *Bank of England Working Paper*, No. 91, January.

Batini, N. and Haldane, A.G. (1999(b)) (forthcoming), 'Monetary policy rules' in Taylor, J. (ed.) *NBER Conference Volume*, University of Chicago Press.

Bean, C. (1998), 'The new UK monetary arrangements: a view from the literature', *Economic Journal*, Vol. 108, No. 451, pp. 1795–1809, November.

Bernanke, B.S. and Woodford, M. (1997), 'Inflation forecasts and monetary policy', *Journal of Money Credit and Banking*, Vol. 29, pp. 653–84.

Britton, E. and Whitley, J. (1997), 'Comparing the monetary transmission mechanism in France, Germany and the United Kingdom: some issues and results', *Bank of England Quarterly Bulletin*, May.

Budd, A. (1998), 'The role and operations of the Bank of England Monetary Policy Committee', *The Economic Journal*, Vol. 108, No. 451, pp. 1783–95.

Czech National Bank (1998), *Czech National Bank: Inflation Report*, Prague, April, July, October.

Di Nardo, J. and Moore, M.P. (1999), 'The Phillips Curve is back? Using panel data to analyse the relationship between unemployment and inflation in an open economy', *NBER Working Paper*, No. 7328, August.

Erceg, C.J., Henderson, D.W. and Levin, A.T. (1999), 'Tradeoffs between inflation and output-gap variances in an optimizing-agent model', Institute for International Economics, *Stockholm University: Seminar Paper*, No. 650.

Gordon, R.J. (1982), 'Why stopping inflation may be costly: evidence from fourteen historical episodes' in Hall, R.E., *Inflation Causes and Effects*, pp. 11–40, Chicago University Press.

Grubb, D., Jackman, R. and Layard, R. (1983), 'Wage rigidity and unemployment in OECD countries' in *European Economic Review*, pp. 11–39.

Hájek M. *et al.* (1997), 'Macroeconomic analysis of the Czech economy', *IECNB Working Paper*, No. 82, Prague.

Hrnčíř, M. (1996), 'Monetary policy in the Czech Republic: strategies, instruments and transmission mechanisms', *Monetary Policy in Transition*, Austrian National Bank.

Haldane, A.G. and Salmon, C.K. (1995), 'Three issues in inflation targets' in Haldane (ed.), *Targeting Inflation*, Bank of England.

Inder, B. (1993), 'Estimating long-run relationships in economics: a comparison of different approaches', *Journal of Econometrics*, 57(1–3), pp. 53–68, May–June.

Ireland, P.N. (1997), 'Stopping inflations big and small', *Journal of Money, Credit and Banking*, Vol. 29, No. 4, pp. 759–82, November.

OECD (1998), *OECD Surveys: The Czech Republic*, OECD, Paris.

Pesaran, H.M., Shin, Y. and Smith, R.J. (1996), 'Testing for the existence of a long-run relationship', Department of Applied Economics, *University of Cambridge Working Papers*, No. 9622.

Pesaran, H.M. (1997), 'The role of economic theory in modelling the long run', *Economic Journal*, 107(440), pp. 178–91, January.

Phillips, P.C.B. and Hansen, B.E. (1990), 'Statistical inference in instrumental variables regression with I(1) processes', *Review of Economic Studies*, 57(1), pp. 99–125, January.

Sargent, T.J. (1982), 'The ends of four big inflations in inflations: causes and effects', Hall, R.E. (ed.), *Inflation Causes and Effects*, pp. 41–97, Chicago: University of Chicago Press.

Svensson, L.E.O. (1998), 'Open economy inflation targeting', manuscript, *IIES*, Stockholm University.

Svensson, L.E.O. (1999), 'Inflation targeting as a monetary policy rule', *Journal of Monetary Economics*, 43, pp. 607–54.

Urbain, J.-P. (1992), 'On weak exogeneity in error correction models', *Oxford Bulletin of Economics and Statistics*, 54(2), pp. 187–207, May.

Vávra, D. (1999), 'Nominal versus real convergence in a CEE transition country: do the Maastricht Criteria make sense for the Czech Republic?' *CERGE-EI Discussion Paper*, No. 1999-16, October.

Woodford, M. (1994), 'Nonstandard indicators for monetary policy: can their usefulness be judged from forecasting regressions?' in Gregory N. Mankiw (ed.) *Monetary Policy*, University of Chicago Press, Chicago, pp. 95–115.

Setting monetary policy instruments in Uganda

Michael Atingi-Ego[1]

1 Introduction

Because Uganda has had an underdeveloped financial system and a fairly substantial public sector, the scope for monetary policy evolution has been limited. However, with ongoing financial sector deregulation and accompanying structural reforms, an increasing use of indirect instruments in the conduct of monetary policy, and declining public-sector involvement, financial deepening is taking place. In this paper we ask: 'What operational, intermediate, and final (domestic) targets of monetary policy would be the most suitable for the developing economic environment of Uganda?'

Uganda offers a fascinating case study for these issues, which have long since occupied the minds of policy-makers elsewhere. In many ways Uganda satisfies the prerequisites that some authors have claimed for inflation targeting (IT). Fiscal policy, for example, has been sound and inflation has averaged less than 10% for the last six years. But there are other unique features of the Ugandan economy that raise many new and interesting questions about the appropriate monetary policy.

Much of the debate over the choice of monetary policy target has focused on the relative parts played by velocity and supply-side shocks. Uganda has experienced both in abundance. Rapid financial liberalisation has made the velocity of money unstable, while quarterly domestic food price inflation has varied from 30% to −15% within six months of changing weather conditions! The VAR results in this paper are in line with the Bank of Uganda's experience that these two sources of shocks explain many of the short-run movements in overall consumer-price inflation.

The broad aim of this paper is to compare alternative domestic monetary policy strategies against this backdrop of velocity and food-price shocks. The method was to construct a small model to capture the main structural and dynamic features of monetary transmission in Uganda and to simulate how different policy reaction functions deal with money-demand and food-price shocks. Carrying out stochastic simulations on macromodels has become a common practice in applied monetary policy research; what is novel about this study is that this technique has rarely been applied to an economy like Uganda's.

The model serves two purposes:

- to establish the transmission from monetary policy instruments to inflation (and growth); and
- to describe the impact of uncertainty in the velocity of money demand and food-price shocks on these final objectives.

This paper evaluates two possible changes to the monetary policy framework. First we analyse the implications of using interest rates rather than base money (as is the current procedure) as an operational target.[2] Second, we compare a strategy that focuses directly on final objectives with an alternative that employs an intermediate money target.

The structure of the paper is as follows. Section 2 begins by describing how monetary policy in Uganda is currently conducted and can evolve. It also discusses the main sources of shocks and how they influence monetary policy. Section 3 describes the model of the Ugandan economy that we use in section 4 to perform experiments about different monetary policy strategies. Section 5 concludes the paper.

2   Monetary policy in Uganda

As in many other countries, the underdevelopment of financial markets has constrained monetary policy in Uganda. Structural problems within the banking system and lingering effects of financial repression have meant that about a quarter of the economy is non-monetised. M2-GDP ratios have been no more than 14%, well below the 39% reported by Fry *et al.* (1996) as the average for a sample of 122 developing countries.

The banking sector has been reluctant to lend to the non-bank private sector and an excess of loanable funds has been kept as free reserves with the Bank of Uganda. It is these reserves that make up the excess liquidity in the banking system.[3] Excess liquidity has meant that monetary policy changes can in some cases be absorbed by variations in these excess reserves (the liquidity conditions) of the commercial banks, and do not always feed through to the spending and pricing decisions of the non-financial sector via market interest rates. This contrasts with the transmission mechanism observed in developed financial markets, where, subject to private-sector expectations, changes in the policy interest rates affect the entire spectrum of interest rates along the yield curve, and thus the economic decisions to consume and invest.

But such banking sector credit as is available, although small in scale by international standards, is still an important source of finance for the government and for prime borrowers in the Ugandan corporate sector, and thus may play an important role in monetary transmission. Any expansion of credit associated with a looser economic policy can boost investment. Conversely monetary policy changes that lead to the banking sector's restricting credit can lend to substantial contractions in real output.[4]

Within these constraints, the monetary authorities have largely concentrated on pursuing their policy objectives through a *reserve money programme*. The first step is to determine a target rate of growth in a broad monetary aggregate that is consistent with the macroeconomic objectives of economic growth and price development. This requires that the velocity of broad money demand can be predicted. With assumptions about the money multiplier and seasonalities, the second step is then to calculate the desired base money levels. The reserve money programme can therefore be summarised as first setting an *intermediate* target for broad money and second relating this to an *operational* target for base money.

Partly as a result of recent financial and money-market reforms,[5] a departure from this way of operating of monetary policy has become feasible. First and most crucially, the fiscal authorities have been successful in avoiding excessive deficits in recent years. Consequently, the government has had less need to borrow from the banking system, leaving more room for an independent monetary policy. Second, there are some reasons to expect the financial market to transmit interest-rate changes more effectively than in the past. In particular, the use of commercial banking has become more widespread, with M2 GDP ratios increasing by about eight percentage points in the last six years. Finally, the money market in which the central bank operates has been reformed. A full recapitalisation of the Bank of Uganda is nearly complete, and the framework for the operationalisation of the repo market has been finalised.[6] With the interest-earning securities and other instruments at its disposal, it is hoped that the Bank of Uganda will be better able to conduct monetary policy.

The ambitions of monetary policy are necessarily constrained, nevertheless, at the lower levels of financial development. For example, until financial markets and monetary instruments become more sophisticated, the financing of the government budget will continue to have a key role in determining bank liquidity.

But the evolution of financial markets may soon reach a stage where, instead of reverting to the reserve money programme of the past, it will be possible to contemplate, for example, setting an operational target for interest rates and letting the market determine the quantities of base money. As a further optional step, the level of interest rates could be set to target directly inflation and growth, thus side-stepping the use of broad money as an intermediate target. Before the cost and benefits of these different strategies are discussed in Section 4, it is important to understand how monetary policy and structural shocks influence inflation and output in Uganda.

2.1 *Some simple VAR analysis of monetary policy and inflation*

Tables 1 and 2 provide some evidence from Granger causality tests on the transmission of monetary policy shocks transmitted to prices in Uganda. The tests use quarterly data for base money, treasury bill rates, and prices, both in levels and as differences.

Table 1 shows that base money has Granger-caused prices in Uganda, both in (log) levels and as rates of change, while Table 2 shows that, in contrast, treasury bill rate movements have not been important. The tentative message is that, mainly by controlling base money movements, monetary policy has been important for inflation in Uganda despite the underdeveloped financial sector.

Table 1 Pair-wise Granger causality test between base money, consumer prices and the treasury bill rate (1982Q1–1997Q4), with base money as causal[*]

To test if → does not Granger Cause ↓	bm			
		2 lags	3 lags	4 lags
p		2.44	3.39	2.99
		(0.09)	(0.02)	(0.02)
r		0.22	1.03	1.06
		(0.80)	(0.38)	(0.39)
To test if → does not Granger Cause ↓	Dbm			
		2 lags	3 lags	4 lags
Dp		4.76	3.43	2.17
		(0.01)	(0.02)	(0.08)
Dr		1.23	0.90	0.91
		(0.30)	(0.44)	(0.47)

* The tables report the F-statistic and below the probability of accepting the null of no Granger causality in brackets. D is the first difference operator, p is the (log of the) consumer price level, bm is (the log of) base money, and r is the three month treasury bill rate.

Table 2 Pair-wise Granger causality tests between base money, consumer prices and the treasury bill rate with the treasury bill rate as causal*

To test if → does not Granger Cause ↓	r			
		2 lags	3 lags	4 lags
p		1.00	0.54	0.17
		(0.37)	(0.65)	(0.95)
bm		1.71	1.45	0.78
		(0.18)	(0.24)	(0.54)
To test if → does not Granger Cause ↓	Dr			
		2 lags	3 lags	4 lags
Dp		0.39	0.15	0.48
		(0.67)	(0.92)	(0.75)
Dbm		0.74	0.32	0.31
		(0.48)	(0.77)	(0.87)

* See Table 1.

Granger causality tests cannot reveal more than this about the nature of the shocks to inflation; a more structural approach is needed. A natural extension is to estimate a VAR with inflation, money growth, treasury bill rates, and output growth,[7] and attribute the variance of inflation at each horizon to shocks arising from these sources. To do this, the system must first be identified by, for example, imposing an ordering of the immediate reactions of macroeconomic variables to these shocks.

For robustness, results are derived from two orderings: (Dp, Dbm, Dr, Dy[8]) and (Dbm, Dp, Dr, Dy). As developed in Christiano *et al.* (1996), these orderings refer to two possible strategies of the monetary authority (Bank of Uganda) that must to maintain price stability.[9] The first ordering suggests a *reactive* stance where the Bank of Uganda reacts only to observed past movements in inflation by adjusting the quantities of base money. These monetary policy changes may then ultimately affect interest rates and consequently output. In the second *proactive* ordering, changes in base money come first, to reflect the assumption that the central bank uses this as a policy instrument as soon as it observes that inflation is likely to rise.

Other possible orderings can be ruled out by making the following assumptions. First, the Bank of Uganda interest rate was not used as an instrument (neither proactively nor reactively) in this sample. Second, the Bank of Uganda does not adjust the money base to react to current output changes. Third, it is assumed that treasury bill rate shock affects output with a lag.

The variance decompositions from the two orderings are shown in Charts 1 and 2.

The pattern that emerges is that inflation movements in the short term are explained by shocks to prices themselves, but after five quarters, shocks in base money become almost as significant. In the reactive stance where the Bank of Uganda is assumed to change base money in response to past inflationary developments (Chart 1), base-money shocks would account for 30% of the long-run changes in inflation while, with the proactive assumption (Chart 2), they explain about 40% of them.

A second interesting result, common to both assumed orderings, is that base money surprises influence the treasury bill rate only in the long run and only slightly. Treasury bill rates are largely determined by their own shocks and by output shocks. On the other hand, treasury bill rate shocks explain about 20% of long-run inflation movements and about 30% of the long-run variance in growth.

These findings about the role of the treasury bill interest rate could reflect the transmission of shocks to the velocity of money under the reserve money programme. Recall that during the programme, money-market shocks would affect the price (the short-term interest rate) rather than the quantity of base money, which was the target. The treasury bill shocks in our VAR may then also reflect shocks to the velocity of broad

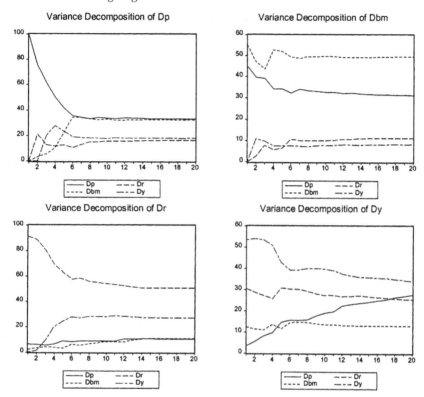

Chart 1 The variance decomposition of a VAR between inflation (Dp), base money growth (Dbm), output growth (Dy) and changes in the treasury bill rate (Dr) (ordering of Dp, Dbm, Dr, Dy) (1982Q1–1997Q4)

money and the money multiplier. The decompositions would then suggest that these velocity shocks can affect output if they are allowed to lead to volatile interest rates, possibly through changes in credit.

Although these preliminary results should be interpreted cautiously (bearing in mind the lack of degrees of freedom), the Granger causality tests and variance decompositions together seem to suggest that base-money growth can affect inflation in the long run. Short-term inflation volatility is dominated by its own shocks, which could represent food-price disturbances.

2.2   Problems with the current monetary framework

From the results of the previous section it would appear that the current framework has been partly able to contain inflation at low levels in Uganda, despite an uncertain economic environment. Two of the most important shocks – an unstable velocity of money demand and volatile food prices – are discussed in this section.

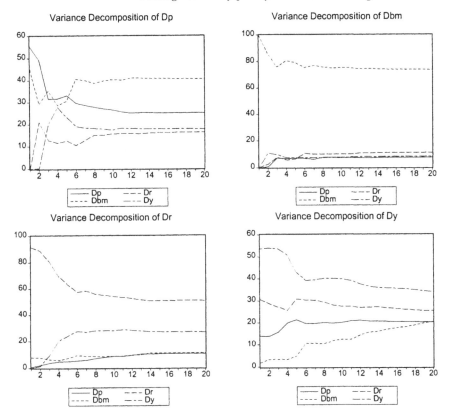

Chart 2 The variance decomposition of a VAR between inflation (Dp), changes in base money (Dbm), output growth (Dy) and changes in the treasury bill rate (Dr) (ordering of Dbm, Dp, Dr, Dy) (1982Q1–1997Q4)

2.2.1 Instability in the velocity of money demand

The behaviour of velocity of broad money is shown in Chart 3. Clearly, the relationship between output and prices on one hand and the broader money aggregates on the other has not been stable. But what has this meant for the authorities' ability to forecast these movements and so implement the reserve money programme? We can glean some insight by comparing the actual macroeconomic performance to the reserve money programme targets agreed to by the government of Uganda and the International Monetary Fund under the Enhanced Structural Adjustment Facility (ESAF) arrangement.

Chart 4 shows that actual broad money growth has always turned out to be higher than programmed. One could conjecture that this is due to the unexpected decline in velocity of broad money circulation that can occur with financial liberalisation. But other explanations are also plausible. Prior to 1996, there was also a higher-than-programmed performance of

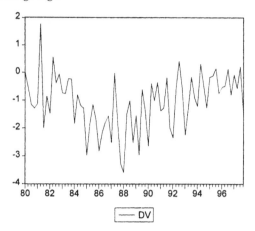

Chart 3 Velocity of broad money (quarter on quarter percentage changes)
        1980–97

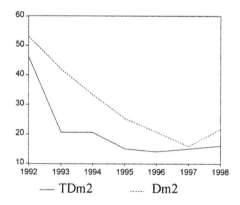

Chart 4 Actual broad money growth (Dm2) vs targeted broad money growth
        (TDm2) (1992–98)

real GDP (Chart 5) following the strong improvement in the terms of
trade associated with a boom in the production of Uganda's main export –
coffee – in 1994 to 1995. To the extent that these shocks were not offset by
a fall in prices, nominal GDP will have been affected.

The next step in the reserve money programme involves relating base
money growth to broad money growth. Chart 6 plots the volatile money
multiplier (M2/base money) in Uganda to explain why, at times, the
central bank was required to revise the base money path that would be
compatible with the programmed growth of the broader monetary aggregate.

Do these results together imply that base money velocity is also unstable? Early work by Musinguzi and Kihangire (1996) suggested a stable
relationship. But more recently Kasekende and Atingi-Ego (1998) have

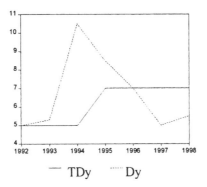

Chart 5 Real GDP growth (Dy) vs targeted real GDP growth (TDy) (1992–98)

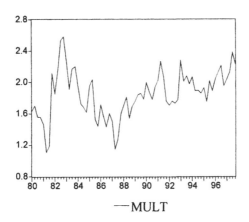

Chart 6 Behaviour of the money multiplier (1980Q1–1997Q4)

suggested that unpredictable volatility has crept into the base money demand function largely because of the excess of free reserves held by the commercial banks. Free reserves represent a large non-discretionary item in the balance sheet of the Bank of Uganda that cannot easily be predicted and offset by changes in the discretionary components of base money.

In summary, an unstable velocity of broad money and money multiplier are likely to have posed problems for monetary policy, but the comparisons of targets and outcomes may also reflect shocks to growth and prices.

2.2.2 Volatility in food prices

The second major source of instability is the behaviour of food prices. Food items account for 33.6% of the weighted consumer price index and are strongly affected by weather patterns. Chart 7 demonstrates that food-price inflation (Df) is extremely volatile, even when compared to its non-food counterpart (Dnf).

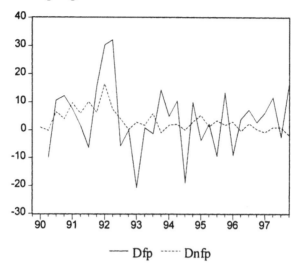

Chart 7 Quarterly food and non-food inflation (1990Q2–1997Q4)

What have food price shocks meant to the performance of headline inflation forecasts embodied in the ESAF programme? We compare the headline inflation target against the headline inflation rate (Chart 8), the non-food price inflation rate (Chart 9), and the food-price inflation rate (Chart 10).

It would appear that since 1994, whenever food-price inflation has been above the desired headline inflation rate, non-food price inflation has been below, and vice versa. The negative correlation between food and non-food prices may reflect the fact that the authorities have pursued the target for headline inflation during food-price shocks. When a drought occurs and food prices rise, the monetary authorities may have squeezed liquidity to act against the rise in overall prices, which could have then deflated non-food prices. A similar scenario may have applied for negative shocks

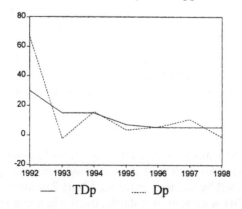

Chart 8 Actual (Dp) vs desired (TDp) headline inflation rate (1992–98)

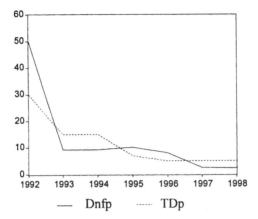

Chart 9 Actual non-food inflation (Dnfp) vs the desired headline inflation rate (TDp) (1992–98)

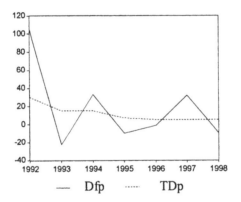

Chart 10 Actual food price inflation (Dfp) vs the desired headline inflation rate (TDp) (1992–98)

to food prices. A glut in food production would tend to lower food prices causing the headline inflation to fall. The Bank of Uganda may then have considered relaxing liquidity, thus raising non-food inflation to compensate for the fall in food-price inflation.

The Bank of Uganda is aware of the difficulties associated with food-price shocks. Indeed that is why the two measures of inflation – the headline and underlying inflation series – are referred to. But could the Bank of Uganda go one step further and target only the non-food rate of inflation? That would depend on the extent to which food-price shocks feed through onto non-food prices in the long run, in the absence of a monetary policy reaction to food-price shocks. Leaving this issue aside, what can be concluded is that food-price shocks are a major source of uncertainty for Uganda, with implications for monetary policy.

3   A model of the Ugandan economy

A small, macroeconomic model of the Ugandan economy was constructed and used as a basis for stochastic simulations that compare operating procedures for monetary policy. In this section the structure of the model is presented. Readers already familiar with this type of model may proceed directly to the simulations in the next section.

Because of structural breaks that occur at different times, the equations of the model were estimated on different samples of quarterly data from the period 1981Q4 to 1997Q4. The long-run relationships were estimated using the Vector Error Correction Mechanism method (Johansen, 1988). For ease of interpretation, the long runs were imposed in an OLS estimation of the short-run dynamics, checking in each case that the long-run parameter estimates did not change significantly. The long-run elasticities of all of the equations are reported in the main text below. The constants and dynamic terms are in the appendix. In what follows, lower-case letters indicate logs, except for the domestic and foreign rate of interest.

We begin our description with two definitions. First we write the real exchange rate as

$$\text{reer} = \text{ner} + \text{pm-p} \tag{1}$$

where pm and p are foreign and domestic consumer prices, respectively, and ner is the nominal exchange rate. A rise in reer indicates a real depreciation.

Real GDP is equal to the sum of real domestic demand and real exports, minus real imports:

$$\text{GDP} = A + (X\text{-}M). \tag{2}$$

Turning to the long-run equations, real domestic demand is determined by real base money (bm) (as a proxy for outside wealth), the *expost* real rate of interest derived from the treasury bill rate (r-Dp), the real exchange rate (reer), and government spending (g) in the long run.

$$a = c_1(\text{bm-p}) - c_2(\text{r-Dp}) - c_3\,\text{reer} + c_4\text{g} + \text{constant} \tag{3}$$

where $c_1 = 1.8$, $c_2 = 0.15$ and $c_3 = 0.21$ and $c_4 = 0.025$.

Real base money (bm-p) affects investment demand through bank credit, with a large elasticity reflecting the importance of credit for investment in an African economy (Oshikoya, 1984). The coefficient on the real treasury bill rate (r-Dp) reflects a combination of two influences. The first is transmission of policy interest rates to market interest rates, which in turn affects agents' decisions to postpone current investment and consumption. This intertemporal substitution may be expected to be weak because of the shallow financial system. But a second, possibly more substantial impact of interest rates on domestic demand may arise from its implications for the availability of bank credit. The real effective exchange rate (reer) shows that real depreciations lower long-run consumption and investment through an income effect. Hemphill (1974) and Moaran (1989) argue that imported raw materials and machinery have few substitutes in developing countries. Following a depreciation, aggregate consumption must be reduced to make foreign exchange available for the more expensive imports. Finally, government spending exerts only a slight influence in the long run and in any case, being assumed exogenous, plays no part in the simulations.

Real exports (x) are largely determined by the real exchange rate based on consumer prices and a weighted export price index (px). This export price term is included, as well as the real exchange rate based on consumer prices, to allow for price differentials between the tradable and non-tradable sectors. The export price term is also significant in explaining the variations in export values in the long run, although the dynamics presented in the appendix show that the real exchange rate explains much of the short-run variations. Foreign incomes of the trading partners are not included, as Uganda's exports are highly income inelastic.

$$x = x_1 \, \text{reer} + x_2 \, \text{px} + \text{constant} \tag{4}$$

where $x_1 = 0.6$ and $x_2 = 1.3$.

Real imports (m) are related to the real exchange rate and domestic absorption:

$$m = -m_1 \, \text{reer} + m_2 a + \text{constant} \tag{5}$$

where $m_1 = 0.50$ and $m_2 = 0.97$.

Because of the income effect in equation (3), the direct effect of a real exchange rate depreciation on imports is accompanied by an indirect effect feeding through lower domestic demand. From equations (5) and (3), a 1% real depreciation lowers long-run imports by about 0.8%, all other things being equal.

The nominal exchange rate (ner) is simply modelled as reflecting backward-looking interest-rate parity:

$$\text{ner}_t = \text{ner}_{t-1} - (r - r^f) + \text{constant}. \tag{6}$$

Equation (7) imposes that food and non-food prices are cointegrated, but the dynamics modelled in the appendix allow food prices to exhibit significant short-run deviations following shocks from, for example, weather conditions. Thus

$$\text{fp} = \text{nfp}. \tag{7}$$

The long run of the non-food price equation implies that non-food price inflation may result from higher foreign raw-material costs as well as a higher price of imported consumer goods:[10]

$$nfp = f_1 ner + constant \tag{8}$$

where $f_1 = 0.23$.

The foreign currency price of imports was not significant, and as they are constant across our simulations, they were simply excluded, leaving only the nominal exchange rate. The appendix shows that an output-gap effect is slightly important for the short-run dynamics of non-food inflation.

Final consumer prices are a combination of food and non-food prices, with weights being approximately equal to their weights in the consumer basket:

$$p = 0.34fp + 0.66nfp. \tag{9}$$

All that is needed to complete the model is the monetary policy rule and the money demand function, which are presented in the next section.

The model is a highly aggregated description of the Ugandan economy. There are many considerations that could not be incorporated mainly because of the limited amount of data available and because much of the transmission mechanism had to be simplified. But the signs and sizes of the parameters are plausible and consistent with what work has been done on the Ugandan transmission mechanism.

4   Model simulations

This section addresses the following two practical questions about the appropriate monetary policy in Uganda:

(i)   How do interest rates compare to base money as operating targets in the face of velocity shocks and under food-price shocks?

(ii)   How does a strategy of using base money as an intermediate target fare against these same shocks?

To begin with, how do base money and interest rates perform as *instruments*[11] of monetary policy? Some simple simulations with our model may help. Chart 11 illustrates the effect of a 1% shock to the treasury bill rate that is sustained for one year with base money determined by the money-market demand function.[12] Chart 12 plots simulations of a one-year 1% shock to base money with interest rates now being set by the money market.[13]

The transmission from an interest-rate instrument change onto inflation

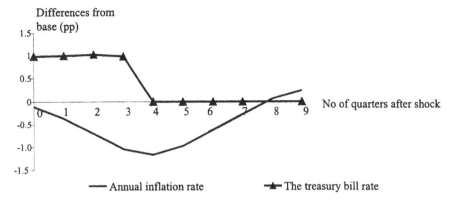

Chart 11 Responses to a treasury bill shock

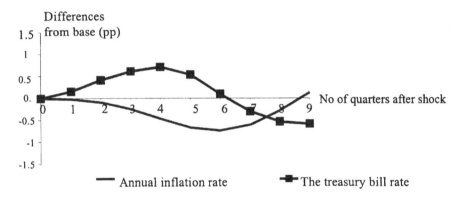

Chart 12 Responses to a money-base shock

in Chart 11 is rapid: the full effect of a 1% rise in interest rates is a 1% fall in inflation in less than six months. When base money is used instead of interest rates, the transmission can be much slower. Chart 12 suggests that it can take a year for the change in the money base to fully affect interest rates through the money market. After this interval has passed, the maximum reduction in inflation takes another three to six months to occur.

Although it is difficult to separate the channels of this transmission in the highly aggregated model, there appears to be a significant difference in time lags with which money and interest rates affect inflation. Does this suggest that the interest rate will be a better operational target than base money? Not necessarily. A good operational target must not only have a short transmission lag to inflation, it must ideally neutralise only the desta-bilising consequences for growth and inflation of the shocks that Uganda faces, and it must do so on a continual basis. Thus to answer questions (i) and (ii), we need to consider monetary policy strategies that set interest rates or base money to keep inflation and growth to their target values over a period when these shocks occur frequently.

The approach followed in this section was to begin by representing each counterfactual operational targeting scheme as a stylised rule.[14] The model was simulated from 1991Q4 to 1997Q4 using this rule, with a different velocity shock hitting long-run money demand (equation 10c) at each quarter. The shocks were drawn from a normal distribution that was scaled to have the same standard deviation as the residuals of the long-run money demand equation (5.4%); that is then our measure of the scale of velocity shocks in Uganda. This simulation was repeated 100 times, with each replication using a different set of velocity of money demand shocks. For each experiment with a different rule, the standard deviations of annual inflation, annual growth and the treasury bill rate across these replications provide a measure of uncertainty or bandwidth in these variables at each quarter. The time average of this standard deviation in inflation and output is used to evaluate the rule. The experiment was then repeated with only food-price shocks, also scaled by their observed historical standard error (10.85%).[15]

As the first step in addressing question (i), an interest-rate operating target regime is stylised as equations 10a, 10b, and 10c below:

$$\Delta i_t = \lambda(\theta(\Delta y_t - tar_y) + \Delta p_t - tar_p); \tag{10a}$$

$$\Delta bm_t = \delta_0 - \delta_3 ecm_{t-1}; \tag{10b}$$

$$ecm_t = (i_t - \alpha_0 + \alpha_1 bm_t - \alpha_2(p_t + y_t)); \tag{10c}$$

where all parameters are positive. Our econometric estimates are that $\alpha_1 = 0.68$, $\alpha_2 = 0.70$, and $\delta_3 = 0.78$ (see appendix).

In this framework, changes in current treasury bill rates (Δi_t) are set by policy-makers to eliminate deviations of overall quarterly consumer price inflation (Δp_t) and current GDP quarterly growth (Δy_t) from their respective target rates (tar_p) and (tar_y). The weight of output in this rule is captured by the parameter θ. The target rates of inflation and output growth are 3.6% and 2%, respectively, their historical averages for this sample. Base-money growth (Δbm_t) is determined by the money market and adjusts according to equation 10b toward the long-run money-demand relationship with interest rates and nominal GDP, given in turn by equation 10c.

This operating system is compared to an alternative money-base operating target system written as equations 11a and 11b below:

$$\Delta bm_t = tar_m - \lambda(\theta(\Delta y_t - tar_y) + \Delta p_t - tar_p); \tag{11a}$$

$$\Delta i_t = \eta_0 + \eta_1 \Delta i_{t-1} + \eta_2 \Delta bm_{t-1} - \eta_3 ecm_{t-1}; \tag{11b}$$

and equation 10c above with all parameters positive and $\eta_3 = 0.34$.

In the base-money operating target system, current base-money growth is set away from its target rate $(tar_m = 6\%)$ to eliminate deviations of overall quarterly consumer-price inflation and deviations of current GDP quarterly growth from the same respective target rates as above. Interest rates are now determined by the money market and adjust according to equation 11b toward the same long-run money-demand relationship as in the previous experiment (10c).

Table 3 presents the results for this first set of experiments. By confirming that the interest-rate rule performs better as an operational target under velocity shocks than the money-base rule, they are in line with Poole's (1970) stylised results on the optimal choice of monetary instrument in a stochastic environment[16] and the experience of many industrialised countries. Even by the standards of these simple experiments, the money rule does particularly badly with velocity shocks: annual inflation has a standard deviation of 9.2%.

Table 3 describes just how much better or worse each operational target does under the very sizable food price shocks that buffet the Ugandan economy. Although neither rule can prevent uncertainty in inflation and growth outcomes, using the interest rate as an operational target does slightly better than using base money, according to the criterion of minimising uncertainty.

Having discussed operational target setting, what can be said about the potential use of intermediate targets in Uganda? To answer this question, the structural model can be used to simulate a base-money intermediate targeting rule in equation 12.

$$\Delta r_t = \lambda(\Delta bm_t - tar_m + \theta(\Delta y_t - tar_y) + \Delta p_t - tar_p). \tag{12}$$

Table 3 Standard deviation of inflation, growth and the treasury bill rate

		Annual inflation		Annual growth		Treasury bill rate	
		Velocity of money demand shock					
Base money operating target	$\theta = 1$	9.35		1.55		16.99	
	0	9.20		1.54		15.56	
Interest rate operating target	$\theta = 1$	0.10		0.44		0.21	
	0	0.00		0.44		0.00	
		Food price shock					
		$\lambda = 0$	$= 0.5$	$\lambda = 0$	$=0.5$	$\lambda = 0$	$= 0.5$
Base money operating target	$\theta = 1$	21.6	24.43	3.82	4.13	11.51	19.12
	0		23.95		4.08		17.78
Interest rate operating target	$\theta = 1$	18.01	17.74	3.12	3.12	9.37	9.96
	0		17.68		3.08		8.55

According to this rule, the treasury bill rate is set as an operational target to affect the intermediate money base growth target. That money target is in turn set to determine final objectives of inflation and growth. Interest rates are set as operational targets, so the actual quantity of base money is determined by the money market according to equations 10b and 10c.

The second experiment compares this rule against a system where interest rates are used as operational targets toward the same final objectives without any intermediate variable – equations 10a, 10b, and 10c. The results reported in Tables 4, 5, and 6 confirm that using the money base as an intermediate target leads to output and inflation instability when there are velocity shocks (only). But when there are food-price shocks (only), an intermediate base money target rule achieves the lowest uncertainty for growth and inflation (standard deviations of 3% and 17.44%, respectively).[17] The differences between the rules in these simulations, however, are small, and they depend on parameter specifications. It is safest to conclude that strategy is particularly effective in the face of the massive food-price shocks witnessed in Uganda.

It could be argued that the model comparisons using base money as an intermediate target are not relevant for the broad money intermediate targeting rule that is followed in Uganda. However, comparing the raw data, base-money velocity in Uganda seems to be at least as stable as broad money velocity. It can therefore be argued that, if anything, the performance of broad money intermediate targeting would be even worse in the face of velocity shocks.[18]

Why are money and interest-rate setting equally (in)effective against the food-price shocks in all our simulations? One explanation is that temporary supply-side shocks, like food-price shocks, distort the signal about long-run inflation that current inflation provides to *both* rules. According

Table 4 Standard deviation of inflation

		$\lambda = 0.25$	0.5	0.75	1
		Velocity of money demand shock			
Base money intermediate target	$\theta = 1$	1.73	3.79	4.41	5.71
	0.5		3.25		
	0		3.21		
Mixed inflation and growth final target	$\theta = 1$	0.04	0.08	1.21	0.16
	0.5		0.04		
	0		0.00		
		Food price shock			
Base money intermediate target	$\theta = 1$	18.32	18.00	17.69	17.44
	0.5		18.06		
	0		17.82		
Mixed inflation and growth final target	$\theta = 1$	18.01	17.88	17.75	17.63
	0.5		17.89		
	0		17.96		

Table 5 Standard deviation of growth

		$\lambda = 0.25$	0.5	0.75	1
		Velocity of money demand Shock			
Base money intermediate target	$\theta = 1$	1.10	1.10	1.30	1.47
	0.5		1.07		
	0		1.14		
Mixed inflation and growth final target	$\theta = 1$	0.46	0.47	0.48	0.48
	0.5		0.47		
	0		0.47		
		Food price shock			
Base money intermediate target	$\theta = 1$	4.26	3.37	3.19	3.00
	0.5		3.42		
	0		3.26		
Mixed inflation and growth final target	$\theta = 1$	6.70	3.32	3.29	3.44
	0.5		3.25		
	0		3.06		

Table 6 Standard deviation of the treasury bill rate

		$\lambda = 0.25$	0.5	0.75	1
		Velocity of money demand shock			
Base money intermediate target	$\theta = 1$	5.17	11.35	18.12	27.37
	0.5		11.34		
	0		11.34		
Mixed inflation and growth final target	$\theta = 1$	0.19	0.25	0.38	0.54
	0.5		0.12		
	0		0.00		
		Food price shock			
Base money intermediate target	$\theta = 1$	7.69	11.73	15.66	20.01
	0.5		11.46		
	0		10.69		
Mixed inflation and growth final target	$\theta = 1$	6.19	10.97	16.47	22.16
	0.5		10.61		
	0		9.97		

to this logic, as the weight of current inflation in the rules diminishes (as λ becomes smaller), interest rates would become more predictable as they respond less to food price shocks. And indeed in Tables 3 and 6, the uncertainty in the treasury bill rates under food-price shocks falls as λ is reduced from 0.5 to 0 in all experiments.

This would suggest that excluding food prices from the targeted inflation rates could be useful in any monetary policy strategy if it improves the clarity of the signal concerning long-run inflation. Simulations with a non-food inflation target in a policy rule could be carried out to see if the uncertain effects of food-price shocks are reduced. But this experiment is beyond the scope of our simple model[19] and is left as a topic for future work.

There are three important caveats that apply to the results. First, we focus on the most important sources of uncertainty (velocity and food-price shocks), whereas a richer description of the potential uncertainty in Uganda would also include, for example, disturbances to financial stability or shocks to world prices.

Second, even though the estimates are derived from recent data, rapid structural change could supersede these values. For example if the efficiency and liquidity of the Ugandan money market improves, then movements in the base money could be more closely reflected in the treasury bill rate, creating a smaller difference between the two as operational targets.

Third, all the results are derived for a period where fiscal policy has a major influence on monetary policy. Any de-linking in this relationship could affect the results.

5   Conclusions

The main objective of this paper was to discuss domestic monetary policy choices in light of identifiable shocks that face the Ugandan economy. This study takes stock of the conduct of monetary policy in Uganda and analyses how interest rates compare to base money as a monetary policy instrument in the face of sizable velocity and food-price shocks. In addition, a strategy of using base money as an intermediate target was tested against these same shocks. To do this, a stylised model of the Ugandan economy that captures its relevant structural and dynamic features was constructed and a general conceptual framework for monetary policy rules was also provided.

The results suggest that the standard prescription, established in the industrialised countries to minimise inflation and output uncertainty in the face of velocity of demand shocks, is also valid for Uganda. Interest rates can be used as an operational target; very short-term forecasts of final objectives of inflation (and output) can be employed to explain outcomes; and less emphasis can be placed on using base money as an intermediate target. Even under food-price shocks, the simulations show that (i) interest rates fare no worse than money as operating target and (ii) using a base-money intermediate target is not much of an improvement on reacting directly to deviations from final objectives. In an environment where both types of shock are common, these results could be used to offer some very tentative support for a planned move to an interest-rate-setting strategy.

There are, however, important caveats to bear in mind. One problem could be the simple nature of the structural shocks we have assumed. The emergence of other structural shocks could distort the picture presented by our stylised comparisons of Ugandan monetary policy strategies. Another problem is that although the parameter values seem sensible, the econometric estimation could be improved when more data becomes available.

APPENDIX 1

Abbreviations of data types

A — Real domestic demand
FP — Food prices
G — Real government expenditure
GDP — Real gross domestic product
M — Real imports
BM — Nominal base money
NER — Nominal exchange rate
NFP — Non-food prices
PM — Weighted trading partners CPI
P — Domestic CPI
PX — Unit export price index ($)
r — Nominal 91-day Ugandan treasury bill rate
r^f — 3-month dollar LIBOR rate
REER — Real effective exchange rate
X — Real exports

APPENDIX 2

Estimates and equations

Table 7 VAR estimates (1991Q1–1997Q4)[†]

OLS	Dp	Dbm	Dr	Dy
Dp(−1)	0.61	1.07	0.19	0.02
	2.20	*1.25*	*0.76*	*0.07*
Dp(−2)	0.56	0.94	0.36	−0.42
	*2.18****	*1.18*	*1.54*	*−1.60*
Dp(−3)	0.06	0.21	−0.16	0.36
	0.28	*0.32*	*−0.83*	*1.67*
Dp(−4)	0.31	0.47	0.15	−0.37
	1.74	*0.84*	*0.90*	*−2.05****
Dbm(−1)	−0.16	−0.23	−0.09	0.08
	−1.35	*−0.65*	*−0.82*	*0.66*
Dbm(−2)	0.07	−0.19	−0.09	0.10
	0.75	*−0.67*	*−1.13*	*1.04*
Dbm(−3)	−0.27	−0.92	−0.12	−0.06
	*−2.45****	*−2.66****	*−1.17*	*−0.56*
Dbm(−4)	−0.29	−0.18	−0.21	0.10
	*−2.42****	*−0.49*	*−1.95***	*0.83*
Dr(−1)	0.72	0.33	0.29	−0.31
	*2.76****	*0.40*	*1.22*	*−1.15*
Dr(−2)	−0.09	−1.15	−0.30	−0.13
	−0.40	*−1.56*	*−1.39*	*−0.53*
Dr(−3)	−0.07	−0.94	0.41	−0.07
	−0.29	*−1.32*	*1.95***	*−0.29*
Dr(−4)	−0.93	−1.00	−0.31	0.44
	*−3.35****	*−1.15*	*−1.22*	*1.55*
Dy(−1)	0.09	1.48	0.15	−0.32
	0.31	*1.70*	*0.59*	*−1.10*
Dy(−2)	1.09	0.88	0.53	−0.45
	*3.20****	*0.83*	*1.70*	*−1.28*
Dy(−3)	0.23	−0.48	0.61	−0.41
	0.75	*−0.49*	*2.15*	*−1.28*
Dy(−4)	−0.64	0.48	0.42	0.42
	*−2.31****	*0.55*	*1.68*	*1.48*
Constant	0.00	−0.01	−0.03	0.04
	0.10	*−0.08*	*−1.59*	*1.91***
R-squared	0.86	0.65	0.72	0.58
R bar-squared	0.66	0.14	0.31	−0.03
Standard error	0.03	0.09	0.03	0.03
Log likelihood	71.24	39.41	73.94	70.53
Akaike AIC	−6.71	−4.44	−6.91	−6.66
Schwarz SC	−5.90	−3.63	−6.10	−5.85

[†] t-statistics in italics, *significance at 10% and **significance at 5%.

The domestic demand equation (1982Q1 to 1997Q4)

Cointegrating equation (estimated in a Vector Error Correction Mechanism with three lags, FIML)

$$ECM1 = a(-1) \quad \underset{-0.83}{-1.8(bm(-1)-p(-1))} \quad \underset{1.5}{+0.15(r(-1)-Dp(-1))} \quad \underset{7.31**}{+0.21\,reer(-1)}$$
$$\underset{-13.13}{}$$

Table 8 The dynamic domestic demand equation estimates (1981Q1–1997Q4)[†]

OLS	Da
ECM1	−0.462
	*−2.78**
Da(−1)	−0.149
	−0.797
Da(−2)	0.062
	0.335
Da(−3)	−0.180
	−1.208
Dbm(−1) − Dp(−1)	0.041
	0.809
Dbm(−2) − Dp(−2)	0.044
	0.841
Dbm(−3) − Dp(−3)	0.081
	1.707
D(r(−1) − Dp (−1))	−0.003
	0.030
D(r(−2) − Dp(−2))	0.021
	0.224
D(r(−3) − Dp(−3))	−0.173
	*−2.011**
Dreer(−1)	0.054
	1.432
Dreer(−2)	0.040
	1.199
Dreer(−3)	−0.027
	−1.095
Constant	−0.445
	*−2.111**
Time trend	−0.001
	−1.752
g	0.058
	*−2.206**
R-squared	0.550
R bar-squared	0.410
Standard error	0.040
Log likelihood	124.43
Akaike AIC	−6.23
Schwarz SC	−5.69

[†] t-statistics in italics, *significance at 10% and **significance at 5%.

The export demand equation (1982Q1 to 1997Q4)

Cointegrating equation (estimated in a Vector Error Correction Mechanism with three lags, FIML)

$$\text{ECM2} = \quad x(-1) \quad\quad \begin{array}{c} -0.64\,\text{reer}(-1) \\ -12.20** \end{array} \quad\quad \begin{array}{c} -1.32\,\text{px}(-1) \\ -21.25** \end{array}$$

Table 9 The dynamic export demand equation estimates (1981Q1–1997Q4)[†]

OLS	Dx
ECM2	−0.64
	*−3.38**
Dx(−1)	0.10
	0.54
Dx(−2)	−0.24
	−1.48
Dx(−3)	−0.48
	*−3.54**
Dreer(−1)	0.37
	1.49
Dreer(−2)	0.26
	1.09
Dreer(−3)	0.50
	*2.68**
Dpx(−1)	0.13
	0.43
Dpx(−2)	−0.51
	*−1.86**
Dpx(−3)	0.27
	1.01
R-squared	0.48
R bar-squared	0.39
Standard error	0.27
Log likelihood	−0.97
Akaike AIC	−2.49
Schwarz SC	−2.16

[†] t-statistics in italics, *significance at 10% and **significance at 5%.

The import demand equation (1981Q4 to 1997Q4)

Cointegrating equation (estimated in a Vector Error Correction Mechanism with two lags, FIML)

$$\text{ECM3} = \quad m(-1) \quad \underset{-13.86**}{-\ 0.97\ a(-1)} \quad \underset{10.96**}{+\ 0.50\ \text{reer}(-1)} + 4.335$$

Table 10 The dynamic import demand equation estimates[†]

OLS	Dm
ECM3	−0.994
	*−3.862**
Dm(−1)	0.304
	1.300
Dm(−2)	0.042
	0.194
Da(−1)	−2.208
	*−3.871**
Da(−2)	−1.261
	*−2.151**
Dreer(−1)	0.158
	0.745
Dreer(−2)	−0.062
	−0.295
Constant	0.073
	*2.748**
R-squared	0.433
R bar-squared	0.364
Standard error	0.165
Log likelihood	29.047
Akaike AIC	−3.485
Schwarz SC	−3.218

[†] t-statistics in italics, *indicates significance at 10% and **indicates significance at 5%.

The food price equation (1991Q2 to 1997Q4)

Table 11 The dynamic food price equation estimates[†]

OLS	Dfp
Constant	−0.118
	*−2.07**
fp(−1) − nfp(−1)	−0.407
	*−2.31**
Dnfp	1.049
	*1.843**
R-squared	0.346
R bar-squared	0.227
Standard error	**0.109**
Log likelihood	24.40
Durbin-Watson stat	1.92
Akaike AIC	−1.44
Schwarz SC	−1.198

[†] *indicates significance at 10% and **indicates significance at 5%.

The non-food price equation (1991Q1 to 1997Q4)

Long run (estimated jointly with short-run dynamics using non-linear least squares)

$$\text{ECM4} = \quad \text{nfp}(-2) \quad - 0.23\,\text{ner}(-2)$$
$$- 0.68$$

Table 12 The dynamic non-food price equation estimates[†]

Non-linear LS	Dnfp
Constant	−2.05
	−1.20
y(−2) − 0.027* trend	0.21
	*1.94**
ECM4	−0.10
	*−3.13**
Dnfp(−1)	−0.26
	*−1.80**
Dner	0.19
	*2.45**
Dner(−1)	0.02
	0.22
R-squared	0.84
R bar-squared	0.77
Standard error	0.0186
Log likelihood	71.43
Durbin-Watson stat	1.68
Akaike AIC	−4.88
Schwarz SC	−4.49

[†] t-statistics in italics, *indicates significance at 10% and **indicates significance at 5%.

The money demand equation – market determination of either base money or the treasury bill rate (1990Q2 to 1997Q4)

Cointegrating equation (estimated in a Vector Error Correction Mechanism with one lag, $p(-1) + y(-1)$ as exogenous variables, FIML)

$$ECM5 = r(-1) \quad + 0.7\,bm(-1) \quad - 0.682(p(-1) + y(-1)) - 3.5$$
$$ 7.7** \quad\quad - 2.77**$$

Log Likelihood	107.240
Akaike Information Criteria	−6.144
Schwarz Criteria	−5.589

Table 13 The dynamic money demand equation estimates[†]

OLS	Dr		Dbm
ECM5	−0.344	ECM4	−0.782
	*−2.838** *		*−2.728** *
Dr(−1)	0.294	Constant	−9.537
	1.640		*−2.709** *
Dbm(−1)	0.105		
	1.634		
Constant	−4.231		
	*−2.843** *		
R-squared	0.240		0.199
R bar-squared	0.155		0.172
Standard error	0.029		0.088
Log likelihood	67.634		33.236
Durbin-Watson stat	2.052		1.513
Akaike AIC	−4.105		−1.952
Schwarz SBC	−3.920		−1.861

[†] t-statistics in italics, *indicates significance at 10% and **indicates significance at 5%.

Notes

1 The views represent those of the author and not the opinions of the Bank of Uganda.
2 Although operational target variables may themselves be monetary policy instruments, this need not always be the case. For example, the level of non-borrowed reserves or base money can be used as an instrument to set interest rates as an operational target. See, for example, Clarida *et al.*, 1998, p. 1046.
3 The Bank of Uganda does not pay interest on commercial banks' reserves.
4 As well as representing the lingering effects of past financial crises, the sensitivity of commercial bank credit to monetary policy may arise from a substantial information asymmetry between commercial lenders and potential borrowers. See Stiglitz and Weiss (1992) for a general exposition and Kasekende and Atingi-Ego (1998) for a discussion of the Ugandan case.
5 The background and early progress of reform in Uganda is reviewed in Sharer and McDonald (1996).

6 The treasury bill secondary market was underdeveloped largely because most investors preferred to hold the bill until maturity and also believe the excessive liquidity prevalent in most commercial banks during this period limited secondary trading.

7 The lag length of the VAR – four quarters – was chosen by minimising the Aikake Information and Schwarz Bayesian Criteria. The VAR estimates are reported in the Appendix 2.

8 D is the first difference operator, p is the log of the consumer price level, bm is the log of base money, r is the three-month treasury bill rate, and y is the log of real GDP.

9 It is noted that the structural identification of shocks based on ordering of reactions may not be appropriate using quarterly data.

10 There are no suitable data on wages and employment in Uganda. If, as seems plausible, Ugandan wages are flexible in nominal terms, we have some justification for not treating the labour market explicitly.

11 See footnote 2.

12 Base money is determined by equation 10b below.

13 Interest rates are determined by equation 11b below.

14 These rules should be interpreted as a benchmark against which we can evaluate the different answers to questions (i) and (ii) rather than a mathematical description of actual policy (Svensson, 1999).

15 We could have also represented the effects of drought by shocking long-run output in the agricultural sector.

16 Poole (1971) obtained the result that relying more on money base rather than interest rates as instruments would be optimal when real spending shocks were more important than velocity shocks in a highly stylised model. Nevertheless, his findings on the inefficiency of money base targets under velocity shocks have proven to be remarkably robust (Blinder, 1998).

17 According to this successful rule, interest rates are adjusted to keep the difference between money-base growth and nominal GDP growth constant ($\lambda = 1$, $\theta = 1$ in equation 12), implying a target of a constant rate of decrease in the velocity of money-base circulation.

18 See also Haldane and Salmon (1995).

19 One difficulty in applying this framework is that the real exchange rate would have to be stated in terms of tradable prices, which may have food and non-food components, rather than consumer prices.

Bibliography

Christiano, L., Eichenbaum, M., and Evans, C. (1996) 'Identification and the effects of monetary policy' in Blejer, M., Eckstein, Z., Hercowitz, Z., and Leiderman, L. (eds) *Financial Factors in Economic Stabilization and Growth*, pp. 36–74, Cambridge University Press.

Blinder, A.S. (1998) *Central Banking in Theory and Practice*, MIT Press.

Clarida, R., Gali, J., and Gertler, M. (1998) 'Monetary policy rules in practice: some international evidence', *European Economic Review*, 42(6), pp. 1033–67, June.

Fry, M.J., Goodhart, C.A.E., and Almeida, A., (1996) *Central Banks in Developing Countries*, Routledge.

Haldane, A. and Salmon, C. (1995), 'Three issues on inflation targets'. In Haldane, A. (ed.), *Targeting Inflation*, pp. 170–202, Bank of England.

Hemphill, W., (1974) 'The effects of foreign exchange receipts on imports in developing countries', *IMF Staff Papers*, 21, pp. 637–77.

Johansen, S., (1988) 'Statistical analysis of cointegrating vectors', *Journal of Economic Dynamics and Control*, 12, pp. 231–54.

Kasekende, L., and Atingi-Ego, M. (1998) 'Conduct of monetary policy in Sub-Saharan African countries: The Case of Uganda', a Collaborative Paper for the African Economic Research Consortium (A.E.R.C.).

Moaran, C. (1989) 'Imports under a foreign exchange constraint', *The World Bank Economic Review*, 3, pp. 279–95.

Musinguzi, P., and Kihangire, D. (1996) 'Estimating a base money demand equation for Uganda', Research Department Bank of Uganda, mimeo.

Oshikoya, T.W. (1994) 'Macroeconomic determinants of domestic private investment in Africa', *Economic Development and Change*, 42, pp. 573–96, April.

Poole, W. (1970) 'Optimal choice of monetary policy instruments in a simple stochastic model', *Quarterly Journal of Economics*, 84, pp. 197–216, May.

Sharer, R., and McDonald, C. (1996) 'Uganda 1987–95' in Hadjimichael, M.T., Nowak, M., Sharer, R. and Tahari, A. (eds) *Adjustment for Growth: The African Experience*, pp. 67–81. IMF Occasional Paper No. 143, International Monetary Fund, Washington D.C.

Stiglitz, J.E., and Weiss, A. (1992) 'Asymmetric information in credit markets and their implications for macroeconomics', *Oxford Economic Papers*, 44, pp. 694–724, October.

Svensson, L. (1999) 'Inflation targeting as a monetary policy rule', *Journal of Monetary Economics*, 43, pp. 607–54.

Monetary policy in a dollarised economy
The case of Peru*

Zenón Quispe Misaico[1]

1 Introduction

Persistent high inflation in Peru during the 1970s led households to hold foreign currency as store of value. This process of dollarisation increased significantly during the hyperinflation of 1988–90. In the years that followed, a wide-ranging package of reforms in the financial system and in the conduct of monetary and fiscal policy were introduced to bring a halt to the hyperinflation. But despite nearly a decade of subsequent economic stabilisation, the decrease in dollarisation has been slow: by June 1999 two thirds of domestic banking deposits were still denominated in dollars, only ten percentage points below their level in 1991.

How has dollarisation affected the efficacy of monetary policy in Peru? In theory, under dollarisation, revisions in expectations of devaluation can lead to instability of the domestic money demand, making monetary control more difficult. But instability in the demand for base money would seem to arise more from a dollarisation characterised by currency substitution (using dollars for transactions) than one characterised by asset substitution (using dollars as a store of wealth).

The second section of this paper characterises the dollarisation process in Peru. We show that agents prefer domestic currency for their current domestic transactions but hold dollars as a store of value: dollarisation reflects asset substitution. Monetary policy may still be effective in influencing nominal domestic transactions through the control of the domestic currency money supply. However, domestic open-market operations may have to be accompanied by foreign-exchange intervention and foreign currency reserve requirements. The subject of this paper is to discuss how a monetary policy that has both domestic and foreign currency dimensions has been effective in dollarised Peru.

The third section describes the recent history of monetary policy in Peru. The fourth section builds on this by using identified Vector Auto-regression Regression (VAR) procedures proposed by Christiano, Eichenbaum, and Evans (1996) and Leeper, Sims, and Zha (1996). It focuses on the role of domestic and foreign components of money aggregates in explaining the variance of inflation. The Conclusions forms the fifth section.

2   Inflation and dollarisation in Peru

2.1   Inflation, hyperinflation, and stabilisation

From the 1950s until 1990, the Peruvian Central Bank financed the public sector and the State Development Banks at subsidised interest rates in order to enhance the output of designated key sectors. These loan policies constituted the main source of base money creation since the 1970s (Chart 1).

The high level of default on development bank credits and the subsidised interest rates meant that the central bank provided a permanent flow of financing to these banks. Since 1985, when external debt service was suspended, the government's access to external financing was greatly reduced and its requirements from the Central Bank increased. The central bank extended subsidised credit to the development banks and implemented a fixed multiple exchange rate regime to promote exports and to subsidise basic imports via exchange-rate differentials. The Central Bank paid more soles per US dollars to exporters and sold the dollars to importers at a lower exchange rate, thus incidentally expanding base money.

This policy increased the inflation rate from an average of 9% during the 1960s to an average of 30% in the 1970s. Monetary policy was eased further after 1985, accelerating money base creation so that a hyperinflation process began in 1988.

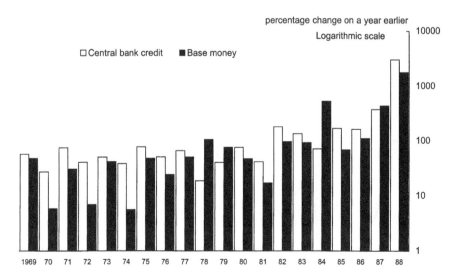

Chart 1 Peru: Central Bank loans to state development banks and the money supply

In August 1990 the policy-induced inflationary process was arrested when a new government implemented a strict control of base-money creation through a drastic stabilisation programme. One component of the reform was the new Peruvian Constitution and Central Bank Charter, which established the autonomy of the central bank and made price stability its sole objective. The Central Bank is forbidden to:

(i) finance the public-sector (indirectly the Central Bank can buy in the secondary market up to 5% of the base money);
(ii) finance any state development bank;
(iii) grant guarantees;
(iv) lend to any particular sector of the economy; and
(v) establish a multiple exchange rates system.

The Central Bank's accountability has been oriented to guarantee its independence; the members of its board of directors may be impeached only by Congress. The transparency of monetary policy is promoted through next-day publication of central bank market operations, weekly publications of macroeconomic statistics, immediate publication of central bank policy statements and the annual publication of the Central Bank Report.

2.2   The dollarisation process

Persistent high levels of inflation of the 1970s, together with underdeveloped capital markets and a repressed banking system that could not offer alternative assets, meant that US dollars became widely held.

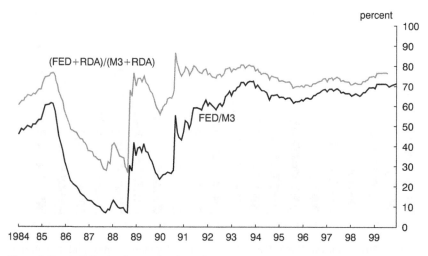

Chart 2 Peru: dollarisation ratio, deposits

The dollarisation ratio can be defined as the ratio of foreign currency deposits in the domestic financial system (FED) plus resident deposits abroad (RDA) (using the data reported by the Bank of International Settlements) to a broad monetary aggregate[2] that includes both foreign and domestic currency deposits home and abroad, (M3 + RDA). This ratio has increased from 37% in 1981 to 65% in 1984. Chart 2 shows that since then, from 1985–8, foreign currency holdings of households in the financial system decreased substantially because the government confiscated foreign currency deposits. Evidently households that could not transfer their assets abroad to avoid confiscation substantially increased their foreign currency cash holdings, despite the opportunity costs involved (foregone interest).

The dollarisation ratio measured by foreign currency deposits in the domestic sector over M3, (FED/M3), has been growing since 1990, in spite of the stabilisation process. It now remains in the region of 65–70%. However, including non-banking sector deposits abroad as part of the private-sector foreign currency holdings and adding them also to the denominator, the new dollarisation ratio ([FED + RDA]/[M3 + RDA]) shows a slight but sustained pattern of decrease since 1991 (10% between 1991 and 1998).

Another important indicator of dollarisation in Peru is the foreign currency lending of the banking system to the private sector. Foreign currency lending in the domestic market (FEDCR/TDCR) increased from around 50% of total domestic lending at the end of 1990 to 80% at the end of 1997. When we include the offshore liabilities of the private sector (ACR), the share of the foreign exchange lending

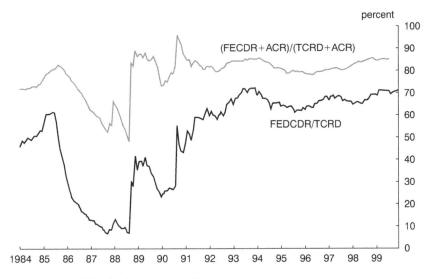

Chart 3 Peru: dollarisation ratio, credits

([FEDCR + ACR]/[TDCR + ACR]) has slightly decreased from around 90% at the end of 1990 to 80% at the end of 1997. This confirms that process followed by the credit dollarisation is similar to deposit dollarisation.

Note also that, for both deposits and borrowing, the spread between the purely domestic rates and the ratio which includes external deposits and borrowing has narrowed substantially. For example many transfers of Peruvian private non-banking sector deposits from abroad back to the domestic financial system took place at the end of 1990 and early 1991, reflecting rising confidence in the Peruvian financial system subsequent to the stabilisation and structural reforms (including financial liberalisation). Despite this, the dollarisation ratio has fallen only modestly as inflation has fallen. There is therefore still a continuing lack of confidence in the domestic currency, due mainly to the recent history of hyperinflation.

2.3   Asset substitution

It is arguable whether dollarisation need affect the conduct of monetary policy substantially. Possibly domestic-currency money demand could destabilise as a result of changes in expectations of devaluation or changes in the relative preferences of assets portfolios. However, the consensus among economists is that it is important to consider the difference between a dollarisation characterised by currency substitution and that characterised by asset substitution.

If current transactions can be paid with either domestic or foreign currency, and if the public chooses to use the latter, then the economy is said to be experiencing *currency substitution*, and the implementation of monetary policy will be more difficult. In the case of *asset substitution*, where the public choose to hold their savings balances, rather than their transactions balances, in foreign currency, monetary policy could still use intermediate targets that are closely related to current transactions and to inflation.

Peruvian economists agree that the dollarisation in Peru is of the asset substitution type rather than the currency substitution type. Current transactions are made in domestic currency, while large transactions are made in foreign currency. Wages are paid in domestic currency. Given the low average income of Peruvian workers, the transaction costs of buying foreign currency are high compared to the benefits of holding them, taking into account the short-run transactions horizon of the average income and the important reduction in the annual inflation rate (to 3.7% in 1999). Domestic currency maintains its role of unit of account and means of payment, whereas foreign currency is used as store of value. In this sense the cash holdings of Peruvian households are a good indicator of current transactions and are a plausible intermediate target of monetary policy.

A useful indicator of asset substitution in the Peruvian economy is

Table 1 Composition of bank deposits (percentages)[†]

	Domestic currency			Foreign currency		
	current account	*savings*	*time deposits*	*current account*	*savings*	*time deposits*
1992	33.0	55.0	12.0	9.0	55.0	36.0
1993	41.0	44.0	15.0	13.0	43.0	45.0
1994	37.2	39.9	22.9	16.6	44.6	38.8
1995	33.4	42.3	24.2	15.2	40.8	43.9
1996	34.9	36.5	28.5	17.4	35.4	47.2
1997	33.4	34.6	32.0	17.5	33.8	48.7
1998	34.4	36.4	29.2	15.8	30.6	53.6
1999	33.0	34.1	33.0	17.1	29.4	53.6

[†] Source: De La Rocha. Javier (1998) and weekly statistics of the Central Bank of Peru

deposit composition (Table 1). In the banking system, domestic currency deposits are mostly checking accounts and savings deposits; foreign currency deposits are mainly savings and time deposits. Furthermore, the withdrawal frequency (defined as a ratio of withdrawals to average balances outstanding) in domestic currency is almost three times as much as in foreign currency. This shows that, again, while foreign currency is demanded for some transactions, its main role is as a store of value.

3   Monetary policy

3.1   Design of monetary policy

The objective of the Central Bank of Peru is to reach international inflation levels in the medium and long term. To do so, it uses base-money growth as the intermediate target. That target is aligned with its inflation goals according to a monetary programme. The programme is reviewed monthly and monitored daily.

The monthly revision of base-money growth target is based on the analysis of indicators such as projected inflation, aggregate demand, inter-bank interest rates, the exchange rate, the fiscal stance, and credit to the private sector. These indicators tell the Central Bank of Peru how far the economy is from its sustainable rate of output growth, the targeted rate of inflation, and the forecast of the velocity of circulation (De la Rocha, 1998) and whether the target should be revised or defended. The base-money growth targets are not made public since technological shocks in the financial system make them subject to revision.

The daily monitoring of monetary policy is based on a careful study of the components of base money, in particular bank reserves, and some components of the banking system balance sheet, together with the evolution of the interbank interest rate, the exchange rate, and other relevant indicators. The demand side of the base money aggregate is mainly composed of the domestic cash holdings of households (75%–80%). The cash

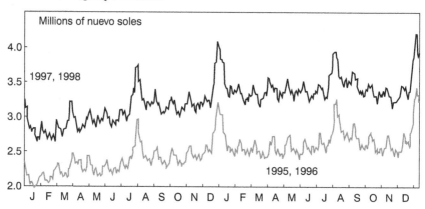

Chart 4 Peru: nominal cash holdings

holdings are good approximation of the current transactions needs of the economy, which are met mainly using domestic currency. Daily cash holdings in domestic currency follow a predictable pattern, as Chart 4 shows.

The Money and Foreign Exchange Commission is in charge of the daily conduct of monetary policy, based on the monetary programme approved by the board of directors of the Central Bank. It meets every morning to decide on actions to be taken. This implementation of monetary policy is primarily carried out with the two market instruments: intervention in the foreign-exchange market and open-market operations (Choy, 1999). Foreign-exchange interventions take two forms. Foreign exchange is purchased as a means of meeting domestic currency needs of financial institutions; US dollars are bought and sold to counteract extreme volatility in the exchange rate. Open-market operations are implemented through the auctioning of Central Bank certificate of deposits. The Central Bank announces the amount of the issue and lets the auction determine the interest rate. Complementary instruments to enhance liquidity in these operations are auctions of repurchase agreements (REPOS) with Central Bank CDs, 'swaps' with foreign currency, and lending through the discount window.

The Central Bank sterilises its net purchases of US dollars in order to keep base money growth under control. Large-scale sterilisation of capital inflows is likely to be ineffective under asset dollarisation, because higher interest rates not only encourage capital inflows (as in other countries) but also lead to portfolio shifts out of dollars into domestic currency deposits. However, intervention is always 'in line with the financial system's liquidity needs and the increase in base money projected in the money programme' (Choy, 1999, page 199). In general, as the government borrows or services its external debt in foreign currency, fiscal discipline and monetary and fiscal coordination are important in avoiding long-run exchange-rate volatility.

Reserve requirements on foreign currency deposits, and the interest rate paid on these reserves, are also used as instruments to prevent the expansion of monetary aggregates denominated in foreign currency.[3] The foreign currency reserve ratio is important because Peru is subject to large capital inflows. Although 70% of these capital flows are estimated to be long term (De la Rocha, 1998, page 187), the scale of inflows is still sufficient to threaten monetary stability.

The foreign currency reserve ratio can also be a buffer against a sudden reversal of these inflows and can encourage the public to hold domestic currency. However, the ratio is not varied systematically for monetary policy purposes and remains a supplementary device. In 1993 the marginal reserve requirement for foreign currency deposits was 45%, but in October 1998 it was reduced to 35% and then to 20% in December 1998. Required reserves are remunerated at a rate of interest related to LIBOR and are computed on the basis of monthly averages. These reserves comprise cash and demand deposits at the Central Bank.

3.2 The role of fiscal policy

The government's commitment to balance its budget is key to achieving inflation goals in an economy with dollarisation. That Peru's budget has been controlled can be observed from the fact that the central government raised, on average, a primary surplus of 1.4% of GDP between 1991 and 1998, with an average fiscal deficit of 1.9% of GDP during the same period (0.7% of GDP in 1998). This commitment lets the Central Bank concentrate on evaluating and avoiding other pressures over prices and revising the monetary targets, as the monetary policy indicators, including the foreign currency aggregates, reveal new information.

Another important factor in the Peruvian economy is the co-ordination of fiscal and monetary policies. The macroeconomic assumptions for the fiscal budget, especially the annual inflation targets, are set by the Ministry of Finance in co-ordination with the Central Bank. A fiscal committee meets monthly to set government expenditures, foreign-exchange purchases, and deposits. The Central Bank attends this committee.

Public-sector financial resources are kept at the Central bank as time deposits at the CD market interest rate. Also, the daily treasury cash surpluses, managed by Banco de la Nación, are deposited at the Central Bank (Choy, 1999, page 195). The revenues (in both foreign and domestic currency) from the privatisation of public enterprises must be deposited in the Central Bank at an interest rate related to LIBOR. The foreign currency needed by the public sector to service its external debts must be bought from the Central Bank to avoid unnecessary volatility in the exchange rate and the liquid assets of the banking system. These operations have to be reconciled with the price stability objective of the Central Bank. But co-ordination enabled the Central

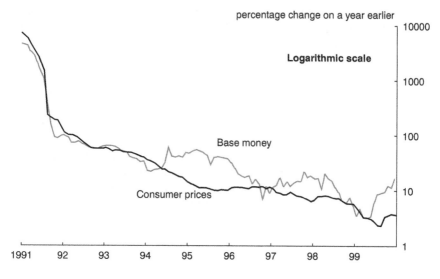

percentage change on a year earlier

Chart 5 Peru: prices and money supply (1991–99)

Bank to intervene and thereby inhibit excess volatility in the foreign-exchange market.

The outcome of this policy mix has been a reduction in the inflation rate: By September 1998, the annual inflation rate had come down to 6.5%.

3.3   The transmission of monetary policy changes

In this paper we are interested in identifying the transmission mechanisms of the monetary policy active in reaching its main goal: the reduction of the inflation rate. The important features of the different channels of monetary policy transmission mechanisms in Peru are described by De la Rocha (1998) and summarised below.

The money channel seems to be effective in Peru because the dollarisation is not of the currency substitution type. Central Bank of Peru estimates have shown that an increase in Central Bank certificate of deposit interest rates tends to feed through to the interbank rate. This can then change longer-term market interest rates and so affect aggregate demand and inflation (De la Rocha, 1998, page 191).

It is less clear whether or not the credit channel is important in dollarised Peru. On one hand, corporations tend to rely on the banking sector for credit, and bank credit is replacing informal funds for investment finance. (It is also worth noting that many non-bank financial institutions have liabilities outside the domestic financial sector.) On the other hand, the access that firms have to foreign credit, and equity finance (on domestic and foreign markets) is becoming ever more important.

The exchange rate would seem *a priori* to be an important means of monetary transmission in Peru. If domestic and foreign assets are highly substitutable, then interest-rate changes can lead to larger swings in exchange rates that can then feed through to domestic prices. The ability of the Central Bank to intervene systematically to control inflation through the exchange rate is, however, weakened by asset substitutability. Hence the Bank of Peru intervenes only to support its monetary targets and to smooth out fluctuations in the exchange rate

4 Analysis of the inflationary process using VARs

Deriving empirical facts about the transmission of monetary policy from raw data cannot be a value-free process. Any results are predicated on identifying assumptions about how the economy works and how monetary policy operates. In the rest of this paper, we will discuss what assumptions are appropriate in Peru and what inferences we can then draw.

As a suitable point of departure, we carry out pair-wise variance decomposition analysis between the inflation rate and the main monetary aggregates,[4] using quarterly data between 1982 and 1998.[5] Pair-wise variance decompositions tell us slightly more than a simple chart of the two series. They measure how much of the inflation variation is explained by each particular monetary aggregate (measured in real terms). But in order to obtain this information, we have to accept two assumptions: that a shock to the money aggregate takes at least one quarter to affect inflation and that money and inflation shocks are not correlated.

The results (reported in Table 2) clearly show that the amount of inflation explained depends on which measure of money is used. Real cash holdings and the broader aggregates M2, M3, and M3a (including residents' deposits abroad) have important explanatory power, whereas intermediate aggregates do not.

Table 2 Pair-wise variance decompositions of inflation

Variance Decomposition of the Inflation Rate					
Quarters	*Cash*	*M0*	*M1*	*M2*	*M3*	*M3a*
1	21.0	2.8	6.4	14.3	11.8	6.4
2	20.4	2.8	11.0	18.5	12.9	8.1
3	20.6	3.2	11.8	19.6	14.0	10.7
4	20.1	3.4	11.8	19.3	14.3	11.3
5	20.9	4.3	11.5	19.0	16.1	18.0
6	20.5	4.2	11.4	18.5	15.8	18.0
7	20.4	4.3	11.4	18.8	17.3	18.5
8	20.3	4.3	11.4	18.8	17.3	18.6
12	20.5	4.0	11.0	18.5	16.3	16.4

How much confidence can we have in these results? These bivariate results can be criticised in that:

(i) they exclude other important monetary policy variables in Peru such as foreign exchange interventions;
(ii) they ignore the relationships among the different monetary aggregates themselves;
(iii) they exclude other non-policy macroeconomic variables that are neither money aggregates nor inflation;
(iv) they do not tell us which components of these aggregates are the most important in explaining inflation;
(v) they depend on identifying assumptions that may not be valid; and
(vi) there are not enough degrees of freedom associated with the estimates.

There is a trade-off in coping with all of these criticisms. Criticisms (i) to (iv) will be dealt with in the following sections by introducing a wider set of variables in our VARs. Yet using more variables consumes more degrees of freedom and requires more identifying assumptions. In order to mitigate problems of type (v), we will try to find robust results by comparing across two different identifying schemes.

4.1   Approaches to identifying VARs in Peru

In this section we will lay out what our different identifying assumptions could mean in the Peruvian context.

Following Bernanke and Mihov (1998), the underlying structure of the economy can be written as

$$P_t = \sum_{i=0}^{k} D_i Y_{t-i} + \sum_{i=0}^{k} G_i P_{t-i} + A^P v_t^P \tag{1}$$

$$Y_t = \sum_{i=0}^{k} B_i Y_{t-i} + \sum_{i=0}^{k} C_i P_{t-i} + A^Y v_t^Y \tag{2}$$

where the vector P represents monetary policy variables. The vector Y contains non-policy macroeconomic variables. Equation (1) are the policy-makers' reaction functions, whereas equation (2) represents the structural relationships that describe the rest of the transmission mechanism. The variables v_t^P and v_t^Y can be naturally interpreted as unobservable structural shocks to the policy variables and the rest of the economic structure, respectively. The system (1)–(2) needs to be identified before the parameters and structural shocks can be estimated.

1   We can assume that v_t^P and v_t^Y are mutually uncorrelated structural error terms. This need only mean that v_t^P is defined as the vector of dis-

turbances to the policy variables that are unrelated to the rest of the economic environment. We can go further and assume that all inter-action between these errors occurs through the dynamics of the system: that A^Y and A^P are both identity matrices. In what follows, we make this assumption.

However, additional, more controversial assumptions are necessary.

2   For example, equation (1) can be identified if in addition we assume that there is only one policy variable; and that the shocks to this vari-able do not affect the given macroeconomic variables within the current period (Christiano, Eichenbaum, and Evans, 1996).

The latter assumption ($C_0 = 0$) is more plausible with high-frequency data. We use monthly data on macroeconomic and financial variables (including the Central Bank of Peru's GDP estimates) that is reliably available since mid-1991. Despite that, with dollarisation, some of the banking-sector series that we could include in the VAR, such as domestic currency deposits, foreign currency deposits, and residents' deposits abroad, can respond within a month to changes in policy.

In the Peruvian case, we cannot make the alternative assumption that the policy-maker does not respond to contemporaneous information: we cannot assume that $D_0 = 0$. Information from macroeconomic variables can quickly lead to monetary policy changes. For example, foreign-exchange intervention is sometimes used to smooth out exchange-rate shocks on a regular basis.

Another problem with these assumptions is that interest rates, cash in circulation, foreign exchange intervention and total reserves can all be used as policy variables in Peru. If each of these variables affect the other macroeconomic variables through different channels, including only a single policy variable in the VAR may be difficult to justify.

4.1.1 Recursive assumptions to identify a role for policy

One general schema for identifying both equations (1) and (2) is to impose a recursive structure on the contemporaneous reaction of all variables to each other (Christiano, Eichenbaum, and Evans, 1996).

Table 3A describes how such a recursive ordering might work, or not work, in the Peruvian case. In terms of equations (1) and (2), Table 3A describes the matrix

$$\begin{bmatrix} B_0 & C_0 \\ D_0 & G_0 \end{bmatrix}.$$

According to Table 3A, the variables in VAR are classified into the following categories:

Table 3A Recursive identifying assumptions for Peru

	GDP	CPI	NER	CDR	M0	CASH	QUASI	FCD	RDA
GDP	C_{11}								
CPI	C_{21}	C_{22}							
NER	C_{31}	C_{32}	C_{33}						
CDR	C_{41}	C_{42}	C_{43}	C_{44}	X	X			
M0	C_{51}	C_{52}	C_{53}	C_{54}	C_{55}	X			
CASH	C_{61}	C_{62}	C_{63}	C_{64}	C_{65}	C_{66}			
QUASI	C_{71}	C_{72}	C_{73}	C_{74}	C_{75}	C_{76}	C_{77}	X	X
FCD	C_{81}	C_{82}	C_{83}	C_{84}	C_{85}	C_{86}	C_{87}	C_{88}	X
RDA	C_{91}	C_{92}	C_{93}	C_{94}	C_{95}	C_{96}	C_{97}	C_{98}	C_{99}

Information variables are used as indicators by monetary policy, and therefore current shocks to these variables feed through immediately to the policy variable. But because these indicators are assumed to be more costly to adjust than the policy variables, they react to policy shocks only after a lag of at least one month. In Peru we can assume that output (GDP), consumer prices (CPI) and, very contentiously, the exchange rate (NER) are examples of information variables. Table 3A explains that, in order to impose a recursive ordering between the variables, we can assume that the exchange rate responds immediately to shocks in all three; price responds immediately to its own shocks and shocks in GDP; and GDP only responds immediately to its own shocks.

Policy variables immediately reflect the monetary policy stance but only respond to the current shocks in information variables. Short-term money-market interest rates, such as the Central Bank Certificate of Deposits rate (CDR), cash (CASH), and money base (M0) are all likely contenders for this designation in Peru.

Banking-sector or money-market variables can respond immediately to all shocks, including policy shocks. Examples for Peru could be domestic currency quasi-money (QUASI), dollar deposits (FCD), and resident deposits abroad (RDA).

We need to make further assumptions about the contemporaneous relationships among the policy variables and among the money market variables. One possibility is to blank out the crosses in Table 3A so as to preserve the recursive structure of our identifying assumptions.

4.1.2 A non-recursive approach to identifying policy

An alternative approach (Leeper, Sims, and Zha, 1996) would be to find enough restrictions on the contemporaneous reactions of variables to each other in Peru without necessarily invoking a recursive ordering.

Table 3B is the adaptation for Peru of this non-recursive VAR identification:

Table 3B Non-recursive identifying assumptions for Peru

	GDP	CPI	NER	CDR	M0	CASH	QUASI	FCD	RDA
GDP	C_{11}								
CPI	C_{21}	C_{22}							
NER	C_{31}	C_{32}	C_{33}	C_{34}	C_{35}	C_{36}	C_{37}	C_{38}	C_{39}
CDR				C_{44}	C_{45}				
M0	C_{51}	C_{52}	C_{53}	C_{54}	C_{55}	C_{56}	C_{57}	C_{58}	C_{59}
CASH	C_{61}	C_{62}	?	C_{64}	C_{65}	C_{66}	C_{67}	C_{68}	C_{69}
QUASI		C_{72}	C_{73}	C_{74}	C_{75}	C_{76}	C_{77}	C_{78}	C_{79}
FCD		C_{82}	C_{83}	C_{84}	C_{85}	C_{86}	C_{87}	C_{88}	C_{89}
RDA		C_{92}	C_{93}	C_{94}	C_{95}	C_{96}	C_{97}	C_{98}	C_{99}

1 GDP and prices are still assumed to be slow to adjust to the other variables, with output unresponsive to current price movements. However, the exchange rate is now allowed to react within a quarter to shocks to any of the other variables in the system. One reason why this happens is that the Bank of Peru intervenes to reduce 'abrupt and transitory changes in the exchange rate' (De la Rocha, 1998, page 186).

2 The assumptions about the response of base money reflect the fact that it is targeted by the Central Bank of Peru. The quarter-on-quarter changes to base money will therefore depend on either temporary deviations from target or revision to this target itself. Money targets can be set and revised during the year to incorporate information from GDP, prices and the exchange rate[6] about future inflationary pressure (De la Rocha, 1998, page 186; Choy Chong, 1999 page 196), and so these variables affect base money in the same period. Interest-rate changes that are understood to represent permanent changes in velocity can also be incorporated in the base-money target.

3 Short-term interest rates (represented by the CD rate) react within a quarter to their own shocks and to shocks to base money only.

4 Money components that are used for transaction purposes (cash holdings of households) may react immediately to current shocks in GDP and prices. But whether cash holdings will be affected by contemporaneous exchange-rate disturbances could depend on how important currency substitution is. A question mark in Table 3B indicates the coefficient over which this decision has to be made.

5 Some banking-sector variables, specifically domestic currency and foreign currency deposits in Peru and residents' deposits abroad, are held primarily as stores of value. Quasi-money, foreign currency deposits, and residents' deposits abroad are therefore assumed to be unaffected by current shocks to GDP. Exchange-rate shocks can, however, quickly feed through to these variables in Peru because of asset substitution. Contemporaneous price shocks are also important, because they could indicate future nominal exchange rate changes.

As above, other restrictions may be needed to identify this system fully; that depends on how many variables are included in the VAR. With these identifications in hand, we now turn to the interpretations of some estimates for Peru.

4.2   Results from VAR estimations and identifications

4.2.1   A VAR with data from the hyperinflation period (recursive assumptions)

We begin by evaluating the role of interest rates, broad and narrow money components together, in determining variations of the inflation rate for the period 1980M1 to 1998M12. An unrestricted VAR is first estimated on two lags of monthly data working with an annual rate of change of all variables except the interest rate. The structural system is identified by ordering the variables as CPI, real output, real exchange rate, real interest rate, and real values of the specific components of the broad monetary aggregate: domestic cash holdings, domestic quasi-money, dollar deposits, and residents' deposits abroad.[7] Real values are used to make the series stationary during the hyperinflation years (see Table 5 in the appendix).

Table 4 reports the variance decomposition analysis of the inflation rate. The most interesting result is that growth in cash holdings explain about 30% of the long-run variance of the inflation rate, even when other money aggregates are included.[8]

Chart 6 reports the impulse response function from this VAR. It is clear that inflationary shocks are persistent. But, after one year, shocks to the cash holdings of the households can also significantly raise the inflation rate. Another influence is the short-lived positive impact of a depreciation

Table 4 Variance decomposition of inflation in a VAR with broad money components

Per cent of inflation variance explained by structural shocks to:	Horizon (months)				
	0	5	10	15	24
CPI*	100	80	66	55	52
GDP	0	4	3	3	2
NER−CPI + USCPI	0	2	2	3	3
CDR−CPI + CPI(−12)	0	4	3	3	3
CASH−CPI	0	5	16	25	30
QUASI−CPI	0	3	6	8	8
FCD−CPI	0	0	0	0	0
RDA−CPI	0	2	3	3	2

* All variables except the real interest rate are measured as annual rates of change in the VAR. Unit root tests of the 12-month variations of the variables except the interest rate (reported in the appendix) show that they are I(0). The lag length of the VAR is chosen to be two months by the Schwarz Bayesian criteria.

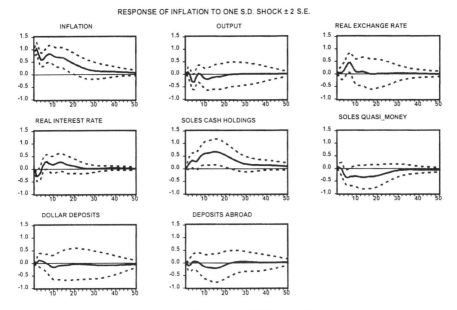

RESPONSE OF INFLATION TO ONE S.D. SHOCK ± 2 S.E.

Chart 6 Impulse response of inflation from a VAR with broad money components including the hyperinflation period

of the real exchange rate. Neither output nor real interest rate shocks have any discernible effect on the inflation rate at any horizon.

4.2.2 A VAR with data from the stabilisation period (recursive assumptions)

To see if money shocks are still important for inflation, we derive estimates of impulse responses of a VAR that is estimated for post-hyperinflation data. A recursive identification of the variables according to the order CPI, GDP, NER, CDR, and M0 is used. That is as reported in the shaded block in Table 3A, with the additional restriction that the interest rate does not respond to current base-money shocks. The estimation sample is restricted to the sample mid-1991 to end-1998, and the VAR was estimated on monthly data using annual rates of change of all variables except the interest rate and by combining data in nominal and real terms.

Positive shocks to base money growth still have a significant effect on inflation. The peak of this effect is reached at its highest level in a year to year and a half. Apart from base-money growth surprises, inflation is driven by its own shocks and by shocks to the nominal exchange rate.

Other responses to a base-money shock seem plausible: a nominal exchange rate devaluation occurs almost within one month and real output falls initially, increases its rate of growth after one quarter, and returns to its original growth rate after three quarters. The interest rate initially

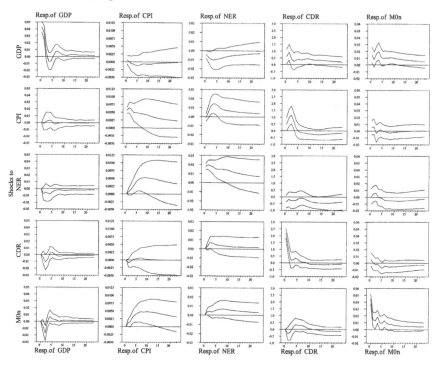

Chart 7 Impulse responses from a VAR (recursive identification)

reduces its level and increases after two months, returning to its former level after one year.

Not all the impulse responses are as intuitive. An interest-rate rise leads to a slight exchange-rate depreciation, for example.

4.2.3 A VAR with data from the hyperinflation period (non-recursive assumptions)

We can compare these impulse responses to what would be obtained from non-recursive assumptions. The same unrestricted VAR estimates are used; all that has changed is the identification scheme. The restrictions are as laid out in the shaded part of Table 3B.

The finding that a positive shock to base money significantly affects inflation after a year or a year and a half is shown to be robust. Many of the other impulse responses are similar, the main difference being that the money base now falls temporarily after a nominal exchange-rate depreciation.

As with the earlier identification, the effect of interest-rate shocks on inflation, the exchange rate, and money-base growth are among the least plausible findings. Another criticism that can be levelled at this VAR is

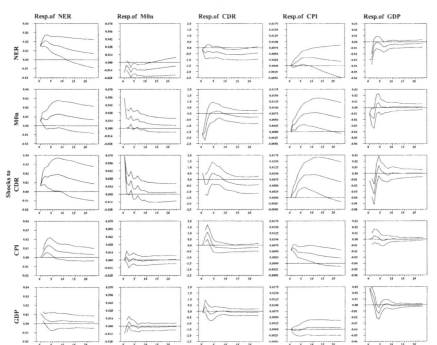

Chart 8 Impulse responses from a VAR (non-recursive identification)

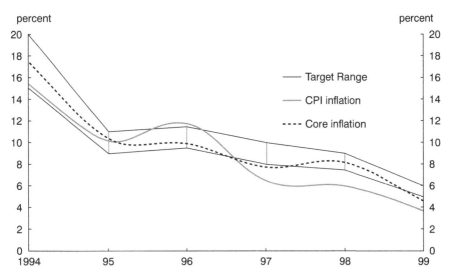

Chart 9 Peru: annual inflation

that, to correctly identify the role of policy, we should disaggregate M0 into its components – cash holdings of households, and total reserves – and also allow for a separate role for the Central Bank CD interest rate. The appendix discusses a scheme by which this could be done in Peru, following the work of Bernanke and Mihov (1998) on US Federal Reserve monetary policy.

But leaving aside these reservations, our results have at least established the robust result that M0 shocks (or possibly just shocks to its cash-holdings component) are responsible for about 30% of long-run inflationary movements.

It is important to recall that, to avoid misunderstandings about the variation of the base money, the Central Bank (in co-ordination with the central government) has been announcing a target range for the inflation rate since 1994. Chart 9 shows low levels of inflation, with only some small deviations from target. Underlying inflation exhibits better performance, although it is used only as an indicator.

In light of this, a possible interpretation of the VAR results is that money-base control has been successful in keeping the evolution of the inflation rate around its target range since 1994.

5   Conclusions

The dollarisation process in Peru is mainly of the asset-substitution type. Domestic currency is used for current transactions and is closely related to the inflation rate. Since cash holdings represent 75% to 80% of base money, there should not be any problem in considering base-money creation an intermediate target.

Fiscal discipline and monetary and fiscal policy co-ordination are the basic conditions enabling the Central Bank to succeed in its inflation objectives.

Shocks to the money base (predominantly domestically denominated cash holdings) explain most of the variance in inflation. Success in keeping to the inflation target could be related to this monetary strategy.

However, we should acknowledge that, to achieve its inflation target, the Central Bank of Peru has been using more than one policy variable. The results could be strengthened by accounting for these multiple instruments in identifying the causes of Peruvian inflation.

APPENDIX

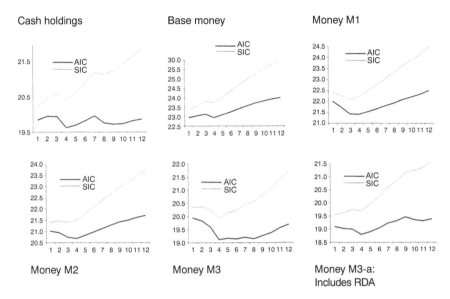

Chart 10 Optimal Lag Identification of the Variation of Real Money Aggregates

Table 5 Unit root tests

Monthly data 1991M1–98M6 Variables	*Augmented Dickey–Fuller*	*Phillips–Perron*
Inflation	−7.36	−17.53
Output growth	−3.26	−3.48
Real exchange rate	−4.50	−4.13
Real interest rate	−8.78	−2.28
Growth of real cash holdings	−3.74	−4.39
Growth of real quasi-money	−3.40	−3.46
Growth of dollar deposits	−2.71	−1.83
Growth of deposits abroad	−2.62	−1.97
Growth of real base money	−2.56	−3.08
Critical values		
1%	−3.51	−3.50
5%	−2.90	−2.89
10%	−2.58	−2.58

Table 6 Pair-wise Granger causality tests

Sample: 1991M1–1998M6, Lags: 2 Null Hypothesis:	F-Statistic	Probability
Growth GDP ⇒ INFL	0.30	0.74
INFL ⇒ Growth GDP	6.05	0.00
Real exchange rate ⇒ INFL	3.06	0.05
INFL ⇒ Real exchange Rate	0.41	0.67
Real Interest rate ⇒ INFL	6.23	0.00
INFL ⇒ Real interest rate	12.81	0.00
Growth cash holdings ⇒ INFL	19.21	0.00
INFL ⇒ Growth cash holdings	1.32	0.27
Growth quasi-money ⇒ INFL	2.45	0.09
INFL ⇒ Growth quasi-money	0.07	0.93
Growth dollar deposits ⇒ INFL	10.07	0.00
INFL ⇒ Growth dollar deposits	14.07	0.00
Growth deposits abroad ⇒ INFL	0.03	0.97
INFL ⇒ Growth deposits abroad	0.00	1.00

The identification of the Central Bank of Peru's operating procedure with many instruments

Bernanke and Mihov (1998) propose that, to identify the optimal monetary policy indicator, it is worthwhile to study the operating procedure of the Central Bank. In Peru, with a banking system that intermediates dollar assets, the Central Bank uses foreign exchange market interventions as an important instrument to provide domestic currency liquidity and issues certificates of deposit to be auctioned in open-market operations, announcing the amount of the auction and letting the market determine the interest rate. These instruments are used to regulate base-money creation through control of the reserves market of the banking system.

In terms of equations (1) and (2) in the main text of this paper, the problem now becomes to identify the impulse responses and structural shocks when there are many policy variables in vector P and when the contemporaneous reaction matrices A_0, B_0, C_0, and D_0 cannot be restricted (as in Table 3A or Table 3B).

The observable residuals in the VAR equation with policy variables, equation (1), contain the component $u_t = (1 - G_0)^{-1}A^P v_t^P$. Bernanke and Mihov suggest that plausible restrictions can be imposed on the matrix $(1 - G_0)^{-1}A^P$, which tells us about how the unobservable policy shocks v_t^P feed onto the policy variables.

In order to show how this can be implemented in Peru, an example can be provided with four policy variables: exchange-rate interventions (e), the money base (M0) and its two components separately: total reserves (TR) and cash holdings of households (CASH). We can write down the plausible set of restrictions between the observable residuals to these variables, VAR equations (the u_t) and the unobservable shocks (the v_t):

$$u_{TR} = -\alpha u_{CDR} + \beta u_e + v^D \tag{A1}$$
$$u_{CASH} = -\gamma u_{CDR} - \delta u_e + v^B \tag{A2}$$
$$u_{M0} = \varphi^D v^D + \varphi^B v^B + \varphi^e v^e + v^S \tag{A3}$$
$$u_e = \theta^D v^D + \beta^B v^B + v^e + \theta^s v^S \tag{A4}$$

Equation (A1) is the banking system total reserves demand, depends negatively on its price and the interest rate of Central Bank CDs,[9] and positively on deviations of exchange-rate devaluation. The positive relationship with the exchange rate comes from the interventions of the Central Bank in the foreign-exchange market.

Equation (A2) describes the household demand for cash holdings that are negatively related to the market interest rate (using as proxy the CD rate) and inversely related to the exchange rate. This relationship comes from the free holdings of currencies in the country.

Equation (A3) reflects the reaction function of the Central Bank to shocks in total reserves demand, to shocks in household cash-holdings demand, and to its own 'monetary policy' shocks.

Equation (A4) relates to the exchange-rate devaluations that are carried out or allowed by the Central Bank. As the exchange rate becomes a policy variable, the restrictions are analogous to equation (A3).

Further identification assumptions

The system has 14 unknown parameters (including the four structural shocks) that have to be estimated from ten variances and co-variances. Just-identification of the system requires four more restrictions: First, we assume that $\alpha = \beta$, which means that the banking system interprets the difference between the nominal interest rate and the rate of devaluation as the cost of total reserves in domestic currency (this assumption is reliable for dollarised economies). The second assumption is that, for monetary policy to be effective in a dollarised economy, there is no currency substitution; a proxy to this assumption is to make $\delta = 0$. Consistent with this approach is to assume that the Central Bank does not react, through exchange-market interventions, to shocks to household demand for cash holdings, that is, $\theta^B = 0$. A fourth assumption comes from the separation of the reaction function of the central bank through exchange-market interventions from the reaction function through the base money creation, that is, $\varphi^e = 0$. This is a necessary assumption, since supply-side base-money creation should include (as a source) the exchange-market interventions of the Central Bank.

With these four assumptions, we can obtain a just-identified system whose estimation provides us with an indicator of monetary policy that is a weighted average of traditional indicators of monetary policy as the CD interest rate.

The solution for the just-identified model will then be:

$$
\begin{bmatrix} u_{CD} \\ u_{TR} \\ u_{CASH} \\ u_E \end{bmatrix} =
\begin{bmatrix}
\dfrac{1 - \theta^D + \alpha\theta^D}{\alpha + \gamma} & \dfrac{(1 - \varphi^B)}{\alpha + \gamma} & \dfrac{\alpha}{\alpha + \gamma} & \dfrac{-(1 - \theta^s)}{\alpha + \gamma} \\
-\dfrac{\alpha[1 - \gamma\theta^D - \varphi^D]}{\alpha + \gamma} & -\dfrac{\alpha(1 - \varphi^B)}{\alpha + \gamma} & \dfrac{\alpha\gamma}{\alpha + \gamma}\alpha\theta^s + \dfrac{\alpha(1 - \theta^s)}{\alpha + \gamma} \\
-\dfrac{\gamma[1 + \alpha\theta^D - \varphi^D]}{\alpha + \gamma} & -\dfrac{\gamma[1 - \varphi^B]}{\alpha + \gamma} & \dfrac{-\alpha\gamma}{\alpha + \gamma} & \dfrac{\gamma(1 - \theta^s)}{\alpha + \gamma} \\
\theta^D & 0 & 1 & \theta^s
\end{bmatrix}
\begin{bmatrix} v^D \\ v^B \\ v^E \\ v^S \end{bmatrix}
$$

Using these reactions, the impulse responses could be derived from a VAR that includes indicators of output, consumer prices, and commodity prices for example.

Notes

*I am indebted to Lavan Mahadeva for his valuable support and excellent revision of this article.

1 The views represent those of the author and not those of the Central Bank of Peru.

2 Household holdings of domestic currency plus current account and time deposits in domestic and foreign currency in the banking system.

3 The importance of the reserve requirement on domestic currency deposits as an instrument of monetary control has diminished, and the ratio currently stands at 7%.

4 We do not have information of market interest rates and market exchange rates for the main part of this period, because of exchange controls and financial repression policies.

5 The optimal lag for these VAR estimations in real terms is 4, using both the Akaike and the Schwarz information criteria. See Chart 10 in the appendix for these results.

6 Net purchases of dollars by the Central Bank of Peru in foreign-exchange intervention are sterilised so as not to affect base money.

7 We consider the lending rate, since the other short-run interest rates, such as the overnight interest rate of the banking system, have been available only since 1994. The interest rate of the central bank certificates of deposit is available since end 1992, however we need to evaluate a market interest rate.

8 Table 6 in the appendix confirms that, in a pairwise Granger causality test, the growth in domestic cash holdings is found to Granger cause inflation.

9 The cost of total reserves for the banking system should be the federal funds rate. However the Peruvian banking system has reported this rate to the Central Bank only since the last quarter of 1995. Instead we use the interest rate of Central Bank CDs. The use of the CDs rate is valid because it is a market rate: the Central Bank auctions announced amounts of CDs and the bidders set the price. We have carried out estimations for a small sample that uses the federal funds rate to test the adequacy of this assumption.

Bibliography

Bernanke, B. and Mihov, I. (1998), 'Measuring monetary policy', *The Quarterly Journal of Economics*, CXIII, pp. 869–902.

Bernanke, B. and Mihov, I. (1997), 'What does the Bundesbank target?' *European Economic Review*, 14, June, pp. 1025–54.

Christiano, L., Eichenbaum, M. and Evans, C. (1996), 'The effects of monetary policy shocks: evidence from the flow of funds', *The Review of Economics and Statistics,* Vol. 78, No. 1, pp. 16–34.

Christiano, L., Eichenbaum, M. and Evans, C. (1998), 'Monetary policy shocks: what have we learned and to what end?' *NBER Working Paper,* 6400.

Choy Chong, M. (1999), 'Monetary policy operating procedures in Peru', in *Monetary Policy Operating Procedures in Emerging Market Economies*, Bank for International Settlements Policy Papers, No. 5.

Cushman, D.O. and Zha, T. (1997), 'Identifying monetary policy in a small open economy under flexible exchange rates', *Journal of Monetary Economics,* 39.

De la Rocha, Javier (1998), 'The transmission mechanism of monetary policy in Peru' in *The Transmission of Monetary Policy in Emerging Market Economies*, Bank for International Settlements Policy Papers, No. 3.

Ishisaka, S., Quispe, Z. (1995), 'Impacto de los shocks de oferta y demanda sobre la inflacion y el crecimiento del producto y mecanismos de transmision de la politica monetaria en el Peru 1991–1995', Central Bank of Peru.

Leeper, E.M., Sims, C.A. and Zha, T. (1996), 'What does monetary policy do?' *Brookings Papers on Economic Activity* 2, Fall, pp. 1–63.

McNeils, P. and Rojas-Suarez, L. (1996), 'Exchange rate depreciation, dollarisation and uncertainty: a comparison of Bolivia and Peru', Inter-American Development Bank.

Ize, A. and Levy-Yeyati, E. (1998), 'Dollarisation of financial intermediation: causes and policy implications', *IMF Working Paper,* WP/98/28.

Savastano, M. (1996), 'Dollarisation in Latin America: recent evidence and some policy issues', *IMF Working Paper,* WP/94/4.

The Balassa-Samuelson effect and monetary targets[1]

Marion Kohler[2]

1 Introduction

Many developing countries have argued that part of the inflation they experience is necessary if they want to 'catch up'. That argument can be supported by the Harrod-Balassa-Samuelson theory. Unbalanced growth leads to dual inflation which, in turn, induces real exchange rate appreciation (measured in CPI terms). In the case of a fixed exchange rate – or, more generally, if the movements in the real exchange rate are not fully compensated by movements in the nominal exchange rate – this will be reflected in higher inflation for higher growth countries.

This model is used frequently in the context of the European Monetary Union (EMU) to argue that inflation differentials may persist because some members have to 'catch up' with the income levels of other countries in EMU. But this explanation of inflation differentials is perhaps even more important for transitional countries now in the process of applying for EMU membership. Not only do they have further to go to catch up, but they will also have to meet the convergence criteria, for both the exchange rate and the inflation rate. Sectorally unbalanced growth provides a potential for a conflict between these two objectives.

Balassa-Samuelson effects are also important for medium- to high-inflation countries. Pegging nominal exchange rates can be an effective device to disinflate a high-inflation country by importing credibility and enforcing wider economic reforms.[3] But Balassa-Samuelson effects may result in CPI inflation – thus affecting the credibility of the new regime. The monetary authority and the public have to be aware that this type of inflation is not a sign of failure of the 'disciplining policy', but it should be expected to occur within limits. For example, Rebelo (1994) argues that this type of real exchange rate movement was responsible for the relatively slow process of convergence of inflation in Portugal in the early 1990s, after Portugal joined the ERM.

But the issue is also important for any monetary authority where the nominal exchange rate is one among the multiple number of targets that are pursued. In the survey responses reported in this volume, 21 out of the

45 central banks which do not keep their exchange rate fixed to within at least a 6% band nevertheless considered the exchange rate to be one of their main objectives.

In the theoretical part (section 2) of this paper I will outline the basic model and clarify the assumptions and their implications for monetary policy. In the empirical part (section 3) I test the validity of Balassa-Samuelson growth for 28 developing and industrialised countries using a panel cointegration analysis. In a second step, the estimation results are used to provide empirical benchmarks of how much inflation can be explained by this type of growth in the different countries. Section 4 contains my conclusions.

2 Theoretical framework

Movements in the long-run real exchange rate result in inflation differentials if the nominal exchange rate does not fully adjust. The Harrod-Balassa-Samuelson model compares movements in the long-run real exchange rate with differences in sectoral productivity growth. Historically, technological progress has been faster in the traded goods sector than in the non-traded goods sector. A rise in productivity will bid up nominal wages in the entire economy because of sectoral labour mobility; producers in the non-traded goods sector will meet the higher wages only if there is a rise in the relative price of non-traded goods. Within a country, differentials in sectoral productivity growth induce dual inflation; across countries, differences in dual inflation translate into real exchange rate variation. If the nominal exchange rate does not fully adjust there is change in the real exchange rate which results in CPI inflation differentials across countries.

The following sub-section sets out the model underlying the Harrod-Balassa-Samuelson effect. Section 2.2 analyses the conditions under which this model is relevant for intermediate policy targets.

2.1 The Harrod-Balassa-Samuelson model

The Harrod-Balassa-Samuelson model focuses on the implications of productivity trends for the long-run real exchange rate, thus abstracting from short-run adjustments arising from nominal rigidities.[4] In this long-run model the relative prices of goods are exclusively determined by the supply side of the economy, without having to specify the demand side or trade balances. To illustrate the Harrod-Balassa-Samuelson effect, consider the following two-sector model. The two production factors, capital (K), and labour (L) are fully employed in the production of two types of goods: tradables (T) and non-tradables (N). The production functions, in terms of the capital-labour ratios (k), are:

$$Y_T = A_T L_T^\theta K_T^{1-\theta} = A_T k_T^{1-\theta} L_T \tag{1}$$

$$Y_N = A_N L_N^\gamma K_N^{1-\gamma} = A_N k_N^{1-\gamma} L_N \tag{2}$$

Perfect competition ensures that factor costs equal the marginal products of the factors. Long-run capital and labour mobility across sectors (within one country) ensure that the marginal product on capital and labour is the same in both sectors.[5]

$$R = (1 - \theta)A_T k_t^{-\theta} P_T \tag{3}$$

$$W = \theta A_T k_T^{1-\theta} P_T \tag{4}$$

$$R = (1 - \gamma)A_N k_N^{1-\gamma} P_N \tag{5}$$

$$W = \gamma A_N k_N^{1-\gamma} P_N \tag{6}$$

Capital is internationally mobile, and (if capital markets are perfectly competitive and integrated), the interest rate (R) *in domestic currency units* is determined by the international financial market (and is *exogenous* to the domestic economy). Capital is fixed one period ahead, but if shocks are anticipated, the first-order conditions (3)–(6) hold. (3) uniquely determines the capital-labour ratio in the tradable sector; (4) determines the *wage (W) in the tradables' sector* (and – due to wage uniformity[6] – also the wage in the *non-tradables'* sector); and (5) and (6) determine the *capital-labour* ratio of the non-tradable sector and the price of non-tradables (P_N) in terms of the price of the tradable good (P_T). Note that this model so far determines only the relative price $\left(\dfrac{P_N}{P_T}\right)$ where P_T is exogenous.

Now consider an anticipated rise in A_T, the productivity in the tradables' sector. Capital intensities in both sectors will rise, wages will rise, and the relative price of the non-tradable goods increase.[7] In contrast, an increase in the productivity of non-tradables while the productivity of tradables remains constant does not affect wages but leads to a fall in the relative price of non-tradables.

Solving (3), (4), (5), and (6) yields an expression for the relative price of non-tradables. Log-differentiating this equation yields the productivity hypothesis: higher productivity growth in the tradable sector will be reflected in higher (relative) inflation in the non-tradables sector. The ratio $\dfrac{\theta}{\gamma}$ is assumed to be larger than one since non-tradables tend to be more labour-intensive than tradables (variables with a ^ denote growth rates).

$$\hat{P}_N - \hat{P}_T = c + \frac{\gamma}{\theta}\hat{A}_T - \hat{A}_N \tag{7}$$

Internationally, purchasing power parity $(P_T = e \cdot P_T^*)$ ensures that the price of the tradable good is the same across countries. If purchasing power parity holds and foreign prices are fixed, equation (7) implies that the real exchange rate of the domestic country measured in consumer prices will appreciate if the relative price of non-tradables in that country rises.

Note that this conclusion is not only independent of demand conditions – it holds for small and large countries alike and is independent of the exchange-rate regime.

2.2 A role for monetary policy?

The Harrod-Balassa-Samuelson model is a highly stylised model that does not provide a role for monetary policy in its original form. But one could imagine that the nominal exchange rate summarises the monetary policy stance. A tightening of monetary policy (for example, by raising the short-term interest rate controlled by the monetary authority) would lead to an appreciation if the nominal exchange rate is determined, for instance, by uncovered interest rate parity. A looser monetary policy would accordingly be reflected in a depreciation of the nominal exchange rate.

2.2.1 Exchange-rate pegging

Under a fixed exchange-rate regime, the objective of monetary policy is to peg the exchange rate. Therefore, the model in the previous section – where the exchange rate is exogenous – need not be modified. Productivity growth in the tradable sector will lead to an appreciation of the real exchange rate, other things being equal.[8] When monetary policy holds the exchange rate constant, an appreciation of the real exchange rate can be secured only if the CPI rises. If a country where productivity in the tradables sector is growing relatively fast has decided to peg its exchange rate (e.g. in order to reduce inflation), as many developing and transitional countries have done, it will persistently exhibit relatively high inflation differentials. It is important for the credibility of this kind of disinflation regime that both the monetary authority and the public are aware of the likely size of this type of inflation differential. It would therefore be of interest to have an empirical estimate of that inflation differential.

2.2.2 Inflation targeting and floating exchange rates

If the exchange rate is allowed to float freely, Harrod-Balassa-Samuelson productivity growth need not imply anything for the inflation rate. An illustrative example is provided by the case where the exchange rate is flexible and the monetary authority instead acts to keep the CPI inflation rate at zero. The CPI inflation rate can be defined by:

$$C\hat{P}I = (1 - \delta)\hat{P}_T + \delta \cdot \hat{P}_N \tag{8}$$

where δ denotes the share of tradable goods in consumption.[9] If productivity in tradables production increases then the relative price of non-tradables will increase (see equation (7)). The money price of tradables is determined by international prices and the nominal exchange rate (PPP); the nominal exchange rate will have to appreciate if CPI inflation is to be avoided. The result of productivity growth and price-stabilising monetary policy are a nominal exchange rate appreciation, deflation in the tradable sector and inflation in the non-traded sector with zero overall inflation. Monetary policy has thus maintained price stability by tightening conditions for the tradable sector – which, however, has also benefited from the rise in productivity.

2.2.3 The intermediate case

A third case lies in between the two alternatives of pegging the exchange rate or keeping inflation at a target rate. In this case the monetary authorities may not want to fully offset the real exchange rate appreciation by a nominal appreciation of the exchange rate, because of considerations that are not captured in the highly stylised framework here. They may dislike nominal exchange rate volatility because they want to create a more stable and favourable environment for investors.[10] Or nominal exchange rate volatility maybe considered undesirable since international competitiveness may be temporarily affected, if nominal rigidities mean that domestic prices do not adjust instantly.[11] Often, there may also be political obstacles to nominal exchange rate appreciation. For any of these reasons, the monetary authorities may therefore wish to accommodate inflation (or part of it) that arises from 'catching up'. If they can predict the scale of this inflation, they can adjust the inflation target thus enhancing credibility by making the trade-off between price stability and an appreciation of the nominal exchange rate explicit.[12]

A different possible reason for neither pegging the exchange rate nor keeping the rate of inflation constant could be that monetary policy has explicit targets for both inflation and the nominal exchange rate. This is the case in countries that have to meet the Maastricht convergence criteria in order to qualify for entry in the EMU. In this case, rapid growth of the Harrod-Balassa-Samuelson type creates a conflict between the two objectives. Knowledge of the likely size of inflation differentials of this type makes it possible to judge how serious the conflict is.

So far, we have neglected a different scenario: if the *non-tradable* sector leads productivity growth, prices in the non-tradable sector will fall. Overall inflation will then be reduced without incurring the potential costs of a higher nominal exchange rate. Monetary policy that was aimed solely at maintaining an inflation target would lead to a depreciation of the real exchange rate. Prices in the tradables sector rise relatively fast.

In this section I have shown that sectoral productivity growth may create a conflict if monetary policy aims at both an inflation target and a nominal exchange rate target. In this situation it is worthwhile to quantify how large the potential for inflation differentials resulting from Harrod-Balassa-Samuelson effects is. The next section will therefore provide empirical estimates for these inflation differentials based on the growth experience of 28 developing and industrialised countries.

3 The empirical analysis

I used an unbalanced panel based on data from 28 countries from 1960 to 1997 (the starting date depends on data availability, as shown in Appendix C) in order to answer two questions:

- How important is sectoral productivity growth of the Harrod-Balassa-Samuelson type in explaining long-run relative price movements of the past?
- How much inflation do these historical trends in productivity growth imply if the nominal exchange rate was held constant?

The first question is addressed by means of equation (7), which has to be modified to yield a testable equation, since it is difficult to obtain reliable estimates of total factor productivity. Data on labour productivity is more readily available, however. I answered the second question by using the estimates provided from the first question and simulating the effects of past productivity trends on CPI inflation. Different data samples and time periods are evaluated in order to assess the robustness of the results.

In the subsection that follows, several data issues will be discussed, including the crucial distinction between tradables and non-tradables. A testable version of equation (7) will also be derived in subsection 3.2 to be estimated in subsection 3.3. Both panel fixed-effects and panel cointegration estimates will be presented. The latter method takes account of a possible non-stationarity of the data and slope heterogeneity across countries. Subsection 3.4 will use these results to determine the implied inflation differentials. Finally, in subsection 3.5, the growth experiences of several selected countries will be discussed. This allows us to draw attention to the heterogeneity of growth experiences across countries. At the same time, it will also shed light on factors which are important for answering the questions asked in this paper, but which have been omitted.

3.1 Data issues

3.1.1 Distinction of tradables and non-tradables

The Balassa-Samuelson model emphasises differences between traded and non-traded goods sectors. Empirical work requires an operationalisation of this distinction. In empirical applications the traded-goods sector (that is, the sector which is exposed to international competition) is usually agriculture and manufacturing, while the non-traded sector is services.[13] I follow this distinction but exclude the public sector from the analysis. The reason for doing so lies partly in the difficulties in measuring productivity and in the considerable share of administered prices in this sector. Therefore, the tradables sector here consists of agriculture and manufacturing, while the non-traded sector covers transportation, retailing, financial and social and personal services.

Of course, a distinction between tradables and non-tradables is never 'perfect'. Rogoff (1996) argues that a non-tradable is a tradable good with infinite transportation costs. A definition based on 'transportation costs' highlights the fact that the distinction is gradual and a classification will always be somewhat arbitrary. Also, a category such as 'transportation or communications' contains sub-categories with quite different degrees of tradability, such as non-tradable local commuter train services and highly tradable telecommunications. Therefore, De Gregorio *et al.* (1994) use a data-driven distinction. They calculate the average share of exports in the overall production in each industry from 1970 to 1985 for 14 OECD countries and assume that an export share of 10% is a reasonable criterion of tradability. They find that manufacturing, transportation, agriculture, and mining belong to the tradable sector, while everything else is non-tradable. The model here was also tested using their classification. The results were similar to those based on the definition discussed earlier as regards the stylised facts and the coefficients of the panel co-integration results, though the De Gregorio definition performed less well with respect to the cointegration tests.[14]

3.1.2 Mismeasurement

Nominal and real value added data (needed to derive labour productivities and implicit prices) have been taken from the OECD database and national statistical sources. Mismeasurement of output and prices may be particularly problematic for services. Julius and Butler (1998) report for example for the United Kingdom that service sector productivity may be underestimated. Actual growth may then be higher and the price deflators lower than implied by the official data. But the degree of mismeasurement varies across different categories within the service sector. It varies also across countries since the bias depends in part on how the data are collected and compiled. As only one data source is available, there is no obvious solution to the problem. It is beyond the scope of this paper to assess the question of mismeasurement in detail, but one should be aware that it is a source of uncertainty in the estimation results.

3.2 A testable equation

Equation (7) provides the theoretical basis for the relationship between relative prices and relative productivities. The productivity parameter in the theoretical model relates to total factor productivity. Total factor productivity could be derived from Solow residuals but this would require data on capital stocks and the labour share of income. Since reliable data on capital stocks is available for only a few countries (and most likely not for the developing countries used in the study here), other studies have proxied total factor productivity with average labour productivity. In the framework here, however, equation (7) can be restated directly in terms of labour productivities.

Consider equations (4) and (6), the first-order conditions for labour. Since marginal productivities in both sectors have to be the same, they can be equated and solved for the relative price of non-tradables. This yields equation (9), which states that the relative output prices are equal to the inverse relative marginal labour productivities. It can easily be shown that in the case of Cobb-Douglas production functions marginal and average labour productivities are equal (compare the term for marginal productivity in equation (4) with equation (1), divided by L_T).[15]

$$\frac{P_N}{P_T} = \frac{\dfrac{\partial Y_T}{\partial L_T}}{\dfrac{\partial Y_N}{\partial L_N}} = \frac{\theta}{\gamma} \cdot \frac{\dfrac{Y_T}{L_T}}{\dfrac{Y_N}{L_N}} \tag{9}$$

Taking natural logarithms results in this testable equation:

$$\ln P_N - \ln P_T = const + \ln Q_T - \ln Q_N \tag{9'}$$

where Q is measured labour productivity. Expressed in first differences, this equation restates an earlier observation: a rise in tradable productivity relative to non-tradable productivity will raise the relative price of non-tradables, *ceteris paribus*. But now the coefficients of the labour productivities are equal because the equation is in terms of labour productivity rather than total factor productivity. The two production functions (1) and (2) do not have to have equal elasticities in order for equation (9)' to be valid.

3.3 Explaining relative prices: the validity of the sectoral productivity approach

The Balassa-Samuelson model has two testable predictions. *Across* countries, relatively fast-growing countries will see real exchange rate appreciations. This hypothesis has been tested – with mixed results – in a number of studies on the determinants of real exchange rates.[16] The second hypothesis, which is the focus of this paper, states that *within* a catching-up country, the inflation of non-tradables relative to tradables varies one for one with labour productivity growth in tradables relative to that in non-tradables. This result, namely that catching-up countries may exhibit persistent inflation differentials when exchange rates are fixed, has been the subject of several studies in inflation divergence in the EMU.[17]

3.3.1 Earlier studies

This study is closely related to those of Canzoneri *et al.* (1999), who explain real exchange rate movements, and of Alberola and Tyrväinen (1998), who evaluate inflation differentials in EMU. While my analysis combines elements from both studies, it also improves upon them in various aspects. In answering the first question, I follow Canzoneri *et al.*, in using a version of equation (9) adapted for labour productivities, and I also use panel cointegration.

Alberola and Tyrväinen have provided an answer to the second question for several member countries of EMU, and their approach is adopted here.[18] Finally, the sample here includes a wide selection of developing countries. Thus, it is also possible to evaluate the growth experiences of developing countries of the 1980s and 1990s, rather than concentrating on the growth experiences of industrialised countries in the 1960s and 1970s, as the other studies do. As will be shown, these experiences were quite different.

Several lessons from previous studies should be emphasised. Nominal rigidities seem to be important in determining real exchange rates in the short run. Therefore, the model outlined here, which abstracts from nominal rigidities, is rather suited to capture medium to long-run movements in real exchange rates and dual inflation.

Second, the assumption of wage uniformity may not hold. Alberola and Tyrväinen (1998) show that for a range of countries the Balassa-Samuelson theory is supported by the data if allowance is made for wage differentials across sectors. Relative wages were included in the estimation where data are available. Since wage data are not available for all the countries in the sample, the panel cointegration tests are of much lower power; consequently non-stationarity of the residuals was more frequently accepted.

A third variable, which other studies control for, is government expenditure. Government expenditure is often used to account for demand shifts toward non-tradable sectors, which may explain a rise in the relative price of non-tradables in the medium term. In the long run, however, these shifts should not have an impact on the relative price of non-tradables (unless they are financed by distortionary taxes). Chinn (1997) finds that fiscal policy is an important determinant of real exchange rates. De Gregorio *et al.* (1995) cannot find strong evidence that demand shifts determine the relative price of tradables. Government expenditure was included in some of the model estimates here (but they have not been reported here). While government consumption seems to be the most important determinant (at the same time highly correlated with money growth) of inflation, no special role could be detected for it in the equations that focus on sectoral productivity. One explanation may be that here (as in De Gregorio *et al.*) annual data is used, and it is the long run rather than the medium term that is captured.

3.3.2 The equation

The equation which is estimated follows from equation (9):

$$\ln P_{rel,it} = \alpha_i + \beta \cdot \ln \frac{Q_{it}^{trad}}{Q_{it}^{ntrad}} + \epsilon_t$$

where $P_{rel,it}$ denotes the relative price of non-tradables to tradables (measured with the implicit sectoral value-added deflators). Q^{tad} and Q^{ntrad} denote labour productivity (measured as real output per employee[19]) in the tradable and the non-tradable sector, respectively. The theoretical model underlying equation (9) predicts that β is positive and equal to one.[20]

Chart 9 in Appendix A shows relative productivity and relative prices for all countries for which data are available. A brief look suggests strong evidence for the hypothesis that relative prices and relative productivity move together.

3.3.3 Results of the fixed-effects model

Given the short data time series for some of the countries, it is most sensible to test for the Harrod-Balassa-Samuelson theory using panel estimation. In a first step, a fixed-effects model was estimated, which allows for heterogeneous intercepts but imposes a common slope. Table 1 in Appendix B reports the results of the estimation. Fixed-effects estimation allows estimating an unbalanced panel, and, hence, I could include all 28 countries over the full-time series length available for each country. The estimation of the balanced panel was included for completeness and allows comparisons with the results of the co-integration panel in Table 2. In a third version of the fixed-effects estimate, I allowed the slope coefficient β to vary over the four decades from 1960 to 1997.[21]

The slope coefficient, with β between 0.53 and 0.71, is positive in all estimates but it is not one, as suggested by the theory. This indicates that one of the basic assumptions may be violated (that is, wage uniformity or profit maximisation). Since we estimate the long-run relationship, it seems more likely that the assumption of wage uniformity rather than the profit-maximisation conditions have failed to hold (particularly since the data are sectoral aggregates, not on a firm level or individual-sector level). Since there are not sufficient data on sectoral wages for the countries considered here, it is not possible to formally test whether this is the case. But this would indeed be consistent with Alberola and Tyrväinen (1998), who find that once they account for an imperfect degree of wage spillovers, they can accept the Balassa-Samuelson hypothesis. They show also that equation (7) holds, albeit to a lesser degree, as long as wage spillovers are positive. Therefore, it is likely that β reflects the degree of wage spillovers.[22]

There may be problems with using a fixed-effects model for two reasons. First, the size of the coefficient β may well be different across countries because in most cases, slope heterogeneity is also required. Second, it has been well documented that the variables used here may be non-stationary. Indeed, a panel unit root test based on the methodology proposed by Im *et al.* (1995 and 1997), shows that the non-stationarity of the series cannot be rejected (see Tables 2, 3 and 4).

3.3.4 Results of the non-stationary panel estimation

Alberola and Tyrväinen (1998) tackle these two problems by estimating the co-integrating vectors separately for each country in their sample. However, given that the data are annual and co-integration tests have notoriously low power in such small samples, this might be inappropriate.

The panel co-integration technique developed by Pedroni (1996) seems a more promising framework for tackling these issues. Panel co-integration has the advantage of increased power if time series are too short for single time series co-integration. It has the advantage over pooled regression of accounting for country heterogeneity (in intercept and slope) by estimating a form of a fixed-effects model.[23]

Technically, Pedroni proposes that the model is estimated by performing a standard OLS regression on each individual country and then testing whether the residuals of this estimation are stationary. The test statistics are derived from a panel estimation. Pedroni offers four panel tests statistics three group tests, based on the similar tests known from time-series regression for one country (augmented Dickey-Fuller, Phillips-Perron, and a modified Phillips-Perron test). The critical values come from the same source (Pedroni, 1998).

The method proposed by Pedroni is based on a balanced panel. Consequently, the available database has to be split up in appropriate panels.[24] This allows us to include every country in at least one panel, while exploiting the full data over time that are available for each country. Comparing the results for an individual country across the different panels allows us to assess the robustness of the estimates as well.

The results of the estimations are reported in Tables 2–4 in Appendix

B. Two versions of the model were estimated: one version assumes that countries have a common trend (a parameter, which may vary over time but not across countries), and another version has no common coefficients across countries. The first version is estimated by demeaning data, and therefore is called the 'demeaned' version. In most of the estimations, the demeaned version was more likely to pass a majority of the co-integration tests. The preferred model is presented in Table 2, which estimates across 18 countries over 18 years. Three of the four panel test statistics and two of the three sets of group statistics reject the hypothesis of non-stationarity on a 10% level.

All countries have a positive slope, but the heterogeneity of the slope across countries is considerable. Australia, Italy, Belgium, and Finland have a slope close to 1. The 'low' coefficient for Germany (0.62) may also be due to the estimation period, which began only in 1976. As explained in more detail in subsection 3.5 on case studies, over the last ten years growth in Germany has been stronger in non-tradables; the long post-war period of a Harrod-Balassa-Samuelson type of 'catching up' is not included in the sample. The low coefficient for Japan (it is actually negative in the third estimation, which considers only the last ten years) appears in the regressions that include a common constant across countries. If this constant that may vary over time is excluded, the coefficient for Japan is considerably higher than 1 (Table 3). Similar results (with 0.3 vs. 0.6) are obtained for Korea. As can be seen in Charts 3 and 4, in Appendix A, both countries have a strong time trend in both relative prices and relative productivities. Once this common constant is allowed for (by demeaning across countries), the remaining variation of the two variables is not very similar. In the case of Chile, the estimated coefficient is very high (2.41). As shown in the case study for Chile in section 3.5, this may reflect the simultaneous effect of a strong growth in non-tradables and a strong appreciation of the nominal exchange rate over the estimation period (that is, effects from nominal rigidities may not have disappeared over the data period) that 'magnify' the effect of falling relative productivity on the relative price. The growth experiences of individual countries will be discussed in subsection 3.5.

For many countries, the estimates of the slope are similar across the three different panels in Tables 2, 3 and 4. Some countries, such as South Africa (which is discussed later), show considerable differences. This is partly due to the differences in behaviour over the different periods considered, but partly it reflects uncertainty about the true parameter. Unfortunately, estimation techniques do not allow us to choose which one is the 'better' estimate; therefore, these results have to be treated with caution.

3.4 The implied inflation rates

Ultimately, with respect to monetary policy, the measured CPI inflation implied by relative productivity growth is of interest. Consequently, this subsection derives a benchmark for the inflation from past productivity growth in the individual countries.

3.4.1 Deriving the benchmark

A positive coefficient in the regression of relative productivity on relative prices does not tell us whether the relative prices have been falling or rising. As shown in the theoretical part, however, falling relative prices of non-tradables decrease inflationary pressure, while rising relative prices increase inflation for a given level of the exchange rate. If equation (9)' were to hold perfectly, I could simply use relative productivity trends to derive the implicit CPI inflation. However, it has been argued in the previous section that equation (9)' does not hold perfectly because some of the model assumptions (in particular wage uniformity) do not hold perfectly. Therefore, I will use the estimated slope-coefficient $\hat{\beta}$ to reflect the degree of 'pass-through' of changes in relative productivity to relative prices.

Equation (8) with equation (9)' in first differences gives:

$$\hat{CPI} = (1 - \delta)\hat{P}_T + \delta \cdot \hat{P}_N = \hat{P}_T + \delta \cdot \beta \cdot (\hat{Q}_T - \hat{Q}_N)$$

We will estimate a benchmark that is the implied inflation rate assuming a constant nominal exchange rate. This gives the equation used for the calculation of the benchmarks:

$$\hat{CPI} = \Delta \ln CPI = \delta \cdot \hat{\beta} \cdot \Delta(\ln Q_T - \ln Q_N) \tag{10}$$

The share of non-tradables in CPI, δ, is approximated by the average of the share of non-tradables in production over the last decade. Changes in relative productivities are measured by the average over the whole sample period. Since the first panel covers almost 20 years, the exercise was repeated for two sub-samples for the same panel. In order to check for robustness, the inflation differentials based on the slope estimates in the other two panels (which are shorter) are also included. Note that not all countries are represented in all panels due to the lack of the respective data.

3.4.2 The implied differentials

The results are recorded in Appendix B, Table 5. The second column contains the estimated shares in CPI. Columns 3 to 7 contain the differences in overall CPI based on past behaviour of sectoral productivity growth. The last column includes actual average inflation over the full sample length. The actual inflation rate also includes changes in the nominal exchange rate (that is, it reflects changes in the stance of monetary policy).

The implied inflation rates range from 2.1% in Italy (however, over the last decade, this rate dropped to 1.3%) to −0.8% in Chile over the last decade. The negative inflation differentials in Chile, Mauritius, and South Africa reflect the strong productivity growth in non-tradables in these countries. Similarly, the inflation differential for Germany is negative due to the higher growth of non-tradables' productivity since the 1980s. This difference became even more pronounced in the last decade, reaching −0.4% in 1985 to 1993.

The results for South Africa are rather uncertain, given that panel 1 in the second sub-period implies a fall in inflation of −0.3% while panel 3 implies a rise of 0.1% over a similar period. Similar conclusions hold for Mauritius, where panel 1 implies −0.3% and panel 3 implies −0.06%.

Another result is worth noting: Japan's implied differential ranges from −0.2% to 1.1% for a similar period, depending on the specification. The charts in Appendix A illustrate that relative prices as well as relative productivity in Japan have been growing strongly. Depending on whether this trend was common to other countries or not, the resulting implied inflation differential for Japan appears to be very different. If the Japanese relative-prices trend follows an international pattern, the implied differential is 1.1%. If the specification does not allow for a common trend across countries, the implied differential is −0.2%. Note however that this result may be an artefact of the large weight of Japan in estimating such a common trend. Hence the results without the common trend may be more plausible. Similar conclusions hold for Korea, where inflation differentials range between 0.1 and 0.6%.

The following subsection will discuss these two cases and the productivity growth experiences of other selected countries in more detail.

3.5   Some case studies

This subsection discusses different growth experiences in the form of case studies. This allows us to set the partial analysis in the previous sections into a broader framework, drawing attention to other factors that may affect the relation between growth and relative productivity growth on the one hand (the phenomenon of 'catching up'), and changes in relative prices and inflation on the other hand. It will become obvious that growth experiences varied quite extensively across countries.

Appendix A contains charts that show productivity and relative price developments in some selected countries. Three types of growth experiences will be discussed:

- the 'classic' case of growth led by tradable productivity growth (Japan and Germany World-War II);
- countries with rapid growth in the 1980s and 1990s: Korea, Chile, Mauritius; and

- countries with low growth in the last decades: South Africa, Zimbabwe, and India.

3.5.1 The 'classic' cases: Japan and Germany

Charts 3 and 7 in Appendix A show the sectoral data and macroeconomic developments for Japan and Germany, which have often been cited as examples of Balassa-Samuelson type growth.[25]

Whole economy productivity in both countries had grown for 20 years at rates between 0% and 5% in the 1960s and 1970s (Charts 3.d and 7.d). In both cases, growth was led by productivity growth in the tradable sector and prices of non-tradables rose faster than those of tradables (Charts 3.a, 3.b, 7.a and 7.b). Relative prices and relative productivity moved closely together over a long period (Charts 3.c and 7.c). Both countries nevertheless exhibited low inflation rates over the same period, the reason may be that the nominal exchange rates appreciated against the United States, one of the major trading partners, thus exerting downward pressure on the price of tradables.[26]

Over the last ten years, relative prices and productivity in Japan diverged, with relative productivity rising less strongly than relative prices. Chart 3b suggests the underlying reason. Although prices in the tradable sector had been flat or even falling, they would have needed to fall faster to keep up with relative productivity growth, but perhaps nominal rigidities have prevented that from happening. The yen appreciated strongly against the US dollar between 1985 and 1990 and CPI inflation was very low. This would support one version of the theoretical model: nominal exchange rate appreciation reduces prices (price inflation) in the tradable sector, which 'balances' the higher inflation in the non-tradable sector.

Over the last ten years, productivity in Germany grew at least as fast in non-tradables as in tradables. This explains why the implied inflation differential in Germany over this time period was negative. Since relative productivity and relative prices continued to move together, relative prices remained broadly stable, consistent with the predictions of the theory.

3.5.2 Countries with rapid growth: Korea, Chile and Mauritius

Korea (until the Asian crisis hit) and Chile, which experienced rapid growth and successful disinflation over the last ten years, have often been cited as examples of countries with rapid growth in the 1980s or 1990s. Mauritius is another example of a developing country with high growth rates in recent years. The stylised facts indicate that the growth patterns are somewhat different from the growth of Japan and Germany after World War II.

Chart 4 shows that Korea experienced a rapid overall growth accompanied by a moderate depreciation *vis-à-vis* the US dollar until 1980.[27] The growth in the tradable sector, however, was initially weaker than in non-tradables. At the same time, inflation was higher in tradables than in non-tradables. Until 1980, relative prices and relative productivity moved closely together, and all prices rose strongly, reflecting high overall inflation. After a slump in 1980, productivity growth in tradables greatly exceeded that in non-tradables. But prices continued to rise in both sectors at the same speeds while the nominal exchange rate depreciated. This was not consistent with the theoretical framework, which predicts that relative productivity growth in tradables leads to a rise in the relative price of non-tradables. Inflation moderated after 1980, the strongly divergent development in relative productivity put some upward pressure on non-tradables inflation.

Chile (Chart 1) is frequently cited as a success story: strong productivity growth (together with prudent fiscal policy), allowed it to pursue an ambitious disinflation programme and an appreciation of the effective exchange rate. Productivity growth in the non-tradables' sector has been stronger than in the tradable sector. In line with the theoretical model, this meant that the relative prices of non-tradables have fallen, though by more than the theory suggests. At the same time, inflation in the tradable sector was restrained by the appreciation of the nominal effective exchange rate in the 1990s (the nominal exchange rate with the US dollar is, in this case, an unreliable indicator). Thus, the strong productivity growth in the non-tradable sector, which was induced by strong foreign direct investment and increased competition in these sectors, has aided the disinflation.

Mauritius (Chart 5) had GDP growth rates around 4% since the 1980s while inflation fell more recently to 5% after an average of 10% from 1977 to 1993. Productivity growth in the 1980s was led by the non-tradables' sector, especially a tourism boom. Tourism is part of our definition of the non-tradable sector as a whole, and therefore there may be a classification issue. Leaving that aside, in the theoretical model, non-tradable sector growth should lead to a lower inflation as in the non-tradable sector, helping to moderate overall inflation as in the case of Chile. However, relative prices have been stable over the period, which indicates that productivity gains were not translated into lower prices of tradables. In fact, unit labour costs in Mauritius had been rising since the 1980s. Wages are set by backward indexation, which makes it difficult to lower inflation unless overall productivity gains are high enough, again, as in Chile. Only since 1992 has growth in the tradable sector (aided by a depreciation of the rupee) picked up. As in Chile, this may have allowed inflation to fall, although the budget deficit in Mauritius is still fairly high.

The stylised facts for fast-growing countries (and, indeed, for some of the industrialised countries) imply that there might have been a change in the type of productivity growth. In the 'classic' cases, productivity growth was almost always led by the tradable sector. Chile and Mauritius (and

Korea until 1980) provide some stylised evidence that productivity growth in the last decade has more often been led by growth in the non-tradable sector than had been the case in the past experience of industrialised countries. This can often be accounted for by an increasing importance of sectors such as telecommunications, business and finance, or tourism for developing countries. There may be more potential for productivity gains in non-tradables today than 40 years ago. For example, the IT revolution over the last 15 to 20 years has transformed the scope for productivity gains in telecommunications and the finance industry. Inference from countries that have 'caught up' after World War II to countries which are developing today may therefore not be straightforward.

3.5.3 Countries with low growth: South Africa, Zimbabwe and India

Some developing countries in the sample have exhibited very low growth. Though they are not obvious places to look for a Balassa-Samuelson effect, it may still be important to analyse differences in sectoral developments in those countries.

Economic growth in South Africa (Chart 6) has lagged behind that of other emerging market economies. One of the reasons was large-scale inefficient capital accumulation, which did not lead to substantial growth in total factor productivity. In the 1990s non-tradables productivity growth started picking up, but at the same time the lifting of international sanctions led to an even larger increase of growth in the tradables sector. Nevertheless, significant barriers to trade (such as tariffs) may explain why growth in the tradables sector has not been stronger. Relative prices of non-tradables increased at the same rate (though overall inflation has fallen since 1993, when labour market rigidities were reduced). This is consistent with the theoretical model.

Zimbabwe (Chart 8) is another country with fairly low growth rates. Tradable sector productivity reflects to a large extent volatile output in the agricultural sector (notably the droughts in 1991 and 1995). Other sectors are affected by droughts as well, due to domestic orientation of the industrial sector, which is a consequence of the international sanctions between 1965 and 1980. Since 1991 the liberalisation of foreign-exchange markets (accompanied by a strong depreciation of the Zimbabwean dollar) led to strong growth in the tourist industry. This explains why productivity had been growing faster in non-tradables than in the tradable sector, which was affected by the droughts. Prices seem not to reflect this difference in relative productivity very much however, probably because many prices are still administered. Although one may interpret the co-movement of relative prices and productivity (with much good will) as evidence of the Balassa-Samuelson theory, administered price and wages, and barriers to trade clearly violate the assumptions of that model.

India (Chart 2) is the only country in the sample where productivity had been falling in both sectors. While much could be said about why this may have happened, there seems to be little evidence of sectoral differences. Consequently, relative prices and relative productivity have been fairly constant over the last 15 years, with non-tradable productivity falling somewhat less than tradable productivity. Although the rupee has appreciated in real terms since 1993, there is not much evidence that this reflects a Balassa-Samuelson effect.

All of these low-growth countries exhibit stronger growth in the non-tradable sector than in the tradable sector. The reasons, however, are often barriers to trade, which prevent gains from international competitiveness and technological spillovers from being reaped.

The evidence presented in the case studies confirm the econometric results: 'catching up' experiences are very diverse across countries, and also across time. There seems to be also some evidence that productivity growth is increasingly biased towards the non-traded sector. Inference from past growth experiences has therefore to be applied carefully.[28] The Harrod-Balassa-Samuelson model for the determination of relative prices works equally well, in whatever direction productivity growth is biased.

4 Conclusions

In real world situations, such as pegging the exchange rate in order to gain credibility or meeting convergence criteria to join EMU, monetary policy has often a dual objective: the inflation rate and the nominal exchange rate. Monetary policy-makers may also care about the level of the exchange rate because of, for example, (short-run) competitiveness or costs of nominal exchange rate volatility. Sectoral differences in productivity growth can then affect overall inflation.

This paper investigates two questions empirically using a panel for 28 developing and developed countries.

- How strong is the link between relative productivity and relative prices? and
- How much inflation is implied by past productivity trends (assuming that monetary policy is unaltered)?

The findings regarding the first question are that there is indeed a positive link between relative prices and relative productivity, as suggested by the Balassa-Samuelson hypothesis. But the strength of this link varies considerably across countries, perhaps reflecting different degrees of sectoral wage spillovers. This makes inference across countries difficult. The results regarding the second question indicate that implied inflation differentials vary between −0.8% and 2% over the last 20 years.

Moreover, inference from the 'catching up' experience of one country to another country is difficult. There is evidence that recent growth trends in some (developing and developed) countries show a dominance of non-tradables growth, in contrast to the post-war experience of Germany and Japan where the tradable sector led growth. Such a shift in sectoral growth can help reduce inflation, contrary to the 'classic' case of strong tradables growth, which can increase domestic inflation. Stronger growth of non-tradables can have different sources: technological changes such as the IT revolution have increased the scope for productivity gains in the non-tradables sector, but also tourism (counted in this study as a non-tradable) may play a stronger role today than it did 40 years ago. In low-growth countries, the dominance of non-tradables growth may reflect barriers to growth in tradables rather than an improvement of the potential for growth in the non-tradables sector.

APPENDIX A

Chart 1a: Sectoral productivity

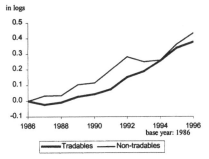

Chart 1b: Sectoral prices

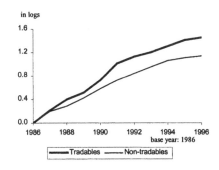

Chart 1c:
Relative prices and productivities

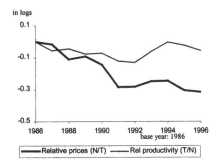

Chart 1d:
Inflation and total productivity growth

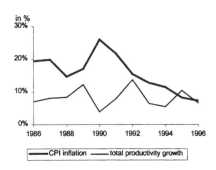

Chart 1e: Exchange rate[1]

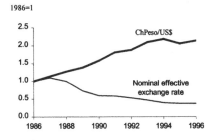

Chart 1 Chile

1   Data for the effective exchange rate comes from the IFS statistics and is 'inverted', such that an appreciation is denoted by a *fall* of the effective exchange rate.

Chart 2a: Sectoral productivity

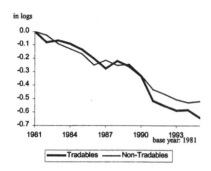

Chart 2b: Sectoral prices

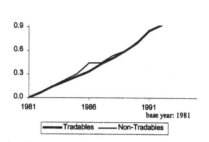

Chart 2c:
Relative prices and productivities

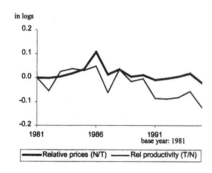

Chart 2d:
Inflation and total productivity growth

Chart 2e: Exchange rate

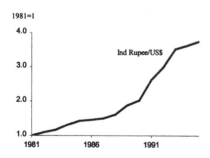

Chart 2 India

Chart 3a: Sectoral productivity

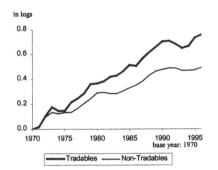

Chart 3b: Sectoral prices

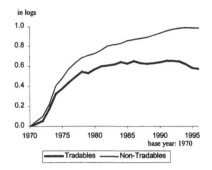

Chart 3c:
Relative prices and productivities

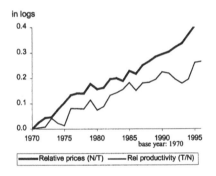

Chart 3d:
Inflation and total productivity growth

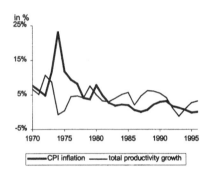

Chart 3e: Exchange rate

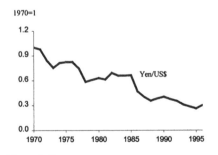

Chart 3 Japan

Chart 4a: Sectoral productivity

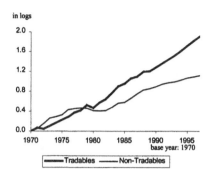

Chart 4b: Sectoral prices

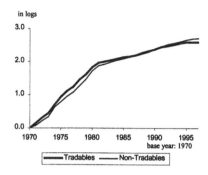

**Chart 4c:
Relative prices and productivities**

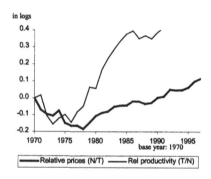

**Chart 4d:
Inflation and total productivity growth**

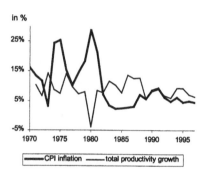

Chart 4e: Exchange rate

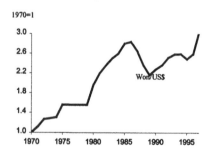

Chart 4 Korea

Chart 5a: Sectoral productivity

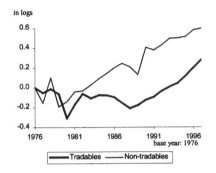

Chart 5b: Sectoral prices

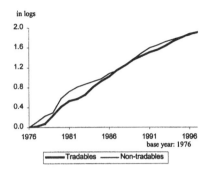

Chart 5c:
Relative prices and productivities

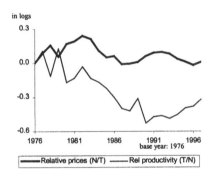

Chart 5d:
Inflation and total productivity growth

Chart 5e: Exchange rate

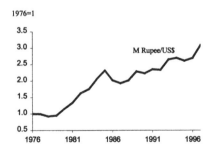

Chart 5 Mauritius

Chart 6a: Sectoral productivity

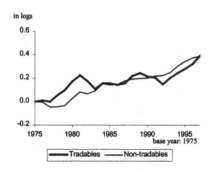

Chart 6b: Sectoral prices

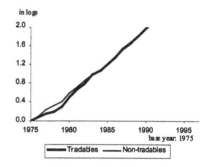

Chart 6c:
Relative prices and productivities

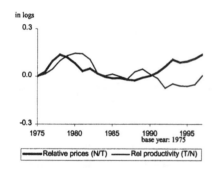

Chart 6d:
Inflation and total productivity growth

Chart 6e: Exchange rate

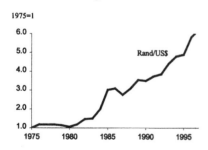

Chart 6 South Africa

Chart 7a: Sectoral productivity

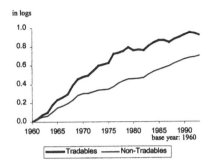

Chart 7b: Sectoral prices

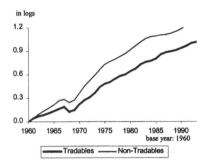

**Chart 7c:
Relative prices and productivities**

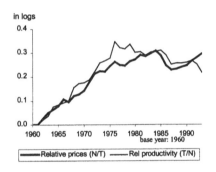

**Chart 7d:
Inflation and total productivity growth**

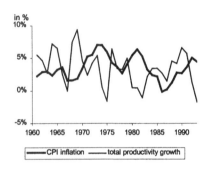

Chart 7e: Exchange rate

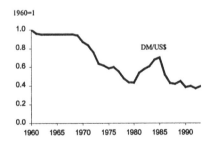

Chart 7 Germany

Chart 8a: Sectoral productivity

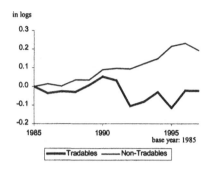

Chart 8b: Sectoral prices

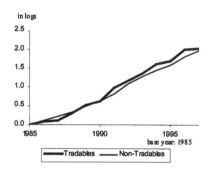

Chart 8c:
Relative prices and productivities

Chart 8d:
Inflation and total productivity growth

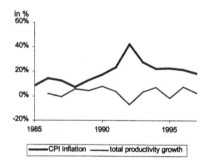

Chart 8e: Exchange rate

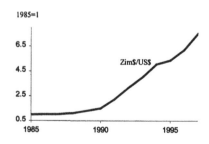

Chart 8 Zimbabwe

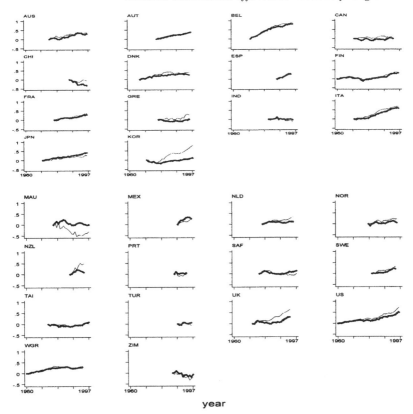

year

Chart 9 Relative prices and relative productivities[1]

1 The relative productivity of tradables to non-tradables is shown as a bold line. The relative price of non-tradables in terms of tradables is shown as a normal line. All variables are annual and logs of the levels (normalised to one in the first period).

APPENDIX B

Table 1 Results of the fixed-effects estimation

$$\ln p_{rel,it} = (\bar{\alpha} + \alpha_i) + \beta \cdot \ln \frac{q_{it}^{trad}}{q_{it}^{ntrad}} + \epsilon_t$$

Fixed effects (within) regression: 1960–97, 28 countries, unbalanced panel

$\ln p_{rel}$	Coeff.	Std. Err.	t
$\ln q^{trad}/q^{ntrad}$	0.62	0.02	33.02
$\bar{\alpha}$	0.006	0.004	1.52

$F(\alpha_i = 0) = F(27,552) = 66\ (Prob > F = 0.0)$ $F(1.552) = 1090\ (Prob > F = 0.0)$
No. of obs = 581   *R-sq within* = 0.66
$N = 28$ *R-sq between* = 0.05
T-avg = 20.8   *R-sq overall* = 0.14

Fixed effects (within) regression: 1977–93, 17 countries, balanced panel

$\ln p_{rel}$	Coeff.	Std.Err.	t
$\ln q^{trad}/q^{ntrad}$	0.53	0.03	18.0
$\bar{\alpha}$	0.02	0.006	3.6

$F(\alpha_i = 0) = F(17,287) = 48.76\ (Prob > F = 0.0)^*$ $F(1,287) = 322\ (Prob > F = 0.000)$
No. of obs = 306   *R-sq within* = 0.53
$N = 18$ *R-sq between* = 0.01
$T = 17$ *R-sq overall* = 0.03

Fixed effects allowing for different slopes in different decades

$$\ln p_{rel,it} = (\bar{\alpha} + \alpha_i) + \beta_1 D_{60} \cdot \ln \frac{q_{it}^{trad}}{q_{it}^{ntrad}} + \beta_2 D_{70} \cdot \ln \frac{q_{it}^{trad}}{q_{it}^{ntrad}} +$$

$$\beta_3 D_{80} \cdot \ln \frac{q_{it}^{trad}}{q_{it}^{ntrad}} + \beta_4 D_{90} \cdot \ln \frac{q_{it}^{trad}}{q_{it}^{ntrad}} + \epsilon_t$$

Fixed effects (within) regression: 1960–97, 28 countries, unbalanced panel

$\ln p_{rel}$	Coeff.	Std. Err.	t
$D_{60} \ln q^{trad}/q^{ntrad}$	0.71	0.03	21
$D_{70} \ln q^{trad}/q^{ntrad}$	0.63	0.02	28.
$D_{80} \ln q^{trad}/q^{ntrad}$	0.59	0.03	22.
$D_{90} \ln q^{trad}/q^{ntrad}$	0.57	0.02	23.
$\bar{\alpha}$	0.008	0.004	2.2

$F(\alpha_i = 0) = F(27,549) = 54\ (Prob > F = 0.0)$ $F(4,549) = 283\ (Prob > F = 0.000)$
No. of obs = 581   *R-sq within* = 0.67
$N = 28$ *R-sq between* =
T-avg = 20.8   *R-sq overall* = 0.16

* Test for fixed effects. H_0 is that fixed effects are zero (data is poolable).

Table 2 Non-stationary panel estimation (18 countries, 1977–93)

Country	Slope	Statistics[†]		
AUS	0.99	*Demeaned data (common time dummies)*		
AUT	0.62	$T = 17$		
BEL	0.83	$N = 18$		
CAN	0.54	*obs* = 306		
DNK	0.22	**panel unit root**	ln p_{rel}	ln q_{rel}
FIN	0.90	*constant only*	0.23	0.54
FRA	0.25	*constant and trend*	1.08	1.56
GRE	0.64	**panel co-integration**		
ITA	0.98	*panel v-stat* = −1.78		
JPN	0.12	*panel rho-stat* = −1.28*		
KOR	0.15	*panel pp-stat* = −1.80**		
MAU	0.33	*panel adf-stat* = −3.54***		
NLD	0.76	*group rho-stat* = 0.21		
SAF	0.64	*group pp-stat* = −1.39*		
TAI	0.58	*group adf-stat* = −5.17***		
UK	0.36			
US	0.64			
WGR	0.62			

[†] All tests are scaled to N(0,1); 10% level is 1.28 (denoted with *), 5% level is 1.64 (denoted with **), and 1% is 2.32 (denoted with ***). For the panel unit root test: The H_0 of non-stationarity is rejected on the extreme LHS. The panel unit root test implemented here is the t-bar-test proposed by Im, Pesaran and Shin (1995) and (1997). For the panel co-integration tests: The H_0 of non-stationarity is rejected on the extreme LHS, except for the panel v-stat where the rejection is on the RHS.

Table 3 Non-stationary panel estimation (17 countries, 1981–95)

Country	Slope	Statistics[†]		
AUS	1.12	*Not demeaned (no common variable)*		
AUT	0.80	$T = 15$		
BEL	0.86	$N = 17$		
DNK	−0.27	*obs* = 255		
FIN	0.92	**panel unit root**	ln p_{rel}	ln q_{rel}
FRA	0.76	*constant only*	3.26	4.28
GRE	0.30	*constant and trend*	0.52	1.28
IND	0.36	**panel co-integration**		
ITA	1.05	*panel v-stat* = −2.31		
JPN	1.46	*panel rho-stat* = −1.39*		
KOR	0.36	*panel pp-stat* = −2.15**		
MAU	0.35	*panel adf-stat* = −3.22***		
NLD	0.07	*group rho-stat* = 0.16		
NOR	0.48	*group pp-stat* = −2.10**		
SAF	−0.28	*group adf-stat* = −7.09***		
TAI	0.72			
US	0.74			

[†] See footnote Table 2.

Table 4 Non-stationary panel estimation (13 countries, 1986–96)

Country	Slope	Statistics[†]		
AUS	0.91	*Demeaned data (common time dummies)*		
AUT	0.27	$T = 11$		
CHI	2.41	$N = 13$		
FIN	0.85	$obs = 141$		
FRA	0.79	**panel unit root**	$\ln p_{rel}$	$\ln q_{rel}$
ITA	1.69	*constant only*	2.85	1.04
JPN	−0.31	*constant and trend*	1.66	−0.09
KOR	0.10	**panel co-integration**		
MAU	0.14	*panel v-stat = −2.68*		
SAF	−0.27	*panel rho-stat = −0.24*		
TAI	0.30	*panel pp-stat = −1.43**		
US	0.63	*panel adf-stat = −2.72****		
ZIM	0.70	*group rho-stat = 1.31*		
		group pp-stat = −0.81		
		group adf-stat = −11.14***		

[†] See footnote Table 2.

Table 5 Simulated annual inflation rates, in %, according to the Harrod-Balassa-Samuelson model

Country	Share δ^{**}	Estimated annual inflation (by Harrod-Balassa-Samuelson productivity growth[*])					Actual inflation
		Panel 1	Panel 1	Panel 1	Panel 2	Panel 3	
		Δp (77–93)	Δp (77–85)	Δp (85–93)	Δp (81–95)	Δp (86–96)	ΔCPI (77–93)
AUS	0.77	1.4	1.5	1.4	1.2		6.9
AUT	0.62	0.7	1.0	0.5	0.8	0.3	3.7
BEL	0.70	1.6	2.5	0.1	1.5		4.2
CAN	0.70	0.1	0.2	0.03			5.8
CHI[†]	0.57					−0.8	14.3
DNK	0.65	0.1	0.2	0.01	0.0		5.8
FIN	0.57	1.0	0.9	1.2	1.2	1.1	6.2
FRA	0.64	0.3	0.3	0.2	0.9	1.2	6.3
GRE	0.61	0.6	0.4	0.9	0.3		17.0
ITA	0.65	2.1	3.0	1.3	2.1	2.0	9.5
IND[‡]	0.45				−0.1		8.7
JPN	0.63	0.0	0.1	−0.003	1.1	−0.2	2.6
KOR	0.50	0.3	0.4	0.1	0.6	0.2	8.5
MAU	0.47	−0.6	−0.6	−0.5	−0.3	−0.06	9.8
NLD	0.48	0.6	0.8	0.4	0.1		3.0
NOR[§]	0.75				0.5		5.2
SAF	0.56	−0.2	−0.1	−0.3	0.2	0.1	13.0
TAI	0.53	0.0	−0.4	0.4	0.2	0.2	–
UK	0.68	0.7	0.5	1.0			7.0
US	0.75	0.8	0.6	1.0	1.7	1.7	5.4
ZIM[§§]	0.70					−0.8	18.7
WGR	0.60	−0.2	−0.05	−0.4			3.2

*   Inflation rates in per cent (differences of logs of the prices).
** δ denotes the share of non-tradables in consumption. The share is approximated with the average of non-tradables in production, 1985–93.
  [†] All values are averages, 1986–96.
  [‡] All values are averages, 1981–95.
  [§] All values are averages, 1981–95.
  [§§] All values are averages, 1986–96.

APPENDIX C

List of countries and length of available time series (annual)

Australia	(74–96)	India	(81–95)	Portugal	(86–93)
Austria	(76–96)	Italy	(70–96)	South Africa	(75–97)
Belgium	(70–96)	Japan	(70–96)	Sweden	(80–94)
Canada	(70–93)	Korea	(70–97)	Taiwan	(73–97)
Chile	(86–96)	Mauritius	(76–97)	Turkey	(88–96)
Denmark	(66–95)	Mexico	(88–96)	United Kingdom	(71–93)
Spain	(86–94)	Netherlands	(77–95)	United States	(60–96)
Finland	(60–96)	Norway	(78–95)	(West) Germany	(60–93)
France	(77–96)	New Zealand	(86–94)	Zimbabwe	(85–97)
Greece	(77–95)				

Data

Variable	Description	Calculation	Source
$\ln p_{rel}$	Relative price of tradables (implicit deflators)	Log (nominal value added/Real VA)$_{non\text{-}tradables}$ − Log (Nominal VA/real VA)$_{tradables}$	OECD National Accounts, International Sectoral Database, National Central Banks
$\ln q^{trad}$ $\ln q^{ntrad}$	Sectoral labour productivity	Log (Real VA/ Employed persons)	Same as relative prices
$D_{60}, D_{70},$ D_{80}, D_{90}	Dummies for decades	1 if year = 60–69, 70–79, 80–89, 90–96; 0 else	
CPI	Annual CPI inflation	$100 * \log(CPI) - \log(CPI(-1))$	IFS line 67
Nom Exrate	Exchange rate (Local currency/ US$)	Normalised to 1 in first year	IFS line rh
Eff Exrate	Nominal effective exchange rate	Normalised to 1 in first year	IFS line xx

Data on overall CPI inflation and nominal exchange rates are from the International Financial Statistics of the IMF. The sectoral data (nominal and real value added, employment, and wages) for almost all OECD countries come form the OECD National Accounts and the OECD International Sectoral Database. In some cases of missing data, data from the national banks could be provided. The sectoral data for Chile, Korea, Mauritius, Mexico, South Africa, Taiwan, and Zimbabwe were provided by the respective central banks.

'Tradables' and 'non-tradables' were identified according to the international sectoral classification standard ISIC. The tradables sector is made up of the 'manufacturing' and the 'agriculture' sector. The non-tradables sector consists of 'wholesale, retail, restaurants and hotel', 'finance, insurance, real estate and business services', 'community, social and personal services' and the 'transport' sector. In an alternative version, the 'transport' sector is considered a tradable instead of a non-tradable. If 'Construction' is included as non-tradable, results do not change.

For most countries, the ISIC classification could easily be identified. For Mauritius, SOC is replaced by 'other services'. Before 1978, the retail sector was included in 'other services'. The share of retail in 'other services' in 1976–8 was assumed to be equal to the share in the subsequent years. For Korea, service-sector employment data previous to 1980 is aggregated in one 'other' category. The breakdown of the employment data was derived from average earnings and compensation of employees, which is available on a sectoral level. For Taiwan, employment data is only available for manufacturing and the four service sectors. Agriculture and construction were therefore excluded from the estimates for this country.

Notes

1 Prepared for the Academic Workshop on Intermediate Policy Targets in Developing, Industrialised, and Transitional Economies at the Centre for Central Banking Studies, Bank of England, 1998.
2 The views expressed are those of the author, not necessarily those of the Bank of England. I want to thank Rebecca Driver especially. Comments of Erik Britton, Jag Chadha, Alex Cukierman, Maxwell Fry, Seamus Hogan, Lavan Mahadeva, Ronald McKinnon, Kateřina Šmídková, Gabriel Sterne, Geoffrey Wood, and participants of the workshop seminar at the CCBS are gratefully acknowledged. My special thanks go to Enrique Ila Alberola and Timo Tyrväinen who provided their sectoral dataset on EMU countries, and the various central banks who provided me with data for their countries. Of course, all remaining errors are mine. Comments are most welcome: marion.kohler@bankofengland.co.uk
3 See Giavazzi and Pagano (1988), Herrendorf (1997).
4 The model here follows the version in Obstfeld and Rogoff (1996), chapter 4.
5 For expositional reasons, the equations are in terms of domestic currency units. Since the model determines only relative prices the price of tradables P_T is often chosen as a *numéraire* for example.
6 Wage uniformity can be justified either because labour is fully mobile between sectors or because of wage spillovers due to strong unionisation of the non-traded sector. Alberola and Tyrväinen (1998) show that the result in equation (7) holds (albeit to a weaker degree) even if there is no wage equalisation, as long as there are positive spillovers.
7 Under the (usual) assumption that the non-tradable sector is more labour-intensive than the tradables sector ($\theta > \gamma$), capital intensity in the tradables' sector will rise more than in the non-tradable sector.
8 This holds, of course, only if domestic productivity growth exceeds productivity growth in tradables abroad.
9 This equation implies that δ remains constant. Of course, the shift in the relative price of the non-traded good can invoke substitution effects, which lead to changes in the consumption pattern. δ is then not exogenous to the sectoral productivity trends. Moreover, most countries adjust the goods basket underlying the CPI frequently to take account of *all* substitution effects. I account for this problem in the empirical part by deriving δ from the production side, rather than using the CPI weights from consumption baskets.
10 For an explicit treatment, see Cukierman *et al.* (1996). Whether nominal exchange rate volatility is damaging will depend crucially on whether investors expect the volatility.
11 The well-documented failure of PPP in the short run is due to such nominal rigidities. See Rogoff (1996).
12 Alternatively, it has been proposed to target wholesale price indices only (see McKinnon, 1996), in the context of EMU. This, however, would lead to neglect of other causes of non-tradable price increases such as demand-side shocks

(such as increased government spending which tends to be biased towards non-tradables).

13 See for example Canzoneri *et al.* (1996) and (1999).

14 Details on the data sources contained in Appendix C.

15 Canzoneri *et al.* (1999) show that this holds also under more general assumptions for the production function.

16 Rogoff (1996) points out that most studies which cannot confirm PPP result from the short time spans used in those studies. Studies which use extremely long time series find that PPP does indeed hold, albeit only in the very long run.

17 See, for example, Canzoneri *et al.* (1996) and (1999), Alberola and Tyrväinen (1998), and Artis and Kontolemis (1998).

18 However, their methodology has several weaknesses. First, they estimate equation (7) using labour productivities instead of total factor productivities. As shown in Canzoneri *et al.* (1999), using labour productivities implies a theoretical restriction on the coefficients for the productivities if the equivalent to equation (7) is estimated. Second, they use the Johanson cointegration methodology in order to overcome problems of non-stationarity of the data. The length of the data available may be too short for this methodology to provide valid estimates. Like Canzoneri *et al.*, I will use panel cointegration techniques to tackle this problem.

19 It would be preferable to measure labour productivity in house worked per employee. Due to restrictions on the availability of this data, I have to assume that average hours worked per employee are constant over time.

20 Note that this result is independent of the exchange rate.

21 In the version where four sub-periods were estimated, β has been positive but decreasing over these periods. I will come back to this result, which may indicate that the translation of relative productivity growth into relative price movements has become weaker over time.

22 It could, of course, also be due to neglected demand-side factors, that is, time-series frequency here captures not only long-run movements. But, as discussed above, proxying demand by government expenditure did not lead to significantly different results.

23 For an extensive discussion of the issues involved in non-stationarity in panel estimation, see Driver and Wren-Lewis (1998). I would like to thank Rebecca Driver for providing the programmes for the panel co-integration.

24 Since the power of the co-integration tests increases faster with time (T) than with countries (N), the panels chosen here have a larger time-series dimension than cross-sectional dimension.

25 All variables are normalised to one in the first year where all variables are available, and are in logs. This allows for comparison of the differences over time across countries.

26 Of course, overall inflation is mainly determined by macroeconomic factors such as fiscal policy stances and money supply growth. The model here explains only the part arising from the interaction of relative prices and the nominal exchange rate.

27 The exchange rate was stable from 1975 to 1980.

28 Given the well-known failure of the PPP hypothesis, the validity of Balassa-Samuelson for developed countries has been doubted, too. See Rogoff (1996) for an assessment. Canzoneri *et al.* (1999) provide empirical evidence for the validity of the part of Balassa-Samuelson under consideration here.

Bibliography

Artis, M.J. and Kontolemis, Z. (1996), 'Inflation targeting and the European Central Bank', *Working Paper in Economics 98/4*, European University Institute.

Alberola, E. and Tyrväinen, T. (1998), 'Is there scope for inflation differentials in EMU? An empirical evaluation of the Balassa-Samuelson model in EMU countries', *Bank of Finland Discussion Papers 15/98*, Bank of Finland.

Balassa, B. (1964), 'The purchasing power parity doctrine: a reappraisal', *Journal of Political Economy*, 72, pp. 584–96.

Canzoneri, M.B., Diba, B. and Eudey, G. (1996), 'Productivity and inflation: implications for the Maastricht convergence criteria and for inflation targets after EMU', *Economic Bulletin*, Banco de España, April, pp. 75–90.

Canzoneri, M.B., Cumby, R.E. and Diba, B. (1999), 'Relative labor productivity and the real exchange rate in the long run: evidence for a panel of OECD countries', *Journal of International Economics*, 47, pp. 245–66.

Chinn, M. (1997), 'Sectoral productivity, government spending and real exchange rates: empirical evidence for OECD countries', *Working Paper 6017*, NBER.

Cukierman, A., Kiguel, M. and Leiderman, L. (1996), 'Transparency and the evolution of the exchange rate flexibility in the aftermath of disinflation', in: Blejer, M., Eckstein, Z., Hercowitz, Z. and Leiderman, L. (eds) *Financial Factors in Economic Stabilization and Growth*, Cambridge University Press.

Driver, R. and Wren-Lewis, S. (1998), 'New trade theory and aggregate export equations', *Discussion Paper*, 99/17 University of Exeter.

De Gregorio, Giovannini, A. and Wolf, H.C. (1994), 'International evidence on tradables and non-tradables inflation', *European Economic Review*, 38 (6), pp. 1225–56.

Giavazzi, F. and Pagano, M. (1988), 'The advantage of tying one's hands: EMS discipline and central bank credibility', *European Economic Review*, 32, pp. 1055–82.

Genberg, H. (1978), 'Purchasing power parity under fixed and flexible exchange rates', *Journal of International Economics*, 8, pp. 247–76.

Halpern, L. and Wyplosz, C. (1997), 'Equilibrium exchange rates in transition economies', *Staff Papers*, IMF, 44 (4), pp. 430–62.

Herrendorf, B. (1997), 'Importing credibility through exchange rate pegging', *Economic Journal*, 107 (442), pp. 687–94.

Hsieh, D. (1982), 'The determination of the real exchange rate. The productivity approach', *Journal of International Economics*, May, pp. 355–62.

Im, K.S., Pesaran, H. and Shin, Y. (1995), 'Testing for unit roots in Heterogeneous Panels', *DAE Working Paper Amalgamated Series No. 9526*, University of Cambridge.

Im, K.S., Pesaran, H. and Shin, Y. (1998), 'Testing for unit roots in Heterogenous Panels', mimeo (revised version).

Julius, D. and Butler, J. (1998), 'Inflation and growth in a service economy', *Quarterly Bulletin*, Bank of England, November, pp. 338–46.

McKinnon, R.I. (1996), *The Rules of the Game*. MIT Press, Cambridge.

Micossi, S. and Milesi-Ferretti, G. (1996), 'Real exchange rates and the prices of non-tradable goods', in De Grauwe, P., Micossi, S. and Tullio, G. (eds) *Inflation and Wage Behaviour in Europe*, Oxford University Press.

Obstfeld, M. and Rogoff, K. (1996), *Foundations of International Macroeconomics*, MIT Press, Cambridge.

Pedroni, P. (1997), 'Fully modified OLS for heterogeneous co-integrated panels and the case of purchasing power parity', mimeo, Indiana University.

Rebelo, S. (1993), 'Inflation in fixed exchange rate regimes: the recent Portuguese experience', in Torres and Giavazzi (eds) *Adjustment and Growth in the European Monetary Union*, Cambridge.

Rogoff, K. (1996), 'The purchasing power parity puzzle', *Journal of Economic Literature*, 34, June, pp. 647–68.

Samuelson, P. (1964), 'Theoretical notes on trade problems', *Review of Economics and Statistics*, 46, pp. 147–54.

Stockman, A. (1983), 'Real exchange rates under alternative nominal exchange-rate regimes', *Journal of International Money and Finance*, 2, pp. 147–66.

Part IV
Country experiences with different monetary strategies

Lessons from the Bundesbank on the occasion of its early retirement

Adam S. Posen[1]

1 Introduction

The Deutsche Bundesbank Act of 26 July 1957 gave birth to the present German central bank. The independent Bundesbank successfully pursued its stated goal of price stability from then until the adoption of the euro, notably maintaining low levels of inflation throughout the post-Bretton Woods period. As with any sustained economic success story, there are lessons to be learnt. While the wealth and stability of post-war Germany provided an easier environment in which to make monetary policy than that facing central banks in many developing and transition economies, the lessons from the Bundesbank properly understood are of relevance for all central banks.

The most important qualities of the Bundesbank, however, are not those normally attributed to it by either its admirers or its critics – it was the transparency and flexibility of its monetary framework that made possible its success. Several central banks founded in the 1990s in the transition economies of eastern Europe and the former Soviet Union (as well as the European Central Bank) explicitly modelled themselves upon the Bundesbank's institutional forms and stated strategy. The most cited aspects to be emulated in all these contexts have been formal independence of the central bank from political control, a legal mandate committing the central bank to price stability as the ultimate goal of policy, and the adoption of monetary targets. This design is usually adopted in a monetary rule-following spirit, signifying a belief that only a strict commitment to single-minded pursuit of low inflation will assure success. Sacrifice of regard for accountability or other economic objectives as required is deemed acceptable in the pursuit of price stability.

These copies of the Bundesbank's form miss the point. According to any strict definition of targeting, the Bundesbank cannot be called a monetary targeter. This does not mean, however, that German inflation remained low either through blind luck or factors beyond the control of the Bundesbank. The historical record shows a different use for announced monetary targets. The Bundesbank consciously used these targets as a framework for signalling its intent and explaining its policies to its constituent public. In consequence, these targets actually granted the German central bank *greater* flexibility in responding to the problems of monetary control and economic shocks than would be available to an idealised monetary targeter or a central bank primarily concerned with credibility problems. The use of monetary targets in Germany has conferred greater transparency on the Bundesbank's monetary policy stances, enhancing flexibility without obvious cost to its independence.

Transparency has always been a sensitive issue for central banks, and it is one issue where the Bundesbank is not usually thought of as a leader. The image usually associated with the Bundesbank (as well as the Swiss National Bank and the United States Federal Reserve) is as the exemplar of independence from political control, and transparency is frequently seen as being traded off against that independence. Yet this is a misleading characterisation both of the Bundesbank's monetary framework and of the choices confronting all central banks. The Bundesbank has been transparent in the most meaningful way – it has publicly announced its goal for policy over the medium term, defined that goal against a measurable standard, and provided the information about its policies and economic outcomes necessary for evaluating its performance in meeting that goal.

The Bundesbank's experience indicates that structured transparency aids rather than hinders the independence of central banks over the long run.[2] What emerges from this analysis is a characterisation of German monetary practice as *disciplined discretion*.[3] Disciplined discretion cannot be construed merely as either a complicated hidden rule, which the Bundesbank strictly follows, or as what occurs when conservative central bankers have autonomy. Disciplined discretion means a system of commitments to clarify publicly and on an ongoing basis the intent and stance of monetary policy with respect to the announced goal. Central bankers are free to set policy so long as those commitments are met.

The German experience with monetary targeting leads to the conclusion that it is not necessary to bind central banks' hands tightly (say, by a fixed exchange rate, gold standard, or specified rule) in order to sustain low inflation. It is crucial, however, that the central bank achieve transparency by stating its goal and providing structured accountability with respect to meeting that goal.

The Bundesbank also teaches us that flexibility and low inflation need not be in conflict. For developing and transition economy central banks, this implies that the goal of their monetary regimes should be to shed excessively binding constraints on policy in so far as possible. This is done by providing information to the public and markets in a manner that builds the central bank's role institutionally and avoids overpromising. Some degree of fiscal sustainability is a prerequisite, because monetary stability cannot be achieved in the face of a complete lack of tax revenues.[4] Once this has been achieved, however, designing an inflation target that acts as an anchor for policy, rather than a straitjacket, is feasible for most economies. Flexibility must be accompanied by transparency in the definition of the target – measure, level, time horizon, and point target (rather than target range) – in the inclusion of information in the forecasting process, and in the handling of the inevitable deviations from the target. When it comes to being flexible in a disciplined manner, communication is necessary, and when it comes to communication, more is more.

2 Bundesbank at 18: coming of age by announcing monetary targets

German decision-makers got involved in the ground stages of the design of a new monetary framework just as the Bundesbank emerged from adolescence. After having been brought up under the relative stability of the Bretton Woods fixed exchange-rate system, the Bundesbank had to begin making monetary decisions for itself at the age of 16, after the system's breakdown in 1973. By its 18th birthday in 1975, the Bundesbank had in place the monetary targeting framework that it followed with minor alterations until the adoption of the euro.[5]

As has been noted, there seems to be a tendency for countries to adopt explicit monetary targets in times requiring toughness on inflation (Bernanke and Mishkin, 1992, page 186), though the Germans seemed to be at least as concerned with bringing inflation expectations rapidly into line once disinflation began. Contemporary documents reveal that there are two principal aspects to the intellectual framework on which monetary targeting was based: the control of inflation through the control of monetary expansion, and the coordination of agents' (especially wage bargainers') expectations through the announcement of quantified policy objectives.

One element that sounds absent from the German discussion of 1973–75 to ears trained by 1990s discussions of monetary policy is any concern about the credibility of the Bundesbank's commitment to low inflation, for example, due to time-consistency problems or troubles verifying central bank preferences. It is important to remember that while the intellectual current of the time was running toward monetarism, and therefore in the direction of rules for monetary policy rather than of discretion, the concern for central bank credibility in the terms now much discussed had not yet been intellectually developed. The German politicians and public accepted the Bundesbank's targeting commitment without feeling any need to tie the hands of the central bank, or to make any institutional provision mandating oversight and accountability. Clearly, the independence of the Bundesbank, and the political coalitions that supported it, contributed to this acceptance.[6]

The second intellectual pillar of the move to monetary targeting was a perception that German wage-inflation expectations had to be locked in even when monetary policy eased, such as after the first oil shock. The generalisation over time of this latter motivation – that the basic challenge of monetary policy is to anchor expectations when responding to shocks – was the true guiding principle of the newly adopted framework's development in Germany. Monetary targeting provided a means of transparently and credibly communicating to wage- and price-setters the relationship between current developments and medium-term goals. For this reason, the move to announced targets was soon accompanied by public reporting mechanisms voluntarily undertaken by the Bundesbank despite the lack of legislated requirement or political pressure to do so. Beyond aiding in the coordination of expectations in Germany's national collective wage-bargaining process, the addition of efforts at transparency to the targeting framework served two other purposes as well. It contributed to the standard of democratic accountability to which the Bundesbank is held. It also gave the central bank a mechanism for publicly identifying, when shocks occurred, to which shocks policy would respond, and to which it would not. Through commitment to transparency, the Bundesbank increased its discipline without explicitly curtailing its discretion.

The actual move to monetary targeting came on 5 December 1974 when the Central Bank Council of the Deutsche Bundesbank announced that 'from the present perspective it regards a growth of about 8% in the central bank money stock over the whole of 1975 as acceptable in the light of its stability goals.'[7] The Bundesbank considered this target to 'provide the requisite scope ... for the desired growth of the real economy', while at the same time the target had been chosen 'in such a way that no new inflationary strains are likely to arise as a result of monetary developments'. Since 1973 the Bundesbank had used the central bank money stock as its primary indicator of monetary developments, but never before had it announced a target for the growth of central bank money or any other monetary aggregate. Although this was a unilateral announcement on the part of the Bundesbank, the announcement stressed that 'in formulating its target for the growth of the central bank money stock [the Bundesbank] found itself in full agreement with the Federal Government'.

Although the Bundesbank chose to base the formulation of its annual monetary targets on the quantity theory, it never was dogmatic in its adherence to the school of thought. Current ECB (and former Bundesbank) chief economist Otmar Issing stated: 'One of the secrets of the success of the German policy of monetary targeting was that ... it often did not feel bound by monetarist orthodoxy as far as its more technical details were concerned.'[8] This statement indicates that the Bundesbank made a link between the success of monetary policy and the practical institutional aspects of policy, rather than ascribing success to simply following a rule. In other words, the visible commitment to price stability by itself is not sufficient; the proper design of the operational framework for targeting is also necessary and that proper design requires a pragmatic approach to targeting.

The second intellectual basis invoked for monetary targeting, the coordination of the expectations of economic agents, was of particular importance at the time when the Bundesbank announced its first target.

> From the immediately preceding period of fixed exchange rates [trade unions and enterprises] were accustomed to the Bundesbank's monetary policy measures becoming ineffective when they resulted in massive inflows of funds from abroad. As a consequence the Bundesbank initially failed to influence wage and price behaviour in the way it wished. In the light of this adverse experience, the Bundesbank, together with the Federal Government and the independent Council of Economic Experts, concluded that it would be useful to explicitly define the 'monetary framework' for the growth of production and prices.
>
> (Schlesinger, 1983, page 6)

When the first oil crisis broke, in October 1973, there were signs that the restrictive policy of the Bundesbank was beginning to slow both inflation, which had peaked at almost 8% in mid-1973, and GDP growth. The Bundesbank's efforts to bring down inflation were thus jeopardised by the oil shock while at the same time output growth was expected to fall drastically. In particular, the Bundesbank was concerned that the oil price increases would quickly lead to a second-round wage price spiral.

Accordingly, by its own account 'the Bundesbank endeavoured to keep monetary expansion within relatively strict limits during 1974. Although it did not expressly commit itself to any quantitative target – as it did later for 1975 – it tried to ensure that monetary expansion was not too great, but not too small either' (BB, 1974, page 17). Despite the fact that a quantitative target was still absent, the Bundesbank was determined to communicate its message of restraint as clearly as possible. It announced:

> It is of the utmost importance that in the field of price and wage policy management and labor behave in a way appropriate to the new situation. In their decisions management and labor will have to consider the fact that if the oil shortage continues, hardly more goods will be available for distribution next year than in 1973.
>
> (BB, December 1973, page 7)

Without the benefit of an explicit numerical target, conveying that policy must be forward-looking and oriented toward inflation expectations was a difficult matter. From April 1974 on the Bundesbank gradually eased monetary policy. At this stage, to anchor expectations, the Bundesbank increasingly rationalised its policy decisions by citing developments in central bank money growth for example (see BB, June 1974, pages 12 to 13). This gradual process culminated in the announcement in December 1974 of a monetary target of 8% growth in central bank money for 1975.

> Under the influence of the growing weakness of business activity and the first signs of progress in fighting inflation, a change was made in the last quarter of 1974; the target became a slightly faster rate of monetary growth, which was publicly announced toward the end of the year.
>
> (BB, 1974, page 17)

Four elements of this quote from the 1974 Bundesbank *Annual Report* announcing the first monetary target are worth noting. First, although the Bundesbank was mostly concerned with reversing the inflationary trend of the previous five years, its new monetary policy framework still did not ignore real activity as a goal of monetary policy. Even its first justification, in 1973, for a 'just right' monetary expansion, neither too great nor too small, reflected its ongoing concern for real-side effects, which translated into gradual disinflation. Second, the Bundesbank did not see it necessary to reverse previous *price-level* increases in order to fulfil its mandate for price stability and anchor expectations. Third, monetary policy was portrayed as acting in a pre-emptive manner, reacting to the 'first signs'. Finally, monetary targets were adopted at a time when inflation and monetary growth were expected to slow, making it easy to meet targets, but also when there was fear that uncertainty about the Bundesbank's long-term policy path might unleash inflationary expectations.

The Bundesbank publicly acknowledged the concern that early easing might lead to the misperception that its resolve to bring down inflation was diminishing. Recent experience had shown that wage setting behaviour in particular was mostly unaffected by the Bundesbank's efforts to reduce inflation.

> [W]age costs have gone up steadily in the last few months, partly as after-effects of [earlier] settlements ... which were excessive (not least because management and labor obviously underestimated the prospects of success of the stabilization policy) ... Despite the low level of business activity and subdued inflation expectations, even in very recent wage negotiations two-figure rises have effectively been agreed.
>
> (BB, December 1974, page 6)

The credibility issue arose as a practical matter in the context of the Bundesbank wanting to stop pass-through of a one-time shock to the price level. This concern for getting the public to distinguish between first-round and second-round effects of a price shock, to avoid lock-in of inflationary expectations, characterises the efforts of 1990s inflation targeters as well.[9]

In particular, before economic research had caught up with events, the Bundesbank appeared to have seen the need for an exception to the pursuit of its long-term targets in the face of the first identified supply shock. The design of a mechanism for making such an exception to the blind pursuit of price stability and explaining the use of such flexibility to the public are inherent challenges to all monetary frameworks. Taken from this perspective, the German monetary target seems to have been adopted, at least in part, to create a necessary means of communication about inflation uncertainty.

3   The Bundesbank as an adult: monetary targeting in operation

From adoption in 1975 to the end of 1998, the Bundesbank adhered to the strategy of publicly announcing numerical monetary targets and the inflation goals underlying their computation. During the first five years, the definition and implementation of the target and the reporting procedures were developed and refined. From 1980 until EMU, however, the operational framework of German monetary targets has displayed a remarkable degree of continuity. Most impressively, repeated overshootings of the target range in the late 1980s and the 1990s, as well as a decision to change the monetary aggregate targeted in 1988 after a large velocity shock, were managed without a persistent rise in inflation or inflation expectations.

The literature on the conditions under which an economic variable constitutes a good intermediate target for monetary policy is too voluminous to be fully summarised here;[10] for purposes of this discussion, it is more important to deflate the myth that the Bundesbank actually set policy solely on the basis of a monetary target at any time.

> Strictly defined, the use of a money growth target means that the central bank not only treats all unexpected fluctuations in money as informative ... but also, as a quantitative matter, changes the interest rate or reserves in such a way as to offset these unexpected fluctuations altogether ... and thereby restore money growth to the originally designated target rate.
>
> (Friedman, 1995, pages 5 to 6)

As will be seen, although the results of announcing monetary targets, and the use made of the information in them, would lead to a positive judgement for its targeting framework, the Bundesbank does not strongly resemble the idealised picture of a monetary targeter. The historical record demonstrates that German monetary policy-making did not behave as though price stability were its sole (short- to medium-term) policy goal, or as though the monetary growth to inflation correlation were strong enough to justify strictly following the targets while ignoring wider information.[11] In fact, the manner in which the Bundesbank conducted policy under the targets implies that monetary targets provide a framework for the central bank to convey its long-term commitment to price stability irrespective of strictness of adherence to the target itself.

From 1975 until 1987, the Bundesbank announced targets for the growth of the central bank money stock (CBM). CBM is defined as currency in circulation plus sight deposits, time deposits with maturity under four years; and savings deposits and savings bonds with maturity of less than four years; the latter three components are weighted by their respective required reserve ratios as of January 1974. From 1988 to 1998, the Bundesbank used growth in M3 as its announced target. Apart from not including savings deposits with longer maturities and savings bonds, the major difference between M3 and CBM is that the latter is a weighted-sum aggregate while the former is a simple sum. The only source of large divergences between the growth of the two aggregates are significant fluctuations in the holdings of currency as compared to deposits.

The Bundesbank always set its monetary targets at the end of a calendar year for the next year. It derived the monetary targets from a quantity equation, in rate-of-change form, stating that the sum of real output growth and the inflation rate is equal to the sum of money growth and the change in (the appropriately defined) velocity. The Bundesbank derived the target growth rate of the chosen monetary aggregate (CBM or M3) by estimating the growth of the long-run production potential over the coming year, adding the rate of price change it considered unavoidable, and subtracting the estimated change in trend velocity over the year.

Two elements of this procedure deserve emphasising. First, the Bundesbank did not employ forecasts of real output growth over the coming year in its target derivation, but instead used estimates of the growth in production potential.[12] This 'potential-oriented approach' was based on the Bundesbank's conviction that it should not engage in policies aimed at short-term stimulation. Not only did this let the Bundesbank claim that it was not making any judgement about the business cycle when it set policy, but it also allowed the Bundesbank to de-emphasise any public discussion of its forecasting efforts, even when they might involve re-estimating or admitting ignorance of the NAIRU, further distancing monetary policy from the course of unemployment. The transparency of the quantity approach therefore removes certain items from the monetary policy agenda (or at least moves in that direction) by specifying the goals for which the central bank regarded itself as responsible.

The second element is the concept of 'unavoidable price increases', where prices are measured by the all-items CPI. These goals for inflation were set *prior* to the monetary target each year; they specified the intended path for inflation, and thus motivated monetary policy.

In view of the unfavorable underlying situation, the Bundesbank felt obliged until 1984 to include an 'unavoidable' rate of price rises in its calculation. By so doing, it took due account of the fact that price increases which have already entered into the decisions of economic agents cannot be eliminated immediately, but only step by step. On the other hand, this tolerated rise in prices was invariably below the current inflation rate, or the rate forecast for the year ahead. The Bundesbank thereby made it plain that, by adopting an unduly 'gradualist' approach to fighting inflation, it did not wish to contribute to strengthening inflation expectations. Once price stability was virtually achieved at the end of 1984, the Bundesbank abandoned the concept of 'unavoidable' price increases. Instead, it has since then included ... a medium-term price assumption of 2%.

(Deutsche Bundesbank, 1995, pages 80 to 81)

By publicly setting the annual 'unavoidable price increase', the Bundesbank made clear several assumptions about the nature of monetary policy: first, that a medium-term goal for inflation motivated forward-looking policy decisions; second, that the medium-term goal of price stability should be operationally defined as a measured inflation rate greater than zero; third, that convergence of inflation to the medium-term goal should be gradual, since the real economic costs of reaching that goal could not be ignored; fourth, that economic events should lead to resettings of the goal (or of the time allotted to reach the goal) in the short run; and fifth, that if inflation expectations remained contained by gradual disinflation, there was no need to reverse prior price-level rises. These aspects of the announced inflation goal, and the fact that the goal was announced, were the true essence of the German monetary framework.

In 1979, two lasting changes to the target formulation were made. First, with the exception of 1989, all targets were formulated in terms of a target range of ±1% or 1.5% around the monetary target derived from the quantity equation.

In view of the oil price hikes in 1974 and 1979 to 80, the erratic movements in 'real' exchange rates and the weakening of traditional cyclical patterns, it appeared advisable to grant monetary policy from the outset limited room for discretionary manoeuvre in the form of such target ranges. To ensure that economic agents are adequately informed ... the central bank must be prepared to define from the start as definitely as possible the overall economic conditions under which it will aim at the top or bottom end of the range.

(Schlesinger, 1983, page 10)

Again, discretion and transparency were advanced in tandem. In moving to a target range rather than a point target, the Bundesbank believed that it could hit the target range by giving itself room for response to changing developments. In fact, the tone of its explanation is that it was conferring some discretion upon itself rather than buying room for error in a difficult control problem. This could reflect actual stability of monetary demand and transmission mechanisms in Germany, or the absence of fears there at the time about central bank error.

The second change was that the targets were formulated as growth rates of the average money stock in the fourth quarter over its counterpart in the previous year. This adaptation was expected to indicate 'the direction in which monetary policy is aiming more accurately than an average target could' (BB, January 1979, page 8).

Even as it implemented the monetary targeting framework, the Bundesbank repeatedly stressed that situations might arise in which it would consciously allow deviations from the announced target path to occur in support of other economic objectives. These allowances were beyond and in addition to those already implicit in the setting of a target range and of a gradual path for disinflation (publicised by movements in unavoidable inflation). In addition, the use of these allowances was not limited to times of overtly recognisable economic hardship. A case in point is the year 1977, when signs of weakness in economic activity combined with a strong appreciation of the DM prompted the Bundesbank to tolerate the monetary target being overshot. As it said at the time:

> However, the fact that the Bundesbank deliberately accepted the risk of a major divergence from its quantitative monetary target does not imply that it abandoned the more medium-term orientation which has marked its policies since 1975. There may be periods in which the pursuit of an 'intermediate target variable', as reflected in the announced growth rate of the central bank money stock, cannot be given priority.
>
> (BB, 1977, page 22)

In other words, the target should not be slavishly adhered to as crises arise and circumstances change. This precept is inherent in any targeting framework so long as the central bank does not totally ignore the short-run effects of unforeseen shocks and cannot be removed by redefining the target aggregate. Neither the Bundesbank nor any major central bank did in fact ignore the short-run effects of unforeseen shocks in the post-war era.[13]

The main reason why CBM was initially chosen as target aggregate was the Bundesbank's perception of its advantages in terms of transparency and communication with the public, not because it was in some control sense the optimal aggregate. The Bundesbank explained its choice of CBM in the following words:

> [CBM] brings out the central bank's responsibility for monetary expansion especially clearly. The money creation of the banking

system as a whole and the money creation of the central bank are closely linked through currency in circulation and the banks' obligation to maintain a certain portion of their deposits with the central bank. Central bank money, which comprises these two components, can therefore readily serve as an indicator of both. A rise by a certain rate in central bank money shows not only the size of the money creation of the banking system but also the extent to which the central bank has provided funds for the banks' money creation.

(BB, 1975, page 12)

This information was to be conveyed not so much to avoid either the public or the central bank making a large mistake about the unclear stance of monetary policy (a major concern in framework design for later inflation targeters who adopted MCIs), as to give rapid feedback about the state of monetary conditions in general. The mindset is that tacking monetary growth against an announced target makes policy appear full of informational content based on as a source of uncertainty itself.

In 1986 and 1987, a strong DM combined with historically low short-term interest rates led to above-target CBM growth of 7.7% and 8% respectively, while M3 grew at 7% and 6% during those two years. This development prompted the Bundesbank to announce a switch from 1988 on to monetary targets for the aggregate M3.

> The expansion of currency in circulation is in itself of course a significant development which the central bank plainly has to heed. This is, after all, the most liquid form of money ... and not least the kind of money which the central bank issues itself and which highlights its responsibility for the value of money. On the other hand, especially at times when the growth rates of currency in circulation and deposit money are diverging strongly, there is no reason to stress the weight of currency in circulation unduly.[14]

The fact that the Bundesbank changed the target variable when CBM grew too rapidly, but did not do so when it grew too slowly (as it did in 1981 and early 1982), can be interpreted as an indication of the importance that the Bundesbank attaches to the communicative function of its monetary targets; allowing the target variable to repeatedly overshoot the target because of special factors might have led to the misperception on the part of the public that the Bundesbank's attitude toward monetary control and inflation had changed.[15]

The Bundesbank's belief that it needed to explain target deviations and redefinitions to the public was reflected in the design of its reporting mechanisms. There is no legal requirement in the Bundesbank Act or in later legislation for the Bundesbank to give a formal account of its policy to any public body. Independence of the central bank in Germany limits government oversight to a commitment that 'The Deutsche Bundesbank shall advise the Federal Cabinet on monetary policy issues of major importance, and shall furnish it with information upon request (Act Section 13)'. The only publications the Bundesbank is required to produce are announcements in the Federal Gazette of the setting of interest rates, discount rates, and the like (Act Section 33). According to Act Section 18, the Bundesbank *may,* at its discretion, publish the monetary and banking statistics that it collects. Any accountability, and therefore legitimacy, that the Bundesbank retained for the exercise of its independence rested upon what use the Bundesbank made of its voluntary communications.

So it is significant that the *Monthly Report* is claimed inside its front cover to be a response to Section 18 of the Bundesbank Act, but does much more than report statistics. Every month, after a 'Short Commentary' on monetary developments, securities markets, public finance, economic conditions, and the balance of payments, two to four articles are published that either cover one-time topics ('The state of external adjustment after German reunification') or are recurring reports such as the annual 'The profitability of German credit institutions' or the quarterly 'The economic scene in Germany'. Before EMU, the monetary target and its justification were printed each year in the January issue (in December from 1989 to 1992).

Similarly, the *Annual Report* gives an extremely detailed retrospective of the economic, not just monetary, developments in Germany for the year, as well as listing all monetary policy moves and offering commentary on the fiscal policy of the federal government and the *Länder*. The vast variety and depth of information provided by the Bundesbank in its *Reports* is clear evidence that a wide range of information variables – far beyond M3, velocity, and potential GDP – played a role in Bundesbank decision-making (the amount of work involved in producing the data and analysis makes it unlikely that it was merely a smokescreen or a public service).

The Bundesbank's commitment to transparency did not come without self-imposed limits to its accountability. Two limitations in particular provided a strong contrast to the inflation report documents prepared by Canada, the United Kingdom, and others in recent years. First, no articles in the *Monthly Report* are signed either individually or collectively by authors, and the *Annual Report* has only a brief foreword signed by the Bundesbank president (although all Council members are listed on the pages preceding it); speeches by the President or other Council members are never reprinted in either document. This depersonalisation of policy was to some extent made up for by the enormously active speaking and publishing schedule in which all Council members (not just the President and Chief Economist) and some senior staffers engaged, but it still distanced the main policy statements from specific responsible individuals.

The second limitation on accountability was that the Reports always dealt with the contemporary situation or assessed past performance[16] – no forecasts of any economic variable were made public by the Bundesbank, and private-sector forecasts and even expectations were not discussed. This is largely the opposite of the practice of contemporary inflation-targeting central banks.[17] The Bundesbank made itself accountable on the basis of its explanations for past performance, but did not leave itself open to be evaluated as a forecaster. In fact, its *ex post* explanations combined with the foundation of its monetary targets on its own estimates of potential GDP and normative inflation, enabled the Bundesbank to generally shift responsibility for short-term economic performance onto factors other than monetary policy.

Nevertheless, those same monetary targets were seen correctly by the Bundesbank as the main source of accountability and transparency because they committed the Bundesbank to explaining policy with respect to a benchmark on a regular basis. Moreover, that explanation of policy to the public was given at length, and with respect to the whole economy (not just monetary developments narrowly defined). This is an explanatory impulse beyond the deceptively uninformative question of whether or not a specific monetary growth target was met at the prescribed time.

4   The Bundesbank at 32: the mid-life crisis of reunification

The greatest challenge to German monetary policy since the adoption of monetary targeting followed the fall of the Berlin Wall in 1989. The Bundesbank's response to the shock of German unification illustrates the exercise of disciplined discretion. The economic situation in the Federal Republic during the two years prior to economic and monetary union with the former GDR on 1 July 1990 (henceforth 'monetary union') was characterised by GDP growth of around 4% and the first significant fall in unemployment since the late 1970s. After a prolonged period of falling inflation and historically low interest rates during the mid-1980s, inflation had increased from −1% at the end of 1986 to slightly over 3% by the end of 1989. The Bundesbank had begun tightening monetary policy in mid-1988, raising the repo rate in steps from 3.25% in June 1988 to 7.75% in early 1990. After the first M3 target (for 1988), of 3% to 6% had been overshot by 1%, the target for M3 growth of around 5% in 1989 was almost exactly achieved, at 4.7%. M3 growth was certainly not high in view of the prevailing rate of economic growth.

In response to the uncertainties resulting from the prospect of German monetary union, long-term interest rates had increased sharply from October 1989 through March 1990, with ten-year bond yields rising from around 7% to around 9% in less than half a year. Combined with a strong DM, this prompted the Bundesbank to keep official interest rates unchanged during the months immediately preceding monetary union. It also did so in the immediate aftermath, despite the fact that the massively expansionary fiscal policy that accompanied unification was beginning to propel GDP growth to record levels.

To some extent the Bundesbank's decision to keep interest rates unchanged for the first months following monetary union was due to the fact that the inflationary potential resulting from the conditions under which the GDR mark had been converted into DM was very difficult to assess. The Bundesbank had been opposed to the conversion rate between Deutsche Marks and Ostmarks agreed to in the treaty on monetary union (overall about 1:1.8), and had been publicly overruled on this point by the Federal Government.[18] During the first months following monetary union the Bundesbank was preoccupied as well with assessing the portfolio shifts in eastern Germany in response to the introduction not only of a new currency, but also of a new financial system and a broad range of assets that had not existed in the former GDR. Thus, the Bundesbank was coping with unprecedented structural uncertainty and publicly visible political pressure.

The Bundesbank therefore continued during the second half of 1990 to calculate monetary aggregates separately for eastern and western Germany, based on the returns of the banks domiciled in the respective parts. Although M3 growth in western Germany accelerated in late 1990, as a result of the moderate growth rates during the first half of the year, growth of western German M3 during 1990 of 5.6% was well within the target of 4% to 6%.[19]

During the fall of 1990 the repo rate had approached the Lombard rate, which meant that banks were increasingly using the Lombard facility for their regular liquidity needs, and not as the emergency facility for which the Bundesbank intended Lombard loans to be used. On 2 November 1990, the Bundesbank raised the Lombard rate from 8% to 8.5%, and the discount rate from 6% to 6.5%. Within the next few weeks, however, as a result of the way that banks were bidding the interest rate, the repo rate rose above the Lombard rate, prompting the Bundesbank to raise the Lombard rate to 9% as of 1 February 1991. With these measures the Bundesbank was reacting to both the tempestuous GDP growth rates and the faster M3 growth in the last part of 1990. Inflation had so far remained fairly unchanged, but it seems likely that the Bundesbank was, at that point, expecting inflationary pressures to develop in the near future, given the fiscal expansion, the pressure on productive capacity in western Germany, and the terms of monetary union.

At the end of 1990 the Bundesbank announced a target for M3 growth of 4% to 6% for the year 1991, applying a monetary target for the first time to the whole currency area. The target was based on the average all-German M3 stock during the last quarter of 1990. As this stock was likely to be still affected by ongoing portfolio shifts in eastern Germany, the target was subject to unusually high uncertainty. It is worth noting that neither of the basic inputs into the Bundesbank's quantity equation, which generates its money-growth targets – 'normative' inflation and the potential growth rate of the German economy – were changed.

> Following German unification, the monetary targets set by the Bundesbank were decidedly ambitious as they left normative inflation, on which these targets are based, unchanged at 2% during this period, even though it was obvious from the outset that this rate could not be achieved in the target periods concerned.
>
> (Issing, 1995b)

The maintenance of the inflation target was a statement of policy that the reunification shock did not fundamentally alter the basic structures of the German economy. Moreover, this was a communication to the public at large that any price shifts coming from this shock should be treated as a one-time event, and should not be passed on into inflationary expectations.

This required faith in the public's comprehension of, and the Bundesbank's ability to credibly explain, the special nature of the period. It is interesting to compare the decision on the 2% medium-term inflation goal after monetary unification with its response to the 1979 oil shock, when, as already noted, unavoidable inflation was ratcheted up to 4%, and both actual and unavoidable inflation were brought down only slowly. Two explanations, not mutually exclusive, of the difference in approach between the 1990–93 and the 1979–86 periods are: that the unification shock was a positive demand rather than a negative supply shock, and so the Bundesbank was correct not to accommodate it; and that, after having lived with monetary targeting for several years, including the time of the oil shocks, the public had been trained by the Bundesbank's transparent explanations of monetary policy to understand the distinction between one-time and persistent inflationary pressures. In any event, the Bundesbank clearly was nuancing its short-term monetary policy so that it could do minimal tightening while continuing to anchor the longer-term goal for inflation.

Following both the Bundesbank's target announcement, in which it stressed its continued adherence to monetary targeting after unification, and the Lombard rate increase on 1 February, long-term interest rates started falling for the first time since 1988. Although the highest inflation rates were still to come, this was the beginning of a four-year downward trend in bond rates. Apparently, at this point financial markets were convinced that the Bundesbank would succeed in containing inflation in the long run, even if not rapidly reducing it in the short run. Through its policy of making clear that it would not accommodate pass-through of inflation in the medium term, the Bundesbank bought itself flexibility for short-term easing without being misinterpreted. This transparency-enhancing flexibility, of course, depended on the credibility of central bank's commitment to price stability, but it emphasises how even a credible central bank may gain through institutional design to increase transparency.

CPI inflation in western Germany had still remained around 3% during the first half of 1991, while GDP growth in the region remained vigorous. By contrast, M3 growth, which had been on an upward trend during late 1990, fell back, partly because of faster-than-expected portfolio shifts into longer-term assets in eastern Germany. These portfolio shifts, as well as the sharper than expected fall in eastern German production potential, led the Bundesbank for the first time ever to change its monetary target on the occasion of its mid-year review. In June, the target for M3 growth for 1991 was lowered by 1% to 3%–5%. Because such a resetting was so unusual, it could be accepted by the public and not regarded as a device whereby the central bank could casually reset goals to match results. In this instance, the Bundesbank was able to make use of its semi-annual review, and, through that formalised process demanding a clear explanation, justify the target adjustment.[20]

Despite the fact that German GDP growth started to slacken during the second half of 1991, M3 growth accelerated. The strong growth of time deposits prompted banks to counter the outflow from savings deposits by offering special savings schemes with attractive terms. The yield curve was inverted for the first time since the early 1980s, and the first time since the Bundesbank had been targeting M3. In this situation, the conflict arose for the Bundesbank that interest rate rises were likely to foster M3 growth. This problem was all the more acute since bank lending to the private sector was growing unabated despite the high interest rates, probably to a large extent due to loan programmes subsidised by the federal government in connection with the restructuring of the eastern German economy and housing sector.

This conundrum – of the Bundesbank's instrument tending to work in the 'wrong' direction for the target variable – brought the underlying conflict of monetary targeting to the fore: the target must be constantly critically evaluated for its relationship to the ultimate goal variable(s), yet if it is constantly cast aside because of changes in that relationship, or because of special circumstances that indicate a role for other intermediate variables, it ceases to be a target and becomes an indicator.

> Strictly defined, the use of a money growth target means that the central bank not only treats all unexpected fluctuations in money as informative in just this sense, but also, as a quantitative matter, changes its instrument variable in such a way as to restore money growth to the originally designated path.
>
> (Friedman and Kuttner, 1996, page 94)

The acceleration in late 1991 notwithstanding, M3 grew by 5.2% during 1991, close to the mid-point of the original target, and just slightly above the revised target.

On 20 December 1991, the Bundesbank raised the Lombard and discount rates by another 0.5%, to 9.75% and 8% respectively, their second highest level since the Second World War.

> In the light of the sharp monetary expansion, it was essential to prevent permanently higher inflation expectations from arising on account of the adopted wage and fiscal policy stance and the faster pace of inflation – expectations which would have become ever more difficult and costly to restrain.
>
> (BB, 1991, page 43)

The rhetoric invoked here by the Bundesbank should be appreciated. Both government policies and union wage demands could be (and were) cited for their inflationary effects – that is, their pursuit of transfers beyond available resources. The Bundesbank may not have been able to override Chancellor Kohl's desired exchange rate of Ostmarks for Deutsche Marks, or his 'solidarity' transfers, but the Bundesbank Direktorium was comfortable in making it clear that the government, and not they, should be held accountable for the inflationary pressures. At the same time, the Direktorium did take on accountability for limiting the second-round pass-through effects of these pressures. In addition to this division of accountability, the Bundesbank also clearly expressed some concern about the persistence of inflationary expectations and the cost of disinflating them (if necessary), thereby making clear some assumptions about the realities of monetary transmission.

The 20 December increase in the Lombard rate proved to be the last one. In 1992, the repo rate peaked in August at 9.7% before starting to fall, as the Bundesbank started to ease monetary policy in response to appreciation of the Deutsche Mark and the emerging turbulences in the European Monetary System. Of course, this interest-rate decline also coincided with the rapid slowdown in German GDP growth. The monetary targets for 1992 and 1993 would not be met, but the mid-life challenge to German monetary policy was over.

> Thus in 1992, for example, when the money stock overshot the target by a large margin, the Bundesbank made it clear by the interest rate policy measures it adopted, that it took this sharp monetary expansion seriously. The fact that, for a number of reasons, it still failed in the end to meet the target ... has therefore ultimately had little impact on the Bundesbank's credibility and its strategy.
>
> (Issing, 1995a)

Monetary policy transparency was explicitly linked to flexibility during monetary unification, and that flexibility was exercised to minimise the short-run real economic and political effects of maintaining long-term price stability. This communication effort anchored inflation expectations in the face of great uncertainty.

5   The Bundesbank at 41: looking back from an early retirement

While the successful record of the Bundesbank's targeting strategy since the collapse of the Bretton Woods regime is indeed impressive, the lessons to be learnt from it are not those commonly held. The primary benefits derived from announced monetary targets in Germany resulted from the transparency that this framework conferred on the exercise of discretionary policy. Neither strict adherence to monetary aggregate growth as a formal intermediate target, nor the rule-like constraint on policy that would imply, played a role in the Bundesbank's success. Even in the face of significant shocks, and periods of temporarily great uncertainty, transparency allowed the Bundesbank to keep expectations anchored. Putting the lessons from the Bundesbank's 40 years in more general terms:

(i) The Bundesbank followed an information inclusive strategy in practice   As discussed above, the announced monetary targets were never slavishly followed in the sense of being actual intermediate target variables in Germany. It is well known that annual target ranges were missed around 50% of the time in Germany in the 1980s and 1990s. Far more significantly, the Bundesbank, both by its own description and as seen in the historical record, took into account a much broader range of information than just CBM or M3 growth when setting policy. When inflation and monetary forecasts diverged, the Bundesbank responded to the former. Moreover, the Bundesbank responded with policy reactions to a number of short-run shocks and challenges even when they had not directly affected inflation or money.

(ii) The key function of the targets was to transparently convey the goal of policy   The primary gains derived from announced monetary targets were generated through their use as a vehicle for regular formal indication of monetary policy stance and intentions with reference to an underlying but public numerical inflation target and not through use as targets *per se*. Pointing to a standard and a goal for forward-looking policy seems to anchor public expectations. Unavoidable deviations from the medium-term goal may then be explained with reference to this standard. This is the reason why the Bundesbank's framework, for all its legal independence and all its accumulation of prestige and support over its 41-year career, included institutionalised structures for explaining policy in an explicit and informative manner on a regular basis. The Bundesbank found very shortly after adopting targets that simply announcing the monetary target and interest-rate numbers alone was insufficient. A concerted

effort to provide greater information about the stance of policy based on the inflation goal and the distance to it was also required.

(iii) Transparency enhanced the discretion of policy-makers to act flexibly Not only did the Bundesbank's targeting framework give wage- and price-setters a better awareness of monetary policy's stance at any given time, it allowed the Bundesbank to distinguish in the public's mind between one-time price-level shifts and other shocks that would require a response irrespective of pass-through. This flexibility tied to transparency was exercised by the Bundesbank during German monetary unification and in the face of the oil shocks and a number of exchange rate swings. In a transparent framework where this information is provided, target-level changes and even target misses have not only proved to have only limited fallout, but have also served an educational function. When the Bundes- bank moved its 'unavoidable inflation' target to 4% in 1979, it informed the public that supply shocks do require a different response than demand shocks, and that there is room for gradualism in disinflation; when the Bundesbank re-named its inflation target of 2% the 'normative rate of price increase' after 1984, it indicated what level of inflation could function as an operational definition of price stability (and why that level was not zero) as well as its likely future stance.

(iv) Flexibility in the face of economic events is not damaging to price stability In fact, while the Bundesbank did not have an explicit numerical 'escape clause' with legal standing, *a la* New Zealand, to allow release from target obligations in the face of severe financial or supply shocks, it exer- cised that flexibility as though it were there. This was in addition to the full advantage the Bundesbank took of the flexibilities built into its target defi- nition by having a target *range* and assessing whether the *trend* of monetary growth fell in it. Binding a central bank's hands extremely tightly does not seem to be a necessary condition for sustained low inflation.

(v) Pursuit of price stability need not be a crusade to be successful The record of policies and performance of the Bundesbank demonstrates as well that the achievement of practical price stability does not require obsessive pursuit of anti-inflationary policies. Germany has shown that a country need not drive inflation all the way down to zero measured change in the CPI – or even make that the announced goal – in order to anchor inflationary expectations. When inflationary shocks occurred in Germany, the Bundesbank disinflated gradually out of consideration for the effects of its policies on real economic performance. As seen in both the after- math of the 1979 oil shock, and the measured response to the inflationary and political uncertainties of monetary union, such gradualism has proved no impediment to the containment of Germany's long-term inflation expectations. Given these results, the Bundesbank has never found it

necessary or in any way advantageous to reverse past inflations to return the price level to its pre-shock level.

6   Practical suggestions for credibly substituting transparency for constraint

Perhaps the success of the Bundesbank in flexibly maintaining price stability seems too easy or preordained to be relevant for most non-OECD countries. Yet, the great monetary divide is between those countries that are trying to re-establish credible stability after a hyperinflation, and all of the rest. Even most high-inflation countries with annual inflation rates of 30% to 60% show some stability in inflation expectations, so long as the fiscal situation is not out of control (see Dornbusch and Fischer, 1994; Fry 1998), and can be thought of as gradually disinflating rather than shock-treatment stabilising. Once there is that minimum stability, any central bank shares with the Bundesbank the basic operational goals of setting a long-run downwards trend for inflation (until 2% is reached) and responding to shocks by deviating from that trend without engendering inflationary spirals or runs on the currency. The key to success is to create a nominal anchor that is credible without setting excessive strictures on behaviour.[21] The message the Bundesbank offers for other central banks is that this creation of a nominal anchor through inflation targeting may be more achievable than is commonly thought.[22]

Surely, German monetary policy choices were eased by the economy's size and development, as well as by the underlying stability present. Nevertheless, the fact that the shocks facing the German economy were less challenging than those faced by many small open economies does not mean they were different in nature, nor that the central bank can just give up when the shocks reach a certain size. What may differ for small open economies are some of the specifics of target design. This can be illustrated by the fact that the Bundesbank and the Swiss National Bank differed widely in the design of their respective specific monetary targets – a range versus a point target for percentage growth, calculated over a one-year versus a five-year time-horizon, defined on a broad versus a narrow aggregate – yet they have achieved similar success in maintaining price stability.[23] And the Swiss National Bank faced a much greater ongoing volatility of capital flows (although, admittedly, not as great a volatility as some transition or developing countries), which had much larger implications for a less-diversified small economy, than the Bundesbank confronted. The key was that the Swiss National Bank employed the same general approach as the Bundesbank as described in the previous section: information inclusion rather than strict monetary targeting, flexibility and gradualism in disinflation, and use of target framework to serve transparency.

In operational terms, the emulation of the Bundesbank's successful monetary framework by a prototypical small open economy depends on several aspects of institutional design. First must come the commitment from the central bank (preferably with explicit government support) to a medium-term inflation target, and the absence of strict commitments to other goals such as the exchange rate. The key recognition is that short-run discretionary monetary policy need not be the same thing as, nor be perceived as, random behaviour – transparency can be a sufficient disciplinary effect on monetary policy to satisfy even financial markets (and, in fact, is usually more credible than strict exchange-rate pegs or other monetary rules that force central bank policy to directly oppose domestic goals in order to avoid speculative attack). If a central bank worries about transparency, its reputation for commitment to price stability will accrue automatically, unless there are fiscal or other real shocks that would overwhelm any monetary regime.

As seen in the Bundesbank's experience, such transparency does not consist simply of the initial announcement of the inflation target and then publication of the inflation series, but rather comprises several institutional aspects. These include the definition of the target measure, the numerical level of the target, and the time horizon of the target; the choice of a point target versus a range target; the revelation of what information has been used for the publication of forecasts; and the public discussion of deviations from the target when they occur.[24] Properly disciplined, short-run policy flexibility can, for the most part, be thought of as increasing hand in hand with transparency.

(i) Target definition   The definition must maximise clarity and awareness to the public, who ultimately are the wage and price expectation setters. This maximisation must be subject to the constraint that the target series be broadly enough based, reasonably accurate (in both the literal sense and the sense of being infrequently revised), and timely in its release. For the Bundesbank, it was easy to pick 'headline CPI' given the diversity and size of the German economy, as well as that measure's role in wage negotiations and legal barriers to indexing in most of the economy. For small open economies, however, the target design must be much more country specific, particularly taking into account the vagaries of the wage-setting system, the extent of indexation in the financial system, and the volatility of import prices. The questions to determine whether something should be excluded from the inflation target series are whether a price jump in that sector (for example, oil or imported food) could reasonably be conveyed to the public as a one-time jump not requiring pass-through to inflation expectations, and whether that kind of volatility is likely to recur. Even very idiosyncratic definitions of the target series are acceptable, as long as the definition remains stable for multi-year periods (no adding or subtracting of excluded sectors) and the series is clearly reproducible by someone qualified outside of the central bank and independent of the central bank's judgement.

(ii) Numerical level of the target   As stated at the start of this section, the main distinction between economies' inflation levels is between hyperinflation (greater than 60% annually, when any anchoring of expectations tends to disappear), moderate-to-high inflation (anything from the mid-teens up to 60% annually), and low inflation (anything from mid-teens down to zero, where disinflation becomes rather costly and inflation becomes rather persistent). The goal should be a long-run, politically sustainable path toward the 'low' tier, since the economic benefits of rapid disinflation (when escaping hyperinflation) are not overwhelming compared to the risks of the central bank being overruled into instability. For Germany after the post-war currency reform, this clearly was no longer an issue, but there are still important lessons to be learnt from its target-setting strategy. One is that there is no substitute for a public numerical target, as discovered by the Bundesbank in the 1973 to 1975 transition. Another is that an eventual goal of 2% inflation is sufficient to achieve practical price stability and anchor expectations. A third is that, even for Germany, rapid movements in the numerical target of several percentage points in response to shocks (remember, the Bundesbank *doubled* its unavoidable rate of inflation in the 1980 post-oil shock) can be made and allowed to persist, so long as they are promptly explained and clearly linked to observable temporary factors. Finally, the numerical target should be seen as binding only in the long run, but as a signal where policy is going in the short run, as was seen in the aftermath of unification when inflation did exceed the normative rate. All of these points are directly relevant for any inflation targeter.

(iii) Time-horizon of the target   Somewhere between one and four years is a practical horizon, given the lags of monetary policy. Too short a time horizon either is directly unattainable or causes instrument instability; too long a time horizon may bring about blows to credibility. The Bundesbank was probably erring too much on the side of appearing credible and too little on the recognition of lags in its own situation by setting a one-year target – this no doubt led to many of the year-to-year target misses, with the alternative being a very high cost in rapid disinflation. For an emerging market, particularly moving away from an exchange-rate commitment (as most inflation targeters do), the one-year target might be a better fit in that the markets and public are accustomed to ongoing assessment of central bank credibility and to rapid adjustment to changes in inflation. Given that a one-year target is likely to be overwhelmed frequently by short-run shocks, the acknowledgement must be made up front that the target is subject to change, but only through a formal and transparent process. The decision of which shocks should be responded to, however, must be made on the basis of severity of harm to the real economy, not just deviation from target: therefore resetting should be rare. This was illustrated by the Bundesbank resetting its mid-year target only one: in 1991 following monetary unification.

(iv) A point target versus a target range   Given the inherent uncertainties of inflation control, no inflation target will ever be hit precisely. The choice is between setting an inflation target as a point, that is a specific number for annual percentage inflation or as a range of inflation values (perhaps as an equal band around a desired point). The advantages of a point target are that the emphasis in public discussion naturally goes to the explanations of why inflation deviated – because it always will – rather than to the numbers; that it admits a great deal of uncertainty but still allows tracking of performance; and that it avoids the possibility of missing an entire range, which looks very bad. The target-range design has three advantages in theory as well: it builds in a zone of flexibility that can be utilised without having to be explained; it can convey information about the extent of uncertainty in achieving the inflation goal; and it might appear more binding and credible *ex ante*. In practice, however, the point target seems to avoid many of the pitfalls that the target range generates, such as the chance of missing the entire range combined with giving the public a false sense of exactitude about the size of the uncertainty. For emerging markets, particularly those coming off of a less credible monetary background and/or an exchange-rate peg, having flexibility that can be exercised without explanation may cause the public to miss a necessary educational exercise, and giving the image of a fixed exchange-rate zone may set up dangerous expectations about defending the bands on the inflation target. For Germany, many of these issues were not as pressing, so the added discretion came in useful compared to the size of the variation. Switzerland, however, as a small open economy went with the point target instead.

(v) Information inclusion and forecasting   There is no question that forecasting of inflation or any other macroeconomic variable is significantly more difficult in a developing or transitional economy than it is in an economy like Germany. Since even those economies' central banks will have to make as good an inflation forecast as they can no matter what, in order to have some guide for policy, they might as well release the forecast. In practice, the release of a forecast that explains the sources of uncertainty (some of which might be political worries about the fiscal process, some of which might be structural terms of trade shocks beyond the country's control) could assist in educating the public about the nature of their economy. Again, it is always helpful to delineate what monetary policy can and cannot do – and it cannot simply wish away major shocks. This was seen in the case of the Bundesbank when it confronted German monetary union in 1989 to 1990. This economic shock was certainly as vast, and as politicised, as any shock confronted by even emerging markets in terms of uncertainty. The amount of error as revealed later, in estimating the size of the GDR's economy, the nature of the portfolio shifts and velocity shocks involved, and in the response of the German government,

was inevitably large. The Bundesbank responded to the situation, as described above, by continuing to make its forecast, by being very conservative in its policy response, and by being open in its expression of concern that its forecast was of limited use. The Bundesbank also spelled out its role and possible realm of control as opposed to that of the government and labour unions. This is a model to follow for all central banks confronted with discrete shocks and transitions involving great uncertainty. And, again relevant to all central banks, the Bundesbank always used as much information as possible to assess progress toward its inflation target, even when times were less uncertain.

(vi) Deviations from target   This topic has already been addressed in the previous five points in terms of showing how transparency enhances flexibility. The key is in identifying and responding to supply shocks: when there is a demand shock, pursuit of the inflation target is clearly stabilising for the real economy. Defining the target, acquainting the public with the uncertainties of a point target, and varying the pace of the long-run disinflationary trend over time all build in some room to deal with supply shocks. It is worth noting that the Bundesbank avoided having a formal legal escape clause for supply shocks (as the Reserve Bank of New Zealand has), which probably made it easier to avoid inflation-only targeting, because the escape clause pressures one to pursue nothing but inflation when one is not 'escaping'. It is better to use target misses as educational opportunities and to reset the target path as needed once the shock is understood.

The bottom-line lesson of the Bundesbank for all inflation targeters, and therefore all central banks extricating themselves from unnecessarily strictured frameworks, is that transparency in the form of communication about a publicly defined numerical goal is the key to anchoring expectations. And when it comes to communication, generally more is more (albeit with some diminishing returns). Most of all, as seen in the Bundesbank's experience, the communication effort's greatest benefits come when the central bank addresses the public at large at least as often as it addresses markets or elected officials. The act of addressing the public builds in itself credibility. Moreover, the public in a broad sense do learn – beyond simple reactions to updated forecasts and estimates of the central bank's preferences.

The key is as it was for the Bundesbank to build a record of achievement against a measurable goal that is easily understood and tracked by the public. Without a clear standard of evaluation, a central bank not only leaves uncertainty about its goals but gains less from its successes, and loses the opportunity to build support from its performance. Central bank independence over the long run is impossible without political support, whatever the legal situation, and, as the Bundesbank's outreach efforts indicate, even where explicit oversight does not exist *de jure* independent central banks will act in line with this reality (Posen, 1993 and 1995). In addition, so acting will force politicians and market critics of the central bank to state their own criticisms in terms of goals or forecasts, rather than just ideological bluff. Institutional design of inflation targets on the Bundesbank model does matter because the central bank must encourage the public discussion of monetary policy to take the form of a substantive interchange rather than just a numerical assessment. This holds particularly true for central banks in developing and transition economies, where both monetary credibility and control will be in short supply.

Notes

1 This paper grew out of a lecture given at the Bank of England's Centre for Central Banking Studies, 'Substituting Transparency for Constraint: Implementing Credible Inflation Targets', 20 November 1998, and an earlier working paper, 'Lessons from the Bundesbank on the Occasion of its 40th (and Second to Last?) Birthday', IIE Working Paper # 97–4. I thank Ben Friedman, Charles Goodhart, Peter Kenen, Mervyn King, Reiner Koenig, Ken Kuttner, Thomas Laubach, Susanne Lohmann, David Mayes, Rick Mishkin, Georg Rich, Lars Svensson, and John Vickers for comments on the research that preceded this paper. The views expressed here, and any remaining errors, are my own and not those of the CCBS or the IIE. Contact aposen@iie.com

2 Bernanke *et al.* (1999) documents this pattern (e.g. Chapter 7 discusses how the Bank of England's inflation-targeting regime contributed to its eventual acquisition of instrument independence). Posen (1998) compares the Bundesbank and the Federal Reserve as models for the ECB in this regard.

3 This term was coined in Laubach and Posen (1997), which gives a more detailed analysis of the historical development of German monetary targeting and of the comparable Swiss framework.

4 See Fry (1998) for empirical evidence to this effect.

5 It is important to acknowledge that the breakdown of Bretton Woods was in part due to the extreme credibility of the Bundesbank's commitment to price stability relative to that of the Federal Reserve, and to the concomitant appreciation of the Deutsche Mark. Under these circumstances, the loss of the exchange-rate anchor was not the sort of credibility crisis with macroeconomic effects demanding an immediate response, as demonstrated by the slow (two-to-three-years long) move to the new framework.

6 See Posen (1993 and 1995) for a general discussion of how central bank independence emerges from political support. Some later observers have imposed the interpretation that one source of monetary targeting was Germans' broad distrust of monetary discretion, but that should not be exaggerated through a contemporary mindset. To most minds, that issue had already been addressed by the granting of independence to the Bundesbank in 1957, the distrust being of the *politicisation* of monetary policy – and, obviously, the Swiss and the United States had no such memories to prompt their contemporaneous moves to similar monetary targeting.

7 The announcement is reprinted in BB, December 1974, p. 8. References to signed articles in the central bank's serials are included in the bibliography. References to unsigned articles are given in the text as follows: quotes from *Annual Reports* of the Deutsche Bundesbank are referred to as BB <year,

page>; quotes from the *Monthly Reports* of the Deutsche Bundesbank are referred to as BB <month, year, page>.

8 Issing (1995b). He accepts the characterisation of the Bundesbank's monetary policy approach as 'pragmatic monetarism' in Issing (1995a).

9 This was seen in the Canadian adoption of inflation targeting at the start of 1991, after a couple years of disinflationary policies and at the time of a one-time rise in inflation due to an increase in indirect taxes. This phenomenon was also seen in the United Kingdom's adoption of inflation targeting in October 1992 following exit from the European ERM, which arguably limited the inflationary pass-through of the one-time shock of devaluation. See Bernanke *et al.* (1999) for a discussion of these events and this pattern of target adoption and use.

10 An authoritative survey on the subject is Friedman (1990).

11 Econometric observers have pointed out these patterns in various data sets. Neumann (1996) and Clarida and Gertler (1996) argue both points, that the Bundesbank has multiple goals and that it doesn't strictly target money. Von Hagen (1995) and Bernanke and Mihov (1996) focus on the latter point.

12 See, e.g. 'Recalculation of the production potential of the Federal Republic of Germany', BB, October 1981.

13 See Bernanke and Mishkin (1992) and Mishkin and Posen (1997).

14 'Methodological Notes on the Monetary Target Variable M3', BB, March 1988, pp. 18–21.

15 Econometric evidence that the Bundesbank has displayed an asymmetry in reacting to target misses is offered in Clarida and Gertler (1996).

16 The *Annual Report* is self-described as 'a detailed presentation of economic trends, including the most recent developments, together with comments on current monetary and general economic problems'.

17 See Bernanke *et al.* (1999) and Mishkin and Posen (1997) for a discussion of inflation-targeting practices.

18 'While officially the question of the correct exchange rate was still under discussion, the German Chancellor announced his decision on the exchange rate without informing Bundesbank President Karl-Otto Pöhl, although they had met only a few hours before' (Hefeker, 1994, p. 383). See Marsh (1992) for a longer historical account.

19 The money stock M3 had increased due to monetary union by almost 15%. This number turned out to be almost exactly right, for while GDP in the former GDR was surprisingly estimated to be only around 7% of the Federal Republic's *ex post*, with the government's transfers to the east, all of the money was absorbed (see König and Willeke, 1996).

20 The discipline of the monetary-targeting framework displayed its disadvantage as well, i.e. the near impossibility of money demand being stable, or at least predicting the changes in demand's relationship to goal variables necessitated by unification.

21 There are, of course, many other challenges facing developing and transition economies, including constraining government fiscal practices, structural or labour market reform, and the need to attract foreign investment. These can only be abetted by monetary stability, which can be achieved by the central bank; they cannot, however, be pursued directly by the central bank. Part of the purpose of a transparent nominal anchor is to prevent central banks from tilting at windmills in these areas. The public must learn what monetary policy can and cannot do (see Mishkin and Posen, 1997).

22 Many developing countries, including Brazil, Chile, and Mexico, have adopted inflation targets in recent years, successfully making a transition from exchange-rate pegs to a domestic flexible nominal anchor. Israel is the paradigmatic case (and discussed in Bernanke *et al.* 1999, Chapter 9).

23 See Laubach and Posen (1997) for an extended discussion of this comparison. This is a further indication that the source of monetary targeting's advantages lies more in the use of a transparent framework than in measurably meeting some specific definition of the target itself.
24 Longer general discussions of these design aspects, but without specific application to emerging market issues, is given in Bernanke *et al.* (1999), Chapter 3, and in Mishkin and Posen (1997).
25 Citations for unsigned central bank documents are given in the main text.

Bibliography

Bernanke, B., Laubach, T., Mishkin, F. and Posen, A. (1999), *Inflation Targeting: Lessons from the International Experience,* Princeton: Princeton University Press.

Bernanke, B. and Mihov, I. (1996), 'What does the Bundesbank target?' *European Economic Review.*

Bernanke, B. and Mishkin, F. (1992), 'Central bank behaviour and the strategy of monetary policy: observations from six industrialized countries', in Blanchard, Oliver and Fischer, Stanley (eds) *NBER Macroeconomics Annual,* 1992, pp, 183–228, Cambridge: MIT Press.

Bundesbank (1995), *The Monetary Policy of the Bundesbank,* Frankfurt, October.

Clarida, R. and Gertler, M. (1996), 'How the Bundesbank conducts monetary policy'. C.V., *Starr Center for Applied Economics Economic Research Reports,* No. 96–14, April.

Friedman, B. (1995), 'The rise and fall of money growth targets as guidelines for U.S. monetary policy', mimeo, Bank of Japan Monetary Conference, October.

Friedman, B. (1990), 'Targets and instruments of monetary policy', in Friedman, Benjamin and Hahn, Frank (eds) *Handbook of Monetary Economics,* Vol. 2, Amsterdam: North Holland.

Friedman, B. and Kuttner, K. (1996), 'A price target for U.S. monetary policy? lessons from the experience with money growth targets', *Brookings Papers on Economic Activity,* 1: 77–146 (Spring).

Fry, M. (1998), 'Assessing central bank independence in developing countries: do actions speak louder than words?' *Oxford Economic Papers,* 50: 512–29, July.

Hefeker, C. (1994), 'German monetary union, the Bundesbank, and the EMS collapse', *Banca National del Lavoro Quarterly Review,* 47: 379–98, December.

Issing, O. (1995a), 'The relationship between the constancy of monetary policy and the stability of the monetary system', mimeo, Gerzensee Symposium of the Swiss National Bank.

Issing, O. (1995b), 'Monetary policy in an integrated world economy', mimeo, University of Kiel, June.

König, R. and Willeke, C. (1996), 'German monetary reunification', *Central Banking,* pp. 29–39, May.

Laubach, T. and Posen, A. (1997), 'Disciplined discretion: lessons from the German and Swiss monetary frameworks', *Princeton Essays in International Finance.*

Marsh, D. (1992), *The Bundesbank.* London: William Heinemann.

Mishkin, F. and Posen, A. (1997), 'Inflation targeting: lessons from four countries', *Federal Reserve Bank of New York Economic Policy Review,* 9–110, August.

Neumann, M. (1996), 'Monetary targeting in Germany', mimeo, Bank of Japan Monetary Conference.

Posen, A. (1993), 'Why central bank independence does not cause low inflation: there is no institutional fix for politics', in O'Brien, Richard (ed.) *Finance and the International Economy,* 7, pp. 40–65, Oxford: Oxford University Press.

Posen, A. (1995), 'Declarations are not enough: financial sector sources of central bank independence', in Bernanke, Ben S. and Rotenberg, Julio J. (eds) *NBER Macroeconomics Annual,* 1995, pp. 253–74, Cambridge: MIT Press.

Posen, A. (1998), 'No monetary masquerades for the ECB', in Meade, Ellen (ed.) *The European Central Bank – How Transparent? How Accountable?* American Institute for Contemporary German Studies, March.

Schlesinger, H. (1983), 'The setting of monetary objectives in Germany', in Meek, Paul (ed.) *Central Bank Views of Monetary Targeting*, pp. 6–17, New York: Federal Reserve Bank of New York.

Schmid, P. (1996), 'Monetary policy: targets and instruments', *Central Banking*, pp. 40–51, May.

Trehan, B. (1988), 'The practice of monetary targeting: a case study of the West German experience', *Federal Reserve Bank of San Francisco Economic Review*, 2: 30–44 (Spring).

Von Hagen, J. (1989), 'Monetary targeting with exchange rate constraints: the Bundesbank in the 1980s', *Federal Reserve Bank of St. Louis Review*, 71: 53–69, September–October.

Von Hagen, J. (1995), 'Inflation and monetary targeting in Germany', in Leiderman, Leo and Svensson, Lars, *Inflation Targets,* London: CEPR.

What can inflation expectations and core inflation tell us about monetary policy in Japan?[1]

Masahiro Higo

1 Introduction

As a primary goal of monetary policy, price stability in Japan is generally considered to include not only stability of current measured inflation rates, but also price stability in the medium to long run. The Bank of Japan has never set a numerical target or monitoring range for a specific price or money index,[2] yet the framework has maintained stability in measured inflation rates since the latter half of the 1980s. At the same time, however, the Japanese economy has experienced turbulence owing to the emergence and collapse of the so-called 'asset price bubble'. Such events provide reasons for the Bank of Japan now to check whether or not its policy approach is appropriate in the pursuit of its ultimate objectives.

This paper argues that volatile inflation expectations may have contributed to such a large swing in real growth rates and in asset prices. As such, it may be useful for the Bank of Japan to consider the introduction of an explicit policy target in order to stabilise the public's inflation expectations. The paper will also investigate some practical difficulties of implementing inflation-targeting that might arise if policy-makers were to use conventional CPI measures. In this regard, the paper proposes excluding from the overall index those inflation fluctuations driven by supply shocks, since these should to some extent be accommodated by monetary policy. At the same time, the paper proposes that trimmed mean CPI inflation be used to improve the accuracy of the forecast values of future inflation.

Section 2 summarises the performance of the Japanese economy and monetary policy since the latter half of the 1980s. Section 3 estimates the expected inflation rate from survey and financial data and analyses characteristics of movements in expected inflation. Section 4 investigates the operational difficulties of implementing inflation targeting and evaluates the usefulness of the trimmed-mean CPI for excluding fluctuations driven by supply shocks from overall inflation and improving the accuracy of forecasts of future inflation. Finally, Section 5 summarises the discussion and comments on the remaining problems.

2   Japanese economic performance and monetary policy since the latter half of the 1980s

2.1   *Japanese economic performance and monetary policy*

From 1979 to 1980, the Japanese inflation rate rose sharply as a result of the second oil price shock, but the Bank of Japan's restrictive monetary policy reduced inflation relatively quickly (Chart 1a). Since the mid-1980s, the annual increase in the CPI has generally been between 0% and 3%.

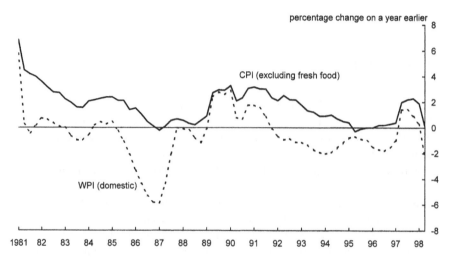

Chart 1a Movement of economic and monetary indicators in Japan – prices

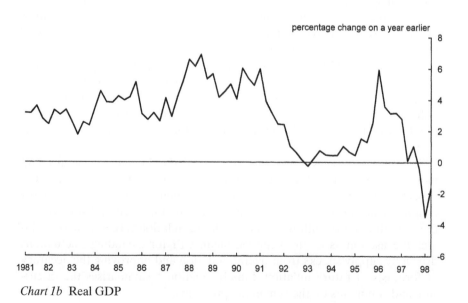

Chart 1b Real GDP

The Bank of Japan has maintained price stability, at least in terms of measured price indexes. In marked contrast, the Japanese economy has experienced large swings in its real growth rate since the mid-1980s (Chart 1b). It has also experienced much greater volatility in asset prices (Chart 1c). Between 1987 and 1990, the real growth rate tended to be above trend, and after that it dropped sharply and remained around zero from 1992 to 1994. More recently, the real growth rate was negative. In brief, the combination of the lower inflation rate and the higher volatility in real growth rate is a conspicuous feature of the Japanese economy in recent years.

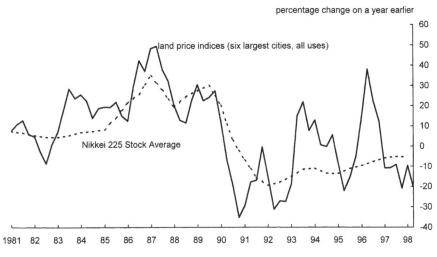

Chart 1c Stock and land prices

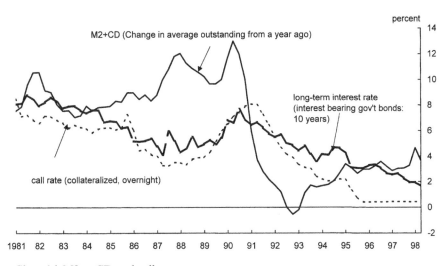

Chart 1d M2 + CD and call rate

The Bank of Japan has responded to large fluctuations in business cycles by changing short-term interest rates (Chart 1d). Between 1985 and 1987 it lowered the short-term interest rate (the overnight call rate) from around 6% to 3%. Although the economy subsequently recovered sharply, the Bank of Japan maintained low interest rates until the end of 1988. In 1989, the Bank changed its policy stance to a strictly restrictive one and increased the short-term interest rate to around 8% by the end of 1990. After the spring of 1991, the Bank eased its policy stance again and lowered the short-term interest rate step by step. It remained at around 0.5% from late 1995 to late 1998 and finally reached 0.15% in February of 1999. Movements in the long-term interest rate (the ten-year government bond yield) have been similar to short-term interest rates, though less marked. After 1991, long-term interest rates continued to fall and in 1998 were less than 1%, the lowest rate in Japanese history.

2.2   *International comparisons of volatility in growth*

Table 1 compares the volatility of the real growth rate in Japan with that of the United States, Germany and the United Kingdom from the first quarter of 1985 to the third quarter of 1998. The real growth rate averaged around 2% in each of the four countries, yet the standard deviation of the Japanese growth rate was significantly higher than the other countries. Furthermore, by using a Fourier transformation, I conduct spectral analysis on the growth rates of real GDP to identify which cyclical components are included in each growth rate (Table 2). In the case of the Japanese growth rate, the power spectrum of irregularly fluctuated components of a cycle of less than one year is large. The power spectrum of business cycle components of cycles of more than two years is also large, at over three times as much as that in the United States, 1.5 times those in Germany, and 20% higher than the United Kingdom.

Volatility in the Japanese CPI is lower than the other three countries for the same period (Table 1). Furthermore, we conduct spectral analysis on

Table 1 Average and variability of real growth rate and CPI inflation rate in selected countries 1985/1Q–1998/3Q

Real growth rate	per cent, quarter on same quarter a year earlier			
	Japan	United States	Germany	United Kingdom
average	2.85	2.80	2.34	2.67
standard deviation	2.57	1.39	2.04	1.39
Inflation rate	per cent, quarter on same quarter a year earlier			
	Japan	United States	Germany	United Kingdom
average	1.09	3.28	2.05	4.45
standard deviation	1.06	1.15	1.29	2.27

Table 2 Contribution to the total variability of real growth rate and CPI inflation rate by cycle period

Real growth rate, 1985/1Q–1998/3Q quarter-on-quarter changes

	Japan	United States	Germany	United Kingdom
total variability	100	24	88	41
more than 2 years	26	8	17	22
more than 1 year	11	3	7	5
less than 1 year	63	12	63	14

Note: Total variability in Japan = 100. All data are seasonally adjusted.

Inflation rate, 1985/Jan.–1997/Mar.   month-on-month changes

	Japan	United States	Germany	United Kingdom
total variability	100	59	73	166
more than 2 years	18	19	25	85
more than 1 year	4	7	3	16
less than 1 year	78	33	45	65

Note: Total variability in Japan = 100. All data are seasonally adjusted.

changes in the CPI to identify which cyclical components show the high-lighted volatility (Table 2). In Japan, the power spectrum of cyclical components of more than two years is small; about 60% of that in Germany and a quarter of that in the United Kingdom, though that of cyclical components of less than one year (caused in part by temporary supply shocks) is larger.

In short, the analysis shows that inflation rate fluctuated less in Japan than in the other three countries but the real growth rate fluctuated more.

2.3 Why is the real growth rate so volatile in Japan?

There are several possible explanations for the very volatile real growth rate in Japan since the middle of 1980s.

The first relates to the large swings in asset prices. Uemura and Kimura (1998) show that share prices lead both real GDP and its private-sector components by testing for Granger causality using a two-variable Vector Auto Regression (VAR) from the first quarter of 1970 to the second quarter of 1997. Positive and negative wealth effects caused by such severe fluctuations in asset prices have greatly influenced business investment and household consumption. Furthermore, because the amount of non-performing bank loans has sharply increased, due in part to the drop in asset prices, many banks have been greatly damaged by the huge losses from such loans; consequently, they do not have the capacity to endure the various financial risks that accompany lending and other financial activities.

The second explanation is that permanent supply-side shocks might have affected the long-run volatility of GDP in Japan since the 1980s. Sterne and Bayoumi (1993) used a structural VAR approach to argue that, in Japan, productivity shocks dominated fluctuations in variations in real GDP, which was different from the case in the United States and the United Kingdom. The contribution of total factor productivity (TFP) to the real growth rate has indeed been larger in Japan than in other countries such as the United States for a few decades (Inoue, 1998). This contribution of TFP increased in the latter half of 1980s, but then decreased in the 1990s. Such a trend parallels that of the real growth rate. Because productivity shocks affect the potential growth rate and maintain the gap between potential and actual output at the same relative level, the fact that the contribution of productivity shocks is large in Japan is partly consistent with the Japanese experience described in Section 2.1. However, it is difficult to explain completely such a large swing of real GDP solely in terms of the change in TFP.

A third possible explanation for volatility in real growth is downward nominal rigidities in wages and prices. By estimating a Phillips-type inflation-forecasting equation, we can calculate the long-run sacrifice ratio (the change of GDP gap relative to the inflation rate). The results show that the sacrifice ratio has increased between 1980 and 1998 (Table 3). As such, recent demand shocks may affect output more and prices less than in previous periods, a result that could be attributable to increased nominal rigidities. However, by analysing a data set from 1976 to 1995, Kimura and Ueda (1997) argue that Japanese wages did not exhibit serious downward rigidity. This result suggests that nominal rigidities may not be very important in explaining the volatility in real growth rates during the 1980s and the first half of the 1990s.

Finally, large swings in inflation expectations may have been a factor causing high volatility in real GDP. As mentioned above, the Bank of Japan has maintained a discretionary policy framework without announcing any numerical policy targets. Under this kind of policy, with no explicit commitment to stabilise inflation over a specified time horizon, the public may have difficulty in forming inflationary expectations. For example, if the economic boom continues for a certain time, the public may be uncertain about the policy reaction and form the expectation that inflation will increase in the near future. If monetary policy lacks credibility, the Bank of Japan may be more likely to attempt to influence expectations through actions than through announcements, for example by raising short-term interest rates markedly and maintaining them at high rates over a period sufficient to control and stabilise expectations of inflation. But by doing so it may temporarily retard real growth and set back asset prices.

Table 3 Long-run sacrifice ratio (change of GDP gap/change of CPI inflation rate)

sample period	1980:Q1–1998:Q3	1987:Q1–1998:Q3	1991:Q1–1998:Q3
sacrifice ratio	1.93	2.14	3.22

To investigate this possibility, it is important for the central bank to understand how inflation expectations have changed and what kind of relationship the movement of expectations had with the change of monetary policy stance in Japan.

3 Interpreting measures of inflation expectations

3.1 Estimation of inflation expectations

To calculate expected inflation, a starting point is to use the Fisher equation to decompose nominal long-term interest rates into the long-term real interest rate and the expected inflation rate:

nominal long-term interest rate = real long-term interest
rate + expected inflation

Japan has no market for indexed government bonds and limited survey data on the expected rate of inflation. It is therefore more difficult than in some other countries to gather direct information about medium- or long-term expectations of inflation. As an alternative, this paper calculates three-year real interest rates using three methods. This makes it possible to estimate expected inflation three years ahead indirectly, by subtracting the real interest rate from a three-year nominal rate. A caveat to this approach is that nominal long-term interest rates include a risk premium for future uncertainty and the expected real growth rate does not. In such circumstances, the expected inflation rate may overstate actual expected inflation. Nevertheless, the paper calculates three-year inflation expectations and real interest rates from 1981 to 1998 on a quarterly basis using the methods described below. Appendix A provides detailed information about the data calculations and sources.

(i) Estimation using survey data about expected real growth rates

The first method involves proxying real interest rates by calculating expected real growth rates of per capita income up to three years ahead.[3] Data are taken from the 'Report of Survey Research Concerning Corporate Behaviour' conducted by the Economic Planning Agency,[4] one in which over 1,300 enterprises are asked directly: 'What do you expect real growth will be in Japan in the coming three years?' Because this survey is conducted in January each year, such survey data is transformed into quarterly data by linear interpolation. Inflation expectations can be estimated from expected growth rates per capita.

(ii) Estimation by using growth rate of potential GDP

The second method is to estimate inflation expectations using growth rates of potential GDP per capita as proxies for real interest rates. The method used is suggested by Watanabe (1997). The procedure is to: (i) estimate a Cobb-Douglas type production function; (ii) estimate the potential labour and capital inputs; and (iii) use these estimates to calculate potential GDP. The results show that the movement in growth rate of potential GDP is relatively smooth and not greatly influenced by the fluctuation in business cycles. The growth rate of potential GDP per capita can serve as a proxy for three-year real interest rates, from which we estimate inflation expectations.

(iii) Estimation by using the rate of return on capital

Theoretically, the real interest rate represents the marginal product of capital. Using the approach of Kitamura and Fujiki (1997), this paper estimates the rate of return on capital as follows.[5,6]

$$MPK_t = 100*(SK_t*\left[\frac{Y_t}{K_t + KG_t}\right])(1 - \tau) - \delta_t - RP$$

where MPK is the rate of return on capital; SK is capital's share of national income; Y is real GDP at factor cost in the calendar year 1990; K is the real private capital stock; KG is the real public capital stock; τ is effective corporate tax rate and δ is the depreciation rate of capital stock.

The estimated value is the rate of return on capital for the private sector, so the rate exceeds the risk-free real interest rate by the default risk premium (RP) for the private sector. To measure the premium, the difference between the average lending rate of the commercial banks and the risk-free interest rate is subtracted from the rate of return on capital, yielding the risk-free rate of return on capital. The movement of the estimated rate of return is smooth and independent of business cycles, though it is estimated on a quarterly basis, so that it is likely to be related to business cycles. Thus the rate is a reasonable proxy for three-year real interest rates, and provides a basis for deriving inflation expectations.

3.2   Characteristics of movement in expected inflation

Chart 2 presents movements in three-year expected inflation rates estimated by the above three methods along with actual inflation. Chart 3 presents movements in the proxies for three-year real interest rates along with actual real GDP. Comparing movements, there appear to be few differences among these estimated rates. Movement in expected inflation has the following three characteristics.

First, these measures of inflation expectations are volatile (Chart 2). All measures of expected inflation rose and maintained an annual rate of around 4% from 1990 to 1991. By contrast, most of them, except those derived from survey data, stayed around 0% from 1986 to 1988, and most

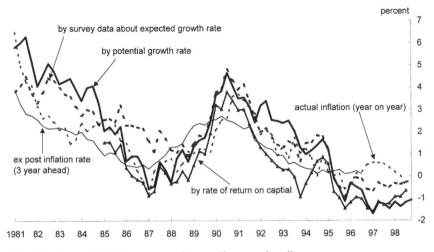

Chart 2 Expected inflation rate estimates (3 years ahead)

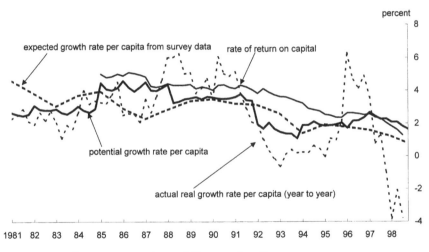

Chart 3 Real interest rate estimated (3 years ahead)

have stayed below zero since 1995. During the last 15 years the difference between maximum and minimum was five percentage points, much larger than that of actual inflation rate.[7]

Second, expected inflation has been close to actual year-on-year inflation rates of one year earlier. This demonstrates that the public has expected current inflation rates to persist for around the next three years. Expectations formation appears to have changed over time. In the first half of the 1980s, expectations of inflation were backward-looking. In contrast, they appear to have become more forward-looking between 1989 and 1991, a period of relatively high inflation.

Third, the short-term real interest rate calculated by deflating the actual

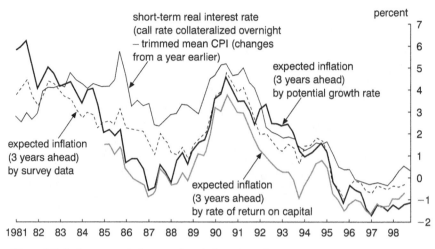

Chart 4 Inflation expectations and real short-term interest rate

inflation rate (trimmed-Mean CPI) of a year earlier continues to be positively correlated with inflation expectations. It seems that expected inflation rates have led short-term real interest rates (Chart 4).

To check the relationship between estimated expectations of inflation and various economic variables we calculate coefficients of time correlation and test with Granger causality using a two-variable VAR from the first quarter of 1983 to the third quarter of 1998. The variables used are the annual change in CPI (the trimmed-mean CPI) and real output. We also include the GDP gap (the difference between potential and actual GDP), short-term real interest rate, and the annual change in stock prices.

The correlation between the variables over time is shown in Table 4. The real growth rate leads expected inflation by 11 quarters and the highest contemporary time correlations are between inflationary expecta-

Table 4 Coefficients of time correlation between expected inflation and economic variables

1983:Q1–1998:Q3	*Expected inflation (3 years)*		
	survey data	*potential growth*	*rate of return*
change of trimmed CPI	0.822 (0)	0.828 (0)	0.859 (−1)
real growth rate	0.470 (+11)	0.450 (+11)	0.477 (+11)
GDP gap	0.658 (0)	0.651 (0)	0.680 (0)
short-term real interest rate	0.920 (0)	0.800 (0)	0.842 (0)
change of stock price	ambiguous	−0.106 (−2)	−0.259 (−2)

1 Figures indicate the largest cross correlation coefficient within twelve quarters before and after the quarter concerned. Figures in parentheses are time lags, and negative figures represent the lead of expected inflation.
2 The change of trimmed CPI, real GDP and stock price is based on annual changes of quarterly data.

Table 5 Results of Granger tests between expected inflation and economic variables
1983/1Q–1998/3Q (F value)

(1) Does expected inflation cause the following variables?

| | Expected inflation (3 years); measured by: | | |
	survey data	potential growth	rate of return
change of trimmed CPI	2.75**	2.39**	1.80*
real growth rate	0.99	0.84	0.42
GDP gap	1.86*	2.19**	1.30
short-term real interest rate	1.29	1.88*	2.80**
change of stock price	1.89*	4.14***	3.18***

(2) Do the following variables cause expected inflation?

| | Expected inflation (3 years); measured by: | | |
	survey data	potential growth	rate of return
change of trimmed CPI	0.52	0.60	0.65
real growth rate	1.14	0.76	0.82
GDP gap	0.45	0.28	0.17
short-term real interest rate	1.23	0.78	0.60
change of stock price	1.26	0.86	1.67*

1 *indicates significance at the level of 10%; **indicates significance at 5%; ***indicates significance at 1%.
2 The change of trimmed CPI, real GDP, and stock price is based on annual changes of quarterly data.

tions and the actual inflation rate, the short-term real interest rate and the GDP gap. Expected inflation has a weak and perverse relationship with changes in stock prices, which in turn lead the real growth rate by three quarters.

The results of Granger causality tests (Table 5) indicate that inflation expectations determine the actual inflation rate, the short-term real interest rate, the GDP gap, and changes in stock prices. It also indicates that the causal relationship between the expectations and the real growth rate is statistically insignificant and almost no variables cause inflation expectations.

The main results to come out of this statistical analysis are that, during the past fifteen years:

(i) the change in the real growth rate influences the expectations of inflation with a long lag,

(ii) inflation expectations lead the movement of other economic variables (with relatively short lags),

(iii) the rise in inflation expectations and actual inflation affects the downward movement of stock prices; moreover, it may also lead to a decline in the real growth rate.

(iv) changes in the short-term real interest rate lag slightly behind inflation expectations.

3.3   Implications for the conduct of monetary policy

What kind of relationship do large-scale fluctuations in inflation expectations have with the conduct of monetary policy? One possible answer is that delayed policy actions may lead to fluctuations in inflation expectations, which in turn may make the economy less stable. Chart 4 suggests that it takes a long time to decrease expected inflation after the Bank of Japan increases the short-term real interest rate. For example, the expected inflation rate continued to jump for more than one year after the short-term real interest rate started to rise in the inflationary phase of 1989. At that time, the Bank of Japan had to raise the interest rate sharply and keep it high for a certain period in order to prevent inflation expectations from accelerating.

One interpretation of the lessons from this experience is that the central bank needs to conduct a more pre-emptive monetary policy. To this end, there may be some benefits in specifying standards for policy judgement, and to clearly demonstrate prior policy objectives or optimal weights among the objectives. To conduct such monetary policy effectively, however, depends on how accurately the bank can forecast inflation in the near future.

The results allow for another possible interpretation of monetary policy implementation. It could be that, in spite of the Bank of Japan's excellent record in controlling inflation, it has not been fully credible in controlling inflation expectations.[8] It is possible that insufficient credibility may have necessitated a more restrictive monetary policy over a longer period than would otherwise have been needed, in order to dampen inflation expectations and fully stabilise inflation. However, this can also damage the real economy. Given these arguments, an effective monetary policy might include the introduction of a policy framework signals a well-timed policy action. This could enhance the Bank's credibility and make it easier for the public to predict the effects of possible future policy actions. This in turn may contribute to more stable inflation expectations.

4   Operational use of the trimmed-mean CPI in implementing inflation targeting in Japan?

4.1   Advantages and difficulties in the implementation of inflation targeting

Inflation targets have been used in several economies to increase the credibility of monetary policy, making the policy more effective and helping to stabilise the inflation expectations of the public. As Bernanke and Mishkin (1997) argue, the inflation-targeting approach has several advantages:

1   it increases credibility by attaching an institutional commitment to the ultimate objective;

2   it increases transparency by clearly stating the specific criteria for monetary policy actions;
3   it decreases the public's uncertainty about the future by improving communication between the central bank and the public.[9]

In Japan, however, there are several operational considerations. One important issue relates to the width of the target range. A range may be needed to provide the flexibility to accommodate fluctuations in inflation caused by supply shocks and to provide room for changes in the relationship between inflation and output. In this way the central bank may be better placed to maintain well-balanced and sustainable growth. However, if the target range for overall CPI inflation since 1985 had been set between 1% and 3% then the policy actually followed would have delivered an inflation rate within the actual target range in most periods. Such a target range may however provide insufficient signals for policy decisions. Another means of providing flexibility might be to exclude from any targeted index that part of inflation caused by supply shocks. In this case, the central bank might consider narrowing the band width of the target in order to enhance its role as a policy guide.

Another important problem in operating an inflation target relates to the accuracy with which the Bank of Japan can forecast inflation. Monetary policy affects inflation, albeit with long time lags. Svensson (1997) argues that the forecast of inflation is the ideal intermediate variable for an inflation-targeting regime because both the public and the central bank can observe the forecast inflation rate contemporaneously, and a rationally formed forecast for inflation incorporates all information currently available.[10] Following this approach, the Bank of Japan would need to forecast inflation rate one or two years ahead as accurately as possible in order to conduct effective policy actions using the inflation-targeting approach.

4.2   How successfully does the trimmed-mean CPI exclude temporary supply shocks?

Many central banks use core measures of inflation in order to improve the clarity of the signal price changes send to policy-makers. This section investigates the extent to which the trimmed-mean CPI might fulfil such a role in Japan through the exclusion of components caused by temporary supply shocks.[11] The trimmed-mean CPI is a price index that excludes outliers in a cross-sectional distribution of individual price changes for each period. Bryan and Cecchetti (1994), Shiratsuka (1997) and Mio and Higo (1999) indicate that this estimator shows moderate fluctuations in line with relevant macroeconomic variations by excluding the components related to temporary shocks.

Chart 5 represents movements in the Trimmed Mean CPI (TM-CPI) calculated on a year-on-year change basis that excludes 30% outliers (15%

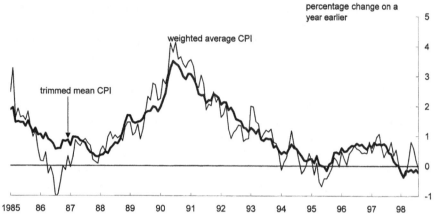

Chart 5 Measures of smoothed inflation

on each side) since 1985. It can be seen that trimming the CPI in this fashion considerably reduces short-run volatility in inflation. The TM-CPI excludes variations caused by temporary supply and external shocks. The excluded components frequently include fresh foods and energy items. Exclusions also include clothes and household electrical appliances influenced by changes in import prices. If it used the TM-CPI as a target or indicator for monetary policy, the Bank of Japan could narrow the band width, rendering inflation targeting more effective and at the same time increasing its own credibility.

4.3   The relative accuracy of inflation forecasting using the trimmed-mean CPI

Can inflation forecasting be improved through the use of the TM-CPI? To investigate further, we separate inflation equations for the overall CPI, the CPI excluding fresh foods, and the TM-CPI. The explanatory variables are estimates of the output gap[1] and rates of inflation lagged by one, two, and three quarters. Table 6 indicates that, when using the TM-CPI, all coefficients of explanatory variables are significant, and the coefficient of determination R^2 is the largest of the three.

Second, we recursively forecast inflation in quarters ahead using the estimated equations and using actual values for the GDP gap in forecast periods. Table 7 shows the results of the standard deviation of prediction errors when doing an out of sample test. When forecasting one quarter ahead, the standard deviation of prediction error obtained by the TM-CPI (0.24%) is less than half of that obtained by the overall CPI (0.54%) and also 10% less than that by the CPI ex-fresh foods (0.27%). As the forecasting period is extended, the difference between the deviation by the TM-CPI and the CPI excluding fresh food increases. In forecasting five

Table 6 Estimates for inflation forecasting function (models for forecasting inflation 1Q ahead)

$$\pi_{t+1} = \alpha_0 + \alpha_1\pi_t + \alpha_2\pi_{t-1} + \alpha_3\pi_{t-2} + \beta_1 GDPGAP_t$$
where π_t = CPI-overall, CPI-ex fresh food, trimmed mean CPI

	α_0	α_1	α_2	α_3	β	Durbin-h	Adj-R^2
CPI overall	0.273$^+$	1.286***	−0.363**	0.025	0.053$^+$	0.004	0.952
CPI ex food	0.213$^+$	1.318***	−0.427***	0.075	0.048$^+$	−0.323	0.963
CPI trimmed	0.215**	0.511***	−0.717***	0.164*	0.046**	−1.487	0.977

Significance level *** = 1% ** = 5% * = 10% + = 20%

quarters ahead, the deviation obtained by the TM-CPI (0.75%) is 20% smaller than that obtained by the CPI excluding fresh foods (0.89%). This may be because the share of various supply shocks except for fresh foods increases with the increase of forecast period. The prediction error for the TM-CPI is markedly smaller than that for other price indices between 1986 and 1987, during the period of the sharp drop in oil prices. Accuracy in forecasting inflation, therefore, is greatly improved by using the TM-CPI. This result suggests that TM-CPI inflation could be of benefit in providing a clear signal to policy-makers attempting to maintain stable inflation now and in the future.

5 Concluding remarks

This paper argues that the Bank of Japan has successfully stabilised consumer price inflation since the 1980s, but has not stabilised inflation expectations to the same extent. As a result, fluctuations in expected inflation may have amplified variations in the real growth in asset prices. Adopting inflation targeting is one possible means of stabilising inflation expectations. However, even if the Bank of Japan were to adopt inflation targets there would remain many issues to be tackled. These relate in particular to the choice of the target band width and how to forecast the target indicator more accurately. Solving these problems requires the effective decomposition of inflation movements into a trend component

Table 7 Standard deviation of prediction error (out of sample test)

	per cent		
forecasting horizon	*CPI overall*	*CPI excluding food*	*CPI trimmed mean*
1Q ahead	0.535	0.270	0.243
2Q ahead	0.685	0.441	0.405
3Q ahead	0.829	0.602	0.507
4Q ahead	1.061	0.774	0.647
5Q ahead	1.179	0.889	0.745
6Q ahead	1.297	0.994	0.809
7Q ahead	1.386	1.101	0.886
8Q ahead	1.447	1.183	0.962
9Q ahead	1.455	1.253	1.023

related to macroeconomic fluctuations which should be controlled by monetary policy, and a component caused by supply shocks, and techniques for forecasting future inflation rates one or two years ahead more accurately. Use of the trimmed-mean CPI would help in developing these tools.

However, even if a device such as the trimmed-mean CPI were effectively utilised, other important issues would need to be tackled if the Bank of Japan were to adopt an inflation targeting approach. First, inflation-targeting does not necessarily stabilise the real growth rate. The legal objectives of the Bank of Japan require it to pursue price stability which contributes to sound development of the economy. Recently in Japan, the sacrifice ratio may have increased. And at the same time, the relationships among economic indicators has been unstable for various reasons. In this kind of situation, it may be difficult to attain sound development of the economy by means of inflation targeting alone. An important question for future work is to examine the extent to which the forward-looking nature of inflation targets is sufficient to smooth output volatility. If the Bank tries to control inflation strictly, it is possible that the real GDP growth rate will fluctuate more widely.

A further issue relates to how the central bank should deal with fluctuations in asset prices that cannot be eliminated merely through stabilising expected inflation. As asserted above, if the central bank introduces inflation-targeting, its monetary policy credibility may in some circumstances increase, which would help to stabilise inflation expectations. However, large variations in asset prices are caused by important factors other than expected inflation. Changes in investor preferences, changes in the age composition of the Japanese population, and changes in regulations and tax systems may all have an important role. It usually takes a long time to reshape these factors, and the role of monetary policy is limited. The long-lasting effects of inflation or deflation in asset prices may exacerbate fluctuations in the real growth rate, and damage financial systems.

In consideration of all these factors, if the central bank were to adopt an explicit target, it might nevertheless take pre-emptive policy actions even in the absence of a forecast that the indicator will overshoot or undershoot the target range.[13]

APPENDIX A

This appendix fully describes the data used in this paper.

(i)   Nominal long-term interest rate (three years)

From Q1 in 1981 to Q4 in 1994: yield of interest-bearing bank debentures (three years)

From Q1 in 1995 to Q4 in 1998: yield of interest-bearing government bonds (three years)

The former yield is the average of the yield at the end of each month of each quarter. The latter yield is the average of the yield for all trading days in each quarter. The main reason why the yield of bank debentures by the end of 1994 is used is because of the availability of data on the basis of compound interest. By the end of 1994, the banks which issued bank debentures maintained high-rank ratings so that the yield of the bank debentures was almost the same as that of government bonds.

(ii)   Capital share of income (SK)

By using National Account Statistics, the share of employee compensation and that of operating surplus and consumption of fixed capital of owner-occupied dwellings in GDP at factor cost are excluded from one as a capital share of income.

(iii)   Real private capital stock (K)

The paper uses the statistics 'Gross Capital Stock of Private Enterprises' from the Economic Planning Agency. This is an estimate of market prices for the 1990 calendar year. This value does not include residential stock.

(iv)   Real public capital stock (KG)

The paper uses statistics estimated by the Economic Planning Agency (1998). These are estimates of market prices for the 1990 calendar year. These statistics are given only at the end of every fiscal year, so the data is transformed into quarterly data through linear interpolation. These statistics cover only the period up to the end of the 1993 fiscal year; therefore the data from 1994–98 are estimated by using the data of gross capital formation by the public sector from National Accounts Statistics.

(v)   Effective corporate tax rate (τ)

The effective corporate tax rate is defined as the direct tax on income of private corporations divided by the sum of the operating surplus and consumption of fixed capital of private corporations.

(vii)   Risk premium of private sector (RP)

As a proxy for risk premium, we calculate the average difference between the average lending rate of commercial banks and the risk-free interest rate from the beginning of 1985 to the end of 1998. The estimated value is 1.21%. The average lending rate is the average contracted interest rate on loans and discounts (total: the average of city banks, regional banks and regional banks II). The risk-free interest rate is the subscriber's yield for the three-month Treasury bill (after 1989) or the three-month yield for government bonds with repurchase agreements (before 1988).

Notes

1 This paper was first prepared for discussion at the Bank of England Workshop 'Choice of Intermediate Monetary Policy Targets', 16–20 November 1998. Views presented in this paper are those of the author, and not necessarily those of the Bank of Japan or the Institute for Monetary and Economic Studies. I would like to thank Lavan Mahadeva (Bank of England), Hasan Bakhshi (Bank of England), Ronald McKinnon (Stanford University), Shigenori Shiratsuka (Bank of Japan) and participants in the Workshop for useful and valuable comments. I am also grateful to Hitoshi Mio (Bank of Japan) and Sachiko Nakada (Bank of Japan) for the helpful support they provided through their empirical analysis.

2 In an announcement of recent monetary policy change (9 September 1998), the policy board stated that: 'The monetary policy objective of Bank of Japan is to pursue price stability, avoiding both inflation and deflation.' However, the board did not comment on any specific price-index targets that might be needed for practical execution of a monetary policy.

3 The following condition for maximising household utility should be satisfied under the neoclassical growth model:

$$r = \rho + \theta * \acute{y}$$

where r is real interest rate, ρ is the rate of time preference, θ is the coefficient of relative risk aversion and $\acute{y}$ is the real growth rate of output (consumption) per capita. Using the expected real growth rate per capita as a proxy for real interest rate implies setting $\rho \to 0$ and $\theta = 1$. To determine whether this assumption is justified additional analysis is needed.

4 The Survey asks the following question to over 1,300 enterprises: 'What growth rate do you expect for the coming three years in Japan?'

5 The rate of return on capital can be considered the average product of capital. If a production function is the Cobb-Douglas type, then the rate of return on capital equals the marginal rate of capital. Kitamura and Fujiki (1996) showed that whichever type is used as a production function, there is little difference between each marginal product of capital.

6 Note that for the purpose of the calculation, the fixed capital of the public sector is added to non-residential fixed capital of the private sector since both contribute to the production of the business sector.

7 This seems to contradict theoretical knowledge that the movement of expected values should be smoother than that of actual values. This implies that the expected inflation estimated here includes a risk premium under future uncertainty that may greatly change during this period.

8 Recently, the expected inflation rate has stayed below zero, although monetary policy has already been fully eased and the short-term interest rate is now around 0%. In this case, perhaps people expect it to be very difficult for the Bank of Japan to conduct additional effective measures by decreasing the interest rate below the zero boundary for nominal interest rates in order to stimulate economic recovery and to increase inflation expectations. Therefore, this situation is somewhat different from the usual case.

9 The Bank of Japan has published a great deal of information for the public in its various announcements, in the minutes of the Monetary Policy Meetings, in

speeches by the Governor at press conferences, in various publications, and so on. The level of public information about monetary policy is comparable to that of other central banks. However, information about the bank's future prospects or its policy actions cannot always be accurately transmitted to the public because the Bank has never published the explicit forecast inflation rate and real GDP growth rate.

10 By contrast, Bernanke and Woodford (1997) assert that the central bank should not target the forecast for inflation as an intermediate variable because targeting the forecast for inflation might make actual inflation and output unstable through the existence of indeterminacy of rational expectations equilibria. Additionally, there would be no incentive for anyone to gather information, so every forecast inflation rate would become uninformative as perfect stabilisation of the inflation forecast was approached.

11 In New Zealand the trimmed-mean CPI has been used as one indicator of underlying inflation (see Roger, 1994).

12 The gap is calculated by the procedure of Watanabe (1997).

13 Regarding the possibility of explicitly incorporating the information inherent in asset price fluctuations, Shiratsuka (1999) discusses as follows. Asset prices can be explicitly incorporated into inflation measures by extending the price index into a dynamic framework so as to trace intertemporal changes in the cost of living. Although such a dynamic inflation measure is highly valued from the viewpoint of theoretical consistency, it is difficult to expect its role to be anything more than a supplementary indicator of inflation pressures. This is because asset price changes do not necessarily imply future price changes since there are many reasons for asset-price fluctuations apart from public expectations of future-price inflation; and secondly, the reliability of asset-price statistics is quite low, compared with existing price indexes.

Bibliography

Bernanke, B.S. and Mishkin, F.S. (1997), 'Inflation targeting: a new framework for monetary policy?' *Journal of Economic Perspectives*, Vol. 11, pp. 97–116.

Bernanke, B.S. and Woodford, M. (1997), 'Inflation forecasts and monetary policy', *Journal of Money, Credit and Banking*, Vol. 29(4), pp. 653–84.

Bryan, M.F. and Cecchetti, S.G. (1994), 'Measuring core inflation', in Mankiw, N.G. (ed.) *Monetary Policy,* University of Chicago Press, pp. 195–215.

Economic Planning Agency (1998), Nippon no shakai shihon (*Public capital stock in Japan*), Toyokeizai Inc. (in Japanese).

Higo, M. and Nakada, S. (1999) 'What determines the relation between the output gap and inflation? An international comparison of inflation expectations and staggered wage adjustment', *Monetary and Economic Studies,* 17(3), Institute for Monetary and Economic Studies, Bank of Japan.

Inoue, T. (1998), 'Impact of information technology and implications for monetary policy', *Monetary and Economic Studies* 16(2), Institute for Monetary and Economic Studies, Bank of Japan, pp. 29–60.

Kimura, T. and Ueda, K. (1997), 'Downward nominal wage rigidity in Japan: is price stability costly?' *Bank of Japan Research and Statistics Department Working Paper,* 97–1.

Kitamura, Y. and Fujiki, H. (1996), 'Keizaiseichoka no jisshitsukinri no sokutei (*Estimation for Real Interest Rate*)' (in Japanese), mimeo.

Kitamura, Y. and Fujiki, H. (1997), 'Supply side jouhou wo riyoushita shohini motozuku shihonshisankakaku moderu no suikei (Estimation for C-CAPM by the real interest rate derived from supply-side information)', *Kin'yu Kenkyu*, 16 (4), Institute for Monetary and Economic Studies, Bank of Japan, pp. 137–54 (in Japanese).

Mio, H. and Higo, M. (1999), 'Underlying inflation and the distribution of price change: evidence from the Japanese trimmed mean CPI', *Monetary and Economic Studies*, 17(1), Institute for Monetary and Economic Studies, Bank of Japan, pp. 103–32.

Roger, S. (1994), 'Alternative measure of underlying inflation', *Reserve Bank Bulletin*, 57(2), Reserve Bank of New Zealand, pp. 109–29.

Shiratsuka, S. (1997), 'Inflation measures for monetary policy: measuring the underlying inflation trend and its implication for monetary policy implementation', *Monetary and Economic Studies*, 15(2), Institute for Monetary and Economic Studies, Bank of Japan, pp. 1–26.

Shiratsuka, S. (1999), 'Asset price fluctuation and price indices', *IMES Discussion Paper Series*, 99-E-21, Institute for Monetary and Economic Studies, Bank of Japan.

Sterne, G. and Bayoumi, T. (1993), 'Temporary cycles or volatile trends? Economic fluctuations in 21 OECD countries', *Bank of England Working Paper*, No. 13.

Svensson, L.E.O. (1997), 'Inflation forecast targeting: implementing and monitoring inflation targets', *European Economic Review*, Vol. 41, pp. 1111–46.

Uemura, S. and Kimura, T. (1998), 'Japanese share prices, the role of asset prices in the formulation of monetary policy, *Conference Papers*, Vol. 5, Bank for International Settlements.

Watanabe, T. (1997), 'Output gap and inflation: the case of Japan', Monetary Policy and the Inflation Process, *Conference Papers*, Vol. 4, Bank for International Settlements.

Inflation and money goals
The recent experience of monetary policy in Mexico

Samuel Alfaro and Moisés J. Schwartz[1]

1 Introduction

On 1 April 1994 Congress granted full autonomy to the Banco de México, with the mandate of procuring price stability. Autonomy gives the Banco de México control over all its credit operations in the widest sense. Thus, the last years have witnessed substantial progress towards the abatement of inflation. Nevertheless, the Mexican experience has clearly shown that there are other factors beyond the direct influence of monetary policy that affect the behaviour of prices. Among these factors are capital flows, movements in the exchange rate, wage negotiations, changes in public or controlled prices, and shocks to aggregate demand and supply.

From 1988 to 1994, economic policy in Mexico was subordinated to the national agreement ('Pacto') among the government, business, and workers. The goal of the agreement was to bring down the level of inflation, by establishing the exchange rate as the nominal anchor of the economy. Under this programme, the Banco de México geared monetary policy to support the exchange-rate regime (a crawling peg that evolved into a target zone in November 1991). The policies implemented brought annual inflation down from 159.2% in December 1987 to 7.1% in December 1994 (see Chart 1). However, the sustainability of the stabilisation effort was ultimately undermined by the inflexibility of the exchange-rate regime in the midst of political uncertainty, banking credit expansion, overvaluation of the currency, and an increasing current-account deficit. These circumstances eventually led to an abrupt devaluation of the peso in December 1994, causing the most severe economic crisis in Mexico's modern history.

After the devaluation a flexible exchange-rate regime was adopted. In March 1995, the Banco de México announced its new monetary strategy, containing an annual inflation objective and quantitative monetary goals. Since then, intermediate money goals have lost significance, while the inflationary objective has gained increasing relevance. Nevertheless, given that inflation in Mexico is determined mainly by factors that are beyond the direct control of monetary policy, the inflationary process in Mexico is

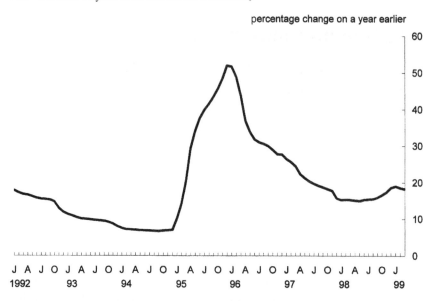

percentage change on a year earlier

Chart 1 Consumer price inflation

still uncertain and subject to substantial volatility. This has been the major obstacle to Mexico adopting a fully fledged inflation-target scheme.

This paper analyses the recent monetary policy strategy implemented by the Banco de México. Section 2 describes the main elements of the monetary programme and the mechanism by which monetary policy is now implemented. Section 3 provides evidence of the relevance of capital inflows to monetary policy implementation under the current floating exchange rate regime. Section 4 describes the main determinants of inflation in Mexico. Section 5 presents some concluding remarks.

2   The implementation of monetary policy in Mexico

Every year the Banco de México publishes the basic guidelines of its monetary programme in the document 'Report on Monetary Policy'. The monetary authorities have acknowledged that a prudent monetary policy is necessary but not sufficient for the fight against inflation. Thus, it is important that monetary policy is co-ordinated with other elements of economic policy, such as fiscal, wage, and public-prices policies.

The monetary programme defines a specific inflation objective for the year. Having defined such an objective, the Banco de México composes its monetary programme based on three governing principles. Table 1 lists each of these principles together with the instruments used to implement them.

Table 1 Principles and instruments of the monetary programme

First		Second	Third
First		**Second**	**Third**
Supply of primary money	= Demand for base money	Discretionary actions	Transparency and surveillance policy
	Accessories		
– Path for money base	– 'Longs'		– Published reports
– Net domestic credit	– 'Shorts'		– Press releases
– Net international assets			

2.1 First principle: As a general rule, the Banco de México will adjust, on a daily basis, the supply of primary money in a way such that supply matches the demand for base money

This basic operational rule provides assurance that the central bank will not create a monetary base surplus. It implies that the central bank will pursue a zero objective for the accumulated balance of commercial banks' accounts at the central bank, and that it will sterilise the monetary impact of variations in net international assets.

A strict application of this rule would entail that the Banco de México passively accommodates any change in the demand for base money. In doing so, it could on occasion satisfy a demand for money consistent with an inflation rate higher than anticipated in the monetary programme. To help detect and alleviate such a possibility, the Banco de México established two quantitative monetary indicators: an annual forecast of the daily monetary base and quarterly limits to domestic credit expansion.

In January of each year, then, the central bank publishes a forecast of the daily path of the monetary base that is consistent with the inflation objective for the year. These money forecasts can be interpreted as a link between the operational rule and the inflation objective. The path is published with certain caveats, using all the information available in January. The announced path does not constitute a formal policy objective a benchmark with which to compare outcomes but serves as its usefulness lies primarily in the information yielded by deviations of observed paths from it.

The Banco de México also examines other indicators that may yield information about future inflation, such as the exchange rate, measures of inflation expectations, and contractual wage negotiations. If, having examined all the evidence, the Banco de México judges that deviations from the forecast are due to additional inflationary pressures, it is likely to adopt a more restrictive policy stance. In this regard, the announced path is an important tool of the first element of the monetary programme (see Chart 2).

Another accessory of the first rule of the monetary programme is the establishment of quarterly limits to the central bank's domestic credit expansion. Such limits are intended to prevent inflationary pressures stemming from excessive growth in the supply of base money. If domestic

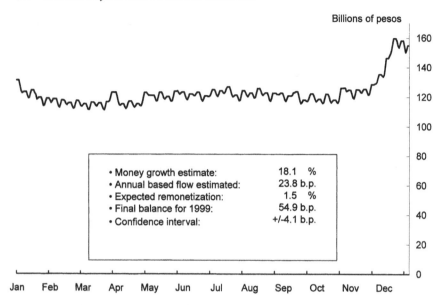

Chart 2 Anticipated path of the monetary base for 1999 (daily balance)

credit surpasses established limits, policy is likely to respond unless the excess is matched by a reduction of net international assets.

Although the monetary programme prevents the Banco de México from producing excess supply in the monetary base, it cannot guarantee the achievement of the desired abatement of inflation. Some inflationary pressures may arise from other sources, such as external shocks that lead to a depreciation of the exchange rate, and from greater-than-anticipated wage inflation. In such circumstances, higher interest rates may be insufficient to ensure that inflation meets the annual target.

2.2 Second principle: The Banco de México may adjust monetary policy, either tightening or relaxing it in the face of unanticipated events

The central bank specifies its operating target as the level of excess reserves in the banking system, indicated by the cumulative balances of banks' current accounts. The level of excess reserves is also the main signal regarding monetary policy direction.

The Banco de México may adjust its monetary policy stance from neutral to restrictive or relaxed, according to the prevailing circumstances. It may adopt a more restrictive policy by leaving the banking system 'short', that is, by operating with an objective of negative accumulated balances in commercial banks and exerting upward pressure on interest rates.

The Banco de México might adopt a 'short' not only to reduce inflation, but also to combat certain disorderly situations in the exchange or money markets. Conversely, the Banco de México may wish to ease monetary policy through the use of 'longs'. In that case, it operates in the open market with an objective of positive accumulated balances in the total current accounts that credit institutions hold with the central bank. Through the use of longs, the Banco de México signals the market that interest rates must be lowered.

2.3   Third principle: The Banco de México will pursue an active communication policy in order to keep the public informed about the use of monetary policy instruments

The Banco de México publishes reports on the implementation of monetary policy. The operative framework is based on the principle that both the interest and exchange rates are market-determined. By following this strategy, the central bank avoids the problem of selecting the combination of interest and exchange-rate movements required to reach equilibrium in the financial markets, particularly at times where markets are volatile. Interest and exchange rates represent the main indicators for monetary policy because of the information they provide regarding participants' perceptions about liquidity and risk.

3   Capital inflows and the floating exchange regime

Capital flows have played a significant role in the choice of policy framework. The 1995 crisis was partly the result of foreign residents withdrawing funds previously invested in Mexico. They reduced their holdings of government securities from \$27.8 to \$2.0 billion between December 1994 and March 1996. During 1995, the absence of foreign-capital inflows forced policy-makers to implement a radical stabilisation programme in order to eliminate the current-account deficit. In this regard, financial authorities view the 1995 crisis to have been partially induced by the lack of flexibility of both the exchange and interest rates.

More flexible exchange rates discouraged speculative foreign investment by increasing the risk of holding peso denominated financial assets. But although foreign investment in government securities has been substantially reduced the levels observed before the 1995 crisis (see Chart 3), in this section we demonstrate that capital flows still have a significant impact on the behaviour of financial markets and therefore on monetary policy.

Government securities have been the main financial instrument used by foreign investors wishing to take Mexican peso risk.[2] However, in order to hedge their exchange-rate risk exposure, market participants may buy forward-dollar contracts. Furthermore, foreign investors may use futures markets to invest in Mexico by selling forward-dollar contracts.

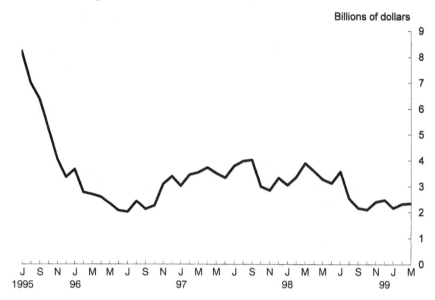

Chart 3 Government securities held by foreigners

Consequently, it is necessary to consider the net position maintained in government securities by deducting the amount of dollars acquired or sold by foreigners through forward and futures contracts from the dollar value of the stock of government debt instruments. Changes in this unhedged position indicate the willingness of foreigners to incur peso risk, so that as investors increase their net position in government securities, the supply of dollars in the exchange market also rises, causing the peso to appreciate. Foreign investment in financial instruments has, however, decreased during the last four years (see Chart 3).

Chart 4 depicts the evolution of the unhedged position in government securities held by foreigners and the nominal exchange rate. The chart shows that there has been a negative relationship between the net position and the nominal exchange rate. Furthermore, in spite of reduced capital flows, there remains a strong correlation (-0.85) between financial investment in Mexican peso risk and movements in the exchange rate.

Granger causality tests also show a statistically significant causality that runs from the unhedged position in government securities held by foreigners to the exchange rate. Table 2 summarises the results obtained from such causality tests, which are the following:

- We cannot reject the null hypothesis that the exchange rate (ERA) does not cause the foreigners' unhedged position in government securities (UPF).

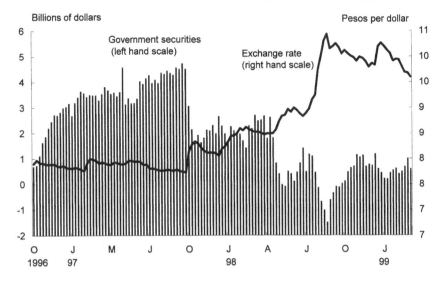

Chart 4 Unhedged position in Government Securities held by foreigners and exchange rate

Table 2 Granger causality test between exchange rate and foreigners' unhedged position

Null Hypothesis	*F-Statistic*	*Probability*
ERA does not cause UPF	0.94550	0.43970
UPF does not cause ERA	3.05183	0.01901

• We can reject the null hypothesis that the foreigners' unhedged position in government securities (UPF) does not cause the exchange rate (ERA).

Although the current regime has deterred capital flows as massive as those experienced from 1990 to 1994, our results suggest that such flows still have played an important role in the foreign-exchange market and hence have affected monetary policy. We therefore analyse further the channels through which foreign financial investment may distort monetary policy evaluation.

Since 1996 there has been a positive correlation between interest rates in the money market and the peso/dollar exchange rate (see Chart 5). From the evidence outlined in both Chart 4 and the Granger causality tests, we concluded that capital flows have recently played a significant role in determining the exchange rate, such that we should expect interest rates to be influenced by such flows. Chart 5 compares the weekly growth of the exchange rate and the weekly difference in the one-month inter-bank interest rate.

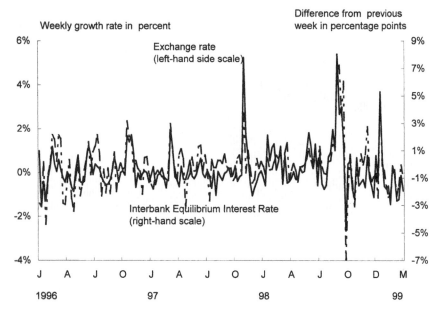

Chart 5 Exchange and interest rates

Chart 5 confirms the positive relationship between changes in the exchange rate and the interbank interest rate – the correlation coefficient between these variables is 0.74. The existence of a positive association between these variables, however, does not necessarily imply that capital flows affect interest rates via the exchange rate. In order to seek further evidence we performed Granger causality tests, summarised in Table 3. The results are:

- We cannot reject the null hypothesis that the interbank interest rate (IBR) does not cause the exchange rate (ERA).
- We can reject the null hypothesis that the exchange rate (ERA) does not cause the interbank interest rate (IBR).

Consequently, the evidence presented in this section points towards a significant influence of foreign financial investment on the exchange rate, which in turn has affected interest rates. Such results are consistent with the Banco de México's declared intention to modify monetary policy stance whenever financial-market behaviour is not perceived to be consistent with macroeconomic fundamentals. Consequently, if foreign-capital flows affect the foreign-exchange market in such a way that alters inflationary expectations, the central bank has to modify its monetary policy stance.

The Banco de México's actions between August and September 1998

Table 3 Granger causality test between exchange rate and interest rates

Null Hypothesis	*F-Statistic*	*Probability*
IBR does not cause ERA	0.2899	0.88421
ERA does not cause IBR	2.2355	0.06762

illustrate the influence of capital flows on monetary policy. The global crisis severely affected Mexican financial markets because of capital flight to the stable markets of Europe and the United States. In particular, after the devaluation of the Russian rouble, investors used Mexican financial markets to hedge their long positions maintained in other countries. The strategy followed by foreign investors is reflected in Chart 4, which shows that there were negative unhedged positions – short positions against Mexican pesos – from the middle of August to the end of September 1998. As a result, the peso depreciated 14.7% from the end of July to the end of September. Since the weakness of the peso was not consistent with macro-economic fundamentals and was also creating additional inflationary pressures, the Banco de México tightened monetary policy: the interbank interest rate was increased 17.0 percentage points from the end of July to reach 38.4% by the end of September. This reaction was just enough to restore order in the financial markets.

Capital flows may cause transitory distortions to the inflation process, mainly through their impact on the exchange rate. Capital flows have affected the mechanics of inflation mainly through aggregate supply affecting productive costs; the impact on aggregate demand has not been significant during the last four years. Before the 1994 crisis it was evident that foreign investment in financial assets had stimulated the expansion of banking credit to the private sector, and in this way influenced domestic demand and the inflationary process. However, the banking crisis led to a credit crunch on private debtors; and as already mentioned, capital flows in recent years have been much smaller than before the 1994 crisis. As a result the influence of foreign capital flows an aggregate demand has recently been negligible.

Since exchange-rate depreciation generates inflationary pressures, on most occasions on which the central bank has tightened monetary policy, the decision was prompted by adverse conditions in the foreign-exchange market. Monetary and exchange rate policy actions also have been required to cope with the volatility of market conditions induced by a reversal of foreign-capital flows. Among such actions implemented by the financial authorities is a mechanism that provides liquidity to the foreign-exchange market by auctioning dollars daily at a minimum price that is 2% above the previous day's level. On the other hand, the Banco de México has not ruled out the possibility of a discretionary intervention in the foreign-exchange market whenever the market is driven by speculative considerations. Nevertheless, financial authorities make no promise to provide liquidity to foreign investors whenever they want to sell their holdings of domestic financial assets. For this reason, there has been a significant reduction in the amount of foreign portfolio investment in comparison with the period of the predetermined exchange-rate regime.

Although the central bank has tightened its policy stance when the exchange rate has depreciated abruptly, it has also recognised the difficulty of fully offsetting the resulting inflationary pressures through monetary policy. In such situations the central bank has to decide whether to accommodate the consumer price increase induced by the exchange-rate movement, or to avoid such inflationary pressures through an even tighter monetary policy that could induce a recession. The Banco de México has generally selected the first alternative.

4   Determinants of inflation

As mentioned earlier in the paper, the inflationary process in Mexico is mainly determined by factors that are beyond the direct control of monetary policy. Among these factors are movements in the exchange rate, wage negotiations and controlled prices. This section presents the results of three papers – Gamboa (1997) and Pérez-López (1996 and 1998) – that analyse the impact of different variables on price behaviour and inflation. Gamboa (1997) focuses on the impact of government controlled prices on inflation and Pérez-López (1996 and 1998) on the behaviour of contractual wages, external inflation, and public prices. Additional empirical studies are presented to assess the influence on the inflation rate of the factors mentioned above.

There are basically three reasons why increments in public prices generate inflationary pressures.[3] First, when controlled prices are indexed to inflation, adjustments in these prices generate inflationary inertia. Second, increments in public prices change the relative price between non-indexed controlled and non-controlled prices, affecting the general level of prices in the long run. Finally, public prices can contain information about future inflation. Gamboa (1997) concludes that public prices – and specifically the variability of the referred adjustments – have a positive effect on inflation.

Pérez-López (1996) models as a weighted average of changes in external prices, measured as the change in the exchange rate multiplied by the external prices index, and the rate of growth of contractual wages (see Chart 6). The study concludes that contractual wages have a larger impact on inflation than external inflation, but the movements in the exchange rate are still an important factor in the determination of inflation. Pérez-López (1998) complements his previous study by introducing public prices; defined as the relative price between controlled and non-controlled prices. His results show that for the period 1985 to 1997, public prices and contractual wages had a major impact on inflation.

The results of these studies show that price behaviour in Mexico is

percentage change on a year earlier

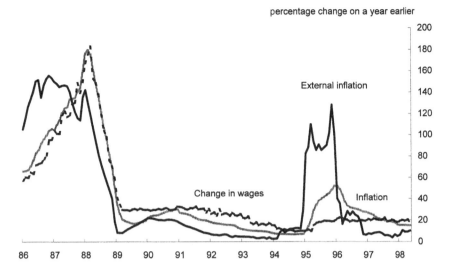

Chart 6 Domestic and external inflation and wage growth

largely explained by factors beyond the direct impact of monetary policy, including exchange-rate movements, contractual-wage negotiations, and adjustments in public prices. Thus, the abatement of inflation in Mexico requires not only a prudent implementation of monetary policy, but also substantial co-ordination between policies, government authorities, and the different sectors of society.

Since the structural reforms of 1990, the number and importance of the goods subject to price controls have been significantly reduced, but there are still some that carry a large weight in the price index. Table 4 shows the annual growth rates of the consumer price index and of specific goods and services subject to official control including tortilla's (TOR), public transportation in Mexico City (MET), gasoline (GAS), and the minimum wage (MIW). The table shows the contrast of the targeted inflation rate with the rate of increase of these controlled prices. This analysis (see Table 4) helps to explain the discrepancies between the observed and targeted inflation rates during 1996 and 1998.

Table 5 reports the results obtained from a regression analysis in which the monthly inflation rate (INF) depends on the evolution of controlled prices: tortillas (TOR), public transportation in Mexico City (MET), gasoline (GAS), the minimum wage (MIW), and the nominal exchange rate (ERA).

The results confirm the importance of exchange-rate movements on inflation. We found that the exchange rate affects the consumer price index not only contemporaneously, but also with one lag – as measured by the coefficients associated with the variables ERA and ERA(−1). Table 5

Table 4 Inflation and controlled prices (rate of growth)

Inflation Date	Targeted	Observed	MET	TOR	GAS	MIW
1996*	20.5%	27.7%	81.7%	25.1%	33.8%	23.4%
1997*	15.0%	15.7%	6.4%	22.4%	14.4%	17.6%
1998*	12.0%	12.2%	10.4%	33.2%	9.0%	15.2%

* Refers to information for the period September 1997 to December 1998, except the targeted level that is the annual inflation rate December 1997–98.

Table 5 Regression of variables affecting the inflation rate

Variable	Coefficient	Std. Error	t-Statistic
TOR	**0.018**	**0.0085**	**2.15**
MIW (1)	0.015	0.0084	1.80
MIW	0.043	0.0088	4.90
GAS	0.103	0.0091	11.34
MET	0.011	0.0031	3.63
INF (−1)	0.543	0.0252	21.59
INF (−5)	0.063	0.0197	3.22
ERA	0.034	0.0043	7.88
ERA (−1)	0.044	0.0044	10.09
R-squared	0.992	F-statistic	159.20
Durbin-Watson stat	1.619	Prob (F-statistic)	0.0000

also shows that large inertial effects characterise inflation in Mexico. In particular, the parameter associated with the monthly inflation rate lagged one period – INF(−1) – is highly significant. Such evidence suggests the importance of implementing a pre-emptive monetary policy, given that abrupt exchange-rate depreciation may affect inflation during a period of several months. Furthermore, among the factors considered in Table 5 that determine the evolution of the monthly inflation rate, the exchange rate is the only variable that can be influenced by the Banco de México.

The results shown in Table 5 strengthen the argument that controlled prices are important determinants of the inflation rate. We found that revisions of gasoline prices (GAS) have had a major impact on the growth rate of the consumer price index. The consumer price index also increases both on the date of the announcement of minimum-wage revisions (MIW + 1, which indicates the growth rate of the minimum wage for the coming month) and when the minimum wage actually changes.

5   Concluding remarks

The considerable abatement of Mexican inflation in recent years shows that the current monetary strategy has worked adequately. The announcement of both inflation and monetary objectives provides a clearer and more transparent framework for monetary policy implementation. The Banco de México's monetary framework includes the following features: (i) an annual objective for the rate of inflation; (ii) some commitments regarding the evolution of monetary aggregates; (iii) the resolve to act in a discretionary way to offset inflationary pressures; and (iv) transparency through the release of reports and press bulletins. In addition, the Banco de México has evolved from reliance on quantitative intermediate targets to a situation in which inflation objectives have gained relevance.

This monetary framework takes into account the fact that price stabilisation is policy's primary goal. Yet the Mexican experience has clearly shown that some factors affecting inflation are beyond the direct influence of monetary policy, especially capital flows, movements in the exchange rate, wages, and public prices. Given this, the inflationary process in Mexico is still subject to volatility. Nevertheless, monetary policy in Mexico is gradually evolving towards a fully fledged inflation-targeting scheme, as inflation objectives gain in relevance and monetary goals reduce in importance in the implementation of policy.

Notes

1 Samuel Alfaro is Manager of Central Banking Operations and Moisés J. Schwartz is Director of Economic Studies. The views expressed in this article are those of the authors and do not necessarily correspond to those of Banco de México. The authors wish to thank Sybel Galván, Laura Greenham and Miryam Saade for their help in the preparation of the article.
2 Foreign investment has also been assigned to the stock market. However, we do not consider such flows in the analysis because of the difficulty to separate the stock price effect in order to obtain the effective flows.
3 Gamboa (1997).

Bibliography

Aboumrad, G. (1996), 'Instrumentacion de la política monetaria con objetivo de estabilidad de precios: el caso de México', *Monetaria, CEMLA, 19.*

Alfaro, S. (1997), 'La demanda oportuna de billetes y monedas en México' in *La Política Monetaria en México, Suplemento, Gaceta de Economía,* ITAM, Año 3, Número 5.

Banco de México, *Informe Anual,* several issues, México D.F.

Banco de México, *Report on Monetary Policy,* several issues, México D.F.

Borio, C.E.V. (1997), 'Monetary policy operating procedures in industrial countries', in Bank of International Settlements, *Implementation and Tactics of Monetary Policy*, Conference Papers, Vol. 3, Basle.

Carstens, A. and Reynoso, A. (1997), 'Alcances de la politica monetaria: Marco Teórico y regularidades empiricas en la experiencia Mexicana', *Documento No. 9705, Serie Documentos de Investigación, Banco de México.*

Escrivá, J.L. and Fagan, G.P. (1996), 'The single monetary policy in stage three',

General Documentation on ESCB Monetary Policy Instruments and Procedures, September.

Freedman, C. (1994), 'The use of indicators and of the monetary conditions index in Canada', in Baliño, T.J.T. and Cottareli, C., *Frameworks for Monetary Stability*, IMF, Washington, D.C.

Gamboa, R. (1997), 'Efecto de los precios administrados sobre la inflacion', *Documento No. 9709, Serie Documentos de Investigación, Banco de México*.

Gil Diaz, F. (1997), 'La política monetaria y sus canales de transmisión', in *La Política Monetaria en México, Suplemento, Gaceta de Economía*, ITAM, Año 3, Número 5.

Goodhart, C.A.E. (1995), 'Money supply control: base or interest rates?', in Hoover K. and Sheffrin, S. (eds) *Monetarism and the Methodology of Economics*, Cheltenham, Glos: Edward Elgar.

Goodhart, C.A.E and Viñals, J. (1994), 'Strategy and tactics of monetary policy: examples for europe and antipodes', *Documento de Trabajo No. 9425, Banco de España*.

Greenham, L.E. (1997), *Mecanismos de Transmisión de Política Monetaria en México*, Tesis, Licenciatura en Economía, ITAM.

Juan Ramon, H. (1996), 'The daily conduct of monetary policy in Mexico'. *IMF Working Paper*.

Leiderman, L., Liviatan, N. and Thorne, A. (1995), 'Shifting nominal anchors: the experience of Mexico', *Economía Mexicana, Nueva Epoca*, Vol. IV, No. 2. México, Segundo Semestre.

Mateos, C. and Schwartz, M.J. (1997), 'Metas de inflación como instrumento de politica monetaria'. *Documento No. 9702, Serie Documentos de Investigación, Banco de México*.

Mateos, C. and Gaytan, A. (1998), 'Medidas alternativas de inflacion'. *Documento No. 9802, Serie Documentos de Investigación, Banco de México*.

Pérez-López, A. (1996), 'Un estudio econometrico sobre la inflación en México'. *Documento No. 9604, Serie Documentos de Investigación, Banco de México*.

Pérez-López, A. (1998), 'La inflación en México'. Internal Document, *Banco de México*.

Svensson, L. (1994), 'Monetary policy with flexible exchange rates and forward interest rates indicators', *Working Paper No. 4633, NBER*, January.

Swank, J. and Van Velden, L. (1997), 'Instruments, procedures and strategies of monetary policy: an assessment of possible relationships for 21 OECD countries', in Bank of International Settlements, *Implementation and tactics of Monetary Policy*, Conference Papers Vol. 3. Basle.

Thorne, A. (1997), 'Assessing the effectiveness of monetary policy', in *Mexico's Monetary Policy*, JP Morgan, Economics Research Note, Mexico City.

Inflation targets and stabilisation in Chile

Oscar Landerretche, Felipe Morandé and Klaus Schmidt-Hebbel

1 Introduction

Among countries that have adopted inflation targets, Chile's stabilisation experience is quite unique for three reasons. First, the Chilean economy appears to be one of the most indexed in the world: backward indexation mechanisms are widespread in many non-traded goods, labour, and financial markets. Even policy instruments are indexed, including income taxes and the monetary policy interest rate.[1] Second, and to a large extent in response to indexation, Chile's programme of price stabilisation has been the world's most gradualist. Inflation has been brought down step by step – almost monotonically – from 30% in 1990 to close to 3.0% in 1999. Third, Chile was among the first countries to adopt a monetary framework based on an explicit publicly announced annual inflation target. The first target was announced in September 1990 for the subsequent calendar year 1991. The (by then only recently independent) Central Bank of Chile (CBC) adopted the target at a time when annual inflation was around 25%, a figure that had been approximately stationary during the 1980s. Chile was among the very few countries (Israel being another case) to adopt inflation targeting when it had an inflation rate that exceeded its long-term inflation goal by 20 or more percentage points. This stands in stark contrast to most other (industrialised) countries that adopted targets when they were close to low, stationary inflation levels.

A major reason for Chile's early adoption of an inflation target was the notion that providing the public with an explicit inflation objective – and committing to its attainment by adopting a supportive monetary policy – would reduce the extent of indexation mechanisms, hence reducing the cost of stabilisation. This paper analyses the features, role, and macroeconomic consequences of inflation targeting in Chile, taking into account the specific conduct of monetary policy in an open economy characterised by strong indexation.

Section 2 describes Chile's experience with inflation targeting, comparing it to that of other countries. Section 3 reviews the conduct of monetary policy and monetary transmission mechanisms. The stabilisation experience of the 1990s is discussed in Section 4. A simple structural model for a small open economy with inflation inertia stemming from indexation is developed next (Section 5), to illustrate the dynamic effects of an inflation target on the main macroeconomic variables. Inflation forecasts from VAR estimates for inflation, the inflation target, and related macro variables in Chile are used in Section 6 to analyse the role of inflation targeting in breaking inflation expectations. The final section provides a brief conclusion.

2   Inflation targeting: International comparison of Chile's experience

A growing number of countries have adopted explicit inflation targeting as their monetary framework during the 1990s (see Table 1). New Zealand (1988), Canada (1991), the United Kingdom (1992), Sweden (1993), and Australia (1993) were the first industrial countries to adopt inflation targets. Among developing countries, Colombia (1991) and Israel (1991) were early inflation targeters.[2] The Central Bank of Chile (CBC) was one of the first central banks in the world (in September 1990) to adopt an explicit and publicly announced annual inflation target (see Table 1). After obtaining its independence in 1990, the CBC had to face a substantial inflation shock caused by expansionary policies adopted in 1989 and the effects of the temporary oil price shock associated with the 1990 Gulf War. In this context, the Bank simultaneously tightened monetary policy and decided to adopt an inflation target as the nominal anchor for the economy and the conduct of its monetary policy.

Inflation targeting along the transition path toward low inflation is markedly different from when inflation starts close to its stationary level. Table 1 distinguishes two groups of countries that use inflation targets. The top part of the table focuses on Chile and Israel, two countries whose initial targets were around 15% above the inflation rates that they eventually attained. Their experience contrasts starkly with that of the five industrial countries included in the bottom part of the table. These countries were much closer to low, stationary inflation rates at the time of adopting inflation targeting. Specific design and implementation features of inflation targeting also differ among converging-inflation and stationary-inflation targeters, as will be discussed next.

Target inflation measure   The inflation target can be defined by the headline CPI or by a measure of underlying or core inflation. The headline CPI is a more comprehensive measure of the cost-of-living index. It is also more widely understood, thus increasing its communicational effectiveness. In countries with significant price and wage indexation, such as Chile and Israel, the (lagged) headline CPI is used as the relevant index. However, headline CPI inflation is much more volatile than any measure

Table 1 International experience with inflation targets

	1. Adoption date, initial target, current target	2. Long term target. Years of convergence from adoption to steady state	3. Index used for targeting	4. Target horizon	5. Exemptions or Escape Clauses
COUNTRIES CONVERGING TO STEADY-STATE INFLATION RATES					
Chile	Started Sept. 1990; initial range 15%–20%. Current target ± 4.3%.	2%–4% for 2001 onwards. 11 years.	Consumer price index	Annual, Dec. to Dec. Until 2000 Unlimited for 2001 onwards	None
Israel	Started 1991; initial target 14%–15%. Current target 4%.	3%–4% (2000–01). 9 years +.	Consumer price index	2000–01	None
COUNTRIES AT STEADY-STATE INFLATION RATES					
New Zealand	Started 1988; initial range 0%–2%. Current range: 0–3%.	0%–3%. 1.5 years.	Consumer price index, excluding various items	Governor's term of office	When target missed, RBNZ presents a *Policy Statement*, announcing corrective measures
Canada	Started Feb. 1991; initial range 2%–4%. Current range 1%–3%.	1%–3%. 1 year.	Consumer price index, excluding various items	1998 to 2001	Target range not absolutely rigid, but deviations expected small and temporary
United Kingdom	Started Oct. 1992; initial range 1%–4%. Current target 2.5%	2.5% ± 1%. 1.5 years.	Retail price index, excluding mortgage interest payments (RPIX)	Parliamentary period	BoE required to write open letter to Chancellor when deviating from target range
Sweden	Started Jan. 1993; initial and current target 2%	2% ± 1%. 1 year.	Consumer price index	Unlimited	Target range not absolutely rigid, but small and temporary deviations expected
Australia	Started Sep. 1994; initial and current range 2%–3%.	2%–3%. 0 year.	Consumer price index (before 1996 excluded various items)	Unlimited	Target must be maintained on average in the medium term; small temporary deviations allowed

of core inflation, and may therefore provide less information content for the conduct of monetary policy. In converging-inflation countries with high indexation like Chile and Israel, the above-mentioned benefits of using headline CPI inflation dominate the costs.

Long-term target level   Theory does not provide a precise answer to the question about the optimal rate of inflation, although it provides a list of potential costs and benefits of inflation. On the cost side – the 'sand in the wheels' argument – inflation raises relative price variability, overall uncertainty, financial and tax distortions, and transaction costs; all this reduces growth and welfare. On the benefit side – the 'grease in the wheels' argument – inflation may contribute to more flexible relative price adjustments when price rigidities are widespread.[3] In addition, it is well established that official CPI inflation measures suffer from positive measurement bias (in comparison to a true welfare-based cost-of-living index) due to changes in product quality, product substitution, and other problems. Recent studies for industrial countries suggest that annual inflation is overestimated by around 1.1%.[4] In practice, the weights given to the aforementioned costs, benefits, and measurement biases of inflation are imprecise. However, most OECD countries – with or without inflation targets – have adopted stationary or long-term CPI inflation targets of 1% to 3% per year, typically slightly higher than their measurement of inflation bias. Chile has recently adopted a stationary annual inflation target range of 2% to 4% (centred on 3%) for 2001 onwards.

Target band-width   The advantages of a target range include the fact that narrow (point) target is extremely unlikely to be hit, and the feasibility of accommodating small short-term shocks within a target range. The costs of a target range include the possibility of sending a less clear signal to the public and the likely perception that policy will in practice be directed at achieving an outcome in the upper part of the range. They also include the likelihood of stronger pressures from the government and the private sector to take larger inflation risks and to accommodate positive inflation shocks. In Chile, target ranges were used both at the beginning and at the end of inflation convergence. In between, at moderately low but not set stationary inflation levels, point targets were adopted to reduce the above-mentioned pressures. However, the recent declines in inflation to the 2% to 4% range and the lengthening of the target horizon from 2001 onwards together imply that the relative volatility of output will decline at the cost of larger price volatility.

Target horizons   Longer or unlimited target horizons are used in countries at steady-state inflation rates. When converging to low inflation, short (annual) horizons help to define a specific path of declining inflation. However, short target horizons may force central banks to overreact to price shocks in order to meet their targets at the cost of causing excessive output volatility, contributing also to more variability of interest and exchange rates. The adoption of annual horizons in Chile during the period 1991–99 may have contributed to greater volatility of the latter variables.

Escape clauses or exemptions　It is unusual to modify a numerical inflation target during the time horizon for which it has been defined. However, most industrial-country targeters at stationary inflation have an escape clause in the sense that deviations are allowed as long as they are small and temporary. These exemptions are institutionalised and monitored strictly in several countries (New Zealand, Sweden, the United Kingdom) where public statements or letters have to be issued by the central bank, providing an explanation of the target misses and spelling out corrective measures aimed at securing a return to the target point or range. Fewer converging economies have established exemptions, probably to avoid abuse of escape clauses and derived weakening of the targeting framework.

Convergence　Industrial-country inflation targeters were generally close to stationary inflation when adopting targeting. Those that were nevertheless somewhat above their long-run target levels converged quickly to the latter levels – it took them at most one to two years (New Zealand and the United Kingdom). In converging economies, however, inflation targeting was actively used as a device to bring inflation down gradually, from more than 20% per year to long-term levels in the 2% to 4% range. Convergence has taken 11 years in Chile and more than 9 years in Israel. Their convergence speed and trajectory to the target have reflected a combination of: (i) initial macroeconomic conditions; (ii) the scope of formal indexation mechanisms and inflation inertia; (iii) credibility of the central bank; (iv) the weight of additional goals (such as deviations of employment and the real exchange rate or current account from long-term equilibrium levels) in the policy-makers' objective function; and (v) the existence of political support for the proposed disinflation path regarding both the speed (reflecting the degree of tolerance to the sacrifice ratio) and the final inflation goal (reflecting the view on the balance of long-term inflation costs and benefits).

We have described the differences in the design and implementation of inflation targeting under disinflation and stationary inflation. Now we briefly review the advantages and rationale of inflation targeting generally to assess its merits as a disinflation device, rather than as a device to hold economies at stationary inflation.

Inflation targeting is superior in various dimensions to alternative frameworks of monetary policy (see Bernanke *et al.*, 1999). An explicit inflation target provides a commitment device that strengthens the credibility of monetary policy. It is also an instrument for communicating the objective of monetary policy: an inflation target helps the public to learn about the central bank's policy reaction function. Regarding central bank independence, an inflation target can be combined with either goal independence (i.e. the central bank specifies its own objective) or only instrument independence (i.e. the central bank has the discretion to adjust monetary policy instruments in pursuit of an objective set by the government). Finally, an inflation target provides a clear benchmark against which the central bank can be held accountable.

When inflation is declining from moderate to low rates, the design features of inflation targets may emphasise the communicational properties of inflation-target design. This has been reflected in the use of the headline CPI. Inflation targets have to be announced for specific time horizons (typically calendar years) because the central bank has to commit to a specific disinflation path and speed. Point (rather than range) targets during disinflation reinforces central bank instrument independence by eliminating the risk of political pressure to bias monetary policy toward the ceiling of any target range. For the same reason, lack of goal independence may reduce the speed of convergence to low inflation. Finally, exemption clauses tend to be absent because they may open the door to larger deviations from target levels.

In sum, the focus of inflation targeting during disinflation is on the attainment of short-term (annual) inflation targets on a preferably monotonic path to low inflation. Success in attaining declining inflation targets reinforces credibility, which in turn makes it easier to achieve subsequent inflation targets. Hence the inflation-targeting framework potentially is a very effective means of initiating a virtuous circle between monetary policy and its ultimate goal. As Chile's and Israel's experience suggest, this device can be extremely successful in breaking with a long past of moderate or high inflation – even in countries where backward-looking indexation is widespread.

3   Conduct of monetary policy in Chile and monetary transmission mechanisms[5]

As discussed above, Chile adopted a monetary framework anchored on an inflation target in 1990. As part of its monetary programming, the Central Bank of Chile (CBC) monitors and projects the main monetary aggregates but does not use them as intermediate targets. Regarding the exchange rate, the CBC adopted a floating exchange rate system in September 1999, suspending the preceding exchange-rate band. Hence, the exchange rate no longer plays any role as intermediate target but is still monitored and projected regularly.

Since the mid-1980s the main instrument or operational objective of monetary policy has been the *real* interest rate. The widespread use of explicit real interest rates in Chilean financial markets has been a market response to historically high inflation and reflects the scope of indexation in Chile. From 1985 through 1995, the CBC used the real rate on indexed CBC paper of 90-day maturity (PRBC-90s or 'Pagarés Reajustables del BCCh a 90 días'). The real rate is applied to the principal that is indexed on a daily basis to a unit of account (the UF or 'Unidad de Fomento'). The latter is indexed daily to the CPI with an average lag of 20 days. Since May 1995, the policy rate is the real (UF-indexed) daily rate paid on overnight interbank loans (the real interbank rate).

The CBC announces its policy rate publicly and guides the market interbank rate toward the policy objective by conducting open-market operations. Since May 1995, with the exception of four months in 1998, the average difference between the policy rate and the actual interbank rate has been only five basis points. Open-market operations are performed by issuing CBC paper and by conducting repos and anti-repos. A monthly programme of CBC paper issues is announced in advance in order to provide markets with information on the stance of monetary policy. Complementary repo and anti-repo operations are conducted during the month in order to satisfy the demand for liquidity that is consistent with the monetary policy interest rate.

Furthermore, two standard facilities are provided by the CBC to financial institutions at their discretion: the line of liquidity credit and the liquidity deposit. The former facility provides CBC credit to individual institutions (subject to quantitative credit ceilings) at marginal interest rates that rise with the amount of the required credit to three successively higher levels. The liquidity deposit is an open window provided to financial institutions to deposit their excess liquidity at a floor interest rate. Chart 1 depicts the evolution of market and policy interest rates in Chile since 1995.

Chile's exchange-rate policy was based on a crawling exchange-rate band from 1984 through September 1999. The main objectives of the band were to maintain international competitiveness and reduce excessive exchange-rate volatility. However, since the start of the band many of its features – including its width, rate of crawl, reference currency basket, degree of symmetry, and central parity level – modified in response to changing policy objectives and market conditions. Intra-marginal foreign-exchange interventions by the Bank were frequent and, at times, intense. Conflicts between the inflation target and the exchange rate band were usually solved in favour of the former during the period September 1990 to September 1999. Chart 2 depicts the evolution of the exchange-rate band and the market real exchange, both in real terms.

Although most of the time the market interbank real interest rate stays close to the monetary policy rate, under exceptional conditions Bank policy has allowed for a temporary wedge between market and policy rates. These conditions have materialised in circumstances when pressures

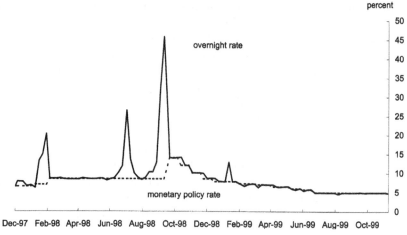

Chart 1 Monetary policy rate and overnight interbank rate (indexed rates)

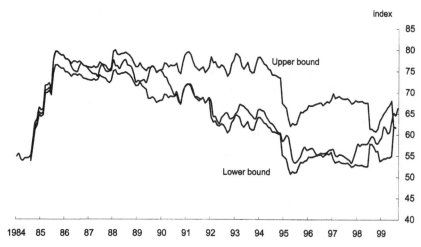

Chart 2 Real exchange rate band and market real exchange rate index

on the domestic currency were deemed to be excessive and temporary. Under such conditions, CBC policy has combined non-sterilised foreign-exchange interventions with a contractionary monetary policy. Such events materialised in 1998, reflecting the turmoil in international financial markets and the widespread flight of capital from all emerging economies. Chile's peso defence gave rise to high market interbank rates observed in the period of December 1997 to January 1998 and during June to September 1998. Both were temporary events after which market rates converged with policy rates, providing support for a gradual exchange-rate depreciation to take place.

The Bank's monetary policy function includes a number of key variables that are closely watched and projected. They include the gap between core inflation and the inflation-target level (projected over the relevant policy horizon), the aggregate spending-income gap (or the current account deficit), the actual to potential output gap, unemployment, monetary growth, wage growth, the exchange rate, the fiscal policy stance, and the market term structure, among other variables.

How does monetary transmission operate in Chile? As in other open economies, the main channels of transmission of a change in the policy rate include market interest rates and the term structure, monetary and credit aggregates, and the exchange rate (see Chart 3). Other relevant transmission mechanisms (not included in the chart) include asset prices and market expectations about the future stance of monetary policy and inflation. All the latter variables act upon (and are also affected by) other macroeconomic aggregates and key prices of goods, labour, and assets. Indexation is a structural feature of the Chilean economy that contributes to price inertia and slows down relative-price adjustment, leading to a quick transmission of exchange-rate and wage shocks to aggregate inflation. Information about the gap between core inflation and the inflation target, as well as about the other variables that were mentioned above, is used by the CBC in reviewing its monetary policy stance.

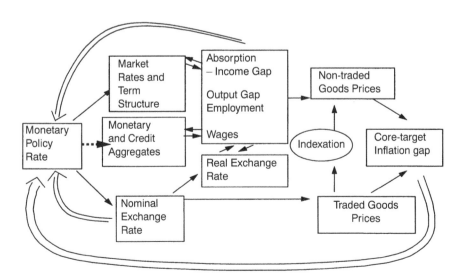

Chart 3 Channels of monetary transmission in Chile

4   Stabilisation and macroeconomic performance

After a decade of moderate but stubborn inflation in 1990, the recently independent CBC faced various choices in its attempts to bring down inflation. Chile's inflation history records two major stabilisation programmes based on a nominal exchange rate anchor: 1959 to 62 and 1979 to 82. Both programmes failed badly – thus reducing the possibility of using the exchange-rate anchor for a third time in order to bring inflation down on a sustained basis. On the other hand, the use of monetary aggregates as an intermediate target would have been difficult in a country with developing financial markets and volatile demands for monetary aggregates. The remaining choice for a monetary framework was inflation targeting.

This new approach has been successful and lasting. Annual inflation has declined from above 25% in 1990 to about 3% in 1999, the lowest level of inflation recorded since the 1930s. An inflation target point of 3.5% has been announced for 2000 (the last year with an annual target) and a target range of 2% to 4% has been announced for an undefined horizon starting in 2001 (see Chart 4).

At the heart of this achievement have been several elements, the most significant relating to the policies implemented by the CBC. Close compliance with annual inflation targets was key in influencing inflation expectations and raising CBC's credibility regarding its commitment to achieving price stability. Several other factors played important supporting roles. Fiscal policy recorded surpluses year after year from the mid-1980s through 1998. On the external side, growing capital inflows from 1989 through 1997 contributed to a real exchange rate appreciation that helped in reducing inflation.

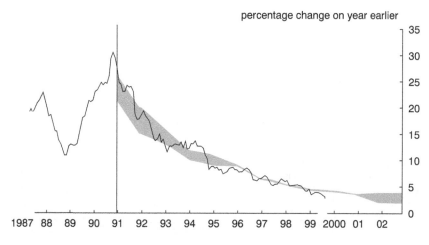

Chart 4 Inflation targets and actual inflation

The ultimate test of the success of disinflation based on inflation target-ing came in 1997 with the Asian crisis. Its real and financial aftershocks in 1998 required a significant real exchange rate depreciation that was gradu-ally accommodated by the CBC. As described above, CBC initially defended the peso against strong speculative pressures through a combina-tion of foreign-exchange interventions and a restrictive monetary policy. This temporary policy mix avoided an overshooting of the nominal exchange rate, allowing for a nominal and real depreciation that was gradual and monotonic.

The large deterioration in the country's terms of trade and lower capital inflows in 1998–99, combined with a restrictive monetary policy in 1999, contributed to a downward correction of aggregate demand and a tempo-rary recession in 1998–99. The reduction in excess spending over income was reflected in a necessary correction of Chile's current account position. In fact, current account deficits had shown a rising trend since the early 1990s, from about 2% of GDP in 1990–92 to a peak of 8% of GDP attained during the first quarter of 1998. The required correction is reflected by a current-account deficit projected at less than 2% of GDP in 1999 (Chart 5). The counterpart to this quantitative correction has been the change in the relevant relative price. After displaying a trend apprecia-tion during 1989–97, the real exchange rate has depreciated by 24% between September 1997 and September 1999 (Chart 2).

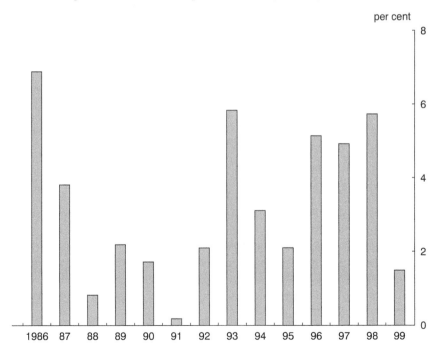

Chart 5 Current account deficit to GDP ratio

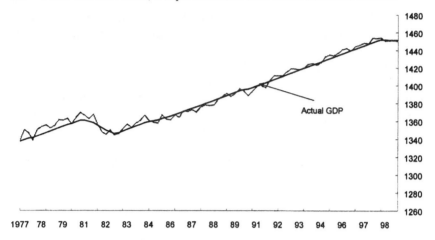

Chart 6 Actual GDP and trend GDP (Chile, 1977–99, in logs)

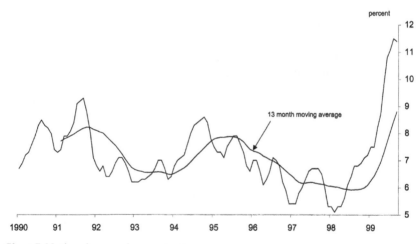

Chart 7 National unemployment rate

After a period of high and sustained real GDP growth at an average of 8.1% during 1989–97, growth declined to 3.4% in 1998 and to a slightly negative figure projected for 1999 (Chart 6). With negative growth recorded between late 1998 and mid-1999, the unemployment rate rose to a peak of 11% in mid-1999 (Chart 7). A recovery from the recent recession is projected to take place in 2000, reflected in positive growth and declining unemployment rates.

The massive adverse shock that hit the Chilean economy during 1997–99, necessitated a major correction in domestic absorption and the external positions. With little contribution from fiscal policy, this correction was sustained by a restrictive monetary policy stance during 1998. The subsequent success in correcting the external imbalance and meeting the inflation target meant that monetary policy could be relaxed in late 1998, and it has continued to be expansionary during 1999. We conclude that the Chilean economy is successfully emerging from the Asian storm and its after-effects. Inflation targeting is passing the test as an effective monetary framework for allowing inflation convergence to low and sustainable inflation in Chile.

5 Inflation targets and stabilisation in an indexed open economy: a model

In this section we develop a simple structural model for inflation in an open economy characterised by both forward-looking monetary equilibrium and backward-looking price rigidities caused by widespread indexation practices in various markets. This model is meant to characterise the process of gradual disinflation under an inflation-target rule in Chile since the early 1990s.

Aggregate inflation (Π) is a weighted average of traded-goods inflation (Π_T) and non-traded-goods inflation (Π_N):

$$\Pi_t = \alpha\Pi_{Tt} + (1 - \alpha)\Pi_{Nt} \tag{1}$$

where sub-index t denotes time period.

Consistent with the weak version of the purchasing-power parity condition, traded-goods inflation is determined by the rate of nominal exchange-rate devaluation (X) and the rate of foreign inflation (Πf):

$$\Pi_{Tt} = X_t + \Pi f_t \tag{2}$$

Nominal devaluation is defined as the sum of the domestic to foreign inflation difference and the rate of real exchange-rate depreciation (approximated by the difference of the log of the real exchange rate, e):

$$X_t = \Pi_t - \Pi f_t + (e_t - e_{t-1}) \tag{3}$$

Real (and hence nominal) exchange-rate depreciation follows a process that is determined in part by a risk-adjusted interest-rate arbitrage condition and in part by the short-term influence of the crawling-peg rule that the central bank applied to determine the central parity of its nominal exchange rate band (abolished in September 1999). The corresponding first-order difference equation for the log of the real exchange rate is:

$$e_{t+1} - e_t = \kappa[r_t - rf_t - \rho(f_t)] + (1 - \kappa)[(\Pi_t - \Pi f_t + ad_{t+1}) + (\Pi f_{t+1} - \Pi_{t+1})] \tag{4}$$

where r (*rf*) is the domestic (foreign) real interest rate and ρ is a risk premium on domestic financial assets factor that depends negatively on the stock of the economy's foreign assets (*f*).

The central parity of the nominal exchange-rate band follows a crawling peg rule such that the rate of the nominal depreciation rule is given by the sum of the one-period lagged domestic to foreign inflation difference and an adjustment factor (*ad*) that reflects an intended real depreciation. In the long term, the latter tends to be equal to the negative of the traded to non-traded productivity growth differential relative to the rest of the world (the Harrod-Balassa-Samuelson effect). This effect is also equal to the real exchange-rate depreciation in the long term, when current and lagged inflation levels are equal to each other. In the short term, however, the real exchange-rate depreciation is influenced by the nominal depreciation rule, implying that lagged domestic inflation will have a temporary effect on the real exchange-rate path.

Non-traded goods inflation reflects the influence of three variables: past aggregate inflation (because of widespread indexation practices in non-traded goods markets), contemporaneous nominal wage growth (Ω) adjusted for non-traded labour productivity growth, and a forward-looking long-term inflation expectations term as of period $t - 1$ (Π^e). The latter expectations term is different from actual inflation expectations (more on this below). Therefore:

$$\Pi_{Nt} = \beta_1\Pi_{t-1} + \beta_2(\Omega_t - \lambda_{Nt}) + (1 - \beta_1 - \beta_2)\Pi^e_{t-1,t} \tag{5}$$

Nominal wage growth reflects the influence of three variables: real growth of aggregate labour productivity (λ, a weighted average of productivity growth in the traded and non-traded sectors), indexation to current and past inflation, and labour market pressures embodied by the deviation of unemployment (*u*) from its natural or full-employment level (*u**). Hence wage growth follows a standard Phillips curve modified to take account of indexation practices:

$$\Omega_t = \lambda_t + \omega\Pi_t + (1 - \omega)\Pi_{t-1} + \sigma(u^* - u_t) \tag{6}$$

Temporary unemployment reflects the influence of the temporary deviation of the domestic real interest, *r*, from its parity level (*rp*). To simplify, the market interest rate is assumed to be equal to the Central Bank policy rate. Therefore unemployment (and hence wage growth) only reflects the stance of monetary policy:

$$u^* - u_t = v(rp_t - r_t) \tag{7}$$

The interest parity level is defined as the foreign real interest rate augmented by the rate of expected real exchange-rate depreciation and the country risk premium factor.

Substituting equations (2) to (3) and (5) to (7) into equation (1) yields the following semi-reduced form for inflation in period t, written in general form as function Π:

$$\Pi_t = \Pi(\Pi_{t-1}, \Pi f_t, e_t - e_{t-1}, ad_t, \lambda_t - \lambda_{Nt}, rp_t, \Pi^e_{t-1,t}) \tag{8}$$

It can be shown that in a steady state, when current and lagged inflation coincide, the combined influence of foreign inflation, real exchange rate depreciation, and the real exchange-rate appreciation factor on inflation is zero. Hence in a steady state, actual (and expected) inflation (Π^*) has to be equal to forward-looking long-term inflation expectations:

$$\Pi^* = \Pi^e_{t-1,t} \tag{9}$$

Now let's focus on the process of formation of long-term inflation expectations that play an important role in non-traded price inflation. In fact, these expectations provide the forward-looking anchor to the process of short-term actual and expected inflation levels. Long-term inflation expectations will be derived as a rational forecast of domestic inflation consistent with monetary equilibrium under rational expectations of backward-looking inflation indexation. A standard form of money demand with constant semi-elasticity of interest and unit income elasticity is assumed:

$$m_t - p_t = -\epsilon[E_t P_{t+1} - p_t + r_t] + y_t \tag{10}$$

where m is nominal money, p is the price level that would prevail in the absence of indexation, y is income, and E is the expectations operator conditional on all contemporaneous information.

By inverting the latter equation we obtain the following stochastic first-difference equation for the price level:

$$p_t = \frac{1}{1+\epsilon}[m_t + \epsilon r_t - y_t] + \frac{\epsilon}{1+\epsilon} E_t p_{t+1}. \tag{11}$$

By forward substitution we obtain:

$$p_t = \frac{1}{1+\epsilon} \sum_{s=t}^{\infty} \left(\frac{\epsilon}{1+\epsilon}\right)^{s-t} E_t[m_s + \epsilon r_s - y_s] + \lim_{T\to\infty} \left(\frac{\epsilon}{1+\epsilon}\right)^T P_{t+T} \tag{12}$$

where the latter limit term is zero, by imposing the condition that rules out speculative bubbles.

Shifting equation (12) one period forward, taking expectations and subtracting equation (12) from the latter, yields long-term rational inflation expectations as a function of the present value of current and future interest monetary growth, real income growth, and real interest rate changes:

$$\Pi^e_{t,t+1} \equiv E_t P_{t+1} - p_t = \tag{13}$$

$$\frac{1}{1+\epsilon} \sum_{s=t}^{\infty} \left(\frac{\epsilon}{1+\epsilon}\right)^{s-t} \{E_t[m_{s+1} - m_s] + \epsilon E_t[r_{s+1} - r_s] - E_t[y_{s+1} - y_s]\}$$

In order to obtain a useful expression for long-term expectations in terms of currently observable variables, we impose the following assumptions about the behaviour of the right-hand variables in equation (13). Note that we specify independent processes for both monetary growth and real interest rates – however, one of them is redundant. In fact, under Chile's real interest rate policy, money supply is the adjusting variable.

Money growth is assumed to follow a weighted average of an AR(1) process of itself and the pre-committed inflation target (added to real income growth):

$$m_{s+1} - m_s = \delta\gamma(m_s - m_{s-1}) + (1 - \delta)[\Pi\tau_{s+1} + (y_{s+1} - y_s)] + \eta_{1,s+1} \tag{14}$$

The AR(1) part of the process has a first-order coefficient of $\chi = \delta\gamma$. If only the inflation target governs monetary policy, δ is equal to zero.

The policy interest rate is defined consistently with the monetary-growth process above. The deviation between the interest rate and its parity level is a positive function of the difference between steady-state $((m - p)^*)$ and actual money holdings:

$$r_s = rp_s + \theta((m_s - p_s)^* - (m_s - p_s)) + \eta_{4,s+1} \tag{15}$$

The central bank determines the inflation target according to the following AR(1) process:

$$\Pi\tau_{s+1} = \psi\Pi\tau_s + \eta_{2,s+1} \tag{16}$$

and income growth also follows an AR(1) process:

$$y_{s+1} - y_s = \mu(y_s - y_{s-1}) + \eta_{3,s+1} \tag{17}$$

Substituting equations (14) to (17) into equation (13) yields the following semi-reduced form for long-term expectations in period t, written in general form as:

$$\Pi^e_{t,t+1} = g(\Pi\tau_{t+1}, rp_t - r_t, m_t - m_{t-1}, y_t - y_{t-1}) \tag{18}$$

As money is endogenous to the setting of the interest rate, it can be substituted as a function of the interest rate (from equations 14 and 15) to obtain a more compact version of the preceding equation:

$$\Pi_{t,t+1}^e = h(\Pi\tau_{t+1}, rp_t - r_t, y_t - y_{t-1}) \tag{18'}$$

The final reduced-form equation for inflation is obtained by substituting forward-looking long-term inflation expectations from equation (18) (or (18')) into equation (8):

$$\Pi_t = f(\Pi_{t-1}, \Pi f_t, e_t - e_{t-1}, ad_t, \lambda_t - \lambda_{Nt}, rp_t - r_t, \Pi\tau_t, rp_{t-1} - r_{t-1}, m_{t-1} - m_{t-2}, y_{t-1} - y_{t-2}) \tag{19}$$

Note that short-term or actual inflation expectations are consistent with the latter expression for inflation. Short-term monetary equilibrium is obtained by substituting the expected value of equation (19) into a monetary equilibrium condition analogous to equation (10).

Finally, consider a standard first-order difference equation for foreign-asset accumulation that reflects the open economy's balance-of-payments equilibrium:

$$f_{t+1} - f_t = nx(e_t, f_t, r_r) + r_t^* f_t \tag{20}$$
$$(+)(-)(-)$$

where f is net foreign assets at the beginning of each period, nx is net exports (a function of the real exchange rate, the domestic real interest rate, and the stock of net foreign assets), and r^* is the foreign real interest rate. Also note that nx is equivalent to the excess supply of traded goods.

Chart 8 depicts monetary and external equilibria in our open economy. The upper panel shows that monetary equilibrium holds along equilibrium schedule MM. This schedule reflects monetary equilibrium (equation 10) corresponding to inflation expectations consistent with equation (19). Steady-state equilibrium is attained when actual inflation coincides with both the inflation target and long-term expected inflation, that is, when the first difference equation implicit in (19) is zero. Note that dynamic adjustment of inflation and monetary holdings affects the external adjustment path and vice versa.

The lower panel shows the combinations of the real exchange rate and the stock of net foreign-asset holdings that satisfy external equilibrium. The corresponding pair of steady-state equilibrium conditions derived from equations (4) and (20) exhibits a saddle-path equilibrium along schedule SS.

Chart 9 depicts the dynamic adjustment to a permanently lower inflation target – supported by a more restrictive monetary policy – in an open economy characterised by sluggish inflation adjustment due to widespread indexation. Under sluggish inflation adjustment, a rise in the central bank's real domestic interest rate could exceed the contemporaneous

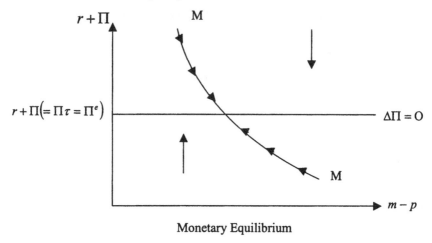

Monetary Equilibrium

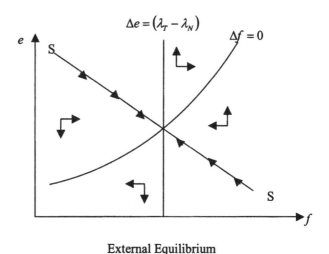

External Equilibrium

Chart 8 Monetary and external equilibria in an open economy

decline in (actual and expected) inflation, implying an increase in the nominal interest rate and hence a decline in real monetary holdings. Therefore, the impact effect is from point A to point B in Panel a. Subsequently inflation starts to decline, allowing a gradual easing of monetary policy. Steady-state convergence is achieved at point C, when inflation has attained the target level and is consistent with long-run inflation expectations, while money holdings have grown accordingly. The real interest rate is back at its initial steady-state level determined by its parity level.

External adjustment (Panel b) involves a real exchange rate appreciation, caused by both the temporary rise in the domestic real interest rate and the influence of lagged inflation (which exceeds contemporaneous inflation), effecting the backward-indexed central parity of the exchange – rate band. Subsequently, the exchange rate appreciates, gradually returning to its initial level at point A. The temporary exchange-rate appreciation causes a temporary current-account deficit, financed by foreign-asset decumulation. Subsequent exchange-rate correction leads to an ultimate reversal in the net foreign-asset position, sending it back to initial equilibrium at point A.

Finally Panel c shows the dynamic adjustment of the model's main variables to the announcement of a lower inflation target.

Note that the non-neutrality of the stabilisation policy – i.e. the result that adjustment takes time and has temporary real effects on asset holdings, relative prices, and employment levels – reflects two key features of the model: (i) inflation sluggishness due to backward indexation in non-traded goods and labour markets as well as the exchange-rate indexation rule, and (ii) the fact that monetary policy follows partly its own history, so that the inflation target plays only a partial role in setting the current policy stance. Therefore, the lower the inflation inertia and the larger the role of the target in setting monetary policy, the quicker and the less costly is the adjustment to a new inflation target.

6 Inflation targets and inflation reduction in Chile during the 1990s

This section assesses the role of inflation targeting in reducing inflation in Chile during the 1990s. The issue is whether the inflation target has been a credibility-enhancing device that has contributed to gradual convergence to low stationary inflation. We address this question by comparing model-based forecasts for future inflation (based on information available just before the announcement of each annual inflation target), with the subsequently known inflation target and actual inflation outcome during the corresponding forecast horizon. If the inflation forecast is systematically above target and actual inflation levels, we infer that (credible) inflation targeting during the decade has helped in Chile's convergence to low inflation at the end of the 1990s.

We inspect the above-mentioned question by using a VAR model with as few restrictions as possible. While this approach is largely non-theoretical, our choice of endogenous and exogenous variables reflects statistical relations that are loosely based on theoretical, common-sense priors. We have explored four alternative VAR specifications: with and without a time trend reflecting the monotonic and downward convergence of inflation to low levels; and with and without the nominal exchange rate as a variable.[6] While this approach lacks a causal and structural interpretation of the variables included in the VAR, it provides potentially more robust

Adjustment to a Low Inflation Target in an Indexed Open Economy

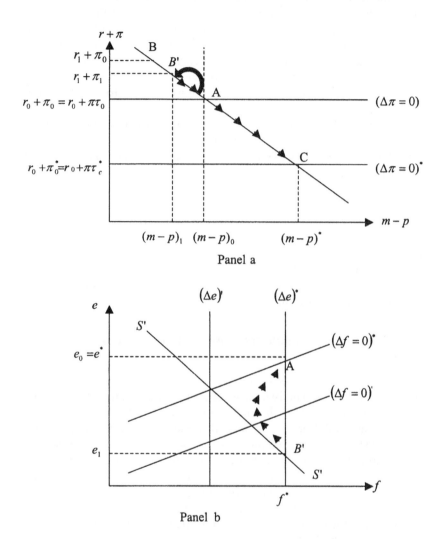

Panel a

Panel b

Chart 9a Adjustment to a low inflation target in an indexed open economy

evidence than that based on a more restrictive structural model.

The monthly data series for the period 1983 to 1998 is depicted in Charts 10a and 10b.[7] The macro variables we plot comprise: headline CPI inflation (IPC), core or underlying CPI inflation (SUBIPC), foreign inflation (IPEXT), nominal exchange rate growth (TCN), nominal wage growth (WAGES), nominal money growth (MONEY), real output growth

Adjustment to a Low Inflation Target in an Indexed Open Economy (continued)

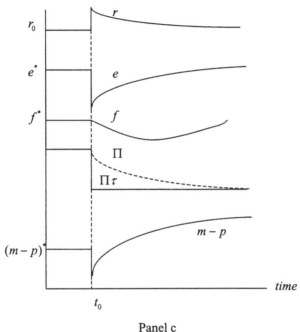

Panel c

Chart 9b

(IMACEC), the indexed interest rate used as the instrument of monetary policy (TASA), and the inflation target (META).

Inspecting the data reveals the cycles and trends of the Chilean economy during the last 16 years. The business cycle is well reflected by the movements of output growth and real wages. With respect to the nominal variables, it is striking that a strong downward trend in all nominal growth rates emerges in 1991. For example, headline and core inflation fall from annual rates of ca. 25% in the 1980s to ca. 5% in 1998. This is a first and casual indication of a regime change that coincides with the adoption of inflation targeting, embodied in a monotonic reduction in pre-announced annual inflation targets. However, the relevant international inflation rate and nominal exchange rate for Chile have also declined during most of the 1990s. Hence simple data inspection does not shed light on the contribution of the inflation target in bringing actual and expected inflation down. In order to identify this effect, we have to consider other determinants of the inflation rate.

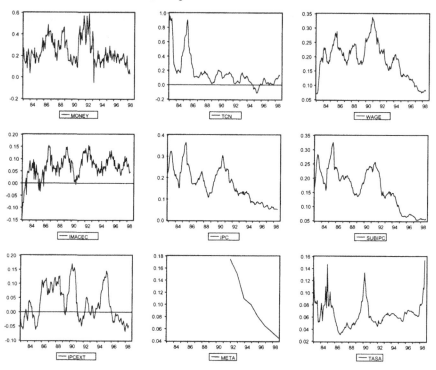

Chart 10a Chile data series

We do this by comparing inflation forecasts based on an unrestricted VAR model with the actual inflation outcome of inflation and the inflation target. Recall that inflation targets are announced by the Central Bank each September and are defined for the subsequent calendar year. The VAR is estimated for each policy announcement using the information available up to the month that predates the target announcement. The forecast is dynamically simulated for 16 months ahead (from September of the current year through December of the next year), and applies to the period of the corresponding target. This means that we estimate seven VARs, each additional one with 12 additional monthly observations, and one VAR for every inflation target announcement of the 1990–96 period.

The unrestricted VAR includes six endogenous variables (interest rate, wages, GDP, CPI, money and nominal exchange rate) and two exogenous variables (terms of trade and relevant foreign CPI). Since we run this VAR to make a forecast, we treat the exogenous variables as endogenous so that they are included in the dynamic forecast. The VAR is estimated with and without inclusion of a trend (as an exogenous variable).[8]

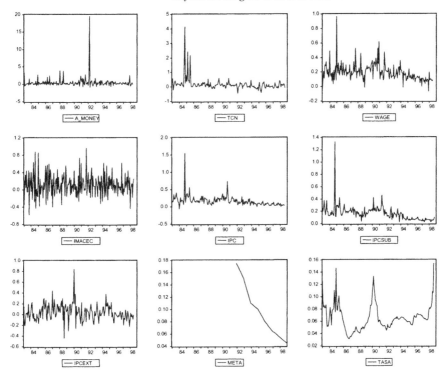

Chart 10b Chile data series

The data we use in the VAR are the following:[9]

1   seasonally-adjusted (sa) monthly real output growth (IMACEC)
2   sa monthly foreign inflation rate (IPCEXT);
3   sa monthly nominal exchange rate growth (TCN);
4   sa monthly inflation rate (IPC);
5   sa monthly money growth (MONEY);
6   sa nominal wage growth (WAGES);
7   90–365 day financial-system interest rate (TASA); and
8   rate of change of the terms of trade (TTRADE).

In order to determine the optimal lags of the model, we first run the VARs over the whole sample period. AIC Akaike (AIC) and Schwarz (SIC) Information Criterion results and likelihood ratio test (LRT) results for the VARs are reported in Table 2. The information criteria and likelihood ratio test results do not provide conclusive answers with respect to the optimal lag structure. AIC signals two lags, while SIC signals one; for VAR1, LRT signals four lags while for VAR2, LRT signals five lags. Since

Table 2 VAR models: information criteria and likelihood ratio test results (Chile, 1983–98)

VAR 1

	AIC	SIC	LRT to MAX	LRT to NEXT
1 lag	−36.53	−35.41*	385.26	200.24
2 lags	−36.89*	−34.91	185.02	123.87
3 lags	−36.83	−34.00	61.14	28.12*
4 lags	−36.65	−32.94	33.01*	25.50*
5 lags	−36.45	−31.85	7.51*	–
6 lags	−36.15	−30.66	–	–

VAR 2

	AIC	SIC	LRT to MAX	LRT to NEXT
1 lag	−36.40	−35.41*	391.50	211.42
2 lags	−36.83*	−34.97	180.07	121.43
3 lags	−36.76	−34.05	58.63	27.33*
4 lags	−36.57	−32.98	31.30*	19.86*
5 lags	−36.34	−31.87	11.43*	–
6 lags	−36.06	−30.70	–	–

Notes: AIC is the Akaike Information Criterion. SIC is the Schwarz Information Criterion. LRT to MAX is the likelihood ratio test with respect to the model with six lags. LRT to NEXT is the likelihood ratio test with respect to the model with one additional lag.
* The null hypothesis that the model with less lags is better cannot be rejected.

there are no major differences in the results between four and five lags, we choose four lags for the VAR dynamic forecast models.

The results are presented in Charts 11 (with time trend) and 12 (without time trend). The grey range or line depicts the inflation target range or target point announced after the last period on which the out-of-sample inflation forecast (the thin black line) is based. Actual inflation is given by the thick black line.

The first and expected result is that the forecasts based on the VARs that include a time trend (in Chart 11) are much closer to actual inflation than the forecasts based on VARs without the trend (in Chart 12). This reflects the negative trend in annual inflation observed during the 1990s.

The second and main result is that inflation forecasts are typically higher than both target and actual inflation rates. This suggests that the systematic attainment of declining annual inflation targets has contributed to a correction of inflation expectations and forecasts. In the absence of credible September announcements of future lower inflation targets, the best (model-based) forecast of future inflation reflects a mean reversion to higher (i.e. historical) rates of inflation in the future. The results suggest that the September target announcements have helped in correcting inflation forecasts downward.

The results are less clear-cut in Chart 11, where inflation forecasts are based on a VAR model that includes a time trend. The latter trend is likely to proxy the markets' expectations about a declining inflation trend,

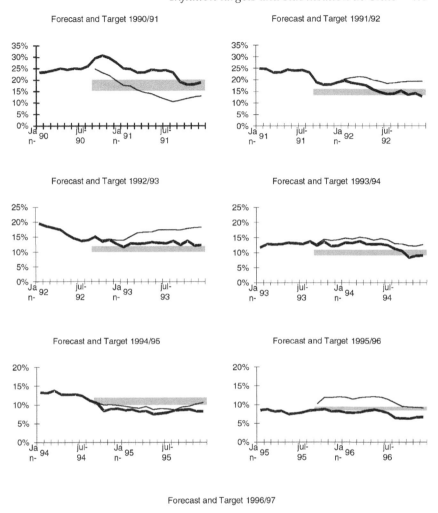

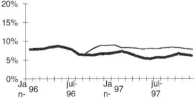

Chart 11

itself a function of the credible attainment of a declining inflation path by the Central Bank. However, the results are very strong in Chart 12, where the VAR model excludes a time trend. Here, in six out of seven cases the out-of-sample forecasts show increasing divergence of inflation forecasts

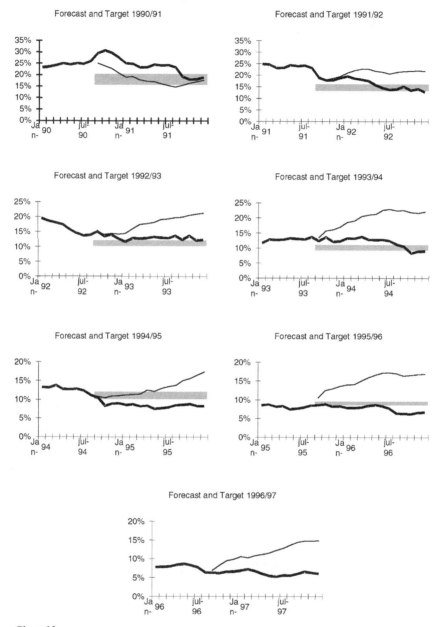

Chart 12

from both actual and target inflation rates over time. This suggests that inflation targeting has allowed a break with inflation history, leading to a gradual downward correction of actual and expected inflation.

We conclude that, for most specifications and sample periods, the inflation target was below the forecast and actual inflation was closer to the target than to the forecast. Although these results do not provide conclusive evidence, they suggest a prominent role played by inflation targeting in reducing inflation. Indeed, a major transmission mechanism of Chile's monetary framework based on inflation targeting may be the credible announcement of the target. The use of a pre-announced inflation objective by a central bank that is strongly committed to its achievement may have overcome the strong mean-reverting effects of inflation inertia in a country with such widespread indexation practices as Chile. The results reported above provide suggestive evidence that the inflation target has performed two roles: a credibility-enhancing device for the conduct of monetary policy, and an effective year-to-year communicator of information from the central bank to the markets.

7 Conclusions

Chile was among the first countries to adopt an inflation target. Its long inflation history had led to widespread backward-looking indexation in goods, labour, and financial markets, as well as in policy instruments. While indexation exacerbates inflation inertia, this paper has provided evidence that adoption of inflation targets by an autonomous central bank since 1990 has made possible a regime change reflected in gradual inflation convergence with international levels. Assessing Chile's targeting experience in an international context and analysing the conduct of monetary policy in Chile provide the background for understanding its recent stabilisation experience. A simple dynamic model was developed to illustrate the role and macroeconomic effects of inflation targeting in a highly indexed open economy. VAR estimations for inflation, inflation targets, and related macro variables support the notion that the introduction of forward-looking inflation targets has contributed to breaking inflation expectations, paving the way for Chile's convergence to sustainable low inflation.

Notes

1 The indexed exchange rate started in 1984 was suspended in September 1999 when a floating exchange rate system was adopted by the Central Bank of Chile.
2 A growing literature on inflation targeting analyses the differences among alternative monetary arrangements and assesses country experiences. Among recent studies are: Leiderman and Svensson (1995), Fischer (1996); Masson, Savastano, and Sharma (1997); Debelle, Masson, Savastano, and Sharma (1998); Bernanke, Laubach, Mishkin, and Posen (1999); and Fry, Julius, Mahadeva, Roger, and Sterne (this volume).
3 Among the recent discussions of the 'sand in the wheels' and 'grease in the wheels' arguments for optimal inflation and empirical results are Card and Hyslop (1996), Feldstein (1996); Akerlof, Dickens and Perry (1996); and

Groshen and Schweitzer (1997).

4　The Boskin commission calculated CPI measurement bias at around 1.1% per year for the United States.

5　A more detailed analysis of monetary policy in Chile is presented by Massad (1998).

6　Below we only report the results of the two VARs that include the nominal exchange rate, because those that exclude the exchange rate are very similar to the former results.

7　We report data for 12-month growth rates and seasonally adjusted (sa) annualised monthly growth rates for most variables in Charts 10a and 10b, respectively. The exceptions are the target inflation rate (which is announced as an annual December-to-December per cent rate of change of the CPI) and the real interest rate. While monthly and quarterly Chilean data are typically reported as 12-month rates of change, the drawback of this choice is that it reflects annual changes and not the corresponding month's change, implying excessive data smoothing. Our alternative sa data present more relevant information on the corresponding month's change, but have the drawback of relying on a particular seasonal adjustment method (the ARIMA X-11 procedure).

8　We do not report confidence intervals for the forecasts based on the VARs. Since the forecasts are dynamic, their variance grows with time: each forecast's precision declines compared to that of the preceding month. Therefore forecast confidence intervals beyond the first month are not meaningful.

9　Data definitions and sources are the following. IMACEC is the Monthly Index of Economic Activity of the Central Bank of Chile. IPCEXT is the Average Price Index for Chilean Trade of the Central Bank of Chile for January 1982 to April 1997; it is the Relevant External Inflation Index for Chile for April 1997 onwards. TCN is the $/US$ nominal exchange rate. IPC is the Consumer Price Index of the National Institute of Statistics. MONEY is M1 published by the IMF (IFS). WAGES is the Nominal Hourly Wage Index of the National Institute of Statistics. TASA is the average real interest rate of the financial system for 90 to 365-day deposits published by the Central Bank of Chile. TTRADE is the terms-of-trade index for export and import prices of the Central Bank of Chile.

Bibliography

Akerlof, G.A., Dickens, W.T. and Perry, G.L. (1996), 'The macroeconomics of low inflation', *Brookings Papers on Economic Activity* (1): 1–76.

Bernanke, B.S., Laubach, T., Mishkin, F.S. and Posen, A.S. (1999), *Inflation Targeting: Lessons from the International Experience*, Princeton University Press.

Card, D. and Hyslop, D. (1996), 'Does inflation "grease the wheels" of the labor market?' *NBER Working Paper*, No. 5538, April.

Debelle, G., Masson, P., Savastano, M. and Sharma, S. (1998), 'Inflation targeting as a framework for monetary policy', *Economic Issues*, 15, IMF.

Feldstein, M. (1996), 'The costs and benefits from going from low inflation to price stability', *NBER Working Paper*, No. 5469, February.

Fischer, S. (1996), 'Maintaining price stability', *Finance and Development*, 33(4): 34–7, December.

Fry, M., Julius, D., Mahadeva, L., Roger, S. and Sterne, G. (2000), 'Key issues in the choice of monetary policy frameworks', this volume.

Groshen, E. and Schweitzer, M. (1997), 'Identifying inflation's grease and sand effects in the labor markets', *NBER Working Paper,* No. 6061, June.

Leiderman, L. and Svensson, L.E.O. (1995), *Inflation Targets,* Centre for Economic Policy Research, London.

Massad, C. (1998), 'La política monetaria en Chile', *Economía Chilena,* 1 (1): 7–27.

Masson, P.A., Savastano, M.A. and Sharma, S. (1997), 'The scope for inflation targeting in developing countries', *IMF Working Paper,* WP/97/130, October.

Monetary policy and disinflation in Israel

Gil Bufman and Leonardo Leiderman[1]

1 Introduction

Disinflation in Israel has been slow and gradual. After inflation reached a peak of 445% in 1984 and following a comprehensive stabilisation programme in July 1985, there have been three major phases. In the first phase, from 1986 to 1991, the rate of inflation stayed in the range of 16%–20%, with an average of about 18% per year. This was followed by a second phase, from 1992 to 1996, in which the average rate of inflation was reduced to about 10% per year. It is evident that Israel has witnessed the emergence of a new (third) phase starting in 1997. The rate of inflation for 1997 declined to 7% and, aside from the last third of 1998, in which inflation was temporarily sent off track by global financial instability, the rate of inflation continued to fall, reaching about 2.5% in 1999. The official inflation target for the years 2000 and 2001 has been set as the range 3%–4% per year.

Monetary policy has played a central role in the process of disinflation. As such, it has been the subject of sharp debate in Israel, part of which reflects major changes in the conduct of such policy. From a highly accommodative policy in the late 1970s and early 1980s, there have been marked changes over time up to the adoption of explicit inflation targets from 1992 to the present. At the centre of the debate are important issues such as: the ability of monetary policy to have an impact on movements in the rate of inflation; the effectiveness of monetary policy in a small open economy operating under a nominal exchange rate commitment; the side effects of monetary policy and the costs of disinflation; and the management of policy under inflation targets.

The purpose of this paper is to provide a body of empirical evidence on the role of monetary policy measures in the process of disinflation in Israel. Establishing a set of basic empirical regularities on these issues is a clear prerequisite for resolving the above-mentioned controversies and for drawing lessons that may be relevant for disinflation in other small, open economies similar to Israel's. The main focus of the paper is *not* on the potential role of monetary policy in a major disinflation programme such as the 1985 economic stabilisation plan – that is aimed at producing a shift from very high to moderate or low inflation. Instead, we concentrate on a given moderate inflation environment – such as the period from the late 1980s to the present – and explore the explanatory role of monetary policy measures for movements in the rate of inflation and, in particular, for disinflation to single-digit rates. Needless to say, a comprehensive analysis of the inflation process would include a discussion of the role of important non-monetary fundamentals such as fiscal policy, wage policy, foreign prices, and so on. These additional fundamentals are especially important when dealing with sharp changes in the inflation environment.[2] While some of these important factors are taken into account in the present paper, the analysis needs to be extended in future work.

The paper is organised as follows. Section 2 briefly describes recent monetary regimes in Israel, including the present system in which an explicit inflation target co-exists with a crawling exchange-rate band. In addition, the section draws on recent work by Lars Svensson to present a basic analytical framework for dealing with forward-looking monetary policy under inflation targets. Section 3 discusses various transmission mechanisms for the impact of money on inflation and documents some basic empirical regularities on the role of monetary aggregates and interest rates in the inflation process. Section 4 presents our main econometric findings on the relation between monetary policy variables, other macro-economic variables, and the rate of inflation. We report estimates of various econometric specifications for inflation equations and discuss how these estimates can be used to forecast inflation in future periods.[3] In Section 5 we present the main conclusions from this research.

2   Monetary policy under inflation targeting

As indicated in the introduction, monetary policy in Israel has gone through major changes in recent years. From a highly accommodative policy in the late 1970s and early 1980s, which supported the escalation of inflation to triple-digit figures, the first phase in the aftermath of the remarkable stabilisation programme of June 1985 featured a policy oriented toward sustaining a fixed but adjustable nominal exchange rate, considered as a key nominal anchor in disinflation. Throughout this first phase, from 1986 to 1991, the rate of inflation stayed in the range of 16%–20% on average per year. This was followed by a second phase, from 1992 to 1996, characterised by the modification of the exchange-rate regime to a crawling exchange-rate band and by the adoption of an explicit inflation target. In this period, the average rate of inflation was reduced to about 10% per year.[4] The data clearly point to a third phase in the disinflation process, starting in 1997, featuring single-digit and declining rates of inflation. That is, the rate of inflation was 7% for 1997, and has declined to about 2.5% in 1999. This decline of the rate of inflation throughout

1997–99 was interrupted temporarily by the volatility in world financial markets during September–November 1998, which had an impact on Israel's exchange rate and on the rate of inflation. Nonetheless, it seems that the impact of the currency depreciation during the last third of 1998 on prices offset by deflationary forces such as the drop in world commodity prices and the slowdown of domestic demand growth and restrictive monetary policy. The rate of inflation reached 8.6% in 1998 (year end), within the official target of 7%–10%. The rate of inflation in 1999, which is expected to be about 2.5%, is lower than the 4% official target. As indicated above, in mid-1999 the government set an inflation target range of 3%–4% for 2000–01. Overall, the evolution of the nominal policy regime after 1985 shows a *gradual shift toward increased flexibility of the nominal exchange rate coupled with increased emphasis on inflation targeting.*

Current monetary policy in Israel is oriented toward achieving the inflation target set by government while at the same time maintaining and supporting the exchange rate's crawling band. When compared to most other countries that adopted explicit inflation targets, Israel's case is unique for at least three reasons. First, it is one of the only cases in which in spite of attempts to keep inflation relatively low, there are still some institutions and modes of operation left over from the era of triple-digit inflation. Second, at variance with other cases, there is a considerable degree of ambiguity about the nature and operational meaning of inflation targets as a pre-commitment device not only for monetary policy but for fiscal policy as well. In part this reflects the fact that, initially, inflation targets were introduced in the somewhat technical context of determining the slope of the crawling exchange-rate band. It is only recently that inflation targets have been given more fundamental importance, as indicated, for example, by the fact that the targets for 1998 and 1999 have been discussed in detail in several cabinet meetings and has been set jointly with the setting of the targets for the government budget for that year. Third, Israel is one of the very few cases where inflation targets coexist with another nominal commitment, namely the crawling exchange-rate band; other such cases have been Chile, Colombia, and Poland. Accordingly, under a considerable degree of international capital mobility, concrete dilemmas about policy have emerged as a result of shocks and developments that gave rise to conflicts between the monetary policy measures required to achieve each one of these two targets.[5]

As in other countries (see, e.g. Leiderman and Svensson, 1995), the explicit inflation target in Israel has become a key nominal anchor in the economy, and as such, it plays two main roles. First, it provides a transparent guide to monetary policy, the commitment, discipline, and accountability of which can be judged according to whether policy actions were taken to ensure that the target is achieved. Second, if credible, it should serve as a coordination device in the wage- and price-setting process and in the formation of the public's inflation expectations. In an economy with a large public sector, such as Israel, the credibility of the inflation target can be strengthened if the specific target that was chosen serves also as a coordination device in the setting of public-sector wages, of prices of public-sector utilities, and of the price deflator used to translate real government spending into nominal government budget figures.

2.1 Inflation targeting: analytical basis

Since inflation targeting is a relatively new framework for conducting monetary policy in Israel, as well as in other countries, it is well to briefly discuss some of the analytical bases underlying such a framework and its policy implications. It is convenient to do so by drawing on the recent important contributions by Lars Svensson (1997a, 1997b). On the motivation for and application of inflation targets in different countries, see Leiderman and Svensson (1995).

Consider the model in Svensson (1997a):

$$\pi_{t+1} = \pi_t + \alpha_1 y_t + \alpha_2 x_t + \epsilon_{t+1} \qquad (2.1)$$

$$y_{t+1} = \beta_1 y_t - \beta_2(i_t - \pi_t) + \beta_3 x_t + \eta_{t+1} \qquad (2.2)$$

$$x_{t+1} = \gamma x_t + \theta_{t+1} \qquad (2.3)$$

where $\pi_t = p_t - p_{t-1}$ is the inflation rate in year t; p_t is the log price level; y_t is the log of output relative to potential output, x_t is an exogenous variable that represents an impulse to aggregate demand (e.g. fiscal policy); i_t is the monetary policy instrument (say, the interest rate on central bank funds); and ϵ_t, η_t, θ_t are i.i.d. random variables with a zero conditional mean. The coefficients α_1 and β_2 are assumed to be positive, the other coefficients are assumed to be nonnegative; β_2 and γ in addition fulfil $\beta_1 < 1$, $\gamma < 1$. The long-run natural output level is normalised to equal zero. Although this is a closed-economy formulation, which can be extended to an open-economy setting (see below), it helps to illustrate the considerations that affect the conduct of monetary policy under inflation targets in both these cases.

From equation (2.1), which is a version of a short-term Phillips curve, the acceleration in the rate of inflation is increasing in lagged output and the lagged exogenous variable. Equation (2.2), which can be viewed as an IS relation, posits that output in the current period depends on output in the previous period, on the lagged real interest rate and the lagged exogenous variable.[6] Equation (2.3) gives the evolution of the exogenous variable as a first-order autoregressive process. It can be seen here that the nominal interest rate set by the central bank affects output with a one-year lag and inflation with a two-period lag. Hence, from the standpoint of influencing the path of inflation, the model embodies a two-period policy lag. That this is the case can be verified by expressing inflation at t + 2 in terms of time t variables:

$$\pi_{t+2} = a_1\pi_t + a_2y_t + a_3x_t - a_4i_t + (\epsilon_{t+1} + \alpha_1\eta_{t+1} + \alpha_2\theta_{t+1} + \epsilon_{t+2}), \quad (2.4)$$

where

$$a_1 = 1 + \alpha_1\beta_2; a_2 = a_1(1 + \beta_1); a_3 = \alpha_1\beta_3 + \alpha_2(1 + \gamma); a_4 = \alpha_1\beta_2 \quad (2.5)$$

Inflation at time t + 2 is increasing in the rate of inflation, the output gap, and the exogenous variable at time t, and is decreasing in the nominal interest rate set at time t. Notice that the equation can be rewritten to include the real interest rate on central bank funds in the right hand side:

$$\pi_{t+2} = \pi_t + a_2y_t + a_2x_t - a_4(i_t - \pi_t) + (\epsilon_{t+1} + \alpha_1y_{t+1} + \alpha_2\theta_{t+1} + \epsilon_{t+2})$$
$$(2.6)$$

How should monetary policy be conducted in this model? Assuming, as in Svensson, that government has set an inflation target of π^*, that the central bank acts to minimise the expected sum of the discounted losses from current and future deviations of the rate of inflation from the inflation target set by government, and that the period loss function is quadratic, the first-order condition for this minimisation problem can be expressed as

$$\pi_{t+2|t} = \pi^* \quad (2.7)$$

where $\pi_{t+2|t}$ is the current (time t) conditional forecast of the rate of inflation at t + 2.

Accordingly, the central bank should engage in what Svensson terms 'inflation forecast targeting', that is, *set the interest rate so as to equate its own two-year forecast of the rate of inflation with the inflation target*. This yields the central bank's optimal interest rate rule:

$$i_t = \pi_t + b_1(\pi_t - \pi^*) + b_2y_t + b_3x_t, \quad (2.8)$$

where

$$b_1 = \frac{1}{\alpha_1\beta_2}; b_2 = \frac{1 + \beta_1}{\beta_2}; b_3 = \frac{\alpha_1\beta_3 + \alpha_2(1 + \gamma)}{\alpha_1\beta_2}, \quad (2.9)$$

which is a reaction function similar to a Taylor (1993) rule. A central bank equipped with this rule will raise the nominal interest rate on its funds in reaction to any one of the following events: a rise in the rate of inflation (above the inflation target), an increase in output relative to potential, and a rise in the exogenous impulse x_t. As stressed by Svensson, the interest rate depends on current values of inflation, the output gap, and the exogenous variable, not because current inflation is targeted, but because in the model these current variables have persistent effects and predict future inflation. In the absence of a monetary policy change, an increase in current output above potential, or a more expansionary fiscal policy (say, an increase in x_t), would imply a future deviation of inflation $(\pi_{t+2|t} - \pi^*)$ from target. Other things being equal, these events call for a rise in the current interest rate in order to achieve (in a conditional-expectation sense) the inflation target.[7] Svensson shows that inflation targeting via an interest rate reaction function is more efficient, in the sense of bringing lower inflation variability, than money growth or exchange-rate targeting.

Although this is a relatively simple model of the economy – one that can be extended to an open-economy framework – it captures the essence of *forward-looking* monetary policy under inflation targets: achieving these targets in the future requires (in the presence of lags) adjusting current monetary conditions in response to current and expected future developments that could lead to deviations of inflation from target. If policy is conducted in this way (via equation 2.4) the inflation forecast equals the target, and ex-post inflation will differ from the target only because of random shocks whose realisation could not be predicted at the time of formulating the policy. Notice that while policy is successful in achieving the target in this case, there will be no simple statistical relation between the interest rate and the rate of inflation: although the inflation rate will be equal, on average, to the target, the interest rate will fluctuate in order to offset potential deviations of inflation from target that may arise due to movements in the output gap (y_t) and in the exogenous variable $(x_t$, due to fiscal policy, for example). Hence, the more fundamental link relates the change in current monetary conditions with the deviation of future inflation from target that would have taken place in the absence of such an adjustment in current monetary conditions. Put differently, the arrival of new information about inflation forecasts which may imply future deviations of inflation from target can trigger interest-rate adjustments aimed at avoiding the emergence of such deviations.

2.2   *Recent inflation performance*

That recent developments featured severe challenges to official inflation targets is evident from Chart 1.[8] This chart depicts the evolution of the rate of inflation, inflation targets, and market-based expected inflation in Israel from 1992 to January 1999. Although there are no explicit multiyear inflation targets in Israel, when the targets were set for both 1997 and 1998 (at 7%–10%), the government added the objectives of having an inflation target for the year 2001 as that common in OECD countries and of continuing the gradual reduction in the rate of inflation to achieve price stability

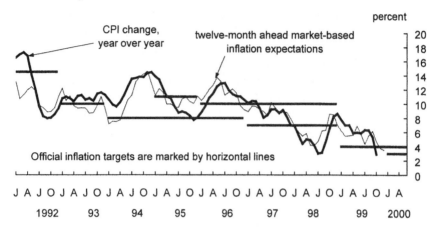

Chart 1 Inflation in Israel – actual, expected and targets

over time as in other industrial countries. As common in Israel, expected inflation is derived from the yields on indexed and non-indexed bonds traded in the local capital market. It can be seen that there have been several periods in which the rate of inflation deviated from target. Measured from December of a given year to December of the previous year, as in the specification of the target, the largest deviation of inflation from target occurred in 1994, when annual inflation reached 14.5% against a target of 8%. However, in the following years of 1995–98 the targets were achieved, and any deviations that occurred were quite minimal. Overall, with a multi-year perspective, it can clearly be argued that *inflation targets have been achieved on average*: the average annual rate of inflation from 1992 to 1999 was 8.9% which was slightly lower than the average annual inflation target of 9%. In addition, the 2000–01 inflation target was set in mid-1999 at 3%–4%, indicating that the government's longer-term objective of convergence with inflation rates in industrial countries to be attainable.

Having established that annual inflation targets were achieved on average in the past six years, it is well to stress that there were four major episodes of acceleration of the rate of inflation within the years well above the target; these occurred in late 1994, in the first half of 1996, in mid-1997, and in late 1998 (see Chart 1). In these cases, the regime was challenged and its credibility was endangered, as suggested by the escalation of inflation expectations to about 15% per year in the first two episodes and to about 8%–10% in the third and fourth episodes.

The developments in the first two episodes, of late 1994 and early 1996, occurred in the face of strong inflationary pressures arising from a relatively overheated economy, in which the rate of unemployment declined markedly, and from a fiscal policy that took an expansionary stance. The fiscal expansion in the period from 1994 to 1996 initially took the form of an increase of government expenditures in 1994 by about NIS six billion (2.7% of GDP) beyond the originally planned level that was the basis for that year's budget law. Then, the budget deficit reached 3.2% of GDP in 1995 compared to the target of 2.75%, and subsequently there was an additional, but sharper, overrun of the budget deficit in 1996, when it reached 4.6% of GDP compared to a target of 2.5%. At the same time, the economy rapidly moved towards 'full employment' and the rate of unemployment declined from a peak of 11.2% in 1992 to 7.8% in 1994, 6.9% in 1995 and 6.7% in 1996. This move was accompanied by demand pressures on Israel's domestic resources, and by a rapid deterioration in the current-account deficit of the balance of payments, which reached 5.6% of GDP in 1996.

These circumstances created a situation where restrictive monetary policy was needed in order to counterbalance expansionary fiscal policy and the demand pressures in an overheated economy as well as to reduce the implied deviation of the rate of inflation from the government's inflation target.[9] There is no doubt that much of the public discussion and debate in Israel about inflation targets has to do with the evaluation of these two salient episodes, which represented a severe challenge to the inflation targets and an overburdening of monetary policy.

The development of mid-1997 occurred after the exchange-rate band had been widened. The immediate reaction of the markets to this change was a drop in the value of the shekel by about 5%, which quickly fed into inflation expectations. In addition, this step was accompanied by a reduction of the interest rate, which soon after was reversed in the face of rising inflation expectations. The development of late 1998 occurred following the rapid depreciation of the shekel in the global financial turbulence that erupted in late August 1998. The exchange rate of the shekel against the currency basket depreciated by 24% from late July 1998 to late October 1998. Both expected and actual inflation responded to the drop of the currency: 12-month ahead inflation expectations rose temporarily from about 4% to about 10% and the CPI rose by a cumulative 6.3% in a matter of four months. Timely and decisive monetary policy was then an important factor in containing the effect of the jolt to the exchange rate on prices: the central bank's fund rate was raised by 400 basis points in a matter of one month. Following these policy steps, and without any central bank intervention in the foreign exchange market, the domestic currency started to appreciate gradually in mid-November 1998. As a result, both actual and expected inflation declined sharply in December 1998 and in early 1999 and the episode turned out to be a one-time jump in the price level but not in the rate of inflation.

The rate of inflation was 7% in 1997, at the bottom of the inflation-target range and 8.6% in 1998, in the centre of the target range (which was 7%–10% for both years). During the second half of 1997 and the first three quarters of 1998, inflation was running at an annual rate as low as 3%, well below the lower limit of the inflation target range for 1998 (7%–10%). Although, in principle, this low rate of inflation during the first three quarters of 1998 pointed to a within-the-year deviation of inflation from target, this development was understood by the central bank as potentially substantial progress toward achieving the government's longer-term target of inflation's convergence to rates in industrial countries. In any case, there was an active public controversy and debate as to how policy should proceed under the circumstances of surprisingly low inflation and whether the existing inflation target of 7%–10% for 1998 should be modified downwards. The drop of the currency in late 1998 turned this debate around and, as a result of three months of relatively high CPI figures, the issue was now whether to adjust the 4% inflation target for 1999 upwards to about 6%. A similar debate took place in mid-1999 regarding the target for 2000, during which there were those who called for a relaxation of the inflation target as a means of boosting economic growth, which had slowed down considerably in 1996–98. Overall it seems that the setting of inflation targets in Israel over the last few years has been an adaptive process in which the target for next year is kept relatively close to the year-over-year rate of inflation in the period prior to the setting of the target.

2.3   The crawling exchange-rate band

Chart 2 gives the evolution of Israel's nominal exchange rate *vis-à-vis* a basket of foreign currencies and of the crawling exchange-rate band. As in the case of the inflation target, the parameters of the exchange-rate regime are set by the government following consultation with the Bank of Israel. This crawling exchange-rate band was introduced in late 1991, in order to help relax the fixity of the previous band system which was based on a fluctuation zone around a fixed central parity rate. The move to a more flexible system came after a series of speculative attacks on the NIS during 1988–91, attacks based mainly on the perception that a fixed exchange rate was not sustainable in view of the persistent domestic-foreign inflation differential. During that period, the interest rate was directed solely to coping with speculative attacks on Israel's foreign currency reserves, rather than achieving a given inflation objective. From 1992 onwards, there were no major threats to the exchange rate regime, and the interest rate gradually gained a central role in the effort to meet the inflation target that was introduced, for the first time, in December 1991 as a part of the new crawling exchange-rate band system.[10]

For most of the crawling band's life until 1996, the central bank operated an inner, intramarginal, intervention band, aimed at keeping the exchange rate relatively close to the central parity rate. During the period when capital inflows grew considerably, in part due to the progress in the

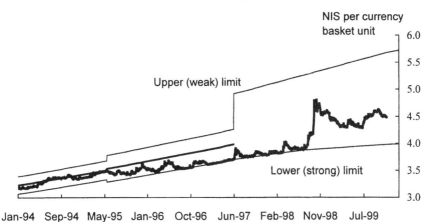

NIS per currency basket unit

Upper (weak) limit

Lower (strong) limit

6.0
5.5
5.0
4.5
4.0
3.5
3.0

Jan-94 Sep-94 May-95 Jan-96 Oct-96 Jun-97 Feb-98 Nov-98 Jul-99

Chart 2 The crawling exchange rate band

Middle East peace process from late 1993 onwards and in part as a result of financial opening and liberalisation measures taken in previous years – this intervention resulted in the Bank of Israel's purchasing the considerable excess supply in the foreign exchange market, with little change in the nominal exchange rate. In late May 1995, the Bank of Israel and the Ministry of Finance announced the widening of the exchange-rate band from 5% to 7% around the central parity rate. The initial purpose of this step was to adjust the exchange rate regime so as to allow greater exchange-rate flexibility. In spite of the potential increase in exchange-rate risk, after a few weeks there was a strong tendency by the exchange rate to appreciate within the band, and the central bank returned to large-scale intervention in the foreign-currency market. It is evident that the perceived implicit commitment by the Bank of Israel to the inner band was interpreted by market participants as a signal that there was little risk associated with exchange-rate fluctuations. The combination of this perception and a sizable domestic-foreign interest rate differential provided an additional incentive for domestic agents to shift from domestic currency denominated credit into borrowing abroad, thus strengthening short-term capital inflows and the pressure toward nominal exchange rate appreciation.

The foregoing developments, together with the objective of making further progress towards capital account liberalisation and deepening of the foreign exchange market, prompted a policy of increased exchange-rate flexibility. Specifically, the inner band was abandoned in February 1996 and, as a result, there was more room for movements of the exchange rate within the announced band. By the summer of 1996, the exchange rate had appreciated to the band's lower (or strongest) limit. With capital inflows and pressure for the nominal exchange rate appreciation continuing, and

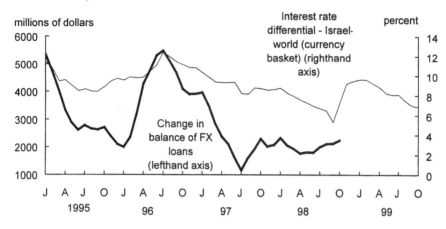

Chart 3 Israel's interest rate differential and the change in the balance of foreign
currency loans, each month, looking 12 months ahead

given the desire to deepen the foreign-exchange market and to make
further progress towards capital account liberalisation, the next and latest
change in the band's parameters occurred in June 1997. Additional room
for exchange-rate flexibility was introduced in the form of enlarging the
band width from 14% to 28%, with provision for further widening over
time. The widening of the band was implemented entirely by raising of the
upper (or weaker) limit. Parallel to the upward widening of the band, the
rate of crawl of the lower limit was reduced to 4% per year, while the
slope of the upper limit was left at 6% per year. In mid-1998, the slope of
the lower limit of the band was reduced even further to 2% while the slope
of the upper limit remained at 6%. This has created a situation where the
band's rate of widening has been stepped up since mid-1998 from 2% to
4% per year, with the band's width already at 35% at the end of 1998.

Following these changes the expansion of the stock of foreign currency
denominated credit slowed down considerably from the second half of
1997 and throughout 1999. This probably indicates a greater perception of
foreign-exchange risk by the private sector, both in view of the wider
exchange rate band and of the developments in global financial markets.
This perception of risk grew considerably during the shekel's rapid depreciation in late 1998. Perhaps the unwillingness of the central bank to intervene in the foreign-exchange market during this episode also contributed
to the public's heightened perception of exchange-rate risk.

As far as pressure on the exchange rate is concerned, while net capital
inflows kept the exchange rate relatively close to the bottom of the band
throughout mid-1998, a moderate reversal of the flows in late 1998 was
enough to cause a substantial depreciation of the shekel (see Table 1). In
the first half of 1999, as the uncertainty in the financial markets subsided,

Table 1 Capital flows of the non-financial, net private sector[a]

$US millions		1995	1996	1997	1998	1/99–10/99
a. Total capital flows to Israel	a = b + c	9,471	6,089	9,123	–367	2,456
b. Capital flows by Israelis		6,460	1,647	4,158	–1,687	–1,306
c. Capital flows by foreign residents	c = d + e + f	3,011	4,442	4,965	1,320	3,762
d. Total financial investment		1,601	3,149	3,435	–36	1,431
e. Direct investments		1,306	1,389	1,455	1,227	2,400
f. Shekel credit received (–) net of increase in shekel deposits		104	–96	75	129	–69

[a] inflows(+)/outflows(−)

and with the aid of tighter monetary policy, the exchange rate started to appreciate once again, though this appreciation was limited and came to a halt in the second half of the year. Overall, for the second half of 1998 and throughout all of 1999, capital inflows to Israel declined at relative to the 1995 to mid-1998 period. The main causes of this reduction were a decrease in the demand for foreign exchange financing by the Israeli business sector, an increase in demand for foreign currency denominated deposits by Israeli residents, and a decline of financial investment by foreigners in Israeli financial assets.

Up to mid-1997, it seemed that the gradualness of the move toward increased flexibility of the nominal exchange rate, in an environment of considerable capital mobility and strong inflationary pressures in the economy, contributed to a conflict in Israeli monetary policy between two nominal goals – the inflation target and the exchange rate band. In other words, the interest rate level required in meeting the inflation target has been higher than the level that would have avoided pressures on the exchange-rate band. When the exchange rate band became a binding constraint, a high degree of sterilised intervention of capital inflows was required – sterilisation that carried a sizable quasi-fiscal cost – and monetary policy could not fully affect inflation developments through the very important exchange-rate channel of the transmission mechanism.

The reduction of the rate of inflation to low single digits, which forced the domestic-foreign interest rate differential downwards, brought a different problem and dilemma, that of foreign exchange market vulnerability. Specifically, the combination of a low interest rate differential and an adverse external financial shock had a powerful impact on the currency market, forcing the central bank to act. Here, the central bank's dilemma was *how* to act – by raising interest rates, by selling foreign exchange, or perhaps by a combination of both. The central bank opted to use the interest rate only, while at the same time allowing market forces to determine exchange rates, without official intervention.

2.4   *Interest rate adjustments*

The implications of the interaction between current and expected future developments on current monetary policy adjustments can be discussed in terms of developments in Israel with Charts 1 and 4. Chart 4 shows are clear the three recent salient episodes of marked interest rate rises by the central bank that occurred in late 1994 and early 1995, in the second half of 1996, and in late 1998. While there is no official or commonly used inflation forecast formulated by the Bank of Israel, market-based measures of inflation expectations are widely used – namely, expectations derived from relative yields on indexed and non-indexed bonds traded in Israel's capital market. In many cases, these expectations, plotted in Chart 4, have performed a similar role to that of the inflation forecast $\pi_{t+2|t}$, a in Svensson's

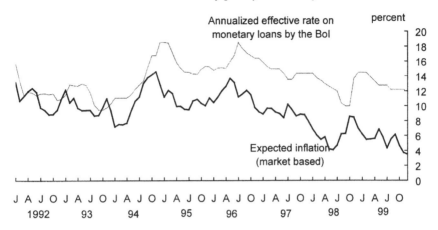

Chart 4 Inflation expectations and the interest rate on Bank of Israel (BoI) funds

model. In fact, the interest rate rises mentioned above were triggered by a combination of factors included in the reaction function (equation 2.8): a rise in expected inflation, a rise in the government's budget deficit, and reductions in the rate of unemployment. Symmetrically, when these factors signalled an easing of inflationary pressures, the central bank adjusted interest rates downward.

Overall, monetary policy developments in Israel illustrate how monetary policy can become severely overburdened in its attempt to achieve the inflation target when other key factors (such as fiscal policy and the state of the business cycle) exert strong upward pressures on the rate of inflation. In addition, these developments illustrate that, under a high degree of capital mobility, the coexistence of an exchange-rate band and inflation targeting may make the job of monetary policy more difficult than in the absence of an explicit exchange rate commitment, especially when the level of the interest rate required by inflation targeting considerations sharply differs from one consistent with avoiding pressures on the exchange-rate band. In order to avoid conflicts among these nominal targets, it would be useful if the authorities could prioritise their objectives in a clear and transparent manner. One possible arrangement is to make official inflation targets the key objective of monetary policy, and to allow for relatively free movements of the exchange-rate. Alternatively, if there are any implicit or explicit exchange rate targets, these could be subordinated to the inflation target. In fact, almost all countries that implement inflation targeting have given primacy to the inflation target over any available intermediate targets.

In discussing the recent reduction in the rate of inflation, the role of monetary policy should be stressed. Since the middle of 1996, the ex ante, expected, real bank rate was maintained at about 6% per year. Yet, as has been typical in other cases of rapid disinflation, the rapid decline in inflation expectations and the slowly changing nominal interest rate on Bank of Israel funds meant that the real rate rose to about 7% per year in early 1998. Moreover, the real rate on central bank funds rose to about 8% in late 1998 and early 1999, after the exchange rate's depreciation had been contained.

3   Monetary factors and the inflation process

In this section we discuss various aspects of the role of monetary factors in the inflation process in Israel. In particular, we present some basic empirical regularities about the link between money and prices and elaborate on changes in monetary policy in the 1990s under inflation targeting.

3.1   *Transmission mechanisms*

There are various channels of transmission from monetary policy variables to movements in the rate of inflation.[11] When policy alters the path of monetary aggregates or of short-term interest rates, this may effect the rate of inflation through at least one of the following channels (some of which were incorporated in the Svensson model of the previous section):

(i) *Long-term interest rates and aggregate demand*   Other things equal, in the short run a rise in short-term interest rates is likely to lead to a rise in long-term rates (the exact impact depends on the term structure of interest rates), which in turn can be expected to lead to slower growth in aggregate consumption and investment, as well as prices.

(ii) *Real balance and wealth effects*   Similarly, a reduction in the rate of growth of outside money may generate real-balance and wealth effects that lead to slower aggregate demand growth. These effects may become particularly strong if there is a large number of liquidity-constrained economic agents.

(iii) *Nominal exchange rates*   In a small, open economy, changes in short-term interest rates can have an immediate impact on the nominal exchange rates of the domestic currency against foreign currencies. Nominal exchange-rate fluctuations, in turn, typically will affect the domestic prices of a large number of goods and services, whose pricing closely follows that in foreign countries, but which are expressed in domestic currency units. Additionally, in the short run, nominal exchange-rate fluctuations can influence the path of domestic currency denominated goods and services such as house prices and rentals.

(iv) *Inflation expectations*   Expectations are a key variable in the dynamics of the inflationary process. Changes in monetary policy can influence the evolution of these expectations, which in turn may affect the price- and wage-setting process as well as the pricing of various assets.

(v) *Credit channel* Changes in monetary conditions may also influence the volume and terms of credit in the economy. On the one hand, there is a credit channel affecting aggregate consumption and investment decisions; on the supply side, shifts in credit may affect production and employment decisions. As in item (ii), the existence of liquidity constraints can strengthen these credit-channel effects.

Previous research has stressed that it is very difficult to determine which of the above channels of transmission is dominant at a given time. First, the various channels may work with different lags. For example, the lag in the impact of nominal exchange rates on impact is likely to be shorter than for real-balance or wealth effects. Moreover, the lags are likely to change over time. Second, the specifics of the transmission mechanism may not be invariant to frequently observed changes in policy regimes and in the structure of the behavioural relations describing the economy. Accordingly, what might have been a strong transmission channel from nominal exchange rates to prices in a high-inflation environment might become much weaker under low inflation. Similarly, substantial changes in the degree of international capital mobility can alter the specifics of the transmission mechanism. Given these complications, it is surprisingly that there are many different views on the specifics of the transmission mechanism for monetary policy.

Nevertheless, there are some basic relations between monetary policy variables and the rate of inflation that can be expected to hold independently of the exact nature of the transmission mechanism. Given the lack of a fully blown structural model of the Israeli economy, we concentrate below on an empirical investigation of some basic relations. In particular, popular macroeconomic models embody a money-market equilibrium condition that can be expressed in dynamic terms as:

$$\pi = \frac{\Delta M}{M} - \frac{\Delta Y}{Y} + \frac{\Delta V}{V} \tag{3.1}$$

where π denotes the rate of inflation, $\dfrac{\Delta M}{M}$ is the rate of growth of the nominal money supply, $\dfrac{\Delta Y}{Y}$ is the rate of growth of output, and $\dfrac{\Delta V}{V}$ denotes the rate of change of velocity of circulation.[12] Other things equal, higher money growth should result in higher inflation. This relation should hold not only for a closed economy but for an open economy operating under a flexible exchange rate, or a fixed-but-adjustable exchange rate. Under strictly fixed nominal exchange rates (e.g. under a currency board), money growth becomes endogenous and domestic inflation cannot differ much from foreign inflation.

Another basic relation from monetary theory is that sustained higher inflation yields higher nominal interest rates. However, in the short run, raising interest rates tends to weaken inflationary pressures.

3.2 Basic monetary regularities

Over the long run there is clear evidence indicating that countries with a high rate of money growth experience a high rate of inflation, and vice versa (see for example, IMF, World Economic Outlook, September 1996)

We begin our discussion of monetary regularities in Israel with Chart 5 which plots the ratio of actual real M1 money balances to GDP against the Bank of Israel interest rate over the period 1989–98. As discussed below, the use of an M1 aggregate is in line with previous research which has documented that of all monetary aggregates, M1 has the closest relationship to inflation and to nominal income in Israel.[13] According to standard monetary theory, the existence of a relatively stable money demand function is an important prerequisite for a well-defined link between money growth and inflation. The impression that the observations in Chart 5 depict a well-behaved money demand function is confirmed by econometric findings, based on quarterly data from 1989 to 1996, which estimated an income elasticity of money demand of about unity, and in an interest-rate elasticity of about -0.2 (evaluated at the sample mean). These parameters were found to be significantly different from zero and we could not reject the hypothesis that they were stable during the sample period.[14]

That Israel is no exception to the general principle that for period averages there is a close link between money growth and inflation is evident from Chart 6, which provides data from 1962 to 1998. It can be seen that for any sub-periods in which there was an acceleration in the rate of inflation, there was an acceleration in the rate of growth of money. And conversely, when the rate of inflation was reduced, money growth was decreased as well. Examining recent periods, note that the escalation of inflation to triple-digit annual rates in 1982–85 was associated with a sharp rise in money growth. In fact, between 1984 and 1985, M1 was growing at an annual rate of about 300%. The period 1986–91 marks the first phase of disinflation, with annual inflation rates of about 16%–18%. At that time, M1 was growing at relatively sizable rates; in particular, M1 growth was about 28% per year in 1991–92. There is reason to believe that these considerable money growth rates had an important explanatory role in accounting for the fact that inflation was *not* reduced below 16%–18% per year at that time. The period 1992–98 is characterised by a lower rate of inflation of about 10% per year. This has been supported by lower money

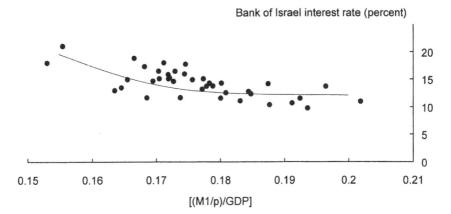

Chart 5 The relation between real money balances and the nominal interest rate
on Bank of Israel funds (1989–98)

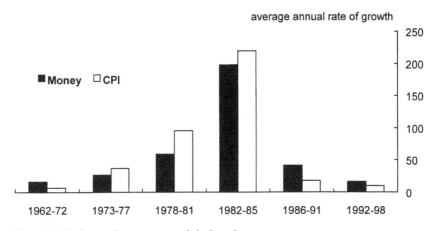

Chart 6 Inflation and money growth in Israel

growth. For example, during 1995–96 M1 grew at about 12% per year,
which is less than one half of the M1 growth rate in 1991–92.

These conclusions on the evolution of monetary policy are strengthened
by examining the (ex ante) expected real interest rate on central bank funds
and by comparing it to real interest rates (or real repo rates) on foreign
central bank funds. As shown in Charts 7 and 8, before 1992 there was a
negative real interest rate on Bank of Israel funds (on average equal to
−2.2% per year for 1989–91), while at the same time real interest rates for
foreign central bank funds were positive. These negative real interest rates
can be taken as another indicator of the existence of a relatively easy monetary policy at that time. This pattern changed after 1992, and especially after
1994, at which time Bank of Israel real rates reached positive territory,

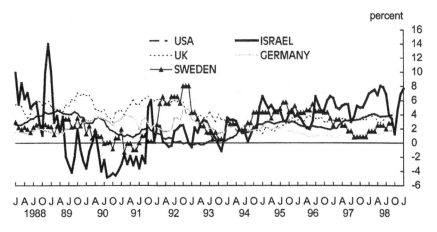

Chart 7 Central bank interest rates, in real terms, Israel and other countries in the world

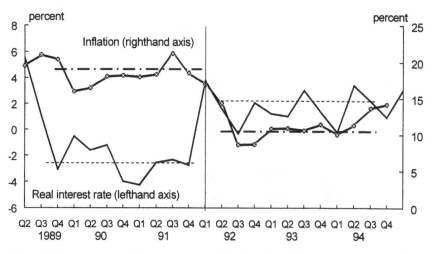

Chart 8 The ex ante real interest rate on Bank of Israel funds and the step-down of inflation in late 1991 (quarterly data)

reaching comparable in magnitude in those abroad, indicating a tighter stance for monetary policy. Since the middle of 1996, and for most of 1997 and 1998, the Bank of Israel maintained its real rate at 5% or more per year, and this contributed (along with other factors) to the reduction in the rate of inflation in 1997 and the first eight months of 1998 to single digits.

3.3 The step-down of inflation: in 1991–92 to about 10% per year; in 1997–98.08 to 7% per year; and in 1999 to about 2.5%

The marked reduction in the rate of inflation to about 10% per year, beginning in late 1991 and early 1992, was the first major development in the process of disinflation since the stabilisation programme of 1985. For more than six years following the initial anti-inflation plan of mid-1985, the rate of inflation had remained in the 16%–20% range, with an average annual rate of 18.1%. Yet from 1992 to 1996, the average annual rate of inflation was about 10%, which coincided with the average upper limit of the government's official inflation target ranges. In what follows we elaborate on some of the factors behind this major development, including the role of monetary variables.

The marked decline in the rate of inflation is documented in Chart 9. After reaching a peak in the third quarter of 1991, the annual rate of inflation fell continuously until the third quarter of 1992. This was true of inflation on a range of definitions, not just of the standard measure based on the consumer price index, such as the wholesale price index, and a measure of underlying inflation which excludes from the CPI highly volatile items such as housing prices and prices of fruits and vegetables, and the shift also applied to forward looking market based inflation expectations.

The explanation for the decline in the rate of inflation to about 10% per year after 1991–92 has become controversial in Israel. It should be emphasised that the reduction in the rate of inflation was *not* the intended result of a pre-conceived set of policy measures undertaken by the authorities. Instead, there is evidence that the reduction in inflation was the outcome of a *combination* of various developments – including monetary and fiscal policies, the labour market, and external fundamentals.

The role of various key economic variables in bringing about disinflation is documented in the six panels in Chart 10. It is possible to group them into four main categories. Consider first external price impulses in the form of

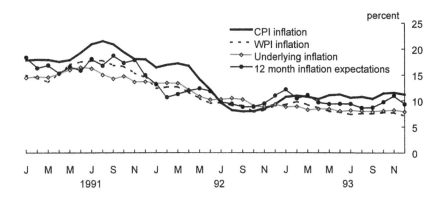

Underlying inflation is a reduced CPI measure that excludes prices of housing, seasonal and volatile items.

Chart 9 The 1991–92 decline in the rate of inflation

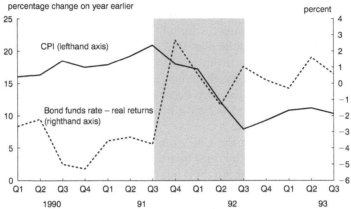

Chart 10a
CPI inflation and the real expected interest rate on BoI funds

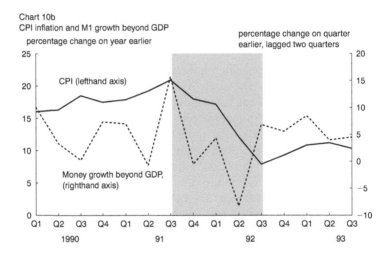

Chart 10b
CPI inflation and M1 growth beyond GDP

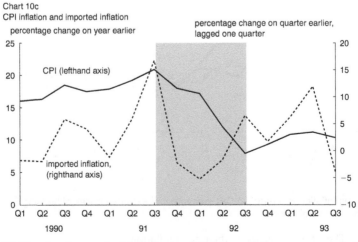

Chart 10c
CPI inflation and imported inflation

Chart 10 The development of inflation and fundamental macroeconomic factors during the 1991–92 inflation step-down

Chart 10d
CPI inflation and quarterly change of public/GDP ratio
percentage change on year earlier

change on quarter earlier,
lagged one quarter

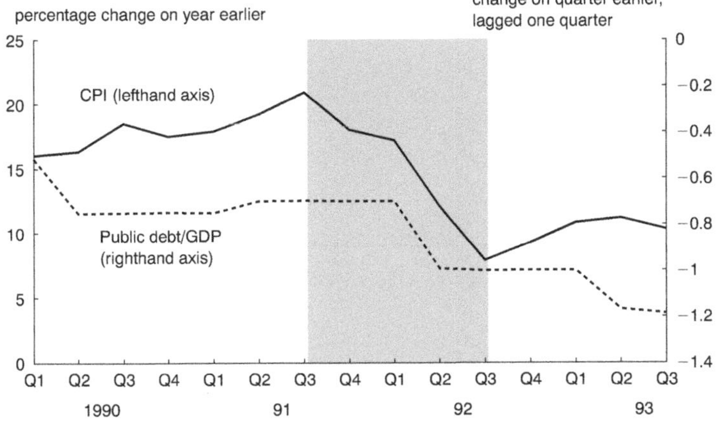

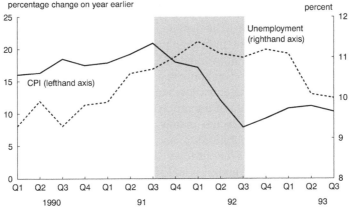

Chart 10e
CPI inflation and unemployment
percentage change on year earlier

percent

Chart 10f
CPI inflation and real wage per employee post
percentage change on year earlier

percentage on tear earlier,
lagged two quarters

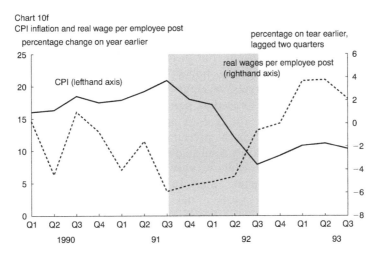

percent

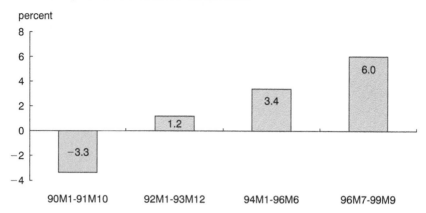

Chart 11 Interest rate on BoI funds, real ex ante terms, annualised period averages[1]

Israel's 'imported' inflation. The decline in Israel's rate of inflation was supported by a substantial drop in foreign price pressures. In fact, import prices
in US dollar terms fell by an average of 5.6% in 1991 and by a further 1.2%
in 1992. A second set of disinflationary factors was related to the labour
market and the state of the economy. Starting in the late 1980s, there was a
considerable rise in the rate of unemployment, from 6.4% in 1988 to 11.2%
in 1992, which initially reflected mainly a major restructuring of business
activities after the 1985 stabilisation, and later reflected the massive inflow
of new immigrants into the labour force. These developments contributed to
attenuate labour market rigidities, and sharply reduced the extent of price
and wage pressures. Accordingly, real wages in the business sector declined
by a cumulative 8% in the period 1989–91, and the official minimum wage
set by government, which was applicable to most of the new immigrants
during their entry into the labour market, declined in real terms for four
consecutive years starting in 1990. Third, as mentioned elsewhere in this
paper, there was an important shift in monetary policy from late 1991 or
early 1992 onward. Specifically, policy began to focus on achieving the
government's inflation targets, which given other developments, required a
tighter stance than in the preceding period. As a result of this shift, there
was a gradual increase in the real, ex ante, interest rate on central bank
funds, from negative levels in the preceding periods to positive rates (Chart
11). This was accompanied by a substantial reduction in the rate of growth
of M1. Last but not least, while various fiscal policy indicators pointed to
continuous tighter discipline after 1985, fiscal policy credibility was
enhanced in 1991 with the passing of the 'law of diminishing budget deficits',
and with a strengthening in the already-existing trend of decline in the ratio
of public-sector debt to GDP.[15]

  To recapitulate, it is hard to find a single economic factor that explains on its own the major reduction in the rate of inflation to about 10% in 1991–92; nor can this reduction be attributed to a single specific decision by the authorities. Instead, foreign price deflation, tight fiscal and monetary policies, and a rise in unemployment, together with a more flexible labour market and the lack of autonomous wage pressures, combined to result in a decline in the rate of inflation, which was then further supported and transformed into a persistent change by the behaviour of fundamentals (and in particular, of monetary policy) in the period that followed.

The second marked reduction in the rate of inflation was from about 10% per year in 1996 to 7% per year in 1997, and to lower than that during most of 1998. The decline of inflation in this episode was rapid and took form in a series of very low CPI inflation figures and even several months of CPI decline in late 1997 and early 1998. In fact, the year-over-year rate of inflation in August 1998 was only 3%.

The marked decline in the rate of inflation is documented in Chart 12. After stabilising during the first half of 1997 at about 10%, the annual rate of inflation started a continued fall. As in the 1991–92 episode, this process was reflected in a range of definitions of inflation, including forward-looking market-based inflation expectations. The decline in inflation continued throughout the third quarter of 1998 and in July 1998 the year over year rate of inflation was only 3%, while market-based inflation expectations were at about 4%, both well below the lower limit of the official 7 to 10% inflation target for 1997–98.

As in the 1991–92 episode, the 1997–98 phase of disinflation occurred with the support of various key economic factors as documented in the three panels in Chart 13. It is possible to group the factors into three main categories. Consider first external price impulses in the form of Israel's 'imported' inflation. As in the 1991–92 episode, the decline in Israel's rate of inflation was supported by a substantial drop in foreign price pressures. A second set of disinflationary factors was related to the state of the

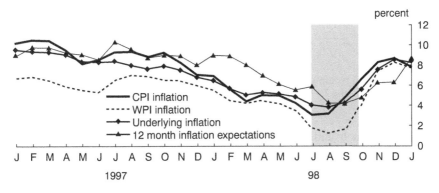

Chart 12 The 1997–98 decline in the rate of inflation

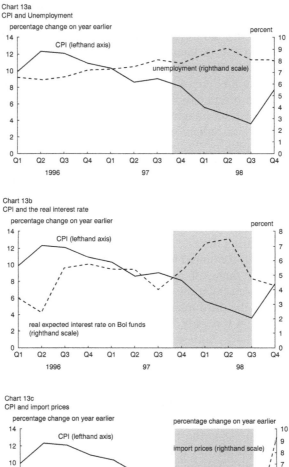

Chart 13a
CPI and Unemployment

Chart 13b
CPI and the real interest rate

Chart 13c
CPI and import prices

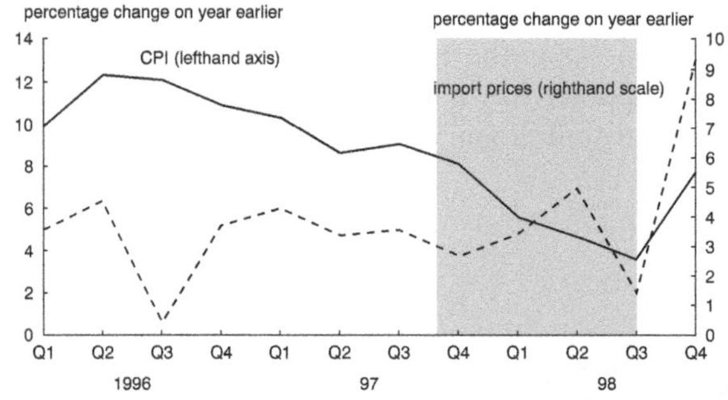

Chart 13 The development of inflation and fundamental macroeconomic factors during the 1997–98 inflation step-down

economy, which had moved away from full employment, and had GDP growth falling from 4.5% in 1996 to only 2% in 1997–98 while unemployment rose from 6.7% in 1996 to 8.7% in 1998. Third, there was an important shift in monetary policy from mid-1996 onward. Specifically, there was a marked increase in the real, ex ante, interest rate on central bank funds,

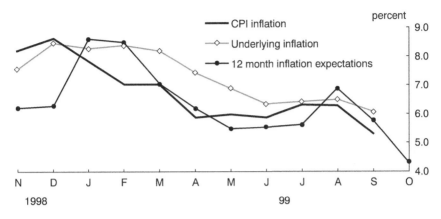

Chart 14 The 1999 decline of the rate of inflation

from about 2% in the first half of 1996 to about 5% to 6% and even higher from mid-1996 onwards. Unlike the 1991–92 episode, the 1997–98 episode did not include a decline of real wages, a factor that seems to have been offset by a greater degree and duration of monetary tightening in the 1997–98 episode than in the 1991–92 episode.

The decline of the rate of inflation in 1998 was interrupted temporarily by the depreciation of the shekel in late 1998. However, following a 4% interest-rate increase and the return to a more tranquil state of affairs in world financial markets, the shekel quickly began to recover. This change, combined with weak growth in domestic demand, enabled the rate of inflation to return to its trend decline, the price level declined in the first half of 1999 (Chart 14).

3.4 A change of monetary regime?

As evident from the discussion in the previous sections, there has been a change in the behaviour of monetary policy in the period from 1992 to the present. In particular, there has been a changing emphasis in the extent to which monetary policy has acted in response to exchange-rate vs. inflation-rate developments. As mentioned before, the advent of inflationary pressures and the absence of foreign exchange market pressures in late 1994 and early 1995 prompted the central bank to act sharply in an attempt to reduce (or eliminate) the deviation of inflation from target.[16] That episode vividly illustrated to the monetary authorities that inflationary pressures might arise through channels other than exchange-rate depreciation and that it would be dangerous to accommodate higher inflation. In a broader sense, this episode marked the transition from a monetary policy focused mainly on maintaining and supporting a nominal exchange rate target (as in the period from 1986 to 1991) to one with the inflation target at its

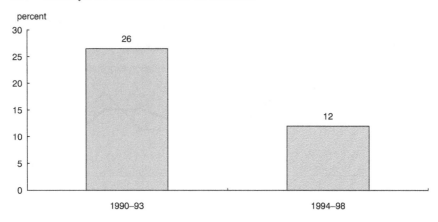

percent

Chart 15 M1 growth, annualised terms

centre. In the latest episode of inflation acceleration, in late 1998, the main focus of the central bank was to limit the impact of the depreciation of the currency to a one-time adjustment of the price level and *not* an adjustment of the rate of inflation. A 400 basis points cumulative increase of the interest rate during this episode helped to curb the rise of 12-month inflation expectations and eventually to return these expectations to a downward path. Charts 11 and 15 document some of the manifestations of that change: the ex ante expected real interest rate on Bank of Israel funds became positive after 1994 and, M1 growth was reduced from 26% on average, per year, in 1990–93 to 11.9% per year in 1994–98. Thus, monetary policy was tighter than before 1992, and helped to consolidate the reduction in the rate of inflation to about 10% per year.

It is useful to discuss further the change in policy focus in terms of a change in the degree of monetary accommodation to present and past changes in the rate of inflation. Monetary theory suggests that a reduction in the degree of monetary accommodation can lead to a reduction in the extent of inflation persistence as well as in the steady-state rate of inflation.[17] In order to assess whether there has been such a change in monetary accommodation, we estimated a bivariate VAR for the rate of inflation and M1 growth using monthly data for two periods, 1988–91 and 1992–98, and we derived impulse responses for the effect of inflation shocks on M1 growth, interpreting these impulse responses as a measure of monetary accommodation. The cumulative impulse responses of M1 to a 1 percentage point shock in the rate of inflation are plotted in Chart 16. The impulse responses for the later period are well below those in the preceding period, thus providing evidence that there is indeed a lower degree of monetary accommodation in the later period than in the earlier period. When added to the previous evidence, this finding provides further

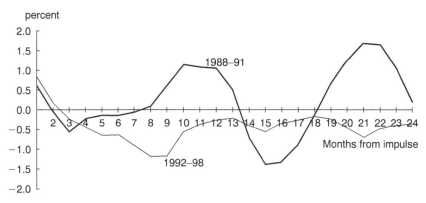

*Based on VARs of M1 growth and inflation for the 1988–91 period and the 1992–98 period

Chart 16 Cumulative response of the rate of change of M1 to a 1% shock to the rate of inflation*

support for the notion that the inflation-target oriented monetary regime of recent years differs significantly from the regime before 1992.

4 Econometric evidence

In this section we provide econometric evidence on the relation between monetary policy variables and the rate of inflation.[18] The first stage in this exploration is to determine which monetary policy variables to use and the lag structure of their impact on the rate of inflation. In the analysis that follows, we used two measures of monetary policy: a monetary aggregate and the ex ante, expected, real interest rate on Bank of Israel funds. As far as the choice of the monetary aggregate is concerned, previous research in Israel has indicated that M1 is the aggregate most closely associated with the rate of inflation. This is confirmed in our work, which shows that there is little additional explanatory power in the non-M1 component of M2. An alternative monetary policy variable was found to have an impact on the rate of inflation, namely the ex ante real interest rate on central bank funds. In summary, over and beyond the role of non-monetary factors in the infla-tion process, our findings indicate that there is a close link between move-ments in the rate of inflation and shifts in money growth in previous periods.

4.1 Estimating inflation equations[19]

The next stage in our research consists of exploring various econometric specifications of the role of monetary and non-monetary variables in accounting for fluctuations in the rate of inflation. Our basic approach is to estimate equations for the rate of inflation as a function of monetary policy variables, the exchange rate, foreign prices, and the rate of unemployment. Although these equations are not formally derived here from a structural model, they represent common reduced-form representations for the rate of inflation that typically arise in standard aggregate demand and supply models of small open economies. Put differently, the estimated equations can be viewed as open-economy empirical counterparts of reduced-form equation (2.4) in Svensson's model of the previous section. Needless to say, a more comprehensive approach would formulate a structural simultaneous equation model of the economy, one in which the exchange rate and the rate of unemployment become truly endogenous variables.

Specifically, equation (4.1), shown in appendix,[20] regresses, by applying instrumental variables and using quarterly data for the period from 1995Q1 to 1999Q3,[21] the rate of inflation of the CPI excluding prices of fruits and vegetables (which in Israel are extremely volatile) against various lags of the following explanatory variables: 'imported' inflation, measured by the rate of change of the nominal exchange rate of the NIS against the US dollar plus the rate of change of the foreign price of imported consumer goods; the rate of change of M1 beyond the rate of real GDP growth, and the rate of unemployment.[22]

The estimated parameters have the expected signs and are significantly different from zero. Specifically, the 'imported' inflation variable affects domestic inflation with relatively short lags; the monetary variable is positive and significant for lags of three and four quarters; and the unemployment variable has a negative sign and appears with a one-quarter lag. The equation's diagnostics indicate the lack of first-order serial correlation in the residuals and a relatively high explanatory power, in spite of the absence of the lagged dependent variable (which was used as an explanatory variable in several previous inflation equations in Israel).

In order to examine the potential explanatory role of a wider monetary aggregate, equation (4.2) (Table 3 of the appendix) expands the previous inflation equation to include the rate of growth of the non-M1 component of M2 beyond the real GDP growth rate. The test for the statistical significance of the block of added variables indicates non-rejection (at standard significance levels) of the hypothesis that these variables have no marginal explanatory power for fluctuations in the rate of inflation. In contrast, when similar tests were conducted separately for the 'imported' inflation and M1-growth variables, the null-hypothesis was rejected, indicating that these variables significantly account for movements in the rate of inflation.

Another extension of the basic inflation equation consists of replacing the previous dependent variable with a rate of inflation that excludes housing prices (in addition to the previously excluded prices of fruits and vegetables). The results of estimating this equation 4.3 are presented in Table 4 of the appendix. Most explanatory variables – including monetary variables – remain with the expected signs and significance as before, yet the coefficients on the 'imported' inflation and monetary variables are now generally lower than in the previous specification.

Turning to the case where monetary policy is represented by the ex ante real interest rate on central bank funds, the basic estimated relation is equation (4.4) estimated in Table 5. The rate of inflation at quarter t is found to be related to the real interest rate at quarter $t-4$, and the estimated coefficient is -0.13. Interestingly, the absolute values of the coefficients on the 'imported' inflation and unemployment variables are similar to those in the previous (M1-growth) specification. The estimated equation diagnostics are satisfactory. This general pattern of results applies to the case in which the dependent variable excludes housing-price inflation; in particular, there is a strong negative and significant effect of the real interest rate on the rate of change of the consumer price index excluding fruits, vegetables, and housing.

4.2   *Inflation rate impulse responses to monetary shocks*

Although a relatively plausible set of results was obtained from the above inflation equations, it was produced in the context of restricted reduced-form specifications. It is well to examine whether similar results about the impact of monetary variables on the rate of inflation arises in more unrestricted specifications, such as in vector autoregressions (VARs). Accordingly, we estimated a four-variable VAR that included current and lagged values of the rate of inflation, imported inflation, money growth in excess of real GDP growth or, alternatively, the ex ante real interest rate on central bank funds, and the rate of unemployment – all defined exactly as they appeared in the foregoing inflation equations. The estimation period was 1990 to 1998 (quarterly). Two systems of VAR were estimated based on the two alternative definitions of the monetary policy variable.

Based on these estimates, impulse responses were derived for the rate of inflation as a function of an innovation (i.e. a unit shock) in the monetary policy variable. These impulse response functions are given in Charts 17 and 18. From Chart 17, we see that a positive unit shock to the rate of growth of M1 net of the rate of growth of real GDP leads to an acceleration in the rate of inflation for a number of subsequent quarters. The peak impact of money growth on inflation arises four quarters after the shock, much as in the above estimated equations. Interestingly, the quantitative impact of the money-growth shock on the rate of inflation is of the same order of magnitude as the estimated coefficients on these monetary variables in the inflation equations.[23] A similar finding arises from Chart 18 for the impact of ex ante real interest-rate shocks. A rise in the real interest rate is associated with a reduction in the rate of inflation in subsequent quarters, and the orders of magnitude are about the same as those in the estimated inflation equations. In conclusion, empirically assessing the

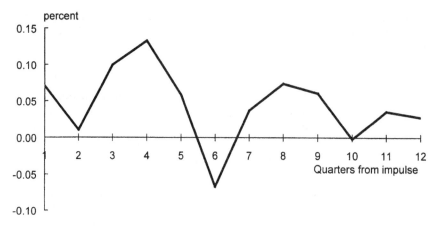

Chart 17 Response of the quarterly rate of change of the CPI excluding fruits and vegetables to a 1% shock to the rate of money growth in excess of real GDP growth

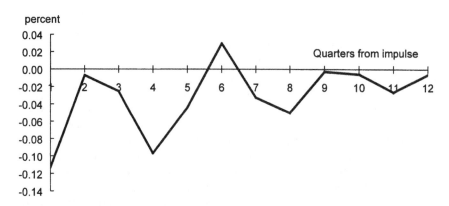

Chart 18 Response of the quarterly rate of change of the CPI excluding fruits and vegetables to a 1% shock to the real, ex ante, interest rate on Bank of Israel funds

impact of monetary policy variables on the rate of inflation in the context of a relatively unrestricted time-series model (such as a VAR) yields results generally similar to those derived from estimating restricted reduced form specifications. Thus, we interpret the findings as providing further support to these specifications.

4.3   *Pass-through from exchange rates to prices*

A common concern in countries that have moved away from tight targeting of nominal exchange rates is that increased variability of exchange rates may be passed on to prices. The concern is especially strong in economies with a high-inflation history, such as several in Latin America as well as Israel. Accumulated evidence from chronic inflation episodes indeed indicates a substantial pass-through from nominal exchange rates to prices. In this section we discuss some new evidence on this issue.

Previous theoretical work has suggested that several considerations determine the degree of pass-through from exchange rates to prices in a given economy. Central among them are market structure, product characteristics, and pricing practices of domestic and foreign firms. In models of imperfect competition and differentiated products, optimal firm behaviour can be characterised by a price-to-market strategy. Accordingly, when exchange rates and costs change, firms will not immediately translate those into price changes, because doing that could reduce market share. Thus, firms' price marginal cost markups absorb some of these fluctuations. The degree of pass-through will depend on a measure of competition and on the relative number of domestic and foreign firms. Other models focus directly on the existence of costs to entry and exit and to changing prices. Given these costs, a key factor that determines the extent of pass-through is whether exchange-rate changes are viewed as permanent or transitory. Other things equal, the degree of pass-through will be higher for permanent than for transitory exchange rate changes. The analysis becomes more complex when taken to the macroeconomic level, because there could be shocks to fundamentals that may alter the equilibrium value of the real exchange rate, in which case there could be incomplete pass-through even under full competition and information. Empirically, most of the evidence suggests that there is less-than-full pass-through across a broad range of countries and products.

It is plausible to hypothesise that the pass-through coefficient might depend on the state of the business cycle; the closer actual output is to potential output, the higher the degree of pass-through. We address this issue in an initial and preliminary way by estimating an inflation rate equation for Israel using two main explanatory variables: the rate of exchange-rate depreciation-to capture *short-term* pass-through effects, and the real interest rate on central bank funds. In order to quantify the notion that the degree of short-term pass-through may depend on the state of the business cycle, we allow for non-linear dependence of the exchange rate depreciation coefficient on a real variable such as the rate of unemployment and/or other indicators of economic activity such as GDP growth. The following equation was estimated for Israel using quarterly data for the period,

$$\pi_t = \beta_0 + (\beta_1 + \beta_2 \bar{U}_{t-1})\Delta\log(e_t) + \beta_3 R_{t-1} + \epsilon_t$$

where π is the rate of quarterly inflation, $\bar{U}$ is a four-quarter moving average of the rate of unemployment, e is the quarterly rate of change of the nominal exchange rate of the NIS *vis-à-vis* the dollar plus the rate of

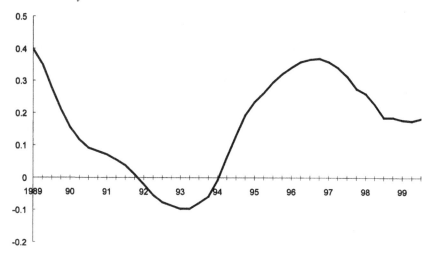

Chart 19 Time varying short-term pass-through coefficient from the exchange rate
to prices

change of the price index of imported private consumption, and R is the
real ex ante rate on central bank funds.

The regression results are shown in Table 6. The estimates indicate that,
other things equal, an increase in the rate of unemployment tends to
decrease the degree of short-term pass-through from the exchange rate to
prices. Chart 19 shows a time-varying pass-through coefficient that is
based on this equation. The value of the coefficient is calculated using the
parameter estimates of β_1 and β_2 and the moving average of the rate of
unemployment. As evident, the rate of short-term pass-through was relatively high during the first few years after the 1985 stabilisation programme
(close to 0.5). The rate of short-term pass-through declined continuously
from 1989 to late 1992 along with increases in the rate of unemployment.
From 1993 through 1996, the degree of short-term pass-through is on an
upward trend parallel to a reduction in the rate of unemployment and a
boom in economic activity. From 1997 onwards the short-term pass-
through coefficient has declined parallel to the slowdown of economic
growth. It appears that the decline of this coefficient has come to a halt in
1998 and that a slight increase may have started to develop in 1999, parallel to the start of a recovery of domestic demand. The main conclusions
from these estimates are that in the short-term, exchange-rate changes are
only partially passed through to prices, and that the degree of pass-
through depends on the state of the business cycle.

5 Conclusions

The Israeli experience with inflation targets offers useful insights for the conduct of monetary policy in both advanced and developing countries. Our first task in this paper was to document a set of basic empirical regularities on the relation between monetary policy variables and the rate of inflation for the period beginning in the late 1980s up to the present. We found that when lags, and the role of other explanatory variables, are properly taken into account, there is a close association between movements in the rate of inflation and shifts in monetary policy variables. In particular, in spite of the well-known turbulence of the Israeli economy over this period, we found that relatively simple econometric specifications of inflation equations, relating the rate of inflation to current and lagged measures of 'imported' inflation, of monetary policy (i.e. the rate of growth of M1 beyond GDP growth, or the ex ante real interest rate on central bank funds), and the rate of unemployment account relatively well for fluctuations in the rate of inflation.

In discussing the evolution of monetary policy regimes in Israel, we then noted that, since the exchange rate based stabilisation programme of 1985, there has been a gradual shift toward increased flexibility of the nominal exchange rate coupled with increased emphasis on inflation targeting.[24] Current monetary policy is oriented toward achieving the inflation target set by government while at the same time, maintaining and supporting the crawling band for the exchange rate of the NIS against a basket of foreign currencies. The inflation target range for the years 2000 and 2001 is 3%–4%, the central bank does not intervene in the foreign-exchange market, and the exchange-rate band has ample width (of close to 40%). Monetary policy is now conducted along the lines of what Svensson (1997a) has termed 'inflation-forecast targeting'; that is, adjustments in monetary policy instruments are made when discrepancies arise between central bank's forward-looking forecast of the rate of inflation in the relevant future and the inflation target. To the extent that these adjustments lead to foreign exchange market pressures on the limits of the exchange-rate band, sterilised intervention in the forex market is implemented in order to support and defend this band. We emphasised that recent experience illustrated some of the difficulties that arise – especially under a high degree of international capital mobility – when one policy instrument (the interest rate on central bank funds, for example) has to support two objectives: the inflation target and the crawling exchange-rate band. However, some of the potential conflicts between these nominal targets have been avoided by expanding the width of the band to the point that currently the official inflation target is the key objective of monetary policy, and the nominal exchange rate has become more of an indicator than an intermediate target.[25]

Special attention was given in our analysis to the reduction in the rate of inflation from about 16%–20% in the period before 1991–92 to about 10% in 1992–96, and further to 7% in 1997 and about 3% in mid-1998 and 1999. We stressed that in these episodes of marked reduction in the rate of inflation there was a combination of fundamentals and other factors – such as fiscal, monetary, labour market, and external developments – that all contributed towards this outcome. Not surprisingly, once the rate of inflation shifted sharply, monetary policy played a key role in consolidating that into a persistent change in the periods that followed.

In addition, the analysis of monetary developments in recent years illustrated how monetary policy can become severely overburdened in an attempt to achieve the official inflation target when other key factors – such as fiscal policy, the state of the business cycle, and public sector wage policy – create strong inflationary pressures. Two salient episodes of such overburdening occurred in late 1994 and in the first half of 1996, when the underlying trends indicated a convergence to annual inflation of about 15%, a figure much higher than the official target. In both of these cases, restrictive monetary policy measures were taken and, for a short time, ex ante real interest rates on central bank funds reached about 5%, or higher, per year. The decision that monetary policy would not accommodate a rate of inflation of about 15%, and the resulting restrictive measures contributed to reducing the rate of inflation toward the official target, so that the deviation from target was merely transitory. As indicated before, much of the public debate in Israel about monetary policy and disinflation was triggered by these two episodes, both of which represented a severe challenge to the inflation targets and an overburdening of monetary policy.

Although the Israeli economy has not been subject to the discipline of the Maastricht convergence criteria, further disinflation is an important policy objective. In setting the inflation target range as 7%–10% for 1997, the government stressed its aim to generate a multi-year gradual convergence of the rate of inflation to that in OECD economies by the year 2001. In setting the same inflation target range for 1998 the government also stressed the aim to make progress at disinflation in 1998, within that range, and to create the conditions for future convergence to the inflation rates of the industrial countries: the inflation target range for the years 2000 and 2001 is 3%–4%. Based on the findings of our research work, monetary policy has a key role to play in achieving convergence of Israel's inflation to that in western economies. However, there are other key policy players whose actions can also contribute to disinflation and can help reduce, as far as possible, the economic and other costs of the convergence process. These are fiscal policy, wage policy, and competition-enhancing structural changes. Israel's experience supports the notion that the greater the coherence between the various types of macroeconomic policies from the standpoint of disinflation – and the smaller the extent of reliance (or overburdening) on a single set of policy measures – the smoother will be the transition to persistent single-digit rates of inflation.

APPENDIX

In this appendix the notations are as follows:

PAIX = Quarterly rate of change of the CPI excluding fruit and vegetables.

PAIXH = Quarterly rate of change of the CPI excluding housing, fruit and vegetables.

DEMP2 = Quarterly rate of change of the exchange rate of the NIS *vis-à-vis* the dollar + the rate of change of the price index of imported private consumption.

DDOL = Quarterly rate of change of the exchange rate of the NIS *vis-à-vis* the dollar.

DIMPRICE = Quarterly rate of change of the price index of imported private consumption (dollar terms).

RMIC = Real ex ante BoI interest rate, in annualised terms.

DMY = Quarterly rate of change of M1/GDP.

DMYA = 2-quarter moving average of the rate of change of M1/GDP.

DM12Y = Quarterly rate of change of (M2 − M1)/GDP.

DM12Ya = 2-quarter moving average of the rate of change of (M2 − M1)/GDP.

MU4 = 4-quarter moving average of the rate of unemployment.

U = Quarterly rate of unemployment.

D2 = Dummy variable for Q2 of each year.

Table 2 Estimates of equation 4.1[*]

Method: Two-stage least squares. Sample (adjusted): 1995Q1–1999Q3. Observations (19).

Regression of PAIX on	Coefficient	Std. Error	t-Statistic	Prob.
Constant	0.077	0.017	4.601	0.0005
DEPM2	0.299	0.067	4.426	0.0007
DEPM2(−1)	0.096	0.042	2.293	0.0391
DMY(−3)	0.091	0.019	4.665	0.0004
DMY(−4)	0.111	0.041	2.679	0.0189
U(−1)	−0.913	0.254	−3.60	0.0032
R-squared	0.74	Durbin-Watson stat		1.72
Adjusted R-squared	0.64			
S.E. of regression	0.0077			
F-statistic	6.58	Prob (F-statistic)		0.003

[*] Newey-West HAC standard errors and covariance (lag truncation = 2). Instruments used are DDOL(−1), DDOL(−2), DDOL(−3), DIMPRICE(−1), DIMPRICE(−2), DIMPRICE(−3), DMY(−2), DMY(−3), DMY(−4), DMY(−5), U(−1), U(−2) and U(−3).

Table 3 Estimates of equation 4.2*

Method: Two-stage least squares. Sample (adjusted): 1995Q1–1999Q3. Observations (19).

Regression of PAIX on	Coefficient	Std. Error	t-Statistic	Prob.
Constant	0.069	0.019	3.537	0.004
DEPM2	0.304	0.047	6.516	0.000
DEPM2(−1)	0.093	0.031	3.031	0.010
DMYA(−3)	0.170	0.055	3.070	0.009
DM12YA(−3)	0.060	0.061	0.989	0.341
U(−1)	−0.839	0.253	−3.318	0.006
R-squared	0.77		Durbin-Watson stat	1.581
Adjusted R-squared	0.68			
S.E. of regression	0.0073			
F-statistic	8.70		Prob (F-statistic)	0.0001
Null hypothesis: DEPM2 DEPM2(−1) are redundant	F-stat 14.307		Prob. (F-statistic)	0.0005

* Newey-West HAC standard errors and covariance (lag truncation = 2). Instruments used are DDOL(−1), DDOL(−2), DDOL(−3), DIMPRICE(−1), DIMPRICE(−2), DIMPRICE(−3), DMY(−1), DMY(−2), DMY(−3), DMY(−4), DMY(−5), DM12Y(−5), DM12Y(−3), DM12Y(−4), DM12Y(−2), U(−2), U(−3), U(−4), U(−5).

Table 4 Estimates of equation 4.3*

Method: Two-stage least squares. Sample (adjusted): 1995Q1–1999Q3. Observations (18).

Regression of PAIX on	Coefficient	Std. Error	t-Statistic	Prob.
Constant	0.063	0.018	3.62	0.003
DEPM2	0.240	0.096	2.51	0.028
DEPM2(−1)	0.107	0.0580	1.84	0.090
DMY(−3)	0.090	0.030	2.98	0.012
DMY(−4)	0.079	0.048	1.65	0.124
U(−1)	−0.713	0.246	−2.90	0.013
R-squared	0.62		Durbin-Watson stat	1.866
Adjusted R-squared	0.46			
S.E. of regression	0.0078			
F-statistic	3.83		Prob (F-statistic)	0.026

* White heteroskedasticity-consistent standard errors and covariance. Instruments used are DDOL(−1), DDOL(−2), DDOL(−3), DIMPRICE(−1), DIMPRICE(−2), DIMPRICE(−3), DMY(−1), DMY(−3), DMY(−4), DMY(−5), U(−1), U(−2), U(−3) and U(−4).

Table 5 Estimates of equation 4.4[*]

Method: Two-stage least squares. Sample (adjusted): 1995Q1–1999Q3. Observations (19).

Regression of PAIX on	Coefficient	Std. Error	t-Statistic	Prob.
Constant	0.079	0.023	3.44	0.004
DEPM2	0.300	0.090	3.32	0.005
DEPM2(-1)	0.126	0.068	1.86	0.085
RMIC(-4)	0.135	0.089	-1.51	0.153
U(-3)	-0.816	0.308	-2.65	0.0191
R-squared	0.67		Durbin-Watson stat	1.570
Adjusted R-squared	0.58			
S.E. of regression	0.0084			
F-statistic	6.216		Prob (F-statistic)	0.004

[*] White heteroskedasticity-consistent standard errors and covariance. Instruments used are DDOL(-1), DDOL(-2), DDOL(-3), DDOL(-4), DIMPRICE(-1), DIMPRICE(-2), DIMPRICE(-3), RMIC(-4), RMIC(-5), RMIC(-3), and M4U(-1).

Table 6 Estimates of equation 4.5[*]

Method: Two-stage least squares. Sample (adjusted): 1989Q1–1999Q2. Observations (42).

Regression of PAIX on	Coefficient	Std. Error	t-Statistic	Prob.
Constant	0.033	0.003	10.858	0.000
DEPM2	1.041	0.341	3.055	0.004
DEPM2*M4U(-1)	-10.185	3.683	-2.765	0.008
RMIC(-1)	-0.311	0.071	-4.388	0.000
R-squared	0.55		Durbin-Watson stat	1.956
Adjusted R-squared	0.52			
S.E. of regression	0.011			
F-statistic	8.16		Prob (F-statistic)	0.000

[*] White heteroskedasticity-consistent standard errors and covariance. Instruments used are DDOL(-1), DDOL(-2), DDOL(-3), DIMPRICE(-1), DIMPRICE(-2), DIM-PRICE(-3), RBI(-1), RBI(-2), U(-1), U(-2), U(-3), and U(-4).

Notes

1 Parts of the paper draw heavily from and extend our previous research paper 'Monetary Policy and Inflation in Israel', Discussion Paper 98.04, Research Department, The Bank of Israel, March 1998. Bufman is a private economic consultant, and Leiderman is Senior Director, Research Department, Bank of Israel, and Professor at the Berglas School of Economics at Tel-Aviv University. The views expressed in the Paper are the sole responsibility of the authors. We thank Yoav Paz and Gil Laufer for their valuable research assistance.

2 On the role of fiscal policy in the inflation process in Israel, see e.g. Bruno (1993), Leiderman (1993), and Dahan and Strawczynski (1997).

3 Some of the specifications that we use are similar to those developed in recent years in important work by Azoulay and Elkayam (see Bibliography).

4 For description and analysis of monetary and exchange rate policies in recent years, see e.g. Bruno (1993), Leiderman (1993), Helpman, Leiderman, and Bufman (1994), Bufman, Leiderman and Sokoler (1995), Leiderman and Bufman (1996), and Sokoler (1997).

5 See Bufman, Leiderman, and Sokoler (1995) for a more detailed discussion of the history of the adoption of inflation targets in Israel.

6 As shown in Svensson (1997a), the model can be extended to incorporate an LM relation through inclusion of the money market. This would enable one to determine a 'steady state' value for the rate of inflation, π.

7 As shown by Svensson, to the extent that the loss function of the central bank includes also deviations of output from potential output, the optimal interest rate rule is of the same form as equation (2.8), yet the absolute value of the b_1 coefficient is smaller, and the absolute value of the b_2 coefficient is larger, than for the loss function in the text. Extending the basic model to a small open economy would introduce additional transmission mechanisms for monetary policy, especially through its impact on nominal and real exchange rates.

8 For a more detailed discussion of these and related developments, see Bank of Israel, *Annual Report*, issues from recent years.

9 In terms of Svensson's model, it is as if all of the right-hand side terms in equation (2.8) increased, thus calling for an upward shift in the central bank nominal interest rate.

10 Specifically, the slope of the crawl (in annual terms) was set equal to the difference between the inflation target and a forecast of foreign inflation.

11 For a detailed discussion of transmission mechanisms in a small open economy, see *The Transmission of Monetary Policy in Canada*, Bank of Canada, 1996.

12 Svensson (1997b) shows that his original model, discussed above, can be extended to incorporate a money market, including a money demand function as implicit in equation (3.1).

13 For example, Cohen and Soreni (1995) found that M1 was the monetary aggregate most closely correlated with nominal GDP.

14 The estimated equation is:

$$Log\left(\frac{M1_t}{P_t}\right) = \frac{-6.564 - 1.416 \cdot i_t + 1.063 \cdot Log(GDP_t)}{(11.897) \quad (5.822) \qquad (19.870)}$$

DW $= 1.420$, Adj. $R^2 = 0.908$. Numbers in parentheses are the t values of the parameter estimates. Sample period: 1990–96, quarterly data.

Similar money demand equations have been estimated in Israel, see for example Azoulay and Elkayam (1996).

15 On the role of fiscal policy variables in the inflation process, see Dahan and Strawczynski (1997).

16 On the changing emphasis see also the detailed discussion by Sokoler (1997).

17 See e.g. the analysis in Obstfeld (1995).

18 For early evidence on the effects of changes in the quantity of money on prices in Israel, from 1955 to 1965, see Kleiman and Ophir (1975).

19 As indicated (see footnote 2), some of the specifications discussed below are similar to those in important previous empirical work by Azoulay and Elkayam (see Bibliography).

20 For convenience, all estimated equations and diagnostics are given in the Appendix.

21 Lengthening the sample period by using an earlier beginning date did not have a substantial impact on parameter stability; see for example equation (4.5). Nonetheless, we preferred the 1995–99 period, as it was more uniform from the perspective of the prevailing inflation environment and the focus of monetary policy.
22 At a preliminary stage of this investigation, we searched various possible lags for the explanatory variables. The specifications reported here and below are those which were found most satisfactory from the goodness-of-fit perspective. Note that the estimated equations typically include a constant term and a seasonal dummy variable for the second quarter of each year.
23 As shown in Chart 20, the cumulative response of inflation to a 1% shock of the rate of money growth is 0.33%. Similarly, the results of the econometric inflation equations (see e.g. equation 4.1), show that the sum of the point estimates of the money growth parameters is 0.34.
24 Similar trends in the evolution of monetary policy and exchange-rate policy have been observed in other countries – such as Chile and Mexico – that undertook exchange-rate-based disinflation programmes.
25 In fact, most inflation targeting countries are now operating under relatively free floating exchange rate regimes. At the same time, it is recognised that the effects of monetary policy on the nominal exchange rate play a key role in the transmission mechanism of this policy.

Bibliography

Adams, C., Mathieson, D. and Schinasi, G. (eds) (1999), *International Capital Markets: Developments, Prospects and Key Policy Issues*, World Economic and Financial Surveys, International Monetary Fund.

Azoulay, Eddy and David Elkayam (1996a), 'The influence of the development of money on inflation in Israel during recent years (1987–1994)', *The Economic Quarterly* (Hebrew), 1/96.

Azoulay, Eddy and David Elkayam (1996b), 'The influence of monetary policy on activity and prices in Israel (1988–1996)', *Internal Discussion Paper,* Monetary Department, Bank of Israel.

Azoulay, Eddy and David Elkayam (1997), 'A model of the effect of monetary policy on economic activity and inflation in Israel, 1988–1996', Bank of Israel, Monetary Department, *Occasional Paper,* No. 1 (Hebrew, forthcoming), June.

Bruno, M. (1993), *Crisis, Stabilization and Economic Reform: Therapy by Consensus,* Oxford: Oxford University Press.

Bufman, G., Leiderman, L. and Sokoler, M. (1995), 'Israel's experience with explicit inflation targets: a first assessment', in Leiderman, L. and Svensson, L.E.O. (eds) (1995).

Cohen and Soreni (1995), 'Identifying an intermediate target for monetary policy in Israel 1988–1994', *Discussion Paper*, 95.13, Research Department, Bank of Israel.

Crockett, A. (1993), 'Monetary policy implications of increased capital flows'. Presented at the symposium on 'Changing Capital Markets: Implications for Monetary Policy', Federal Reserve Bank of Kansas City, Jackson Hole, August.

Dahan, M. and Strawczynski, M. (1997), 'Fiscal policy and inflation in Israel', *Working Paper,* Research Department, Bank of Israel.

Helpman, E., Leiderman, L., and Bufman, G. (1994), 'A new breed of exchange rate bands: Chile, Israel, and Mexico', *Economic Policy*, 19, pp. 259–306, October.

Kleiman, E. and Ophir, T. (1975), 'The effects of changes in the quantity of money on prices in Israel, 1955–65', Bank of Israel, *Economic Review*, 42, pp. 15–45, January.

Leiderman, L. (1993), *Inflation and Disinflation: The Israeli Experiment*, Chicago: University of Chicago Press.

Leiderman, L. and Svensson, L.E.O. (eds) (1995), *Inflation Targets*, London: CEPR.

Leiderman, L. and Bufman, G. (1996), 'Searching for nominal anchors in shock-prone economies in the 1990s: inflation targets and exchange rates bands', in Hausmann, R. and Reisen, H. (eds) (1996), *Securing Stability and Growth in Latin America: Policy Issues and Prospects for Shock-Prone Economies*, OECD, Paris, France.

Obstfeld, M. (1995), 'International currency experience: new lessons and lessons relearned', *Brookings Papers on Economic Activity*, 1, pp. 119–96.

Poole, W. (1994), 'Monetary aggregates targeting in low inflation economies', in Fuhrer, J.C. (ed.) *Goals, Guidelines, and Constraints Facing Monetary Policy-makers*, Federal Reserve Bank of Boston.

Sokoler, M. (1997), 'Credibility half-won in an ongoing battle: an analysis of inflation targets and monetary policy in Israel', Working Paper joint with members of the Monetary Department, Bank of Israel.

Svensson, L.E.O. (1997a) (forthcoming), 'Inflation forecast targeting: implementing and monitoring inflation targets', *European Economic Review*, 41 (6). June, pp. 1111–46.

Svensson, L.E.O. (1997b), 'Inflation targets: some extensions', *NBER Working Paper*, 5962.

Taylor, J.B. (1994), 'Discretion versus policy rules in practice', *Carnegie Rochester Conference Series on Public Policy*, 39 (Autumn), pp. 195–214.

Inflation targeting in the Czech Republic

Miroslav Hrnčíř and Kateřina Šmídková[1]

1   The search for a new strategy

In December 1997, the Czech National Bank (CNB) announced a switch to inflation targeting. After eight years of relying on three strategies based on intermediate targets (see Table 1 for summary[2]), this represented an historic change in the strategy of Czech monetary policy with regard to the way in which policy reacts to economic shocks. The long-run strategy has not changed as much, however, as the stability of the Czech koruna has been the ultimate monetary policy target of the CNB since the very beginning of the Bank's existence[3] and its monetary strategies have always been derived from the necessity of ensuring disinflation subject to the constraints imposed by the process of transition.[4]

Between 1993 and 1995 the koruna was pegged to a basket of currencies, and the money supply was used as a complementary intermediate target.[5] In 1996, the stability of both the money supply and the exchange rate were affected by large capital inflows as well as by financial innovations, and liberalisation. The koruna was still pegged to a basket, but the fluctuation band was widened as a response to the capital inflows, and intervention on the foreign-exchange market became rare. The monetary target gained in importance. In May 1997, after exchange-rate turbulence,[6] the CNB let the koruna float and undertook an intensive search for a new monetary policy strategy.

At that time there were three major arguments in favour of inflation targeting. First, after having hovered around 9%–10% for three years, inflation increased in late 1997 and was well above single digits in early 1998. Consequently, the key policy issue became the need to provide an anchor for inflation expectations. Previous strategies had been insufficient to reduce inflation expectations[7] in the changing conditions of successive of economic transition stages. A new strategy was needed, and inflation targeting offered an attractive option. Unlike previous non-binding annual forecasts, inflation targeting involved the public commitment by the CNB to the unambiguous declaration of the medium-term disinflation path. Accordingly, economic agents would be provided with a new

Table 1 Targets and inflation forecasts 1993–97

	Forecast of CPI inflation (%)	Intermediate Target: Money supply growth (%)	Intermediate Target: exchange rate peg	Operational target
1993	15 (18)	complementary 16 ± 1 (21)	'92' peg fluctuation band 0.5%	monetary base
1994	10 (10)	complementary 13.5 ± 1.5 (22)	'92' peg fluctuation band 0.5%	free reserves
1995	9 (9)	complementary 15.5 ± 1.5 (19)	'92' peg fluctuation band 0.75%	free reserves with overriding rule
1996	9 (9)	15 ± 2 (8)	'92' peg fluctuation band 7.5%	short-term rates
1997	8 (9)	10 ± 2 (10)	'92' peg fluctuation band 7.5% May: koruna floats	short-term rates

Note: Annual Reports data are from CNB and annual monetary documents prepared each December. Although some targets were modified during the year, we do not report the modifications here for the sake of simplicity. For example, in 1994, the target for money-supply growth was modified upwards owing to capital inflows, but the growth exceeded the upper limit. Outcomes are in parentheses. CPI inflation deviated from the forecast in two periods when monetary policy decisions were subject to uncertainty: after the VAT reform in 1993 and during the exchange-rate turbulence in 1997.

medium-term nominal anchor on which they could base their expectations and decisions. This new nominal anchor would also supply economic agents with a longer time horizon than annual forecasts.

A second argument in favour of inflation targeting is that under conditions of financial openness and 'transitional' innovation, the intermediate targets used previously showed increased inconsistency with the long-term target of price stability (see Chart 1). Specifically, the open-capital account and increasingly liberalised and innovative financial markets made massive capital flows possible. Such flows started to dominate exchange-rate developments, especially in the short run. Defending the peg thus implied increased volatility in other important macroeconomic indicators, and subsequently caused deviations from the desired disinflation path. The links between money supply, which was the operational target and inflation, became difficult to predict. In addition to the impact of capital flows, velocity was affected by profound changes to financial markets within a relatively short time span. Consequently, monetary targeting was not a reliable basis for the medium-term disinflation strategy. Inflation targeting, on the other hand, provided a framework for integrated a broader set of economic indicators (including the previously used intermediate targets).[8]

Chart 1 illustrates the contradiction between signals sent by the CPI forecast and the intermediate targets. In 1993, both intermediate targets were met but the CPI inflation exceeded the forecast. In the following three years, the koruna index remained within its bands and the CPI inflation was in accordance with the forecasts but monetary targets were over-

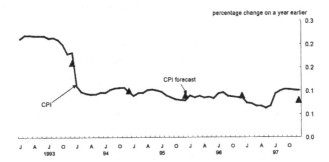

Chart 1a Inflation and the inflation forecast (1993–97)

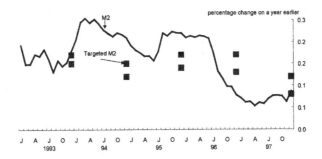

Chart 1b Intermediate M2 targets (1993–97)

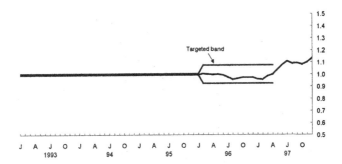

Chart 1c Koruna index (1993–97)

shot. In 1996, there was an appreciation of the koruna after the bands had been widened and CPI inflation was in accordance with the forecast but the monetary target was undershot. In 1997 the lower band of the monetary target was hit and CPI inflation was in accordance with the forecasts, but there was a depreciation of the koruna after the bands had been abandoned in May.

Third, the type of inflation targeting adopted by CNB has provided a scheme for filtering out transitional price shocks from 'market' inflation pressures. The concept of *net inflation* used for target purposes excludes from the CPI the primary impact of changes in administered prices as well as the effects of changes in indirect taxes. Consequently, targeting net inflation helped monetary policy to accommodate the primary inflation impulses of transitional shocks and to smooth their secondary effects. This function is still important as there remains much uncertainty regarding the scale and speed of future adjustment of administered prices.

2   Implementation of inflation targeting in the Czech Republic

The implementation of inflation targeting in the Czech Republic has had two important features. First, in December 1997, targets were specified explicitly in terms of net inflation, which excludes the first-round effects of changes in administered prices and indirect taxes. The exclusion of regulated prices was supported by the fact that the data available at the time clearly demonstrated that there had been different short-run dynamics in the two price segments (Chart 2). It was expected that such differences would continue for several years and that the effect would diminish gradually over the medium term as regulated prices converged with competitive levels. With elections scheduled for June 1998, uncertainty about adjustments to regulated prices was relatively high.

For the purposes of inflation targeting, the Czech Statistical Office calculated an historical net inflation index. The consumer basket was adjusted to exclude items with regulated prices and prices affected by other administrative measures. As currently defined, the net inflation index represents approximately 82% of the consumer price index. It covers 663 of its 754 items.[9] The weights and components of this index can be changed from year to year if there is a change in the government's approach to price adjustments.[10]

As a result of short-run deviations between administered and free prices shown in Chart 2 the forecast of overall CPI inflation is not considered the most reliable indicator of the medium-term inflation outlook. The divergence of the two inflation indicators in 1995, 1997, and again in 1998 has shown net inflation to be a useful tool for policy-makers.

The second feature of the Czech approach to inflation targeting stems from the necessity of declaring the targeted disinflation path. After the Czech National Bank Board meeting on 21 December 1997, the Board committed to a net inflation target of 6% ± 0.5% by end 1998 and 4.5% ± 1% by end 2000. In 1997, there was still a gap between Czech inflation and long-term target, which is benchmarked as inflation prevailing in European Union countries.[11] Two options were considered in tackling this issue: (i) the CNB could announce a medium-term benchmark as its target and specify a time horizon (e.g. five years) within which inflation

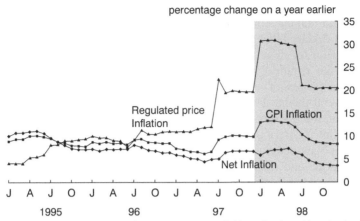

percentage change on a year earlier

Note: The shaded area shows which information was not available at the time of introducting inflation targeting.

Chart 2 Inflation indicators: 1995–96

should have converged with the target, or (ii) the CNB could define the targeted disinflation path for the next several years.

The latter option was chosen for the following reasons. First, announcing a target one year ahead corresponds better to the monetary policy lags in the Czech Republic. Second, the shorter horizon has increased the efficiency of the strategy by giving a nominal anchor for each year to economic agent. This is important since inflation expectations have not settled on the disinflation path, and nominal contracts, especially wage contracts, have been relatively rigid. Third, the target set for three years ahead (for the year 2000) allowed it to be set at a level higher than the benchmark without losing credibility, since in the medium-term, inflation could be expected to converge with the benchmark according to the declared slope of the disinflation path. The smoother disinflation path[12] may be less costly in terms of short-term volatility of output if expectations are adaptive. Fourth, it is thought that measurement errors in CPI inflation differ between the benchmark countries and the Czech Republic. This has been to a large extent due to the catch-up effect.[13] Consequently, rapid convergence of observed inflation rates could imply deflation in some sectors.

The three-year target for the end of 2000 was declared a 'key' target, the aim of which was to provide a framework for decision-making. The one-year target announced for the end of 1998 was declared to be an 'orientation' target whose aim was to provide a nominal anchor for economic contracts, whose horizons do not usually exceed one year. In previous years, these contracts were often linked to annual inflation forecasts published by various institutions, including the CNB.

An increase in the transparency of the decision-making process has been an important aspect of the new framework. In early 1998, the CNB explained the decision-making strategy at several press conferences and in press releases. It declared that achieving the net-inflation targets was to be the ultimate criterion for monetary policy decisions. Decisions would be taken by analysing the conditional inflation outlooks and comparing them to the targets. The process of constructing the inflation outlooks has been described to the general public. The CNB has begun to publish the minutes of board meetings on the Internet two weeks after each meeting. The minutes include a fairly detailed description of the discussion as well as the reasoning behind monetary policy decisions. The CNB now publishes Inflation Reports that focus on price and monetary developments, including descriptions of the inflation outlook and explanations of monetary policy measures.

During the first year of inflation targeting, one could distinguish three periods during which different factors affected the decision-making process.[14] Until March 1998, inflation expectations were not in line with the targeted disinflation path, even though the economic fundamentals, for example as the trade deficit and consumption, were becoming more sustainable![15] This inconsistency was due to backward-looking expectations as well as inflation signals sent by the January adjustment of administered prices, the secondary impact of deregulation, and increased exchange-rate uncertainty. As a result, the inflation outlook was revised upwards and the REPO rate was increased by 0.25% to 15% in March.

In the second period, up until July, several factors caused a reduction in inflation. One was weaker domestic demand. Furthermore, the koruna appreciated,[16] owing to a falling current-account deficit as well as to the narrowing of the gap between productivity growth and wage increases. More importantly, other external factors started playing an important role. The exogenous reduction in inflation caused by the fall in world commodity and producer prices was named 'borrowed disinflation'.[17] During this period the REPO rate remained unchanged.

In the third period, the economy slowed down and domestic demand pressure reduced. According to the Czech National Bank estimates, the external price shock slowed inflation by 1%–2%. The speed of disinflation was fairly rapid. In this period, the CNB started to adjust the REPO rate downwards as expected inflation fell. The changes in the market were attributed to the falling inflationary expectations, the temporary impact of borrowed disinflation, and the domestic economic slow down.

3   Lessons from the Czech case

The experiences of the Czech Republic provide lessons because this was the first economy in transition to adopt inflation targeting as the explicit framework for its monetary policy. Most countries switched to inflation targeting only after inflation was under control and on a decreasing path.[18] Generally, countries implementing inflation targeting had one-digit infla-

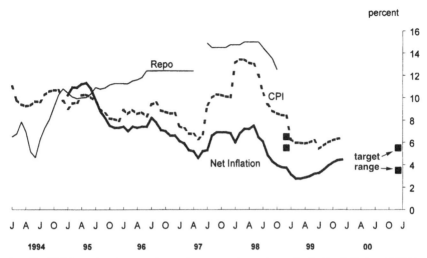

Note: The REPO rate has been used as an instrument of monetary policy by the CNB since 1996 (the volatility of the rate in 1994–95 was due to the use of volume instruments). The targets for net inflation were announced in December 1997: 6% ±0.55 (end 1998) and 4.5% ±1% (end 2000). The information on net inflation is separated into three parts: data calculated backwards in 1997 (period 1995–97), observed values of 1998 (period of 1998:1 to 1998:10) and the outlook (period of 1998:11 to 1999:12). The CPI inflation and outlook are included for comparison.

Chart 3 REPO rate, inflation targets and inflation outlook

tion, and in the majority of cases, their central banks placed more emphasis on reducing inflationary volatility than inflation itself. The first lesson from the Czech case is that certain preconditions enabled the effective implementation of this strategy. Second, there have been important gains even in the first year of implementation. Third, several problems have led to increased uncertainty, making targets more difficult to reach. These problems would have constrained any monetary strategy, however, and have not been caused by the switch to inflation targeting.

3.1 Conditions for implementation

Outlining the preconditions is important since their absence would reduce the advantages of inflation targeting. A distinguishing feature of the Czech reform strategy has been the priority attached to domestic price stability.[19] In choosing a framework, some other countries in the region placed emphasis on the balance of payments and external competitiveness.[20] The monetary strategy in the Czech Republic was in keeping with society's preferences for a stable currency; such support for a strategy can overcome the adverse impact of any short-term costs.

In the Czech case, the institutional preconditions have been met as well. The central bank conducts its monetary policy with a fairly high degree of independence. According to the Constitution and the central bank law, the

CNB is independent of the government and has sole responsibility for the conduct of monetary policy. During the course of transition, this independence has been exercised with respect to both instruments and goals. Furthermore, there has been no loss of fiscal discipline, which might have limited policy effectiveness. A balanced-budget has been maintained throughout the recent past, so that extensive public borrowing from the banking system has not constrained monetary policy.[21] One of the most important benefits of inflation targeting has been the increasingly efficient formation of expectations, which has reduced the costs of disinflation.[22] Another precondition, which has been met in the Czech Republic, is that of adequate development of financial markets. With a floating exchange rate, there is a need for a foreign-exchange market that is deep enough so that short-term volatility of capital flows need not lead to excessive turbulence in the real economy.

For example, instruments reducing exchange rate uncertainty are available to economic agents. Similarly, the instruments needed for the central bank to transmit its monetary policy decisions effectively are available. The foreign exchange and money markets were relatively well developed in 1997. Finally, it was important that in the initial stages of inflation targeting, external factors such as import prices did not damage the credibility of targets. In fact, lower import prices helped to reduce inflation expectations.

3.2   Gains from the new strategy

The CNB's internal and its external communications have become increasingly transparent. Internally, the decision-making process has come to focus squarely on inflation developments. The conflict between intermediate and long-term targets – a disadvantage of earlier strategies – has been eliminated. The importance of various indicators has been unambiguously (although implicitly) determined by their weight in the transmission from the interest-rate to the inflation outlook. Changes in instruments have been based on the deviation of the inflation outlook from the targeted path.

Monetary policy has also become more transparent to the general public. The policy moves of the CNB have become smoother and more predictable because of clear defined targets and instruments. Publishing minutes of the board meetings 'opened the kitchen' of the central bank. By the same token, decisions are now more exposed to the reactions of professional economists and the public.

In the Czech case, an increase in inflation was envisaged in early 1998, and market expectations for the future rate of inflation were quite unstable, with little public confidence that the disinflation process would be re-established in the foreseeable future. Public commitment to the explicit disinflation target and the related resolute policy stance were aimed at reversing expectations and reassuring the markets and the public. Given the situation of increased political uncertainty, with the government having resigned, the independent central bank's commitment to sound, transparent, long-term goals was of utmost importance.

The introduction of net inflation has been the third important gain from the introduction of inflation targeting, helping to avoid a counter-productive reaction in monetary policy. As can be seen from Chart 2, in 1998 the initial shock from administered price adjustments was significant.[23] Had CPI inflation been targeted, monetary policy could have over reacted to a temporary increase in inflation; alternatively, the credibility of the new strategy might have been compromised. In this case, one of the most important gains would have been lost since expectations would not have settled in line with the targeted disinflation path.

3.3   The 1998 dilemmas

The first year of inflation targeting has brought three dilemmas for the central bank. First, the reduction of borrowed disinflation caused net inflation to deviate from its targeted path. Second, financial factors determining exchange-rate movements increasingly. Third, it has become more difficult to assess the inflation outlook owing to increased uncertainty about the medium-term fiscal outlook.

In the Czech case the large impact of external factors on domestic inflation has presented a challenge to policy-makers. *Ex ante*, it was clear that there would be a choice to be made in specifying inflation targets between an index covering a narrow basket of goods and services that would be less vulnerable to exogenous shocks, and a broader index that would better represent consumers' actual cost of living and the public's inflationary expectations. Two types of exogenous shocks have been classified as most important to monetary policy decisions: (i) administered price corrections; and (ii) external price shocks.

In 1997, the CNB opted for providing as powerful a nominal anchor as possible. Net inflation was designed to filter out primary transitional price shocks, on the publicly-announced assumption that CPI inflation and net inflation would converge in the medium run, after administered prices had been completely corrected. An unanticipated fall in world commodity prices in 1998[24] reaffirmed the need to incorporate some mechanism for dealing with external shocks into an inflation-targeting framework. Credibility would be best served if this were done when the framework is introduced instead of when the shock arrives. The solution to the problem of borrowed disinflation remains an issue for future research. It is not clear whether the gain of reduced expectations will last, nor whether it will outweigh the loss of credibility caused by the deviation from the originally announced disinflation path.

The strong exchange rate has had a powerful impact on net inflation in 1998 because Czech economy is very open to trade. The Czech economy is also highly open to capital flows, which have increasingly dominated short-term exchange-rate developments. Economies in transition that have wide interest rate differentials over industrialised economies and volatile risk premiums may contribute to exchange-rate volatility. This volatility arises as a response to various international shocks, new economic and political data, and the changing and occasionally erratic perceptions of investors.

In such circumstances, some issues related to the exchange rate within the framework of inflation targeting require clarification. The level of the exchange rate can be neither an explicit nor an implicit objective of monetary policy. This is because control of the exchange rate is neither feasible in current conditions nor consistent with an inflation-targeting framework. Accordingly, external imbalances must be addressed by a combination of macroeconomic policies. Foreign-exchange interventions can cause the transition from one exchange-rate level to another and reduce volatility in the market for the koruna.

Yet for a small, open economy, movements in the exchange rate are a significant factor in the decision-making process of the central bank. Consequently, foreign investors try to anticipate the strategy of the central bank towards these changes and to use these implicit bands to reduce foreign-exchange risk when speculating on the foreign-exchange market. Analogously, market participants tend to forecast the behaviour of the central bank by comparing their own inflation forecasts with the targeted disinflation path, which can be interpolated from the explicit short- and long-run inflation targets. Increased credibility of the inflation target may in itself lead to nominal exchange-rate appreciation and potentially to loss of competitiveness. If the inflation forecast is in accordance with the target, then uncertainty about possible future cuts in domestic interest rates is reduced. Hence the risk premium falls, and all things being equal, the currency appreciates.

The Czech experience offers an important lesson about 'domestically produced' uncertainties. While the dilemmas of dealing with external factors are common to open economies that target inflation, the central bank may confront additional economic uncertainty during transition, making it difficult to project the medium-term fiscal outlook. Specifically, a reform strategy can be changed, with consequent changes in the prospects for administered price corrections and tax reforms. As a result, the inflation target can turn out to be the only medium-term economic policy target that is announced publicly. Hence, instead of having a reliable fiscal outlook to use as an important source of information, the central bank has to make only its own forecasts of fiscal policy on which to base future policy. The central bank has to consider whether this type of uncertainty should be reduced by initiating the co-ordination of economic policies, with the necessary institutional structure, even if it is not a standard role of an independent central bank.

Notes

1 Miroslav Hrnčíř and Kateřina Šmídková work for Czech National Bank. Their e-mail address is smidkova@cnb.cz. The views expressed in the paper are those of the authors and do not necessarily represent those of the Czech National Bank.

2 All three strategies used a similar framework. Each year, specific intermediate targets were announced together with a forecast of CPI inflation that was projected in accordance with these targets.

3 The Czech National Bank was established on 1 January 1993, after the dissolution of Czechoslovakia, succeeding the State Bank of Czechoslovakia (see Constitutional Act No. 542/1992 Coll., on the Dissolution of the Czech and Slovak Federal Republic, adopted 1 January 1993). Act No. 130/1989 Coll., on the State Bank of Czechoslovakia, adopted on 15 November 1989, created the preconditions for the two-tier banking system.

4 The transitional period imposes various types of constraints on monetary policy. For example, market instruments are introduced gradually and become efficient only after financial markets progress from their embryonic stage.

5 In the first years of transition, it was possible to target both money and the exchange rate owing to the low degree of koruna convertibility. The intermediate monetary target was important because due to embryonic financial markets, the only available operational targets were quantitative ones. Only in 1996, did short-term interest rates start playing the role of operational target.

6 For more information on the May exchange rate turbulence, see the CNB working paper, *Koruna Exchange Rate Turbulence in May 1997.*

7 In particular, wage negotiations continued to be based on a double-digit assumption despite the fact that the koruna had been pegged to the basket of DEM and USD since 1992 with no change in central parity until May 1997 (see Pohledy [1997] for the inflation forecast by Czech–Moravian Confederation of Trade Unions). Growth in average nominal wage was 25% in 1993, 17% in 1994, 18% in 1995, 14% in 1996, and 12% in 1997.

8 Inflation targeting is not, however, a panacea for all the instabilities of transition. For example, corrections to administered prices and tax reforms may lead to volatility in overall inflation.

9 The items excluded from the consumer basket are: (i) prices regulated by the Ministry of Finance or local authorities (weight in CPI is 7.4%); (ii) prices affected by other administrative measures (weight in CPI is 6%); and (iii) administrative fees (weight in CPI is 4.4%).

10 For example, in 1997, local authorities began to regulate taxis, so the price of taxi fares was excluded from the net-inflation index.

11 The inflation rate of European Union countries was used as a long-term benchmark in order to ensure convergence of financial indicators that would smooth the entry of the Czech Republic into the Union.

12 The term 'smoother path' is meant to stress a difference between defining a disinflation path by two subsequent targets (this implies the 1% annual reduction) and defining a targeted jump from observed levels of inflation to a benchmark inflation level (with approximate scale of 6% without specifying time distribution of disinflation).

13 During transition, productivity grew faster in some sectors of the Czech economy than in the benchmark countries, due to the catch-up effect. Since the CPI measure does not record each innovation as a change in the consumption basket, a part of the inflation differential reflects a difference in speed of innovations and should be allowed for in the medium term.

14　See minutes of the Board meetings (Inflation Reports) for detailed descriptions of the decision-making process.

15　One can compare inflation targets as shown in Chart 3 with inflation forecast by trade unions (Pohledy, 1997) for end of 1998 that predicted 14% CPI inflation. In May 1998, their prediction was 11% CPI inflation

16　The appreciation was partially an endogenous process linked to improvement in domestic economic fundamentals. But it was also a consequence of exogenous factors, since crises in some emerging markets made the koruna relatively more attractive to foreign investors.

17　The term 'borrowed' refers to the fact that the external positive shock has been viewed as temporary. The medium-term scenario used for outlooks assumed that an international fall in prices would be corrected for later on. There has, however, been a permanent gain in terms of reduced expectations.

18　In the Czech case, there were three detectable inflation episodes. In 1993, inflation was created by the VAT reform. In 1995, the impact of capital inflow on demand started to affect inflation. In 1997, the exchange-rate turbulence and consequent depreciation of the koruna was a significant factor in the development of inflation.

19　The remarkable stability of the Koruna has not been limited to recent developments. After World War I, the currency of the newly formed Czechoslovak Republic was the only country in the region to avoid hyperinflation. After World War II, the relatively modest monetary overhang was a favourable feature of the macroeconomic situation.

20　For example, Hungary and Poland used crawling-peg regimes.

21　Nevertheless, the revealed hidden debt of institutions during transformation inflated the previous officially declared debt level.

22　Implementation of the new strategy contributed to a change in the mode of expectations. In the past, expectations were mainly adaptive. After the declaration of targets, they have become gradually more forward-looking. This has been a very important achievement. Should wages be negotiated under a strictly backward-looking mode of expectations, the costs of disinflation would be much higher and the risk of reappearance of the external imbalance would increase.

23　Chart 2 also shows that the net inflation has been influenced by the secondary (spillover) effect from the segment of regulated prices to other price segments. However, this factor has been considered in making monetary policy decisions.

24　See Chart 3 for illustration of this positive price shock. The 1998 target will be undershot significantly. The impact of a fall in world prices has been estimated from 1 to 2%.

Bibliography

Annual Reports, 1993–98, Czech National Bank, Prague.

Inflation Reports, 1998, Czech National Bank, Prague.

Pohledy (1997), *Prognóza makroekonomického vývoje v roce 1998*, October.

Pohledy (1998), *Zastavíme další prohlubování ekonomické krize*, May.

Šmídková, *et al.* (1998), *Koruna Exchange Rate Turbulence in May*, Czech National Bank, Prague, Working Paper No. 2.

Part V
Specifying and using targets

Core inflation as an indicator in monetary policy rules

Seamus Hogan[1]

1 Introduction

In an inflation-targeting regime, future inflation is the final target, but current inflation is a determinant of future inflation and thus can be used as one of a set of indicators to suggest whether policy should be tightened or loosened now in order to achieve the final target in the future. This is explicit in a Taylor rule, which specifies the monetary policy reaction as a function, in part, of the deviation of current inflation from its target.

Such considerations raise the question of what measure of inflation would be the best to use as this indicator. Most inflation-targeting countries employ a definition of 'core' or 'underlying' inflation that seeks to capture the underlying trend in inflation. Typically, measures of core inflation remove or reduce the weight of some items in the Consumer Price Index (CPI) basket in order to downplay the influence of those forces thought to be transitory. In many countries, inflation targets are defined in terms of the 'headline' CPI (that is, the regular CPI reported by the country's statistical agency), but measures of core inflation are used as indicators to help guide monetary policy. In Canada, for instance, the *operational* inflation target is expressed in terms of a particular measure of core inflation, even though the end objective of the inflation-targeting regime is stability in the headline rate of inflation. In addition, the Bank of Canada uses several other measures of core inflation as indicators.

This paper examines the idea of core inflation as an indicator, with particular reference to the measures of core inflation that are constructed by the Bank of Canada and their potential inclusion in Taylor-type rules. The next two sections describe the theoretical framework used in this paper. Section 2 outlines a simple model within which core inflation can be defined and motivated. Section 3 discusses when definitions of core inflation improve monetary policy performance, as would be described by an optimal Taylor-type monetary policy rule. Sections 4 and 5 are empirical, with Section 4 describing some of the measures of core inflation constructed by the Bank of Canada and Section 5 analysing the potential role those measures could play as indicators of future inflation. Section 6 contains some brief concluding remarks. The body of the paper makes no explicit reference to the role of the exchange rate in the analysis of core inflation and policy rules, but the analysis transfers naturally to an open economy. This extension is described in the appendix.

2   Core inflation

Core inflation is a difficult concept to define precisely. At its most general level, the concept of core inflation rests on the premise that in the long run it is monetary policy that determines the price level, but in the short run transitory shocks can divert the price level away from its long-run, monetary policy determined path. Core inflation refers to this long-run unobserved path. Exactly what this means, however, depends on how shocks affect inflation in the short run, how policy is assumed to affect prices in the long run, and on what role the concept of core inflation plays in informing these policy actions. In any discussion of core inflation measures, therefore, it is crucial to state carefully the context motivating the measures. Ideally, the following elements should be specified: a formal model of price determination that defines the core conceptually and explains the process by which observed inflation may differ from the core; a statement of the end use to which we wish to put a measure of the core; a motivation for why the model-derived definition might be interesting in terms of this end use; and an operational *measure* of the core (distinct from the definition) that uses the model to describe the time-series and/or cross-section properties of the difference between actual and core inflation and thus provides a way of estimating it. In the remainder of this section we specify a framework along these lines.

2.1   A model of price determination

We use a version of the standard aggregate-demand/Phillips-curve formulation of inflation, given by the following equations:

$$\text{Aggregate demand } \frac{Y_t}{Y_{t-1}} = f(R_t - \pi^e_{t+1}, \pi_t) + \delta_t \tag{1}$$

$$\text{Potential output } Y^*_t = Y^*_{t-1}(\gamma + \sigma_t) \tag{2}$$

$$\text{Phillips curve } \pi_t = \pi^e_t + g\left(\frac{Y_{t-1}}{Y^*_{t-1}}\right) + \epsilon_t \tag{3}$$

$$\text{Inflation expectations } \pi^e_t = \alpha\bar{\pi} + (1 - \alpha)\pi_{t-1} \tag{4}$$

Equation (1) expresses the growth in aggregate demand as a function of the monetary policy instrument (the nominal interest rate, R_t, minus this period's expectations of next period's inflation) and the current inflation rate (which determines where along the aggregate demand curve the economy will be). Equation (2) describes the evolution over time of potential output, Y_t^*. Equation (3) is a Phillips curve, where Y_{t-1}/Y_{t-1}^* is the lagged output gap and π_t^e is the momentum built into the inflation rate at time t. Equation (4) can be derived from a simple model where wages and prices are set for fixed periods. In our illustrative model, we shall refer to π_t^e as expectations of inflation at time t formed at time $t - 1$. These inflation expectations comprise partly backward-looking inflation expectations and partly the inflation target, $\bar{\pi}$, with α being a measure of central-bank credibility. An alternative interpretation of inflation momentum would be that the lagged-inflation term in equation (4) reflects the fact that it takes time for inflationary impulses to work through the production chain of intermediate goods so that cost-push influences continue to act on inflation for some time after an initial impulse.

Equations (1), (3), and (4) together imply that as long as there is inertia in inflation expectations, monetary policy changes will have implications for aggregate output in the short run.

The error terms in equations (1) and (2) represent important *output uncertainties* facing a central bank. The demand shock, δ_t, captures the idea that the relationship between monetary policy instruments and aggregate demand is uncertain, and the aggregate supply shock, σ_t, represents the volatility in potential output growth.

The price error term in the Phillips-curve equation, ϵ_t, is key to our discussion of core inflation. It represents *price uncertainties,* which are changes to the price level that arise for reasons other than an output gap or inflation expectations. In particular, the price shock captures a large discrete change to the relative price of some commodity that has an effect on the aggregate price level. In principle, there is no reason for there to be any relationship between relative prices and the aggregate nominal price of a commodity basket; the latter should depend only on monetary factors. In a non-tâtonnement economy, however, particularly one with menu costs, a large change in the relative price of a good with respect to all other goods will initially affect only the nominal price of that good. It is only when that change feeds into other prices through the effects of a reduced aggregate quantity demanded that the quantity signals will induce other prices to adjust relative to their trend.

These shocks (σ_t, δ_t, and ϵ_t) may of course be correlated; a taste or technology shock affects demand or supply as well as the relative price of a particular commodity. For instance, a bad harvest that causes an increase in food prices reflects a temporary loss of production potential in the economy as a whole. This will not necessarily be the case, however. For instance, a general increase in productivity could affect δ_t but not ϵ_t. It is therefore important to define the price shock independently from the other two shocks. The distinction is important because, as we shall see in

Section 3, price shocks have very different implications for monetary policy than do shocks to aggregate demand or potential output.

2.2   *Permanent and transitory price level shocks and core inflation measures*

The importance of price shocks to inflation and output stability will thus depend in part on whether they are permanent or transitory. To formalise this, let us decompose the price-shock term in equation (3) into two components: $\epsilon_t = \mu_t + \eta_t$. The first component, μ_t, represents $I(0)$ shocks to the price level and so produces a negative moving average process in the inflation rate. It is intended to capture temporary relative price shocks, such as those affecting the volatile components of food and energy. This component will also pick up any random measurement error in the CPI. The second component, η_t, represents $I(1)$ shocks to the price level, and hence $I(0)$ shocks to inflation. It represents permanent relative price shocks. For our purposes here, we can define as permanent any shock that lasts for a period of time greater than the monetary policy lag, say 18 months.

This decomposition of the price shock suggests two definitions of core inflation:

$$\pi_t^{c_1} = \pi_t^e + g\left(\frac{Y_{t-1}}{Y_{t-1}^*}\right) + \eta_t, \tag{5}$$

and

$$\pi_t^{c_1} = \pi_t^e + g\left(\frac{Y_{t-1}}{Y_{t-1}^*}\right) \tag{6}$$

The first of these definitions removes price-level shocks that are temporary; i.e. it removes the inflation surprises that are self-reverting and that should not feed through into permanent changes in inflation expectations and headline inflation. The second core definition removes all influences on the inflation rate that are not due to expectations or an output gap.

2.3   *End uses of a core inflation measure*

There are three principal ways in which the above definitions of core inflation can be useful to inflation targeting.

First, measures based on these definitions of core inflation may be more informative as one of a set of predictors of future headline inflation than the current headline inflation rate would be in the same role; as such, the core inflation rate would be more useful to a central bank seeking to target the headline inflation rate. Which of the two definitions of core inflation would be appropriate as an indicator depends on whether price-level shocks revert quickly or not. When a relative price shock has only a temporary effect on the aggregate price level, π_t^{c2} might be a preferred indicator. On the other hand, if price-level shocks are non-reverting and inflation expectations are backward-looking, then π_t^{c1} might be a preferred target measure.

Second, the welfare costs of inflation that motivate the policy of inflation targeting apply more to the *underlying* inflationary pressures than to the headline rate. Core inflation would then constitute the final target of monetary policy π_t^{c2}.

Finally, even if stability in headline inflation is the final objective of monetary policy, it may still be advantageous for central banks to target core inflation. One reason for this is that the central bank may have multiple policy objectives. That is, even if it is the headline CPI in which low and stable inflation is desirable, there may be other economic costs, such as excessive output variability, to maintaining that stability in the face of particular shocks. In this case, defining core inflation in such a way that the central bank does not have the obligation to try to negate certain types of shocks to the aggregate price level could reflect this policy trade-off between competing objectives. Here, π_t^{c2} might be a preferred target measure.

The idea of multiple economic objectives for monetary policy underlies the literature on optimal policy rules.

3 Optimal policy rules

A 'monetary policy rule' describes the relationship between current data and monetary policy instruments that a central bank follows to achieve its objective. If a central bank has more than one objective and only one policy instrument, then it needs an explicit or implicit objective function weighting the multiple objectives. The solution to the resulting constrained optimisation problem produces what has been termed in the literature an 'optimal policy rule'.

Although one can imagine a large number of objectives that a central bank might have, the literature on optimal policy rules has concentrated on two: to minimise the variance of inflation around its target rate, and to minimise the variance of output around its potential level. The motivation behind the desire to minimise output variability can be justified in two ways. First, output fluctuations are not borne evenly across society and so have implications for income inequality. Second, if there are asymmetries in which the costs from output falling below potential are stronger and longer-lasting than are the benefits when output rises above potential, then greater output variability implies lower average output over time.

The potential tension between the two objectives of inflation and output-gap stabilisation can be illustrated neatly using the standard aggregate model outlined in Section 2.1. This then leads naturally into a discussion of the Taylor rule and the role of core inflation.

3.1 Policy rules in the standard model

Recall that there are two classes of shocks in the model: shocks to aggregate demand and potential output, and shocks to the price level. Now consider the response to these two kinds of shocks by a central bank that seeks to minimise both the variance of output around potential and the variance of inflation around its target level.

Shocks to aggregate demand or potential output present no strategic problems to a central bank. If such shocks cause aggregate demand to grow faster than potential output plus the target rate of inflation, then the objectives of stabilising inflation around its target level and output around potential both require the same response – to adjust monetary conditions to eliminate the excess demand. Of course, there is still the operational problem that the bank needs to be able to identify shocks to aggregate demand or potential output quickly enough to be able to make the required response, but, once identified, these shocks do not force the central bank to trade off competing objectives.

A price-level shock, however, is more problematic. When a relative price shock has an effect on the aggregate price level, a central bank that sought only to keep output at potential would want to fully accommodate the price shock.[2] If, on the other hand, the central bank wishes to counteract the effect of the relative-price shock on aggregate prices, then it must allow the output gap to deviate from zero. However, the lags between the adjustment of a monetary policy instrument and its effect on the output gap, and hence inflation, is such that a central bank will not be able to react to a surprise aggregate price shock in order to counteract its effect on inflation during the period over which inflation is measured in the inflation-targeting rule (usually 12 months). The policy objective of targeting the rate of inflation rather than targeting the price level implies, then, that there is no need, in principle, to avoid accommodating a price level shock. The problem arises when price-level shocks are non-reverting (that is, they arise from permanent relative-price shocks) and when the weight on lagged inflation in the inflation-expectations term in equation (4) is high. In this case, a one-time price-level shock will set in place ongoing inflation that can be eliminated only by the creation of a non-zero output gap. In this case, inflation stabilisation and output stabilisation are competing objectives.

In this framework, a good policy rule needs to do two things. First, it needs to be able to distinguish shocks to aggregate demand and potential output from shocks to the aggregate price level. Second, it needs to specify a stronger response to the former than the latter, where the difference in the response strength will depend partly on the importance of lagged inflation in the Phillips curve, as well as the weight the policy-maker puts on output stability over inflation stability. An example of such a rule is that proposed by Taylor (1993).

3.2 Taylor-type rules and core inflation

Taylor's proposed monetary-policy feedback rule describes short-term interest rates as a linear function of the difference between current inflation and its target level and of the output gap:

$$r_t = \bar{r} + \beta(\pi_t - \bar{\pi}) + \gamma\left(\frac{Y_t}{Y_t^*}\right), \tag{7}$$

where r_t is the current value of an interest rate or some other indicator of monetary policy that is directly controlled by the central bank, and $\bar{r}$ is the steady-state level of that indicator. Taylor's original rule used the federal-funds rate as the indicator of monetary policy and imposed values of 0.5 for both β and γ, but the term 'Taylor rule' is now used more generally to indicate any rule of the form of equation (7).

Taylor proposed his rule as a description of monetary policy rather than as a prescription for what monetary policy should be. Svensson (1997), however, has shown that, in a simple model, a Taylor rule can be the optimal reaction function for an inflation-targeting central bank that seeks to minimise a weighted sum of the variance of both inflation around its target and output around potential. In more complicated models, where the optimal rule is correspondingly complicated, a Taylor-type rule may still provide a simple approximation to the optimal rule and hence a useful guide to monetary policy. Taylor-type rules have therefore played a prominent role in the numerical literature analysing optimal-policy rules (for example, see Black, Macklem, and Rose, 1998).

Why the Taylor rule may be a reasonable rule for central banks that seek to stabilise both inflation and the output gap is as follows. The coefficient on the inflation gap links the inflation target to the immediate policy instrument. If this weight on inflation deviations were zero, then any change in inflation that became embedded in inflationary expectations would become permanent. Such a shock to inflation could arise from either the monetary policy's failure to maintain a zero-output gap or from a price-level shock. In either case, a policy that continued to respond only to deviations of output from potential would lead to inflation having a unit root.

At the other extreme, it may also not be optimal to place a zero weight on the output gap. This is partly because the output gap is an early-warning indicator of future inflation, and so a higher weight on the output gap produces a faster response to deviations of inflation from target that are the result of excess demand or supply. More important, the output-gap term in the Taylor rule produces a response only to inflation driven by excess demand, while the inflation-gap term produces a response to inflation caused by either a non-zero output gap or a price-level shock. As a result, putting a weight on the output-gap term produces a stronger response to output-gap inflation than to inflation resulting from a price-level shock, as required by an optimal rule.

Building on this, the potential tension between the objectives of inflation and output-gap stabilisation in the context of price-level shocks can be described by a Taylor rule that explicitly includes core inflation terms:

$$r_t = \bar{r} + \beta^0(\pi_t - \bar{\pi}) + \beta^1(\pi_t^{c1} - \bar{\pi}) + \beta^2(\pi_t^{c2} - \bar{\pi}) + \gamma\left(\frac{Y_t}{Y_t^*}\right). \tag{8}$$

Two factors are important for determining the weight of the core inflation terms (π_t^{c1} and π_t^{c2}) in this rule.

(i) Any measure of core inflation that is a better indicator of underlying inflation pressures than the current headline rate should then receive more weight than current headline inflation than the headline rate in the Taylor rule. π_t^{c1} could have an advantage over π_t^{c2} insofar as it allows pre-emptive action to be taken against price-level shocks that will feed into inflationary expectations. More generally, when the extent to which price shocks have more permanent inflationary effects is uncertain, an optimal rule might put some weight on both core inflation gap terms.

(ii) As a separate issue, π_t^{c2} filters out that component of inflation that arises from price-level shocks while maintaining the component that was the result of the output gap and inflationary expectations. The output gap has an advantage over core inflation in that it provides an earlier warning of inflationary pressures, given that it is the lagged output gap that affects inflation in the model. The output gap, however, is notoriously difficult to measure. If π_t^{c2} could be measured reasonably accurately, putting some weight on both it and the output gap could be a way of avoiding large policy mistakes due to measurement error.

4   Summary of core inflation measures considered by the Bank of Canada

The theoretical section of this paper outlined how, conceptually, the use of core inflation should improve the performance of a Taylor-type rule. The natural empirical question, then, is which, if any, of the available measures of core inflation would furnish such a benefit.

Many of the measures of core inflation proposed by the literature can be understood as attempts to measure either one of the two conceptual measures of core inflation defined in this paper. The techniques used to obtain a measure of core inflation include *aggregate filters,* in which the inflation series is smoothed to uncover a trend; *re-weighters,* which look at the individual components of the basket of goods used to construct headline inflation measures and reduce or eliminate the weight on some components; and *event adjusters,* in which information about the economy outside of the price data is used to infer the impact on inflation of some event known to represent a price shock, such as a change in indirect taxes.

The Bank of Canada follows a number of measures of core inflation that employ some or all of these techniques. The two most important of these are the following:

(i) *Year-Over-Year Headline CPI* (CPI y/y)   *Statistics Canada* publishes the CPI monthly and reports both the monthly and the year-over-year inflation rate calculated from it. The year-over-year CPI can be thought of as a measure of core inflation, as it applies a 12-month one-sided moving-average filter to the monthly inflation rates.

(ii) *CPI Excluding Food, Energy, and the Effect of Indirect Taxes* (CPI × FET)   *Statistics Canada* constructs a filtered re-weighter measure that is the year-over-year change in the CPI once all food and energy items have been removed from the CPI basket (CPI × FE). In 1991, the Bank of Canada constructed an historical series that added an event adjuster to CPI × FE by removing the contribution of changes in indirect taxes to measured inflation. The Bank publishes this series in its quarterly publication, *The Bank of Canada Review,* and releases its value to the news media on the day that *Statistics Canada* releases the monthly CPI.

CPI (y/y) and CPI × FET have a formal role in Canada's inflation-targeting framework. The official inflation targets have been announced in terms of the year-over-year growth in the headline CPI, as this is the measure of inflation with which the public is most familiar. However, CPI × FET is the *operational* target for policy in the sense that the Bank states that it will focus on this measure as long as movements in both it and CPI (y/y) are the same beyond the short run. CPI × FET is referred to officially as 'core CPI inflation'.

In addition to these two measures of core inflation that help define the official inflation-targeting policy, Bank staff have constructed three other measures that are used purely as indicators. These derive from the work of Laflèche (1997a) and (1997b), who investigated a class of re-weighter measures in which information from the historical CPI series is used to determine the weights.[3] The first two measures (CPIW and CPIX) are published in the *Weekly Financial Statistics* and the quarterly *Bank of Canada Review.* The Bank does not publish the third (CPIT), but it does compute it monthly and track it as part of the Bank's monitoring of inflation trends. All of these measures are year-over-year measures of inflation and exclude the effect of the introduction of a value-added tax in 1991.

(i) *Double-Weighted CPI* (CPIW)   CPIW does not remove any components from the CPI basket, but it down-weights volatile components by multiplying the weight applied to each commodity in the CPI basket by a second weight equal to the reciprocal of the historical standard deviation of the relative price change of that component, and then normalising the weights to one.

(ii) *CPI Excluding the Eight Most Volatile Components* (CPIX)   CPIX excludes from the CPI basket the eight sub-indices that have been particularly volatile. These eight are fruit, vegetables, gasoline, fuel oil, natural gas, mortgage interest costs, inter city transportation, and tobacco products. In addition, CPIX adjusts for the effect of changes to indirect taxes. The advantage of this measure over CPI × FET is that it excludes only those components of the food and energy sub-groups that in the past have generated the high volatility of prices in those groups. That is, it is a more finely targeted re-weighter than CPI × FET, with only 15.8% of the CPI basket excluded in CPIX, compared to 25.3% in CPI × FET.

(iii) *Trimmed Mean CPI* (CPIT)   This measure gives the weighted mean of the distribution of the year-over-year growth rates of the 54 components of the CPI, trimmed to exclude the components with year-over-year growth rates (in absolute value) greater than 1.5 standard deviations from the mean growth rate. The difference between CPIT and the other re-weighter measures is that the set of goods whose inflation rate is weighted to zero changes from month to month, with the weights in any particular quarter depending on the cross-section distribution of inflation rates that quarter.

Charts 1 and 2 show how these measures of inflation have evolved over time using quarterly data. Chart 1 shows both the quarterly and year-over-year inflation in the headline CPI. The quarterly inflation is seasonally adjusted and expressed as an annual rate. Included on the graph is the target band for inflation for the period that Canada has had a formal inflation target. When the inflation targets were first announced in February 1991, the joint announcement by the Minister of Finance and the Governor of the Bank of Canada specified a target range for inflation of plus or minus 1 percentage point around mid-points of 3.0% to be achieved by the end of 1992, 2.5% by the middle of 1994, and 2.0% by the end of 1995. Further joint announcements in 1995 and 1998 have extended the 1%–3% control bands to 2001.

The graphs in Chart 2 show the other measures of core inflation with year-over-year CPI inflation included on each graph for comparison. The big fall in inflation in 1994 in the graphs for the headline CPI reflects a substantial reduction in the indirect tax on tobacco products that year. With their event adjustment for the effect of indirect taxes, CPI × FET and CPIX show stable inflation for 1994. The remaining two measures do

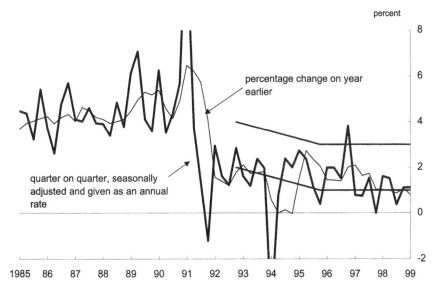

Chart 1 Consumer prices, 1985Q1–99Q1

not explicitly remove the effect of indirect taxes other than the introduction of a value-added tax in 1991. They are defined in such a way, however, that the tobacco tax shock does not affect the measure of core inflation. For instance, CPIW puts a low weight on tobacco products, and CPIT eliminates the effects of components whose inflation rates lie in the tails of the inflation distribution.

Table 1 shows the mean and variability of these different measures over time. The variability is defined as the root mean squared difference between the measure of inflation and the three-year centred moving average of headline CPI inflation. We include these for the full data period of 1985Q1 to 1999Q1, and also for the sub-period from 1992Q1. This latter period constitutes a single regime during which monetary policy has been formally directed towards maintaining stable inflation, following a period of rapid disinflation. It is notable that the filter provided by using a 12-month moving average removes between a third and a half of the variability in the quarterly measure, and that the additional adjustments contained in the remaining core measures provide only small marginal reductions in variability.

5 Core inflation as an indicator in practice

The literature on comparative policy rules tends to use artificial economies calibrated to the real world that can be simulated using different policy

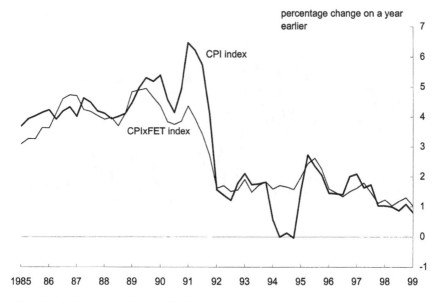

Chart 2a–d Measures of core inflation

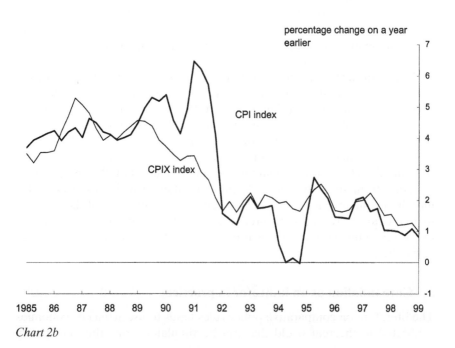

Chart 2b

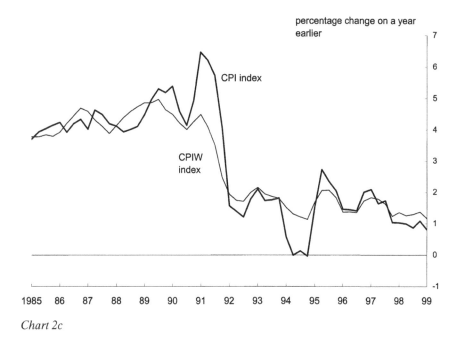

Chart 2c

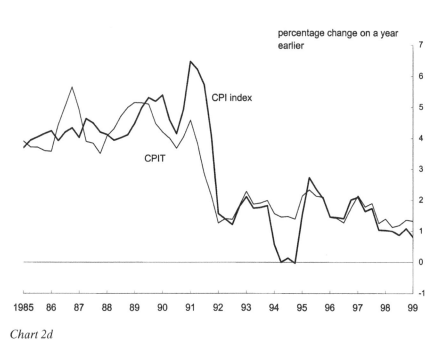

Chart 2d

Table 1 Mean and variability of core inflation measures

Inflation measure	85Q1 to 99Q1*		92Q1 to 99Q1*	
	Mean	Variability	Mean	Variability
CPI (q/q saar)	2.91	1.76	1.43	1.37
CPI (y/y)	2.95	0.84	1.39	0.89
CPI × FET	2.80	0.69	1.62	0.71
CPIW	2.89	0.55	1.61	0.61
CPIX	2.83	0.82	1.81	0.74
CPIT	2.89	0.76	1.65	0.78

* Quarterly data. End of sample for variability measure is 98Q1 to allow for three-year centred moving average.

rules to compare performance according to some objective function. This kind of simulation exercise is useful for enhancing our understanding of the theoretical properties of different classes of policy rule. The key question with measures of core inflation, however, is not the theoretical one of whether an ideal measure of core inflation would improve the performance of a Taylor rule – it seems clear that this would be the case – but rather whether any of the available real-world measures of core inflation captures underlying inflation sufficently to be useful.

It is extremely difficult, however, to construct a counterfactual exercise to ask how different real-world core inflation measures would have performed if used in a Taylor rule in a real-world economy. In an earlier version of this paper, we tried estimating Canadian Taylor rules using the different measures of core inflation described in the previous section, and then asking if the deviation of actual from estimated interest rates could explain the deviation of inflation from target after six or eight quarters. However, over the period that Canada has had formal inflation targets, inflation has been very stable, and the movement in interest rates in that time has been dominated by specific international shocks (the Mexican peso crisis in 1995 and the Asian crisis in 1998). As a result, the signal-to-noise ratio in any exercise seeking to estimate a Taylor rule is very low.

In this section, then, we eschew the attempt to analyse directly the role of measured core inflation in a Taylor rule, and instead ask the question, Which measures of core inflation have been the best leading indicators of future inflation in Canada during the period of inflation targeting?

Table 2 shows the simple correlation coefficients of the different indicators and the lead values of CPI (y/y) and CPI × FET, which constitute the official and operational target measures of inflation, respectively. The indicators are the quarterly inflation rate, the five measures of core inflation discussed above, and the output gap. The output gap variable is taken from the Bank's Quarterly Projection Model. It is constructed from a multivariate filter that combines structural information and mechanical filters with the components of a neoclassical production function before applying

Table 2 Correlation between current indicators and future target inflation

Inflation after	4 quarters Sample 92Q1–98Q1		6 quarters Sample 92Q1–97Q3		8 quarters Sample 92Q1–97Q1	
Indicator	CPI (y/y)	CPI × FET	CPI (y/y)	CPI × FET	CPI (y/y)	CPI × FET
CPI (q/q)	−0.02	−0.05	−0.25	−0.51	−0.06	0.06
CPI (y/y)	−0.49	−0.67	−0.18	−0.29	−0.02	0.16
CPI × FET	0.07	−0.01	0.41	0.17	0.26	0.08
CPIW	−0.42	−0.34	−0.21	0.06	0.01	0.45
CPIX	−0.24	−0.24	0.22	0.18	0.29	0.27
CPIT	−0.45	−0.3	−0.08	−0.04	0.41	0.29
Output Gap	−0.03	−0.36	0.09	−0.5	0.32	−0.53

the function to obtain a measure of potential output.[4] As a result of the filtering methodology, estimates of historical output gaps change over time. The measure of the output gap at time t that is used in this paper is the real-time estimate made at time t and so reflects information available to the monetary authority at that time.

The correlations in Table 2 are taken over the period that the Bank has had a formal inflation target, excluding the initial 12-month period of disinflation. We consider leads of four, six, and eight quarters. The maximum correlation in each column is indicated by heavy shading, and the minimum correlation by light shading. This identifies, respectively, the indicators that are the best and worst indicators of future inflation for each of the two target measures of inflation.

For a lead of four quarters, the inflation indicators are mostly negatively correlated with the lead values of the two target rates. This suggests that there has been a substantial effect from reversible price shocks in the CPI. The only measure of inflation in which there is no negative correlation with the four-quarter lead CPI is the Bank's standard core measure, CPI × FET.

For a lead of six quarters, the correlations between the five measures of core inflation and target inflation are all substantially higher, suggesting that the tendency of the price level to revert to its trend following a shock occurs within four to six quarters after a shock. The Bank's standard core measure continues to be one of the best indicators of future inflation, whereas the headline year-over-year CPI is a poor indicator.

This relative performance of the different measures changes somewhat when considering leads of eight quarters. In this case, CPI × FET performs relatively badly as an indicator and the more recently constructed measures – CPIW, CPIX, and CPIT – perform relatively well. One has to be careful in interpreting the numbers in this table, however, due to an endogenous policy response. It is generally thought that monetary policy takes about six to eight quarters to affect inflation. If monetary policy is successfully acting to bring inflation back to the mid-point of the target range within eight quarters, then we would expect to see a zero correlation between any indicator and future targeted inflation. After eight quarters, the correlation between current and future CPI × FET is close to zero. This may simply reflect the fact that CPI × FET is the operational target for the Bank, so there is an automatic policy-induced tendency for this measure to revert to its mean within eight quarters. The higher correlations between the other measures of core inflation and the eight-quarter lead of CPI × FET, however, suggests that there has been some unexploited information in those measures.

Finally, it is notable in Table 2 that the output gap is a very poor indicator of future inflation, particularly over the policy horizon of six months. If we could assume that the poor correlation of the output gap is not due to an endogenous policy response, then these results suggest that it would be better to place greater weight on core inflation and less weight on the output gap in a Taylor rule.

6   Conclusions

In this paper, we have provided two model-derived definitions of core inflation and outlined how accurate measures of these could be useful as both targets and indicators in an inflation-targeting framework. Incorporating these measures into a monetary policy rule such as the Taylor rule illustrates their potential utility.

It is difficult, however, to find accurate measures of these conceptually defined notions of core inflation and to assess their usefulness to real-world monetary policy. Some simple empirical work using the measures of core inflation employed by the Bank of Canada suggests that those measures do provide a better indicator of future inflation pressures than quarterly headline inflation, but the difference between the core measures is not great. In particular, the Bank's traditional measure of core inflation – year-over-year inflation in the CPI excluding food, energy, and the effect of changes in indirect taxes – seems to be at least as effective as some of the more sophisticated measures, although there may be some unexploited information in those measures after eight quarters.

APPENDIX

Extension to the open economy

In the body of the paper, we made little reference to the role of exchange rates in the inflation process for an open economy. This was largely for expositional convenience: open-economy considerations fit easily into the framework described above. In this appendix, we briefly outline the role of the exchange rate in this framework.

1   *Exchange-rate derived price shocks*

If changes in the exchange rate pass through quickly into consumer prices, then exchange-rate shocks are an example of the relative price shocks that cause the error term in the Phillips curve. For instance, exchange-rate movements that are associated with changes in capital flows are an example of shocks that shift demand from some commodities onto others, say from investment goods to exports; shocks to the exchange rate that arise from changes in the terms-of-trade shocks are examples of shocks that simultaneously affect the aggregate price level and potential output; and so on.

2   *The exchange rate in the Taylor rule*

Ball (1999) has extended the closed-economy models of Ball (1997) and Svensson (1997) to formally model the role of the exchange rate in the transmission mechanism from monetary policy to aggregate demand and in generating price shocks. He finds that, with this extension, the appropriate measure of monetary policy on the left-hand side of a Taylor rule is a real 'monetary conditions index'; that is, a weighted average of real interest rates and the real exchange rate. He also finds that the appropriate measure of inflation to use on the right-hand side of the rule excludes the effect of reversible exchange-rate shocks. This is consistent with our conclusion in Section 3.1 that an ideal Taylor rule would eliminate the effect of reversible price shocks from the measures used to determine the current inflation gap and with the statement above that exchange-rate shocks can be thought of as a form of relative price shock.

Notes

1   At the time of writing, Research Department, Bank of Canada. I would like to thank Bob Amano, Marianne Johnson, Dave Longworth, Tiff Macklem, and Gerald Stuber for many helpful comments, and Jason Allen and Frederic Beauregard-Tellier for excellent research assistance. The views expressed in this paper are those of the author alone and do not necessarily reflect those of the Bank of Canada.
2   In the case of a supply-derived relative price shock, this may require no change in policy, as the effect of the price-level change on the aggregate quantity demanded may exactly match the change in potential output associated with the supply shock. In the case of demand-derived relative price shocks, accommodation will require an active policy response.
3   For a recent examination of these measures, see Johnson (1999).
4   For a complete description of the multivariate filter, see Butler (1996).

Bibliography

Ball, L. (1999), 'Policy rules for open economies', in Taylor, J. (ed.) *Monetary Policy Rules*, Chicago University Press: Chicago.

Ball, L. (1997), 'Efficient rules for monetary policy', *NBER Working Paper,* No. 5952.

Black, R., Macklem, T. and Rose, D. (1998), 'On policy rules for price stability', in *Price Stability, Inflation Targets and Monetary Policy*, Ottawa: Bank of Canada.

Butler, L. (1996), 'A semi-structural method to estimate potential output: combining economic theory with a time-series filter – the Bank of Canada's new quarterly projection model, part 4', *Bank of Canada Technical Report,* No. 77.

Johnson, M. (1999), 'Core inflation: a measure of inflation for policy purposes', in *Measures of Underlying Inflation and Their Role in the Conduct of Monetary Policy*, proceedings of the workshop of central-bank model builders held at the BIS on 18–19 February 1999, Basle: Bank for International Settlements.

Laflèche, T. (1997a), 'Mesures du taux d'inflation tendanciel', *Bank of Canada Working Paper,* 97–9.

Laflèche, T. (1997b), 'Statistical measures of the trend rate of inflation', *Bank of Canada Review* (autumn), pp. 29–47.

Srour, G. (1999), 'Inflation targeting under uncertainty', *Technical Report,* No. 85, Bank of Canada.

Svensson, L.E.O. (1997), 'Inflation targeting: some extensions', *Scandinavian Journal of Economics*, 101 (3), pp. 337–61.

Taylor, J.B. (1993), 'Discretion versus policy rules in practice', *Carnegie-Rochester Conference Series on Public Policy,* 39: pp. 159–214.

Specifying an inflation target

The case of administered prices and other candidates for exclusion

Uros Cufer, Lavan Mahadeva and Gabriel Sterne[1]

1 Introduction

In defining an inflation target, policy-makers have frequently chosen to exclude certain measurable components from the consumer-price basket. The types of goods excluded have differed significantly across countries targeting inflation (Table 1). Among industrialised economies that directly targeted inflation in 1995, six made a combined total of nine separate exclusions from their indices. And more recently, the increasing focus of policy on inflation targets in a number of developing and transitional economies has renewed a global interest in the issues of target specification, including exclusions, bandwidth, and the time horizon over which the target should be met. This paper suggests a framework by which the various potential costs and benefits of exclusions may be more systematically examined, and uses it to apply a battery of econometric tests to Slovenian administered and free prices.

Policy-makers may contemplate excluding components of the consumer price index when they are volatile, unresponsive, or even perversely responsive to monetary policy changes.[2] Exclusion of these components may improve the clarity of the signal sent by changes in prices. Yet the exclusion may also reduce the extent to which the index accurately measures changes in the true cost of living. In choosing whether or not to exclude a component from the price index, policy-makers are therefore attempting to trade off the *clarity* and *comprehensiveness* of the index that is used to form a target.

In the next section we demonstrate how econometric tests can help quantify the net gains to clarity and the costs to comprehensiveness of excluding price components. The candidate we test for possible exclusion is administered prices in Slovenia, which make up over a quarter of the retail-price basket (Table 2).[3] Section 3 interprets the econometric results

Table 1 Exemptions from consumer price indices in eleven inflation-targeting countries

Main exemptions from broadest measure of consumer prices	Do these countries make the exemptions?**											Total
	Australia	Canada	Finland	NZ	Czech	Spain	UK	Chile	Poland	Israel	Sweden	
1 Mortgage & other interest	yes			yes		yes	yes					4
2. Government controlled prices	yes	?		yes	yes							3
3. Indirect taxes		yes	yes		yes							3
4. Energy prices	yes	yes			yes*							3
5. Government subsidies			yes									1
6. Housing capital costs			yes									1
7. Commodity prices				yes								1
8. Food prices		yes										1
Total number	3	3	3	3	3	1	1	0	0	0	0	17

* Gas and electricity prices are administered in the Czech Republic

** Data are for 1995 except Czech Republic, Poland (1999), and Chile (1999). Australia no longer makes these exclusions, although the headline consumer price index does not include mortgage interest payments.

Sources: Haldane (1995); Czech National Bank *Inflation Report* (April 1998), Landerretche, Morandé and Schmidt-Hebbel (this volume).

with reference to a detailed consideration of how administered prices are actually set in Slovenia, and Section 4 offers a conclusion.

It is important to interpret carefully the econometric findings because there are a variety of reasons why the relationship between free and administered prices can have changed in Slovenia:

(i) The relative movement of administered versus free prices in a former socialist country reflects the process of *price liberalisation* (De Broek *et al.*, 1997; Koen and de Masi, 1997; and Ross, 1998). In order to converge to market levels during transition, administered prices should be expected to rise faster than free-prices.

(ii) The smoothness and predictability of administered-price adjustments depends on *how administered prices are set*. The prices of goods supplied by private sector producers with monopoly power are set by an appointed regulator in several countries. In the UK and Chile for example, they are set according to predictable formulae based on the consumer price index and changes in producers' costs. In other economies, including Slovenia, changes in administered prices may reflect relative shifts in government preferences toward keeping the prices of staple goods low on the one hand, and improving the fiscal position by removing subsidies on the other. Furthermore, when a fiscal tightening is implemented through a reduction in administered price subsidies, the increase in prices may (like other adverse supply shocks) provide a perverse signal to a monetary policy targeting inflation.

(iii) The impact of administered-price changes on other economic variables depends upon *the nature of products* whose prices are administered. For example, utilities that are important for production or have few substitutes in consumption, have prices that are typically administered. Increases in the price of these non-substitutable goods may be passed quickly and fully into free-price inflation as price and wage-setters seek to restore their real incomes. Hošek (1998) argues that increases in administered prices in the Czech Republic may have precipitated an increase in wages and other prices, as consumers have tried to offset falls in their real incomes. Such income effects may be strong in the Czech Republic because the basket of administered-price goods includes many staple products.

2 Costs and benefits of exclusions: a framework and test results

The tests in this paper are based on measuring how an exclusion would affect the two following desirable properties of a price index that is used as an inflation target:

- *Comprehensiveness of the index* An index should include a range of products whose prices fully describe changes in the cost of living. Our yardstick is that the overall index with no exclusions is the most comprehensive index.[4]

- *Clarity of the price signal*   Changes in the price index should provide a clear indication of present and future monetary conditions.

This section employs various tests that identify *net gains* to clarity and *losses* to comprehensiveness from excluding a price component.

The choice of annual inflation rates

The econometric tests of this section use annual, rather than monthly, inflation rates – measured as 12-month changes. This choice reflects the focus of policy-makers and wage-bargainers on annual rates. Using annual rates can also remove seasonality. Regressing annual inflation rates against each other with monthly data could, however, induce serial correlation. To check for this, tests were carried out on the residuals of all econometric relationships; no significant serial correlation was uncovered. Furthermore, Cufer (1997) established econometric results using monthly inflation rates that are broadly in line with those that follow.

2.1   The impact of exclusions on the comprehensiveness of the price signal

Excluding a component from the index can reduce its comprehensiveness in both the short run and the long run. This section assesses each of these factors in turn:

(i)   The short-run correlation between the excludable component's price and the overall index

If administered prices are excluded, the targeted price index will deviate from the overall cost of living in the short run. The larger the weight of administered prices in the overall basket and the greater the short-run deviation between changes in free and administered prices, the greater this temporary discrepancy between the targeted price index and the overall cost of living. In Slovenia, administered-price goods account for up to 30% of the Slovenian consumer-price basket (Table 2). The correlation coefficient between annual inflation in free and administered-prices is 0.65.[5] Chart 1 illustrates that short-term movements in administered price inflation diverged markedly from those of free price inflation on several occasions between 1992 and 1997. The chart therefore suggests that free prices did not comprehensively capture short-term changes in the cost of living over the sample period.

Table 2 The weight of administered prices in the Slovenian consumer-price basket*

Component	weight (%)
Total	**30.2**
Energy	17.0
Municipal services	2.9
Transport and communication	2.1
Basic foodstuffs	3.5
Other administered prices	4.8

* Sources: Slovenia SORS, IMAD, and Bank of Slovenia.

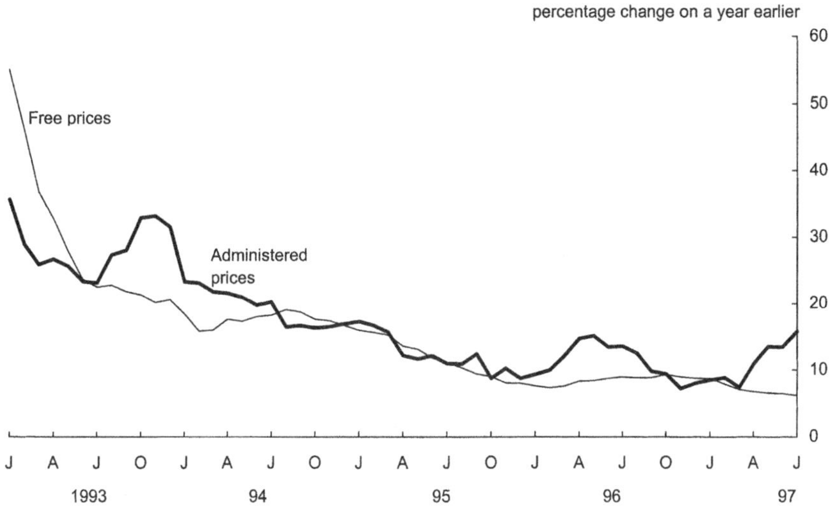

Chart 1 Components of the RPI in Slovenia

(ii) The long-run correlation between the excludable component's price and the overall index

If policy-makers exclude an item whose inflation rate does not move in line with the remainder of the index over a long horizon, this may result in the remainder of the index being a poor proxy for long-term changes index (Yates, 1995). Jacob Frenkel argues that this was a factor in determining the Bank of Israel's decision not to exclude any items from their index:

> If one decides to exclude some items from the index, one technical statistical test should be made. Any excluded item should be one that may have a larger noise, but not a fundamentally different rate of inflation than the average rate of inflation. Otherwise you are excluding something which is more fundamental.
>
> (Frenkel, 1996, page 141)

This discussion suggests the following test for long-run comprehensiveness: if the excludable component does not cointegrate with the other component, then omitting it implies that policy is not targeting an index that reflects long-term movements in the cost of living.

Table A1 in the appendix presents results regarding the time-series properties of the two series. Tests performed on data that leave out the early years of transition suggest that administered-price inflation is stationary but that free price inflation may be non-stationary. One implication is that the two variables may not be cointegrated, thereby highlighting the Bank of Slovenia's dilemma. Another inference, given the lower power of unit root tests, is that we need to use techniques that are not sensitive to assumptions about the stationarity of these two component rates of inflation.

In order to secure more robust results, we performed a variety of cointegration tests on the annual rates of inflation. We estimated the possible cointegrating relationships between the two inflation rates using two single-equation methods as well as the likelihood ratio test for the number of cointegrating vectors within a Vector Error Correction Mechanism (VECM) (Johansen, 1988). The results are presented in Table A6 of the appendix. The single-equation test suggested by Pesaran, Shin, and Smith (1996) provides a result that seems to be robust to whether or not the series are stationary. This and the VECM test both indicate a unique stable long-run equilibrium relationship between administered and free price inflation. Thus, excluding administered prices over the estimation period would not have provided a misleading signal regarding long-term movements in the overall index.

2.2   Impact of exclusions on clarity of the price signal

Policy-makers generally wish to focus attention on an index that provides the most accurate indication of monetary conditions. This section suggests various tests for determining the extent to which the exclusion may affect the clarity of the price index.

(i)   Effect of the exclusion on the volatility of the targeted index

The inclusion of products with noisy prices in the index may send an unclear signal to monetary policy. An exclusion may therefore increase the clarity of the price signal if it reduces its volatility. Table 3 provides various measures of volatility for total free and administered price inflation. The unconditional standard deviation is not a good measure of volatility when the series are non-stationary, so we prefer to measure volatility using conditional standard deviations. Table 3 illustrates that administered price inflation is subject to more short-run 'surprises'. The conditional standard deviation of administered-price inflation is almost

Table 3 Measures of volatility of annual inflation rates

Inflation measured by percentage change from previous year, 1994–97	Unconditional standard deviation	Conditional standard deviation*
Total	4.1	0.7
Free	4.4	0.6
Administered	*4.3*	*1.7*
Difference in volatilities		
Total – Free	−0.3	0.1

* Standard deviation of the residual in a regression of inflation on a constant, one lag of inflation, and time trend.

three times that of free-price inflation. However, excluding administered prices does *not* markedly reduce the conditional variance of inflation. The conditional standard deviation of total inflation is only 0.1 higher than free price inflation.[6] There is therefore not much evidence that the exclusion enhances the clarity of the signal.

(ii) Prices may be excludable because they react 'perversely' to monetary policy changes (e.g. interest payments, or fiscal policy, e.g. indirect taxes)

Certain prices *increase* in response to tighter fiscal or monetary policy, leading to potentially misleading signals as to the stance of either monetary or fiscal policy. Six of the 17 examples of excluded components in Table 1 are mortgage interest payments or indirect tax prices that may demonstrate such a perverse reaction to policy. Changes in government-controlled prices reflect such a desire to tighten fiscal policy if, for example, governments wish to reduce subsidies provided to producers of these products (Schaffer, 1997). In Slovenia, we were unable to find a good measure of fiscal policy with which to compare changes in administered prices. We instead used M0, a variable that may be directly affected by the fiscal stance. M0 showed no evidence of being associated with changes in administered prices, providing tentative evidence that over the sample period there had been little reaction of administered prices to changes in fiscal requirements.

(iii) Extent to which administered prices are affected by monetary policy

When monetary policy can do little to affect administered prices, excluding them may improve the clarity of the index because it avoids the necessity of monetary policy having to react with excessive vigour to changes in a variable over which it has no effect. Hrnčíř and Šmídková (in this volume) argue that targeting net inflation in the Czech Republic – excluding administered prices – 'helped monetary policy to accommodate the primary inflation impulses of transitional shocks and to smooth their secondary effects'. According to Hrnčíř and Šmídková, this is partly because 'the forecast of overall CPI inflation has not been viewed as the most reliable indicator of the medium-term inflation outlook'.

Such arguments lead us to test for different measures of the exogeneity of administered-price inflation.[7] To begin with, we use a single-equation version of a test for simultaneity bias (Spencer and Berk, 1981), to find that *current* administered price inflation is exogenous in an equation where the current free-price inflation is the dependent variable (Table A5 in the appendix).

Administered prices could also be exogenous in the sense that past administered-price inflation affects current free-price inflation but current administered-price inflation does not depend on past free-price inflation. This Granger-Sims causality is tested for on an unrestricted Vector Autoregression (VAR) (Table A3 in the appendix) estimated between the two inflation rates. The results in Table A4 confirm that administered-price inflation Granger causes free price inflation but that the reverse is not true. As a further step, administered-price inflation would be *weakly* exogenous when the series is unaffected by past deviations from the long-run cointegrating relationship (Urbain, 1992). Table A9 confirms that the adjustment coefficient in the VECM equation for administered-price inflation is not significant. Table A10 suggests that unexplained movements (shocks) to administered-price inflation are unrelated to free price inflation. These three results together imply that administered prices are strongly exogenous to the equation that determines free-price inflation: the two series are cointegrated only because free prices adjust toward the exogenous administered-price series.

The exogeneity tests illustrate that current and lagged values of free price inflation do not affect administered-price inflation. Insofar as administered-price inflation is not affected by developments in other prices, it fails to provide a clear signal as to what monetary policy can affect.

(iv) Extent to which the excludable component has leading indicator properties over free prices

If administered-price changes feed rapidly and strongly into free prices, leaving them out of the targeted index may leave out information about the second-round effects of administered-price shocks on free prices.

Using our preferred unrestricted VAR estimates, we test how much of the variance of free-price inflation in the past is due to administered-price surprises. The variance decomposition shown in Chart 2 below illustrates that the contribution of administered price inflation shocks to free-price inflation is significant (explaining about 40%–50% of its variance after six months).

Excluding the first-round effects of administered prices may therefore

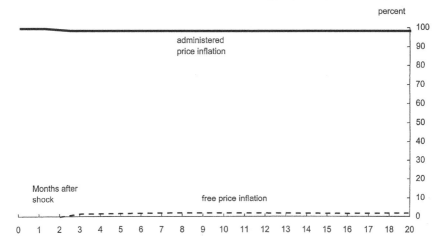

Chart 2a Variance of annual administered price inflation due to shocks in administered or free price inflation

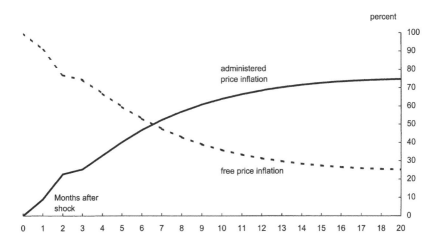

Chart 2b Variance of annual free price inflation due to shocks in administered or
free price inflation

worsen the clarity of the index by making it less of a leading indicator of
future monetary conditions.

(v) The exclusion may reduce the impact of supply shocks on the
targeted index and increase the sensitivity to demand shocks

There are strong arguments for policy to accommodate the impact of
supply shocks, such as a change in the terms of trade. Failure to accommodate such a shift may result in falling output and rising prices (stagflation).

Yet a rigid interpretation of inflation targeting would make it difficult to accommodate such a shock. Excluding the direct effects of a supply shock may increase the clarity of the price signal by dampening the tendency for prices to signal a tightening (or loosening of policy) in the face of negative (or positive) supply shocks.

Conversely, policy *should* respond to demand shocks. A positive demand shock increases prices and output. The inflation target should signal such a shock in prices as fully as possible. The exclusion may therefore have beneficial properties if it results in policy targeting a price index that is more reflective of demand shocks and less contaminated by supply shocks.

In order to identify more clearly the role of administered prices in the economy, we distinguish between shocks that have a permanent effect on unemployment (permanent shocks) from those that have a transitory effect on unemployment (temporary shocks). Both shocks may have an impact on nominal variables such as prices. These shocks can be obtained from estimates of a VAR with two lags between the unemployment rate and total RPI inflation in Slovenia from 1994M1–1997M10 (Table A11 of the appendix). The effect of the temporary and permanent shocks on overall RPI inflation can be extracted from the VAR estimates after imposing the restriction that the two types of shocks are uncorrelated and that one shock does not have a permanent effect of the variance of unemployment (Blanchard and Quah, 1989).[8] The results are shown in Chart 3 and Table 4.

The permanent-shock component of overall inflation is strongly correlated with annual administered-price inflation. The contemporaneous

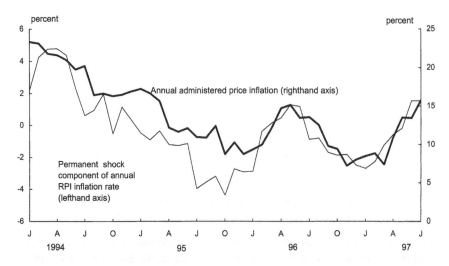

Chart 3 Permanent shocks and administered prices

Table 4 Correlations between annual free and administered-price inflation and temporary and permanent-shock components of annual overall inflation (1994M1–1997M10)

	Temporary shock	*Permanent shock*	*Administered price inflation*	*Free-price inflation*
Temporary shock	1.00	−0.39	−0.22	0.16
Permanent shock		1.00	**0.85**	0.47
Administered-price inflation			1.00	0.69
Free-price inflation				1.00

correlation coefficient between administered-price inflation and permanent supply shocks (as identified by our structural assumptions) is 0.85. This is much higher than the correlation of 0.45 between permanent shocks and free-price inflation. This strong result is consistent with the view that changes in administered prices largely reflect relative-price adjustments. Revisions to administered prices are not so much motivated by nominal changes such as the passing on of changes in the overall price level. This *relative* price-setting behaviour would make administered-price shocks analogous to shocks in the terms of trade of consumers.

The results suggest that the Bank of Slovenia is justified in drawing a clear distinction between movements in administered and free-price inflation in their analysis of monetary conditions. The findings also suggest that it may be advantageous for monetary policy to accommodate the first-round effects of changes in administered-price inflation, since these are akin to permanent supply shocks.

2.3 Summary of econometric results

The balance of tests is summarised in Tables 5 and 6. The implications are left open to interpretation. The exercise is useful in identifying more precisely the net advantages from excluding administered prices, and the following section provides practical insights into the formulation of Slovenian administered prices in order to facilitate a more informed decision.

3 Administered price policy in Slovenia: cause and effect

Administered-price behaviour has been a key consideration in the setting of monetary policy in Slovenia. The econometric results therefore need to be viewed in conjunction with a discussion both of how administered prices are determined and of their impact on the economy. This discussion will focus on the following questions:

Table 5 Summary of results for comprehensiveness

Issue	Include or Exclude?
• Administered price goods comprise a very large part of the Slovenian consumer basket, and price changes deviate significantly in the short run.	**Include:** large potential loss to comprehensiveness if excluded
• In the long run, administered prices have moved broadly in line with free prices, indicating that meeting targets for free prices may also imply achieving similar inflation rates for administered prices.	**Can be excluded:** potential loss to comprehensiveness small, *but subject to change in the relationship in 1997.*

Table 6 Summary of results for the effect of the exclusion on clarity of the price index

Issue	Include or Exclude?
• The volatility of free-price inflation is not markedly lower than the volatility of the overall index.	**Little grounds to exclude.**
• There is evidence that administered prices react perversely to policy.	**No grounds to exclude** (but the test is weak).
• Administered prices have predictive powers over free prices.	**Include,** excluding them could delay policy response.
• Administered-price inflation is not caused by free prices, and administered-price inflation is exogenous to developments in free-price inflation.	**Exclude:** policy is unable to affect administered free prices.
• Administered prices correlated highly with permanent (supply) shocks.	Direct effects imply **exclusion.** Indirect effects imply **inclusion.**
• Administered prices react less than free prices to demand shocks.	No significant losses from **excluding.**

• Are the results in Section 2 validated by our practical knowledge of the setting of administered prices?
• Will the economy be subject to further structural change that will limit the usefulness of analysis of historical data?

3.1   Legal framework for price control

The Prices Law was adopted on 15 May 1991 and published in the Official Gazette of the Republic of Slovenia (UL RS 1/91-I). It defines both the prices that are included in the price-control regime and the conditions under which the government can put certain free prices under its control. It also defines methods of price control as well as the time limitation of the controls. The stated purpose of this price control is to eliminate the inconsistencies in price formation, which can appear because of market imperfections or monopoly positions. In practice, approximately one quarter of all retail prices is subject to price control, which can be imposed on a permanent or temporary basis.[9]

3.2 Composition of administered price index

From the retail price index we have constructed two indices: of administered prices and of free prices (Appendix 2). The Institute for Macroeconomic Analyses and Development (IMAD) in Slovenia classifies administered prices into five major groups (Marzidovsek, 1995). Table 7 presents the weights of administered prices by category and as a total.

3.3 The formation of administered prices

The formation of administered prices has changed over time; we can consider two distinct periods:

(i) From 1992 to 1997, government policy on administered prices was partially influenced by a desire to offset inflation in free prices

For example in 1992–93, the administered-prices policy contributed considerably to the lowering of the inflation rate and inflation expectations. The implication is, as Chart 1 shows, that only between 1995 and 1996 did the two series grow in parallel. Over this period, the administered-price increases (decreases) that were not wholly reflected in free-price increases (decreases) would have had the effect of altering *relative* prices.

(ii) From 1997, the government adopted the policy of equalising the prices of energy (petroleum, gas, and electricity) with average European levels

Significant discrepancies between the inflation rates appeared in the first part of 1997. Table 8 shows that administered prices increased by 16.1% in 1997 and contributed 4.6 percentage points to an overall inflation rate of 9.4% in 1997. One reason for the increases was that the levels of some particular administered prices in Slovenia were previously below the average European levels so that a 'level-equalising policy' leads to sharp price increases.

Fiscal policy also helps to explain the rapid growth of administered prices in 1997. The budget memorandum for 1997 referred to the increase of administered prices as a necessary element of fiscal reform. For example the tax-driven increase in oil derivative prices contributed greatly to the increase in tax revenue.

If such a policy is sustained, however, administered-price inflation may cease to be cointegrated with other domestic prices. This would happen if

Table 7 Weights of administered prices by category[*]

Shares in percentages	1992	1993	1994	1995	1996	1997	1998
Energy	16.4	13.7	13.6	12.9	12.8	15.3	17.0
– petroleum products	13.4	10.9	9.5	8.7	8.4	12.3	13.7
– electricity for households	3.0	2.8	4.0	4.3	4.4	3.1	3.3
Municipal services	2.4	2.4	2.5	2.7	2.9	2.1	2.9
Transport and communication	3.2	2.2	2.2	2.5	2.5	2.6	2.1
Basic foodstuffs	4.3	4.4	4.0	4.4	4.0	3.6	3.5
Other administered prices	7.4	7.6	7.3	7.1	7.2	4.6	4.8
Total of administered prices	33.7	30.3	29.6	29.6	29.4	28.3	30.2

[*] Source: SORS (Slovenian statistical office) IMAD (Price Regulator) and own calculations.

Table 8 Weight and contribution of administered and free prices to overall inflation in 1997

	Weight in price index (in %)	Contribution to inflation p.p.	(in %)	Price growth (in %)
Administered price index	28	4.6	48	16.1
Free price index	72	4.9	52	6.9
Retailed price index	100	9.4	100	9.4

Contribution is defined as the relative importance (growth multiplied by its relative weight) of price sub-index to the inflation, in p.p. and in percentage.

free prices (having already caught up more quickly to world levels) are more closely anchored to world levels. Thus administered prices may increase more quickly than free prices during the period in which they catch up with free prices. For example, in order to reach European Union levels, the prices of petroleum products and electricity for households should increase substantially in the next three years. For the price of electricity, the increase should be about 7% in real terms, which amounts to approximately 15% to 16% in nominal terms.[10]

This discussion helps in the interpretation of the econometric tests that featured in the previous section. Clearly the behaviour of administered prices over the sample reflected different influences. However, we can conclude that, for whatever reason, a significant proportion of the administered-price adjustments was not aimed at maintaining a constant relative-price ratio.

This suggests the following conclusions about administered prices and monetary policy implementation in Slovenia.

(i) *It is harder for the central bank to control the entire price index if a large proportion of administered prices is set exogenously.*

(ii) *It is important for the central bank to understand how inflation pressures are affected by the relationship between administered and free prices.* Cufer (1997) has suggested that the monetary policy stance has been restrictive after allowing for the direct impact of administered prices on free prices. He argues that, as the central bank would be resisting a supply shock, the tightening of monetary policy could be excessive and cause weaker economic activity growth.

(iii) *The process of administered price convergence implies that free prices will not provide a comprehensive proxy for overall changes in the cost of living. While free prices have already reached world levels, administered prices may catch up to those levels in the future. Thus free and administered prices are unlikely to cointegrate as they have in the past. This implies that the exclusion of administered prices will increase the extent to which comprehensiveness is eroded.*

4   Policy implications and conclusions

The preceding analysis has identified a policy dilemma. In the face of supply shocks, there may appear to be good reasons to accommodate the increase in the overall price level. Yet the final decision is a matter of taste: the exclusion may be insufficient to prevent monetary policy from having to react because for horizons longer than six months at least 40% of annual free-price inflation may be explained by shocks to administered prices. A goal of policy in Slovenia and other transitional economies is to accommodate some of the impact of price liberalisation while maintaining a credible policy peg. Thus the practical options may be the following:

- Exclude administered prices from the targeted index to minimise target misses, but ensure that policy anticipates their impact on the free-price index; or
- Include administered prices in the targeted index, but implement policies that aim to preserve credibility in the face of unavoidable target misses when administered-price shocks occur. Such policies might involve using relatively wide bands, publishing regular forecasts, and other communications strategies.

Between the extremes of excluding administered prices from any policy reaction function and treating them like any other price movement, there are various ways for policy to partially accommodate such supply shocks in an inflation-targeting framework. The main focus of the paper is, however, the framework rather than the results. Our tests quantify the main economic arguments that have been proposed in favour of or against the exclusion of administered prices from a targeted index. This method could be applied to a wide range of potential candidates for exclusion.

APPENDIX 1. ECONOMETRIC RESULTS

Unit root tests

We perform three types of unit root tests on the annual inflation rates:

(i)   augmented Dickey Fuller tests using a sequential testing procedure to determine whether a constant or a time trend should be included (Dolado, Jenkinson, and Sosvilla-Rivero, 1990);
(ii) the Phillips-Perron non-parametric test that is robust to higher-order serial correlation (Phillips-Perron 1988) and;
(iii) a unit root statistic that tests the null hypothesis of stationarity against the alternative of non-stationarity (Kwaitkowski *et al.*, 1992).

Table A1 Unit root tests for stationarity[1]

Unit root test	ADF test	Phillips-Perron	Kwaitkowski et al.	Summary
Null hypothesis:	Unit root	Unit root	No unit root	
Free-price inflation 1993M1–1997M10	−6.92**[2]	−8.98 **[3]	0.164**	stationary/unit root
Administered-price inflation 1993M1–1997M10	−2.70[4]	−1.98[5]	0.157**	unit root
Free-price inflation 1994M1–1997M10	−1.81[6]	−1.46[7]	0.107	stationary/unit root
Administered-price inflation 1994M1–1997M10	−4.11***[8]	−3.762**[9]	0.106	stationary

[1] Rejection level of null hypothesis: ** at 5%; * at 10%.
[2] constant, time trend and one lag of the dependent variable.
[3] constant, time trend and one lag of the dependent variable.
[4] constant only.
[5] constant only.
[6] constant and time trend.
[7] constant and time trend.
[8] constant only.
[9] constant only.

Lag length

Table A2 The optimal lag length by criteria for a VAR in annual free and administered-price inflation[†]

SBC	AIC	LR test of extra lags (testing sequentially shortest to largest[‡])	Q-Statistic for correlogram (order 13) residuals of 4-lag VAR
2–4	2–4	1	Admin. price inflation equation. 9.05
			Free-price inflation equation. 17.04

[†] Rejection level of null hypothesis: ** at 5%; * at 10%.
[‡] See Greene (1997), p. 817 and Lutkephol (1990).

From Table A2, a lag length of three to four months would be favoured by both the Aikake Information and the Schwartz Bayesian Criteria. The Q-statistics show that the residuals in the favoured four-lag VAR are not significantly autocorrelated with any past residuals up to and including 12 months ago. This provides some evidence that working with annual inflation rates using monthly data does not imply significant serial correlation.

Unrestricted VAR estimates and Granger causality

Building on the previous findings, a VAR with four lags in annual free and administered-price inflation was estimated and used to carry out Granger-Sims causality tests (see Charezma and Deadman, 1997).

Exogeneity tests

An unrestricted VAR does not tell us whether or not current administered-price inflation would be exogenous to current free-price inflation in a structural system. To test this concept of exogeneity, a general structural equation was estimated where current free-price inflation is determined by *current* and lagged administered-price inflation and lagged free-price inflation. The restriction that the current administered-price inflation term is exogenous can be tested using Spencer and Berks' (1981) single-equation version of the Hausman (1993) test for simultaneity bias (see Greene, 1991, page 764). The statistic reported is a Chi-squared statistic with one degree of freedom. A symmetrical test can be carried out on a structural equation with current administered-price inflation as the dependent variable and current free-price inflation as the (potentially endogenous) dependent variable.

Cointegration tests and estimates of long-run relationships

Three different cointegration tests are performed on the two series. The first, the well-known Engle-Granger two-step test, is assessed with refer-

Table A3 Unrestricted VAR estimates for free-price inflation (ADRPIF) and administered-price inflation (ADRPIA)[†]

Estimation method: Least squares Sample: 1994M1–1997M10 (observations: 46)			
Regression of ADRPIA on	*Coefficient*	*Std. Error*	*t-statistic*
ADRPIA(−1)	0.77	0.16	4.87**
ADRPIA(−2)	0.18	0.20	0.91
ADRPIA(−3)	−0.16	0.19	−0.84
ADRPIA(−4)	0.02	0.14	0.16
ADRPIF(−1)	0.03	0.55	0.05
ADRPIA(−2)	0.03	0.68	0.04
ADRPIA(−3)	0.55	0.67	0.82
ADRPIA(−4)	−0.61	0.39	−1.57
Constant	0.03	0.01	2.71**
Regression of ADRPIF on	*Coefficient*	*Std. Error*	*t-statistic*
ADRPIA(−1)	0.12	0.04	2.95**
ADRPIA(−2)	0.01	0.05	0.10
ADRPIA(−3)	−0.11	0.05	−2.26**
ADRPIA(−4)	0.09	0.04	2.50**
ADRPIF(−1)	0.99	0.14	6.97**
ADRPIF(−2)	−0.02	0.18	−0.12
ADRPIF(−3)	0.15	0.17	0.84
ADRPIF(−4)	−0.22	0.10	−2.18**
Constant	0.00	0.00	−1.77
	Regression of ADRPIA	*Regression of ADRPIF*	
R-squared	0.918	0.99	
S.E. of regression	1.740	0.45	
Durbin-Watson stat	1.973	2.09	

[†] Rejection level of null hypothesis: ** at 5%; * at 10%.

ence to critical values provided by Davidson and MacKinnon (1993). The Pesaran *et al.* test has the advantage of being robust to whether the variables are I(1) or I(0). It is based on two statistics: a Wald test (W) and an F-statistic (F) whose critical values are given in Pesaran, Shin, and Smith (1996). Finally, the Johansen cointegration trace test is carried out, assuming a time trend in the variables, and an intercept but no time trend in the cointegrating vector.

We now derive the long-run coefficients of the relationship between free and administered-price inflation. Four different methods are used. First, we estimate a Vector Error Correction Mechanism (VECM) with three lags in each variable, assuming a time trend in the data and an intercept but no time trend in the cointegrating vector. The estimated coefficients are reported with the *t*-statistics based on Newey-West standard errors. Second, we use Inder's (1992) version of the Phillips-Hansen fully

Table A4 Granger causality tests on annual free and administered-price inflation[†]
Sample: 1994M1–1997M10 (observations: 46)

Lag length of VAR	1	2	3	4
Sims GMD Test (CHISQRD 2)				
NULL: free not gcause admin	4.30	6.42*		
NULL: admin not gcause free	9.72**	8.85**		
Granger Causality (CHISQRD 1)				
NULL: free not gcause admin	0.26	0.66	0.33	0.16
NULL: admin not gcause free	4.14**	5.03**	2.99**	4.4**

[†] Rejection level of null hypothesis: ** at 5%; * at 10%.

Table A5 Tests for simultaneity bias between annual administered and free-price inflation[†]

Null hypothesis is exogeneity of administered-current:	Dependent variable: free-price inflation	Dependent variable: price inflation
Administered-price inflation	0.529	
Free-price inflation		0.08

[†] Rejection level of null hypothesis: ** at 5%; * at 10%.

modified estimator (1990), which is meant to have better small-sample properties as it estimates the long and the short-run coefficients together. We also obtain estimates by regressing the exogenous variables of the equation in unrestricted lagged levels and differences: the autoregressive distributed lag (ARDL) format. Finally, we can obtain estimates of the long-run coefficients and Newey-West standard errors by imposing the non-linear restriction implied by cointegration.

The next table presents the estimates of the VECM between the two series.

Weak and strong exogeneity

Is administered-price inflation affected by a tendency to preserve the long-run cointegrating relationship? This hypothesis can be directly tested by checking whether the cointegrating relationship is significant in determining administered-price inflation in a VECM (Table A9).

We also check whether the residuals from the administered-price inflation equation are independent (orthogonal) of the residuals from the free-price inflation, by testing whether the residuals from the administered-price equation (without a long-run term) are significant in a dynamic free-price inflation equation. The results of these tests are

Table A6 Cointegration tests on annual inflation rates (1994M1–1997M10)[†]

Regression of annual inflation rates	Engle-Granger test statistic	Pesaran et al. (1996): Fstat and Wald test reported	Johansen Trace test (with VECM of 3 lags)	Summary
Free on admin.	−1.76	10.86(F), 21.73(W) **	6.62**	cointegrated
Admin. on free	−2.23	4.42(F), 8.85(W)		not cointegrated

[†] In all three tests, the null is that the series are not cointegrated
Rejection level of null hypothesis: ** at 5%; * at 10%.

Table A7 Estimates of the long-run coefficient between administered-price inflation (ADRPIA) and free-price inflation (ADRPIF)[†]

Equation D(ADRPIF) = −c1*(ADRPIF(−1) − c2*ADRPIA(−1)) + lagged free and administered-price inflation acceleration terms	Coefficient c1	Coefficient c2
Johansen	−0.08 (−4.29)	1.27 (5.43)
Inder	NA	1.28 (3.01)
ARDL	−0.062 (−2.88)	1.333
Non-linear	−0.062 (−2.264)	1.28 (3.01)
Equation D(ADRPIA) = −c3*(ADRPIA(−1) −c4*ADRPIF(−1)) + lagged free and administered-price inflation acceleration terms	Coefficient c3	Coefficient c4
Johansen	−0.158 (2.09)	
Inder	NA	0.216 (0.70)
ARDL	−0.27 (−2.93)	0.216
Non-linear	−0.27 (−2.93)	0.216 (0.70)

[†] Rejection level of null hypothesis: ** at 5%; * at 10%.

reported in Table A10 and confirm that the errors from the equations determining free and administered-price inflation are orthogonal.

Finally, we report the estimates of the VAR that we used to derive the permanent and temporary shock component of Slovenian retail-price inflation.

Table A8 Vector Error Correction Mechanism between administered-price inflation (ADRPIA) and free-price inflation (ADRPIF)[†]

Estimation method: FIML
Sample: 1994M1–1997M10 (observations: 46)
Standard errors and t-statistics in parentheses

Cointegrating Eq:	ECM =	
ADRPIF(−1)	1.00	
ADRPIA(−1)	−1.277	
	(0.24)	
	(−5.43**)	
Constant	6.74	

Error Correction:	D(ADRPIF)	D(ADRPIA)
ECM	−0.08	0.16
	(0.019)	(0.075)
	(−4.30**)	(2.10**)
D(ADRPIF(−1))	0.07	−0.123
	(0.132)	(0.533)
	(0.56)	(−0.23)
D(ADRPIF(−2))	0.07	0.063
	(0.109)	(0.439)
	(0.67)	(0.14)
D(ADRPIF(−3))	0.218	0.607
	(0.10)	(0.404)
	(2.18**)	(1.50)
D(ADRPIA(−1))	0.029	0.055
	(0.036)	(0.146)
	(0.787)	(0.376)
D(ADRPIA(−2))	0.034	0.243
	(0.04)	(0.143)
	(0.97)	(1.71)
D(ADRPIA(−3))	−0.08	0.05
	(0.036)	(0.144)
	(−2.31*)	(0.353)
Constant	−0.109	−0.044
	(0.078)	(0.315)
	(−1.40)	(−0.140)

R-squared	0.520	0.275
Sum sq. resids	7.73	126.08
S.E. equation	0.45	1.82
Log likelihood	−24.24	−88.46
Akaike AIC	1.40	4.194
Schwarz criteria	1.72	4.512
Log likelihood		−112.67
Akaike information criteria (system)		5.68
Schwarz criteria (system)		6.40

[†] Rejection level of null hypothesis: ** at 5%; * at 10%.

Table A9 Weak exogeneity of administered-price inflation (ADRPIA)

Estimation method: Least squares Sample: 1994M1–1997M10 (observations: 46) D(ADRPIA) on	Coefficient	Std. error	t-statistic
Constant	−0.02	0.33	−0.07
D(ADRPIA(−1))	0.14	0.15	0.95
D(ADRPIA(−2))	0.24	0.15	1.59
D(ADRPIA(−3))	−0.01	0.15	−0.08
D(ADRPIF(−1))	−0.19	0.37	−0.51
D(ADRPIF(−2))	−0.04	0.28	−0.16
D(ADRPIF(−3))	0.25	0.24	1.08
ADRPIA(−1)−1.28*ADRPIF(−1)	**−0.09**	**0.08**	**−1.21**
R-squared	0.10		
S.E. of regression	2.11		
Sum squared resid	205.10		
Log likelihood	−112.66		
Durbin-Watson stat	1.91		

Table A10 Test of orthogonality of residuals from administered-price inflation (ADRPIA) and free-price inflation (ADRPIF) equations[†]

Estimation method: Least squares Sample: 1994M1–1997M10 (observations: 46) D(ADRPIF) on	Coefficient	Std. error	t-statistic
Constant	−0.109	0.079	−1.38
D(ADRPIA(−1))	0.008	0.038	0.21
D(ADRPIA(−2))	0.006	0.037	0.17
D(ADRPIA(−3))	−0.097	0.037	−2.60**
D(ADRPIF(−1))	0.172	0.124	1.38
D(ADRPIF(−2))	0.088	0.110	0.80
D(ADRPIF(−3))	0.194	0.101	1.93*
ADRPIA(−1)−1.28*ADRPIF(−1)	0.086	0.021	4.03**
residual from administered price equation	**−0.027**	**0.039**	**−0.70**
R-squared	0.52		
S.E. of regression	0.4568		
Sum squared resid	7.79		
Log likelihood	−24.44		
Durbin-Watson stat	2.30		

[†] Rejection level of null hypothesis: ** at 5%; * at 10%.

Table A11 VAR estimates for annual inflation rate (ADRPI) and unemployment as a percentage of population of working age (UNEMP)[†]

Estimation Method: Least squares
Sample: 1994M1–1997M10 (observations: 46)

Regression of UNEMP on	Coefficient	Std. error	t-statistic
CONSTANT	1.63	0.858	1.90**
UNEMP(–1)	1.25	0.126	9.91**
UNEMP(–2)	–0.36	0.132	–2.69**
ADRPI(–1)	–0.11	0.046	–2.31**
ADRPI(–2)	0.10	0.043	2.33**

Regression of ADRPI on	Coefficient	Std. error	t-statistic
CONSTANT	–8.46	2.493	–3.39**
UNEMP(–1)	–0.74	0.367	–2.01**
UNEMP(–2)	1.37	0.383	3.56**
ADRPI(–1)	0.85	0.135	6.34**
ADRPI(–2)	0.03	0.126	0.21

	Regression of UNEMP	Regression of ADRPI
R-squared	0.902	0.981
S.E. of regression	0.192	0.558
Durbin-Watson stat	1.998	1.743

[†] Source of employment and working-population data: SORS. Rejection level of null hypothesis: ** at 5%; * at 10%. Lag length chosen by minimising AIC and SBC and likelihood ratio tests.

APPENDIX 2. THE COMPOSITION OF THE RETAIL PRICE INDEX IN SLOVENIA

The retail price index (RPI) was used as an official measure of inflation until the end of 1997, since then the consumer price index (CPI) has been followed more closely. This analysis is based on the retail price index. The Statistical Office of the Republic of Slovenia (SORS) calculates and publishes the price index. In the index calculation of retail prices it takes into account the retail price growth from the 21st of the previous month until the 20th of the current month. The calculation takes into consideration the importance of individual products and services. The calculated retail price index is then considered as the official inflation figure of the current month. Information about inflation is made public on the last working day of each month. There are no privileged parties – no one receives any advance information: neither the government, nor the central bank, the ministries' or other institutions.

The index consists of approximately 500 retail products and services, which are classified into groups. The first two levels of retail price index division are shown in Chart 4. The basic price index division is the division

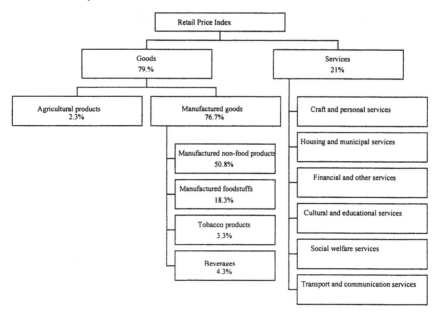

Chart 4 Breakdown of the Slovenian Retail Price Index

into the goods price index and the services price index. The sub-indexes are further divided into more detailed price indexes, SORS groups prices into price indexes up to ten levels. It also determines the influence of each product or service on the total price index. Weights change once yearly (at the beginning of the year) and remain unchanged within the year. Weights for individual products and services are calculated on the basis of their share in the common retail sale of goods and services. SORS publishes only the weights of the main sub-groups of the retail price index.

Notes

1 The authors are grateful for helpful comments made by Maxwell Fry, Tibor Hledik, and Vincent Labard. The arguments represent the views of the authors and not those of the Bank of Slovenia or the Bank of England.
2 We do not discuss components of the consumer price basket, such as the price of future goods (Alchian and Klein, 1973), whose prices are excluded from an inflation target because they are difficult to measure.
3 Administered prices are defined to be prices whose values are wholly set by the general government.
4 Consumers may themselves filter noisy (uninformative) components in their perceptions of inflation. A comprehensive index may not then be what is relevant for economic agents' welfare. But for simplicity we abstract from such considerations and assume that the true cost of living that should be stabilised is captured by the fully comprehensive index.
5 There were no significant cross-correlations between *monthly* changes in free and administered prices at any lag.

6 The result is very similar if we condition on another measure of trend inflation, such as the Hodrick-Prescott filter.
7 We are assuming that if administered-price inflation is exogenous to free-price inflation, it is not affected by monetary policy. In this sample, we failed to detect a *direct* statistical relationship between any monetary policy variable and administered prices.
8 See also Sterne and Bayoumi (1995) for an international comparison of supply and demand shocks based on these identifications.
9 Temporary price controls are limited to four months, but this tenure can be prolonged. In the event, the decrees that classified prices as being temporarily controlled were prolonged after their validity expired. So, the estimates assume no difference between the direct and the indirect control.
10 The price increase is calculated on the basis of an expected inflation rate of 8% to 9%.

Bibliography

Alchian, A. and Klein, B. (1973), 'On a correct measure of inflation', *Journal of Money, Credit and Banking,* Vol. 5, No. 1, pp. 173–91.
Bakhshi, H. and Yates, A. (1998), 'Are inflation expectations rational?', *Bank of England Working Paper No. 81,* July.
Barth, R.C., Roe, A.R. and Wong, C-H (eds) (1994), *Coordinating Stabilization and Structural Reform,* IMF.
Blanchard, O. and Quah, D. (1989), 'The dynamic effects of aggregate demand and supply disturbances', *The American Economic Review,* September, Vol. 79, No. 4, pp. 655–73.
Cagan, P. (1979), *Persistent Inflation: Historical and Policy Essays,* Colombia University Press.
Central Bank of Sri Lanka, *Annual Report (*1997), pp. 92–3.
Charemza, W.W. and Deadman, D.F. (1997), *New Directions in Econometric Practice,* Edward Elgar.
Czech National Bank, *Inflation Report* (1998), April.
Cufer, U. (1997), 'Administered prices in Slovenia', paper presented to CEFTA Workshop, Poland.
Davidson, R. and MacKinnon, J.G. (1993), 'Estimation and inference in econometrics', Oxford University Press, New York.
De Broeck, M., De Masi, P. and Koen, V. (1997), 'Inflation dynamics in Kazakhstan', *Economics in Transition,* Vol. 5(1), pp. 195–213.
Dolado, J.J., Jenkinson, T. and Sosvilla-Rivero, S. (1990), 'Cointegration and unit roots: a survey', *Journal of Economic Surveys,* No. 4, pp. 249–76.
Frenkel, J. (1996), 'Israel's experience with inflation' in '*Achieving Price Stability*', a symposium sponsored by the Federal Reserve Bank of Kansas City, Jackson Hole, Wyoming, 29–31 August, pp. 139–46.
Goodhart, C.A.E. and Viñals, J. (1994), 'Strategy and tactics of monetary policy: examples from Europe and the Antipodes', *LSE Financial Markets Group Special Paper,* No. 61, August.
Greene, W.H. (1991), *Econometric Analysis,* Prentice Hall, New York.
Hausman, J. (1983), 'Specification and estimation of simultaneous equations models' in Griliches, Z. and Intriligator, M. (eds) *Handbook of Econometrics,* Amsterdam: North Holland.

Hošek, J. (1998), 'Czech inflation and the income effect of price deregulation: the theory and reality', Czech National Bank, unpublished memo.

Johansen, S. (1988), 'Statistical analysis of cointegration vectors', *Journal of Economic Dynamics and Control,* 12, pp. 231–54.

Inder, B. (1993), 'Estimating long-run relationships in economics', *Journal of Econometrics,* 57, pp. 53–68, North Holland.

Koen, V. and De Masi, P. (1997), 'Prices in the transition: ten stylized facts', *IMF Working Paper,* WP/97/158.

Kwiatowski, D., Phillips, P.C.B. and Schmidt, P. (1992), 'Testing the null hypothesis of stationarity against the alternative of a unit root', *Journal of Econometrics,* 54, pp. 159–78, North Holland.

Lutkepohl, H. (1991), *Introduction to Multiple Time Series Analysis,* Springer-Verlag, Berlin.

Marzidovsek, N. (1995), *Politika cenovnega nadzora v Sloveniji v letih 1991 do 1995,* UMAR Delovni zvezek st. 9, letnik IV, December.

McNeilly, C.J. and Schiesser-Gachnang D. (1998), 'Reducing inflation: lessons from Albania's early success', *IMF Working Paper,* WP/98/78.

OECD (1997), *OECD Economic Surveys, Slovenia,* OECD, Paris.

Phillips, P.C.B. and Hansen, B.E. (1990), 'Statistical inference in instrumental variables regression with I (1) processes', *Review of Economic Studies,* 57, pp. 99–125.

Phillips, P.C.B. and Perron, P. (1988), 'Testing for a unit root in time series regression', *Biometrika,* 75, 335–46.

Pesaran, M.H., Shin, Y. and Smith, R.J. (1996), 'Testing for the existence of a long-run relationship', *Department of Applied Economics, University of Cambridge, Working Papers,* No. 9622.

Reserve Bank of India, *Annual Report* (1996–97), p. 65.

Ross, K. (1998), 'Post stabilization inflation dynamics in Slovenia', *IMF Working Paper,* WP/98/27.

Spencer, D. and Berk, K. (1981), 'A limited information specification test', *Econometrica,* 49, No. 4, July, pp. 1079–85.

Schaffer, M. (1997), 'Government subsidies to enterprises in Central and Eastern Europe. Budgetary subsidies and tax arrears' in Newbury, D. (ed.) *Tax and Benefit and Central Europe.*

Sterne, G. and Bayoumi, T. (1993), 'Temporary cycles or volatile trends? Economic fluctuations in 21 OECD countries', *Bank of England Working Paper,* No. 13, April and (1995) *The Manchester School,* March.

Urbain, J-P. (1992), 'On weak exogeneity in error correction models', *Oxford Bulletin of Economics and Statistics,* 54(2), May, pp. 187–207.

Woodford, M. (1997), 'Nonstandard indicators for monetary policy: can their usefulness be judged from forecasting regressions?' in Mankiw, G. (ed.) *NBER Studies in Business Cycles,* Vol. 29, University of Chicago Press.

Yates, A. (1995), 'On the design of inflation targets' in Haldane, A.G. (ed.) *Targeting Inflation,* pp. 135–69.

Exchange rate considerations in a small open economy

A critical look at the MCI as a possible solution

David G. Mayes and Matti Virén[1]

1 Introduction

In a regime of floating exchange rates and mobile capital, both the interest rate and the exchange rate are important components in the transmission of monetary policy to inflation. Central banks in small open economies have little choice over the specific combination of the two components, but larger economies such as the United States and the euro area can make a choice, especially if they co-ordinate their actions.[2] The more 'open' the economy, the greater the importance of the exchange rate tends to be. Central banks have undertaken to estimate the effect of exchange rates and communicate it to financial markets. A common communication device employed by central banks, international organisations, and private-sector financial institutions has been to combine interest rates and the exchange rate into a single indicator of monetary conditions, an MCI (monetary conditions index). MCIs are weighted sums of the variables that the central bank influences directly by monetary policy. As a means of summarising the setting of monetary pressures on the economy, they may be superior to referring to central bank instruments alone. The variables chosen reflect the main channels of transmission of monetary policy through to inflation. The weights reflect their relative importance. In practice most MCIs include just a short interest rate and a measure of the exchange rate,[3] both usually in real terms, although some private-sector organisations have begun to add other asset prices.[4]

MCIs have the advantage of simplicity. However, they also present difficulties in estimation and interpretation. This paper, therefore, explores the definition of MCIs. It suggests how the difficulties of estimation can be addressed by illustrating a set of new estimates for 12 EU countries over the period 1972 to 1997. With the aid of experience from central banks in Canada, Finland, New Zealand, Norway, and Sweden, we explain how an MCI might best be used to inform monetary policy-making in other small open economies.

In Sections 1 and 2, we define MCIs and explain the motivation for their use. Section 3 then surveys existing estimates and reviews the problems that MCIs pose for estimation, providing a basis for our empirical work in Section 4. Using a data set covering all the EU countries (except Luxembourg and Greece), we explain the variation among existing estimates and provide new estimates over our own. These estimates suggest that an MCI ratio – defined as the ratio of the interest rate coefficient to the exchange-rate coefficient in the MCI – of the order of 3.5 might be an appropriate description of the average position in the European Union at present. In Section 5 we explore the practical experience of using MCIs, particularly among central banks. The last section draws together the lessons and offers conclusions for other open economies seeking to achieve and maintain price stability through targeting inflation.

There is considerable debate over how MCIs should be used in the formulation of monetary policy.[5] Our conclusion is that MCIs can have an important role to play, particularly in the period between full revisions of a central bank's forecasts (usually at three- or six-month intervals), when sources of changes in monetary conditions are difficult to identify. However, as with many indicators, they should come with a 'health warning'. Because they can lack robustness and do not reflect the total of all influences on price stability, they need to be used in combination with other information. Moreover, comparisons of MCI values for different time periods are difficult, because each value is affected by the whole range of external factors that influence inflation in each of the periods and not just by monetary policy.

2   The motivation for monetary conditions indexes

A monetary conditions index summarises, in a single series, the value of the variables that the central bank can influence directly with monetary policy, which also play a clear role in affecting the central bank's target for policy. In a simplistic framework we would be able to set this up like a control problem.

In Chart 1 the central bank's policy instruments affect the variables to be included in the MCI directly, and these in turn affect the bank's target, but much more indirectly. As long as we know the relationships between the instrument, usually a short-run interest rate, and the variables directly affected, such as other interest rates and exchange rates, and the relationships between the variables directly affected and the target (inflation), it is possible to decide how to set the instrument.[6] The variables directly affected are weighted in the MCI according to their impact on the target. We can take the simple case where there are only two such variables, an interest rate and the exchange rate. If a 1 percentage point change in the interest rate has twice the effect on inflation as a 1% change in the exchange rate, the interest rate has twice the weight in the MCI as

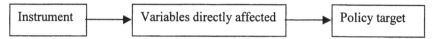

Chart 1 The monetary transmission mechanism

the exchange rate (i.e. a weight of two thirds, against one third for the exchange rate).[7]

The reasons for splitting this control problem into two steps and not just moving straight from the instrument to the target are threefold. First, it takes some time for policy to affect the target, whereas the variables in the MCI can be observed currently. Second, a wide range of other variables in the economy and abroad also affect both the variables in the MCI and the target, but not necessarily in the same proportions. Some of these other variables may themselves be affected by the central bank's actions. Third, central banks seek to influence monetary conditions by other means, such as speeches, as well as the usual monetary instruments. They may also choose to run a somewhat passive policy, allowing influences outside their immediate control to have an affect on the target as well as intervening directly themselves. Between them, these three factors illustrate both the usefulness of MCIs and the caution about their use. They are forward-looking indicators of the impact of monetary influences on the economy, but they do not just depend on the direct actions of the central bank.

The control problem is thus more complicated than the above example suggests. The central bank can only choose to set its instrument appropriately in the light of its forecast of all the other influences on the target. Many of these influences will actually be future events, and the relationships themselves will be only imperfectly understood. Indeed, using the word 'control' is not really appropriate, as the central bank can only influence, not control, financial variables in a market economy. An MCI will only indicate that part of the influence on the target that comes through variables included in it. The first step, therefore, in setting up an MCI is to decide which variables to include.

Following the pattern set up above, an MCI is normally defined as

$$MCI_t = \Sigma_s w_s (P_{st} - P_{s0}) \tag{1}$$

where the P_s are variables directly affected by monetary policy actions A_j (j indicating the actions available) and thought to affect demand (Y) or inflation (π).[8] It is more common to express MCIs in terms of the effects on demand, rather than on inflation directly, as there is also a range of supply-side influences on inflation that are best captured in a separate manner. Second there will be the relationships of the form

$$Y = f(P_{1,..,s}, \mathbf{X}), \quad (\text{or } \pi = g(P_{1,..,s}, \mathbf{X})) \tag{2}$$

between the components of the MCI and the 'target', where **X** represents all the other variables in the model that also have an impact on demand (or inflation). The weights w_s will be computed from the partial derivatives of the appropriate elements in $f(.)$ or $g(.)$, including due allowance for the dynamic structure, as there is no reason to expect that the different components of the MCI will have same time lags in influencing the target. The deviations of the Ps in period t from the base period 0 are weighted by w_s and summed to form the index. The index is usually normalised in the base period.

MCIs are conditional on the particular model of the economy that is chosen.[9] The model will affect both the choice of the variables to be included in the MCI and the weights that these variables have in the index as a whole. The appropriate model needs to be large enough to incorporate the principal channels of influence of monetary policy and to handle the other influences (the variables **X**), in a satisfactory manner. In the cases considered in this paper, in line with most MCIs that are currently in use, only short interest rates *(i)*, and exchange rates *(e)*, are normally included, both usually expressed in real terms as this is the basis of the relationship in the underlying model. However, we do conduct some experiments to see whether additional information can be obtained by including a long as well as a short rate of interest. The inclusion of other financial prices, such as the stock market index, has been contemplated (Roger, 1993, 1995; Mayes and Razzak, 1998). Even if the stock market index has a weight as low as 0.1 in the MCI, it can have striking effects on the overall assessment of monetary conditions (Roger, 1998).

The more complex the model – particularly if it contains a monetary policy reaction function and model-consistent expectations, as is the case with most of the central-bank models considered here – the more complex the meaning of the MCI becomes. On the other hand, if the model is too simplified and key characteristics of behaviour are left out, then the estimation of the weights will tend to have rather poor econometric properties, as pointed out by Eika *et al.* (1996).[10]

Although we have described the derivation of the MCI algebraically, MCIs are often presented visually. The track of an MCI over time indicates the pressure that monetary conditions are exerting on the economy. Take Chart 2, for example, which illustrates an MCI for the euro area. The chart shows the path of an MCI for the period January 1979 to April 1999, based on estimates derived in Section 4. Over the first four months of the euro area (up to the end of April 1999) the MCI fell by 2.2%. If we were merely to concentrate on the conventional interest rate measure, we would not find such a substantial effect (Chart 3).[11] Interest rates fell by only about 0.5%. The extra contribution came from the real exchange rate (Chart 4), which fell by almost 6% during the same period. Even though the exchange rate has a weight

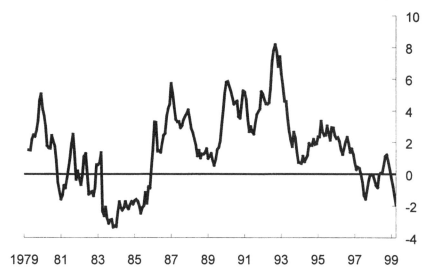

Chart 2 The monetary conditions index for the EMU area (weight = 3.5)*

* Source: Bank of Finland. Data are monthly averages, using the euribor (previously ecu) three-month rate as the interest rate and the euro exchange rate using the BIS trade weights. Real values are obtained by deflating by the three-month rate of inflation in HICP and its foreign counterparts. The index is the sum of the percentage deviation of the real exchange rate from its base, which is 1990, and the real interest rate.

of only 0.222 in this particular index (a 3.5% change in the real exchange rate has the same effect on future demand as a 100 basis point change in the real interest rate), its fall accounts for three quarters of the weakening in monetary conditions.

Public commentary may have substantially underestimated the extent to which the ECB has let monetary conditions ease because the ECB has focused on interest rates alone and did not consider an MCI. The distinction between an MCI and monetary policy actions is also clear.[12] During the first few months of 1999, the ECB's only significant monetary policy action[13] was to reduce its interest rate from 3% to 2.5% in April. The yield curve responded immediately, as this change was not anticipated by the market. Otherwise interest rates fluctuated little. However, monetary conditions eased throughout the period, mainly through the exchange rate. After April inflation expectations and consequently longer interest rates increased, reducing the likely impact of the easing.

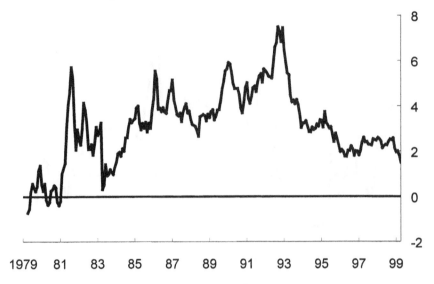

Chart 3 The real interest rate in the EMU area*

* Source: Bank of Finland. See Chart 2.

3 Survey of methods of estimating MCIs and their results

In the sections that follow we consider estimates of MCI ratios by other authors before proceeding in Section 4 to discuss our own new estimates. We explore the region in which reliable estimates appear to lie. To make this process as clear as possible, we have summarised the various estimates in Table 1. Column 1 shows the results obtained by Dornbusch *et al.* (1998). Column 2 lists the results from a study using the NiGEM model by the EMI (Kennedy and van Riet, 1995), which has since been published by the Banque de France, 1995.[14] Column 3 shows the results of a study by Peeters (1998) using NiGEM and the Dutch central bank's EUROMON model. The last column, with multiple entries, is derived from the survey of previous work by Ericsson *et al.* (1997) and other examples.

The most appealing method for estimating MCIs is through the sorts of macroeconomic models that central banks and other forecasters normally use. Such models embody the sort of detail and complexity considered appropriate for analysing monetary policy for other purposes. However, most work on MCIs, particularly outside central banks, has been undertaken with rather simpler models. Some private-sector institutions merely assume that using the share of trade in GDP gives the appropriate weight for the exchange rate. We have therefore structured this survey in order of increasing complexity of models but excluded the examples where the values are largely assumed.

Table 1 Previously estimated MCI ratios

	Dornb[*] [1]	NIGEM[**] [2]	Other[†] [3]
Austria			3.3(4)
Belgium		(1.5)	0.4(6)
Denmark			1.9(6)
Finland			2.5(6)
France	2.1	3.0(2.0)	3(2), 4(3), 3.4(4), 2.1(5), 3.5(6)
Germany	1.4	4.0(6.1)	2.5, 4(2), 4(3), 2.6(4), 4.2(5), 2.3(6)
Italy	2.9	0.1(1.8)	3(2), 4(3), 6.6(4), 6(5), 4.1(6)
Netherlands		(3.0)	3.7(4), 0.8(6)
Spain	1.5	1.3	1.5(3), 2.5(4), 4.2(6)
Sweden	8.1		3–4(1), 1.5(3), 0.5(4), 2.1(6)
UK		6.2(4.6)	3(2), 4(3), 14.4(4), 5(5), 2.9(6)
Australia			2.3(3), 4.3(6)
Canada			2.3(1), 4(2), 2.3(3), 4.3(5), 2.7(6)
Japan			10(2), 4(3), 8.8(5), 7.9(6)
New Zealand			2(1)
Norway			3(1), 1.4(6)
Switzerland			6.4(4), 1.7(6)
United States			10(2), 9(3), 39(5), 10.1(6)

[*] Drawn from Dornbusch *et al.* (1998), Table 10.
[**] Drawn from Banque de France (1996), Table 1. Numbers in parentheses are drawn from Peeters (1998), Table 5. Peeters also provides estimates from EUROMON: Belgium, 6.7; France, 3.5; Germany, 9.0; Italy, 5.7; Netherlands, 8.1; and UK, 3.0.
[†] Drawn from Ericsson *et al.* (1997), Table 1. Numbers in parentheses denote sources of estimates as follows: (1) central banks, (2) IMF, (3) OECD, (4) Deutsche Bank, (5) Goldman Sachs, and (6) JP Morgan.

3.1   *Reduced form estimation*

Customary practice is to use simple models, usually in reduced form.[15] Duguay (1994), in what appears to be the first published estimates of the Bank of Canada's MCI, uses simply an IS curve of the form

$$y_t^d = a_0 - a_1 r_t + a_2 q_t + a_3 y_t^* + v_t \tag{3}$$

where domestic output (y_t^d) depends on the real rate of interest (r_t), the real exchange rate (q_t) and foreign demand (y_t^*) and

$$q_t \equiv e_t + p_t^* - p_t \tag{4}$$

where p_t^* is the price of foreign goods and services, p_t the price of domestic goods and services, e_t the nominal exchange rate, and v_t the domestic demand disturbance. The United States is the 'foreign country' in the model rather than some weighted aggregate as would be more appropriate for most euro countries. The lag structure is also a little more complex in the estimated equation,

$$\Delta GDP_t = \quad 0.13 + 0.52\Delta GDP_{USt} + 0.45\Delta GDP_{USt-1} - 0.40r_t + 0.15q_t$$
$$\qquad\quad (1.0) \quad (4.8) \qquad\qquad (4.2) \qquad\qquad\quad (1.8) \qquad (1.3)$$
$$\bar{R}^2 = 0.64, \text{SEE} = 0.62, \text{DW} = 1.96, \text{sample 1980Q1 to 90Q4}$$

Δ denotes the quarterly growth rate, r is the eight-quarter moving average of the quarterly change in the 90-day commercial paper rate less a one-quarter lag of the four-quarter growth rate of the GDP deflator, and q is the 12-quarter moving average of the quarterly growth rate in the real Canada and US exchange rate (defined in terms of relative GDP deflators), with t-ratios in parentheses. From this Duguay concludes that the value of the MCI ratio for policy purposes should be approximately 3 as the ratio of coefficients is 0.4/0.15 in the above equation.

The main source of the estimates for the RBNZ MCI ratio that is used in practice (Dennis, 1996b) also follows this reduced-form approach, as does the Norwegian MCI ratio based on the work of Jore (1994). Sveriges Riksbank (Sweden) goes a little further in adding an inflation equation (Hansson, 1993; Hansson and Lindberg, 1994), where inflation depends on its own lags, the output gap, and current and lagged foreign inflation. These results are shown in column 3 of Table 1 (marked (1) for central banks' estimates).[16] The estimated values fall in a narrow range, and all show that exchange rates exert more influence than is implied by the foreign trade share in total activity. Ericsson *et al.* show, however, that the 95% confidence intervals for the MCI ratios are wide (Canada – 1.72 to 8.85; New Zealand – 0.16 to 3.66; Norway – 0.94 to 5.23), except for Sweden (1.17 to 2.87).[17]

Dornbusch *et al.* (1998) seek to refine the estimation process by estimating a two-equation model composed of a monetary policy reaction function and an output-growth function for Germany, France, Italy, Spain, the United Kingdom, and Sweden. The reaction functions differ in form according to the regime deemed to be in place over the estimation period (1987 to 96). They assume that the central banks set short-run interest rates according to the deviation of the exchange rate, inflation rate, and output growth from their respective targets, with a lagged dependent variable to allow for instrument smoothing. Germany is assumed to be setting policy based on the trade-weighted exchange rate with respect to the other European currencies, a quadratic output trend, and stable inflation. France, Italy and Spain are assumed to be targeting the Deutsche Mark and German inflation and output growth.[18] The United Kingdom and Sweden are included as inflation targeters in their own right.[19]

Output-growth functions are then estimated using the fitted values of the monetary policy reaction function as one of the arguments. The other explanatory variables are inflation and its lagged value and seven to 12

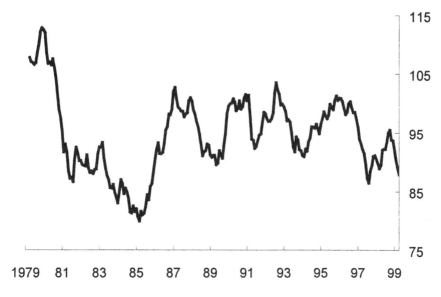

Chart 4 The real exchange rate in the EMU area (1990 = 100)*

* Source: Bank of Finland. See Chart 2.

lags on the exchange rate (data are monthly).[20] Taking these results together gives the MCI ratio estimates shown in column 1 of Table 1. Considering the MCIs alone omits useful information in the detail of their estimates, as shown in Table 2. These expose two characteristics that are important for the successful use of an MCI. First, the elasticities with respect to the interest and exchange rates individually are not large. Second, with the exception of Sweden, the MCI ratio, both as a point estimate and as an interval, lies within a somewhat narrower interval than Ericsson, *et al.* (1997) found in their study of Canada, New Zealand, Norway, Sweden and the United States.[21] However, the data periods are very different, and Dornbusch, *et al.* use monthly rather than quarterly data. As we show in the next section, the results can be quite sensitive to the choice of data period, typically it is the longer period that gives the weaker results as it tends to include regime shifts.

Peersman and Smets (1998) have produced results from output-growth equations for Austria, Belgium, France, Germany, Italy, and the Netherlands that suggest that the US$/DM rate is unimportant. Their model also includes foreign output growth, real interest rates in the domestic economy and in Germany, and the exchange rate of the national currency against the Deutsche Mark. The model is estimated on quarterly data for the period 1978 to 1995. Numerical estimates are not given, but these results differ sharply from the Dornbusch, *et al.* (1998) findings.[22]

Table 2 Estimates of the MCI from Dornbusch *et al.* (1998)

Country	Exchange rate elasticity	Interest rate elasticity	MCI ratio	95% confidence interval for MCI ratio
Germany	1.01	1.40	1.39	0–2.8
France	0.73	1.54	2.10	0.35–3.85
Italy	0.74	2.14	2.89	0.59–5.29
Spain	1.05	1.54	1.46	0–2.9
Sweden	0.29	2.36	8.13	−3.0–19.2

3.2   Use of VAR (Vector Autoregression Regression)

A second route for trying to obtain useful estimates for an MCI, when lag structures are important and there are multiple relationships among the key variables, is to use a VAR with sufficient identifying restrictions to distinguish the key relationships.[23] This is the approach of Dennis (1996a), Gerlach and Smets (1997), Smets (1997), and Jacobsen *et al.* (1998). It has the great advantage of not needing to be so specific about the exact structural relationships that are thought to underlie behaviour. The effect of shocks to either interest rates or the exchange rate can be derived from impulse-response functions. Most of the literature relates to the United States, and some of that undertaken for Europe (see Ramaswamy and Sloek, 1998, for a well-known example) concentrates on interest rates alone and hence does not permit the calculation of MCIs.[24] Jacobsen *et al*'s (1998) analysis relates to Sweden, which is outside the initial euro area.

The use of VARs to measure monetary policy is controversial (see Rudebusch, 1998, for example, and Bagliano and Favero, 1997, for a clear exposition of the issues).[25] Estimates are rather fragile. It is questionable whether the residuals from the interest-rate equation could be interpreted as monetary policy shocks. The key issue for interpretation is identification. However, even if the interpretation is problematic, the VAR approach still provides a helpful description of the characteristics of the data.

Jacobsen *et al.* (1998) go further by introducing the cointegrating relationships in a VECM framework with seven variables, adding 'foreign' real GDP, prices and nominal interest rates to the same domestic variables and the nominal exchange rate.[26] The estimated MCI ratio that emerges for Sweden from their model is 2.875, in line with other estimates.

However, the discussion in their paper also provides a strong reminder that different shocks have different implications for aggregate demand and inflation. That the level of the monetary conditions index has moved does not imply a uniform future impact of monetary conditions. The outcome depends on the source of the shock: monetary policy itself will react differently to demand and supply shocks.

3.3 Small structural models

VARs have the disadvantage of a rather opaque structural basis, which makes it difficult to understand the relative importance of the various channels of the transmission mechanism of monetary policy to inflation and the real economy. The obvious solution, therefore, might appear to be to use a small structural model of about the same dimension as the VAR. However, while this is potentially a helpful route, small structural models which are analytically tractable yet large enough to cover all the key features of the transmission mechanism, have tended to have too simple a lag structure to make estimation of an MCI very illuminating (Nadal De Simone, 1996; Collins and Nadal De Simone, 1996). An exception is Britton and Whitley (1997), which uses a small model very effectively to study different transmission mechanisms. However, these models do illustrate that the time horizon over which the MCI is estimated is important. If the time horizon is only two to four quarters ahead, then the relative importance of the exchange rate will be considerably greater than over a horizon of six or more quarters that is more commonly used for monetary policy decision-making. After six quarters or so, the MCI ratio tends to stabilise and changes little as the horizon is extended.

3.4 Using a complex macro-model

The obvious approach for estimating an MCI is to derive it from the macroeconomic model that the central bank uses for forecasting and monetary policy analysis. However, most current central bank models in the euro area have not been published. De Nederlandsche Bank's EUROMON (De Bondt *et al.* (1997)) and the Bank of Finland model BOF5 (Willman *et al.* (1998)) are available. The BOF5 model implies a MCI ratio of 1.8 to 2 over the policy horizon when simulated into the future. The interest-rate shock is temporary (for a period of eight quarters) since a permanent shock would be inconsistent with the long-run equilibrium of the model, and fiscal transfers and taxes are indexed. A further complication with many complex macro-models, including BOF5, is that the simulation results vary according to the data period over which the model is run. In this case the model has been run with the spring 1998 forecast as the baseline with unanticipated shocks being applied as from 2001(Q1). Trade outside the euro area is growing relative to GDP in Finland, so the external exchange rate is attaining increasing importance as time passes.

A smaller model of the Finnish economy, QMED, also used in the Bank (Hukkinen and Virén, 1998) shows a nominal MCI ratio of 2.3 (the individual interest-rate and exchange-rate effects differ more between these models). However, the relative effect on inflation from the exchange rate over the same horizon as for BOF5 is much more substantial with an MCI ratio of 0.6 (Hukkinen and Virén, 1998).

EUROMON, on the other hand (Peeters, 1998), shows very limited effects for the exchange rate in some countries using nominal rates. MCI ratios over a two-year horizon are: United Kingdom 3; France, 3.5; Italy, 5.7; Belgium, 5.9; Netherlands, 8.1; Germany, 9; and 19 for the five last-named countries combined.[27] Since this is a complex model it is not possible to track down the source of differences from other estimates without considerable extra information on its detail.

MCIs can, however, be computed from other macro-models of the EU countries that are available for public access. Kennedy and van Riet (1995) use the NIESR NiGEM model to provide estimates for France, Germany, Italy, Spain, and the United Kingdom (shown in column 2 of Table 1). This form of analysis typically yields MCI ratios in the range 1 to 5 for European economies. Peeters (1998) compares the results from NiGEM with EUROMON and derives an MCI ratio of 4.1 for the euro area.[28] The MCI ratios computed by Kennedy and Van Riet from NiGEM for the impact on *inflation* are much lower than those on output, being in the range of 0.1 to 1.6.

In recent years macro-models have become more complete in two senses. They have incorporated forward-looking expectations and they have incorporated reaction functions that set out policy-makers' stylised reactions to shocks. These changes mean that the coverage of the transmission mechanism is more complete; agents can base today's actions on what they expect to happen tomorrow.[29] Thus asset prices can move very quickly in response to news. In particular, they would respond to an announced or perceived change in the objectives of monetary or fiscal policy. Normally such responses are progressive, either because it takes some time for agents to work out ('learn') what the shock implies or because some agents are constrained from reacting immediately. This alters the profile of the response to a shock considerably (see Willman *et al.* (1998) for the impact on BOF5). Thus the level of the MCI will be affected (increased) over shorter time horizons, and the ratio may be affected if the impact on the two components is different. In BOF5, for example, the MCI ratio increases after the first few quarters as the weight on the forward-looking element of expectations rises.[30]

The existence of these mechanisms poses a problem for simulations. If the authorities always react to exogenous shocks so as to neutralise their impact on forecast inflation (or whatever is the target variable), then we would have difficulty in tracing out the components of an MCI.[31] Similarly, models will posit a link between domestic and foreign asset prices, say, through uncovered interest parity, so a shock to either the exchange rate or domestic interest rate would tend to elicit a response from the other. These responses will vary depending upon whether the response is perceived to be permanent or temporary. Indeed the authorities' response will also depend upon that perception. Generally, monetary authorities will tend to accept a 'supply-side' shock, such as a change in commodity

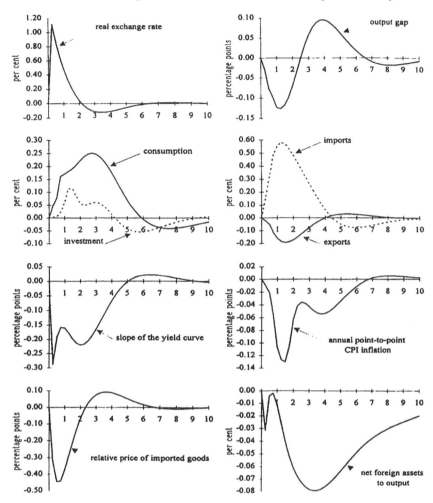

Chart 5 A temporary real exchange rate appreciation[*]

[*] Source: Black *et al.* (1997), Figure 5.7. Time scale is in quarters.

prices, as being a relative price shock that they have to accommodate, and they will respond only to demand shocks.

In calibrated models such as the Bank of Canada's QPM and the Reserve Bank of New Zealand's FPS, the direct and indirect channels of influence on prices are deliberately accounted for. In Chart 5 (from Black *et al.* 1997) the effect of a temporary real exchange-rate shock has twin peaks on inflation. The direct feed-through into the relative price of imports occurs almost immediately but has been completely reversed after two years, by which time the exchange-rate shock itself has dissipated. The demand effects, however, take about six years to flow through the economy completely. Although the initial output-gap response is negative (as we would expect from an MCI related to output), a positive output gap emerges after two to three years, largely because monetary policy responds to the initial exchange-rate shock and short-run interest rates are lowered. In MCI terms the initial shock is negative, as interest rates cannot offset the effects of the exchange-rate shock immediately, and hence a positive MCI is required later.[32]

3.5   An assessment of methodological issues and estimation problems

Whatever the uses to which MCIs are put, their construction requires estimation of the impact of the interest-rate and exchange-rate channels of monetary policy. Methods of estimation are complex, and none is totally satisfactory (Ericsson *et al.* 1997; ECB; 1998). Our prime concern in developing estimates for the euro area in this paper is to establish the relative importance of the exchange rate in the transmission mechanism, rather than to establish its exact magnitude or time profile. However, focusing on relative impact does not evade all of the problems, and estimates of the ratio typically tend to have larger variances than their component parts.

Using the definition of an MCI given in Section 2, a ratio of X to 1 in an MCI implies that a change in the exchange rate by X per cent has an impact equivalent to a 100 basis point change in the interest rate. Thus the larger the ratio, the *weaker* is the relative impact of the exchange rate. As is clear from Table 1, large, relatively closed economies such as the United States or Japan are thought to have ratios around 10 to 1, and very open economies, around 2 or 3 to 1. However, there is no very precise correlation with either economic size or trade shares. Estimates for the relative size of the interest-rate and exchange-rate impacts in the euro area range from a ratio of 2 to 1 by Dornbusch *et al.* (1998) to 10 to 1 by Peersman and Smets (1998), but the bulk of the estimates for the various component countries and our own lie well within these extremes.

The time paths for the impact through the exchange rate and the interest rate are likely to be different. Existing evidence (see ECB (1998) for an example) and the results summarised later in this paper suggest that there is considerable variation in the impact of both interest rates and the exchange rate across Western European countries. This variation affects both the extent of the impact for a given change in the two variables and the length of time it takes. However, our analysis suggests that there is far less variation in the *ratio* of the impact through the exchange rate to the impact through the interest rate in three respects: across the various countries; across different sources of estimates; and over time after the first few quarters. Thus, while there may be considerable uncertainty about the *extent* and the *timing* of the impact of monetary policy through these channels, there is likely to be rather less about the *relative* impact of the exchange rate and interest rate. In order to compile an MCI, one only requires estimates of the ratio.

The caution about how MCIs should be used and computed is well summarised by Ericsson *et al.* (1997) who point out six possible drawbacks:

- There are several relationships between the key variables involved (output, inflation, interest rates, and the exchange rate) that must be specified if the estimates are to be unbiased.
- Assumptions about exogeneity of the instruments of monetary policy and other variables must not be too strong.
- Normal considerations of cointegration should be applied; many MCIs in practice have confused levels and differences of variables in their structure. The dynamics of the relationships are important and need to be carefully modelled.
- The impact of the components of an MCI varies over time, so an MCI needs an explicit time horizon.
- The coefficients of MCIs are not stable over time, partly because of failure to allow for the first three problems listed above.
- Estimates are subject to wide variances.

Generally, the simpler the model, the more of these six difficulties are likely to occur.

4   New estimates of MCIs for the euro area

In the light of previous experience and the difficulties for estimation that have been exposed, we develop a new set of estimates for the euro area in this section. In order to show how our estimates fit into the existing pattern, we follow the same process of exploring simple reduced-form models first before moving on to VARs and to complex macro-models.

4.1   *Using reduced-form models*

Although estimating straightforward IS curves of the form shown in equation (3) presents a range of problems, it is the method used for the construction of a number of MCIs used in current practice (Canada, New Zealand, Sweden, Finland, and Norway). Therefore we begin our analysis by obtaining directly comparable estimates from our wider data set of 13 EU countries (covering the period 1972Q2 to 1997Q4).[33] We have considered the MCI only in real terms and have used only a limited specification search, in order to provide robust estimates. We searched up to eight lags for each variable except the dependent variable, where only two lags

Table 3 New MCI ratio estimates*

| | long | short | short | short | short | short |
| | | sample | + prices | ΔGDP | SURE | + bondr |
	[1]	[2]	[3]	[4]	[5]	[6]
Austria	14.3	2.4	3.1	1.3	1.2	14.4
Belgium	60.1	60.6	88.9	6.4	6.2	2.2
Denmark	3.6	8.3	9.6	−13.3	14.4	−4.1
Finland	8.9	3.1	3.2	3.3	3.4	4.3
France	19.2	2.5	1.9	2.5	3.4	2.1
Germany	29.7	3.6	2.5	4.9	3.4	2.7
Italy	17.7	7.8	8.4	2.4	4.3	13.1
Netherlands	12.8	2.3	2.3	2.8	1.2	3.4
Portugal	−4.6	11.6	5.6	2.3	14.8	3.6
Spain	−2.1	0.8	0.8	0.6	0.5	3.7
Sweden	5.2	1.2	1.3	0.7	1.2	0.8
UK	0.8	1.5	0.3	1.5	1.1	0.9
Ireland		2.0	1.5	1.9	1.1	−1.7

* See explanation in text.

were considered.[34] Since we are interested in MCIs as an indicator for
future policy, they need to relate to the euro area. We have therefore considered only the bilateral exchange rate with the US dollar in the initial
estimates. Our foreign demand variable relates to the OECD as a whole in
all cases, and we have not attempted to obtain more specific measures
related to each individual country's trade pattern. The resultant estimated
MCI ratios are shown in column 1 of Table 3 and the equation estimates
themselves in Table 4.[35]

With other EU countries being the most important markets for both
imports and exports for many of these countries, one might expect that the
DM exchange rate would act as a better explanatory variable then the US
dollar rate. This possibility was explored for each country (except
Germany). This does indeed result in an increased role for the exchange
rate in some cases, but it has very little impact on the overall fit (see Mayes
and Virén, 1998). Table 5 shows that, as might be expected, the DM and
US$ exchange rates are only weakly correlated, so one would expect their
explanatory roles also to be decidedly different. Table 5 also explores the
impact of including both variables (for a shorter data period, 1987Q1 to
1997Q4). Significance levels tend to be rather weak, but in only three cases
(out of eleven) does addition of the DM exchange rate increase the relative importance of the exchange-rate channel.[36] In four cases it renders the
total effect perverse.

The US dollar does not cover all the external trade and transactions of
the euro countries. The yen, sterling, the Swiss franc, and for Finland, the
Swedish krona all play a significant role. It would obviously be more

Table 4 IS curve estimates for 1972Q2–1997Q4[*]

Name lags	∇y_{t-1}	∇y_{t-2}	rr_{t-k}	re_{t-k}	$OECD_{t-k}$	R^2 (SEE)	DW	λ
Austria	.587		−.040	.003	.216	.495	2.01	14.3
2,1,2	(7.10)		(1.59)	(0.60)	(2.37)	(0.84)		
Belgium	1.289	−.616	−.024	.001	.199	.885	1.85	60.1
3,1,1	(17.88)	(9.20)	(1.74)	(0.16)	(3.71)	(0.42)		
Denmark	−.904	−.160	−.050	.014	.182	.726	2.02	3.6
2,3,1	(5.41)	(0.98)	(1.21)	(2.52)	(0.86)	(1.16)		
Finland	.641	.120	−.111	.013	.427	.726	1.87	8.9
3,2,2	(5.66)	(1.36)	(2.73)	(1.20)	(2.15)	(1.43)		
France	.983	−.231	−.037	.002	.106	.747	2.03	19.2
3,2,2	(9.82)	(2.26)	(1.91)	(0.50)	(1.58)	(0.56)		
Germany	.666	.188	−.156	.005	.062	.816	2.11	29.7
3,1,1	(5.06)	(1.72)	(4.50)	(1.29)	(0.70)	(0.90)		
Italy	1.245	−.593	−.015	.001	.208	.828	2.31	17.7
3,8,2	(14.03)	(6.63)	(0.91)	(0.19)	(2.12)	(0.62)		
Neths	.411		−.075	.006	.501	.498	1.92	12.8
2,7,1	(2.93)		(2.37)	(1.10)	(2.96)	(0.91)		
Port	1.066	−.203	−.021	−.005	.259	.911	2.03	−4.6
3,2,2	(5.79)	(1.25)	(1.25)	(1.15)	(3.19)	(0.53)		
Spain	1.661	.783	−.005	−.002		.960	1.69	−2.1
1,1	(19.28)	(9.05)	(1.11)	(1.70)		(0.22)		
Sweden	.426	.278	−.071	.014	.179	.576	1.98	5.2
2,2,2	(3.41)	(2.49)	(4.08)	(1.83)	(1.56)	(0.96)		
UK	.783		−.008	.010	.098	.727	1.77	0.8
3,3,2	(10.04)		(0.50)	(1.27)	(1.07)	(0.97)		

[*] The dependent variable ∇y is the output gap constructed by the HP filter. rr is the real interest rate, re the real exchange rate with respect to US. OECD denotes the output gap for OECD GDP. λ is the ratio between interest rate and exchange rate elasticities. Lags indicate the lag length for rr, re, and oecd (in this order), respectively. The data are quarterly and cover the period 1972:2–1997:4. For the UK, the US output gap is used instead of the OECD output gap. The Portuguese equation also includes an additional inflation term for lag 8 (the respective coefficient estimates are −0.030 (2.60) and −0.024 (2.93)). The German equation includes a level and one period dummies for the unification period (1991:1–1997:4). All estimates are OLS.

accurate to create weighted indices, using, say, trade weights. As the problem is likely to be greatest for Finland, we used this as an illustration. For the shorter time period, the estimate of the MCI ratio is increased from 3.1 to 4.4. This result is largely to be expected, as the Swedish krona and sterling moved in a similar pattern to the markka in the currency crisis of 1992 before recovering. This swing will have an important impact on the variance for the period as a whole. Only the other countries that depreciated substantially in 1992 will have experienced this particular narrowing of the variance of the exchange rate. In general it would be more likely that the MCI ratio would fall rather than rise as the overweighting of the US dollar will probably have exaggerated the fluctuations in the exchange

Table 5 The DM real exchange rate as an additional variable[*]

Country	r_1	r_2	λ	$REGER_{t-k}$	$\lambda(sum)$
Austria	.33	−.26	2.4	−.062 (0.59)	−0.3
Belgium	.52	−.09	59.1	−.032 (0.90)	−1.9
Denmark	.33	−.13	7.7	+.011 (0.33)	4.9
Finland	.29	.84	2.7	−.062 (2.39)	9.0
France	−.17	−.25	2.0	+.019 (0.75)	1.2
Italy	.21	.73	4.7	−.020 (2.14)	14.5
Netherlands	−.03	.20	1.1	+.030 (1.17)	0.4
Portugal	−.42	.76	4.7	−.024 (2.59)	−16.3
Spain	.52	.64	1.0	−.003 (0.60)	1.4
Sweden	−.27	.35	1.1	−.111 (1.20)	−1.1
UK	.26	.57	1.5	−.003 (0.49)	1.7

[*] r_1 (r_2) denotes the correlation between US$ and DM real exchange rates for 1972–97 (1987–97). Estimation period is 1987Q1–1997Q4. REGER is the real exchange rate with respect to DM. Inside parentheses are the respective t-values. The lag length k is the same as with the US$ real exchange rate. $\lambda(sum)$ denotes the ratio between the real interest rate elasticity and the sum of real exchange rate elasticities.

rate. With the exception of Ireland, where trade with the United Kingdom has a substantial though declining role, the changes for other countries, whichever the direction, would tend to be small.

On the whole our results over the full data period are less well determined, and suggest rather higher MCI ratios, than others have found (Table 1). One reason appears to be simply the length of the sample used. We used all the data available; arguably however, the move toward monetary union in the late 1980s meant that estimating across that change would likely give poorly determined coefficients. We therefore reduced our time period to cover only the quarters since the beginning of 1987 to match the time period shown in Dornbusch *et al.* (1998). The results are shown in Table 6. As can be seen from a comparison with the long period estimates (column 5 vs. column 1 in Table 3), more of the results fall in the plausible range, and the size of the estimated MCI ratios has fallen, indicating a greater importance for the exchange rate and the greater opening of the economies.

Table 6 OLS estimation results for the 1987Q1–1997Q4 period[*]

Name lags	∇y_{t-1}	∇y_{t-2}	rr_{t-k}	re_{t-k}	$oecd_{t-k}$	R^2 (SEE)	DW	λ
Austria	.729	−.095	−.021	.009	.338	.660	1.90	2.4
2,2,2	(6.39)	(0.74)	(0.91)	(0.65)	(0.65)	(0.58)		
Belgium	1.145	−.457	−.046	.001	.334	.882	1.81	41.7
4,3,2	(6.60)	(2.85)	(1.28)	(0.08)	(1.55)	(0.40)		
Denmark	.105		−.152	.018	.065	.261	1.96	8.3
1,3,1	(1.02)		(1.77)	(1.51)	(1.12)	(0.84)		
Finland	.773	−.158	−.152	.048	.406	.881	1.99	3.1
3,2,2	(5.36)	(1.00)	(2.36)	(3.90)	(0.83)	(1.19)		
France	.960	−.274	−.069	.027	.305	.871	1.94	2.5
4,2,2	(6.64)	(1.56)	(2.06)	(1.99)	(1.35)	(0.44)		
Germany	.545	.181	−.072	.020	.123	.911	1.53	3.6
7,3,2	(2.73)	(1.23)	(0.87)	(0.84)	(0.57)	(0.81)		
Ireland	.970	−.298	−.056	.028	.788	.867	1.81	2.0
1,3,2	(7.18)	(2.63)	(1.73)	(1.56)	(3.09)	(0.72)		
Italy	.701		−.095	.012	.332	.767	1.97	7.8
3,2,1	(8.88)		(1.90)	(1.43)	(2.35)	(0.50)		
Neths	1.077	−.381	−.037	.016	.259	.824	1.86	2.3
1,2,2	(11.41)	(4.72)	(1.53)	(1.76)	(2.34)	(0.39)		
Port	.447	.135	−.081	.007	.747	.901	1.95	11.6
3,1,1	(3.47)	(1.30)	(2.87)	(1.24)	(3.74)	(0.48)		
Spain	1.518	−.595	−.008	.009	.115	.982	1.44	0.8
1,2,1	(15.98)	(6.53)	(1.16)	(3.01)	(1.85)	(0.18)		
Sweden	.537	.226	−.065	.052	.604	.809	2.33	1.2
1,2,2	(5.21)	(1.70)	(5.21)	(4.05)	(2.30)	(0.77)		
UK	.981	−.175	−.033	.022	.262	.950	1.83	1.5
1,1,1	(10.50)	(1.86)	(1.84)	(2.96)	(4.34)	(0.40)		

[*] Notation is the same as Table 5.

In estimating an IS curve of this fairly simple form, we are clearly omitting other information that may be relevant. In order to cover at least some of this we also estimated the equations using SURE (Table 7). As might be anticipated, the relatively well determined estimates change little (columns 1 and 2 in the Table and columns 2 and 5 in Table 3). Only four countries lie outside the range of 1 to 5 for the MCI ratio. The Spanish result is less than 1, the result for Belgium just over 6, and those for Denmark and Portugal 14 to 15. It is thus clear, that for the twelve countries as a whole, the US dollar exchange rate was important in the determination of inflationary pressure over the period 1987 to 1997. A mean value of 3 to 4, depending on the weights used, would seem to describe the results. The last two countries in the table, Sweden and the United Kingdom, are not part of the euro area at the outset, and their exclusion raises the overall average within that range.

It has been argued that the long rate of interest should also be included

Table 7 The weight parameter and its standard deviation[*]

Country Period	λnls 1987:1–1997:4	λsur 1987:1–1997:4	λnls 1972:1–1997:4
Austria	2.4	1.2	14.3
	(4.9)	(1.8)	(42.1)
Belgium	60.6	6.2	60.1
	(353.6)	(5.9)	(3500)
Denmark	8.3	14.4	3.6
	(5.8)	(19.4)	(37.9)
Finland	3.1	3.4	8.9
	(1.9)	(1.8)	(8.9)
France	2.5	3.4	19.2
	(1.2)	(1.4)	(37.8)
Germany	3.6	3.4	29.7
	(4.9)	(2.3)	(22.6)
Ireland	2.0	1.1	
	(2.1)	(1.1)	. . .
Italy	7.8	4.3	17.7
	(7.3)	(4.3)	(93.1)
Netherlands	2.3	1.2	12.8
	(1.7)	(1.2)	(17.1)
Portugal	11.6	14.8	−4.6
	(3.7)	(11.6)	(3.6)
Spain	0.8	0.5	−2.1
	(0.8)	(0.8)	(18.3)
Sweden	1.2	1.2	5.2
	(0.5)	(0.5)	(2.7)
UK	1.5	1.1	0.8
	(1.3)	(1.0)	(2.0)

[*] Numbers in parentheses are standard deviations. In the case of non-linear least squares, they have been computed by using the Newey-West correction with the lag length equalling 3.

in the MCI (Kennedy and van Riet, 1995; Peeters, 1998, for example) either directly or through the yield gap. We therefore re-estimated the models using the difference between the ten-year bond rate and the short rate as an additional variable (column 6 of Table 3). In general these results show considerable robustness for the estimates of the MCI ratio, defined as the ratio of the sum of the coefficients on interest rates to the coefficient on the exchange rate.[37] However, in some cases the coefficients are rather poorly determined, perhaps reflecting the interrelation between long and short rates, and the sign on the long rates was perverse. In the case of Austria and Italy, the estimated ratios rise to implausible levels, but this is offset by the decline in the ratios for Denmark and Portugal from implausible levels when only the short rate was included, to values that are in line with the other countries. Lag structures became more

Table 8 SUR and NLS estimates for λ for different estimation periods[*]

	SUR87	NLS87	SUR85	NLS85	SUR83	NLS83	SUR81	NLS81
Austria	1.2	2.4	−120.3	−0.9	7.6	1.1	2.1	2.3
Belgium	6.2	60.6	−4.8	−9.5	−15.2	−20.7	−20.7	−37.3
Denmark	14.4	8.3	−0.6	4.6	6.5	5.7	3.2	3.3
Finland	3.4	3.2	10.9	6.0	12.7	4.6	6.3	1.9
France	3.4	2.5	−13.7	14.5	22.0	8.4	12.3	6.5
Germany	3.4	3.6	3.3	3.6	2.9	5.7	12.7	−262
Ireland	1.1	2.0	...	...	...	...	...	...
Italy	4.3	7.7	30.3	5.1	−483	11.0	−1515	8.3
Neths	1.2	2.3	3.8	4.0	2.9	6.1	9.4	4.2
Port	14.8	11.6	−8.3	−8.5	−4.0	−5.1	−5.7	−9.7
Spain	0.5	0.8	1.3	0.2	1.0	−4.0	−2.2	13.2
Sweden	1.2	1.2	11.1	2.9	9.3	3.8	3.8	2.0
UK	1.1	1.5	5.5	3.7	6.8	5.3	3.7	3.7

[*] SUR denotes the Seemingly Unrelated Regression (Aitken) estimator, NLS the non-linear least squares estimator. In the case of SUR87, the sample period is 1987Q1–1997Q4. SUR85 indicates 1985Q1–1997Q4 and so on.

complex. Taken together, the inclusion of long rates had little impact on the relative importance of interest rates but provided further evidence of the sensitivity to specification.

To assess the merits of beginning at 1987, we re-estimated the model over periods covering 1985, 1983, and 1981 (Table 8). Here the results become fragile for most countries, even when only two years are added to the data period, suggesting that there was indeed an important shift in regime or other structural break(s) in the earlier period. This is consistent with more direct information on the changes in monetary policy regimes being applied in several of the countries over the period.

Comparing these findings with the earlier estimates by other authors, shown in columns 1 to 3 of Table 1, it is clear that the results obtained for the MCI ratio from estimating simple IS curves are sensitive to the choice of variables and estimation period. This is not especially surprising for a ratio, but it does mean that it is relatively easy to find support for most plausible hypotheses in terms of point estimates by choosing an appropriate specification. Moreover, the variance of the individual estimates is such that, like Ericsson *et al.* (1997), we have to be cautious about the significance we attach to any specific value of the MCI in the plausible range. Individual coefficient estimates, other than lagged values of the dependent variable, tend to be weakly determined. Furthermore, the implied elasticities of output with respect to both interest rates and the exchange rate tend to be rather lower than normally expected.

However, having weakly determined estimates does not mean that the appropriate assumption for the null hypothesis for decision-making should be an MCI ratio of either zero or the inverse of the trade share. Most of the results are mutually consistent. The combined evidence from the previous studies and our results is quite persuasive and points to values for all the countries in our sample between 1 and 4, with a preponderance toward the upper half of that range.

Impulse response functions for the IS curves[38] indicate that, with the exception of Finland, the main impact of either an exchange-rate or an interest-rate shock is largely complete by the end of two years. In this simplified structure, therefore, the change in the MCI ratio over the time horizon of the impact of a shock is not really important if the focus of policy is on the impact around two years ahead. As noted by Ramaswamy and Sloek (1998), however, the level of the impact varies fairly considerably from one country to another, with the impact of interest rates being greatest in Germany, the United Kingdom, Austria, Finland, and Belgium and lowest in Sweden, Italy, France, and Spain.[39] The largest effects are around twice as large as the smaller. Hence similarity in MCI ratios (i.e. the relative impact) does not necessarily entail similarity in the absolute impact of monetary policy.

We can, however, draw some clear lessons: (i) If the estimation period is extended backwards before the mid-1980s, it becomes much more difficult to get plausible estimates. Like Smets (1996), among others, we interpret this as suggesting that there have been regime shifts, which make the function misspecified; (ii) If the DM exchange rate is used instead of the US dollar exchange rate over the longer period, the estimates become more plausible for some countries. Over the shorter period the DM exchange rate is not a very helpful additional explanatory variable; and (iii) Introducing inflation into the estimating equation has little impact on the outcome. Over the longer period, inflation acts as an indicator of the regime in place at the time.

More recently we have extended the analysis by arranging the data in the form of a panel and estimating the reduced-form model under the hypothesis of common coefficients (Mayes and Virén, 1998). For the euro countries this gives an estimate of 3.3 for the MCI using GLS and 3.1 using SUR.[40] These estimates are not weighted and cover the period 1987Q1 to 1997Q4, with a total of 440 observations. The subject of weighting and compiling aggregate estimates both for the MCI and for the non-linear Phillips curve is the subject of ongoing research. The hypothesis of common coefficients is, not surprisingly, rejected. Nevertheless, it would be possible to group the countries, at least with respect to some parameters, and hence produce a more parsimonious specification.

4.2   Using VARs

We have conducted two experiments with VARs. The first was simply to see if the impulse-response coefficients looked plausible for various specifications of the VAR. Taking a simple two-lag, four-variable VAR (ordered output, prices, the US$ exchange rate, and the short interest rate) with prices, the exchange rate and GDP (output) in logarithmic form showed that the results are not unduly sensitive with respect to the way in which the time series are made stationary (Mayes and Virén, 1998).

Second, Chart 6 shows impulse-response graphs from a two lag four variable 'real' VAR (ordered output gap, US$ real exchange rate, short real interest rate, and exogenous lagged OECD output in the Cholesky decomposition) estimated over the period 1987Q1 to 1997Q4. Two graphs are shown for each country, the response of the output gap (HPR + country mnemonic) to a real exchange rate (RE) shock on the left-hand side of the page and to a real interest rate (RR) shock on the right, conformable with Ramaswamy and Sloek (1998).

The results vary quite substantially over countries, suggesting that both the magnitude and dynamics of the real exchange rate and the real interest rate effects are different. Moreover, the results are quite imprecise, so that the implied values of the MCI ratio have very large confidence intervals. In most cases the signs of the effects are, however, expected, although Germany represents a notable exception in terms of the real interest rate effects. An obvious reason is unification: if we extend the estimation period back to 1972, the results are quite similar to other countries. The Finnish (and partly also Swedish) real exchange rate impulses also look rather extreme, probably reflecting the extraordinary nature of the recession of the early 1990s.

All in all, the results with the simple VAR models are largely consistent with the IS curve estimates. Because the data sample is so short, it is no surprise that the VAR model results show more variability and less accuracy. Notice also that the impulse responses reflect the effects of policy shocks, not permanent changes in the respective variables. In spite of, or perhaps because of, that, the VAR model results may be useful in providing additional information on the dynamics of monetary policy effects.

4.3 Using complex macro-models

In order to bring work on the complex macro-model approach up to date, we have conducted new simulations with the most recent available version of NiGEM (version of the first half of 1998).[41] These show MCI ratios with respect to GDP in a range from 1.5 to 7.3, with an average of 4.1 for a two-year horizon (0.4 to 3.2 with an average of 1.5 for inflation). This version also permits simulations with a constrained system for the euro 11 countries as a whole, which produces rather larger values after eight quarters.

Response to One S.D. Innovations ± 2 S.E.

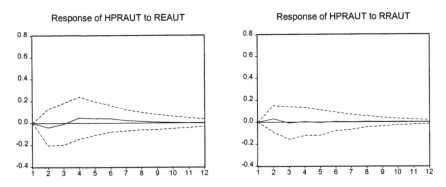

Response to One S.D. Innovations ± 2 S.E.

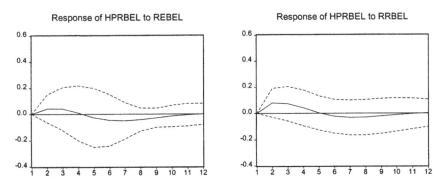

Response to One S.D. Innovations ± 2 S.E.

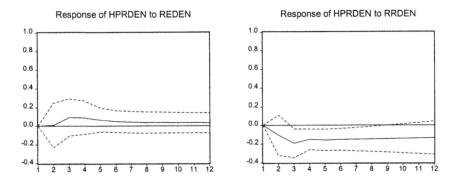

Chart 6 Impulse response graphs from unrestricted real VAR[*]

[*] For explanation of the notation, see text. Time scale is in quarters.

Response to One S.D. Innovations ± 2 S.E.

Response of HPRFIN to REFIN

Response of HPRFIN to RRFIN

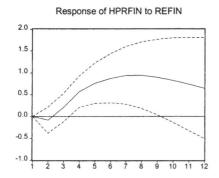
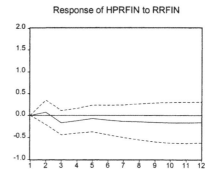

Response to One S.D. Innovations ± 2 S.E.

Response of HPRFRA to REFRA

Response of HPRFRA to RRFRA

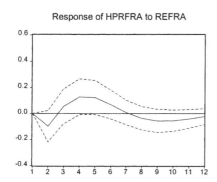
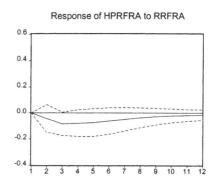

Response to One S.D. Innovations ± 2 S.E.

Response of HPRGER to REGER

Response of HPRGER to RRGER

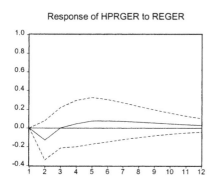
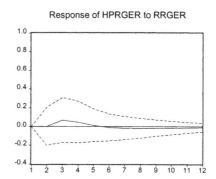

Chart 6 continued

Response to One S.D. Innovations ± 2 S.E.

Response of HPRIRL to REIRL

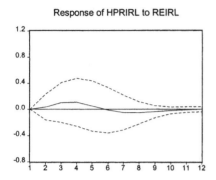

Response of HPRIRL to RRIRL

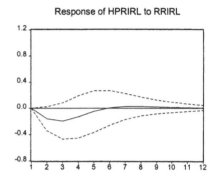

Response to One S.D. Innovations ± 2 S.E.

Response of HPRITA to REITA

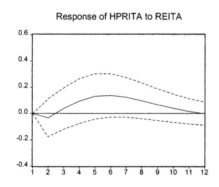

Response of HPRITA to RRITA

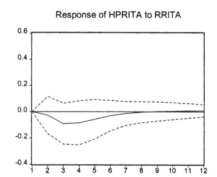

Response to One S.D. Innovations ± 2 S.E.

Response of HPRNET to RENET

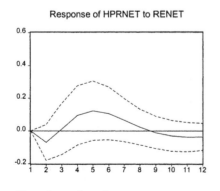

Response of HPRNET to RRNET

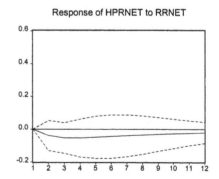

Chart 6 continued

Response to One S.D. Innovations ± 2 S.E.

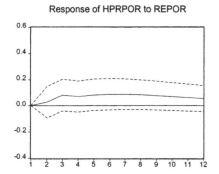

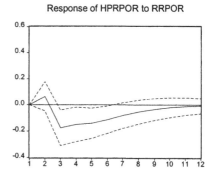

Response to One S.D. Innovations ± 2 S.E.

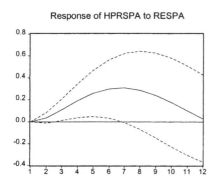

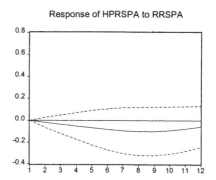

Response to One S.D. Innovations ± 2 S.E.

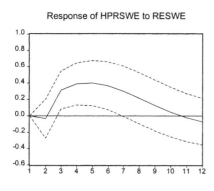

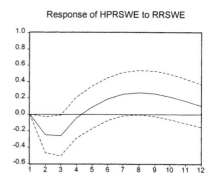

Chart 6 continued

Response to One S.D. Innovations ± 2 S.E.

Response of HPRUK to REUK

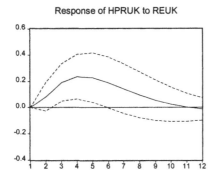

Response of HPRUK to RRUK

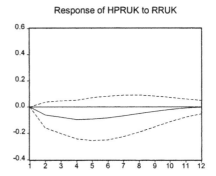

Chart 6 continued

5   Using an MCI in practice

MCIs have been used by three main groups:

(i)   International organisations trying to assess macroeconomic policy both across countries and over time.[42]
(ii) Private-sector financial institutions in their descriptions and forecasts of economies and monetary authorities' actions;[43] and
(iii) Monetary authorities themselves, in trying to assess how to set policy and in communicating the needs of policy to the private sector.

In each of these cases the MCI provides a convenient way of summarising information.

5.1   Use of MCIs by the private sector and international financial institutions

Most private sector users and international organisations use MCIs in an indicator role. The IMF and OECD set out tracks for the level of MCIs in the main countries and measure the evolution of monetary policy against them.[44] However, while the IMF uses the MCI to reveal relatively short-run changes, OECD considers the evolution over the latest several years.[45] The information is interpreted in two main ways: first, as an indicator of how pressures on the economy are changing and, second, as an indicator of the central bank policy stance.

The central bank itself does not have to be using an MCI for the private sector or other agencies to compute and use them. Indeed, most central banks do not use MCIs explicitly. Furthermore, even if a central bank does use an MCI, it may not be using the same one as the external observers and it may not be using MCIs in the same sort of way. Since the relative importance of the components of the MCI is determined on the basis of empirical investigation, the MCI an organisation uses will depend on the estimates it thinks appropriate.[46] Such a proliferation of MCIs is analogous to the proliferation of different models of the same economy.

5.2   Use of MCIs by central banks[47]

Central banks have used MCIs in two main ways:

- as an indicator to assist policy-making, particularly in the interval between full economic forecasts; and
- to help communicate needs for changes in monetary policy, as well as the bank's intentions.

(i) The MCI as an aid to policy-making

A change in the level of the MCI can indicate either of two things. It can imply that there has been a 'shock' to the economy that has caused markets to change their view of prospects and hence to alter asset prices. It can also imply, in the absence of any such shock, that the prospects for aggregate demand and hence for inflation have changed. In either event the central bank will wish to consider whether to change the setting of its own policy instrument. Indeed, the change in the MCI will incorporate the market's guess as to how the central bank is going to react when it next reappraises the setting of its policy instrument. When it comes to explain the setting of its policy instrument, the central bank can talk in terms of the MCI that would be appropriate in the new conditions for achieving its target.

(ii) The MCI as an aid to communication

Central banks have found MCIs helpful in communication because they make clear the relative importance of the exchange rate in the transmission of monetary policy. There are several circumstances in which this has been found particularly useful. Three that we highlight here are:

- in projecting paths of monetary conditions over the future;
- in explaining the setting of central bank interest rates;
- and in explaining what short-run fluctuations in exchange rate and market-determined interest rates might threaten price stability.

Since some international organisations and private financial institutions use MCIs, simply speaking in that language might assist central banks in their explanations.

5.2.1   The general picture

The Bank of Canada was not only the first central bank to publish an MCI
but has gone furthest in its use, in effect having an MCI as an operating
target for policy (Freedman, 1994). The Reserve Bank of New Zealand
has used an MCI to help inform markets about its wishes for monetary
policy since 1996, having used them internally before then (Mayes and
Razzak, 1998). The Norges Bank and the Sveriges Riksbank use an MCI
to inform policy but without such a direct role, while the Bank of Finland
computed two MCIs for internal use in the same manner (Chart 7).

Central banks tend to be rather cautious in their use of MCIs
(Pikkarainen and Ripatti (1995), for example, set out the concerns of the
Bank of Finland). The level of an MCI tells us the pressure of monetary
policy on demand in the economy only if all other influences on exchange
rates and interest rates are held constant. Significant events like the rapid
depreciation in the markka as part of the ERM crisis in September 1992

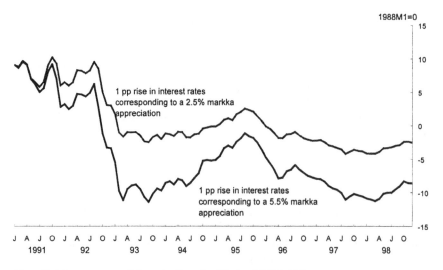

Chart 7 Monetary conditions indices for Finland 1991–98*

* Data drawn from Bank of Finland database. Index is the real 3-month interest rate plus the
weighted real exchange rate, 1991M1 = 100. The chart plots computed MCIs using 2.5:1 and
5.5:1 ratios of changes in the nominal exchange rate to changes in the short interest rate both
daily and monthly. The value of 2.5:1 was estimated in Pikkarainen (1993) (see Pikkarainen
and Ripatti, 1995 for an explanation in English), whereas the 5.5:1 index was computed by
the IMF. The Bank of Finland's models suggest values within in the range; BOF4, for
example, implies a ratio of 3.5 to 1. Since the advent of the euro area, attention in the Bank
of Finland has switched to the euro but as Finland's exposure both to euro interest rates and
to the real exchange rate differ from that of the euro area as a whole, MCIs still have a role
to play in considering monetary policy in Finland. A falling curve indicates a tightening.

did not feed through to the extent that the MCI might have implied. The existence of substantial, recently acquired, foreign currency denominated debt dampened the impact, for instance. Exploiting the full usefulness of the MCI as a leading indicator of the pressures on inflation entails also making a rather wider macroeconomic assessment so that other influences are not neglected.

Freedman (1994) explains that the MCI helped the Bank of Canada to judge how to respond to shocks to demand or to changes in one or other of the two components of the MCI. In the case of a demand shock, the Bank could judge how much the weighted sum of the two MCI elements should change, to keep inflation within the target. However, it could not judge in advance how that change would be distributed between the two elements, because this depends on the market. Similarly, in the case of an exchange-rate shock, the Bank could estimate how much the interest rate would have to change to offset it (and vice versa). The explanation was thus very much in terms of clarity of policy to the Bank itself. It was an aid to policy, not a mechanical rule.

Other central banks that compute MCIs are less explicit about their use but appear to treat them as one among a number of indicators of the stance of policy. If our interest is only in short-run (between-forecast) changes, the MCI will still indicate the broad direction of the changes, even if the MCI ratio is chosen with fairly different values in the plausible range (Chart 7).[48,49] While policy may be robust over a wide range of weights, ignoring the exchange rate altogether (assigning it a zero weight in the MCI) can result in monetary conditions appearing to have changed in one direction when in fact their joint movement is in the opposite direction.

Levels of the MCI can, on the other hand, diverge rapidly in a projection across several time periods, if the weights differ. Moreover, the impact of a particular level of the MCI will differ across time as the other factors (the X variables in equation (2)), that affect demand and inflation also vary. Discussion of the level of the MCI thus makes greatest sense when comparing one scenario with another, where differences in the X variables can be set out and their impact explained.

MCIs are thus most useful for policy-making when explicit assumptions can be made about the rest of the influences on inflation. They are useful indicators of the change in monetary pressures in the short run between forecasts, when other influences are largely unchanged. They are also useful in simulating the impact of different policy choices with the central bank's model(s). However, changes in the MCI itself act as an indicator of shocks to the economy and of financial market appraisal of the likely future impact of those shocks on the economy.

5.2.2   *The Reserve Bank of New Zealand*

The Reserve Bank of New Zealand used an MCI largely in response to difficulties in explaining to market participants the difference between changes in the *mix* of monetary conditions and changes in the *level* of monetary conditions. Its use was thus motivated more by the requirements of clear external *communication* than internal decision-making. Nevertheless, MCIs were considered in the weekly discussions of the Bank's Monetary Policy Committee.[50]

Financial markets found it difficult to interpret statements by the central bank about interest rates that were contingent upon the level of the exchange rate, and vice versa. The market began to talk about unconditional 'floors' and 'ceilings' for the interest rates that the Bank was supposed to be prepared to tolerate, which did not exist in reality (Mayes and Riches, 1996). Such confusion was incompatible with the Bank's requirements for transparency in the setting of policy.

The RBNZ went into the use of MCIs with considerable caution, as it was well aware of the difficulties both in determining the appropriate values and in using a rather unsophisticated indicator of policy. It was therefore not until the end of 1996 that an MCI was published after two years of research (documented in Mayes and Razzak, 1998). Even then, MCIs were only accorded a limited role, which can be explained in the context of the simple 'control' problem we outlined in the previous section.

The Reserve Bank of New Zealand used MCIs in two ways:

- It provided a projection of an MCI that was consistent with the rest of its forward assessment of the New Zealand economy.[51]
- It stated a level for the current MCI that the RBNZ thought appropriate for price stability and the value of the MCI that it was using.

A specific MCI in nominal terms, combining the 90-day bank bill rate and the TWI (trade-weighted exchange rate),[52] is published by the Reserve Bank and updated by the market.[53] It is this MCI that was used in the statement about what monetary conditions would be appropriate in the current quarter, and it is this number that is used by financial markets.[54]

In its projection, the Reserve Bank uses a real MCI, based on the same quarter, with the 90-day rate deflated by the annual inflation in the target (CPIX)[55] and the TWI deflated by the appropriate GDP deflators. The RBNZ's projection, which is produced quarterly, is based on the Bank's own published model (Black *et al.*, 1997).[56] More specifically, the Bank's quarterly projections are not run on the basis of some assumed track for policy variables such as interest rates. The model itself computes the values of interest rates necessary to achieve the goal of continuing price stability, consistent with the endogenously determined values for the exchange rate and the rest of the model.[57]

The aim of monetary policy is to bring inflation into the middle of the Bank's annual inflation target of 0% to 3%, six to eight quarters ahead. This can be achieved by varying short-term domestic interest rates. Projections follow the standard pattern of setting assumed values for foreign demand, foreign inflation, and foreign interest rates, based on Consensus Forecasts that are external to the Bank. Domestic long-run interest-rates are assumed to follow the rest of the world, with a risk premium and uncovered interest rate parity through the exchange rate. The long-run exchange rate achieves asset balance.

The resultant paths for the interest and exchange rates are then combined into an MCI in the manner described. Thus the MCI does not add anything to the model, as it is computed by combining the interest rates and exchange-rate paths that the model projects. The projection would be unchanged if the concept of an MCI did not exist.

The reason for reporting the outcome in MCI form is simply that any combination of interest rates and the exchange rate that delivered the same MCI would also be consistent with maintaining price stability. In practice, all sorts of small factors cause relative financial market prices to move in the short run, and many exchange-rate tracks would be plausible. Indeed, the choice is beyond the influence of policy. Publishing an MCI track gives the market an idea of the likely profile that monetary policy must take if all the assumptions behind the projection actually come about. Here the appropriate MCI ratio relates to the impact over that horizon six to eight quarters ahead. The index is in real terms because real interest rates and the real exchange rate are thought to have the impact on inflationary pressures and not their nominal counterparts, whose impact will vary with the level of (expected) inflation.

Thus far the process is generalisable and could be used by any central bank trying to run an independent monetary policy in an open economy. Other central banks seeking to use an MCI in this way might need to follow a somewhat different path. First, if they do not have an explicit reaction function in their modelling, such as an inflation target, they will have to use less transparent methods in deriving a suitable path for monetary conditions. This will make it harder to describe the needs of monetary policy beyond the immediate future.

Second, the New Zealand arrangements differed in one respect from those in most other countries. Most central banks set a short-run interest rate as their instrument. Until March 1999, the RBNZ did not. The RBNZ ran policy in a more market-driven manner. It achieved the outcomes it wanted largely through setting out the monetary conditions it wanted to see and explaining why. It did not normally have to enforce its wishes by explicit actions, although it could do so by altering the amount of cash available for interbank settlement at the end of each trading day.[58] It made, and continues to make, an extensive statement and explanation quarterly, when it publishes a projection of the future and an assessment of the risks that monetary policy will face.[59] It normally expects that there will be insufficient new information between statements to warrant any great change in the monetary conditions it wants to see. As part of the March 1999 changes, it has announced that it will only normally consider making changes at six-week intervals.[60] However, it is prepared to accept some variation in monetary conditions round the desired level, as a range of MCIs would be consistent with inflation remaining near the middle of the target range six to eight quarters ahead. Should there be substantial news, the Bank would issue another statement about the new conditions it wanted. Since March 1999, a short-run interest rate has been set at a level thought likely induce the desired monetary conditions, and the MCI, forms part of the explanation, rather than the being single direct indicator to the market.

It is apparent in the RBNZ's explanation of the March 1999 changes that the introduction of the MCIs raised some problems (Hunt and Orr, 1999). In the two years after the RBNZ first published MCIs, exchange rates were much more volatile – with consequent volatility of interest rates if the Bank tries to stabilise monetary conditions. However, it is not yet possible to attribute volatility to a particular cause, because this same period coincided with the Asian crisis, which had a major impact on financial markets' perceptions of the prospects for the New Zealand economy. Market perceptions shifted considerably during this period, first treating the crisis as of limited importance, then taking a much more serious view before converging toward an intermediate position. Furthermore, the market and the RBNZ did not always share the same perception. As a result, over a period of 18 months the New Zealand dollar depreciated by 30% before recovering somewhat. This is a severe test for any monetary policy.[61]

6   Lessons and conclusions

The survey of previous work in Section 3 and our own estimates for 13 European countries, shown in Section 4, suggest that it is possible to compute satisfactory estimates of monetary conditions indexes for a wide range of OECD countries despite the extensive range of practical difficulties involved. Although some estimates are poorly determined, the estimates for the euro area lie in a fairly narrow range. MCIs are not independent of the models used to derive them. They also vary according to how far ahead one wants to look for the impact of monetary policy, as the interest-rate and exchange-rate channels of the transmission mechanism tend to operate at different speeds. Typically, in the OECD countries, the main impact lies one to three years ahead, so our estimates mainly look at the horizon of two years ahead.

Monetary conditions indexes are only summary statistics. They do not present information that is not otherwise available from the economic models on which they are based. However, the virtue of such a summary is that it can convey the information in a simpler and more readily understandable form. Our review of MCIs in practice in Section 5 suggests that MCIs can play a helpful role in the setting of monetary policy and more widely in the understanding of monetary policy and the monetary pressures on the economy. MCIs summarise the likely joint pressure on demand from changes in exchange and interest rates. The IMF, OECD, European Commission and an increasing number of major private-sector institutions use them, as do some central banks. The ability to refer to an MCI makes it easier to explain the consistency of decisions when the exchange rate moves, as has been clearly illustrated in the first few months of the euro's existence, when three quarters of the easing of the monetary stance came through the exchange rate.

In particular, the MCI is an important source of high-frequency information about the level of monetary conditions and their potential impact. Central banks typically take decisions at discrete intervals (every month or six weeks in most cases) unless there is an unusual shock (Woodford, 1999). Thus, as illustrated particularly by the experience of the Bank of Canada and the Reserve Bank of New Zealand, if the MCI changes significantly between forecasts, then the central bank will try to find out why. If the cause can be identified with particular shocks to the economy, then the bank will want to recompute its view of the future, using whatever methods it thinks appropriate. If that recomputation indicates a significant change in the prospects for price stability, then the setting of monetary policy will probably also need to change. If it cannot identify a shock and hence cannot see any other factors other than the relative movement in the exchange rate that will affect future inflation, then it should act to keep that relative movement from having a significant impact on future price stability. The MCI ratio helps determine the size of the necessary response.

Hunt and Orr (1999) emphasise that the central bank should seek to offset exchange-rate shocks only if there is no other observable source of a simultaneous macroeconomic shock. Using simulations with FPS, they show that if a fixed MCI is used as a *target* for monetary policy between forecasts, without regard to the source of the shocks, then this policy will be inferior either to fixing interest rates or to allowing a wide band for the permitted fluctuation of the MCI over the period.

Both the Bank of Canada and the Reserve Bank of New Zealand have used discussion of MCIs as a communication device to help make their assessments of the requirements for monetary policy clearer. However, they have not always been successful.[62] Financial markets respond continuously, including trying to anticipate what the central bank will do in future decision-making meetings (Mayes and Tarkka, 1999). Following a shock, or perceived shock financial markets will drive monetary conditions toward the level they think appropriate, which will be closely related to the level they think that the central bank will try to achieve at subsequent meetings. Part of the reason for moving to setting a cash rate in New Zealand in March 1999 was to emphasise that the MCI was not an intermediate target.

If monetary conditions are used in some sense as a target then financial markets' attempts to anticipate what the central bank will do next will pose a dilemma. Either the central bank will have to allow monetary conditions to move outside the range it thinks appropriate for maintaining price stability until it next changes the setting of its instrument, or it will have to bring forward the resetting of the instrument, either to validate or contradict financial markets' views. A central bank may be reluctant to take the second course without the benefit of having the opportunity to compile enough information to make a considered judgement and to rerun its projections. However, the first course can also be unattractive if delay lets the change in inflation expectations become more embedded and hence more expensive to shift when the time to change the policy setting is reached.[63]

APPENDIX

The data

The following quarterly time series are used in the empirical application:

- GDP (Y)
- Consumer prices (CP)
- Interest rates (money market rates; in addition also the long rates) (R)
- Exchange rates *vis-à-vis* US dollar and German Deutsche Mark (E)
- World (OECD) output (OECD)

The GDP series come from the NiGEM model data bank and the other series from the IFS (from lines are, 64, 60B and 61, respectively). The GDP data are seasonally adjusted. The data cover the period 1972Q1 to 1988Q4. With Ireland, Portugal, and Spain, the series are somewhat shorter (1984:1, 1981Q1; 1978Q1–1997Q4, respectively). The number of data points for individual countries is thus about 100. In the empirical analysis, GDP, consumer prices, and the exchange rates are expressed in logs; the log differences have been multiplied by 100. Thus output is given by $y = \log(GDP)$ and the output gap by $\nabla y = y - HPTREND(y)$, similarly for the OECD output gap, $\nabla OECD$. Inflation is $\Delta p = 100*\log(CP/CP(-1))$, the real interest rate is $rr = R - 400*\log(CP/CP(-1))$, and the real exchange rate is $re = 100*\log(E \cdot (CP_{US}/CP_i))$ where CP_{US} denotes US consumption prices.

Lack of suitable data obliged us to drop Greece and Luxemburg from the sample. The following countries are included (abbreviations in parentheses):

Austria (Aut)

Belgium (Bel)

Denmark (Den)

Finland (Fin)

France (Fra)

Germany (Ger)

Ireland (Irl)

Italy (Ita)

Netherlands (Net)

Portugal (Por)

Spain (Spa)

Sweden (Swe)

United Kingdom (UK)

Notes

1 The views expressed here are personal.

2 Central banks in largely closed economies may still find MCIs helpful if they relate to the term structure or to stock market prices. Although the focus is normally on the exchange rate other relative prices may be of use.

3 This reflects the way the asset side is treated in most estimated macroeconomic models.

4 Goldman Sachs (1999), for example, has recently introduced an FCI (Financial Conditions Indicator), which adds a long corporate interest rate and the ratio of the total market capitalisation of the equity market to nominal GDP to the normal short interest rate and exchange-rate terms.

5 Banque de France (1996) provides a helpful summary of the uses of MCIs and the problems associated with them. See also Ericsson *et al.* (1997).

6 If the central bank is targeting some intermediate current variable such as the exchange rate or a monetary aggregate and not price stability directly, then the problem is much simpler to set out and only the first stage in the transmission mechanism through to inflation need be spelt out.

7 We would also need to specify the time horizon; the weights and the ratio might not be the same for all time horizons.

8 While it is normal to include the level of interest rates in P, exchange rates are normally included in log form.

9 In practice central banks tend to choose robust values for the MCI weights that are consistent with quite a wide range of plausible models.

10 There are wider problems in estimation (Ericsson *et al.*, 1997) including difficulties stemming from non-stationarity (Mayes and Virén, 1998), as we explain in Section 3.5.

11 As is conventional, we have calibrated the MCI so that it can be compared directly with interest-rate changes.

12 See, for example, 'Euro's fall seen reducing need for rate cut', *The Wall Street Journal*, 10 February 1999; 'Weakness is a strength', *The Financial Times*, 30 March 1999; 'Pedal to the metal. ECB cuts rates by Half a point in bid to spur growth', *The Wall Street Journal*, 9 April 1999.

13 There have been some minor technical adjustments, particularly to the range of interest rates, as part of the process of seeking a smooth introduction for the euro.

14 These include the sum of the short and long interest-rate effects.

15 These approaches are, however, much more open to the criticisms of Ericsson *et al.* (1997).

16 Except for Sweden, where the Riksbank publishes an estimate of 3 to 4 as opposed to the value of 2 estimated in Hansson and Lindberg.

17 Ericsson *et al.* use three bases for calculating confidence intervals for the MCI ratio. We report those based on the Wald statistic primarily because this makes them comparable with the estimates used by Dornbusch *et al.* (1998).

18 Our results show that the explicit 'foreign' demand variable matters. With an area as large as the euro area, assuming that even OECD GDP is the appropriate variable may be mistaken.

19 However, Sweden has the same specification as France, Italy and Spain.

20 The exchange rate is with the Deutsche Mark except in the case of Germany, where it is with the US dollar.

21 In fact Sweden was the only case where Ericsson *et al.* obtain closely determined estimates.

22 In earlier work, discussed in Mayes and Virén (1998), Smets (1996) finds both elasticity and VAR estimates for MCIs that are substantially lower than those implied by trade shares.

23 As set out in Bernanke (1986), Blanchard and Watson (1986), and Sims (1986), *inter alia,* and reviewed in Cechetti (1996).

24 Ramaswamy and Sloek (1997) only include an exchange rate in their VAR as the last step in examining robustness in their appendix. Even then it is the bilateral rate with the Deutsche Mark in all cases except Germany. The exchange rate with countries outside the euro area is important in our case; moreover, the DM exchange rates have not proven very important sources of independent variation in VARs for the EU countries. However, the Ramaswamy and Sloek results are interesting in that they suggest that the 12 EU countries that they study can be placed into two distinct groups according to the extent of the impact of monetary policy on them. The effects of a monetary policy shock on Austria, Belgium, Finland, Germany, the Netherlands, and the United Kingdom take almost twice as long to occur and are almost twice as large as those experienced by Denmark, France, Italy, Portugal, Spain, and Sweden. These groupings contradict other evidence repeated in Dornbusch *et al.* (1998), *inter alia,* that the United Kingdom is likely to be more responsive because of the high proportion of variable-rate mortgages. Our own results also show substantial variations among countries. Some countries, such as Denmark and Portugal, that are very open in terms of trade shares are nevertheless relatively unresponsive to changes in the exchange rate.

25 See Mayes and Virén (1998, pp. 33 and 34) for a discussion of the difficulties of using VARs to measure monetary policy.

26 The estimation period runs quarterly from 1973Q2 to 1996Q4. Germany is used for 'foreign' GDP and interest rates, while the IMF's Total Competitiveness Weights for Sweden's 20 largest trading partners are used for the exchange rate and the foreign price.

27 Shocks are imposed for five years.

28 Very similar to our own round estimate of 3.5, derived in Section 4.

29 The effect on expectations is a key feature of the monetary transmission, which is one reason for describing it first. If policy-makers can commit themselves to act in a credible manner, then the changes in the settings of the instruments of monetary policy can be smaller to achieve any desired change in forecast inflation or output (Mayes and Tarkka, 1999).

30 At the same time, the effects of policy come through much faster and smaller policy responses are required to any given shock.

31 This finding was noted over 25 years ago during an attempt to measure the effectiveness of fiscal policy (Blinder and Solow, 1973).

32 In real terms there is actually a third phase of a negative MCI, again to help damp out the cycle. The return to asset equilibrium takes even longer and is still not complete by the end of the ten-year period, as can be seen in the last graph in Chart 5.

33 We use quarterly data, as it is not possible to interpolate GDP data in a satisfactory manner to compare with the United States. The use of industrial production as a substitute output variable is likely to introduce a range of complications with the switch to outsourcing and substantial changes in public and privately provided services in the EU countries. However, the use of longer time periods makes the identification of the lag structure a little more problematic, as a quarter may be long enough to permit 'contemporaneous' policy reactions to some shocks. The problem may be limited; the monetary authority faces not the final published data used in this analysis but first and partial estimates, which may in fact turn out to be rather different (see Mayes, 1981, for an extreme case with UK national accounts data).

34 We began our analysis with the usual cointegration inspection to check that the statistical properties of the data were likely to be consistent with obtaining usable estimates. The respective results are reported in Mayes and Virén (1998).

35 The lag for the interest rate, exchange-rate and foreign demand variable are shown in order under the country mnemonic in column 1 of Table 4. Thus, in the case of Austria, the sequence 2,1,2 that is shown indicates a two-quarter lag on interest rates, a one-quarter lag on the exchange rate and a two quarter lag on foreign demand.

36 The DM exchange rate shows a coefficient different from zero only at the 5% level in the case of Finland, Italy, and Portugal.

37 In contrast to Peeters (1998), where including long rates separately substantially increases the interest-rate effect.

38 Available from the authors on request.

39 According to the VARs that include the exchange rate. Ehrmann (1998) suggests that there may be even greater differences among the EU countries and places them in five rather than two groups on the basis of an SVAR model.

40 The ordinary least squares estimate was 4.2, but this is an inappropriate method because the errors are clearly heteroscedastic. For the whole sample, including Sweden, Denmark, and the United Kingdom the MCI is somewhat lower (2.6 GLS, 2.1 SUR).

41 Detailed in Mayes and Virén (1998).

42 Both the IMF and the OECD use MCIs in order to summarise the stance of monetary policy (see IMF *World Economic Outlook* and *OECD Economic Outlook*).

43 Ericsson *et al.* (1997) quotes MCIs computed by Deutsche Bank, Goldman Sachs, and JP Morgan, while BNP and Morgan Stanley Dean Witter, for example, use MCIs in their regular briefings. Goldman Sachs now uses a broader FCI (Goldman Sachs, 1999).

44 Shown in the IMF *World Economic Outlook* and the OECD *Economic Outlook*.

45 Private-sector financial institutions tend to follow a format similar to the IMF (see, for example BNP, 1998; MSDW, 1998).

46 There are no specific agreed rules for the detailed construction of MCIs, and there are very few examples of MCIs that have 'official' status in a market and are hence used by most market participants. The base and scale of MCIs are open for decision even if people agree about the relative importance of their components. Published absolute numbers may differ even where their interpretation will be identical.

47 The Bank of Canada and the Reserve Bank of New Zealand dominate this section, having taken the use of MCIs furthest and also having published most about how they use them. It is no surprise that these very open economies, running independent monetary policies should have taken the lead, nor that Finland, Norway, and Sweden should also have moved in the same direction when faced with similar problems. Some of their concerns are not generalisable to the euro area, but, while that may reduce the significance of the MCI, it by no means eliminates it.

48 The Finnish result seems to be typical (Mayes and Virén, 1998).

49 As Mayes and Razzak (1998) explain, the RBNZ was able to operate satisfactorily in the face of small shocks although it had not made up its mind where the MCI ratio was in the range 1 to 3.

50 Mayes and Razzak (1998).

51 This use continues.

52 The TWI is also computed and published by the Reserve Bank. The trade weights of the five largest trading partners are used with the weights recomputed every three months.

53 It is based on the average of the daily values for the December 1996 quarter of 8.71% for the 90-day rate and 67.11 for the TWI being set equal 1000. It is then calibrated so that one basis point on the 90-bill rate equals one point on the MCI. A 2% change in the TWI has the same effect on the index as a 100 basis point change in the 90-day rate (i.e. the MCI *ratio* is 2).

54 This system was changed in March 1999, when the Reserve Bank changed from setting cash targets in the overnight market to setting an interest rate. Since then it is this instrument that has been the key indicator of the monetary stance, and the MCI has played a secondary role.

55 The consumer price index excluding Credit Services (as published by Statistics New Zealand, for the past; the RBNZ uses its own projections for future values).

56 This model, which includes all the main elements of the transmission mechanism, also contains reaction functions for both fiscal and monetary policy. This feature has a number of important consequences. The model has expectations consistent with policy.

57 In its *Inflation Reports* the Bank of England now provides a projection of the path for the exchange rate that might emerge but this is based on the assumption of unchanged interest rates and hence will in effect be a counterfactual if maintaining inflation within the target range implies policy actions (Mayes and Tarkka, 1999).

58 The last time this was required, before the system was changed, was in August 1995; before that, in late 1993. This process is explained in more detail in Mayes and Razzak (1998).

59 These are colloquially referred to as 'open mouth operations' (see, for example, Guthrie and Wright, 1997).

60 At Monetary Policy Committee meetings immediately after each quarterly projection is finalised and at a review midway between these projections.

61 It is interesting to note that the Australian dollar underwent a very similar cycle at the same time.

62 As shown, for example, in the Monetary Policy Statements issued in 1998 and the beginning of 1999.

63 Central banks like the Bank of England and the Swedish Riksbank, which show a probability distribution for the expected outcomes on which they are basing policy, may find it rather easier to explain how they are responding to shocks.

Bibliography

Armstrong, J., Black, R., Laxton, D. and Rose, D. (1995), 'A robust method for simulating forward-looking models, the Bank of Canada's new quarterly projection model, Part 2', *Technical Report,* No. 73, Bank of Canada.

Bagliano, F.C. and Favero, C.A. (1997), 'Measuring monetary policy with VAR models: an evaluation', *CEPR Discussion Paper,* No. 1743, November.

Bank of Finland (1990), 'The BOF4 Quarterly Model of the Finnish Economy', D: 73, Bank of Finland.

Banque de France (1996), 'Les indicateurs des conditions monetaires', *Bulletin de la Banque de France*, No. 30, pp. 99–111, June.

Banque National de Paris (1998), *Market Outlook,* 15, September.

Bernanke, B.S. (1986), 'Alternative explanations of the money-income correlation', in Brunner, K. and Meltzer, A. (eds) *Real Business Cycles, Real Exchange Rates and Actual Policies,* Carnegie-Rochester conference series on Public Policy, No. 25, Amsterdam: North Holland.

Bernanke, B.S. and Blinder, A. (1992), 'The federal funds rate and the channels of monetary transmission', *American Economic Review,* Vol. 82, pp. 901–21, September.

Bernanke, B.S. and Mihov, I. (1995), 'Measuring monetary policy', *NBER Working Paper,* 5145, June.

Black, R., Laxton, D., Rose, D. and Tetlow, R. (1994), 'The steady-state model: SSQPM, the Bank of Canada's new quarterly projection model, Part 1', *Technical Report,* No. 72, Bank of Canada.

Black, R., Cassino, V., Drew, A., Hansen, E., Hunt, B., Rose, D. and Scott, A. (1997), 'The forecasting and policy system: the core model', *Reserve Bank of New Zealand Research Paper,* 43.

Black, S. (1989), 'Transaction costs and vehicle currencies', mimeo, University of North Carolina, Chapel Hill, September.

Blanchard, O. and Watson, M. (1986), 'Are business cycles all alike?' in Gordon, R.J. (ed.), *The American Business Cycle: Continuity and Change*, Chicago: University of Chicago Press for NBER.

Blinder, A.S. and Solow, M. (1973), 'Does fiscal policy matter?' *Journal of Public Economics*, Vol. 2, pp. 319–37.

Bowden, R.J. and O'Donovan, B. (1996), 'Financial markets: volatility and policy', chapter 9, in Silverstone, B., Bollard, A. and Lattimore, R. (eds) *A Study of Economic Reform: the Case of New Zealand*, Amsterdam: North Holland.

Britton, E. and Whitley, J. (1997), 'Comparing the monetary transmission mechanism in France, Germany and the United Kingdom', *Bank of England Quarterly Bulletin*, Vol. 32(2).

Butler, L. (1996), 'A semi-structural method to estimate potential output: combining economic theory with a time series filter, the Bank of Canada's new quarterly projection model, Part 4', *Technical Report,* No. 77, Bank of Canada.

Cechetti, S.G. (1996), 'Practical issues in monetary policy targeting', *Federal Reserve Bank of Cleveland Economic Review*, Q1, pp. 2–15.

Christiano, L.J., Eichenbaum, M. and Evans, C.L. (1996), 'Identification and the effects of monetary policy shocks', in Blejer, M., Eckstein, Z., Hercowitz, Z. and Leiderman, L. (eds) *Financial Factors in Economic Stabilisation and Growth*, pp. 35–74, Cambridge: Cambridge University Press.

Christiano, L.J., Eichenbaum, M. and Evans, C.L. (1997), 'Monetary shocks: what we have learned and to what end?' *Handbook of Macroeconomics.*

Coletti, D., Hunt, B., Rose, D. and Tetlow, R. (1996), 'The dynamic model: QPM, the Bank of Canada's new quarterly projection model, Part 3', *Technical Report,* No. 75, Bank of Canada.

Collins, S. and Nadal De Simone, F. (1996), 'Selected policy issues under inflation targeting in a small open economy', in *The Impact of Financial Market Development on the Real Economy,* pp. 209–39, Monetary Authority of Singapore.

Dennis, R. (1996a), 'Monetary conditions and the monetary policy transmission mechanism', *Reserve Bank of New Zealand Working Paper.*

Dennis, R. (1996b), 'A measure of monetary conditions', Reserve Bank of New Zealand Discussion Paper, G97/1.

Dornbusch, R., Favero, C. and Giavazzi, F. (1998), 'Immediate challenges for the European Central Bank', *Economic Policy,* No. 26, pp. 15–64.

Duguay, P. (1994), 'Empirical evidence on the strength of the monetary transmission mechanism in Canada: an aggregate approach', *Journal of Monetary Economics,* Vol. 33, pp. 39–61.

Ehrmann, M. (1998), 'Will EMU generate asymmetry? Comparing monetary policy transmission across European countries', *European University Institute Working Paper,* ECO 98/28.

Eika, K.H., Ericsson, N.R. and Nymoen, R. (1996), 'Hazards in implementing a monetary conditions index', *Oxford Bulletin of Economics and Statistics,* Vol. 58, No. 4, pp. 765–90.

Ericsson, N.R., Jansen, E.S., Kerbeshian, N.A. and Nymoen, R. (1997), 'Understanding a monetary conditions index', mimeo, Federal Reserve Board.

Evans, C.L. and Kuttner, K.N. (1998), 'Can VARs describe monetary policy?' mimeo, Federal Reserve Bank of New York.

Freedman, C. (1994), 'The use of indicators and of the monetary conditions index in Canada', in Balino, T.J.T. and Cottarelli, C. (eds) *Frameworks for Monetary Stability,* Washington: IMF.

Gali, J. (1992), 'How well does the IS-LM model fit postwar US data?', *Quarterly Journal of Economics,* Vol. 107, No. 2, pp. 709–38.

Gerlach, S. and Smets, F. (1996), 'MCIs and monetary policy in small open economies under floating rates', mimeo, BIS.

Goldman Sachs & Co. (1999), *Global Economics Paper,* No. 26, 17th September.

Grenville, S. (1995), 'The monetary policy transmission process: what do we know? (And what don't we know?)', *Reserve Bank of Australia Bulletin,* pp. 19–33, September.

Grilli, V. and Roubini, N. (1990), 'Capital mobility, vehicle currencies and exchange rate asymmetries in the EMS', mimeo, Yale University, March.

Guthrie, G. and Wright, J. (1997), 'Market-implemented monetary policy with open mouth operations', mimeo, University of Canterbury, July.

Hansson, B. (1993), 'A structural model', in Sveriges Riksbank, *Monetary Policy Indicators,* June.

Hansson, B. and Lindberg, H. (1994), 'Monetary conditions index – a monetary policy indicator', *Sveriges Riksbank Quarterly Review,* No. 3, pp. 12–17.

Hukkinen, J. and Virén, M. (1998), 'How to evaluate the forecasting performance of a macroeconomic model?' *Bank of Finland Discussion Papers,* 5/98 and *Journal of Policy Modelling* (1999), 21(6), November, pp. 753–68.

Hunt, B. and Orr, A. (1999), 'Inter-forecast monetary policy implementation: responding to unexpected exchange rate developments', *Reserve Bank of New Zealand Bulletin*, Vol. 26(1), pp. 62–74.

Jacobsen, T., Jansson, P., Vredin, A. and Warne, A. (1998), 'A VAR model for monetary policy analysis in a small open economy', Sveriges Riksbank, August.

Jore, A.S. (1994), 'Calculation of an indicator for monetary policy', Norges Bank, Penger og Kreditt, No. 2, pp. 100–5.

Kennedy, N.O. and van Riet, A.G. (1995), 'A monetary conditions index for the major EU countries: a preliminary investigation', EMI.

Kool, C. and Tatom, J. (1994), 'The P-star model in five small economies', *Federal Reserve Bank of St Louis Review*, pp. 11–29, May–June.

Leeper, E.M., Sims, C.A. and Zha, T. (1996), 'What does monetary policy do?' *Brookings Papers on Economic Activity*, No. 2, pp. 1–63.

Mayes, D.G. (1981), 'Assessing economic models and economic forecasts', *National Institute Economic Review*, No. 95, pp. 21–31.

Mayes, D.G. and Razzak, W. (1998), 'Transparency and accountability: empirical models and policy making at the Reserve Bank of New Zealand', *Economic Modelling*, Vol. 15, pp. 377–94.

Mayes, D.G. and Riches, B. (1996), 'The effectiveness of monetary policy in New Zealand', *Reserve Bank of New Zealand Bulletin*, Vol. 59, No. 1, pp. 5–20.

Mayes, D.G. and Tarkka, J. (1999), 'The value of publishing central bank forecasts of inflation', *Bank of Finland Discussion Paper*, 22/99.

Mayes, D.G. and Viren, M. (1998), 'The Exchange Rate and Monetary Conditions in the Euro Area', *Bank of Finland Discussion Paper,* 27/98.

McCallum, B.T. and Nelson, E. (1997), 'An optimizing IS-LM specification for monetary policy and business cycle', *NBER Working Paper,* No. 5875.

Mishkin, F. (1995), 'The channels of monetary transmission: lessons for monetary policy', *NBER Working Paper,* No. 5464.

Morgan Stanley Dean Witter (1998), *Weekly International Briefing*, 16 October.

Nadal De Simone, F., Dennis, R. and Redward, P. (1996), 'A monetary conditions index for New Zealand', *Discussion Paper,* G96/2, Reserve Bank of New Zealand.

Norges Bank (1995), 'Norges Bank's monetary conditions index', *Norges Bank Economic Bulletin*, Vol. 66, No. 1, p. 33.

Obstfeld, M. and Rogoff, K. (1996), *Foundations of International Macroeconomics*, Cambridge MA: MIT Press.

Page, S.A.B. (1981), 'The choice of invoicing currency in merchandising trade', *National Institute Economic Review*, Vol. 85, pp. 60–72.

Peersman, G. and Smets, F. (1998), 'The Taylor rule: a useful monetary policy guide for the ECB?', mimeo, BIS.

Peeters, M. (1998), 'Monetary conditions in Europe: a methodological analysis', *mimeo*, De Nederlandsche Bank.

Pikkarainen, P. (1993), 'Rahapolitiikan välitaoitteet, indikaatorit ja viritys', *Kansantaloudellinen aikakauskirja* (Finnish Economic Journal), No. 4.

Pikkarainen, P. and Ripatti, A. (1995), 'The role of monetary indicators in the design of monetary policy', *Bank of Finland Bulletin*, Vol. 69, No. 8, pp. 3–8, August.

Ramaswamy, R. and Sloek, T. (1998), 'The real effects of monetary policy in the European Union: What are the differences?', *IMF Staff Papers,* Vol. 45(2), pp. 374–96.

Roger, S. (1993), 'Asset prices and monetary policy', mimeo, Reserve Bank of New Zealand.

Roger, S. (1995), 'Monetary conditions and monetary policy', *Research Memo,* M95/49, Reserve Bank of New Zealand.

Roger, S, (1998), *Internal memorandum,* Reserve Bank of New Zealand, July.

Rudebusch, G.D. (1998), 'Do measures of monetary policy in a VAR make sense?' mimeo, Federal Reserve Bank of San Francisco.

Sims, C. (1980), 'Macroeconomics and reality', *Econometrica,* Vol. 48(1), pp. 1–48.

Sims, C. (1986), 'Are forecasting models usable for policy analysis?', *Federal Reserve Bank of Minneapolis Quarterly Review*, pp. 2–16 (winter).

Smets, F. (1996), 'Measuring monetary policy in the G7 countries: interest rates versus exchange rates', BIS.

Smets, F. (1997), 'Measuring monetary policy shocks in France, Germany and Italy: the role of the exchange rate', *BIS Working Paper,* No. 42.

Strongin, S. (1992), 'The identification of monetary policy disturbances: explaining the liquidity puzzle', *Working Paper,* 92–27, Federal Reserve Bank of Chicago, November.

Tarkka, J. and Willman, A. (eds) (1985), *The BOF3 Quarterly Model of the Finnish Economy*, D: 59, Bank of Finland.

Willman, A., Kortelainen, M., Männistö, H-L. and Tujula, M. (1998), 'The BOF5 macroeconomic model of Finland, structure and equations', *Bank of Finland Discussion Paper,* 10/98.

Winkelmann, L. (1996), 'A study of pass-through elasticities for New Zealand import markets', *Reserve Bank of New Zealand Discussion Paper,* G96/5.

Woodford, M. (1999), 'Optimal monetary policy inertia', mimeo, Princeton University.

Index

For Product Safety Concerns and Information please contact our EU
representative GPSR@taylorandfrancis.com Taylor & Francis Verlag GmbH,
Kaufingerstraße 24, 80331 München, Germany

Printed and bound by CPI Group (UK) Ltd, Croydon, CR0 4YY
08/05/2025
01864499-0003